Mastering
Turbo Assembler

R E L A T E D   T I T L E S

Mastering
Turbo Assembler

Tom Swan

HAYDEN BOOKS

A Division of Macmillan Computer Publishing
11711 North College, Carmel, Indiana 46032 USA

International Standard Book Number: 0-672-48435-8
Library of Congress Catalog Card Number: 89-60591

Acquisitions Editor: *Richard K. Swadley*
Development Editor: *James Rounds*
Manuscript Editor: *Sara Bernhardt Black*
Production Coordinator: *Marjorie Jo Hopper*
Cover Artist: *Celeste Design*
Indexer: *Brown Editorial Service*
Technical Reviewer: *Charles P. Jazdzewski*
Compositor: *Impressions, Inc.*

Printed in the United States of America

Trademarks

Overview

PART I Programming with Assembly Language

PART II Multilanguage Programming

PART III Reference

*For my mother-in-law, Adriana Baldisseri Oehme,
and my father-in-law, J. Herbert Oehme.*

Preface

Programmers are always arguing about which language is the best. Try to win C programmers over to Pascal and they'll tell you to go eat quiche. Try to get Pascal pundits to recognize the fresh look of BASIC and you'll probably be told where to GOTO. And don't even think of suggesting to Forth fans that theirs is an obscure language, hardly suitable for any "serious" work—unless, that is, you're prepared to be threaded up and tarred right out of town.

I try to avoid getting into such arguments, which I find to be more amusing than significant. What if, instead of programmers, the debaters were chefs arguing about whether a souffle will be more heavenly if the recipe is written in French, English, or Spanish? Of course, that's silly—you'll get the same results no matter what language spells out the ingredients. Flour is flour, right?

The same is true in programming. All high-level languages must translate their instructions into native machine code to run on computer processors such as the IBM PC's 8086, 8088, 80286, or 80386 microprocessors, covered in depth in these pages. With this in mind, it's easy to see that, when stripped bare (as the cover seems to suggest), all programming languages actually speak the same tongue—forked as it may be in some cases.

So, no matter what high-level language you favor, it makes sense to learn assembly language, the only computer language that lets you talk to a naked computer in its own dialect. In the following chapters, I'll concentrate mostly on how to write entire programs in assembly language, paying special attention to developing reusable library modules. There are chapters that explain how to add optimized assembly code to Turbo C and Turbo Pascal, plus a tear-out assembly language reference card that will serve you long after you master the tutorial.

To the beginners among you, I add this note: If you've heard that assembly language is difficult, don't believe it. With Turbo Assembler's many features including the all-new Ideal mode, and with the guiding hand of the marvelous Turbo Debugger, you'll soon be twiddling bits with the best of them. Quiche indeed!

Tom Swan

Acknowledgments

To my wife and assistant Anne Swan, who kept me going for the months it took to research and write this book, thank you for understanding. To Bill and Carmen Alexander and their family, who made room for all my "stuff" in their homes in Taxco, Mexico, thank you for being there. To my mother Mary P. Swan and father Reyer O. Swan, thank you for your support and love (and the honey!). To David, Barb, and Collin Swan, thank you for the ice cream, which helped keep me cool. To Sara Black, thank you for your keen eye and a "high-energy" editing job. To Richard Swadley, Jim Hill, Glenn Santner, Jim Rounds, Marj Hopper, Wendy Ford, Damon Davis, and Jim Irizarry, thank you for fine food, fine wine, fine company, and your very fine help. And, to everyone else at Howard W. Sams & Company, especially the guys in the back who showed me how the web press works, thanks for doing your parts so that I may continue doing mine. Also, a special thank you to everyone at Borland International and to Chuck Jazdzewski for many fine suggestions.

Contents

PART II   Multilanguage Programming

PART III   Reference

Tables

Programs

I Programming with Assembly Language

Chapter *1 Introduction*

3

1 **Introduction**

In This Chapter

Why you should learn assembly language; what to expect from reading this book; machine code versus assembly language; how assembly language differs from other computer languages; using Turbo Debugger as a teaching tool; advantages of Turbo Assembler's Ideal mode; advantages and disadvantages of programming in assembly language; this book's hardware and software requirements; selecting a programming editor; how to get the most from this book; chapter organization and contents; library modules included in chapters; how to organize floppy and hard disks; how to enter example programs; how to get answers to your questions

Learning Assembly Language

I remember when I discovered assembly language. The nearest I've come to experiencing the same elation was the day I first balanced a two-wheeler, wiggling my way down our street, my father's thumb no longer snagging my belt, my fear of falling melting like bee's wax in the sun.

Mastering assembly language gives many programmers the same sort of astonished joy. Why? Because assembly language is the only computer language that lets you talk to a computer in its native tongue, commanding the hardware to perform exactly as you say. If you like to be in charge, if you like to control things, if you're interested in details, you'll be right at home with assembly language.

My goal in writing this book is to offer a guiding hand as you find your own balance in assembly language programming. Read the rest of this chapter for suggestions on how to prepare your disk and how to make the best use of the book's various parts and pieces. Enter the examples—or examine the files if you purchased the disk—puzzle through the exercises and projects at the end of each chapter, and don't be afraid to experiment on your own. Above all, have fun! (If you become frustrated, see "How To Get More Help" later in this chapter.)

**You Take the High
Level and I'll Take
the Low Level**
Even though it may appear as though a computer "understands" high-level languages such as BASIC or Pascal, all computer programs actually run in *machine language,* the coded bytes that drive the computer's central processing unit (CPU). For this reason, *machine code* is a better term for this lowest of low-level computer languages—the only language the CPU knows. Because CPUs can't directly execute C and Pascal statements, programs in these and other high-level languages must be *compiled* (translated) to machine code before the programs can be used. Similarly, a program written in an interpreted language like BASIC or LISP must be translated to machine code, although in these cases, the translation happens invisibly while the program runs, usually one statement at a time.

Assembly language programs are also translated to machine code by a program called an *assembler.* Despite this similarity with other languages, assembly language is neither high nor low level; it's sort of stuck in between. Unlike C and Pascal statements, which might translate to dozens of machine-code bytes, assembly language instructions directly relate to individual machine codes—the major distinction between assembly language and high-level computer languages. All languages have their good points, but only assembly language allows you to write programs directly in the CPU's indivisible instruction set.

Note: Experienced C programmers may be frowning because they know that some C statements—also some Turbo Pascal statements—translate to single machine codes. Forth language fans may also argue that their lexicon provides direct low-level access. Even so, while C and Forth may not be the highest of high-level languages, they're still miles above assembly language's special access to the CPU.

By the way, shaded boxes like this one are used throughout this book to point out interesting views and other scenery as you travel through the chapters.

If assembly language and machine code enjoy a one-to-one relationship, why not program directly in machine code? The answer is: Machine code is just too cumbersome. While it's true that very early computer programs were programmed in machine code, today this is almost never done—and with good reasons. For example, many machine codes depend on their relative positions in memory. Also, in pure machine code, there are no named variables, and there is no way except by fixed addresses to tell a program where values and subroutines are stored. This means that, if you change one instruction in a 10,000-byte machine-code program, you may have to modify 9,000 other codes as well!

Obviously, such hard labor lacks appeal for fun-loving programmers, whose brains, despite popular opinion, are not bit mapped and wired with AND gates. Programming directly in machine code is drudge work. Programming in assembly language gives you the best of two worlds, combining direct access to the computer's lowest levels with features like named variables and numeric expressions that make programming in high-level languages practical and enjoyable. With assembly language, you can change one instruction and then feed the modified code to Turbo Assembler, which translates the entire program to machine code. Some people say that assembly language is only one step above machine code. That's true, but it's a *big* step.

Developing Mental Pictures

Because assembly language statements directly translate to the CPU's fundamental machine codes, the best way to become a crack assembly language programmer is to develop good mental models of a computer's inner workings. The more you know about how your computer is constructed and the more familiar you are with the functions in DOS and the ROM BIOS on PCs, the better you will be able to apply your knowledge of assembly language when writing computer programs.

In later chapters, I'll concentrate on subject areas that explain in detail how to control various parts of a PC's hardware. For example, one chapter deals with the keyboard and display, while another chapter explains serial communications. The goal in these chapters is to help you develop mental models of what really goes on inside your computer, while showing how to control the computer's devices with assembly language statements.

> Note: As you probably know, MS-DOS and PC-DOS are pretty much birds of the same feather. To keep things simple, this book uses *DOS* to mean both of these Disk Operating Systems. The BIOS, for *Basic Input-Output System,* refers to routines—yes, in machine code—stored in Read-Only Memory chips. Generally speaking, the BIOS is responsible for driving the computer hardware, while DOS is responsible for providing a standard interface to that hardware, which may vary from system to system.

Preventive Debugging

Some people find it difficult to make the intuitive leap between a program's written statements and the actions that occur when the program runs. This is especially so with cryptic assembly language instructions such as mov ax,bx and xor cx,cx, which appear to have no connection with displaying characters on screen, printing text, and dialing up remote systems via modems. Comprehending a program by executing out-of-context assembly language statements mentally can frustrate even the most mechanical of thinkers. But don't let such moments ruin your day. This is hard for *everybody.*

Using a program such as Turbo Debugger, included in the Turbo Assembler package, is one way—maybe the best way—to improve your ability to understand an assembly language program's actions. Many people consider a debugger to be useful only for helping to fix a broken program. But a debugger can offer preventive medicine as well as a cure. With Turbo Debugger, you can peer into memory as your program runs, watch processor registers change, see memory bytes take on values, and step through a program's actions in slow motion. You can also view your assembly language statements along with the corresponding machine code, seeing exactly what Turbo Assembler generates from your program text.

Using Turbo Debugger to examine running programs will help you to understand the purpose of specific assembly language statements. In future chapters, I'll often suggest using Turbo Debugger to check registers and flags, to examine sections of memory, and to run your program up to temporary stopping places, letting you reflect at your own speed on what the program is doing every step of the way.

> Note: I used two undefined terms in the preceding section, *register* and *flag*. A register is a small amount of volatile memory inside the CPU processor. As you'll learn, various machine-code instructions operate directly on CPU registers. A flag is a single-bit switch, also inside the processor and also directly affected by certain machine codes. We'll take a closer look at these items later.

Striving for the Ideal   Turbo Assembler is actually two assemblers in one. Normally, Turbo Assembler processes programs written in the popular *MASM syntax*. For assembling programs downloaded from bulletin boards, copied from time share systems, or gleaned from MASM books, this is the method to use.

Examples in this book use Turbo Assembler's *Ideal mode,* which I believe to be superior to MASM syntax—especially for writing stand-alone assembly language programs. With Ideal mode, programs assemble faster and are less prone to developing bugs that can result from MASM's many known quirks and syntactical freedoms. (The Turbo Assembler User's Guide spells out the differences between MASM and Ideal mode instructions.)

In addition to extra speed and the absence of quirky behavior, Ideal mode offers other advantages. Structures (similar to Pascal records or C structures) can repeat member field names. Assembler directives are easier to remember and use. Equated symbols and expressions always have predictable values. And formats for various memory-addressing modes must conform to generally recognized guidelines. If you don't yet grasp the significance of some of these items, you'll have to trust my opinion: Ideal mode is what PC assembly language programmers have needed for years.

Don't be concerned that, by learning Ideal mode, you'll be shut out from using the thousands of lines of MASM code in the public domain. After learning Ideal mode, you'll be able to read and understand MASM-mode programs with little effort. Most differences between the two modes are subtle—a spelling change here, an operand reversal there. I regularly read and work on programs in both syntaxes without difficulty, but I prefer using Ideal mode for new projects.

Advantages of Assembly Language

Many books list in detail the advantages and disadvantages of programming in assembly language. The advantages are rather obvious and well known: low-level access to the computer and the promise of top speed that comes from total control over the CPU. High-level language programs tend to run more slowly than assembly language programs because of the way a C or Pascal compiler uses standard methods to read and write variables, to call subroutines, and so on. In assembly language, if you want to store a variable in a readily accessible processor register, that's your business.

Despite many claims to the contrary, there is no guarantee of speed in assembly language programming. An experienced C or BASIC programmer can write programs that run circles around bungled assembly language jobs. Assembly language gives you nothing more than the *opportunity* to write programs with optimum efficiency—a worthy goal that requires time and patience to achieve in practice. But if speed is your aim, you can at least be sure of one thing. You've come to the right race track.

Disadvantages of Assembly Language

The main disadvantages of assembly language programming most often cited are: increased risk of bugs, reduced portability, and the absence of library routines to perform tasks such as displaying strings or reading disk-file data. Let's take these one by one.

Increased risk of bugs   I don't agree with this criticism. Bugs are the result of carelessness, not the result of features in a computer language. You can write buggy programs in any language, and you can write bug-free programs in assembly language. I do agree that simple bugs in assembly language programs are often more serious than mistakes in C or Pascal. Because assembly language gives you complete control of the CPU, a single haywire statement can cause a system crash more readily than in high-level languages, where a compiler generates the machine code for you. One way to deal with this problem is to run your programs under the control of Turbo Debugger, which can help reduce the likelihood of a crash.

> Note: Several months ago when I began writing this book, I experienced what many assembly language programmers expect as routine—crash after crash, requiring me to reboot or switch off power to recover. Then, as I became more familiar with Turbo Debugger, my frequent crashes practically disappeared! Today, I won't run a new section of code until it passes the Turbo Debugger crash test.

Reduced portability   By nature, assembly language is tied to the CPU for which a program is designed. Assembly language instructions translate directly to machine code and, therefore, will run only on computers using a compatible CPU. *Porting* (transferring) an assembly language program from one computer to another with a different processor usually means starting over from scratch. I have to agree with this gripe. To gain the advantages of assembly language, you must give up the ability to port programs easily to other systems. You can't have it both ways.

Absence of library routines   All high-level languages have commands to perform common jobs such as displaying strings, printing text, and processing disk files. Also, high-level languages let you write mathematical expressions such as (x * 2 + 8). Assembly language lacks such niceties, requiring you to write custom code for these and other tasks. While this fact is true, the argument misses the primary point of gaining total control over a computer's resources compared with giving up that control to a high-level language's run-time library—the opportunity to achieve optimum efficiency and top speed. Furthermore, many assembly language libraries are available containing routines to perform typical high-level operations. You may have to work a little harder, but there's nothing you can do in a high-level language that you cannot do in assembly. Besides, if you must use certain features in C or Pascal, you can always combine high-level languages with assembly language, as chapters 12 and 13 explain.

Hardware Requirements

To make the best use of this book, at a minimum you should have the following equipment:

▷ IBM PC, XT, AT, PS/2, or compatible

▷ 384K memory (256K if you don't use Turbo Debugger)

▷ One or two floppy disk drives

▷ Monochrome or color display

For simplicity, I'll use *PC* to refer to this basic system, which is perfectly suitable for entering and running all of the examples in this book. You'll probably find the going easier if you also have any of the following optional equipment:

▷ Printer

▷ Hard disk drive

▷ Additional memory

Almost all the programs in this book will run on any IBM computer with an 8086, 8088, 80286, or 80386 processor. A few programs in chapter 11 require an 80286 or 80386.

Note: For simplicity, I frequently refer to the "8086 processor" and discuss "8086 programming" methods. Except where specifically noted, such references apply equally to the logically equivalent 8088 and to the newer 80286 and 80386 processors—all of which recognize the same 8086 instruction set. Some books, tutorials, and articles use terms such as *80x86, 8086/88,* and *iAPX-86* to refer to the family of Intel processors found in all PCs. This book uses the simpler *8086* instead.

Software Requirements

In addition to the required hardware listed in the previous sections, at a minimum you need to have the following software:

▶ Turbo Assembler 1.0 and Turbo Debugger 1.0

▶ DOS 2.0 or a later version

For entering program listings, you also need a text editor, which is not supplied with Turbo Assembler. You can use EDLIN as explained in your DOS manuals, although there are far better choices than this ancient, line-oriented editor, designed more for dumb terminals than sophisticated PC displays. Any one of the following editors will work just fine:

▶ The editor in Turbo Pascal, C, BASIC, or Prolog

▶ Brief

▶ VEdit Plus

▶ ME (Microsoft Editor)

▶ Epsilon

▶ WordStar (in nondocument mode)

▶ SideKick or SideKick Plus notepad

▶ Microstar from the Turbo Pascal Editor Toolbox

If you have Turbo Pascal, C, or any other Borland language, use the editor built into the integrated version of your compiler. You can also use any plain ASCII text editor, but don't use a word processor such as WordPerfect, which adds formatting codes to text.

After entering each program, use your editor's "exit-to-DOS" command to return to the DOS prompt and then follow the instructions listed and explained before each program example. After assembling and experimenting with the program, type EXIT and press Enter to return to editing. If your text editor lacks a similar command to return to DOS, you'll have to quit the program, assemble, and then reload your editor to enter the next example. Some editors such as Brief can run Turbo Assembler directly, but you still have to exit to DOS to run the resulting programs.

To more easily return from DOS to editing, you can program a function key to type the EXIT command. I do this by including the following lines in my AUTOEXEC.BAT file in my disk's root directory:

```
echo on
prompt $e[0;66;"Exit";13p
prompt $p$g
```

You could also insert these lines into another batch file, which you can then run before each session with Turbo Assembler. The `prompt` statements program function key F8 to issue the EXIT command. To use this idea, you must load the driver ANSI.SYS from your DOS disks. Assuming this file is in the directory C:\DOS, insert the following line in your root directory's CONFIG.SYS file:

```
DEVICE=C:\DOS\ANSI.SYS
```

How to Use This Book

Beginners should read this book from front to back. The text and program examples were carefully selected to avoid using terms not yet introduced. If you read chapters out of order, be aware that many program examples use the modules introduced earlier. For example, you won't be able to run all the programs in chapter 9 before entering the modules from previous chapters. To find hints about specific topics, refer to the table of contents, the program index, and the subject index.

About the Chapters   Each chapter in this book follows the same general organization, designed so that you can use the book both as a tutorial and as a reference. A shaded flyleaf page lists the chapter's major topics. Chapters begin with a section titled "In This Chapter," forming a terse but detailed reference to the subjects covered in the chapter. Following this comes the chapter text, which ends with a summary, plus a list of at least ten exercises to test your knowledge and, except for this chapter, at least six projects. Answers to all exercises are included near the back of the book.

The book is divided into three parts. Part I, Programming with Assembly Language, is a tutorial on 8086 assembly language. Part II, Multilanguage Programming, describes how to add assembly language to Turbo Pascal and Turbo C, emphasizing optimization techniques. Part III, Reference, lists processor and Turbo Assembler instructions. The following notes briefly describe each chapter.

▶ Chapter 1, *Introduction,* introduces concepts of assembly language programming, explains how to use this book, and makes other suggestions, as you no doubt know if you've read this far!

▶ Chapter 2, *First Steps,* describes the parts of an assembly language program, gets you started using Turbo Assembler and Turbo Debugger commands, and explains how to create .EXE and .COM code files on disk.

▶ Chapter 3, *A Bit of Binary,* reviews the basics of the binary number system, concentrating on concepts that are vital in assembly language programming. Beginners: Don't skip this chapter! Experts: Skim the material for a quick refresher.

▶ Chapter 4, *Programming in Assembly Language,* explores the difficult subject of memory segmentation and introduces most of the 8086 instruction set.

▶ Chapter 5, *Simple Data Structures,* explains addressing modes and shows how to reserve memory for variables. You'll also learn how to use the TLIB utility program to construct a library file containing this book's modules, required by examples in future chapters.

▶ Chapter 6, *Complex Data Structures,* expands on the topics introduced in chapter 5, showing how to create advanced multifield structures, unions, arrays, and packed bit-field records.

▶ Chapter 7, *Input and Output,* gives advice on reading the keyboard and writing text to the standard output file (usually the display) from assembly language. Some examples call DOS and ROM BIOS routines for these tasks. Others show how to improve display performance by writing directly to video RAM buffers.

▶ Chapter 8, *Macros and Conditional Assembly,* explains how to combine repetitive instructions into macros, adding custom commands to assembly language. Also discussed are conditional assembly techniques for writing multipurpose programs that assemble differently on demand.

▶ Chapter 9, *Disk-File Processing,* covers assembly language techniques for creating, reading, and writing file data stored on disk. Reading disk directories is also explained.

▶ Chapter 10, *Interrupt Handling,* dives into the intricate and often confusing subjects of writing interrupt service routines, tapping into the PC timer, and accessing serial I/O ports.

▶ Chapter 11, *Advanced Topics,* discusses some of the less frequently used (and, perhaps, poorly understood) 8086 instructions, and explains how to use special 80286 and 80386 registers and features.

▶ Chapter 12, *Optimizing Pascal with Assembly Language,* unravels the tricky secrets of mixing assembly language with Turbo Pascal, with the goal of optimizing program performance.

▶ Chapter 13, *Optimizing C with Assembly Language,* shows how to mix assembly language with Turbo C, emphasizing optimization as in chapter 12.

▶ Chapter 14, *8086/88, 80286, 80386 Reference Guide,* is an alphabetic reference to the instruction sets for these four processors (excluding protected-mode instructions, not used in application programming).

▶ Chapter 15, *Turbo Assembler Reference,* lists the syntax for 8086, 80286, and 80386 non-protected-mode instructions and Turbo Assembler's predefined symbols, operators, MASM- and Ideal-mode equivalents, and directives.

About the Modules   Many of the programs are constructed as separate modules, which you can assemble and store in a library file for other programs to share. Instructions are given for creating and using a suggested library file named MTA.LIB, but feel free to store the modules in another file if you prefer.

A program index at the front of this book lists all the program examples, demonstrations, shells (ready for filling with your own code), Pascal and C external routines, macros, and other files. In addition to the book's many tested examples, major library modules include:

▶ STRINGS.ASM: package of ASCIIZ string subroutines

▶ STRIO.ASM: routines for reading and writing ASCIIZ strings

▶ BINASC.ASM: conversion utilities for strings and numbers

▶ SCREEN.ASM: memory-mapped video procedures

▶ KEYBOARD.ASM: routines for reading key presses including function keys

▶ DOSMACS.ASM: macros for calling DOS functions

▶ DISKERR.ASM: routines for deciphering disk errors

▶ PARAMS.ASM: routines to read DOS command-line parameters

▶ ASYNCH.ASM: interrupt-driven serial I/O routines

How to Organize Your Disks

Floppy-Disk Systems

Follow the installation instructions in the Turbo Assembler and Turbo Debugger User Guides to prepare your boot disks. Depending on your disk drive's capacity, you may be able to create one boot disk containing both the assembler and debugger, or you may have to create two disks, one for each. Either setup will work. Install your text editor on the same disk as the assembler. Also format one or two blank disks for storing the programs you enter. When one disk becomes full, start another. Be conscious of DOS limitations on the number of files in a directory. You may run into this limit with assembly language, which tends to generate lots of short disk files, long before you run out of disk space.

If you have two floppy-disk drives, create or edit a plain ASCII text file called AUTOEXEC.BAT on each boot disk. Into this file, insert the line:

```
PATH=A:\;B:\
```

This tells DOS to look for files in both drives A: and B:, no matter which drive is current. With this setup, you can type B: and press Enter to make B: the current drive but still run programs stored in drive A:. You don't have to preface the program name with a drive letter and a colon. The only disadvantage is that you must be sure to have formatted disks in all drives at all times, or you may receive a "Not ready" error. If this happens, press R to Retry after inserting a disk into the drive.

> Note: In chapter 5, you begin storing separate modules in a library file named MTA.LIB. Floppy-disk users may find it easiest to store this file on the disk that contains the Turbo Linker, TLINK.EXE. In that case, change all *MTA* references to *d:MTA*, where *d* is the disk-drive letter.

Hard-Disk Systems

Follow the installation instructions in the Turbo Assembler and Turbo Debugger User Guides to prepare subdirectories on your disk containing the necessary files to run the assembler and debugger. In your root directory, usually C:\, insert the following line into your AUTOEXEC.BAT text file:

```
PATH=C:\DOS;C:\TASM;C:\TDEBUG
```

Replace TASM and TDEBUG with the subdirectory names you specified during installation. The reference to C:\DOS assumes that you store miscellaneous DOS utility programs such as XCOPY in this directory. The PATH list lets you change to another directory with the DOS CD command and still be able run the assembler, debugger, and other programs by simply entering the program names.

It's probably best to store this book's examples in a single subdirectory named MTA (or any other name you like). Later, you can transfer individual programs and modules to separate directories. To create the subdirectory, assuming your disk drive is labeled C:, issue the DOS commands:

```
c:
cd \
md mta
cd mta
```

Entering Program Listings

Using your favorite text editor, enter the example programs exactly as printed, except for the numbers and colons at the left. *These numbers are for reference only—don't type them.* Try to match the indentations in the listings. You don't have to indent every line exactly as printed, but you should try to keep the columns aligned more or less as they are in the book. Use your editor's tab key to save typing time.

Programs were fully tested on at least two and sometimes four different computers. The program listings were inserted directly into the text for typesetting, and then, after editing, copied out of these files and assembled again to ensure that no lines or characters were accidentally dropped. In addition, many pairs of eyes have carefully scrutinized every line for errors; therefore, I can say with near 100% certainty that if you type the programs correctly, they *will* assemble.

Each example program is numbered by chapter (1-5, 4-3, etc.) with the name of the disk file shown next to the program number (BINASC.ASM, ASYNCH.ASM, etc.). Save each program with the suggested disk-file name. Some programs depend on these file names; therefore, if you change the name of one program file, you may have difficulty running other programs later.

Note: For those who don't relish typing thousands of lines of code, a disk containing this book's programs is available. See the order form inside the back cover for details on how you can purchase a copy.

Getting More Help

If you need more help, if you have a burning question, if you find a mistake (horrors!) in this book, what should you do? First, don't panic. Second, don't phone. Sorry, but if I took the time to speak to all who telephone, I'd never get books like this one finished. That doesn't mean I don't want to hear from you. I love to receive letters from readers, and I always write back. Limit your questions to one or two, but don't send disks—I can't return them. If you want to get in touch, here's how:

▶ Write to Swan Software, P.O. Box 206, Lititz, PA 17543

▶ Or send an MCI-Mail or BIX electronic letter to TSWAN

▶ Or send Compuserve Email to 73627,3241

Summary

The purpose of this book is to guide you through the often difficult world of assembly language programming for IBM PCs and compatibles running DOS. Learning assembly language does not have to be difficult, despite what you may have heard. This book's many examples and topics will help you to acquire programming skills that even many professional programmers lack. The published programs are modular and well tested, and many can be extracted for use in your own work.

Assembly language is a convenient method for writing machine-code programs. Although early programmers wrote computer programs directly in low-level machine code, few programmers would do the same today. Assembly is one step above machine code, while C, Pascal, BASIC, Prolog, and others are high-level languages. Because assembly language is closely tied to the machine code of the computer processor, a good way to learn assembly language programming is to develop useful mental models of the computer's inner workings. Also, using Turbo Debugger as a teaching tool helps explain how assembly language programs operate.

Turbo Assembler runs in two modes, MASM and Ideal. The example programs in this book are all written in Ideal mode, superior in many ways to the older MASM syntax.

Assembly language—like all computer languages—has its advantages and disadvantages. The major advantages are the promise of extra speed plus the ability to program the computer's processor directly. The major disadvantage is that assembly language programs will run only on the processor for which they are written.

Line numbers added to all example programs in this book are purely for reference. When entering listings, don't type the numbers and colons.

Exercises

1-1. Why is "machine language" an improper term?

1-2. What is meant by the terms "high level" and "low level" in describing computer languages?

1-3. What is the major difference between a high-level language and assembly language?

1-4. Why don't programmers write software directly in machine code anymore? Why do you think they ever did?

1-5. How can a debugger help you to learn assembly language?

1-6. What is a register?

1-7. What is a flag?

1-8. What are some of the advantages of Turbo Assembler's Ideal mode?

1-9. What are the main advantages of programming in assembly language?

1-10. What are the main disadvantages of programming in assembly language?

Chapter **2 *First Steps***

Chapter *2* *First Steps*

In This Chapter

The parts of an assembly language program; all about labels, mnemonics, operands, and comments; how to assemble a program; what the linker does; dealing with errors; introducing Turbo Debugger; making .COM and .EXE code files; how to create and print listing files

Assembly Language: Parts and Pieces

Assembly language is an odd-looking computer language. The program source-code text is sprinkled with three- and four-character unpronounceable words like cli, movsb, and sbb, appearing to the untrained eye to follow no preplanned order or to have any relationship with one another. And no matter how long you stare at the programmer's comments—the text preceded by semicolons at the ends of most assembly language lines—the words often seem to have no connection with the program's instructions.

One reason for this apparent (but deceiving) disarray is the lack of built-in control structures in assembly language. There are no REPEAT-UNTIL or WHILE constructions to group repetitive actions. There are no IF-THEN-ELSE or CASE statements to make decisions, and there is no assignment symbol to initialize named variables. Performing such high-level actions requires you to construct programs from a single set of low-level machine-code instructions, giving the assembly language source-code text a homogenized sameness that tends to hide the inner meaning of what the program is doing. Also, assembly language is line oriented, not statement oriented as are C, Pascal, and BASIC. Consequently, many lines of code are usually needed to perform even simple operations like adding numbers or initializing variables.

There is order in the apparent jumble, however. Even though Turbo Assembler permits programmers to organize their code in numerous styles, most assembly language programs naturally divide into five main sections: *header, equates, data, body,* and *closing.* (These are my own terms, by the way—there are no standard names for the parts of an assembly language program.) The *header* contains setup information. The *equates* area declares symbols to which you assign various expressions and constant values. The *data* section declares variables to be stored in memory. The *body* contains the actual program code. The *closing* marks the end of the source code text. Let's examine each of these parts more closely.

The Header   The header begins an assembly language program. In the header are various commands and directives, none of which produces any machine code in the final product. The header instructs the assembler to perform certain actions, generating the finished code file according to various options at your disposal.

Figure 2-1 shows a sample header, similar to the header at the beginning of most example programs in this book. (This isn't a complete program—so don't bother trying to assemble it.) The optional %TITLE line describes the purpose of the program, causing the text between quotes to print at the top of each listing page—that is, if you ask Turbo Assembler to print a listing. The IDEAL directive switches on Turbo Assembler's Ideal mode. Leave this out to assemble a program written in Microsoft Macro Assembler (MASM) syntax.

```
%TITLE "Test Header--Don't Assemble!"
IDEAL
DOSSEG
MODEL    small
STACK    256
```

Figure 2-1 *Typical assembly language header.*

Introducing Memory Models

The DOSSEG directive in Figure 2-1 tells the assembler how to order the program's segments—areas in memory addressed by segment registers, a subject you'll learn more about in later chapters. If you don't understand what segments are, for now, just think of them as variable-size chunks of memory assigned a specific purpose. You can choose to order a program's segments in different ways, although knowing the actual segment order is rarely as important as many programmers believe. In my programming, I almost always let the assembler figure out the segment order in memory, letting me concentrate more on what the program does. I suggest you do the same, using the DOSSEG directive to store segments in memory in the same order used by most high-level languages.

Next comes the MODEL directive, optionally preceded by DOSSEG. MODEL selects one of several memory models (see Table 2-1), most of which are used only when combining assembly language with Pascal or C. In stand-alone assembly language programming, the *small* model is usually the best choice. But don't be fooled by the name. The *small*-memory model gives you up to 64K of code plus another 64K of data for a total maximum program size of 128K—practically a bottomless pit in the memory-efficient world of machine code.

The STACK directive in Figure 2-1 reserves space for the program's stack, an area of memory that stores two kinds of data: values temporarily

Table 2-1 *Memory Models*

Name	Description
tiny	Code, data, and stack in one 64K segment. Subroutine calls and data references are near. Use for .COM programs only.
small	Code and data in separate 64K segments. Subroutine calls and data references are near. Use for small- to medium-size .EXE programs. Best choice for most stand-alone assembly language programs.
medium	Unlimited code size. Data limited to one 64K segment. Subroutine calls are far; data references are near. Use for large programs with minimal data.
compact	Code limited to one 64K segment. Unlimited data size. Subroutine calls are near; data references are far. Use for small- to medium-size programs with many or very large variables.
large	Unlimited code and data sizes. Subroutine calls and data references are far. Use for large program and data storage requirements, as long as no single variable exceeds 64K.
huge	Unlimited code and data size. Subroutine calls and data references are far. Use for largest programs where one or more variables exceed 64K.
tpascal	Assemble with Turbo Pascal segments—similar to small model, but with multiple code segments. Normally not used for stand-alone assembly language programs.

stored by or passed to subroutines and the addresses to which subroutines return control. (Stacks also come into play during interrupts, a subject for chapter 10.) Manipulating the stack is an important assembly language technique, which I'll cover in more detail in the chapters to come. The value after the STACK directive tells Turbo Assembler how many bytes to reserve for the stack segment—256 bytes in Figure 2-1. Most programs require only a small stack, and even the largest programs rarely require more than about 8K.

Equates   After the program header come various constant and variable declarations. In assembly language, constant values are known as *equates,* referring to the EQU directive that associates values with identifiers such as MaxValue and PortAddress. Turbo Assembler allows you to use EQU or, for numeric values only, an equal sign (=).

> Note: Equates may appear anywhere in a program without restriction. To make your programs more readable, however, place most equates just after the program header.

Using equated identifiers instead of "magic" numbers like 0100h and 0B800h lets you refer to expressions, strings, and other values by name, making programs easier to read and modify. (Literal values are magical because of the way they can hide a program's secrets.) Here are a few sample equates that could follow the header in Figure 2-1:

```
Count      EQU   10
Element    EQU   5
Size       =     Count * Element
MyBoat     EQU   "The Ugly Duckling"
Size       =     0
```

Although most equated symbols simply stand in place for their associated values and expressions—similar to the way constants are used in Pascal and C—there are several tricky rules to remember when creating and using assembly language equates:

▶ After declaring a symbol with EQU, you cannot change the symbol's associated value. Redefining an equated symbol (changing Count to 11, for example) is never allowed.

▶ The same rule is not true for symbols declared with an equal sign (=), and you can change these values as often as you like. Notice how the sample equates change the value of Size from 50 to 0. This can be done anywhere in the program, not just in the equate section.

▶ EQU can declare all kinds of equates including numbers, expressions, and character strings. The equal sign (=) can declare only numeric equates, which can be literal values like 10 and 0Fh, or expressions such as Count * Size and Address + 2.

▶ Equated symbols are not variables—neither the symbols nor their associated values are stored in the program's data segment. Assembly language instructions can never assign new values to equated symbols, regardless of whether EQU or = was used to declared the symbols.

▶ Although you can declare equates anywhere in your program, it's usually best to place them near the beginning where they are most visible. An equate buried deeply inside the program's code can easily become the source of a hard-to-find bug.

▶ Expressions declared with EQU are evaluated later when the equated symbol is used in the program. Expressions declared with an equal sign (=) are evaluated at the place where the equated symbol is defined. The assembler stores the equated *text* of EQU symbols but stores only the *value* of = symbols.

This last rule is easier to understand by examining a few more examples. Suppose you have the following three equates:

```
LinesPerPage   =    66
NumPages       =    100
TotalLines     =    LinesPerPage * NumPages
```

Obviously, TotalLines equals the result of multiplying LinesPerPage times NumPages, or 6,600. (As in most computer languages, an asterisk (*) indicates multiplication.) Because TotalLines is declared with the equal sign (=)—indicating a numeric value—the expression is evaluated immediately, associating the result of the expression with TotalLines. If you assign a new value to NumPages later on, the value of TotalLines will not change. A different effect occurs, however, if you declare TotalLines with EQU:

```
TotalLines      EQU  LinesPerPage * NumPages
```

Internally, Turbo Assembler stores the actual text, not the calculated result, of an expression along with all EQU symbols—in this case, the text of the expression LinesPerPage * NumPages. Later in the program when you use TotalLines, the assembler inserts this text as though you had typed those characters at this place in the source code. The expression is then evaluated to produce a final value. If you previously changed one or both of the values in the expression—either NumPages or LinesPerPage—the evaluated result changes accordingly.

This ability to affect the result of equated expressions can be useful. You can program one module with an equated expression that changes value depending on equates in other modules. Be aware of the subtle difference between = equates and those that you create with EQU. This is a feature that can also create bugs if used carelessly.

The Data Segment

A program's data segment usually appears between the equates and the program's instructions. It's possible, but rarely useful, to declare data segments elsewhere and to have multiple data segments strewn throughout the program text. Despite this feature, your assembly language programs will be easier to read and modify if you follow the simpler plan suggested here, declaring all your variables between the equates and code.

Begin your program's data section with the DATASEG directive. This tells the assembler to store variables inside the program's data segment, which can be as large as 64K in the small memory model. The data segment can store two kinds of variables: *initialized* and *uninitialized*. When the program runs, initialized variables have preassigned values, which you specify in the program text and which are stored inside the program's code file on disk. These values are automatically loaded into memory and are readily available when the program runs. Uninitialized variables are identical to initialized variables in every way except that uninitialized variables do not occupy space in the program's code file and, consequently, have unknown values when the program runs. Because of this, declaring a large uninitialized variable—an array of consecutive values or a large buffer to be filled from a disk file, for example—will reduce the size of the program's code file.

> Note: To prevent uninitialized variables from being stored inside the assembled code file, the variables must be declared after the last initialized variable in the program source-code text. Uninitialized variables declared between other initialized variables take up space in the assembled code and needlessly increase the program's code-file size on disk.

Reserving Space for Variables

Although chapter 5 describes in detail how to declare variables in a program's data segment, a few simple examples introduce several important concepts that you need to know now. Here's a typical data segment as it might appear after the program's header and equates:

```
DATASEG
numRows          DB    25
numColumns       DB    80
videoBase        DW    0B00h
```

First comes the DATASEG directive, informing Turbo Assembler to allocate space for the program's data segment. Three variables are then declared: numRows, numColumns, and videoBase. As a rule, I prefer to capitalize my equated constants (Count, NumPages, etc.) and to begin variables with lowercase letters as shown here. This is an arbitrary convention, and you can type symbols in uppercase or lowercase as you prefer. Also, some programmers use underline characters to make multiword identifiers more readable, for example, writing num_rows and video_base instead of the mixed case style shown here.

DB (define byte) and DW (define word) are the two most common directives used to reserve space for a program's variables. You'll use these directives repeatedly. Unlike high-level languages where the actual location of variables in memory is usually unimportant, in assembly language, you must reserve space in memory for your variables and, in the case of uninitialized variables, assign values to that space. Be sure that you understand how this differs from equated symbols, which are associated with values and expressions in the source-code text only. Variables have space reserved in the program's data segment in memory. Equated symbols do not.

The symbols associated with variables—numRows, numColumns, and videoBase in the previous samples—are called *labels*. A label points to the item that it labels—in this case the reserved memory space for a variable's value. Program's can refer to this space by using the label as a *pointer* to the value in memory. In the assembled program, labels are translated to the memory addresses where variables are stored, a process that allows you to address memory by the names you invent rather than by literal memory addresses.

> Note: If you were programming directly in machine code, you would have to specify actual addresses instead of labels. One of assembly language's major advantages is the use of symbolic labels to identify locations in memory.

Variables are guaranteed to follow each other inside the data segment—knowledge that you can use to perform various tricks. For example, these declarations:

```
DATASEG
aTOm        DB    "ABCDEFGHIJKLM"
nTOz        DB    "NOPQRSTUVWXYZ"
```

seem to be creating two character strings labeled aTOm and nTOz. In memory, however, the characters A to Z are stored consecutively, creating one string containing the letters of the alphabet. The label nTOz simply points to the middle of this string—there aren't really two separate entities in memory.

Careful readers may be thinking, "But wait! If DB means 'define byte,' what's it doing declaring character strings?" Good question. DB has the special ability to reserve space for multiple-byte values, from 1 to as many bytes as you need. A string is composed of individual ASCII characters, each occupying 1 byte; therefore, DB is simply assembly language's tool for declaring character strings, which, after all, are merely series of ASCII byte values stored consecutively in memory. You can use DB to declare individual characters and byte values, separated by commas:

```
DATASEG
perfectTen    DB    1, 2, 3, 4, 5, 6, 7, 8, 9, 10
theTime       DB    9, 0        ; i.e., 9:00
theDate       DB    12,15,88 ; i.e., 12/15/1988
```

And, you can also combine character and byte values, creating a two-line string variable with the ASCII codes for carriage return and line feed stuck in between. As the following example shows, you can use either single or double quotes around character strings:

```
combo         DB    'Line #1', 13, 10, "Line #2"
```

Some languages—most notably Pascal—differentiate between single characters and strings of multiple characters. In assembly language, the difference between a character and a string is one of size only. There are no extra values, length bytes, or termination characters in assembly language strings, unless, of course, you put them there.

You'll learn more about strings later when examining assembly language instructions specially designed to manipulate byte strings in memory. For now, remember that, unlike most high-level languages, strings are simply consecutive values in memory, created with the DB directive.

The Program Body

After the data segment comes the program's body, also known as the *code segment*—the memory chunk that contains your program's assembled code. Inside this area, assembly language text lines are further divided into four columns: *label, mnemonic, operand,* and *comment.* Each column has an important function, best described by example. In the program text, by the way, the amount of spacing between columns is not important. Most people align the columns by simply pressing their editor's tab key once or twice.

Note: If your editor allows you to choose between inserting tab control characters and inserting spaces, choose the tab controls and specify tab settings at every eighth column (the default in most editors). Inserting tab control characters makes it easy to keep columns aligned. Many times, with this arrangement, you can edit the text in one column without affecting another's alignment. If you prefer, though, you can insert spaces between columns. Turbo Assembler doesn't care.

Although you haven't met any actual assembly language instructions yet, examine the sample data and code segments in Figure 2-2 and try to pick out the four columns. (This is not a complete program—so don't bother trying to assemble it.) Although short and sweet, the example contains the essential elements of a complete assembly language code segment. To provide some data to use, a data segment also declares a single-byte variable named exitCode, initialized to 0.

After the CODESEG directive in Figure 2-2 are several lines divided into label, mnemonic, operand, and comment columns. In the first column are two labels Start: and Exit:. Labels mark the places in a program to which other instructions and directives refer. Lines that don't need labels have blanks in this column. In the code segment, a label always ends with a colon (:). In the data segment, a label must not end with a colon. (See the exitCode label, for example.) You just have to memorize this rule, which admittedly makes little logical sense.

In the second column are mnemonics, literally "formulas for remembering things." (By the way, the word "mnemonic" has a fascinating history. In Greek mythology, Mnemosyne—pronounced nee-mos'-in-nee—is the goddess of memory, the bride of Zeus, and the mother of the Muses. While trying to memorize assembly language mnemonics, a silent offering to Mnemosyne may not help, but it can't hurt.) Each mnemonic formula in the second column in Figure 2-2 refers to one machine-code instruction—mov for Move, jmp for Jump, and int for Interrupt. Some mnemonics are easy to remember: dec for Decrement, shl for Shift Left, and ror for

```
Label       Mnemonic  Operand        Comment
------------------------------------------------------------------------
            DATASEG
exitCode    DB        0              ; A byte variable
            CODESEG
Start:      mov       ax, @data      ; Initialize DS to address
            mov       ds, ax         ;  of data segment
            jmp       Exit           ; Jump to Exit label
            mov       cx, 10         ; This line is skipped!
Exit:
            mov       ah, 04Ch       ; DOS function: Exit program
            mov       al, [exitCode] ; Return exit code value
            int       21h            ; Call DOS. Terminate program
            END       Start          ; End of program / entry point
```

Figure 2-2 *The four columns of an assembly language program.*

Rotate Right. Others look like the handiwork of a crazed typesetter: jcxz for Jump if cx is Zero, and rcr for Rotate through Carry Right. A few rare cases are actually full-blown words: out for Out, push for Push, and pop for Pop. Even so, as you can clearly see, assembly language is abbreviated to the extreme. It will take time and patience to learn the name and purpose of each mnemonic. You'll meet the full set of mnemonics in chapter 4. Also, chapter 14, the 8086/88, 80286, 80386 Reference Guide, lists every mnemonic along with full names and descriptions of how the associated instructions operate. Refer to these sections often and memorize as many mnemonics as you can. When reading through a program, always pronounce a mnemonic's full name. In time, this will help make assembly language, if not easy reading, at least more understandable.

The third column in Figure 2-2 contains the operands—the values on which the preceding mnemonic instruction operates. A few instructions require no operands and, in these cases, the third column is blank. Many instructions require two operands; others take only one. No 8086 instruction requires more than two operands. The first operand is usually called the *destination*. The second operand (if there is one) is called the *source*. Operands take many forms; therefore, it's best to learn the different forms as you meet each mnemonic instruction.

The fourth and final column is always optional and, if included, must start with a semicolon (;). Turbo Assembler ignores everything from the semicolon to the end of the line, giving you a place to write a short comment describing what this line does. Nearly every line of every example program in this book ends with a comment, which you can leave blank to save typing time if you want. In your own work, be sure to add clear comments that fully describe your program. As you are no doubt beginning to realize, especially if assembly language is new to you, this language is cryptic and hard to read. You can't add too many comments.

A Few Comments on Comments

Sometimes you'll see an assembly language line that begins with a semicolon in the first column. Most programmers write their more lengthy comments this way, identifying various program sections and describing tricky sections. (As with comments at the ends of lines, you can leave these longer comments blank to save typing time when entering this book's examples.) Many programmers begin their programs with a multiline identifying comment like this:

```
;-------------------------------------------------
; PURPOSE: Predict winning lottery numbers
; SYSTEM:  IBM PC / Turbo Assembler Ideal Mode
; AUTHOR:  Ivan the Unlucky
;-------------------------------------------------
```

Another kind of comment exists in MASM mode but, unfortunately, not in Ideal mode. In MASM mode, you can start a large comment with the COMMENT directive, followed by a character called the *comment delimiter,* in turn followed by your comment, and ending with a second instance of the same delimiter. To do this in Ideal mode, temporarily switch to MASM mode:

```
MASM

COMMENT /* This is a comment, which can
stretch over several lines and which you
can easily reformat with your editor's
paragraph command. */

IDEAL
```

After the MASM directive enables MASM mode, the COMMENT directive begins a multiline comment, defining a backslash as the comment delimiter character. A second backslash ends the comment. (The asterisks are purely for show here—I use them only to help my eye pick out comments in the text and to make the comments resemble those in C.) Finally, the IDEAL directive returns Turbo Assembler to Ideal mode. The blank lines after MASM and before IDEAL let me reformat the entire comment block using my editor's reformat-paragraph command, making it easier to edit a lengthy note in the program text. You may want to try this trick if your editor has a similar command.

The Closing   The final part of an assembly language program is the closing, a single line that tells Turbo Assembler it has reached the end of the program. There is only one directive in the closing: END. Repeating the last line from Figure 2-2, a typical closing is:

```
END    Start          ; End of program / entry point
```

The END directive marks the end of the program source-code text. The assembler ignores any text below this line—a good place to stick additional notes, by the way. To the right of END, you must specify the label where you want the program to begin running. Usually, this label should be the same as the label that precedes the first instruction following the CODESEG directive. You can start a program elsewhere, although I can't think of any good reasons for doing so.

Assembling a Program

Now that you know the form of an assembly language program, the next step is to learn how to assemble a program text file to produce a running code file on disk. Use your text editor to type in Program 2-1, FF.ASM. (Remember: Don't type the reference numbers and colons at the left. Type only the text to the right of the colons.) Try to align the four columns similarly to the printed text. You don't have to be too exacting—close is good enough. To save time, leave out the comments. Quit your editor (or temporarily return to DOS if your editor has such a command) and type these lines:

```
tasm ff
tlink ff
```

The `tasm` command runs Turbo Assembler, which reads FF.ASM and, provided you entered the program text correctly, creates a new file FF.OBJ, containing the assembled code in raw form—not yet ready to run. If you receive any errors, check your typing and try again. The `tlink` command runs the Turbo Linker, which reads FF.OBJ and creates the executable code file FF.EXE. Notice that neither command requires you to type the file name extension (.ASM or .OBJ). You can type these extensions if you want, but why work harder than necessary?

Now turn on your printer. (If you don't have a printer, you can't use this program. Sorry!) Type FF at the DOS prompt and press Enter to send a form-feed command to the printer, advancing the paper to the next page. Copy FF.EXE to the directory where you store your other utilities and run this program instead of reaching for your printer's form-feed button. (My printer is across the room, and I originally wrote FF years ago so I wouldn't have to get out of my chair just to advance the paper. So call me lazy.)

Program 2-1 *FF.ASM*

```
 1:   %TITLE "Send Form-Feed Command to Printer"
 2:
 3:           IDEAL
 4:           DOSSEG
 5:           MODEL   small
 6:           STACK   256
 7:
 8:   ;-----  Equates
 9:
10:   ASCIIcr         EQU     13          ; ASCII carriage return
11:   ASCIIff         EQU     12          ; ASCII form-feed control code
12:
13:           CODESEG
14:
15:   Start:
16:           mov     ax, @data           ; Initialize ds to address
17:           mov     ds, ax              ;  of data segment
18:
19:           mov     dl, ASCIIcr         ; Assign cr code to dl
20:           mov     ah, 05h             ; DOS function: Printer output
21:           int     21h                 ; Call DOS--carriage return
22:
23:           mov     dl, ASCIIff         ; Assign ff code to dl
24:           mov     ah, 05h             ; DOS function: Printer output
25:           int     21h                 ; Call DOS--form feed
26:
27:   Exit:
28:           mov     ax, 04C00h          ; DOS function: Exit program
29:           int     21h                 ; Call DOS. Terminate program
30:
31:           END     Start               ; End of program / entry point
```

Understanding Object Code

Program 2-1 requires two steps—assembling and linking—to translate an assembly language program from text form into an executable program. Turbo Assembler never directly creates a program in ready-to-run form but instead generates an intermediate file containing the assembled program in a form called the *object code.* Before you can run the program, you must further process the object code with a linker, which creates the executable .EXE file on disk.

For simple programs, this may seem like two steps too many, but there is a good reason for dividing the process into assembly and link steps. As you will learn in later chapters, Turbo Linker (as well as other linkers) can combine multiple object-code files to produce a single executable program. This ability lets you program a large project in small pieces, assemble the pieces to create separate object-code files, and then link all the pieces with one command. The individual pieces, or modules, can share data and call subroutines declared in other modules. Most programmers build libraries of assembled object-code modules, collecting their favorite and well-tested building blocks, ready for constructing new programs. For some strange reason, in many high-level languages, writing programs in separate pieces this way is difficult and requires unusual commands and other incantations to get the job done. Luckily, as you will see, linking separately assembled object-code modules created by Turbo Assembler is simple.

Inside the object-code file are the machine-code instructions, translated from your assembly language text. Also in the object code are various text symbols that you want to share with other modules plus optional information that Turbo Debugger requires. It's not necessary to understand every last detail of what's inside an object-code file. Just be aware that Turbo Assembler creates this file, always ending in .OBJ, and never directly creates the finished executable code. Only Turbo Linker can do that.

By the way, Turbo Assembler's object-code files end in the standard .OBJ, and you can link these files with other linkers (such as the one supplied on your DOS disks) and with object-code files produced by languages from other companies (for example, Microsoft C). You can, of course, link Turbo Assembler's object-code files with those produced by other Turbo Languages. Always use Turbo Linker for this purpose.

Note: In the future, carefully read your User's Guide and README file on disk for notes concerning compatibility between Turbo Linker and other linkers. Object-code file formats are constantly evolving, and anything I say here may be out of date six months from now.

Command-Line Options

Both Turbo Assembler and Turbo Linker allow you to specify options on the command line to select various features during assembling and linking.

Type `tasm` and press Enter to list Turbo Assembler's command-line options. Type `tlink` and press Enter to list Turbo Linker's command-line options.

Options are represented by one or two letters, sometimes followed by other information. To select an option, type a dash and the option letter or letters between the `tasm` or `tlink` commands and the file name of the program you are assembling or linking. For example, to assemble Program 2-1 and create a listing file, use the command:

```
tasm -l ff
```

You can type this and all other command lines in uppercase or lowercase. You can also use a forward slash instead of a dash if you prefer. The option `-l` tells Turbo Assembler to generate a listing file in addition to assembling the program, creating both FF.OBJ and FF.LST on disk. Try this command and then examine FF.LST with your text editor. Inside, you'll find a complete listing of the program along with line numbers, the object-code bytes, and, at the end, a listing of the program's symbols. You might want to print a copy of this file for reference.

> Note: Don't create a listing file every time you assemble a program—this can slow even the speedy Turbo Assembler to a crawl. Most programmers create and print a listing file only after finishing a program or, sometimes, when a problem develops and they want to examine the object code that the assembler creates.

When assembling a program, you can string multiple command-line letters together, optionally separated by spaces. Here are a few more samples:

```
tasm /h
tasm -l-c ff
tasm /l /c ff
tasm -zi ff
tasm -l -iC:\INCLUDES ff
```

Try these on your system. Instead of assembling a program, the first command tells Turbo Assembler to display a list of command options. For a printed reference, type `tasm /h >prn`. The second line creates a listing file with cross-referenced line numbers (#10, #25, etc.) at the end. The third command does the same but shows how to use slashes instead of dashes to specify the option letters. The fourth line adds to FF.OBJ information for Turbo Debugger. The last line creates a listing file and specifies a path name for include files. (Include files are separate text files that you want Turbo Assembler to insert into your program. Program 2-1 doesn't use any include files; therefore, this sample command has no practical effect.)

Turbo Linker also has various command-line options given in the same way, except that you must use a slash—a dash will not work. (Software specifications change, however, and this is the kind of detail that may be different in a future version of the linker. You can always try to use dashes—someday, they may work!) Here are several examples of Turbo Linker command-line options:

```
tlink /v ff
tlink /m/l ff
tlink /x ff
```

The first line gives the /v option to prepare FF.EXE for use with Turbo Debugger. The second line specifies two options, selecting an extended map file (saved to FF.MAP on disk) and adding to this file additional line number information (/l). After trying this command, examine FF.MAP with your text editor. The third line tells Turbo Linker not to create a map file, saving a small amount of disk space and a tiny bit of time during linking. Use this command if you don't need the map file, which shows the memory organization of the program and is generally used by debuggers and as part of a program's documentation.

Dealing with Errors

If to err is human, programmers must be superhuman beings. No matter how careful we are, no matter how diligent, we all make plenty of mistakes in our day-to-day work. But you can't fool Turbo Assembler. At least, you can't force the assembler to accept an illegal construction. If you try—whether intentionally or not—you'll receive an error message, a warning, or both. The distinction between errors and warnings is important:

▶ Errors are fatal. The resulting object code—if created—will not link and will not run.

▶ Warnings are not fatal. The resulting object code probably will link but may or may not run correctly.

Let's make a few intentional errors now so you'll know how to deal with your own mistakes later on. If you're using an editor such as Brief that can automatically run Turbo Assembler, press the Alt-F10 keys to assemble the next few examples. The error message will then appear at the bottom of your screen, and the cursor will rest on the offending line. If you are assembling by typing commands at the DOS prompt, you'll have to reload the program text, fix the error, exit to DOS, and try again.

When it finds an error, Turbo Assembler displays an error message along with the line number in parentheses. Some programmers save these messages in a disk file or print them for reference, using commands such as:

```
tasm ff>err.txt        (save errors in err.txt)
tasm ff>prn            (send errors to printer)
```

Without the redirection symbol (>) and a file name, error messages appear on screen. Unless the errors scrolled off screen, you can still print a copy of the display by pressing your Shift and PrtScr keys. To experiment with errors, copy FF.ASM (Program 2-1) to a new file, FF2.ASM. Then modify line 3 to read `IDEA.` (Remove the capital L.) Because Turbo Assembler has no idea what an `IDEA` is, assembling the program produces:

```
Assembling file:   FF2.ASM
**Error** FF2.ASM(3) Illegal instruction
Error messages:    1
Warning messages:  None
Remaining memory:  432k
```

The error message after the "Assembling file . . ." line tells you in which file the error occurred, shows the line number in parentheses, and gives a brief message about the error. If you need more help, look up the error message in the alphabetized list near the end of your Turbo Assembler Reference Guide. Changing `IDEA` back to `IDEAL` fixes the mistake. Do that and then make another error, deleting the colon from the `Start` label at line 15. Assembling this file produces:

```
Assembling file:   FF2.ASM
**Error** FF2.ASM(15) Illegal instruction
**Error** FF2.ASM(31) Undefined symbol: START
Error messages:    2
Warning messages:  None
Remaining memory:  432k
```

Although you've made only one mistake, Turbo Assembler displays two error messages, one at line 15 because of the missing colon, and another at line 31, which refers to the `Start` label. Because the first error makes the `Start` label unrecognizable—labels in the code segment must end with colons, remember—the later reference also fails. This is an example of *error propagation:* one error causing others to occur or to propagate. In a large program, the little buggers can sometimes propagate all over the place. If this happens, and especially if you suddenly begin receiving errors in sections that previously assembled just fine, try fixing only the first couple of reported errors and reassemble. Often, the remaining errors will then be gone.

Returning to our mistake-ridden example, replace the colon at the end of line 15. Then, add to line 14 the two words `PROC DUMMY.` Don't worry what this means. I just want to show you something. Assembling the program now gives:

```
Assembling file:   FF2.ASM
*Warning* FF.ASM(31) Open procedure: DUMMY
Error messages:    None
Warning messages:  1
Remaining memory:  432k
```

Similar to an error message, a warning tells you something is wrong at a certain line. Notice that, in this case, the reported line number is 31, not 14 as you might have expected. A `PROC` directive specifies the start of a *procedure,* a group of instructions that your program treats as a complete routine. Turbo Assembler expects all **PROC** directives to have matching **ENDP** (End Procedure) directives. Because it finds no such directive by the time it reaches the end of the program, the assembler warns you that a procedure was left open somewhere.

Because this is a warning and not an error, you can link and run the resulting program. In this case, the nonexistent open procedure does no harm. In fact, there is no effect whatsoever on the resulting code. This may not always be true, however, and you are living dangerously if you ignore Turbo Assembler's warnings. For example, a missing **ENDP** may result from leaning on your text editor's delete-line key—or perhaps you accidentally left a procedure unfinished. Turbo Assembler is very forgiving of such errors, giving you the freedom in many cases to make gross mistakes— the price you pay for the low-level access and potential speed available only in pure assembly language. The assembler is smart enough to warn you about potential dangers, but intimate knowledge of your program is still the only way to know for certain whether a warning is significant or can be safely ignored.

Note: If you've been following along, you can delete your FF2.* test files now. You won't need them again.

Introducing Turbo Debugger

Although you can fix syntax errors by reading Turbo Assembler's error messages and then examining your text to find typos and illegal constructions, fixing logical errors is not so easy. Turbo Assembler knows how to assemble a syntactically correct program, but it doesn't understand what the program is supposed to do. Often, your programs will not do what you think they should. In this event, you can get some much needed help from a program specifically designed to help you find and repair logical errors: Turbo Debugger.

Like all debuggers, Turbo Debugger serves as a kind of supervisor, taking control of a program and letting you examine variables in memory and run the code in slow motion. You can tell Turbo Debugger to run a program up to a certain point or until a certain event occurs. You can change values in memory, temporarily try out new instructions, and change register and flag values. You can also use Turbo Debugger to program in machine code, occasionally useful for trying out ideas as long as the number of instructions is not too large.

Such a versatile program is extremely helpful in assembly language programming, where a program's logic is difficult to discern from the program's text. Turbo Debugger can also help you to find errors in Turbo C and Turbo Pascal programs, although we'll concentrate here on assembly language debugging. As I mentioned in chapter 1, Turbo Debugger also makes an excellent teacher, giving you the opportunity to examine your program and observe the effects of various instructions. One of the best ways to learn about individual mnemonic instructions is to write a short test program, load the program into Turbo Debugger, and examine the results in slow motion. If you make the effort to do this every time you have a question about a certain instruction, you'll be amazed at the amount of information you'll pick up just by watching the instruction in action.

Debugging with an 80386 Processor

If your system has an 80386 processor, you can take advantage of special features in Turbo Debugger. If your system has an 8086, 8088, or 80286 processor, you can't use these special features. Even so, Turbo Debugger is a powerful program, having many commands that you can use to debug programs on any PC. If your system does have an 80386, or if you have an installed 80386 circuit board, insert the following command in your root directory's CONFIG.SYS file, specifying the correct path name to locate the TDH386.SYS device driver file:

```
DEVICE=\TDEBUG\TDH386.SYS
```

This enables Turbo Debugger to use special debugging registers available only inside the 80386 processor. These registers give Turbo Debugger the ability to stop a program when any bytes in a specified memory range are changed or even if these bytes are merely examined by a program. You can also run your program in virtual memory, exactly simulating how your program will run as a stand-alone DOS application. Without an 80386, your program necessarily shares memory with the debugger. As a result, some bugs—especially those that depend on the program's location in memory—may disappear under control of the debugger and then reappear when running the program normally, a tricky problem that can be difficult to fix.

With the device driver installed, you can use the virtual-memory version of Turbo Debugger TD386.EXE in place of the standard version TD.EXE. (You can still use the standard version.) Whenever this book tells you to type TD, type TD386 instead.

Turbo Debugger as Teacher

To demonstrate how to use Turbo Debugger as an assembly language teacher, let's examine Program 2-1 under control of the debugger. First, copy FF.ASM to LF.ASM and load the copy into your text editor. Then change three lines as follows:

```
1: %TITLE "Send line feed command to printer"
11: ASCIIlf    EQU  10        ; ASCII line feed control code
23:       mov  dl,ASCIIlf      ; Assign lf code to dl
```

These modifications convert the form-feed program into a line-feed program, which you can use to advance your printer one line at a time. This may not be that useful of a utility program to keep around, but these changes will save paper for the upcoming tests.

After saving LF.ASM, assemble and link the program with options that add debugging information to the .OBJ and .EXE files. This information tells Turbo Debugger about the program's symbols, locations of variables, segment organization, and so on. Type these commands to prepare the program for debugging:

```
tasm /zi lf
tlink /v lf
```

If you don't use the /zi and /v options as shown here, Turbo De-bugger can still load your program, but the debugger will be able to show only the disassembled machine code. With the command-line options, the debugger can show labels, variable structures, source-code lines, and other information. In future example programs, whenever I suggest examining a program with the debugger, use these same options during assembly and linking.

> Note: Using the /zi and /v options can greatly increase the size of a program's .OBJ and .EXE disk files. After debugging, reassemble and link without these options to shrink disk-file sizes back to normal.

After assembling and linking with the /zi and /v options, make sure you have at least the LF.ASM and LF.EXE files on disk and then load the program under Turbo Debugger's control with the command:

```
td lf
```

Remember: If you installed the TDH386.SYS device driver and have an 80386 processor in your system, you can use the virtual-memory version of Turbo Debugger by giving the alternate command:

```
td386 lf
```

In a moment, you should see Turbo Debugger's display, showing the program's source code. (If Turbo Debugger can't find the program's .ASM file, it will be unable to display the source-code window.) Use the cursor keys to move the flashing cursor up and down, examining the program text. You can also use the PgUp, PgDn, Home, and End keys to move around in the source-code window. You can only view this text; you can't edit any mistakes you may find. To do that, you have to quit Turbo De-bugger and use your text editor.

> Note: For more help, press F1 (the Help key) and read the window that pops up on screen. At any time when using Turbo Debugger, you can get help on the current window by pressing F1.

For a different view of your program, press Alt-V-C, selecting the View-CPU-Window command. Press F5 to toggle this window to full screen. The CPU window shows your program's source code in an abbreviated form, the actual machine code as stored in memory, the values of registers and flags, and a dump of the memory bytes. Besides showing many more details, there's an important difference between this window and the previous one. In the source-code window, you are seeing a copy of the program text. In the CPU window, you are peering directly into memory, seeing the actual byte values that are there. The CPU window takes you on a kind of fantastic voyage, miniaturized in the style of an Isaac Asimov novel and injected into your computer's RAM. Naturally, when performing surgery on bytes in memory, you want to be careful not to kill the patient. Turbo Debugger helps prevent catastrophes, but you can still get into trouble by fooling around indiscriminately.

Press the cursor up and down keys to move the highlighted bar to different instructions. Diamonds mark the instructions that belong to your program. Notice that, unlike the source-code window, you can view other areas outside of these marked lines. Press the Tab key to move the cursor to other sections of the CPU window. You'll do this from time to time to change register values and to modify bytes in memory. (Don't change anything this time.)

Press the Tab key until the highlighted bar reappears in the large section. To change the appearance of this window, press Alt-F10 and select the Mixed command (press M or move the bar to Mixed and press Enter). You can give this same command more easily by pressing Ctrl-M, too. The command has three settings: No, Yes, and Both. The settings change the view of your program as follows:

▶ **No** shows a disassembly of the machine-code bytes in memory, looking similar to assembly language instructions. It is convenient for viewing code when you don't have the corresponding .ASM file. This view is less cluttered than the others, and, for that reason, many prefer it.

▶ **Yes** shows your source code along with the disassembled machine code. It is used to display high-level language lines along with the compiled machine code. Normally, you won't use this setting to view assembly language programs.

▶ **Both** is the default and probably the best view in the CPU window, showing the machine-code bytes in the left column along with the source-code lines that created the code. It doesn't display blank lines.

Besides showing you different views of your program and memory, Turbo Debugger can execute your code in various ways. For practice, turn on your printer (if you have one) and then follow these numbered steps to execute the program under Turbo Debugger's control:

1. Press F9 to run the program to completion. The paper should advance one line. Use this command to run a program and then examine the state of memory, registers, and flags after the program finishes.

2. After running the program, press Ctrl-F2 to reset. This reloads the program from disk, resetting Turbo Debugger to its original start-up condition. (If you forget this step and press F9 to run

again, you'll see a message asking if you want to reload the program.)

3. Press F6 twice to get back to the source-code window.

4. Press Alt-V-R to select the View-Registers command. If necessary, press the Scroll Lock key and use the arrow keys to move this window to the far right, uncovering your program's instructions. Press Scroll Lock again to lock the window in its new position. The registers window shows the values of the registers and flags inside your computer's processor. This window is extremely useful for examining the results of various machine-code instructions, most of which affect the values in one or more registers.

5. A dark arrow to the left of the program's first instruction, `mov ax, @data,` tells you that this is the next instruction to be executed. Press F8 to execute this instruction. When you do this, two things happen: The dark arrow moves down to the next instruction, and the value of the `ax` register in the registers window changes. The instruction "moved" a value into the register—you saw it happen. Stepping through individual instructions with F8 lets you run your program in slow motion, executing one instruction at a time and pausing to let you view the effects of each machine code.

6. Press F8 again, executing the next instruction, `mov ds, ax.` Watch the registers window—you should see the value of the `ds` register change to the same value now in `ax`. The `mov` instruction moved the value of `ax` into `ds.` Again, for the time being, don't be too concerned with why the program does this.

7. Press F6 until the flashing cursor reappears in the source-code window. The register window is now covered by this window. (F6 switches among all open windows—you can also press Alt-# where # is the window number 1–9.)

8. Move the flashing cursor down to the line that reads `mov dl, ASCIIlf`—three instructions beyond the current instruction marked by the dark arrow. Press F4 to run the program from the current instruction down to the instruction at the flashing cursor. Use this method to execute small sections of code when you don't want to pause after each instruction.

9. Press F6 repeatedly until the registers window reappears. Then press F8 twice, executing the next two instructions. Watch the value of the `dx` register—you should see a part of this value change.

10. The dark arrow should now point to the `int 21h` instruction (at line 25 in Program 2-1). This instruction calls a function in DOS, activating one of the operating system's many routines, in this case, sending a character to the printer. Press F8 to execute the instruction. If your printer is on, the paper should advance one line.

11. There's no need to run the program to completion as the remaining instructions simply return control to DOS—or, in this case, to Turbo Debugger. Press Alt-X to quit the debugger and end the session.

Turbo Debugger has many other commands to let you examine, execute, and modify your program. But the preceding steps are all you need to know to run most assembled examples in this book, examining the effects of various instructions. In future examples, I'll tell you how to use other Turbo Debugger commands. As you can see, a debugger can help you examine your program in ways that otherwise would be impossible. When it comes to helping you learn assembly language, Turbo Debugger is indeed a great teacher.

Writing .COM and .EXE Programs

You probably know that there are two kinds of executable code files: those that end in .COM and those that end in .EXE. You can write assembly language programs to create both types. Although most example programs in this book are of the .EXE variety, at times you may want to produce a .COM file instead.

Note: Microsoft has indicated its desire to kill the .COM file format, but it has so far been unsuccessful in the attempt. If you write your programs in this format, be aware that you may be making a lot of work for yourself in the future should Microsoft succeed in its effort to banish .COM files from the face of the Earth.

Rather than start new programs from scratch, you may find it helpful to begin with a template containing the bare necessities required by .COM and .EXE programs. Program 2-2 lists a shell for .COM programs. Program 2-3 lists the corresponding .EXE shell. You can use the .EXE shell to save typing time when entering example programs in other chapters. Each template has several comments beginning with semicolons and suggesting where to place equates, variables, and other items, some of which will be new to you. You may remove these comments when starting a new program with a copy of one of the templates.

Program 2-2 *COMSHELL.ASM*

```
1:  %TITLE "Shell for .COM Code Files"
2:
3:          IDEAL
4:          DOSSEG
5:          MODEL   tiny
6:
```

```
 7:  ;-----  Insert INCLUDE "filename" directives here
 8:
 9:  ;-----  Insert EQU and = equates here
10:
11:          DATASEG
12:
13:  ;-----  If an error occurs and the program should halt, store an
14:  ;       appropriate error code in exitCode and execute a JMP Exit
15:  ;       instruction.
16:
17:  exitCode        DB      0
18:
19:  ;-----  Declare other variables with DB, DW, etc., here
20:
21:          CODESEG
22:
23:          ORG     100h                ; Standard .COM start address (origin)
24:
25:  Start:
26:
27:  ;-----  Insert program, subroutine calls, etc., here
28:
29:  Exit:
30:          mov     ah, 04Ch            ; DOS function: Exit program
31:          mov     al, [exitCode]      ; Return exit-code value
32:          int     21h                 ; Call DOS. Terminate program
33:
34:          END     Start               ; End of program / entry point
```

Program 2-3 *EXESHELL.ASM*

```
 1:  %TITLE "Shell for .EXE Code Files"
 2:
 3:          IDEAL
 4:          DOSSEG
 5:          MODEL   small
 6:          STACK   256
 7:
 8:  ;-----  Insert INCLUDE "filename" directives here
 9:
10:  ;-----  Insert EQU and = equates here
11:
12:          DATASEG
13:
14:  ;-----  If an error occurs and the program should halt, store an
15:  ;       appropriate error code in exitCode and execute a JMP Exit
16:  ;       instruction. To do this from a submodule, declare the Exit
17:  ;       label in an EXTRN directive.
18:
```

```
19: exitCode        DB      0
20:
21: ;----- Declare other variables with DB, DW, etc., here
22:
23: ;----- Specify any EXTRN variables here
24:
25:         CODESEG
26:
27: ;----- Specify any EXTRN procedures here
28:
29: Start:
30:         mov     ax, @data           ; Initialize ds to address
31:         mov     ds, ax              ;  of data segment
32:
33: ;----- Insert program, subroutine calls, etc., here
34:
35: Exit:
36:         mov     ah, 04Ch            ; DOS function: Exit program
37:         mov     al, [exitCode]      ; Return exit-code value
38:         int     21h                 ; Call DOS. Terminate program
39:
40:         END     Start        ; End of program / entry point
```

Writing .COM Programs

Program 2-2 shows the correct format for writing .COM programs in Ideal mode. Line 5 selects the tiny memory model, which combines the program's variables, code, and stack into one 64K memory segment. Because of this, .COM programs occupy 64K of memory (or all available RAM, whichever is less), regardless of the program's size on disk. This little-known fact is the reason that .EXE programs are preferred. Although .EXE code files may take up more room on disk (because additional information about the program's organization is included in the file), most small .EXE programs take up much less memory during execution than the equivalent .COM programs.

Line 23 shows another characteristic of a .COM program. The ORG (origin) directive tells Turbo Assembler that this program's first instruction is to be loaded at address 100h (the small *h* stands for hexadecimal), relative to the beginning of the program's *code segment*—the chunk of memory designated to hold the assembled machine code. This value is the same as the load address for programs written for the CP/M operating system, upon which much of DOS is based and which usually ran on computers having a *total* memory size of 64K. Under DOS, .COM programs operate in a kind of pseudo-CP/M address space, despite the fact that most modern PCs have ten times the memory capacity (640K) or more. Today, there's almost no good reason to use this ancient code-file format.

In chapter 4, you'll meet most 8086 instruction mnemonics; therefore, I won't explain here what Program 2-2 does at lines 30–32. The effect of this code is to return control to DOS when the program is finished. All .COM programs must end with these instructions (or an equivalent variant).

Assembling .COM Programs

To assemble a .COM program requires slightly different commands than described earlier. You must tell the Turbo Linker with the **/t** option letter that this is a tiny model program. For practice, assemble and link Program 2-2 with these commands:

```
tasm comshell
tlink /t comshell
```

It Ain't Over Till ... Actually, It Ain't Ever Over

This is a good time to introduce a most important point: All assembly language programs must return control either to another program or to DOS, using commands specifically provided for this purpose. This concept frequently confuses programmers who have written programs in other languages like C, Pascal, and BASIC, where programs simply end. Assembly language programs never end—they just fade away—that is, they relinquish control to another running program.

You can understand the purpose behind this idea if you remember that the computer's processor is always processing. As long as the plug is in and the switch is on, there is never a time when a computer isn't computing. Even when the DOS prompt silently waits for your next command, the computer processor is whizzing away, performing billions of cycles, constantly processing the instructions that only appear to make the computer pause. Doing nothing takes a great deal of effort for a computer!

Because of the processor's incessant cycling, a program can never simply end—it has to hand over control to another program to give the processor something to do. Forgetting this step almost always has drastic results. If you fail to hand over control to another program, the processor will continue to process whatever is in memory after the physical end of your program. That memory might contain anything—leftover code and data from other programs or just the random bit patterns that exist when you switch on power. The result of processing this unknown information is usually a spectacular crash, garbage on screen, or worse, the permanent destruction of data on disk. Use the templates in Programs 2-2 and 2-3, which include the necessary instructions to return control to DOS. That way, you won't accidentally forget this important step.

When most programs end, they give DOS a command to reload a program called COMMAND.COM, located on your boot disk. COMMAND.COM is a program just like any other but with the special purpose of letting you give commands to DOS. When you run a program from DOS, COMMAND.COM loads your code and passes control to your program's instructions. When your program ends, it must return control to COMMAND.COM for the DOS prompt to reappear. Be sure you understand this process—it is vital to your ability to write assembly language programs.

Writing .EXE Programs

Writing a program in .EXE format takes a little more work than writing COM programs, but the result is usually worth the effort. The .EXE format occupies only as much memory as required to run your program, leaving the most room possible for storing data, creating large arrays, and sharing space with other .EXE programs in a multitasking operating system. (DOS does not have multitasking abilities—that is, the ability to run two or more programs simultaneously, although you can add this ability to DOS with add-on software such as DesqView, VM386, and Carousel. Writing programs in .EXE format lets these programs organize memory more efficiently.)

The reason that .EXE programs require more work is that variables, the stack, and the machine code are stored in separate memory segments, occupying up to a total of 128K under the small memory model. (The small memory model combines the stack and data segments; other models allow larger amounts of code and data.) In Program 2-3, the size of the stack is specified by the STACK directive (line 6). The size of the data segment is calculated from the combined sizes of the program's variables. The size of the code segment depends on how many instructions are in your program.

Because variables are stored apart from the program's code—unlike in the .COM format, where data and code share the same memory segment—the first job in all .EXE programs is to initialize the data segment register ds. Lines 30–31 accomplish this task in Program 2-3, assigning the built-in symbol @data to register ax (line 30) and then assigning ax to ds (line 31). The reason this takes two steps is that you cannot assign values like @data directly to segment registers—you can assign values only from other general-purpose registers such as ax.

Ending an .EXE program is identical to ending a .COM program, as lines 36–38 show. Again, don't be too concerned here with what these instructions do. Remember, though, that the purpose is to pass control back to COMMAND.COM, using a special DOS function. To assemble and link Program 2-3, use these commands:

```
tasm exeshell
tlink exeshell
```

Printing Listings   Now that you know how to enter, assemble, and link programs, you may want to print reference listings of the sample programs in this chapter. Because assembly language listings tend to produce lines longer than the standard 80-character width of most printers, the first step is to write a program to select your printer's compressed style, usually extending the limits to 132-character lines and, on some printers, even more.

Program 2-4, PR132.ASM, is a simple .EXE style program that selects 132-character output on most Epson-compatible printers. Assemble and link the program with these commands:

```
tasm pr132
tlink pr132
```

Program 2-4 *PR132.ASM*

```
1:  %TITLE "Select Compressed 132-Character Printer Output"
2:
3:          IDEAL
4:          DOSSEG
5:          MODEL   small
6:          STACK   256
7:
```

```
 8:          DATASEG
 9:
10:    ; Insert the codes that select your printer's 132-character (or
11:    ; greater) output style, sometimes called "compressed" mode.
12:    ; The values below should work with most Epson-compatible printers.
13:    ; The last value must be 0!
14:
15:    prCodes       DB        27, 15, 0        ; Must end in 0!
16:
17:          CODESEG
18:
19:    Start:
20:          mov       ax, @data              ; Initialize ds to address
21:          mov       ds, ax                 ;  of data segment
22:
23:          cld                              ; Clear df--auto increment si
24:          mov       si, offset prCodes     ; Point si to prCodes
25:    Next:
26:          lodsb                            ; Load next code into al
27:          or        al, al                 ; Is al = 0?
28:          jz        Exit                   ; If yes, jump to exit
29:          mov       dl, al                 ;  else assign al to dl
30:          mov       ah, 05h                ; DOS print char function
31:          int       21h                    ; Call DOS. Print char.
32:          jmp       Next                   ; Do next code.
33:    Exit:
34:          mov       ax, 04C00h             ; DOS function: Exit program
35:          int       21h                    ; Call DOS. Terminate program
36:
37:          END       Start              ; End of program / entry point
```

After assembling PR132.ASM, try an experiment. Turn on your printer and type DIR>PRN to print a listing of the current directory in your printer's default style. Type PR132 and press Enter. Then, type DIR>PRN again, this time printing a directory in compressed style. If this doesn't work, you'll probably have to modify the codes in line 15 for your printer. Check your manual for the correct values to use. After the DB directive, you can specify codes in decimal, hexadecimal (start the value with 0 and end with h), or characters (surround one or more characters with double or single quotes). Some printer manuals list hexadecimal codes with preceding dollar signs, as in $1F. Rewrite such codes in assembly language style: 01Fh. For example, if your printer specifies the sequence Escape-C,$1F, you could use any one of the following lines in place of line 15:

```
prCodes    DB    27, 67, 31, 0            ; decimal
prCodes    DB    01Bh, 043h, 01Fh, 0      ; hexadecimal
prCodes    DB    27, 'C', 01Fh, 0         ; decimal, char, hex
```

The last value must be 0, marking the end of the sequence. This format—a list of bytes ending with 0—is a typical construction in assembly language programs, allowing the list to contain any number of items—as long as no other value is 0, of course.

Unless you've written programs in assembly language before, you probably won't understand the instructions in PR132.ASM. This is not too important. The purpose of this chapter is to get you started, giving you practice entering, assembling, and linking programs—valuable experience that you will draw upon later. Even so, you should at least be able to understand the idea of this program by reading the comments. The plan is simple: get each of the prCodes bytes in turn and send each value to the printer until reaching the 0 byte, marking the end of the list. Then, return control to DOS.

Listing PR132   After entering PR132.ASM, assembling, linking, and testing, you're ready to print a reference listing. Turn on your printer and type PR132 to select compressed output. Then reassemble the program, this time using the command:

```
tasm /l PR132
```

As an alternative, to include a cross reference of symbols at the end of the listing, use the command:

```
tasm /l/c PR132
```

Either of these commands creates PR132.LST, called the *listing file,* ready to print. To print the listing file, type the command:

```
type pr132.lst>prn
```

The listing file contains form-feed control characters to skip page perforations, and for this reason, you probably shouldn't print listing files with a word processor, as these programs usually handle paging automatically. You might also send the listing to a print spooler, allowing you to run other programs while printing continues. Unless you are logged onto a network, use the DOS command to spool a listing file:

```
print pr132.asm
```

If this is the first time you gave a print command, you'll be asked to supply an output file. Usually, just press Enter to select the default file PRN. Refer to your DOS manual for more information about using the print spooler. You can print multiple listings by separating their names with spaces on the command line—a real time saver if you need to print several listing files and want to continue editing and assembling other programs. You can print multiple files by separating their names with spaces or by giving separate print commands. Assembly language listings tend to be much longer than those produced by high-level languages, and a print spooler is a practical necessity for assembly language programmers.

After printing, copy your listing files to a floppy disk along with the other files related to each program. Most people save the listing files for future reference. If you're tight on space, you can delete the files ending in .LST.

Note: Because the %TITLE directive line is not included in the listing file, the line numbers printed in this book do not match the line numbers in a printed listing. Line 3 in the book is line 2 in the listing, and so on. To refer to your own printed listings while reading this book, subtract 1 from line number references. (In other words, if I say "see line 20," refer to your listing file line 19.)

Summary

Assembly language programs roughly divide into five sections: header, equates, data, body, and closing. The body is further divided into four columns: label, mnemonic, operands, and comment. Labels refer to the positions of variables and instructions, represented by mnemonics. Operands are required by most assembly language instructions, giving instructions data to process. Comments, always optional, help you to remember the purpose of various instructions.

Assembling programs produces object code, which must be linked to create an executable file, ending either in .EXE or .COM. You can use special option letters to select features in Turbo Assembler and Turbo Linker. Turbo Assembler reports errors and warnings on screen during assembly.

Turbo Debugger can run an assembled program in slow motion and can let you peer into memory to see the actual bytes that form your program's code and data. You can use Turbo Debugger to help pinpoint bugs and also as your personal assembly language teacher, which can run test programs and let you observe the effects of executing individual machine-code instructions. On systems with 80386 processors, you can optionally use the virtual-memory version of Turbo Debugger.

The .COM code file format is a carry-over from the CP/M operating system. While useful in some cases, this format is not recommended for PC programs. All code, data, and the stack in a .COM program occupy one 64K memory segment. The .EXE code-file format is more efficient, even though programs may occupy slightly more room on disk. In memory, .EXE programs occupy only as much memory as needed. Writing .EXE programs takes a little more effort because you are responsible for specifying a program's data, code, and stack segments.

Assembly language programs don't end—they pass control to another program, usually COMMAND.COM. Forgetting this step can cause serious problems by executing random instructions in memory following the physical end of your program.

A listing file documents a program. Most programmers print listing files of their finished programs for future reference. You can use the DOS print spooler to print long listings while you continue working.

Exercises

2-1. Referring to Program 2-3, what are the line numbers of the header, equates, data, body, and closing?

2-2. What is the name of the variable in Program 2-4?

2-3. How many comments are there in Program 2-1?

2-4. What characters precede option letters for Turbo Assembler and Turbo Linker?

2-5. Suppose you have a program text file named BUGABOO.ASM. What are the assembling and linking steps required to create the necessary files to debug BUGABOO with Turbo Debugger?

2-6. Which program do you use, Turbo Assembler or Turbo Linker, to create object code? Which do you use to create executable code? What is the purpose of creating object code?

2-7. What is the difference between an error and a warning? What should you do if you receive an error or a warning?

2-8. How do .COM and .EXE code files differ?

2-9. Suppose you have a program named LISTME.ASM. What are the steps required to assemble and print a listing file of this program?

2-10. What is the correct way to end an assembly language program?

2-11. What does the DB directive do? What kinds of data can you create with DB?

Projects

2-1. Print a reference copy of Turbo Assembler's option letters.

2-2. Make a copy of Program 2-4 and rename the copy PR80.ASM. Modify this program to select your printer's 80-column output style.

2-3. Create and print listing files for Programs 2-1 through 2-4.

2-4. Start a floppy disk for saving your assembled example programs. Create individual subdirectories for each program, naming the directories the same as the programs. Then copy all files for each program to the appropriate subdirectory. For example, to save Program 2-1, you could create a subdirectory named FF and copy to FF the files: FF.ASM, FF.OBJ, FF.EXE, FF.MAP, and optionally FF.LST.

2-5. Execute Program 2-4 under control of Turbo Debugger. Press the F8 key to run the program a single step at a time. Watch carefully the repetitive action of the instructions from line 26 through 32 as the program reads each printer code until reaching the 0, marking the end of the list. Bring up the register window and watch the ax register, especially for the instruction at line 26. What do you think is happening here?

2-6. Rewrite Program 2-1 and assemble to a .COM code file.

Chapter *3* **A Bit of Binary**

Chapter **3 A Bit of Binary**

In This Chapter

Readin', writin', and 'rithmetic in binary; all about bits, bytes, words, and other multibyte values; the power of 2 explained; converting among hexadecimal, decimal, and binary; two's complement notation; representing negative values in binary; how to use the logical AND, OR, and XOR operators to perform binary surgery; using bit shifts to multiply and divide

Memorabilia

Bits and bytes are an assembly language program's fuel. The more you know about bits, bytes, and the arithmetic and logic operations you can perform on binary values, the more energy you'll be able to squeeze from this power source of all digital computing—the lowly binary digits, or *bits*, 0 and 1.

Physically, of course, there are no binary digits in memory or in the computer's processor—there are only electric charges that are on (energized) or off (not energized). For the purposes of programming, however, it's convenient to ignore this fact and pretend that there are indeed ones and zeros stuffed into the computer's circuit board. Groups of binary digits can then represent values, which in turn can stand for all sorts of items: ASCII characters, printer control codes, checkbook balances, the date and time, and so on. Other binary values might be used to read and write values to input and output ports, which appear to programs like other values in memory but which might actually be switches that activate and deactivate various circuits that control devices attached to the computer. Storing bits to these locations is equivalent to flipping a light switch on and off. In assembly language, simply writing a certain value to a specific location can turn on motors, display characters, send values to remote systems, and make sounds.

With such an important role for binary values to play—especially in assembly language programming—it's important to be intimately comfortable with binary arithmetic and logic. That doesn't mean you have to be able to add columns of hexadecimal numbers by hand. For this, you may as well use a programmer's calculator. (After all, that's what most professional programmers do.) Even so, a working knowledge of binary principals is vital to your ability to write good assembly language programs. By all means, use your calculator, but don't ignore learning the basics. Every minute you spend learning these subjects will save you from hours of puzzlement in the future.

Note: Because a good understanding of binary arithmetic and logic operations is so important to assembly language programming, this chapter reviews the fundamentals from the beginning. If you know your way around the binary number system, you may want to skim this material (and look for more advanced tips near the end).

How Many Bits in a Byte?

Let's start with a quick review. There are 8 bits in a byte; 2 bytes in a word; 4 bytes in a doubleword; 6 bytes in a farword; and 8 bytes in a quadword. Bits are numbered from right to left—bit 0 is always farthest to the right and is called the *least significant digit* (LSD). The bit farthest to the left is called the *most significant digit* (MSD). Figure 3-1 illustrates typical ways of representing the bits in byte and word values.

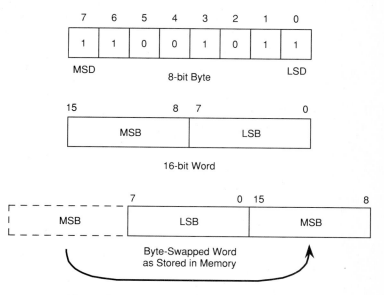

Figure 3-1 *Typical byte and word diagrams.*

In memory, bytes are stored consecutively one after the other. Each byte has an associated address, a unique number that pinpoints this byte's location from all others. To read and change byte values in memory, assembly language programs specify a value's starting address, usually but not always in the form of a named label such as `temperature` or `numCumquats`. Being able to use readable labels instead of actual adress values like 0F00:0014 is one of the main advantages offered by assembly language.

In 8086 programming, word values are stored in byte-swapped order, with the word's *most significant byte* (MSB) at a higher address than the *least significant byte* (LSB). In assembly language listings, word values are shown in reverse order from the order that the bytes are actually stored in memory. (For example, see Figure 3-1, bottom.) This byte-swapped order makes arithmetic easier to perform on multibyte values because the least significant bytes, which must be added first, are at lower addresses. But the swapped order can also lead to confusion for people who have to read the listings and relate printed values to those in memory. To locate a word in memory equal to hexadecimal 0201, for example, requires searching for the two consecutive bytes, 01 and 02, not for 02 and 01.

Binary Arithmetic and Logic

Because large values can take many bits to represent, calculating complex equations directly in binary is tedious. Fortunately, you don't need to become so fluent in binary arithmetic that you can instantly convert a grocery cash register tape from decimal to binary, compute the sum, and convert back to decimal all in your head. Some books require you to learn how to add, subtract, multiply, and divide directly in binary—operations that programmers in the real world would rather do on a computer. My hat's off to you if you find such operations easy. For most purposes, the well-versed assembly language programmer needs to know how to perform only four fundamental operations:

▶ Count from 0 to 16 in binary without help

▶ Convert values into binary, hexadecimal, and decimal

▶ Understand the logical operations AND, OR, and XOR

▶ Understand how signed (positive and negative) and unsigned (positive only) values differ in their binary representations

Counting in Binary

Table 3-1 lists the binary, hexadecimal, and decimal values from 0 to 16. Try to memorize this table and mark this page. You'll need these values time and again.

It's easy to learn how to count and add in binary if you remember one simple fact about adding two values expressed in any number system: When you run out of symbols in a column, carry a 1 to the left. You know

Table 3-1 *0–16 in Binary, Hexadecimal, and Decimal*

Binary	Hexadecimal	Decimal
0000	00	0
0001	01	1
0010	02	2
0011	03	3
0100	04	4
0101	05	5
0110	06	6
0111	07	7
1000	08	8
1001	09	9
1010	0A	10
1011	0B	11
1100	0C	12
1101	0D	13
1110	0E	14
1111	0F	15
1 0000	10	16

how to do this in decimal. But with only two symbols in binary—or *base two*—values, a carry from one column to the column on the left occurs sooner in binary than in decimal, which has ten symbols and, therefore, can represent larger values with fewer numbers of digits. Adding 1 + 1 in decimal requires no carry:

$$\begin{array}{r} 1 \\ + \ 1 \\ \hline 2 \end{array}$$

In decimal, the result can be represented by a single symbol (2). In binary, a single digit can be only 0 or 1; therefore, it takes an additional digit to represent a count of two things. Adding 1 + 1 in binary, then, forces a carry to the column on the left:

$$\begin{array}{r} 1 \\ + \ 1 \\ \hline 10 \end{array}$$

The result is *not* ten. The result is *two* expressed as the base two value 10. As you know, adding 1 to decimal 9 (the highest single digit in base ten) gives 0 in that column with a carry to the next column to the left. Likewise, adding 1 to binary 1 (the highest single digit in base two) gives 0 in that column with a carry to the next column to the left. Adding in binary is no different from adding in decimal—you just run out of symbols more quickly and, as a result, have to carry a 1 to the left more frequently. With this rule in mind, you can add any two binary values. Let's try this with a more complex addition, writing the carries above the values being added:

$$
\begin{array}{rl}
11\ \ 1\ 11 & \text{(carries)} \\
0110\ 1010 & \text{(first value)} \\
+0010\ 1110 & \text{(second value)} \\
\hline
1001\ 1000 & \text{(sum)}
\end{array}
$$

The Power of 2   In most number systems (at least in those of the modern world), the position of a digit represents a value equal to the digit multiplied by the column's significance, or *power*. In decimal, for instance, the 3 in 300 stands for the number of hundreds—the power of the third column to the left. The rightmost column represents 10 to the zero power, written 10^0. The second column to the left represents 10^1; the next represents 10^2; and so on. To find the power of any column, write the number of the column's position (starting with 0) as the exponent to the number base. Then, multiply that many base values to find the significance of the column. For example, the value 10^3 equals $(10 \times 10 \times 10)$, or 1000.

> Note: Any base value to the zero power (n^0) is traditionally considered to equal 1. Technically speaking, the value of a digit in the rightmost column equals the value of that digit times 1.

Binary values are positional, too. Because binary values are expressed in base 2, binary columns represent the powers of 2. In binary, the 1 in 100 stands for one count of the third column's power, or 2^2, which in decimal equals 4 (2×2); therefore, 100 in binary is equivalent to 4 in decimal. 1000 in binary equals 2^3, or 8 ($2 \times 2 \times 2$), and so on.

Finite Values   Computer programs usually represent numbers with fixed numbers of bits in one or more bytes. This makes it practical to store numbers in memory, which is divided into byte-size pieces. At the same time, a fixed number of bits places a limit on the number of values that can be expressed. A single byte of 8 bits, for example, can express values from 0 to 255. A 16-bit word can express values from 0 to 65,535, and so forth. To express higher values requires more bits.

To calculate the maximum value that can be expressed within a fixed number of bits n, use the formula $2^n - 1$. For example, if n is 8, then the maximum value you can express in 8 bits equals ($2 \times 2 \times 2 \times 2 \times 2 \times 2 \times 2 \times 2$) $- 1$, or 255. Counting 0, there are 256 values in the range 0 to 255; therefore, the formula for the *number* of values that a fixed number of bits n can express equals 2^n. Know these boundaries well. You'll bounce into them all the time.

The K Game   Most people use a convenient shorthand to represent 1,000-byte, or *kilobyte,* quantities of memory as in 64K, 128K, and 640K. These convenient powers of 2—in all cases equal in binary to a 1 followed by several zeros—have been adopted by computer users everywhere as accurate measurements of RAM, despite the fact that a 64K computer actually has 65,536 bytes—the full number of values that can be expressed in 16 bits, or 2^{16}.

The address range of the 8086 processor, by the way, is 2^{20}, or 1,048,576 bytes—a so-called *megabyte* plus change. As you'll learn in later chapters, the 8086 uses some hocus-pocus to reduce two 16-bit address values down to a 20-bit physical address that actually locates individual bytes within this memory range.

When working with address values in binary, try to get used to thinking in powers of 2. Measuring memory in K is quick and easy, but it is just too vague for the exacting world of assembly language programming.

Binary and Hexadecimal

Hexadecimal values are represented in base 16—in other words, with the 16 symbols 0, 1, 2, 3, 4, 5, 6, 7, 8, 9, A, B, C, D, E, and F. The hexadecimal digits are made up of the ten decimal digits 0 to 9 plus the six letters A to F.

> Note: Some early computer texts used a different set of six letters in place of A to F. One suggested U, V, W, X, Y, and Z. Another proposed lowercase t, e, d, h, f, i. Believe it or not, you were supposed to remember t for tens, e for elevens, d for dozens, h for thirteens, f for fourteens, and i for fifteens! Fortunately, this didn't become one of computerdom's more popular standards.

Counting in hexadecimal is easy (see Table 3-1) if you remember that 1 + F equals hexadecimal 10 (16 in decimal). Remember, 1 plus the last symbol in any positional number system equals the symbol 10 expressed in that number system.

> Note: To avoid confusion, don't say "hundred" for hexadecimal 100 or "ten" for hex 10. Say "one-zero-zero" and "one-zero" pronouncing each digit. Hexadecimal 100 equals 256 decimal, not "one hundred."

Because the hexadecimal number system contains 16 symbols and because 16 is a power of 2 (2^4), values in binary are easily converted to and from hexadecimal by substitution. Plainly, it's easier to write and remember hex values like B800 than it is to write and remember the binary equivalent: 1011 1000 0000 0000. Here's another example:

```
0100   1111   0101   1100
  4      F      5      C = 4F5C
```

The binary value (top) converts to hex (bottom) by substitution from Table 3-1. To convert from hex to binary, substitute in the other direction, replacing hex digits with their 4-bit binary equivalents.

Converting Hexadecimal and Decimal Values

Converting between hexadecimal and decimal is not as simple as converting between hexadecimal and binary values. The easiest way to accomplish such conversions is to use a programmer's calculator designed for this purpose. Or, use a software calculator such as the one in Borland's SideKick. That way, you can pop up the calculator in the middle of typing a program, do the calculation, and go right back to work.

For the times when you can't get to your calculator, it pays to know how to convert hexadecimal and decimal values by hand. This is not as difficult to do as you may think. As in binary and decimal, hex digits are positional, representing increasing powers of 16 from right to left. Knowing this provides a quick trick for converting any 16-bit value from hexadecimal to decimal, requiring you to memorize only these four values:

$$16^0 = 1$$
$$16^1 = 16$$
$$16^2 = 256$$
$$16^3 = 4,096$$

The exponents represent column positions in the hexadecimal value, numbered from right (0) to left (3). To convert hexadecimal to decimal, multiply the value of each hex digit by the power of its column. Add the multiplications, and you're done. For example:

$$8B92 = (8 \times 4096) + (11 \times 256) + (9 \times 16) + (2 \times 1) = 35,730$$

The hexadecimal value 8B92 equals 35,730 in decimal. For the hex digits A–F, use Table 3-1 to convert mentally to decimal before multiplying. In this example, $(B \times 256)$ is equivalent to (11×256). To convert from decimal to hexadecimal, reverse the process, dividing by powers of 16. Although this is a little more difficult, you can do the calculation by hand this way:

$(35,730/4096) = 8.72\ldots$	$(8 \times 4096) = 32,768$	$(35,730 - 32,768) = 2962$
$(2,962/256) = 11.57\ldots$	$(11 \times 256) = 2816$	$(2,962 - 2,816) = 146$
$(146/16) = 9.125$	$(9 \times 16) = 144$	$(146 - 144) = 2$
$(2/1) = 2$	$(2 \times 1) = 2$	$(2 - 2) = 0$

$$8, 11, 9, 2 = 8B92$$

Don't be overwhelmed—this isn't as confusing as it probably looks. Reading each row from left to right, look at how the expressions divide a decimal value by decreasing powers of 16, throw out the remainder, multiply the whole number by the same power, and subtract the result from the total. Then the next line uses the result of this calculation in the next division, repeating the process until reaching 0. If the first division is greater or equal to 16, start with a higher power. If a subsequent division is greater or equal to 16, you've made a mistake. Written down, the expressions seem to be a frightening load of work. But with practice and an inexpensive decimal calculator, you can do the conversion in a few seconds. Notice how the hex digits pop out of the divisions—8, 11 (B), 9, 2, or hexadecimal 8B92.

Two's Complement Notation

Unsigned integers include 0 and all positive whole values. Signed integers include the unsigned integers plus whole values less than 0. Within a fixed number of bits, there are a fixed number of signed and unsigned values. For instance, in 4 bits, the smallest value is 0000; the largest unsigned value is 1111. Converting to decimal, this equals the range of 0–15—a total of 16 possible values including 0. In 8 bits, the largest unsigned value is 1111 1111, or 255 decimal—making a total of 256 possible values in one 8-bit byte. The whole numbers in mathematics may be infinite, but in computer programming, whole numbers have definite limits.

Because you can express only a fixed number of values within a fixed number of bits, representing negative values in signed binary requires some trickery. A value's sign is either positive (+) or negative (−); therefore, a single bit can represent the sign of an integer—1 for negative and 0 for positive. That leaves the rest of the bits to represent the signless *absolute value*. This observation leads to a convenient representation for negative integers in binary, called the *two's complement*.

> Note: For simplicity, 0 is considered to be a positive value even though, strictly speaking, 0 is neither positive nor negative.

In two's complement notation, if the leftmost bit is 1, the value is negative. If the leftmost bit is 0, the value is positive or 0. To convert between positive values and two's complement notation, first negate each bit (step 1 below)—changing the ones to zeros and the zeros to ones—forming an intermediate value called the *one's complement*. Add 1 to this value (step 2 below), forming the final two's complement result:

```
  0110 1010   (original value)
  1001 0101   (1. negate each bit—one's complement)
+         1   (2. add 1)
  ─────────
  1001 0110   (two's complement)
```

The steps are reversible. To convert a two's complement value to its absolute value, perform the same steps. For example:

$$
\begin{array}{lll}
& 1111\ 1110 & \text{(two's complement)} \\
& 0000\ 0001 & \text{(1. negate each bit)} \\
+ & \underline{\qquad\quad 1} & \text{(2. add 1)} \\
& 0000\ 0010 & \text{(absolute value)}
\end{array}
$$

As this example shows, the absolute value of the 8-bit two's complement 1111 1110 equals 0010, or 2. In other words, 1111 1110 is decimal −2, represented as a signed binary, two's complement value. The conversion steps work no matter how many bits are in the value—4, 8, 16, or more. The leftmost bit always indicates whether a value is positive (0) or negative (1). If negative, performing the two's complement operations finds the absolute value.

> Note: Another way to form the two's complement is to subtract a binary value from 0, although negating and adding 1 is simpler to do by hand.

A good way to understand the purpose of the two's complement is to remember the number line you no doubt learned in math class. (See Figure 3-2.) Values to the right of 0 are positive; values to the left are negative. The line extends in two directions farther than human minds can imagine.

With a fixed number of positions for digits—as in a computer's memory—you might imagine the familiar number line to be circular. (See Figure 3-3.) The binary values (outside the circle) orbit sequentially to the right. Adding one to the highest value (1111) returns to 0. Signed decimal equivalent values are inside the circle; unsigned values are outside, with the binary values written under their decimal counterparts. This figure assumes four binary digits are available, although the same idea holds for any fixed number of bits.

From Figure 3-3, you can see that exactly half of the signed values are negative (−1 to −8). The other half are positive (0 to 7). The unsigned values (0 to 15) use the same binary values as the signed quantities, a fact that leads to an important rule to remember: *Negative binary values are negative by convention only.* Within a fixed number of bits, all unsigned values have corresponding signed values represented by the identical bit patterns such as (9, −7), (13, −3), and (15, −1). The binary values for the negative numbers are simply represented in two's complement form.

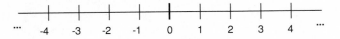

Figure 3-2 *Signed-integer number line.*

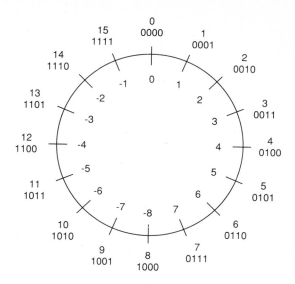

Figure 3-3 *With a fixed number of binary digits available, it's convenient to imagine the familiar number line as a circle.*

Note: A common misconception is that there is one more negative value than there are positive values in signed, two's complement notation. Considering that 0 is positive, this is not true—there are equal numbers of positive and negative values. Count them in Figure 3-3.

Subtracting by Adding

Two's complement notation is important in binary arithmetic because it gives computer circuits the ability to subtract by adding. Also, performing the two's-complement steps—negating the bits and adding 1—makes it easy to find the absolute value of negative binary values expressed in two's complement notation. If you understand the idea of a circular number line (Figure 3-3), you can easily grasp these ideas. Obviously, adding decimal 1 + 9 equals 10, equivalent to the signed value −6 on the circular number line—the identical result received by subtracting 1 − 7. Therefore, instead of subtracting 1 − 7, you can instead add 1 + 9 and then look up the negative value on the circular number line as the two's complement of the result.

Fortunately, in 8086 assembly language, you don't have to subtract by adding two's complements because the processor has instructions for subtracting values. Even so, it pays to understand the mechanism. The rule is: To subtract one binary value from another, convert the second value to two's complement notation and add. For demonstration, let's start with a simple subtraction that produces a positive result:

$$
\begin{array}{ccc}
1001 & 1001 & 9 \\
-\ 0101 & +\ 1011 & -\ 5 \\
\hline
0100 & 1\ \ 0100 & 4
\end{array}
$$

On the left, 5 (0101) is subtracted from 9 (1001) directly. In the middle, the two's complement of 5 (1011) is added to 9. The right column shows the subtraction in decimal. The two calculations give identical results, but with a carry out of the middle column for the two's complement addition, indicating the result is positive. Now watch what happens when you subtract 5 − 9, giving a negative answer:

```
   0101        0101
 − 1001      + 0111   (two's complement of 1001—9 decimal)
  ?100       0 1100   (two's complement of 0100—4 decimal)
```

The left column requires a borrow where none is to be had. On the right, subtracting by adding the two's complement of 9 decimal to 5 gives 1100, which you know is negative because the leftmost bit in 1100 is 1. The two's complement of this is 0100, or 4, the absolute value of −4, which is the result of subtracting 5 − 9. In this way, the system of two's complements allows you to subtract binary values by adding—simple as 1, 10, 11.

> Note: The 8086 processor line contains two instructions to create the one's and two's complements of binary values. The **not** instruction forms the one's complement. The **neg** instruction forms the two's complement. You'll meet these instructions again in chapter 4.

Logical Operators

Three logical operations—AND, OR, and XOR (exclusive or)—are as common in assembly language programming as weeds in a garden. (On second thought, they're not as common as weeds in our garden.) AND, OR, and XOR give you total control over manipulating the individual bits in binary values. You can set and reset single bits without affecting others, isolate one or more bits from bytes and words, and perform other operations.

Table 3-2 lists the truth tables for AND, OR, and XOR, showing the effects that a logical operation has on 2 bits. AND is represented by &, OR by |, and XOR by ⊗.

Table 3-2 *AND, OR, XOR Truth Tables*

AND (&)	OR (|)	XOR (⊗)
$a \& b = c$	$a \mid b = c$	$a \otimes b = c$
$0 \& 0 = 0$	$0 \mid 0 = 0$	$0 \otimes 0 = 0$
$0 \& 1 = 0$	$0 \mid 1 = 1$	$0 \otimes 1 = 1$
$1 \& 0 = 0$	$1 \mid 0 = 1$	$1 \otimes 0 = 1$
$1 \& 1 = 1$	$1 \mid 1 = 1$	$1 \otimes 1 = 0$

Study Table 3-2 carefully. The result of ANDing two bits equals 1 only if bit *a* and bit *b* also equal 1. The result of ORing two bits is 1 if bit *a* or bit *b* equals 1. The result of XORing two bits is 1 only if bit *a* or bit *b* exclusively equals 1.

Masking with AND

AND is most often used to mask (isolate) bits in byte and word values. Referring to the AND truth table in Table 3-2, you can see that a 1 passes through from *a* to *c* only if there is a corresponding 1 in column *b*. You can use this observation to create *filters* to extract bits from bytes. Here's a typical example:

```
  0101 1101    (original value)
& 0000 1111    (AND mask)
  0000 1101    (result)
```

The mask is 0000 1111, or 0F hexadecimal. Because ANDing 2 bits gives a 1 only if both bits are 1, only the least significant 4 digits on the right pass through the mask unchanged. The most significant 4 digits on the left are masked out by the zeros in the AND mask. Perform the truth table operations on each column of this example to prove to yourself that the mask works.

Another typical use for AND masks is to test the value of single bits. First, create a mask with a 1 in the test bit position. Then, AND this mask with the test value, allowing a candidate bit to pass through. For example, suppose you want to test the leftmost bit, perhaps to determine whether a value is negative in two's complement notation:

```
  0111 1010      1001 1111    (original values)
& 1000 0000    & 1000 0000    (AND masks)
  0000 0000      1000 0000    (results)
```

The mask (80 hexadecimal) isolates the most significant digit—the one farthest to the left. If the original value has a 0 in this position, the result equals 0. If the original value has a 1 in this position, the result is not 0. Following the AND operation, testing if the result is 0 tells you whether the original value is negative (in two's complement notation). In 8086 programming, as you will learn, there are other ways to test for negative values. Even so, masking single bits this way is an important technique to know.

Setting Bits with OR

Contrasting the action of AND, logical OR is most often used to change the value of individual bits without affecting other bits in a byte. As Table 3-2 shows, a 1 bit in column *b* always results in a 1 bit in the result *c*, while an 0 in column *b* allows the original bit value from column 1 to pass through to the result. Notice that this pass-through action is the opposite of the AND operation, where a 1 bit in the mask allows bit values to pass through. These facts allow OR to set any bit in a byte, as this example demonstrates:

```
  0010 1011   (original value)
| 1000 0000   (OR mask)
  1010 1011   (result)
```

The OR mask (80 hexadecimal) changes the most significant digit in the original value from 0 to 1. (If that bit was already 1, then it passes through unchanged.) Referring to the OR truth table in Table 3-2, perform the OR operation on each column in this example to prove to yourself how this works.

Combined with AND, OR is frequently used to change the settings of a device's switches, economically represented as single bits in memory, perhaps stored in registers inside the device's interface card plugged into the computer. (A register is a small amount of special-purpose memory, usually inside an integrated circuit chip. The 8086 processor as well as other chips on your PC's circuit board have many such registers to hold meaningful values.) To see how AND and OR can be used to control devices, imagine a light attached to your computer and suppose that bit 3 of a certain register byte value represents the switch to turn the light on (1) and off (0). Bits 5, 6, and 7 represent the light's intensity in eight steps from 000 (dim) to 111 (bright). Other bits have other meanings and you must be careful not to change bits that are of no concern to you. Representing the taboo bits as question marks, the intensity as v, and the switch as s, the following operations turn on the light and change the intensity to 3:

```
  7654 3210   (bit position numbers)

  vvv? s???   (original settings)
& 0001 0111   (AND mask)
  000? 0???   (result of AND)
| 0110 1000   (OR mask)
  011? 1???   (result)
```

First, an AND mask strips the original value of any 1 bits in positions 7, 6, 5, and 3—the bits to be changed to the new settings. The ones in the AND mask preserve the original values in the forbidden positions—4, 2, 1, and 0—that must not be changed. After this, an OR mask sets bits 7, 6, and 5 to 011 (3 decimal) and also sets bit 3 to 1. Notice how zeros in the OR mask allow the values of the preserved bits (?) to pass through unharmed. Now, compare the bottom and top lines. The intensity value vvv is changed to 011 and the switch s to 1. The bits that control other devices are undisturbed.

> Note: When setting individual bits in bytes, you'll almost always use an AND followed by an OR. This is one of assembly language's most fundamental sequences, and you should learn it by heart.

The Exclusive OR Club The third common logical operator, XOR, is similar to OR but with one important difference. As you can see from Table 3-2, the result *c* equals 1 only when one but not both of the original two values is 1. If both of the original two bits are the same, then the result of XOR is 0. This property provides a handy tool for toggling individual bits on and off—without having to know beforehand what the original bit values are. As with OR, a 0 in the XOR mask allows an original bit value to pass through. This example helps explain the idea:

$$
\begin{array}{ll}
\ 1010\ 0010 & \text{(original value)} \\
\otimes\ 1110\ 1011 & \text{(XOR mask)} \\
\hline
\ 0100\ 1001 & \text{(result)}
\end{array}
$$

Applying XOR to these two values, when both bits are equal, the result is 0. When both bits are different, the result is 1. Using Table 3-2 as a guide, verify that each of the columns in this example is correct. Then watch what happens when the XOR mask has a 1 bit in every position:

$$
\begin{array}{ll}
\ 1010\ 0101 & \text{(original value)} \\
\otimes\ 1111\ 1111 & \text{(XOR mask)} \\
\hline
\ 0101\ 1010 & \text{(result)}
\end{array}
$$

Compare the top and bottom lines. Each bit in the original value is reversed in the result. All the ones are converted to zeros; all the zeros, to ones. (Adding 1 to this result gives the two's complement of the original value. How interesting.) What's more astounding about XOR is that, as if by magic, repeating the identical operation restores the original value:

$$
\begin{array}{ll}
\ 0101\ 1010 & \text{(result from previous example)} \\
\otimes\ 1111\ 1111 & \text{(same XOR mask, too)} \\
\hline
\ 1010\ 0101 & \text{(original value!)}
\end{array}
$$

You can understand this apparent sleight of hand by observing that, if an XOR mask toggles every bit in the original for which there is a corresponding 1 in the mask, then reapplying that same mask to the result has to again toggle every bit back to its original value. This action—the ability to combine a value via XOR and then restore the original value with a second XOR—is frequently used in graphics software to allow objects, represented by bit patterns, to pass through each other harmlessly. Other uses for this property are found in communications and encryption software.

As a kind of side show effect—because of XOR's toggling action—every 1 bit in the mask toggles the corresponding bit in the original value on or off. Exclusively ORing any value with itself always gives 0. For example:

$$
\begin{array}{ll}
\ 0111\ 1101 & \text{(original value)} \\
\otimes\ 0111\ 1101 & \text{(same value as an XOR mask)} \\
\hline
\ 0000\ 0000 & \text{(result)}
\end{array}
$$

Remember: The result is 0 when two exclusive-ORed bits have the same value. Obviously, XORing two identical values can have only one effect—all zeros in the result. By the way, you'll see this trick often in 8086 assembly language programs. There are other ways to change a byte to 0, but XORing a value with itself is one of the fastest methods available.

> Note: Subtracting a value from itself also produces 0. For an interesting experiment, try adding the two's complement of a value to itself. What do you get for the result? As you can see, there is more than one way to skin a byte.

Returning to the example of a light attached to a computer, you could perform this XOR operation to toggle the light on and off without affecting the other bit values:

```
      vvv? s???   (original settings)
  ⊗   0000 1000   (XOR mask)
      vvv? x???   (result)
```

A 1 bit in the XOR mask toggles the corresponding bit *s* in the original value to its opposite value *x* in the result without affecting any other bits. The importance of this operation is that the program doesn't have to know the original value *s* to toggle the value. All that's known is that the result is opposite of the original. If the light was on, now it's off. If it was off, now it's on.

Shifting and Rotating

Shifting bits left and right is another common operation performed on binary values. A shift to the left typically moves a 0 bit into the LSD position, pushing the former MSD off the edge of the cliff at the far left. A shift to the right does the same, but moves a 0 bit into the MSD position, losing the former LSD. Variations on this theme store the lost bit and move the value of another single-bit flag into the new LSD or MSD position. Other variations move the LSD or MSD around to the other end—or through a single-bit flag—causing the bits to rotate.

Because bit shifting is such a common operation in assembly language programming, we'll pick up this discussion again when meeting the 8086 shift and rotate instructions. But, for now, there are two concepts you should understand: multiplication by shifting left and division by shifting right. To understand how it is possible to multiply and divide by shifting, examine this addition:

```
    0110 1011   (original value)
  + 0110 1011   (added to itself)
    1101 0110   (shifts value left!)
```

As the top and bottom lines indicate, adding a value to itself causes the bits to shift one position to the left. Stated differently, a binary multiplication by 2 is equivalent to shifting the bits in the value once to the left. Continuing to shift the bits left multiplies the result again by 2, thus multiplying the original value by 4, or 2^2. This leads to a general rule: To multiply any value by a power of 2, shift the value left by the exponent's value. To find x times 2^4—that is, to multiply x by 16—shift x left 4 bit positions.

Apparently, if shifting left multiplies binary values by successive powers of 2, shifting right divides values by 2, 4, 8, and so on. To find the result of 1010 1111 (AF hexadecimal, or 175 decimal) divided by 4, just shift the bits right twice:

```
1010 1111   (original value)
0101 0111   (divided by 2)
0010 1011   (divided by 2 more)
```

The result, 0010 1011 (2B hexadecimal, or 43) equals the result of 175 divided by 4—throwing away any remainder, that is. Similar to multiplication, to divide by any power of 2, shift the original value right by the exponent's value.

There are several catches to these tricks. For one, you can multiply and divide only unsigned values by powers of 2. For another, the product must fit within the size of the destination. (Multiplying 1111 1111 by 2, for example, is *not* equal to 1111 1110—a ninth bit is needed to represent the correct result.) And, because bits are lost off the forward end of the shift—with 0 bits coming in from the leading edge—dividing ignores any remainder in the result. Despite these restrictions, because shifting bits is one of the fastest operations a digital computer processor can perform, whenever you can multiply or divide by shifting, it pays to do so. In future chapters, you'll see programming examples that prove this point.

Summary

Bits and bytes fuel the computer processor. There are 8 bits in a byte; 2 bytes in a word; 4 bytes in a doubleword; 6 bytes in a farword; and 8 bytes in a quadword. In memory, bytes are stored consecutively, each byte precisely located by a unique address. Word values are stored in byte-swapped order with the most significant bytes at higher addresses.

Well-dressed assembly language programmers need only four binary basics in their wardrobe: counting from 0 to 16 in binary; converting among binary, hexadecimal, and decimal values; understanding logical AND, OR, and XOR operations; and representing negative values in two's complement notation.

As in other positional number systems, columns from right to left in binary represent increasing powers of the number base. Because 16 is a power of 2, hexadecimal notation gives programmers a convenient way to represent binary values by substitution. Converting between hexadecimal and binary is easy. Converting between decimal and hexadecimal is more difficult—probably best handled by a programmer's calculator. Even so, you should learn how to do the conversion by hand, which is not so difficult once you know the tricks.

Negative values in binary are represented in two's complement notation. A negative number's MSD always equals 1. For simplicity, 0 is considered to be a positive value. Two's complement notation allows processors to subtract by adding and also makes it easy to find the absolute value of any negative number expressed in two's complement form.

The three logical operations AND, OR, and XOR are typically used to manipulate individual bits in binary values without disturbing other bits. AND masks combine with binary values to isolate one or more bits. OR masks can set individual bits to 1. XOR masks can toggle bits from 1 to 0 and back regardless of the original value. AND followed by OR is one of assembly language's most common sequences and is typically used to change specific bit values without disturbing other bits in bytes.

Shifting bits left multiplies unsigned binary values by successive powers of 2. Shifting bits right divides unsigned binary values by powers of 2, throwing away any remainder. Because computers can shift bits very quickly, using these operations can help speed binary math in assembly language programs.

Exercises

3-1. What does the word "bit" stand for?

3-2. How many bits are there in a byte? How many bytes are in a word? How many words are in a quadword?

3-3. What do MSD, LSD, MSB, and LSB stand for?

3-4. What is the sum of the two binary values 0110 1011 1111 1001 and 1010 1011 1100 1000?

3-5. What are the hexadecimal equivalents of the binary values in question #4 (including the sum)?

3-6. How much in decimal does 2^7 represent? What column (bit number) in a binary value has the power of 2^7?

3-7. How much is 3BF9 in decimal? How much is decimal 12,152 in binary? Try doing this by hand, even if you have a programmer's calculator. (Hint: Convert the decimal value to hexadecimal and then to binary by substitution.)

3-8. What AND mask would you use to isolate bits 5, 3, and 2 in an 8-bit byte? What OR mask would you use to set bits 7 and 6 to 1? What XOR mask would you use to toggle a byte's MSD on and off?

3-9. [Advanced] Given the job of setting bits 3 and 7 to 1 while toggling bit 2 on/off and preserving all other bits in a byte, what combination of masks and logical operators would you use?

3-10. How many bits are there in 2,048 farwords?

3-11. What are the one's and two's complements of the binary values 1011 1111, 0000 0001, 1000 0000, 1110 0001, and 1111 1111?

3-12. What is the decimal equivalent of the signed binary value 1111 1001? What is the decimal equivalent of these same bits as an unsigned binary value?

3-13. What is the maximum value that you can express in 6 bits? How many values can you express in 9 bits?

3-14. Multiply 0011 1001 by 4 using a bit shift. Divide 1001 1100 by 8 using bit shifts. Check your answers in decimal. Why can't you multiply 0101 0101 by 8 using bit shifting?

Projects

3-1. Count in binary and hexadecimal from 0 to 16 without referring to Table 3-1. Create your own binary-to-hex pocket reference.

3-2. Devise number circles similar to Figure 3-3 for 3- and 5-bit binary values.

3-3. Why do you suppose processors like the 8086 require words to be stored in byte-swapped order?

3-4. Write the bit numbers for a 16-bit word as depicted on the top of Figure 3-1.

3-5. Write the truth tables for AND, OR, and XOR without referring to Table 3-2.

3-6. Add several binary values to themselves. What do the results suggest?

Chapter *4* **Programming in Assembly Language**

4 Programming in Assembly Language

In This Chapter

How memory segments divide memory; the difference between logical and physical addresses; the 8086 processor registers and flags; instruction groups and concepts; how stacks operate; signed and unsigned integer mathematics; shift and rotate instructions; subroutines; jump instructions; introducing strings and repeat prefixes; plus several example programs demonstrating most of the 8086 instruction set

Memory Segmentation

Before learning about 8086 processor registers and the instruction set, it's helpful to understand how the 8086 addresses memory using a system of *segments* and *offsets*—two terms that have caused more than their fair share of confusion.

Representing address values internally in 20 bits, the 8086 processor can directly access up to 1 megabyte of memory. Because DOS, the ROM BIOS, and a few other items occupy some of that space in PCs, most software has to run in a smaller space of about 256K to 512K. If you want your programs to run on as many PCs as possible, limit your memory requirements to this range.

No matter how much memory the processor can address, and no matter how many memory chips are installed inside the computer, the smallest memory unit remains the 8-bit byte. As mentioned earlier, each byte has a unique location, called the *physical address,* which programs specify to read and write the bytes they need. Obviously, you need a greater number of bits to represent the physical addresses of greater amounts of memory. If your computer had only 64K, then the address of any byte would comfortably fit in 16 bits, which can represent values from 0 to 65,535 ($2^{16} - 1$)—or 64K in round numbers. To address the PC's maximum 1 megabyte of memory requires a minimum of 20 bits. ($2^{20} - 1$ equals

1,048,575, or hexadecimal FFFFF.) The problem is: 8086 registers are only 16 bits wide. How is it possible for the 8086 processor to access the full megabyte of memory in a typical PC?

The answer is *memory segmentation,* a method the 8086 uses to divide its large address space into logical 64K chunks. With this method, the address of a specific byte can be expressed in two values: the address of the chunk, or segment, plus a 16-bit offset from the beginning of the segment. Together, the combination of segment and offset values is called the *logical address.* The first byte in a segment is at offset 0000, the second at offset 0001, the third at 0002, and so on—no matter where the segment physically begins in memory. Figure 4-1 illustrates this idea, showing that each location in memory has both a physical address (right) and a logical address (left), expressed as an offset from the beginning of a segment boundary. With segmentation, the 8086 processor can efficiently address up to 1 megabyte of memory while using relatively small, 16-bit registers. As an additional benefit, segmentation makes it easy to move programs to new physical locations by changing only the segment base address. The offset values within a segment require no adjustments, allowing for *relocatable programs* that can run identically in different memory locations.

Paragraphs, Segments, and Offsets

To locate the beginnings of memory segments, the 8086 processor contains four 16-bit segment registers. Internally, the processor combines the value of one segment register with a 16-bit offset (the logical address) to create a 20-bit physical address. It does this by first multiplying the segment value by 16 and then adding the offset to the result. Because of the multiplication—equivalent to shifting the bits left four times, as you recall from chapter 3—segment boundaries fall on physical address multiples of 16 bytes. Each of these 16-byte memory tidbits is called a *paragraph.* A simple calculation proves that there are a maximum of 65,536 paragraphs—and, therefore, an equal number of segment boundaries—in the 8086's 1-megabyte address space (1,048,576/16). (Notice that this also equals the

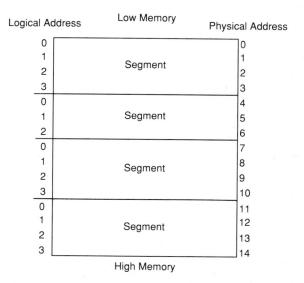

Figure 4-1 *Logical addresses all have equivalent physical addresses in memory.*

number of values you can express in one 16-bit segment register.) Here are a few other important facts about segments to keep in mind:

▶ Segments are not physically etched in memory—a common misconception. A segment is a logical window through which programs view portions of memory in convenient 64K chunks.

▶ A segment's starting location (that is, the segment's logical address) is up to you and can be any value from 0000 to FFFF hex. Each logical segment value (0, 1, 2, . . . , 65,535) corresponds to a physical paragraph boundary (0, 16, 32, . . . , 1,048,560).

▶ Segments can be as small as 16 bytes or as large as 64K (65,536 bytes). The actual size of a segment is up to you and your program.

▶ Segments do not have to butt up against each other physically in memory, although they often do.

▶ Segments can overlap with other segments; therefore, the same byte in memory can have many different logical addresses specified with different but equivalent segment and offset pairs. Even so, each byte has one and only one 20-bit physical address.

This last point confuses almost everyone on their introduction to memory segmentation. Two different segment and offset pairs can (and often do) refer to the same byte in memory. If you remember how the processor creates a 20-bit physical address—multiplying the segment value by 16 and adding the offset—you can see that the segment:offset hexadecimal values 0000:0010 and 0001:0000 refer to the same physical location. Duplicating in decimal how the 8086 processor converts these logical addresses to physical addresses, each calculation—$(0000 \times 16) + 16$ and $(0001 \times 16) + 0$—gives the same result, 16.

Note: By custom, a segment and offset logical address is written with two 4-digit hexadecimal numbers separated by a colon, for example, 0140:001A and F000:0010. When you see values like these, you should assume they are hexadecimal. This is easy to forget with addresses like 0100:1024 and 0000:0010, which are not obviously in hexadecimal.

8086 Registers

Figure 4-2 illustrates the 8086 registers. The same registers are available in all 80x86 models. (The 80386 has additional registers and extensions that don't concern us here.) If you limit your register use to those listed in Figure 4-2, your programs are guaranteed to run on all PCs. The registers are grouped into five categories:

▶ General-purpose registers (ax, bx, cx, dx)

▶ Pointer and index registers (sp, bp, si, di)

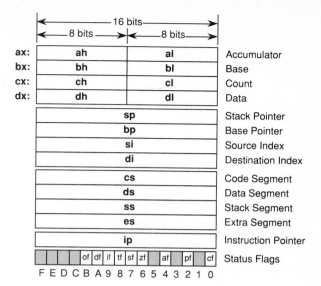

Figure 4-2 *8086 registers.*

▶ Segment registers (cs, ds, ss, es)

▶ Instruction pointer (ip)

▶ Flags (of, df, if, tf, sf, zf, af, pf, cf)

All 8086 registers are 16 bits wide. In addition, the four general-purpose registers—ax, bx, cx, and dx—are subdivided into high and low 8-bit halves. The 16-bit ax register, for example, is composed of two 8-bit parts, ah and al. Register bx is divided into bh and bl; cx, into ch and cl; and dx, into dh and dl. This flexible arrangement lets you operate directly on the full 16-bit register width or work separately with the register's two 8-bit halves. Remember that changing the value in the 16-bit ax also changes the register's two 8-bit halves al and ah. Likewise, changing the value in cl also changes the value of cx.

Note: In this text, registers are written in lowercase—cs, ax, si, etc. In programs and in other references, you'll often see the same registers in uppercase as in AX, BX, DH. Both forms are correct.

General-Purpose Registers

Assembly language programs refer to registers by their mnemonics, ax, cl, ds, and others. But the registers also have less familiar names as shown to the right of Figure 4-2. (The names are never used directly in programs, though.) The *accumulator* ax is usually used to accumulate the results of additions, subtractions, and so forth. The *base* register bx often points to the starting address (called the base) of a structure in memory. The *count* register cx frequently specifies the number of times some operation is to repeat. And the *data* register dx most often holds data, perhaps passed to a subroutine for processing. These definitions are by no means fixed, and most of the time it's up to you to decide how to use a general-purpose register. For example, just because cx is called the count register, there's no reason you can't count things using bx. In some cases, however, certain 8086 instructions require specific registers.

Pointer and Index Registers

Contrasting the four general-purpose registers, other 8086 registers in Figure 4-2 are closely related to specific operations. The *stack pointer* sp always points to the top of the processor's stack. (We'll tackle stacks in detail a bit later.) The *base pointer* bp usually addresses variables stored inside the stack. *Source index* si and *destination index* di are known as *string registers.* Usually, si and di serve as work horses for easing the load of processing byte strings.

> Note: A byte string is not the same as a high-level language's character string data type. In assembly language, a string is simply a series of consecutive bytes. To avoid confusion, I'll use the term *character string* to refer to an ASCII string as found in most high-level languages. A plain string can be any sequence of bytes, which might also represent characters.

Segment Registers

The four segment registers—cs, ds, ss, and es—locate the start of four 64K segments in memory, as illustrated in Figure 4-3. A program is free to allocate more than four segments but, in that case, has to swap the correct values in and out of one or more segment registers to address the additional segments.

Segment registers are highly specialized. You can't directly perform math on segment registers or use them to hold the results of other operations. The *code-segment register* cs addresses the start of the program's machine code in memory. The *data-segment register* ds addresses the start of the program's variables. The *stack-segment register* locates the start of the program's stack space. The *extra-segment register* es locates an additional data segment if needed, although in many programs, es and ds address the same memory, facilitating some operations tied to these registers. Actual segment order does not have to match the order shown in Figure 4-3. As explained before, segments may be stored anywhere in memory and in any order.

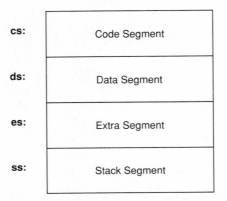

Figure 4-3 *Segment registers address four memory segments.*

Instruction Pointer

The special-purpose *instruction pointer* ip specifies the next machine-code instruction to be executed, relative to the segment located by cs. You'll rarely (if ever) refer to ip directly. Instead, you'll use instructions that change ip (and possibly cs) to alter the location of the next instruction to be executed, thus changing the flow of the program. For example, calling a subroutine causes the address of that routine to be loaded into ip (or into the cs:ip pair).

Flags

Although the *status flags* register is 16 bits wide, only 9 bits are used. (See Figure 4-2.) The other 7 bits are of no use to programs. Individual flag bits are represented by single letters o, d, i, t, s, z, a, p, and c. Some references (including this one) frequently refer to these as of, df, if, and so on. Table 4-1 list the full names of each flag bit.

Most of the time, the 8086 flag bits reflect the result of various instructions and operations. For example, after an addition, the carry flag cf indicates if the result generated a carry. The overflow flag indicates if the result of a signed addition cannot be represented correctly within a certain number of bits. Flags also serve multiple purposes. For instance, you might shift a register's bits left, transferring the former MSD into the carry flag cf for inspection. Other instructions can then take action based on the setting of this and other flag bits. Or you might use cf as a single-bit warning device to indicate that an error occurred, allowing other parts of the program to be aware that something is amiss. As you learn each assembly language instruction, you'll also learn the various roles that flags play in a program's actions.

Table 4-1 *8086 Flags*

Symbol	Full Name
o or of	Overflow flag
d or df	Direction flag
i or if	Interrupt enable flag
t or tf	Trap (single-step) flag
s or sf	Sign flag
z or zf	Zero flag
a or af	Auxiliary flag
p or pf	Parity flag
c or cf	Carry flag

Instruction Groups and Concepts

All 8086 instructions are divided by function into six categories. The rest of this chapter examines each of these groups and lists short programs that you can use to view the operation of many 8086 instructions. (Future chapters will introduce the remaining instructions.) The six groups are:

▶ Data transfer instructions

▶ Arithmetic instructions

▶ Logic instructions

▶ Flow-control instructions

▶ Processor control instructions

▶ String instructions

Note: Chapter 14's 8086 reference lists each instruction with programming examples and full descriptions of the kinds of data elements that instructions can process. Please refer to chapter 14 for additional details as you meet new 8086 instructions here.

Data Transfer Instructions

Table 4-2 lists the 8086 data transfer instructions. There are four subdivisions in this group: General, Input/Output, Address, and Flag. The operands to the right of each mnemonic specify the data elements required by the instruction. Most instruction mnemonics specify destination and source operands. Others require one or no operands.

Let's look at the first data transfer instruction mov and see how it works. Probably, mov appears in assembly language programs more frequently than any other instruction. From Table 4-2, you see that mov requires a source

Table 4-2 *Data Transfer Instructions*

Mnemonic/operands	Description
General Instructions	
mov *destination, source*	Move (copy) byte or word
pop *destination*	Pop data from stack
push *immediate*	Push data onto stack
xchg *destination, source*	Exchange bytes and words
xlat/xlatb *table*	Translate from table
Input/Output Instructions	
in *accumulator, port*	Input (get) byte or word
out *port, accumulator*	Output (put) byte or word
Address Instructions	
lds *destination, source*	Load pointer using ds
lea *destination, source*	Load effective address
les *destination, source*	Load pointer using es
Flag Instructions	
lahf	Load ah from (some) flags
popf	Pop flag register from stack
pushf	Push flag register onto stack
sahf	Store ah into (some) flags

and a destination operand. Notice that the source is written after the destination, implying that mov operates this way:

```
mov  destination <-- source
```

The source data moves in the direction of the arrow, from right to left. Be careful not to reverse the operands, a typical and potentially disastrous mistake. In assembly langauge programs, the following instruction moves the value of the bx register into the ax register:

```
mov  ax, bx     ; ax <-- bx
```

If ax equals 0000 and bx equals 0123h, then this instruction sets ax equal to 0123h. The value of bx does not change. Some programmers like to use a comment to clarify the direction that the data moves. Here's an example:

```
mov  cx, [numPages]    ; cx <-- [numPages]
```

This mov instruction moves the value stored at numPages into the cx register. The brackets around numPages are important. The label numPages specifies a memory address. But, with brackets, [numPages] stands for the data stored at that address. This concept—that a label specifies the address of data stored in memory—is vital to your understanding of assembly language programming. At all times, you must be careful to specify whether an instruction is to operate on an address value or on the data stored at that address. Brackets are simple tools for this purpose, but you must remember to use them correctly.

You can move data from registers to memory, too. For example, this copies the value in the 8-bit register dl to the address specified by level:

```
mov  [level], dl        ; [level] <-- dl
```

From the brackets, you know that the value of dl moves to the location to which level points. Moving data around this way— copying one register value to another and transferring data from a register to a location in memory—is one of the most common operations in assembly language programming. One thing mov can't do, however, is transfer data directly between two memory locations. This never works:

```
mov  [count], [maxCount]      ; ???
```

To move the value stored at maxCount into the location addressed by count instead requires two steps, using a register as an intermediate holding bin:

```
mov  ax, [maxCount]    ; ax <-- [maxCount]
mov  [count], ax       ; [count] <-- ax
```

A Moving Example   Program 4-1 demonstrates how mov works. Assemble, link, and load the program into Turbo Debugger with the commands:

```
tasm /zi mov
tlink /v mov
td mov
```

Program 4-1 *MOV.ASM*

```
 1:  %TITLE "MOV Demonstration"
 2:
 3:          IDEAL
 4:          DOSSEG
 5:          MODEL   small
 6:          STACK   256
 7:
 8:          DATASEG
 9:
10:  exitCode       DB      0
11:  speed          DB      99              ; One-byte variable
12:
13:          CODESEG
14:
15:  Start:
16:          mov     ax, @data             ; Initialize ds to address
17:          mov     ds, ax                ;   of data segment
18:
19:          mov     ax, 1                 ; Move immediate data into
20:          mov     bx, 2                 ;   registers
21:          mov     cx, 3
22:          mov     dx, 4
23:
24:          mov     ah, [speed]           ; Load value of speed into al
25:          mov     si, offset speed      ; Load address of speed into si
26:
27:  Exit:
28:          mov     ah, 04Ch              ; DOS function: Exit program
29:          mov     al, [exitCode]        ; Return exit code value
30:          int     21h                   ; Call DOS. Terminate program
31:
32:          END     Start         ; End of program / entry point
```

Running MOV in Turbo Debugger   You should now have the MOV program loaded into Turbo Debugger. Follow these numbered steps for a few experiments that will help you to understand what the instructions do:

1. Press Alt-V-C to open the CPU window and press F5 to zoom the window to full screen. Because the CPU window shows many important details on one display—the stack, registers, flags, memory, and instructions—this is the window you should use to run most assembly language programs in this book.

2. Press F8 to run the program a single step (instruction) at a time as you read the following descriptions. (Line numbers refer to the numbers printed in this book along with Program 4-1's listing.)

3. Lines 16–17 initialize the ds segment register, first assigning to ax a predefined value @data and then assigning this value to ds. (You can assign only values from a general-purpose register, a

memory variable, or the stack to a segment register—you can't directly assign literal values to segment registers.)

4. Executing lines 19–22 assigns literal values 1, 2, 3, and 4 to the general-purpose registers `ax`, `bx`, `cx`, and `dx`. Stop pressing F8 when Turbo Debugger's instruction arrow (to the right of the addresses such as `cs:0011`) points to the `mov ah, [speed]` instruction. (If you accidentally go too far, press Ctrl-F2 to reset and then press F8 until you get back to the right spot.)

5. The `mov ah, [speed]` instruction at line 24 loads the value stored at the location addressed by `speed` into the 8-bit register half `ah`. Near the top of the display in the double-line border, look for the text that reads `ds:0001 = 63`. This tells you the value in hexadecimal (63) that is about to be loaded into `ah`. The `ds:0001` notation indicates the address at which this value is stored. Like all addresses, the address has two components: a segment value (held by register `ds`) and an offset 0001.

6. Press F8 to execute the instruction at line 24 and watch the value of the `ax` register change in the upper right corner of the display. Notice that the `ds:0001=63` is now gone. To see this again, use the up and down arrow keys to move the highlighted bar up and down. You can always move the bar to any individual instruction to see the effect of values about to be loaded into registers or written to memory.

7. Find register `si` near the upper right third of the CPU window. Press F8 again, executing the instruction at line 25, `mov si, offset speed`. As you can see, this instruction sets register `si` to 0001, the offset value of the address in the previous step. The `OFFSET` keyword in the `mov` instruction tells the assembler you intend to use the offset address of a label. (`OFFSET` may be in lowercase—`offset`—on your screen.)

8. Continue to press F8 until the program ends. Lines 28–30 perform three steps that end every EXE program. First, the value of the DOS exit operation (04Ch) is loaded into `ah`. Then, `al` is assigned the contents of variable `exitCode`, which a program can pass back to DOS as an error indicator. A zero value means no error. The `int 21h` instruction at line 30 calls DOS with these parameters in `ah` and `al`, ending the program.

9. Press Esc followed by Alt-X to quit Turbo Debugger.

> Note: The lowercase *h* at the end of values like 21h and 04Ch tells Turbo Assembler that these values are expressed in hexadecimal, always beginning with decimal digits. In other words, you cannot write FFFh. Instead, you must write 0FFFh.

Stacking the Deck   A stack is a special segment of memory that operates in conjunction with several 8086 instructions. As with all segments, the location of the stack and its size (up to 64K) is up to you and your program to determine. In assembly language programs, the easiest way to create a stack is to use the **STACK** directive, as in most example programs in this book. If you don't create a stack, you'll receive a warning from Turbo Linker. A stack has three main purposes:

▶ To preserve register values temporarily

▶ To store addresses to which subroutines return

▶ To store dynamic variables

The last of these comes into play more often in high-level language programming, where variables are passed via the stack to and from functions and procedures. Similarly, temporary variables may be stored on the stack. These uses are rare in pure assembly language programming, although you can certainly store variables in stack memory this way if you want.

How Stacks Operate

Conceptually, a stack is like a spring-loaded bin of dishes in a restaurant kitchen. The top dish on the stack is readily available, but to get to the dishes below, other dishes above must first be removed. Placing a new dish on the top of the stack is called a *push*. Removing a dish from the top of the stack, causing other dishes below to move up a notch, is called a *pop*. Because of the way the last dishes pushed onto the stack are the first dishes to be popped, this kind of a stack is called a LIFO stack, for "Last-In-First-Out."

Unlike dishes, values in computer memory can't physically move up and down. Therefore, to simulate the action of a moving stack of values requires using registers to locate the base address of the stack and the offset address of the top dish—that is, the location where the top value of the stack is stored. In 8086 programming, segment register **ss** addresses the stack segment base. Register **sp** addresses the top of stack offset in that segment.

Figure 4-4 illustrates how a small stack of 12 bytes appears in memory. Register **ss** addresses the base of the stack at segment address 0F00. Register **sp** addresses offsets from this starting address, ranging from 0000 to 000A. The last byte in the stack is at offset 000B (in the figure, just to the right of the byte at 000A). Items in the stack occupy 2-byte words. The program that prepares this stack would declare a **STACK 12** and let the assembler, linker, and DOS calculate exactly where in memory the stack will be stored. You don't have to initialize registers **ss** and **sp**. DOS does that for you when it loads your assembled program. In the figure, **sp1** shows where **sp** points when the program begins running. Notice that the logical address in **ss:sp** points to the byte *below* the last byte in the stack.

> Note: Because the bottom of an 8086 stack is at a higher memory address than the top of the stack, terms like "bottom," "above," and "below" can be confusing. Because these terms are so common when discussing stacks, there's nothing to do but live with the ambiguities. Just remember that in memory, stacks grow toward lower memory addresses and shrink toward higher ground.

Refer again to Figure 4-4. Several actions occur if you execute these instructions:

```
mov   ax, 100
push ax                    ; sp2
mov   bx, 200
push bx                    ; sp3
```

The **push** instruction performs two steps:

1. 2 is subtracted from **sp**
2. The specified register value is copied to [**ss:sp**]

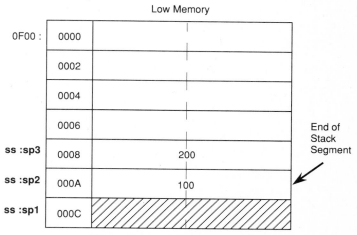

Figure 4-4 *The stack segment.*

The order of these steps is important. A **push** first subtracts 2 (not 1) from **sp**. In Figure 4-4, the first such **push** leaves **sp** at **sp2**, where the value of register **ax** is then stored. Notice that this action leaves the stack pointer addressing the most recently pushed word value on the stack.

Note: Become familiar with the notation [**ss:sp**], which refers to the contents at the offset of **sp** inside the stack segment. Remember that the brackets refer to the value stored in memory at a specified address.

A Stack Demo   You can use Turbo Debugger to watch a stack in action—a great way to learn how stacks operate. For this purpose, use Program 4-2, which demonstrates one of the stack's most common uses—to preserve register values. Assemble, link, and load the program into Turbo Debugger with the commands:

```
tasm /zi pushpop
tlink /v pushpop
td pushpop
```

After the listing are step-by-step instructions for running the program under control of Turbo Debugger.

Program 4-2 *PUSHPOP.ASM*

```
 1:  %TITLE "PUSH/POP Demonstration"
 2:
 3:          IDEAL
 4:          DOSSEG
 5:          MODEL   small
 6:          STACK   256
 7:
 8:          DATASEG
 9:
10:  exitCode        DB      0
11:
12:          CODESEG
13:
14:  Start:
15:          mov     ax, @data       ; Initialize ds to address
16:          mov     ds, ax          ;  of data segment
17:
18:          push    ax              ; Save ax and bx
19:          push    bx              ;  on the stack
20:
21:          mov     ax, -1          ; Assign test values
22:          mov     bx, -2
23:          mov     cx, 0
24:          mov     dx, 0
25:
26:          push    ax              ; Push ax onto stack
27:          push    bx              ; Push bx onto stack
28:          pop     cx              ; Pop cx from stack
29:          pop     dx              ; Pop dx from stack
30:
31:          pop     bx              ; Restore saved ax and bx
32:          pop     ax              ;  values from stack
33:
34:  Exit:
35:          mov     ah, 04Ch        ; DOS function: Exit program
36:          mov     al, [exitCode]  ; Return exit code value
37:          int     21h             ; Call DOS. Terminate program
38:
39:          END     Start           ; End of program / entry point
```

**Running the
PUSHPOP Demo**
You should have PUSHPOP running in Turbo Debugger. Follow these
steps to see a stack in action:

1. Open and zoom the CPU window with Alt-V-C and F5. Press F8
    twice, stepping to line 18. Note the values of the **ax** and **bx**
    registers.

2. Watch the stack values in the lower right corner—the window
    with addresses that begin with **ss:**. Press F8 once to push the
    value of **ax** onto the stack. Press F8 again to push the value of

bx. The top of the stack is marked with an arrow at the bottom of the window. (Only Turbo Debugger's designers know why the "top" of the stack appears at the "bottom" of this window. I told you such terms tend to be confusing.)

3. Press F8 four times, executing lines 21–24 and loading registers ax, bx, cx, and dx with test values.

4. Press F8 again to execute line 26, pushing the value of ax onto the stack. Observe the stack contents and the value of sp before and after the push. Press F8 once more to push bx.

5. Lines 28 and 29 pop the stack, removing the value at [ss:sp] and adding 2 to sp, addressing the next word. Press F8 twice to execute the two lines. Notice that you can pop values from the stack into registers other than the ones you pushed earlier.

6. Press F8 twice again to execute lines 31–32. These instructions restore the values of bx and ax to the values they had before executing lines 18–19.

7. Quit Turbo Debugger with Alt-X. You don't have to run the program to its completion.

Stack Management

The goal of good stack management is simple: For every push in a program, there must be a balancing pop. Matching your pops and pushes keeps the stack pointer "right"—in other words, in synch with the program's ability to store and retrieve the values it needs.

> Note: There are exceptions to the rule that every push must be balanced with a pop. For example, you can add and subtract values from sp, perhaps to reserve stack space for storing temporary values. And you can end a program with DOS function 4C even if the stack is not in synch. But in general, try to keep the stack in a known state at all times. Careless stack management is one of the leading causes of serious bugs.

Consider what happens if you fail to execute a matching pop for every push. In this case, future pushes will cause the stack to grow larger and larger, eventually overflowing the segment space allotted by your program. This serious error usually results in a crash as areas in memory are overwritten by the runaway stack pointer. A similar error occurs if you execute more pops than pushes, causing a stack underflow and also usually resulting in a crash.

A good way to prevent such problems is to write your programs in small modules, or subroutines. In each module, push onto the stack all the registers you plan to use. Then, just before this section of code ends, pop the same registers off the stack but in the reverse order. For example, here's how you might construct a typical section:

```
push ax          ; Save ax, bx, dx on the stack
push bx
push dx


; ---- Programming goes here


pop dx           ; Restore dx, bx, ax from the stack in reverse order
pop bx
pop ax
```

Presumably, the instructions between the push and pop instructions will use ax, bx, and dx; therefore, these registers are pushed onto the stack to preserve the register values. Later, the same registers are popped from the stack in reverse order, restoring the original register values and keeping the stack in synch. Recalling the analogy of the stack of dishes, you can see that popping in reverse order is necessary to restore the previously saved values to the correct registers. The last value pushed onto the stack (dx) is the first to be removed, while the first dish pushed (ax) is the last to be popped.

> Note: After popping a value from the stack, don't attempt to subtract 2 from sp and reread that same value in the future. This is always illegal, even though you may notice while viewing the stack in Turbo Debugger that the popped values appear to remain in the stack memory at address offsets lower than sp. Only the values located from sp to the bottom of the stack are guaranteed to be preserved. All other values in the stack segment are subject to being overwritten, possibly by DOS and, even more likely, by interrupts that run concurrently with your program. (Chapter 10 explains more about interrupts and stack handling.) Breaking this rule is a sure way to break your code. Don't do it!

Exchanging Data   Let's examine another instruction from Table 4-2, xchg, which swaps two register values or a register value and a byte or word stored in memory. Suppose you want to exchange the values in dx and ax. With xchg, you simply write:

```
xchg ax, dx      ; ax <- dx; dx <- ax
```

Even though Table 4-2 lists source and destination operands for xchg, the order of operands doesn't matter as the instruction swaps the value of one operand with the other. Without xchg, swapping two registers requires either a push onto the stack or a third register. For example, here's a less efficient method to exchange two 16-bit registers using the stack as an intermediate way station for one value:

```
push ax          ; stack <- ax
mov  ax, dx      ; ax <- dx
pop  dx          ; dx <- stack (original ax)
```

Swapping two 8-bit values takes a third register because you can't push bytes onto the stack—you can push and pop only 16-bit words. Without xchg, to swap two bytes in al and ah, you could write:

```
mov bh, ah      ; bh <- ah
mov ah, al      ; ah <- al
mov al, bh      ; al <- bh
```

Of course, with xchg, none of this is necessary. (It is instructive to understand how the stack and other registers can be used this way, however.) In addition to swapping register values, xchg can also swap the value in a register with a value stored in memory. Here are two examples:

```
xchg ax, [things]       ; ax <--> [things]
xchg [oldCount], cx     ; cx <--> [oldCount]
```

The first line swaps the value of ax with the value stored at things. The second line swaps cx and oldCount. Again, the order of operands is unimportant.

Note: Exchanging full 16-bit register values when one of those registers is the accumulator ax executes a tiny bit faster than instructions that exchange other registers. Turbo Assembler correctly assembles instructions such as xchg ax,bx and xchg cx,ax into fast, single-byte machine-code instructions. Other exchanges that don't involve ax take 2 bytes of machine code. Be aware that all assemblers are not as smart as Turbo. For example, the assembler in DOS DEBUG requires ax to be specified last to generate the single-byte machine-code form. Also, pure register exchanges are many times faster than exchanges between registers and values in memory. Paying attention to small details like these will help you to squeeze extra speed from your code.

Arithmetic Instructions

Most computers are great at math; therefore, it may come as a surprise that assembly language has only a few relatively primitive math operators. There are no exponentiation symbol, no floating point, no square root, and no SIN and COS functions built into the 8086 instruction set. Mathematics instructions in assembly language are restricted to adding, multiplying, dividing, and subtracting signed and unsigned binary integer values. Table 4-3 lists the 8086 math instructions.

There are two ways to increase the math power of assembly language programming. First, you can purchase (or write) a math package with routines that implement the high-level functions you need. Another solution is to purchase a math coprocessor chip for your PC, although this can be expensive if your computer has an 80286 or 80386 processor, which requires a complementary 80287 or 80387 math chip. Third, and probably

Table 4-3 *8086 Arithmetic Instructions*

Mnemonic/Operands	Description
Addition Instructions	
aaa	ASCII adjust for addition
adc *destination, source*	Add with carry
add *destination, source*	Add bytes or words
daa	Decimal adjust for addition
inc *destination*	Increment
Subtraction Instructions	
aas	ASCII adjust for subtraction
cmp *destination, source*	Compare
das	Decimal adjust for subtraction
dec *destination*	Decrement byte or word
neg *destination*	Negate (two's complement)
sbb *destination, source*	Subtract with borrow
sub *destination, source*	Subtract
Multiplication Instructions	
aam	ASCII adjust for multiply
imul *source*	Integer multiply
mul *source*	Multiply
Division Instructions	
aad	ASCII adjust for division
cbw	Convert byte to word
cwd	Convert word to doubleword
div *source*	Divide
idiv *source*	Integer divide

best, is to use a high-level language such as Turbo Pascal or Turbo C to code your floating point expressions. These languages come with automatic detectors to sniff out the presence of a math coprocessor and can switch to a software emulator for systems lacking the optional chip. After writing your program, you can combine the compiled high-level code with your assembly language program (see chapters 12 and 13). Because math coprocessors have strict requirements about data and instruction formats, most compilers generate optimized machine code, and there's little advantage to writing floating point expressions directly in assembly language.

But don't take this as a negative pronouncement on assembly language math. Even without a math library or coprocessor, you can do plenty with the 8086's built-in integer instructions. In fact, most programs get along just fine without any higher math abilities. You certainly don't need floating point numbers to total the bytes in a disk directory or to count the number of words in a text file. For these and other operations, integer math is more than adequate. In pure assembly language, such jobs frequently run more quickly than equivalent code of compiled high-level languages.

Addition Instructions   Table 4-3 lists five addition instructions. Two of these, `add` and `adc`, sum 2 bytes or words. `Inc` (increment) is a fast instruction to add 1 to a register or value in memory. (The other two instructions `aaa` and `daa` make adjustments to values stored in *binary-coded-decimal* format, which you'll meet again later on.) To add an 8-bit value in `ah` to the 8-bit value in `bh`, you can write:

```
add ah, bh        ; ah <- ah + bh
```

As with `mov`, the `add` instruction requires source and destination operands. The instruction sums these two values and stores the result in the specified destination, replacing the original value. In this example, the result is stored in `ah`. The `adc` instruction operates similarly but adds in the value of the carry flag `cf` to the result:

```
adc ah, bh        ; ah <- ah + bh + cf
```

If `cf` equals 1, the result is the same as adding 1 to the sum of `ah` and `bh`. After a previous `add` operation, `cf` is set to 1 if an overflow occurred; therefore, `adc` is most often used after an initial `add` when summing multibyte values, picking up the possible carries while individually adding each byte in turn. Although you can add words directly, you could use these instructions to add the individual bytes of a 16-bit value stored at `sum` to register `ax`. These instructions double the word at `sum`:

```
mov ax, [word sum]        ; Set ax to value of [sum]
add al, [byte sum]        ; Add LSBs
adc ah, [byte sum + 1]    ; Add MSBs with possible carry
mov [word sump], ax       ; Store value back in memory
```

Remember that words are stored in byte-swapped order. In this sample, the first line loads the word value into `ax`. The second line adds the least significant bytes together, storing the result in `al` and setting `cf` to 1 if the addition generates a carry. The third line adds this possible carry to the sum of the most significant bytes. Finally, the fourth line stores the final result back in memory. Because the 8086 can manipulate word values directly, you can perform this same addition with the simpler instructions:

```
mov     ax, [word sum]  ; Set ax to value of [sum]
add     [word sum], ax  ; Add [sum] to itself
```

True for all 2arg cmds   You must load [sum] into a register before adding because `add` cannot directly add two values stored in memory—at least one register must be specified. Notice that in these examples the `word` and `byte` operators tell the assembler what kind of data `sum` addresses. In some cases, the assembler can figure this out on its own. In others, you need to use the operators. There's no harm in using them, however. (Chapter 5 explains data formats and operators in more detail.)

Both `add` and `adc` can add immediate (literal) values to registers and values in memory. For example, this adds 5 to the current value of `bx`, storing the result in `bx`:

```
add bx, 5          ; bx <- bx + 5
```

When you need to add only 1 to a value, use inc instead of add—it's faster. Notice from Table 4-3 that inc requires only one operand. The following instructions increment four general purpose registers by 1:

```
inc ax             ; ax <- ax + 1
inc bx             ; bx <- bx + 1
inc cx             ; cx <- cx + 1
inc dh             ; dh <- dh + 1
```

The last of these samples increments dh, leaving the value of dl alone. The other three samples increment the full 16-bit registers specified. Remember that you can operate on either of a general-purpose register's 8-bit halves without affecting the other half.

Subtraction Instructions

Subtracting in assembly language is similar in form to adding. The sub instruction subtracts two byte or word values. The sbb does the same but takes into account a possible borrow from a previous subtraction of multibyte or multiword values. An example shows how to subtract bx from ax and store the result in ax:

```
sub ax, bx                 ; ax <- ax - bx
```

As with add and adc, you can subtract two registers or a register and a value stored in memory. You can also subtract immediate values. You should be able to understand the following samples by reading the comments to the right of each line:

```
sub cx, 5              ; cx <- cx - 5
sub dx, [score]        ; dx <- dx - [score]
sub [answer], 3        ; [answer] <- [answer] - 3
sub ax, 1              ; ax <- ax - 1
```

You can replace the last of these samples with the faster dec instruction, which decrements by 1 a register or value in memory. You can decrement byte and word values, as these samples show:

```
dec   ax               ; ax <- ax - 1
dec   dl               ; dl <- dl - 1
dec   si               ; si <- si - 1
dec   [balance]        ; [balance] <- [balance] - 1
```

Add and Subtract Demonstration

Program 4-3 demonstrates the four instructions add, sub, inc, and dec. Assemble, link, and run the program under control of Turbo Debugger with the instructions:

```
tasm /zi addsub
tlink /v addsub
td addsub
```

Program 4-3 *ADDSUB.ASM*

```
 1:   %TITLE "ADD, SUB, INC, DEC Demonstration"
 2:
 3:           IDEAL
 4:           DOSSEG
 5:           MODEL   small
 6:           STACK   256
 7:
 8:           DATASEG
 9:
10:   exitCode      DB      0
11:   count         DW      1
12:
13:           CODESEG
14:
15:   Start:
16:           mov     ax, @data       ; Initialize ds to address
17:           mov     ds, ax          ;  of data segment
18:
19:           mov     ax, 4
20:           mov     bx, 2
21:           add     ax, bx          ; ax <- ax + bx
22:
23:           mov     cx, 8
24:           add     cx, [count]     ; cx <- cx + [count]
25:
26:           add     [count], cx     ; [count] <- cx + [count]
27:
28:           inc     [count]         ; [count] <- [count] + 1
29:           dec     [count]         ; [count] <- [count] - 1
30:           inc     ax              ; ax <- ax + 1
31:           dec     cx              ; cx <- cx - 1
32:
33:   Exit:
34:           mov     ah, 04Ch        ; DOS function: Exit program
35:           mov     al, [exitCode]  ; Return exit code value
36:           int     21h             ; Call DOS. Terminate program
37:
38:           END     Start           ; End of program / entry point
```

Running the ADDSUB Demo Press Alt-V-C to view the CPU window and watch the register values change as you single step through the program by pressing F8 while reading the following descriptions. Try to predict register and memory values before executing each instruction.

Lines 19–21 show how to add the values in two registers ax and bx, storing the result in ax. Try changing the initial values (4 and 2) and rerun the program. Lines 23–26 add register cx and variable [count] together. Notice that you can store the result in a register (line 24) or back in memory (line 26). To experiment with sub, change all add instructions to sub, reassemble, link, and run under Turbo Debugger's control. (If you purchased the disk, do this to a copy of ADDSUB.ASM.)

Lines 28–31 demonstrate how inc and dec increment and decrement variables and register values. To see the values in memory change, watch the upper middle of Turbo Debugger's CPU window. You should see the value stored at [count]. Unfortunately, after executing line 29, this value disappears (because the next instruction makes no reference to count's location). The next section explains a method to make watching variables easier.

> Note: Quit Turbo Debugger now with the command Alt-X.

Watching Out for Number One

Turbo Debugger has a "watch window" for viewing variables. As you execute instructions that change values in memory, the values listed in the watch window also change. This makes it easy to observe the effects on variables of executing assembly language instructions. Load Program 4-3 with the command td addsub, but don't open the CPU window just yet. Then follow these steps to inspect the value of count (line 11):

1. Press Ctrl-F7, type count, and press Enter. Turbo Debugger locates the count variable in memory and shows count's initial value in the watch window at the bottom of the display.

2. Press F8 until reaching line 26 (add [count],cx). Then press F8 again and watch the value of count in the watch window change.

> Note: With the CPU window visible, you can also watch variables using these same techniques, but to make the watch window visible, you might have to press F6 several times or press Alt-2.

When running other example programs in this book, you can add variable names to the watch window. Also, there are other ways to view memory with Turbo Debugger—for example, the bottom left corner of the CPU window shows successive bytes from any starting location. But the watch window is easy to use and has the advantage of showing variables by name. Even better, you can change the values of variables without having to reassemble the program. To try this, press Ctrl-F2 to reload ADDSUB (or start Turbo Debugger with td addsub) and follow these steps:

1. Press F6 until the watch window borders change to double lines, indicating this window is active. Type count and press Enter. This demonstrates another way to enter variable names to watch. (If count is already in the window, you can skip this step.)

2. Press Ctrl-C (the watch window's "Change" command) and enter a new value for count. Instead of count's initial value (1) as listed in the program (line 11), the program now begins with your new count value.

3. Step through the program with F8. The instructions use the new

count value. Press Ctrl-F2 to reload the program, use F6 to make the watch window active if necessary, and enter new values for count until you're familiar with this option.

These Turbo Debugger commands save time by giving you the ability to change variable values and run test programs without having to reassemble your code. When changing variable values, you can enter new numbers in hexadecimal, decimal, or binary. In all cases, the first character must be a decimal digit. The last character can be *d* for decimal, *h* for hexadecimal, or *b* for binary. The default is hexadecimal. Here are a few sample values as you might enter them into the watch window:

```
100      hexadecimal (256 decimal)
OFFh     hexadecimal (255 decimal)
256d     decimal
1001b    binary (9 decimal)
FFh      error--first character must be 0-9     no longer true
```

Sneaky Subtractions

From Table 4-3, you might think the instructions neg and cmp are out of place. Neg negates a binary value. Cmp compares two values. So, what do these instructions have to do with subtraction?

In the case of neg, the 8086 processor internally subtracts from 0 the value to be negated. This value might be stored in a register or in memory. Subtracting a value from 0, as you recall, forms the two's complement of that value—identical to toggling all the zeros to ones and the ones to zeros, and then adding 1. In 8086 assembly language, it's simpler just to use neg to do the same thing. Here are two samples:

```
neg     ax          ; Form two's complement of ax
neg     [value]     ; Form two's complement of [value]
```

The relation between cmp and subtraction is not as obvious—that is, until you understand that most digital processors perform comparisons between two values by subtracting one value from the other and then throwing away the result. The reason for performing comparisons this way is to set various flag bits that indicate the condition of the result—for example, whether the result is zero, negative, or positive. Cmp performs a subtraction identically to sub but saves only the flag values, which other instructions can inspect. (Later in this chapter when we get to flow-control instructions, this will make more sense.) For now, just remember that a cmp is the same as a sub with no result, only a possible change to various flags.

Multiplying and Dividing Unsigned Values

Multiplication and division require extra care to perform properly. You must be certain to place values in the correct registers. After the operation, you must be careful to extract the answer from the right places. The best way to learn the ropes is to run an example program in Turbo Debugger and demonstrate how mul, imul, div, and idiv operate. Assemble and link Program 4-4 and load the code into Turbo Debugger with the commands:

```
           tasm /zi muldiv
           tlink /v muldiv
           td muldiv
```

                      unsigned
                      ⁀‿‿⁀   **Program 4-4 *MULDIV.ASM***

```
 1:    %TITLE "MUL, DIV, IMUL, IDIV Demonstration"
 2:                            signed
 3:            IDEAL
 4:            DOSSEG
 5:            MODEL   small
 6:            STACK   256
 7:
 8:            DATASEG
 9:
10:    exitCode     DB      0
11:    opByte       DB      8
12:    opWord       DW      100
13:    sourceByte   DB      64
14:    sourceWord   DW      4000
15:
16:            CODESEG
17:
18:    Start:
19:            mov     ax, @data       ; Initialize ds to address
20:            mov     ds, ax          ;  of data segment
21:
22:            mov     al, [opByte]
23:            mul     [sourceByte]    ; ax <- al * [sourceByte]
24:
25:            mov     ax, [opWord]         dx, ax
26:            mul     [sourceWord]    ; ax,dx <- ax * [sourceWord]
27:
28:            mov     ax, [opWord]         dx, ax
29:            mul     ax              ; ax,dx <- ax * ax
30:
31:            mov     ax, [opWord]
32:            div     [sourceByte]    ; al <- ax div [sourceByte]  ≡ quotient
33:                                      ah ← remainder
34:            mov     ax, [opWord]    ; least significant word
35:            mov     dx, 0           ; most significant word
36:            div     [sourceWord]    ; ax <- ax,dx div [sourceWord]
37:
38:    Exit:
39:            mov     ah, 04Ch        ; DOS function: Exit program
40:            mov     al, [exitCode]  ; Return exit code value
41:            int     21h             ; Call DOS. Terminate program
42:
43:            END     Start           ; End of program / entry point
```

Running the
MULDIV Demo

In addition to the exitCode, MULDIV declares four test variables at lines 11–14. Add these variable names to Turbo Debugger's watch window. (Quick tip: Press F6 and type the variable names.) Then, open the registers window or view the CPU window, whichever you prefer. Press F8 to step through each instruction. To start over, press Ctrl-F2. Experiment with different values as you follow these suggestions:

1. Lines 22–23 multiply two unsigned bytes. One byte must be in register al. The other can be in memory, as in this example, or in another 8-bit register. The result of the multiplication is stored in the 16-bit register ax. Overflow is not possible as 255 * 255 equals 65,025—well within the maximum range of a 16-bit word. Prove this to yourself by changing opByte and sourceByte to 0FFh and rerun the program.

2. Lines 25–26 are similar but, this time, multiply two 16-bit word values. Two registers, dx and ax, hold the result, which can be up to 32 bits long. dx holds the most significant part of the result; ax, the least significant part. As with byte multiplication, overflow cannot occur.

3. Lines 28–29 square the value of a register, multiplying ax by itself. You can also square an 8-bit value by multiplying al by itself. You can't do this with any other registers—you can use only ax and al.

4. Lines 31–32 demonstrate unsigned division. The source data to the div instruction divides into the 16-bit dividend in ax. The whole number quotient is placed in al with any remainder in ah.

5. Lines 34–36 perform a similar division, this time dividing a 32-bit value in dx and ax by the 16-bit word value of sourceWord. Register dx holds the most significant word of the original value, and ax holds the least significant word. After the division, the whole number quotient is stored in ax with any remainder in dx.

> Note: While experimenting with new values, don't attempt to divide by 0. Doing so causes the processor to generate a signal called the "divide-by-zero" interrupt (see chapter 10), halting the program. Actually, this condition is misnamed as it can occur any time the result of a division is too large to fit in the specified destination. For example, the "divide-by-zero" interrupt occurs at lines 31–32 when opword = 0F000h and sourcebyte = 1 because 0F000h is larger than the maximum value that a single byte can express. If this condition occurs while running Turbo Debugger, try resetting with Ctrl-F2 or quit and reload.

As you can see from these experiments, unsigned multiplication and division is somewhat unfriendly in 8086 assembly language. You must use only the specified registers, and you must be aware that 32-bit results and operands are stored in two registers dx and ax. The source operand to mul and `div` (see lines 23, 26, 29, 32, and 36) can be a memory location as in most of these examples or any general-purpose register. Because the size of the source operand determines the size of the result, you should also be aware that accidentally multiplying a word variable (as in line 26) when you think you are multiplying a byte variable will cause `dx` to change.

Multiplying and Dividing Signed Values

The signed multiply (`imul`) and divide (`idiv`) instructions operate similarly and use the same registers as `mul` and `div`. (The *i* in the mnemonics stands for integer, indicating that signed positive and negative values are allowed.) The only difference is in the range of values allowed:

▶ Signed bytes range from −128 to +127

▶ Signed words range from −32,768 to 32,767

Try a few experiments by modifying Program 4-4 to use `imul` in place of `mul` and `idiv` in place of `div`. Enter various positive and negative test values, either by editing lines 11–14 or by typing new values in Turbo Debugger's watch window. As you will see from your tests, using signed multiplication and division requires some care. If you get stuck, the following notes should help:

▶ Remember that negative results are in two's complement notation.

▶ Any remainder (`ah` for 8-bit divisions and `dx` for word divisions) has the same sign as the quotient.

▶ An interrupt 0 is generated, possibly halting the program, if you attempt to divide by 0 or by any divisor that produces a result larger than the specified destination can hold.

Converting Bytes, Words, and Doublewords

When using signed binary values, you often need to convert an 8-bit byte value to a 16-bit word, perhaps to prepare for a multiplication or division. Because the value may be a negative number in two's complement notation, this can be tricky as you must take care to preserve the orginal value and its sign. To make this easy, use `cbw` (convert byte to word) and `cwd` (convert word to doubleword). For an example of how these instructions work, insert the following lines into Program 4-4, replacing lines 22–36. Assemble and run under control of Turbo Debugger, experimenting with different values for `sourceByte` and `sourceWord`:

Sign Propagation

```
mov    al,[sourceByte]      ; Load source byte into al
cbw                         ; Extend sign to ax
mov    ax,[sourceWord]      ; Load source word into ax
cwd                         ; Extend sign to dx,ax
```

Try setting `sourceByte` to −3 decimal and executing the first two of these instructions. Before `cbw`, `al` equals hexadecimal FD. After, `ax` equals FFFD—the same value (−3 decimal) expressed in 16 instead of 8 bits. The `cbw` instruction *extends* the 8-bit value (including the sign) to the 16-bit destination. Similarly, `cwd` extends 16-bit values to 32-bit doublewords. Except for the number of bits involved, the two instructions perform the same job.

When using these instructions, you must observe a few restrictions. The source value for `cbw` must be in `al`. The 16-bit result always appears in `ax`. The source value for `cwd` must be in `ax`. The 32-bit result always appears in `dx` and `ax`. Normally, you'll use `cbw` and `cwd` along with `imul` and `idiv` when you have byte values to multiply or divide into words. But you're certainly free to use these instructions in other ways, too.

Logic Instructions

Table 4-4 lists the 8086 logic instructions, organized in two subdivisions: Logical and Shift/Rotate instructions. Logical instructions combine bytes and words with AND, OR, and other logical operators. Shift/Rotate instructions shift and rotate bytes and words. These concepts were introduced in chapter 3.

The simplest logical instruction `not` toggles the bits in a byte or word from ones to zeros and from zeros to ones. As you know, this is called the one's complement. (Adding 1 to this result forms the two's complement, although it's much easier to use `neg` for this purpose.) One way to use `not` is to toggle true and false values. If a zero value represents false and a nonzero value represents true, then the following instruction flops register `dh` from true to false and then back to true:

```
mov dh, -1      ; Set dh to true
not dh          ; Set dh to "not true," i.e., false
not dh          ; Set dh to "not false," i.e., true
```

Table 4-4 *8086 Logic Instructions*

Mnemonic/Operands	Description
Logical Instructions	
and *destination, source*	Logical AND
not *destination*	Logical NOT (one's complement)
or *destination, source*	Logical OR
test *destination, source*	Test bits *(does AND)*
xor *destination, source*	Logical Exclusive OR
Shift/Rotate Instructions	
rcl *destination, count*	Rotate left through carry
rcr *destination, count*	Rotate right through carry
rol *destination, count*	Rotate left
ror *destination, count*	Rotate right
sar *destination, count*	Shift arithmetic right
shl/sal *destination, count*	Shift left/arithmetic left
shr *destination, count*	Shift right

neg is two's complement (handwritten annotation)

> Note: Remember that **neg** subtracts a value from 0; **not** toggles the bits in a value on and off—two very different operations. Take care not to confuse the two instructions. A mixup is almost sure to lead to a hard-to-find bug.

Logical Combinations

Chapter 3 explains the ins and outs of the logical AND, OR, and XOR operations on binary values. The 8086 instructions of the same names perform these logical jobs, combining byte and word values according to the rules of the truth tables in Table 3-2. Program 4-5 demonstrates how the instructions work in assembly language. Assemble, link, and run with Turbo Debugger using the commands:

```
tasm /zi andorxor
tlink /v andorxor
td andorxor
```

Program 4-5 *ANDORXOR.ASM*

```
 1:  %TITLE "AND, OR, XOR Demonstration"
 2:
 3:          IDEAL
 4:          DOSSEG
 5:          MODEL   small
 6:          STACK   256
 7:
 8:          DATASEG
 9:
10:  exitCode     DB     0
11:  sourceWord   DW     0ABh         ; 16-bit source value
12:  wordMask     DW     0CFh         ; 16-bit mask
13:
14:          CODESEG
15:
16:  Start:
17:          mov     ax, @data        ; Initialize ds to address
18:          mov     ds, ax           ;   of data segment
19:
20:          mov     ax, [sourceWord] ; Set ax, bx, cx, and dx
21:          mov     bx, ax           ;   to [sourceWord]
22:          mov     cx, ax
23:          mov     dx, ax
24:
25:          and     ax, [wordMask]   ; ax <- ax AND mask
26:
27:          or      bx, [wordMask]   ; bx <- bx OR mask
28:
29:          xor     cx, [wordMask]   ; cx <- cx XOR mask
30:
31:          xor     dx, dx           ; dx <- 0000
32:
```

```
33:  Exit:
34:          mov     ah, 04Ch              ; DOS function: Exit program
35:          mov     al, [exitCode]        ; Return exit code value
36:          int     21h                   ; Call DOS. Terminate program
37:
38:          END     Start                 ; End of program / entry point
```

**Running the
ANDORXOR Demo**

With the assembled ANDORXOR program loaded into Turbo Debugger, follow these steps to see the 8086 and, or, and xor instructions in action:

1. Open Turbo Debugger's CPU window (Alt-V-C) and zoom to full screen (F5).

2. Watch (Ctrl-F7) variables sourceWord and wordMask to make it easy to enter new test values. Press F6 if necessary to bring the watch window into view.

3. Press F8 to step through the program, stopping after executing the xor instruction in line 31. Try to predict the results of the and, or, and xor instructions in lines 25–29, comparing your predictions with the register values ax for and, bx for or, and cx for xor.

4. To experiment with new test values, press Ctrl-F2 to reset the program. Then, with the watch window active, position the selector bar on the variable you want to change and press Ctrl-C. Enter a new value and press Enter. Then repeat from step 3.

The xor instruction in line 31 of Program 4-5 sets register dx to 0, a frequently used trick in 8086 programming. Try line 31 with different test values to prove that this line always produces a zero result.

**Testing 0001
0010 0011**

ANDing two bits produces 1 only if both bits equal 1; therefore, the and instruction is often used to test whether one or more bits equal 1 in a byte or word value. For example, if you need to determine whether bit 2 is set, you can use a mask of 4:

$$
\begin{array}{ll}
0011\ 0111 & \text{(Value to test)} \\
\underline{0000\ 0100} & \text{(AND mask)} \\
0000\ 0100 & \text{(Result)}
\end{array}
$$

If the result equals 0, then bit 2 in the original value must be 0. If the result does not equal 0 as in this sample, then bit 2 of the original value must equal 1. Unfortunately, the and instruction destroys the original value in the process. To perform this operation while preserving the test value—perhaps to test several single bits in succession without having to reload a register—use the test instruction instead of and:

```
mov  ah, [testValue]    ; Load [testValue] into ah
test ah, 04h            ; Test if bit 2 is set

;----- take action here on bit 2
```

```
mov   dh, 80h              ; Load mask into dh
test  ah, dh               ; Test if masked bit is set

;----- take action here on bit 7

test  ah, [testBit]        ; Test bit with variable mask

;----- take action on the test bit
```

As these samples show, you can test literal (also called *immediate*) values such as 04h and 80h, values in registers, or values in memory. Test performs a logical and on the operands but throws away the result, leaving the destination operand unchanged but setting the flags exactly the same as and. After the test instruction, you would normally use a jump instruction (explained later) to take an appropriate action based on the test result. Note the similarity between test and cmp, which performs a subtraction but throws out the result. The test instruction performs an and but throws out the result.

Shifting Bits Around

Several shift-and-rotate instructions are available in the 8086 instruction set. As Table 4-4 shows, there are instructions to shift bits left and right and to rotate values through the carry flag cf. The instructions further divide into four subgroups:

▶ Plain shifts (shl, shr)
▶ Plain rotations (rol, ror)
▶ Rotations through cf (rcl, rcr)
▶ Arithmetic shifts (sal, sar)

Each of these groups follows a different rule for shifting the bits in bytes and words left or right. Despite their subtle differences, the instructions take the same number and types of operands. Once you learn how to use one, you know how to use them all. Let's use the most common shift shl for demonstration. It specifies a register or memory location plus a count, n:

```
shl   ax, n       ; Shift ax left by n = 1 bits
```

Strangely enough, n must equal 1, or you'll receive an error. (On 80186/286/386 systems, n may be an unsigned 8-bit constant.) The only legal form of this kind of shift in 8086 assembly language is:

```
shl   ax, 1       ; Shift ax left by 1 bit
```

To shift values by more than 1 bit at a time on the 8086 requires two steps: first load a count value into cl and then specify cl as the second operand to the shift instruction:

```
mov   cl, 5       ; Load count into cl
shl   ax, cl      ; Shift ax left by cl bits
```

You must use cl for this—no other register will work as the second operand. You can also shift memory locations and 8-bit register halves. For example:

```
mov   cl, 2           ; Load count into cl
shl   bh, cl          ; Shift bh left by cl bits
shl   [seconds], 1    ; Shift [seconds] left by one bit
shl   [minutes], cl   ; Shift [minutes] left by cl bits
```

A few experiments and diagrams will clarify the differences between the various shift instructions. Use the following commands to assemble and run Program 4-6 with Turbo Debugger:

```
tasm /zi shift
tlink /v shift
td shift
```

Program 4-6 *SHIFT.ASM*

```
 1:  %TITLE "Shift Instruction Demonstration"
 2:
 3:          IDEAL
 4:          DOSSEG
 5:          MODEL   small
 6:          STACK   256
 7:
 8:          DATASEG
 9:
10:  exitCode        DB      0
11:  operand         DB      0AAh
12:
13:          CODESEG
14:
15:  Start:
16:          mov     ax, @data      ; Initialize ds to address
17:          mov     ds, ax         ;   of data segment
18:
19:          shl     [operand], 1   ; Shift left
20:          shr     [operand], 1   ; Shift right
21:          rol     [operand], 1   ; Rotate left
22:          ror     [operand], 1   ; Rotate right
23:          rcl     [operand], 1   ; Rotate left through carry
24:          rcr     [operand], 1   ; Rotate right through carry
25:          sal     [operand], 1   ; Shift arithmetic left
26:          sar     [operand], 1   ; Shift arithmetic right
27:
28:  Exit:
29:          mov     ah, 04Ch       ; DOS function: Exit program
30:          mov     al, [exitCode] ; Return exit code value
31:          int     21h            ; Call DOS. Terminate program
32:
33:          END     Start          ; End of program / entry point
```

Running the SHIFT Demo   The following steps assume that you have assembled SHIFT.ASM and loaded the program into Turbo Debugger. These experiments will help clarify several tricky points about the 8086 shift instructions:

1. Program 4-6 executes each of the seven 8086 shift instructions from Table 4-4. For reasons I'll explain later, shl and sal are two names for the identical instruction; therefore, while there are eight shift mnemonics, there are only seven actual shift instructions.

2. Figure 4-5 illustrates how the plain shift instructions shl and shr operate. Step through (F8) lines 19–20 to experiment with these. Each bit in the destination operand shifts one or cl positions to the left or right. For shl, bit 7 (MSD) moves into the carry flag (cf), while a 0 bit shifts in from the right. For shr, bit 0 (the LSD) moves into the carry flag, while a 0 bit shifts in from the left.

Note: Although Figures 4-5 through 4-8 show only 8-bit bytes, all shift instructions can operate on 16-bit values, too. For this reason, bit numbers are not shown in these diagrams.

3. Figure 4-6 shows how the rotation instructions rol and ror differ from plain shifts. They do not shift a 0 bit in from the right or left; instead, the MSD and LSD values rotate around to the opposite end. The other bits shift in the indicated direction. With rol, the original MSD rotates around to become the new LSD. With ror, the original LSD rotates around to the MSD position. These *same* bits also move into the carry flag, just as they do with shl and shr. Step through lines 21–22 to experiment with these instructions.

4. Figure 4-7 illustrates the rotate-through-carry instructions, rcl

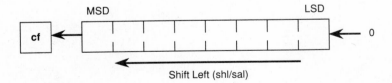

Shift Left (shl/sal)

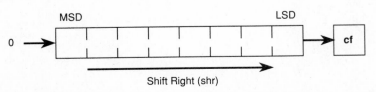

Shift Right (shr)

Figure 4-5 *The shl/sal and shr plain shift instructions.*

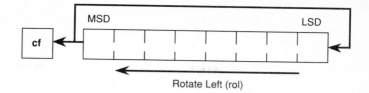

Rotate Left (rol)

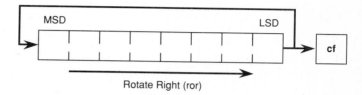

Rotate Right (ror)

Figure 4-6 *The rol and ror rotate instructions.*

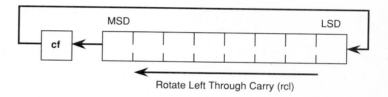

Rotate Left Through Carry (rcl)

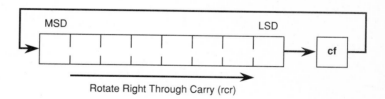

Rotate Right Through Carry (rcr)

Figure 4-7 *The rcl and rcr rotate-through-carry instructions.*

and rcr. For both of these instructions, the 1-bit carry flag serves as an extension to the register or memory location being rotated. With rcl, the MSD shifts into the carry flag while the old carry flag value moves into the LSD position. With rcr, the LSD shifts into the carry flag while the old carry flag moves into the MSD position. The other bits shift in the indicated direction. Step through lines 23–24 to experiment with rcl and rcr.

5. Figure 4-8 illustrates the final shift instruction sar, which is a strange bird. Sar operates identically to shr except that the MSD retains its original value. Additionally, the MSD is copied to the bit on the right. This is easier to see with a few example binary values:

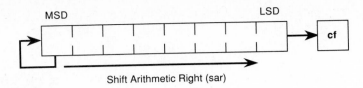

Shift Arithmetic Right (sar)

Figure 4-8 *The sar instruction.*

propagates the sign bit

```
10001000
11000100
11100010
11110001
11111000
```

Starting with the second value, each successive line shows the result of applying sar to the value above. The bits shift right just as with shr, but the MSD retains its value and is copied to the right. As a result, sar is useful for dividing two's complement negative numbers by powers of 2. For example, expressed in hexadecimal, successive sar instructions produce this sequence:

```
8000    −32768
C000    −16384
E000     −8192
F000     −4096
F800     −2048
  :
  :
FFFE        −2
FFFF        −1
```

Additional sar instructions have no effect on hexadecimal FFFF—unlike idiv, which if used to divide −1 by 2 gives 0, as you'd expect.

Unlike other shift instruction pairs that match a right shift with a similar left shift, sar does not have a left-handed partner. Instead, the shl instruction is given a second mnemonic sal, making up for the deficiency. The reason that an arithmetic shift left is no different from a logical shift left is evident by examining the previous hexadecimal sequence in reverse. If we work from the bottom up, these are the same values that applying shl would produce. (Try converting the hex values to binary if you have trouble visualizing this.) In a nutshell, sar is already balanced by shl/sal, which can multiply negative two's complement values by powers of 2, and there's no need for a separate instruction.

Note: When viewing sal instructions in Turbo Debugger, some of the CPU window options display this instruction as shl. This happens because the debugger can't know the context in which you are using one or the other mnemonic; therefore, it displays the more common name.

Why Shift? There are many reasons for programs to employ shift instructions, although two reasons stand out:

> ▷ To move bits into specific positions
> ▷ To multiply and divide by powers of 2

Moving bits into specific positions and then using logical operators to pack the shifted result into other values is a typical assembly language operation. For example, suppose dh initially equals 3, dl equals 5, and the program requires these two numbers to be packed into dh with the 3 in the most significant bits and the 5 in the least significant portion of the byte. Here's how you might proceed:

```
mov  dh, 3      ; dh <- 3
mov  dl, 5      ; dl <- 5
mov  cl, 4      ; Load count into cl
shl  dh, cl     ; Shift dh left four bits
or   dh, dl     ; dh <- dh OR dl
```

Note: If you have trouble following the logic of this example, replace lines 19–26 in Program 4-6 with these five instructions and run the program in Turbo Debugger. Watch register dh as you single step through each line. The shl instruction shifts dh left 4 bits, moving the lower 4-bit value to the upper position and shifting in zeros from the right. Then the or instruction combines the shifted value with dl, packing the two 4-bit values into one 8-bit byte.

Shifty Multiplies and Divides A useful technique to know is how to multiply and divide by powers of 2 using only shift instructions. (You learned the basics of this in chapter 3.) Most of the time, shifts are much faster than mul, imul, div, and idiv instructions; therefore, you should always use shifts when appropriate. To multiply a value by 8 (or 2^3), for example, you need only to shift that value left 3 times:

```
mov  ax, 6      ; ax <- 6
mov  cl, 3      ; Load count into cl
shl  ax, cl     ; ax <- ax * 8
```

Or to divide by 16 (2^4), shift right 4 times:

```
mov  cl, 4      ; Load count into cl
shr  ax, cl     ; ax <- ax / 16
```

One problem with multiplication is the possibility of overflow, ignored in these samples. If the carry flag equals 1 after a shl by 1, then the result is too large to fit in the destination register or memory location. Overflows from shifting by more than 1 are difficult to detect. Also, with division, any remainder is lost—dividing 2 into 3 by shifting 3 right equals 1 and the remainder is nowhere to be found.

Flow-Control Instructions

Table 4-5 lists the 8086 flow-control or *jump* instructions, those that allow programs to change the address of the machine code to be executed next. Without flow-control instructions, a program would simply start at the top and run at breakneck speed toward the bottom, with no stops, loops, or side trips along the way. With flow-control, programs can make decisions,

Table 4-5 *8086 Flow-Control Instructions*

Mnemonic/Operands	Description
Unconditional Transfer Instructions	
call *target*	Call procedure
jmp *target*	Jump unconditionally
ret *value*	Return from procedure
retn *value*	Return from near procedure
retf *value*	Return from far procedure
Conditional Transfer Instructions	
ja/jnbe *short-target*	Jump if above/not below or equal
jae/jnb *short-target*	Jump if above or equal/not below
jb/jnae *short-target*	Jump if below/not above or equal
jbe/jna *short-target*	Jump if below or equal/not above
jc *short-target*	Jump if carry
je/jz *short-target*	Jump if equal/0
jg/jnle *short-target*	Jump if greater/not less or equal
jge/jnl *short-target*	Jump if greater or equal/not less
jl/jnge *short-target*	Jump if less/not greater or equal
jle/jng *short-target*	Jump if less or equal/not greater
jnc *short-target*	Jump if no carry
jne/jnz *short-target*	Jump if not equal/0
jno *short-target*	Jump if no overflow
jnp/jpo *short-target*	Jump if NOT parity/parity odd
jns *short-target*	Jump if NOT sign
jo *short-target*	Jump if overflow
jp/jpe *short-target*	Jump if parity/parity even
js *short-target*	Jump if sign
Loop Instructions	
jcxz *short-target*	Jump if cx equals 0
loop *short-target*	Loop while cx <> 0
loope/loopz *short-target*	Loop while equal/0
loopne/loopnz *short-target*	Loop while not equal/not 0
Interrupt Control Instructions	
int *interrupt-type*	Interrupt
into	Interrupt on overflow
iret	Interrupt return

u = unsigned data
S = signed data
f = flag

(handwritten margin annotations next to conditional transfer rows: u, u, u, u, f, f, s, s, s, s, f, f, f, f, f, f, f, f) inspect flags, and take actions based on previous operations, bit tests, logical comparisons, and arithmetic. Also, flow-control instructions give programs the ability to repeat instructions based on certain conditions, conserving memory by looping through the same sections of code over and over.

Although there may seem to be an overwhelming number of jump instructions in Table 4-5, the forest has only a few easily identified species to memorize. This chapter concentrates on the first two categories: conditional and unconditional jumps. Later chapters introduce loops and the interrupt control instructions.

Unconditional Transfers

An *unconditional transfer* changes the address of the next instruction to be executed. It operates like an exit-only ramp on a highway—once you're in the lane, you're going that-a-way, whether you want to or not. And once the processor executes an unconditional transfer, the destination instruction will be the next to execute without exception. Unconditional transfers load new address values into the `ip` register and, in some cases, into the `cs` code-segment register, too. Together, `cs:ip` specify the address of the next instruction to execute. Changing either or both registers changes the address of this instruction, altering the normal top-to-bottom program flow.

Calling Subroutines

One of assembly language's most useful devices is the *subroutine,* a collection of related instructions, usually performing one repetitive operation. A subroutine might display a character string on screen, add a series of values, or initialize an output port. Some subroutines live grandiose lives: making a chess move or logging on to a remote computer. Others play more humble roles: displaying a single character or reading a key press from the keyboard.

Some programmers write long subroutines that perform many jobs on the theory that multiple subroutines can make a fast program run slowly. Don't do this. You may gain a tiny bit of speed by combining operations into a massive subroutine, but you are more likely to end up with a buggy and hard-to-maintain program over which you will ponder your original intentions while questioning the sanity of your decision to become a programmer.

The best subroutine does one and only one job. The best subroutine is as short as possible and only as long as necessary. The best subroutine can be listed on one or two pages of printout paper. The best subroutine begins, not with code, but with comments describing the subroutine's purpose, results, input expected, and registers affected. The best subroutine can be understood out of context by someone who has no idea what the entire program is doing. In other words, the best subroutine is short and sweet and neat.

Program 4-7 demonstrates how to write a subroutine in assembly language. Assemble, link, and load into Turbo Debugger as you have the other examples in this chapter, using the commands:

```
tasm /zi subdemo
tlink /v subdemo
td subdemo
```

Program 4-7 *SUBDEMO.ASM*

```
 1:  %TITLE "Subroutine Demonstration"
 2:
 3:          IDEAL
 4:          DOSSEG
 5:          MODEL   small
 6:          STACK   256
 7:
 8:          DATASEG
 9:
10:  exitCode        DB      0
11:
12:          CODESEG
13:
14:  Start:
15:          mov     ax, @data       ; Initialize ds to address
16:          mov     ds, ax          ;  of data segment
17:
18:          mov     al, 1           ; Load AL - DL with values
19:          mov     bl, 2           ;  to add
20:          mov     cl, 3
21:          mov     dl, 4
22:          call    AddRegisters    ; AX <- AL + BL + CL + DL
23:          call    AddRegisters    ;  again
24:          call    AddRegisters    ;   and again!
25:
26:  Exit:
27:          mov     ah, 04Ch        ; DOS function: Exit program
28:          mov     al, [exitCode]  ; Return exit code value
29:          int     21h             ; Call DOS. Terminate program
30:
31:  ;------------------------------------------------------------
32:  ; AddRegisters           Sum al, bl, cl, and dl
33:  ;------------------------------------------------------------
34:  ; Input:
35:  ;       al, bl, cl, dl = Four 8-bit values to add
36:  ; Output:
37:  ;       ax = al + bl + cl + dl
38:  ; Registers:
39:  ;       ax, bh, ch, dh changed
40:  ;------------------------------------------------------------
41:  PROC    AddRegisters
42:          xor     ah, ah          ; Set ah equal to 0
43:          xor     bh, bh          ; Set bh equal to 0
44:          xor     ch, ch          ; Set ch equal to 0
45:          xor     dh, dh          ; Set dh equal to 0
46:          add     ax, bx          ; AX <- AX + BX
47:          adc     ax, cx          ; AX <- AX + CX + CF
48:          adc     ax, dx          ; AX <- AX + DX + CF
49:          ret                     ; Return to caller
```

```
50:   ENDP    AddRegisters
51:
52:          END     Start          ; End of program / entry point
```

Running the SUBDEMO Program

The main portion of the SUBDEMO program is at lines 14–29. The subroutine is at lines 31–50. There are several new items in the code:

▶ The comments at lines 31–40 describe the subroutine's name, purpose, input, output, and affected registers. The dashed outlines are optional, serving mostly to mark the beginnings of many subroutines in a long listing. For many programmers, a personal subroutine header style is a valued trademark. If you want to use your own format, that's fine—just be sure to include at least the information shown here.

▶ The PROC and ENDP directives (lines 41, 50) mark the subroutine's beginning and ending. *Not necessarily in col 1.*

▶ The ret instruction (line 49) must be included in every subroutine, but not necessarily on the last line as in this example.

The PROC and ENDP directives are optional, but I strongly suggest you use them to mark the beginnings and endings of all your subroutines. PROC and ENDP are directives to Turbo Assembler—they are not 8086 instructions and do not generate any code. The PROC directive comes first, followed by the subroutine's name, which labels the address of the first instruction, here at line 42. The ENDP directive comes last, optionally followed by the same label name as in the preceding PROC. Including the name here shows which subroutine is ending, but you can leave the name blank if you prefer. In line 22, the main program *calls* the subroutine by using the call instruction along with the label AddRegisters. Two important actions take place when call executes:

▶ The address of the next instruction following the call is pushed onto the stack.

▶ The address of the subroutine is inserted into register ip or, in some cases, into the register pair cs:ip.

Before starting to run the called subroutine, the 8086 processor pushes the address of the instruction following the call onto the stack. This address is called the *return address* because it marks the location to which the subroutine should eventually return control. In this example, the first such return address is that of the instruction at line 23, another call. After pushing this address, the processor jumps unconditionally to the called label, executing the instruction at line 42. The program then continues running from that point, executing the instructions in the subroutine.

The reason for pushing the return address onto the stack becomes clear when the subroutine's ret instruction at line 49 executes. Like call, ret causes two important actions to occur:

▶ The return address is popped from the stack into register ip (or into cs:ip).

▶ The program continues running with the instruction following the call that previously activated the subroutine.

Figure 4-9 illustrates the action of the three call instructions in lines 22–24 of Program 4-7. Each call causes the subroutine's instructions to begin running until reaching the ret instruction, which returns control to the instruction immediately after the call. Different places in the program can call the same subroutine. To view this action on your computer, load Program 4-7 into Turbo Debugger and follow these steps:

1. From the CPU window, press F8 six times, stopping just before you execute the call instruction at line 22. Notice that registers al, bl, cl, and dl are loaded with values to pass to the subroutine for processing.

2. Instead of pressing F8 to execute the call instruction, press F7, the "trace into" key. You should see the instruction marker jump to the xor instruction at line 42, indicating that the subroutine code is ready to run. If you're quick, you might also see the return address pushed onto the stack (lower right corner of the screen).

3. Press F7 repeatedly until you get to the ret instruction in line 49. Then press F7 again, executing ret and returning control to the instruction following the call in line 22.

4. Press F7 to again call the same subroutine. And then press F7 repeatedly as you did before, stopping after executing the ret instruction for a second time.

5. The instruction marker should now be poised on line 24, ready to execute the final call. This time, instead of F7, press F8—the

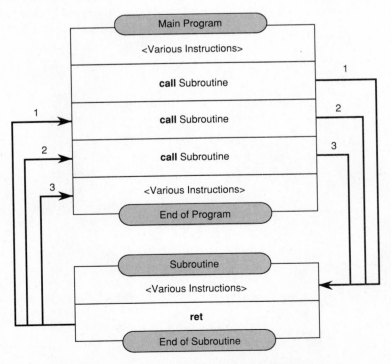

Figure 4-9 *Subroutine calls and returns.*

key you normally use to single-step through programs. F8, the "step over" key, executes the subroutine at full speed, stopping only after the subroutine returns rather than showing you the individual instructions. Remember, to step *through* a subroutine, press F7 at the `call` instruction. To step *over* a subroutine, press F8. F8 is useful when you're positive that a subroutine is functioning correctly and you don't want to waste time single-stepping through the routine's instructions.

You should be able to understand how the `AddRegisters` subroutine works in Program 4-7. Read the comments if you need help—there aren't any new instructions here. The `xor` instructions at lines 42–45 clear any extraneous values in the upper halves of the registers to be added. Then `add` and `adc` add the four values in `al`, `bl`, `cl`, and `dl`, placing the sum in `ax`.

The Long and Short of It

Although Table 4-5 lists three return instructions—`ret`, `retf`, and `retn`—there actually are only two: `retf` and `retn`. The generic `ret` mnemonic allows Turbo Assembler to decide which of the other two returns is appropriate for the memory model in use. To understand the difference between `retf` and `retn`, you first have to understand the difference between an *intrasegment* and *intersegment* subroutine call:

▶ An intrasegment subroutine call activates a subroutine in the same code segment as the `call` instruction. In other words, upon transferring control to a new location, segment register `cs` remains unchanged; therefore, it's necessary to change only `ip` to run the subroutine. An intrasegment return address is a 16-bit word.

▶ An intersegment subroutine call activates a subroutine in a different code segment from the segment containing the `call`. In this case, both `cs` and `ip` must be changed to the new location and the full 32-bit return address of the instruction following the call is pushed onto the stack.

There is only one `call` mnemonic because the assembler knows whether a called subroutine is near (in the same segment) or far (in a different segment) when it assembles the `call`. But there are two return mnemonics—`retn` for *near,* intrasegment calls and `retf` for *far,* intersegment calls—to allow you to write near and far subroutines as you choose, changing the default instruction that Turbo Assembler generates for `ret`. The best way to avoid confusion with these details is to let Turbo Assembler generate the correct codes for you. (After all, that's one reason for using an assembler in the first place.) To define a near subroutine, use the `NEAR` operator in the `PROC` definition:

```
PROC    SubName         NEAR
;-----  insert subroutine instructions here
        ret
ENDP    SubName
```

To write an intersegment subroutine, change NEAR to FAR. Turbo Assembler will then assemble far calls to this subroutine and replace the ret instruction with retf.

> Note: When using the small-memory model, as in most of this book's example programs, subroutines are assumed to be near (in the same code segment as calls to the subroutines). Consequently, specifying the NEAR operator in the PROC declaration is unnecessary.

Passing Values to and from Subroutines

From Program 4-7, you can see that subroutine AddRegisters requires four 8-bit registers to hold values to add. The subroutine returns the sum of this addition in ax. Passing values in registers to subroutines and receiving results of operations in other registers is the most common method for giving subroutines data to process. Two other methods are:

▶ Storing data in global variables

▶ Passing data on the stack

Subroutines may operate directly on variables declared in the data segment, for example, the exitCode byte at line 10. Usually, though, this is not a wise choice. Changing global variables from inside subroutines can lead to confusion over which subroutine changed which values when. In a complex program with hundreds or thousands of subroutines, many of which call each other in various sequences, two subroutines that affect the same global values may introduce a dangerous kind of bug called a *side effect* into your program. This problem develops when a program (or another subroutine) calls a subroutine that changes a global value currently used for other purposes.

Passing data on the stack is a good solution, especially when a subroutine requires many parameters. You could modify Program 4-7 to follow this scheme. Before each call (lines 22–24), instead of loading registers al, bl, cl, and dl with data to process, you might use these instructions:

```
mov  ax, 1      ; First element
push ax         ; Push onto stack
mov  ax, 2      ; Second element
push ax         ; Push onto stack
mov  ax, 3      ; Third element
push ax         ; Push onto stack
mov  ax, 4      ; Fourth element
push ax         ; Push onto stack
call AddValues
```

Notice that you must load a register (ax here) and then push that register onto the stack—you can't push literal values directly onto the stack. In the subroutine, you may think the first job is to pop the parameters from the stack. But this doesn't work:

```
PROC AddValues
    pop  dx    ; ???
    pop  cx
    pop  bx
    pop  ax
    :          ; Subroutine instructions
    ret
ENDP AddValues
```

The first pop accidentally removes the return address pushed by the call instruction, causing the subroutine to add the wrong values and to lose its ability to return to the calling place. The solution is to remove the return address, pop the parameters, and then replace the return address back onto the stack. This takes another register:

```
PROC AddValues
    pop  si    ; Save return address in si
    pop  dx    ; Pop 4 parameters
    pop  cx
    pop  bx
    pop  ax
    push si    ; Replace return address
    :          ; Subroutine instructions
    ret
ENDP AddValues
```

See USES directive!

This works but, as you can see, passing values on the stack is not as easy as passing values directly in registers. It is possible to address parameters on the stack using a method employed in high-level languages, explained in chapters 12 and 13. As you'll see, a special form of the ret instruction can remove the pushed parameters before popping the return address, eliminating some of the complexity of the method described here.

To Push or Not to Push

Program 4-7's comment at line 39 tells you that ax, bh, ch, dh, and various flags are changed by the subroutine. If the calling program uses any of these registers or flags for its own purposes, you now have a conflict to resolve. There are two solutions:

▶ Save the original register values before the call
▶ Save the original register values inside the subroutine

Ask six programmers, and you shall receive six opinions about which of these two methods for preserving registers is best. The first plan saves registers currently in use before calling subroutines that change those registers. In Program 4-7, for example, if the calling program is using bh and ch, it might call the subroutine like this:

```
push bx           ; Save bx on the stack
push cx           ; Save cx, too
call AddRegisters ; Call subroutine
pop  cx           ; Restore cx from the stack
pop  bx           ; Restore bx, too
```

You must push the entire register (ax, bx, etc.), even if you need to preserve only the 8-bit halves (ah, bl, etc.). Pushing the registers onto the stack before the subroutine call saves the register values temporarily on the stack, from where the same register values are later restored after the subroutine finishes. Notice that the pop instructions must be in the reverse order from the push instructions.

The second school of thought on register preservation makes each subroutine responsible for saving and restoring the registers it changes—except, of course, for registers used to pass values back to callers. With this approach, you could revise AddRegisters (lines 41–52) as follows:

```
PROC AddRegisters
      push bx    ; Save changed registers
      push cx
      push dx
      pushf      ; Save flags, too
      :          ; Subroutine instructions
      popf       ; Also restore flags
      pop  dx    ; Restore saved registers
      pop  cx
      pop  bx
      ret        ; Return to caller
ENDP AddRegisters
```

The calling program now can freely call the subroutine, which guarantees that, if it uses any registers for its own purposes, it will restore those registers to their original values before returning. This example also saves the flags with pushf and then restores the flags with popf just before the subroutine ends. This works because call, push, and ret (among others) do not change the flag values. Even so, saving and restoring flags this way is probably unnecessary, and few programs actually do this. If you need to save flag values, however, this is how to do it.

Which is the best method? Should the caller or the "callee" save registers affected by the subroutine? In practice, I usually make the subroutine responsible for saving the registers it changes—probably the preferred method of most assembly language programmers. This does entail some wasted effort, however, as the subroutine might needlessly save the value of a register that isn't being used by the program that calls the subroutine. Even so, in a typical program with dozens of subroutines, many of which call each other in unpredictable sequences, it's simply more practical if not 100% efficient to let the subroutines save and restore their modified registers. Sometimes, however, and especially where top speed is needed, I'll ignore this rule of thumb and make the caller responsible for saving needed values. If you do this, be sure to carefully document which registers are changed inside the subroutine, or bugs are almost sure to surface later.

Jumping Unconditionally

The 8086 has well over a dozen different jump instructions (see Table 4-5). One of these, jmp, is an *unconditional jump*; the others are all *conditional jumps*. The difference between the two jump types is important:

▶ An unconditional jump always causes the program to start running at a new address

▶ A conditional jump causes the program to start running at a new address only if certain conditions are satisfied. Otherwise, the program continues as though the conditional jump instruction did not exist

The unconditional `jmp` works identically to `call`, except that the return address is not pushed onto the stack. The `jmp` instruction takes a single parameter: the label of the location where the program is to transfer control. For an example of how this works, modify Program 4-7, inserting the following instructions between lines 21 and 22:

```
jmp  Exit
```

When you single-step the modified program in Turbo Debugger, you'll see the `jmp` instruction skip the three `call`s in lines 22–24, jumping directly to the `mov` instruction at the `Exit` label. That's all `jmp` does. Use the instruction anytime you want to jump from somewhere to somewhere else. As with `call`, that somewhere else may be in the same code segment or in a different segment. Turbo Assembler implements the correct `jmp` for you, making either an intrasegment jump (to a different offset in the same code segment, changing only the `ip` register) or an intersegment jump (to a different segment and offset, changing both `cs` and `ip`). Most of the time, you'll use `jmp`s to locations in the same code segment—almost always the case with the small-memory model.

> Note: Use `jmp` sparingly to avoid creating that well-known blue plate programmer's special, *spaghetti code*, where imaginary lines from numerous `jmp`s to their target addresses entwine like pasta in a pot. You may as well play pickup sticks with wet noodles than figure out what such a program does.

Jumping Conditionally

Table 4-5 lists the 8086's 18 conditional jump instructions, many of which have two mnemonics representing the same instruction, for example, `je`/`jz` and `jg`/`jnle`, making a total of 30 mnemonics. This may seem to be an overwhelming number of conditional jumps to learn, but, like verb conjugations, the different forms are easy to remember if you separate the root (always *j* for jump) from the endings (*a, nbe, e, z,* etc.). Each of these endings represents a unique condition as listed in Table 4-6. Once you memorize these meanings, you'll have little trouble differentiating among the many kinds of conditional jumps. In the table, the endings on the right are negations of the endings on the left. (Two conditional jump mnemonics, `jpe` and `jpo` do not have negative counterparts.)

All conditional jumps require a *target address*—a label marking the location where you want the program to continue running if the specified condition is met. For example, following a comparison of two registers with `cmp`, you might use `je` (jump if equal) to transfer control to a location if the values in the registers are equal. To demonstrate this, suppose you need a subroutine to return `cx` equal to 1 if `ax` = `bx` or to 0 if `ax` <> `bx`. This does the job:

```
PROC RegEqual
      mov  cx, 1          ; Preset cx to 0001
      cmp  ax, bx         ; Does ax equal bx?
      je   Continue       ; Jump if ax = bx
      xor  cx, cx         ; Else, set cx to 0000
Continue:
      ret                 ; Return to caller
ENDP RegEqual
```

Table 4-6 *Conditional Jump Endings*

Ending	Meaning	Ending	Meaning
a	above	na	not above
ae	above or equal	nae	not above or equal
b	below	nb	not below
be	below or equal	nbe	not below or equal
c	carry	nc	not carry
e	equal	ne	not equal
g	greater	ng	not greater
ge	greater or equal	nge	not greater or equal
l	less	nl	not less
le	less or equal	nle	not less or equal
o	overflow	no	not overflow
p	parity	np	not parity
pe	parity even	—	
po	parity odd	—	
s	sign	ns	not sign
z	zero	nz	not zero

First, cx is preset to 1, the result that indicates ax equals bx—a fact the subroutine doesn't know just yet. Next, a cmp compares ax and bx. Remember that cmp performs a subtraction (ax - bx) but throws away the result, setting the zero flag zf to 1 if the result is zero, or to 0 if the result is not zero. The je conditional jump tests the zero flag, transferring control to the Continue label if the condition is met—namely that zf = 1, indicating that ax equals bx and, therefore, preserving the preset value in cx. If the condition is not met (zf = 0), then the xor instruction sets cx to 0. In either case, the ret instruction executes last, returning control to the location after the call instruction that activated the subroutine.

A downward jump as in this example—skipping an assignment to a register or, perhaps, a call to another subroutine—is probably the most typical use for conditional jumps. But you can also jump up to create loops in programs. For example, this fragment increments ax by 1, calling a subroutine Print (not shown here) until ax equals 10:

```
      xor   ax, ax            ; Preset ax to 0000
Count:
      inc   ax                ; ax <- ax + 1
      call  Print             ; Call subroutine
      cmp.  ax, 10            ; Is ax = 10?
      jne   Count             ; Jump if ax <> 10
      :                       ; Program continues here
```

The loop extending from `Count` to `jne` executes repeatedly as long as `ax` is not equal (*ne*) to 10. As in the previous example, the `cmp` instruction sets the flags for the following conditional jump to test. If the condition is not met—in other words, if `ax` does not yet equal 10—control transfers back up to `Count`, starting the loop over from the `inc` instruction. When `ax` hits 10, the condition fails, and `jne` does not transfer control to the target label, continuing instead with the next instruction below.

Double Jumping

As you can see from Table 4-5, many conditional jumps have two names for the same instruction. In all cases, you can use either mnemonic interchangeably. For example `je` and `jz` assemble to the identical machine code.

Why, then, do you need the two different names? The answer is: Simply to make programming easier. Literally translated, `jz` means "jump if the zero flag equals 1" while `je` translates to "jump if equal." The reason for the two different translations is more obvious when you consider how this jump instruction is used. After a `cmp` operation, if the result is 0, then the zero flag is set to 1. Knowing this, you could use `jz` to test the zero flag and jump to another location.

To avoid forcing you to perform similar mental gymnastics at every step in a program, the 8086 instruction set provides alternate mnemonics that make more sense in given situations. After a `cmp`, you simply use `je` to test if the operands were equal. Or you can use `jne` to test if the operands were not equal. In most cases, you don't even have to be aware of which flags are set and tested.

Note: Sometimes, of course, you'll want to know which flags are being tested by a conditional jump. At these times, look up the instruction's mnemonic in chapter 14. Also listed in this chapter are the exact combinations of flag bits inspected by each conditional jump instruction.

Using Conditional Jumps

Learning which conditional jump to use in a given situation takes practice. Reading assembly language programs will help, and, as you read through this book, you'll see most of the conditional jumps in action. Be sure to memorize the endings in Table 4-6. Also, understand the difference between the two phrases *above-below* and *less-greater,* as used in instructions such as `jb` and `jge`. Remember these two points:

▸ Use above-below jumps such as `ja` and `jbe` with *unsigned* values

▸ Use less-greater jumps such as `jle` and `jg` with *signed* values

Very Important:
(common source of errors!)

Because of the wrap-around effect in arithmetic operations on binary values expressed within fixed numbers of bits, the difference between comparisons of signed and unsigned values is important. (Adding 1 to hexadecimal FFFF, for example, equals 0000 within 16 bits. In decimal, this is equivalent to the strange but true equation, $65{,}535 + 1 = 0$.) A few examples help clarify this important detail. Suppose you subtract two registers and want to jump to a certain location if the result is less than 0. This is the correct way to accomplish your goal:

```
sub  ax, bx    ; ax <- ax - bx
jl   Negative  ; Jump if ax < bx
```

If the subtraction of bx from ax results in a negative value, then the condition of jl succeeds, and control transfers to the address of the Negative label. Obviously, if ax < bx, then the result of subtracting bx from ax will be negative. Replacing jl with jb, though, does not work:

```
sub  ax, bx    ; ax <- ax - bx
jb   Negative  ; ???
```

The above-below conditional jumps test the results of comparisons and other operations on unsigned, positive whole numbers. Even if bx > ax, the result of subtracting unsigned bx from ax is still an unsigned value. To test whether the unsigned ax is greater than unsigned bx, you can write:

```
cmp  ax, bx    ; Is unsigned ax > bx?
ja   Greater   ; Jump if ax > bx
```

The ja (jump if above) instruction correctly tests the result of a comparison between two unsigned values. Only if ax is greater than bx does the jump occur. If ax is below or equal to bx, then the jump does not occur. On the other hand, if ax and bx were signed values, then ja would not be appropriate here—instead, you'd probably want to use the signed conditional jump, jg.

> Note: Get into the habit of using "above-below" for unsigned comparisons and "greater-less" for signed comparisons. Do this in your programs, in your speech, and in your notes and comments. There's no easy trick to learning the differences—you just have to memorize the rules.

Conditional Restrictions

All conditional jumps have one major restriction: They can transfer control only a very short distance away—exactly 128 bytes back (to a lower address) or 127 bytes forward (to a higher address) from the first byte of the instruction immediately *following* the jump. Counting the 2 bytes that each conditional jump occupies, you can jump a tiny bit farther ahead than back—a small detail that rarely matters very much. Don't worry, Turbo Assembler will tell you if you try to jump too far.

The conditional jump target in the range of −128 to 127 bytes is called the *displacement,* a value calculated for you by the assembler from the label you supply in your program's text. The displacement—not the actual address of the target label—is inserted into the assembled machine code for this jump instruction. You never have to calculate the displacement manually, but you should be aware that, because the target address is expressed as a displacement, conditional jumps have the marvelous property of executing identically at any memory location without change, leading to an interesting fact about 8086 programming:

Note: Code that uses only conditional jumps can execute anywhere in memory. Such code is relocatable—able to be relocated in memory and then executed without change.

Although relocatable conditional jumps are usually advantageous, when you absolutely must jump conditionally to a far-away location, the limited displacement range can be troublesome. To jump farther than about 127 bytes away requires a combination of conditional and unconditional jumps. For example, suppose you want the program to jump to an Error routine if dx equals 1, perhaps halting the program with a message. You could write:

```
          cmp   dx, 1          ; Is dx = 1?
          jne   Continue       ; Jump if dx <> 1
          jmp   Error          ; Error, halt (dx = 1)
Continue:
          :                     ; No error, continue program
```

If dx equals 1, then the jne condition fails, executing the unconditional jmp, which transfers control to Error, presumably out of range of jne. When combining jumps this way, carefully think through the logic—it's easy to pick the wrong conditional, a common source of bugs. To avoid confusion, remember this hint:

Note: Use the opposite conditional jump than you normally would use if the target is within range. Then follow with an unconditional jmp to that target.

You can see how this hint works by examining the code for the previous example if the Error label is in range of the conditional jump. The much simpler program now becomes:

```
cmp   dx, 1      ; Is dx = 1?
je    Error      ; Error, halt (dx = 1)
```

Obviously, this fragment jumps to Error if dx equals 1. To jump conditionally to an out-of-range label requires the opposite conditional (jne instead of je) followed by the unconditional jmp to the target.

To learn more about how each conditional jump instruction operates, try running some of the previous examples in Turbo Debugger. You should be able to do this on your own by now. Just take one of the test programs you entered earlier and replace the guts with the programming from this text—or, even better, make up your own examples. (You'll have to supply labels for any subroutine calls and jumps.)

Chapter 14 lists each conditional jump in detail. Refer to this chapter to learn which flag bits are affected by each instruction. Above all, think logically. After a comparison, question your motives. Do you want to jump if the result is less or greater (signed), or if the result is above or below (unsigned)? Keep your jumps to the minimum distances possible and avoid using too many jumps. A typical mistake is to write code like this:

```
        cmp   bx, 5         ; Is bx = 5?
        jne   Not5          ; No, jump to Not5
        mov   ax, [count5]  ; Yes, load ax with [count5]
        jmp   Continue      ; Jump to skip next instruction
Not5:
        mov   ax, [count]   ; Load ax with [count]
Continue:
        :                   ; Program continues here
```

This fragment requires two labels and two jump instructions just to load ax with a different value depending on whether bx equals 5. Try not to hop around so much. Preloading ax with one of the two possible results eliminates a label and the unconditional jump:

```
        mov   ax, [count5]  ; Preset ax <- [count5]
        cmp   bx, 5         ; Is bx = 5?
        je    Continue      ; Yes, ax is correct, so jump
        mov   ax, [count]   ; No, load ax with other value
Continue:
        :                   ; Program continues here
```

Not only is this shorter and easier to read, the code operates more quickly when bx does not equal 5. (A jmp instruction as used here takes more processor time to execute than a mov between a register and memory location; therefore, the two movs are not as wasteful as you may think on a casual reading.)

Processor Control Instructions

The set of 8086 instructions listed in Table 4-7 directly operate on the processor. In all cases but one, these processor control instructions assemble to single-byte codes and require no operands. Most of the instructions set or clear individual flag bits. Others synchronize the processor with external events and, in one case, nop actually does nothing at all.

Table 4-7 *8086 Processor Control Instructions*

Mnemonic/Operands	Description
Flag Instructions	
clc	Clear carry
cld	Clear direction (auto-increment)
cli	Clear interrupt-enable flag
cmc	Complement carry
stc	Set carry
std	Set direction (auto-decrement)
sti	Set interrupt-enable flag
External Synchronization Instructions	
esc *immediate, source*	Escape to coprocessor
hlt	Halt processor
lock	Lock the bus
wait	Wait for coprocessor
Miscellaneous	
nop	No operation

Flag Operations   The first group of instructions in Table 4-7 sets and clears individual flag bits. A flag is set when it equals 1. It's clear when it equals 0. You can set and clear the carry flag (stc and clc), the direction flag (std and cld), and the interrupt flag (sti and cli). You can also complement the carry flag with cmc, toggling cf from 1 to 0 or from 0 to 1.

The direction flag instructions are used exclusively with the string instructions in Table 4-8. Chapter 5 explains how to use these instructions. The interrupt flag bit is normally set or cleared inside interrupt service routines, as chapter 10 explains. In general, sti allows most kinds of interrupts to occur, while cli prevents their occurrence.

One typical use for stc and clc is to set the carry flag to pass back a result from a subroutine. For example, you could write a routine to test whether a certain bit is set in a value passed in register dl:

```
PROC TestBit
     test dl, 08h      ; Test bit 3
     jz   Exit         ; Exit if bit 3 = 0
     stc               ; Set carry flag
Exit:
     ret               ; Return to caller
ENDP TestBit
```

This procedure tests whether bit 3 equals 1, setting the carry flag to 1 only if it does. The test instruction resets the carry flag regardless of the operand values, but it also sets the zero flag to 1 only if the result is 0—indicating in this example that bit 3 in dl is 0. In that event, the jz instruction jumps directly to Exit, leaving cf = 0. Otherwise, the stc instruction sets the carry flag, returning cf = 1. The main program might call the subroutine this way:

```
mov  dl, [testvalue]    ; Load test value into dl
call TestBit            ; Call test subroutine
jc   BitIsSet           ; Jump if bit 3 = 1
:                       ; Program continues if bit 3 = 0
```

After calling TestBit, the jc instruction transfers control to BitIsSet only if cf = 1. Passing the carry flag back from a subroutine this way is common in assembly language programming. Also, you'll often see routines that use cf to indicate whether an error occurred. For example, to call a hypothetical routine DiskRead and check for an error, you might write something like this to jump to your error handler if the subroutine fails:

```
    call DiskRead       ; Read the disk (subroutine not shown)
    jnc  Continue       ; Continue program if no error (CF = 0)
    jmp  Error          ; Else, jump to error handler (CF = 1)
Continue:
    :                   ; Program continues here
```

Getting In Synch

The 8086 external synchronization instructions are rare birds for which you'll probably have only occasional uses. Hlt brings the processor to a screeching halt, continuing only after receiving one of two kinds of interrupts. (See chapter 10 for more information about interrupts.) The most typical use for hlt is to force the processor to wait for a signal from an external device, continuing only when the device gives the processor the green light to proceed.

Wait and esc are used to interface the 8086 with a math coprocessor. Esc is the only processor control instruction that requires operands.

Lock causes the 8086 to assert (turn on) a signal that interface circuits can recognize as a notice that the *bus* is in use. (The bus is the collection of lines to and from the processor, memory, and elsewhere, over which data bits travel their various routes.) Lock is not really a separate instruction, but a prefix for another instruction, most often xchg. In a computer with multiple processors accessing the same memory locations, you can use lock to avoid the potential conflict of both processors writing to the same location simultaneously. If you need this capability, refer to Intel's documentation (see Bibliography). In most PC programming, lock isn't needed.

Something for Nothing

Nop is perhaps the strangest of all 8086 instructions. From the instruction's name, you may think that nop doesn't do anything. And so it doesn't! Executing nop is like accelerating a car in neutral—push the pedal to the floorboards and you're still going nowhere fast. But in the sometimes whacky world of assembly language programming, even nothing has its purposes. Nop comes in handy usually in two ways:

▶ To remove another instruction temporarily
▶ To save space for a forward jmp

Nop is most useful when you want to remove an instruction from a program without having to reassemble and link. Poking a few nop machine codes (hexadecimal 90) over other instructions is a useful debugging trick. When trying to locate the source of a bug, try replacing a suspect instruction or two with nops in the hope that this will reveal hidden mistakes.

Often, removing instructions is a good way to learn what effects those instructions have. For example, suppose you want to examine what happens in Program 4-7 (SUBDEMO) if line 42 does not zero ah. You could remove the instruction in the text, reassemble, link, and test. Or you can just load the already assembled code into Turbo Debugger and follow these steps:

1. Open the CPU window and move the selector bar to the xor instruction at the beginning of AddRegisters. Note the address to the left, probably something like cs:001D.

2. Tab to move the cursor to the memory dump area in the CPU window's bottom left corner.

3. Press Ctrl-G to select the Goto command. Then enter the address from step 1, for example, cs:001Dh. (Remember to add the *h* for hexadecimal!)

4. The cursor should now be positioned on the first of two bytes, 32 and E4, the binary machine codes for the xor ah,ah instruction. Verify this by comparing the bytes in the memory dump area with the disassembled code above.

5. Change the byte values by typing 090h 090h and watch the disassembled code above when you press Enter. The 2-byte xor instruction instantly changes to two single-byte nops.

6. Use F7 to step through the modified program, observing what happens (or, rather, doesn't happen) to ah when the nops execute. When the subroutine ends (at the ret instruction), ax no longer correctly holds the sum of the four registers. As this test proves, zeroing ah is necessary to ensure an accurate result.

7. To reset the program, press Ctrl-F2 or replace the nops with their original machine codes, 032h and 0E4h.

Saving Jump Space

Turbo Assembler will occasionally insert a nop to reserve space for a jmp instruction. Earlier, you learned that jmp transfers control unconditionally to a target address. But, depending on how far away you are jumping, Turbo Assembler generates one of several machine code forms for jmp, adding from 2 to 5 bytes to the assembled program. Normally, you can ignore this fact and just let the assembler choose the most efficient form, which it will always do. Even so, because Turbo Assembler is a one-pass program—reading your source code only one time to generate object code— a problem develops with instruction sequences such as:

```
          or    ax, bx         ; Does ax = bx?
          jz    Skip           ; Jump if yes
          jmp   Elsewhere      ; Else jump to Elsewhere
Skip:
          mov   ax, 1          ; Set ax to 1 if ax = bx
          jmp   Continue       ; Skip next command
Elsewhere:
          mov   ax, 2          ; Set ax to 2 if ax <> bx
Continue:
          :                    ; Program continues
```

Although this sequence has no practical purpose, it demonstrates a typical problem. When Turbo Assembler reaches the first jmp instruction—which in this case jumps forward to a higher memory location—the assembler doesn't yet know how far it is from the jmp to the target address at Elsewhere. Always the pessimist, Turbo Assembler assumes the worst—that Elsewhere will be greater than 127 bytes ahead. Therefore, the assembler reserves space for a 3-byte jmp, which has a reach of about ±32K. Upon reaching Elsewhere, Turbo Assembler realizes its error—Elsewhere is close enough for the shorter 2-byte jmp to reach, within 128 bytes back or 127 bytes forward. Because the 2-byte jmp operates more quickly than the 3-byte version, Turbo Assembler goes back and changes the jmp to the 2-byte model. To avoid having to reassemble the other instructions between this jmp and Elsewhere, the assembler changes the now extra third byte to a nop, then continues on with the rest of the program. If you assemble this short example, you'll see code that looks something like this:

```
cs:0000    EB 04      jmp Elsewhere
cs:0002    90         nop
```

The inserted nop does nothing but occupy space. Because of the preceding unconditional jmp, the nop never even executes. To get rid of the do-nothing nop, saving 1 byte, place a **SHORT** directive before the jmp target address:

```
jmp   SHORT Elsewhere
```

This forces Turbo Assembler to use the 2-byte jmp version. Of course, if Elsewhere later turns out to be farther than 127 bytes away, you'll receive an error and will have to remove the **SHORT** directive.

Using the JUMPS Directive

If you insert a JUMPS directive on a line somewhere early in your program, Turbo Assembler allows you to use conditional jump instructions to locations that are farther away than the normal restriction of about 127 bytes. There's a catch with this directive, however. Suppose you write:

```
      JUMPS
      or    ax, ax       ; Is ax = 0?
      je    There        ; Jump if ax = 0
      mov   ax, 5        ; Else set ax to 5
There:
```

With the JUMPS directive in effect, when Turbo Assembler assembles the je instruction, it actually inserts:

```
      je    There
      nop
      nop
      nop
There:
```

The three nops reserve space for alternate code that the assembler inserts if the target label There is farther away than je can normally reach:

```
        jne   Temp
        jmp   There
Temp:
```

Instead of assembling the je that you wrote, Turbo Assembler inserts the opposite instruction jne followed by an unconditional jmp—exactly the same as explained earlier. The Temp label is just for illustration—a label isn't actually inserted into the program. The problem with JUMPS is those extra nops, which are inserted whether or not they are needed. For this reason, I prefer to write double jumps explicitly. The JUMPS directive does come in handy as a temporary tool, though. After finishing a program design, you can convert the long jumps to explicit double jump instructions and remove the JUMPS directive for the final assembly. This will eliminate the wasteful nops.

String Instructions

The 8086 string instructions in Table 4-8 are powerful little engines for processing all kinds of data—not just strings. Remember that strings in assembly language are sequences of bytes that may or may not represent

Table 4-8 *8086 String Instructions*

Mnemonic/Operands	Description
String Transfer Instructions	
lods *source*	Load string bytes or words
lodsb	Load string bytes
lodsw	Load string words
movs *destination, source*	Move string bytes or words
movsb	Move string bytes
movsw	Move string words
stos *destination*	Store string bytes or words
stosb	Store string bytes
stosw	Store string words
String Inspection Instructions	
cmps *destination, source*	Compare string bytes or words
cmpsb	Compare string bytes
cmpsw	Compare string words
scas *destination*	Scan string bytes or words
scasb	Scan string bytes
scasw	Scan string words
Repeat Prefix Instructions	
rep	Repeat
repe/repz	Repeat while equal/0
repne/repnz	Repeat while not equal/0

ASCII characters. Despite their suggestive names, the 8086 string instructions don't care what the bytes mean. String instructions divide into three groups:

▶ String transfer instructions

▶ String inspection instructions

▶ Repeat prefix instructions

String transfer instructions move bytes and words from memory to a register, from a register to memory, or directly from memory to memory. *String inspection* instructions let you compare and scan bytes and words, searching for specific values. *Repeat prefix instructions* can be attached as prefaces to other string instructions, creating single commands that repeat a number of times or cycle until a specified condition is met. A prefixed string instruction can quickly fill thousands of bytes with values, copy strings from one location to another, and search large memory blocks for values.

Despite the many mnemonics in Table 4-8, there are actually only five string instructions: `lods`, `stos`, `movs`, `scas`, and `cmps`. The others are shorthand mnemonics for these same commands. As you can see in the table, the shorthand names such as `lodsb` and `cmpsw` require no operands and, therefore, are easier to use. Similarly, there are only two repeat prefixes: `rep` is identical to `repe` and `repz`. And `repne` and `repnz` represent the same prefix. The interchangeable names are provided merely to help you document exactly what your program is doing.

String Index Registers

All string instructions use specific registers to perform their duties. Unlike other instructions that let you decide which registers to use, string instructions are finicky, always operating with the same combination of registers `ds:si` and `es:di`—the source and destination string index registers, which specify offsets in the data and extra segments.

> Note: If `ds` and `es` address the same data segment, as they often do, then you don't have to be concerned about addressing the correct memory segments during string operations. When `ds` and `es` address different segments, you must be careful to reference the correct segment for the operations you want to perform. Also, the destination index `di` is always relative to the segment addressed by `es`. The source index `si` is normally relative to the segment addressed by `ds` unless you override this by using `es` explicitly as in `es:si`.

The five string instructions load, store, move, compare, and scan bytes and words. While performing these jobs, each string instruction also increases or decreases the registers they use. Byte operations subtract or add 1 to `si` or `di` (or both); word operations add or subtract 2. For example, if `si` equals 0010 hexadecimal, then after a `lodsw` operation, `si` would be advanced to 0012 (or retarded to 000E, depending on the direction of the string operation). Because of this effect on the index registers, by adding a repeat prefix to a string instruction, programs can process whole sequences of data with a single command.

The direction flag df specifies whether string instructions should increase or decrease si and di. If df = 1, then the indexes are decreased toward lower addresses. If df = 0, then the indexes are increased toward higher addresses. Use cld to clear df, automatically incrementing si and di toward higher addresses. Use std to set df, automatically decreasing si and di toward lower addresses.

> Note: Although you can set or clear df at the beginning of a program, because df could be changed by another routine, the safest course is always to set or clear the direction flag immediately before every string instruction. This takes very little time and is good preventive medicine against bugs.

Loading Strings

The lods instruction loads data addressed by ds:si or es:si into al for byte operations or into ax for word operations. After this, si is increased or decreased, depending on the setting of the direction flag df. Byte operations adjust si by 1; word operations, by 2. With this instruction, you can construct a simple loop to search for a byte value:

```
        cld                      ; Auto-increment si
Repeat:
        lods [byte ptr ds:si]    ; al <- [ds:si]; si <- si + 1
        or   al, al              ; Is al = 0?
        jne  Repeat              ; Repeat if al <> 0
```

First, cld clears df, preparing to auto-increment si after each lods, which copies into al the byte addressed by ds:si. Then si is advanced to address the next byte in memory. After loading each byte, an or instruction tests if al equals 0. If not, the jne jumps back to label Repeat:, thus repeating this sequence until finding a zero byte. (If no zero byte exists in the segment at ds, by the way, this loop will repeat "forever." Take care that you don't introduce a bug into your programs with loops such as this.)

> Note: Auto-incrementing or decrementing si and di past the edge of a segment causes the registers to "wrap around" to the other segment end. In other words, if si or di are equal to 0FFFFh, adding 1 "advances" the registers to 0000. Likewise, if the registers equal 0000, subtracting 1 "retards" the registers to 0FFFFh.

Using Shorthand String Mnemonics

Because lods normally operates on the value addressed by ds:si, Turbo Assembler gives you two shorthand mnemonics that do not require operands, lodsb and lodsw. The *sb* in this and other shorthand string mnemonics stands for *string byte*. The *sw* stands for *string word*. Table 4-9 lists the equivalent longhand forms for all the shorthand mnemonics.

Addressing String Labels

Turbo Assembler allows you to specify data labels in the long forms of the string instructions in Table 4-9. For example, to load into al the first byte of a string s1, you can write:

```
DATASEG
string  db  'This is a string', 0

CODESEG
mov si, offset string              ; Assign address of string to si
lods [string]                      ; Get first byte of string
```

Table 4-9 *String Instruction Shorthand*

Shorthand	Equivalent String Instruction
lodsb	lods [byte ptr ds:si]
lodsw	lods [word ptr ds:si]
stosb	stos [byte ptr es:di]
stosw	stos [word ptr es:di]
movsb	movs [byte ptr es:di], [byte ptr ds:si]
movsw	movs [word ptr es:di], [word ptr ds:si]
scasb	scas [byte ptr es:di]
scasw	scas [word ptr es:di]
cmpsb	cmps [byte ptr ds:si], [byte ptr es:di]
cmpsw	cmps [word ptr ds:si], [word ptr es:di]

But the instruction lods [string] does not assemble as you may think. Instead, Turbo Assembler converts this instruction to lodsb, assuming that you previously loaded the offset address of string into si. Remember that all string instructions require specific registers to address the data on which the instructions operate. Even when you specify a variable by name as in this example, you still have to load si or di with the appropriate addresses for the instruction. Specifying a variable by name merely lets Turbo Assembler verify that this variable is probably addressable by the appropriate registers. The assembler doesn't initialize the index registers for you.

Storing Data to Strings

Stos and the shorthand mnemonics stosb and stosw store a byte in al or a word in ax to the location addressed by es:di. As with lods, stos increments or decrements di by 1 or 2, depending on the setting of df and whether the data is composed of bytes or words. Combining lods and stos in a loop can transfer strings from one location to another:

```
    cld                    ; Auto-increment si and di
Repeat:
    lodsw                  ; ax <- [ds:si]; si <- si + 2
    cmp  ax, 0FFFFh        ; Is ax = 0FFFFh?
    je   Exit              ; Jump if ax = 0FFFFh
    stosw                  ; [es:di] <- ax; di <- di + 2
    jmp  Repeat            ; Repeat until done
Exit:
```

In this example, first the cld instruction prepares to auto-increment si and di. Then, lodsw loads into ax the word addressed by ds:si, also incrementing si by two. If ax equals the value 0FFFFh—presumably placed into memory by another routine as an end-of-data marker—the je instruction exits the loop. Otherwise, stosw stores the word in ax to the location addressed by es:di, also incrementing di by 2. The final jmp repeats these actions until detecting the 0FFFFh marker. Once again, the danger here is that 0FFFFh does not exist in the data segment. As you'll learn later, there are other ways to code this operation that eliminate this problem.

Moving Strings

Use movs or the shorthand forms movsb and movsw to move bytes and words between two memory locations. Because these instructions do not require an intermediate register to hold data on its way from and to memory, they are the fastest tools available for moving data blocks. As with other string instructions, you can use the longhand form along with operands, or, as most programmers prefer, you can use the simpler shorthand mnemonics.

Movsb moves 1 byte from the location addressed by ds:si or es:si to the location addressed by es:di, incrementing or decrementing both index registers by 1. Movsw moves a word between the two locations, incrementing or decrementing the registers by 2. Although you can use these instructions alone to transfer one byte or word—or construct a loop to transfer many successive values—you'll most often add a repeat prefix as in this sample:

```
cld                   ; Auto-increment si, di
mov   cx, 100         ; Assign count to cx
rep   movsb           ; Move 100 bytes
```

These three little instructions move 100 bytes of memory starting at ds:si to the location starting at es:di. The repeat prefix rep repeatedly executes movsb, subtracting 1 from cx after each repetition, and ending when cx equals 0. You must use cx for this purpose. Without a repeat prefix, you'd have to write the instructions this way:

```
      cld             ; Auto-increment si, di
      mov   cx, 100   ; Assign count to cx
Repeat:
      movsb           ; [es:di] <- [ds:si]; advance si & di
      dec   cx        ; Count number of loops done
      jnz   Repeat    ; Repeat loop if cx <> 0
```

But, with a repeat prefix, there's no need to go to all this trouble; furthermore, handling the counting chores yourself results in slower code.

Strange but True Department: Some perfectly valid repeated string instructions produce senseless code. For example, you can write rep lodsb, loading cx successive bytes into al. Because each new value erases the previous value in al, there's never a good reason to perform such a wasteful instruction.

Filling Memory

The stos instruction makes filling memory with a byte or word value easy. Be careful with this one. It can erase an entire memory segment in a flash.

For example, this stores 0 bytes in a 512-byte block of memory, starting at the label `Buffer`:

```
mov   ax, SEG Buffer      ; Assign segment address of Buffer
mov   es, ax              ;  to extra segment register es
mov   di, OFFSET Buffer   ; Assign offset address to di
xor   al, al              ; Assign value to store in memory
mov   cx, 512             ; Assign count to cx
cld                       ; Prepare to auto-increment di
rep   stosb               ; Set 512 bytes to zeros
```

First `es` is assigned the segment address of the variable to be erased to all zeros. The `SEG` operator returns the segment portion of a variable, here `Buffer`. This value is first assigned to `ax`, which is then assigned to `es`. (The two steps are necessary because of the restriction against moving literal values directly into segment registers such as `es`.) After this, `di` is initialized to address the beginning of `Buffer`, `al` is set to the value to store in memory, and the number of bytes is loaded into `cx`. Finally, after `cld` sets `df` to 1, preparing to auto-increment `di`, the repeated `stosb` instruction fills `Buffer` with zeros. By changing only the value assigned to `cx`, this same sequence can fill up to 65,535 bytes. (Set `cx` to 0ffffh to repeat a string instruction this maximum number of times. To fill 65,536 bytes, add an additional `stosb` instruction after `rep stosb`.)

Scanning Strings

Use `scas` to scan strings for specific values. As with other string instructions, you can use the longhand or shorthand forms `scasb` and `scasw`. Each repetition of `scas` compares the byte value in `al` or the word value in `ax` with the data addressed by `es:di`. Register `di` is then incremented or decremented by 1 or 2.

This is counter-intuitive! Should use si but they don't!

Because you can compare single bytes and words with a `cmp` instruction, the scan instructions are almost always prefaced with `repe` (repeat while equal) or `repne` (repeat while not equal)—or with the mnemonic aliases `repz` (repeat while `zf` = 1) and `repnz` (repeat while `zf` = 0). For each repetition, these prefixes decrement `cx` by 1, ending if `cx` becomes 0. (Remember that `repe`, `repz`, and `rep` are the same instruction.) When these prefixes are used with `scas` or `cmps` (or any of their shorthand equivalents), repetitions also stop when the zero flag `zf` indicates the failure of the scan or the compare. For example, a simple sequence scans 250 bytes looking for a 0:

```
cld                       ; Auto-increment di
mov   di, OFFSET Start    ; Address starting location with es:di
mov   cx, 250             ; Set cx to maximum count
xor   al, al              ; Set al = 0, the search value
repne scasb               ; Scan memory for a match with al
je    MatchFound          ; Jump if a 0 was found at es:di - 1
```

jCXZ is also useful here

After clearing `df` with `cld`, causing `scasb` to auto-increment `di`, which is initialized to address the label `Start`, `cx` is loaded with the maximum number of bytes to scan, 250. Then, `al` (holding the search value) is zeroed with an `xor` instruction. The `repne scasb` instruction scans up to 250 bytes, decrementing `cx` after each repetition, and cycling while `cx` is not 0 and while zf indicates that a match has *not* been found. (You would use repe or repz to cycle until a mismatch is found.) After the repeated scan, an optional je jumps to MatchFound (not shown) only if the search byte was located. The address of that byte is at es:di - 1.

When Zero Means Zero

If cx equals 0, repeated string instructions cycle 65,536 times. But when you want 0 to mean "perform this operation zero times," you must test whether cx is 0 before starting the repeated string instruction. You could do this with an or followed by a jump:

```
       or    cx, cx      ; Does cx = 0?
       jz    Skip        ; Jump if yes (cx = 0)
       rep   stosb       ; Else repeat stosb
Skip:
```

This sequence jumps to label Skip if cx is 0. Only if cx is not 0 does the rep stosb instruction execute. This prevents accidentally repeating the string operation 65,536 times—unless, of course, that's what you want to do. Instead of this sequence, however, you can use a special conditional jump instruction provided for this purpose:

```
       jcxz  Skip        ; Jump if cx = 0
       rep   stosb       ; Else repeat stosb
Skip:
```

The jcxz instruction performs the same function as the or and jz instructions in the previous example.

Comparing Strings

To compare two strings, use cmps or the shorthand forms cmpsb and cmpsw. The instructions compare two bytes or words at es:di and ds:si or es:si. As Table 4-9 shows, the operands are reversed from the similar operands for movs—an important distinction to keep in mind. The cmps comparison subtracts the byte or word at es:di from the byte or word at ds:si or es:si, saving the flags of this subtraction but not the result—similar to the way cmp works. After the comparison, both si and di are incremented or decremented by 1 for byte compares and by 2 for word compares. These instructions are almost always prefaced with a repeat prefix as in this sample:

```
cld                      ; Auto-increment si, di
mov   si, OFFSET s1      ; Address first string with ds:si
mov   di, OFFSET s2      ; Address second string with es:di
mov   cx, strlength      ; Assign string length to cx
repe  cmpsb              ; Compare the two strings
jb    Less               ; Jump if s1 < s2
ja    Greater            ; Jump if s1 > s2
je    Equal              ; Jump if s1 = s2
```

jcxz will catch the end of string cond when s1 & s2 are identical.

This sequence assumes that string s1 is stored in the segment addressed by ds and that string s2 is stored in the segment addressed by es. If ds = es, then the two strings would have to be stored in the same segment. After the initializing steps—clearing df with cld, assigning the string addresses to `si` and `di`, and setting `cx` to the maximum number of bytes to compare—the `repe cmpsb` repeated string instruction compares the two strings, ending on the first mismatched byte found. (You could also use `repne` here to compare two strings, ending on the first match found.) After the repeated instruction, the flags indicate the final result, which you can test by any of the three conditional jumps as shown here.

Note: The string comparison method shown in the previous sample requires knowing the length of the strings being compared. If the strings are of different lengths, you must set `cx` to the number of characters in the shorter string. When it's not practical to calculate the string lengths ahead of time, different methods are required to compare strings. Chapter 5 describes these techniques in more detail.

Summary

Segments divide the 8086's large address space into manageable 64K-maximum size chunks, allowing programs to address memory using efficient 16-bit pointers. Segment registers point to the start of segments in memory. Segments can overlap and can begin at any 16-byte paragraph boundary.

There are five categories of registers in the 8086 design: the general-purpose registers (`ax, bx, cx, dx`), the pointer and index registers (`sp, bp, si, di`), the segment registers (`cs, ds, ss, es`), the instruction pointer (`ip`), and the flags (`of, df, if, tf, sf, zf, af, pf, cf`). Some registers have specific purposes; others are free to be used however you wish.

Six main groups divide the 8086 instruction set into data transfer instructions, arithmetic instructions, logic instructions, flow-control instructions, processor control instructions, and string instructions. Many instructions require one or two operands, usually labeled the destination and the source. Other instructions require no operands.

Stacks in memory resemble a stack of dishes where the last dish placed onto the stack is the first to be removed. This is known as a LIFO (Last-In-First-Out) structure. In the 8086, the `ss:sp` register pair locates the base and top of stack in memory. Programs use the **STACK** directive to allocate stack space at run time.

Subroutines help divide a large program into modules. Programs run subroutines with `call` instructions. Subroutines must end with a `ret` instruction to return to the instruction following the `call`. By using the **PROC** and **ENDP** directives around subroutine code, Turbo Assembler automatically assembles the correct calls and returns for intrasegment (same `cs`) and intersegment (different `cs`) subroutines.

Jump instructions change program flow, altering which instruction is to execute next. There are two kinds of jump instructions, conditional and unconditional. Conditional jump target addresses are limited to about 127 bytes away. The unconditional `jmp` instruction has no range limit.

Exercises

4-1. What are the minimum and maximum sizes of a memory segment?

4-2. List several ways to set register `ax` equal to 0.

4-3. Using `push` and `pop`, how can you duplicate the effect of the instruction `mov ax,dx`?

4-4. Describe the difference between `neg` and `not`.

4-5. What combination of instructions can rotate a 16-bit register enough times to restore completely the original value in that register? Which shift or rotate instructions will also preserve the value of the carry flag?

4-6. Write a routine to unpack two 4-bit values from an 8-bit byte into two 8-bit bytes. For example, if the original value equals 5F hexadecimal, then the two results should equal 05 and 0F. Assume that the original value is in register `ah` and that the result is to be stored in `dh` and `dl`.

4-7. How might you use a shift instruction to test whether a certain bit, say number 5, is set in register `dh`?

4-8. Suppose that the label `Target` is farther away than the conditional jump `jl` can reach. How can you recode the following instruction to avoid an error from Turbo Assembler?

```
jl Target        ; Jump to Target if less
```

4-9. Without using `neg` or `not`, write instructions to form the one's and two's complements of values in `bx`.

4-10. Write your own `nop` instruction. No registers or flags should change by executing your custom `nop`. Can you find more than one way to do nothing? (Your answer can take more than a single byte of assembled code.)

4-11. What do string repeat prefixes do?

4-12. What instructions would you use to scan 65,536 bytes of memory?

Projects

4-1. Write a subroutine to unpack any number of bits from a word, returning those bits in the lower portion of a register. In other words, the caller to this subroutine should be able to pass a value containing bits, say, in positions 4, 5, and 6. The subroutine should return those bits in positions 0, 1, and 2, setting all other bits to 0.

4-2. Write a subroutine to do the reverse of project #1. That is, the routine should be able to pack any number of bits into a certain position in a word, without disturbing other bits already there.

4-3. Create templates on disk for your future programs and procedures. Decide what information you will place in your subroutine headers.

4-4. Write a subroutine to scan memory for a specific byte value, stopping if that byte is not found within a certain number of memory locations. Use string instructions from Table 4-8.

4-5. Write subroutines to copy blocks of memory from one location to another, correctly handling variables in the same or in different segments. Use string instructions in your answer.

4-6. Write a routine to change all the characters in an ASCII string to uppercase or lowercase. Write your answer with and without string instructions.

Chapter *5* *Simple Data Structures*

5 Simple Data Structures

In This Chapter

Ways and means of addressing data in memory; explanation of addressing modes; how to write expressions and use operators; declaring simple variables; the difference between initialized and uninitialized data segments; all about string variables; using local labels; adding an ASCIIZ string package to your library; how to assemble and link separate modules; how to use TLIB to create and manage an object-code file library; reading and writing string variables; more details on the 8086 string instructions

Addressing Data in Memory

Of all the subjects in 8086 assembly language programming, the many ways of addressing data in memory are probably some of the most difficult to learn. But you'll avoid a lot of head scratching if you remember that all data references take one of these three forms:

▶ Immediate data references   *1 mode*

▶ Register data references   *1 mode*

▶ Memory data references   *7 modes*

Immediate data are values stored directly in the machine code of an instruction. For example, when you write:

```
mov  ax, 5     ; ax <- 5
```

the assembler generates a machine-code variant of the mov instruction that loads the *immediate* value 5 into ax. The 5 is stored directly in the mov instruction's assembled machine code. In most cases, immediate data is the only operand or is the second of two operands. (An exception is out, which allows immediate data as the first of two operands.) You can never change the value of immediate data when the program runs.

Explain pitfalls of self-modifying code.

> Note: You can, of course, write programs to change machine-code instructions stored in memory. Using this technique, you could locate the place where an immediate value is stored and change it before the instruction operates. Pulling this trick is generally considered to be bad form. Such *self-modifying* code is often difficult to debug and, worse, cannot be stored in ROM, where memory values are permanently etched in silicon. Also, because the 8086 family of processors preloads several instructions at once into a small amount of internal memory called the *instruction cache*, modifying code on-the-fly is unreliable at best. Resist the temptation to write self-modifying programs. There are few times (if any) when the results are worth the risks.

Register data refers to data held in processor registers. You've already seen many examples of this kind of data reference. The machine code generated by the assembler for register data includes appropriate values to cause the instruction to operate on the specified registers, as in:

```
add   ax, bx      ; ax <- ax + bx
```

Memory data is the third kind of data reference, of which there are several variations. To avoid confusion when learning these variants, remember that the goal is to help the processor calculate a 16-bit, unsigned value called the *effective address*, or EA. The EA represents an offset starting from the base of a segment addressed by one of the four segment registers: cs, ds, es, and ss. As you recall from chapter 4, a segment register and offset form a 32-bit logical address, which the 8086 further translates into a physical 20-bit address, uniquely locating any byte in memory.

You never have to be concerned about calculating an EA or forming the physical 20-bit address—these are the processor's jobs. Your responsibility is to give the processor the data necessary to calculate the EA, locating your variables in memory. To do this, you can use one of seven memory modes, as described next.

> Note: Chapter 14's 8086 reference lists the memory-addressing modes available for each instruction. Consult this reference when you are unsure whether an instruction recognizes a specific mode.

Memory-Addressing Modes

Table 5-1 lists the seven memory-addressing modes available in 8086 programming. Except for string and I/O port addressing, which have special requirements, these addressing modes can be used in all instructions that allow referencing data in memory. For instance, although the mov instruction is used in the examples in Table 5-1, you can use similar references with other instructions such as add, inc, and xor. The following sections

Table 5-1 *8086 Addressing Modes*

Addressing Mode	Example
Direct	`mov   ax, [count]`
Register-indirect	`mov   ax, [bx]`
Base	`mov   ax, [record + bp]`
Indexed	`mov   ax, [array + si]`
Base-indexed	`mov   ax, [recordArray + bx + si]`
String	`lodsw`
I/O port	`in    ax, dx`

describe the first five addressing modes, leaving string and I/O port addressing for later.

Direct Addresses   A *direct address* is the literal offset address of a variable in memory, relative to any segment base. For example, to refer to variables in the data segment, you can write instructions such as:

```
inc   [MyMoney]          ; Add 1 to value of [MyMoney]
```

The notation `[MyMoney]` is assembled to the offset address where the variable `MyMoney` is stored. All such direct address references are permanently fixed in the assembled code and can't be changed by a running program. (Self-modifying programs can change a direct address reference, but, for the reasons already described, this is a poor and unreliable technique.)

Note: Only the offset address of a direct memory reference is cut into stone. The segment in which the variable `MyMoney` is stored may begin at any paragraph boundary; therefore, there's no guarantee that `MyMoney` will be stored at a predetermined physical address.

Overrides   Direct address references are normally relative to the segment addressed by `ds`. To change this, you can specify a *segment override* as in:

See FARDATA and @fardata directives!

```
mov   ch, [es:OverByte]
```

This instruction loads a byte at the label `OverByte` stored in the segment addressed by `es`. The override instruction `es:` is required to defeat the processor's normal use of the default segment base in `ds`. You can apply similar overrides to access data in other segments, too. Here are three more examples:

```
mov   dh, [cs:CodeByte]          ; dh <- byte in code segment
mov   dh, [ss:StackByte]         ; dh <- byte in stack segment
mov   dh, [ds:DataByte]          ; dh <- byte in data segment ???
```

The first line loads into dh a byte located in the code segment. Because most variables will be in a data segment, referring to data stored in the code segment is only occasionally useful. The second line loads a byte located in the stack segment. While permissible, this is rarely done in practice. The third line unnecessarily specifies ds—direct data references normally refer to the segment addressed by ds. Here are a few additional hints that will help you to use overrides correctly:

▷ Even though you specify an override as part of the data reference, an override actually occupies a byte of machine code and is inserted just before the affected instruction. Overrides are instruction prefixes that change the behavior of the next instruction to be executed.

▷ The effect of an override lasts for only one instruction. You must use an override in every reference to data in a segment other than the default segment for this instruction.

▷ In Turbo Assembler's Ideal mode, the entire address reference including the segment override must be in brackets. Although MASM mode allows a more free-form style, Ideal mode's clearer syntax requirements are fully compatible with MASM mode.

▷ It is your responsibility to ensure that variables are actually in the segments you specify and that segment registers es and ds are initialized to address those segments. Stack register ss and code segment cs do not require initialization.

Register-Indirect Addresses

Instead of referring to variables in memory by name, you can use one of three registers as a pointer to data in memory: bx, si, and di. Because a program can modify register values to address different memory locations, *register-indirect addressing* allows one instruction to operate on multiple variables. After loading an offset address into an appropriate register, you can refer to the data stored in memory with instructions such as:

```
mov  cx, [WORD bx]    ; Copy word at [bx] into cx
dec  [BYTE si]        ; Decrement byte at [si]
```

The WORD and BYTE operators are required when Turbo Assembler is unable to know whether the register addresses a word or a byte in memory. In the first line here, data addressed by bx is moved into the 16-bit register cx; therefore, the WORD operator is not needed because the assembler knows the size of the data reference from the context of the instruction. Specifying the operator as in this sample does no harm, though. In the second line, the BYTE operator must be included because the assembler has no other way of knowing whether dec is to decrement a byte or a word.

Note: In instructions such as `inc [si]`, Turbo Assembler displays a warning but still assembles the program, assuming that `si` addresses a word in memory even if this is not what you intend. Always use the **WORD** and **BYTE** operators to remove all addressing ambiguities and to reduce the likelihood of introducing hard-to-find bugs.

Register-indirect addressing defaults to the segment addressed by `ds`. As with direct addressing, you can use overrides to change this default to any of the other three segments. A few examples make this clear:

```
add   [WORD es:bx], 3      ; Add 3 to word at es:bx
dec   [BYTE ss:si]         ; Decrement the byte at ss:si
mov   cx, [cs:di]          ; Load a word from code segment
```

As explained earlier, when using overrides this way, you must be sure that the data you are addressing actually exists in the segments you specify. And, even though overrides to the stack segment as in the second sample are allowed, they are rarely of much practical use.

Note: String instructions use `es` as the default segment register for index `di`. Register-indirect addressing uses `ds` as the default segment for `di`. Don't confuse these two completely different addressing modes, even though they use the same register.

Base Addresses

Base addressing employs the two registers `bx` and `bp`. References to `bx` are relative to the data segment addressed by `ds`. References to `bp` are relative to the stack segment `ss` and are normally used to read and write values stored on the stack. You can use segment overrides as previously described to refer to data in any of the other segments.

Base addressing adds a *displacement* value to the location addressed by `bx` or `bp`. This displacement is a signed 16- or 8-bit value representing an additional offset above or below the offset in the specified register. A typical use for base addressing is to locate fields in a data structure. For example:

```
mov   bx, OFFSET Person    ; Point to start of Person
mov   ax, [bx + 5]         ; Get data 5 bytes beyond
```

After assigning to `bx` the offset address of a variable named `Person` (not shown), a second `mov` loads into `ax` a value stored 5 bytes from the start of `Person`. Similarly, you can use instructions to reference variables on the stack, as in:

```
inc   [WORD bp + 2]        ; Increment word on stack
dec   [BYTE bp - 8]        ; Decrement byte on stack
```

Remember that references to `bp` are relative to the stack segment `ss`. (Chapters 12 and 13 describe in more detail how to use `bp` and base addressing to access stacked variables.) The displacement value may also be negative as the second line shows. Because displacements are 16-bit values, the effective range is −32,768 to 32,767 bytes away from the offset addressed by bx or bp.

why bp is not listed in reg.-indirect mode.

> Note: When the displacement is 0, base addressing is identical to register-indirect addressing for register **bx**. Knowing this, Turbo Assembler reduces references such as [bx + 0] to the more efficient [bx] (no displacement). The same is not true for references that use bp as in [bp + 0] for which [bp] is merely a synonym, not a different addressing mode. (Some references confuse this point and list **bp** as a register-indirect mode register, although this is technically incorrect.)

Indexed Addresses

Indexed addressing is identical to base addressing except that si and di hold the offset addresses. Unless you specify a segment override, all indexed address references are relative to the data segment addressed by ds. Normally, indexed addressing is used to access simple arrays. For example, to increment the fifth byte of an array of 8-bit values, you can write:

```
inc   [BYTE si + 4]      ; Add 1 to array element number 5
```

Because si + 0 locates the first array element, a displacement of 4 and not 5 must be used to locate the fifth byte in the array. Also, as with base addressing, displacements are signed values and, therefore, can be negative:

```
mov  dx, [WORD di - 8]  ; Load word 8 bytes before di
```

> Note: When the displacement is 0, base addressing is identical to register-indirect addressing for the two registers si and di. Knowing this, Turbo Assembler reduces references such as [si + 0] and [di + 0] to the more efficient register-indirect equivalents, [si] and [di].

Base-Indexed Addresses

Base-indexed addressing combines two registers and adds an optional displacement value to form an offset memory reference—thus coupling the features of the base- and indexed-addressing modes. The first register must be either bx or bp. The second register must be si or di. Offsets in bx are relative to the ds data segment; offsets in bp are relative to the ss stack segment. As with other addressing modes, you can use overrides to alter these defaults. A few examples help explain this valuable addressing technique:

```
mov  ax, [bx + si]      ; Load data segment word into ax
mov  ax, [bx + di]      ;       "        "         "
mov  ax, [bp + si]      ; Load stack segment word into ax
mov  ax, [bp + di]      ;       "        "         "
```

Turbo Assembler allows you to reverse the order of the registers, for example, writing [si + bx] and [di + bp]. But these are not different addressing modes—just different forms of the same references. You can also add an optional displacement value to any of the four previous variations:

```
mov   ax, [bx + si + 5]   ; Load displaced data segment word into ax
mov   ax, [bx + di + 5]   ;       "         "         "
mov   ax, [bp + si + 5]   ; Load displaced stack segment word into ax
mov   ax, [bp + di + 5]   ;       "         "         "
```

In addition, you can add overrides to any of these eight basic base-indexed addressing variants to refer to data in segments other than the defaults:

```
mov   ax, [es:bx + si + 8]      ; Use es instead of ds default
mov   ax, [cs:bp + di]          ; Use cs instead of ss default
```

Base-indexed addressing is the 8086's most powerful memory reference technique. With this method, you can specify a starting offset in bx or bp (perhaps the address of an array), add to this an index value in si or di (possibly locating one element in the array), and then add a displacement value (maybe to locate a record field in this specific array element). By modifying the base and index register values, programs can address complex data structures in memory.

referencing an array of records:
bx = start of array
si = index into array
8 = field offset into record.

Note: In MASM mode, base-indexed address references (and other addressing methods) can have a more free-form appearance such as 5[bx + si] and 5[bp][di], leading many people to assume that these are unique and mysterious addressing forms. This is not so. There are only eight basic forms of base-indexed addressing, as listed earlier. You'll avoid much confusion (and lose nothing in the process) if you stick to the standard forms described here and required by Ideal mode.

Using the ASSUME Directive

An ASSUME directive tells Turbo Assembler to which segment in memory a segment register refers. The purpose of ASSUME is to allow the assembler to insert override instructions automatically when needed. Always remember that ASSUME is a command to the assembler and does not generate any code.

When using simplified segment addressing—as in most of this book's examples—you'll rarely need to use ASSUME. And, by explicitly using segment overrides, you can eliminate the need for ASSUME altogether. Even so, it pays to understand how this directive works. Suppose you write:

```
CODESEG
      jmp   There       ; Skip declaration of v1
v1    db    5           ; Store a 5 in the code segment
There:
      mov   ah, [cs:v1] ; Load 5 into ah
```

This code snippet illustrates one way to store data inside the code segment—an unusual but allowable practice. The `jmp` instruction skips over the declaration of a byte variable `v1`. (When mixing data and code, you certainly don't want to accidentally execute your variables as though they were instructions.) The `mov` instruction uses a segment override (`cs:`) to load the value of `v1` into `ah`. The override is required because direct data references normally default to the `ds` data segment.

Because Turbo Assembler knows that `cs` refers to the code segment, it allows you to replace the `mov` instruction with the simpler instruction:

```
mov  ah, [v1]       ; Load 5 into ah from code segment
```

Even though an explicit override is not used, Turbo Assembler checks its list of variables, detects that `v1` is stored in the code segment, and *automatically inserts the required override.* In other cases when Turbo Assembler doesn't know which segment registers refer to which memory segments, you must either use an explicit override or tell the assembler what's going on with an **ASSUME** directive. Here's another example:

```
CODESEG
     jmp   There          ; Skip declaration of v1
v1   db    5              ; Store a 5 in this location
There:
     mov   ax, @code      ; Assign address of code segment
     mov   es, ax         ;  to es register
ASSUME es:_TEXT
     mov   ah, [v1]       ; Load 5 into ah from extra segment
```

Again, a 5 byte is stored directly in the code segment. In this example, segment register `es` is initialized to address the code segment, assigning the predefined symbol `@code` to `ax` and then assigning this value to `es`. The **ASSUME** directive tells Turbo Assembler where `es` now points, using the small memory model's name for the code segment `_TEXT`. Finally, the `mov` loads the value of `v1` into `ah`. Although this appears identical to the earlier example, because of the **ASSUME** directive, the actual instruction assembled is:

```
mov  ah, [es:v1]
```

Because `v1` is stored in the code segment, however, both `[es:v1]` and `[cs:v1]` correctly locate the same variable. All that **ASSUME** does is allow the assembler to insert the override instructions automatically.

Note: Segment names such as `_TEXT` are listed with the MODEL directive in your Turbo Assembler Reference Guide. Using simplified memory models as explained in chapter 2 usually makes it unnecessary to refer to these names or to use **ASSUME** directives.

Expressions and Operators

Expressions in assembly language have one purpose: to make programs easy to understand and, therefore, easy to modify. For example, you might have several equates, associating optional values with symbols such as:

```
RecSize   EQU  10
NumRecs   EQU  25
```

Elsewhere you can use the equated symbols in expressions, perhaps to store in memory a value equal to RecSize times NumRecs:

```
BufSize   dw   RecSize * NumRecs
```

When Turbo Assembler processes this directive, it multiplies RecSize by NumRecs and stores the resulting constant (250) in the word variable BufSize. It's important to understand that this calculation occurs during assembly—not when the program runs. All expressions evaluate to constants in the assembled code. In high-level languages, expressions such as (Columns * 16) are evaluated at run time, possibly with a new value for a variable named Columns entered by an operator. In assembly language, expressions reduce to constant values when you assemble the program text, not when the program runs. The difference can be confusing at first, especially if you're more accustomed to high- than low-level programming.

Table 5-2 lists Turbo Assembler's Ideal-mode expression operators, which you can use to calculate constant values of just about any imaginable type. MASM-mode operators (listed in Turbo Assembler's Reference Guide) are similar. Don't confuse operators such as AND, OR, XOR, and NOT with the assembly language mnemonics of the same names. The assembly language mnemonics are instructions that operate at run time. The operators are for use in expressions, calculated at assembly time. In this and in other chapters, you'll meet many of these operators in action.

Simple Variables

Earlier program examples created simple variables with db and dw directives. These directives belong to a family of similar commands, all having the same general purpose: to define (meaning to reserve) space for values in memory. The directives differ only in how much space they can define and the types of initial values you can specify. Table 5-3 lists all seven of these useful directives ranked according to the minimum amount of space each reserves. Also listed are typical examples, although the directives are not limited to the uses shown here. You can type any of these directives in uppercase or lowercase. DB and db have the same meaning.

Wide Open Spaces   To create large amounts of space, you can string together several db, dw, or other define-memory directives, or you can use the DUP operator, which is usually more convenient. DUP has the following form:

```
[label] directive count DUP (expression [,expression]...)
```

Table 5-2 *Expression Operators*

Operator	Description	Operator	Description
( )	Parentheses	MOD	Division remainder
*	Multiply	NE	Not equal
/	Divide	NEAR	Near code pointer
+	Add/unary plus	NOT	Ones complement
—	Subtract/unary minus	OFFSET	Offset address
.	Structure member	OR	Logical OR
:	Segment override	PROC	Near/far code pointer
?	Uninitialized data	PTR	Expression size
[ ]	Memory reference	PWORD	32-bit far pointer
AND	Logical AND	QWORD	Quadword size
BYTE	Force byte size	SEG	Segment address
DUP	Duplicate variable	SHL	Shift left
DWORD	Force doubleword	SHORT	Short code pointer
EQ	Equal	SHR	Shift right
FAR	Far code pointer	SIZE	Size of item
FWORD	Farword size	SMALL	16-bit offset
GE	Greater than or equal	SYMTYPE	Symbol type
GT	Greater than	TBYTE	Ten-byte size
HIGH	Return high part	THIS	Refer to next item
LARGE	Force 32-bit offset	TYPE	Type of item
LE	Less than or equal	UNKNOWN	Remove type info
LENGTH	Number of elements	WIDTH	Bit field width
LOW	Low part	WORD	Word size
LT	Less than or equal	XOR	Exclusive OR
MASK	Record-field bit mask		

Table 5-3 *Define-Memory Directives*

Directive	Name	Minimum Bytes Allocated	Typical Use
db	Define byte	1	Bytes, strings
dw	Define word	2	Integers
dd	Define doubleword	4	Long integers
dp	Define pointer	6	32-bit pointer
df	Define far pointer	6	48-bit pointer
dq	Define quadword	8	Real numbers
dt	Define ten bytes	10	BCD numbers

To create a multibyte space, start with an optional label and a define-memory directive from Table 5-3. Follow this with a count equal to the number of times you want to duplicate an expression, which must be in parentheses. The DUP keyword goes between the count and the expression. For example, each of these directives reserves a 10-byte area in memory, setting all 10 bytes to 0:

```
Ten1    dt   0              ; Ten zero bytes
Ten2    db   10 DUP (0)     ; Same as above
```

Separating multiple expressions or constant values with commas duplicates each value in turn, increasing the total size of the space reserved by the count times the number of items. Despite a count of 10, therefore, the following directive creates a 20-byte variable—ten repetitions of the two bytes 1 and 2:

```
Twenty1   db   10 DUP (1,2)   ; 20 bytes--1, 2, 1, 2, ..., 2
```

You can also nest DUP expressions to create large buffers initialized to a constant value. For example, each of the following directives reserves a 20-byte area with all bytes equal to 255:

```
Twenty2   db   10 DUP (2 DUP (255))   ; 20 bytes of 255
Twenty3   db   20 DUP (255)           ; Same as above
```

These same examples work with any of the define-memory directives to reserve different amounts of space. Most often, though, you'll use **db** and **dw** for integer, string, and byte variables, putting the other directives to work only for the special purposes listed in Table 5-3. But you are free to use these directives as you please. To create a 20-byte variable of all zeros, for example, you could use **db** as before or **dt** like this:

```
Twenty4   dt   2 DUP (0)
```

Of all the define-memory directives, only **db** has the special ability to allocate space for character strings, storing one ASCII character per byte in memory. Here's a sample, ending in a zero byte, a typical construction called an *ASCIIZ string*:

```
AString   db   'String things', 0
```

Combining **db**'s string ability with the DUP operator is a useful trick for filling a buffer with text that's easy to locate in Turbo Debugger's dump window. You might code a 1,024-byte buffer as:

```
Buffer    db   128 DUP ('=Buffer=')   ; 1024 bytes
```

DUP repeats the 8-byte string in parentheses 128 times, thus reserving a total of 1,024 bytes. In Turbo Debugger, use the View-Dump command, zoom to full screen with F5, press Alt-F10, and select Goto to view the program's data segment at DS:0000. Then use the PgDn key to hunt for this or a similar buffer in memory. There are other ways to find variables with Turbo Debugger, but this age-old debugging method is still a useful trick.

Initialized vs Uninitialized Data

When you know your program is going to assign new values to variables and, therefore, don't care what the initial values are, you can define uninitialized variables—those that have no specific values when the program runs. To do this, use a question mark (?) in place of the define-memory constant:

```
stuff      db   ?     ; Byte of unknown value
moreStuff  dw   ?     ; Word of unknown value
anyStuff   dt   ?     ; Ten bytes of unknown values
```

To create larger uninitialized spaces, use a question mark inside a DUP expression's parentheses, a useful technique for creating big buffers such as:

```
BigBuf     db   8000 DUP (?)   ; 8000-byte buffer
```

The 8,000-byte buffer created by this command contains bytes of no specific values when the program runs. Whatever was in the memory occupied by the buffer when DOS loads your program is what the buffer will contain.

> Note: When assembling and linking programs with the commands **tasm /zi <filename>** and **tlink /v <filename>** for running in Turbo Debugger, uninitialized data is filled with zero bytes, although this is not a documented feature. Do not rely on it. When assembling and linking without these switches, uninitialized variables have indeterminate values.

The main reason for declaring uninitialized variables is to reduce the size of the assembled code file. Instead of storing useless bytes on disk, uninitialized space is allocated at run time. For this to work, you must follow one of two rules:

▷ Place all uninitialized variables last in the data segment

▷ Or preface uninitialized variables with **UDATASEG**

Usually, the easiest plan is to place uninitialized variables last in the data segment, after variables with initial values. When this isn't practical, use the **UDATASEG** directive to tell Turbo Assembler to relocate an uninitialized variable to the end of the last initialized variable in the data segment even though the uninitialized variable appears elsewhere in the program text. For example, you can write:

```
DATASEG
var1     db    1
var2     db    2
UDATASEG
array    db    1000 DUP (?)
DATASEG
var3     db    3
```

The UDATASEG directive places array after var3 in memory, just as though you had declared the large uninitialized variable last instead of between the two initialized variables var2 and var3. Without UDATASEG, the large array would be "trapped" between var2 and var3, unnecessarily increasing the size of your code file by 1,000 bytes.

> Note: Many public domain assembly language source-code listings contain uninitialized variables between other initialized variables. When you find such a program, try relocating the uninitialized variables to the end of the data segment. Chances are this will reduce the size of the assembled disk code file, sometimes dramatically.

Be careful when using UDATASEG not to assume that one variable physically follows another in memory, as variables normally do. Some programs expect variables to be ordered in memory the way they are declared in the program text and, in these cases, relocating the variables is a big mistake. Avoid this problem in your own programs—and add clarity to your source code—by organizing your data segment like this:

```
DATASEG
; initialized variables
UDATASEG
; uninitialized variables
```

String Variables

While db can create character-string variables, assembly language has no built-in character-string commands to read and write strings, to delete characters, or to compare one string with another. Program 5-1 adds these and other routines to assembly language programs. But first, let's examine a few typical string formats.

Probably the most common string format is the *ASCII$ string*—a series of ASCII characters ending in a dollar sign. Use db this way to create an ASCII$ string:

```
myString        db    'Welcome to my program', '$'
```

You don't have to separate the dollar sign from the main string—you could just add $ between the "m" and the closing single quote. Separating the characters as shown here emphasizes that the dollar sign is a string terminator—not just another character. To display this string, use DOS function 09:

```
mov  dx, OFFSET myString    ; Address string with ds:dx
mov  ah, 09                 ; Specify DOS function 09
int  21h                    ; Call DOS to display string
```

The first line assigns the offset address of myString in the program's data segment addressed by ds. The 09 assigned to ah is the number of the DOS "Output character string" function, which int 21h activates. The int (software interrupt) instruction operates similarly to a subroutine call and, after DOS finishes executing the function specified in ah, returns control to your program starting with the instruction that follows int 21h. Chapter 10 discusses this and other kinds of interrupts in more detail.

> Note: Consult the Bibliography for references that list other DOS functions that you can call in assembly language programs.

The major problem with ASCII$ strings is obvious—there's no easy way to display a dollar sign! Also, it's difficult to read characters from the keyboard or from disk files into such strings. For these reasons, I rarely use ASCII$ strings. Instead, I prefer ASCIIZ strings ending in a zero byte—the same format used by most high-level language C compilers. With AS-CIIZ strings, you might create an error message by writing:

```
diskErr    db    "Disk read error!", 0
```

ASCIIZ strings can be as long as you need—from a single character up to thousands. The first byte at the string label is either an ASCII character or a zero byte, also called an ASCII *null character*. If the first byte is 0, then the string is empty. This fact leads to an easy way to create zero-length string variables with the DUP operator:

```
stringVar db   81 DUP (0)      ; 80-character string + null
```

When creating strings this way, always set the DUP count to one more than the maximum number of characters you plan to store in the string, leaving room for the null, which must always end the string. The only disadvantage of ASCIIZ strings is that DOS has no standard routines for reading and writing string variables in this format. The string packages later in this chapter fix this deficiency with routines that you can use to read and write ASCIIZ strings.

Quoting Quotes   For all strings declared with db, you can surround characters with either apostrophes (') or double quotes (") as long as you begin and end with the same symbols. (In the ASCII character set, an apostrophe and a closing single quote are the same characters. On your keyboard and in this book, the symbols are printed with straight up and down lines. But on your display, the single quote apostrophe symbol probably hooks down to the left.)

Note: Don't surround strings with opening single quotes ('), usually created by pressing the key in the upper left corner of most PC keyboards. Opening quotes are not allowed as string delimiters.

To include a quote mark inside a string, you have several options. The easiest method is to use one type of quote mark around the character string containing the other type:

```
Quote     db    'When "quoting" speech, you can surround', 0
Unquote   db    "the text with 'quote marks' like this.", 0
```

The double quotes in the first string are inserted as characters. The single quotes in the second string are also inserted as characters. Another method is to repeat the same quote used as the string delimiter. This is useful for creating strings that contain both single and double quotes:

```
CrazyQuotes db 'This ''string'' contains four "quote" marks', 0
```

The repeated single quotes around the word "string" are inserted as single quote mark characters even though the entire string is delimited by these same characters. You can do the same with double quotes, too.

Local Labels

Up until now, program examples used code segment labels like `Start:` and `Repeat:`. Such labels are global to the entire program that declares them. In other words, if you label an instruction `Here:` at the beginning of the program, that label is available to `call`, `jmp`, and other instructions anywhere else throughout the code. One problem with this is that you constantly have to think up new names to avoid conflicts with labels you've already used. For short hops, this is a major inconvenience, as in this short sample:

```
        cmp   ax, 9      ; Does ax = 9?
        je    SkipIt     ; Skip add below if ax = 9
        add   cx, 10     ; Else add 10 to cx
SkipIt:
```

Short jumps such as the `je` to label `SkipIt:` are common in assembly language programming. Most probably, no other instruction will need to jump to this same label; therefore, `SkipIt:` isn't needed beyond this one place. A large program might make hundreds or thousands of similar hops, requiring you to invent new names for each one! To reduce this burden, Turbo Assembler lets you create *local labels,* which exist only in the sections of code that need them.

A local label is identical to any other code label but begins with two "at signs," `@@`. Examples of local labels include such names as `@@10:`,

@@Here:, @@Temp6:, and @@x:. The life of a local label extends only forward and back to the next nonlocal label. Because this includes labels defined in PROC directives, if you surround your procedures with PROC and ENDP, local labels in subroutines are visible only inside the routine's code. You can then reuse the same local labels elsewhere without conflict. An example helps make this clear:

```
        jmp   There           ; Jump to global label
@@10:
        inc   ax
        cmp   ax, 10
        jne   @@10            ; Jump to local label above
There:
        cmp   ax, 20
        je    @@10            ; Jump to local label below
        xor   cx, cx
@@10:
```

Don't try to run this example—it's just for illustration. The first jmp jumps to the global label There:—you can jump to global labels from anywhere in a program. The next jne jumps to local label @@10:. But, which one? There are two. The answer is, the first @@10:, which extends only down to the global label There:. Consequently, the jne can "see" only the first @@10:. For the same reason, the later je instruction jumps down to the second @@10: because the global There: above blocks the view of the first local label. Some of the advantages of local labels follow:

▷ Local labels save memory by letting Turbo Assembler reuse RAM for other local labels. Global labels are permanently stored in memory during assembly, even if the labels are used only once. Local labels are thrown away every time a new nonlocal label is encountered.

▷ Local labels improve program clarity. For example, a quick scan of a program easily picks out the global and local labels.

▷ Local labels help reduce bugs by making it more difficult to write long-distance hops from one place in a program to another. If you surround your procedures with PROC and ENDP directives, you won't be tempted to jump to a temporary label in the midsection of a subroutine—a generally recognized source of bugs.

Note: Like global labels, local labels must end with colons as in @@ABC:. When an instruction refers to a local label, the label must not have a colon, as in jmp @@ABC.

An ASCIIZ String Package

Chapter 4 introduced the 8086 string instructions. Program 5-1 (STRINGS.ASM) is a package of 12 ASCIIZ string routines, many of which put these string instructions to good use. Lines 18–29 list the names and give brief descriptions of the routines in the package, which is organized a little differently from listings you've seen up to now. STRINGS.ASM is a *library module* that you must assemble separately and then link with another program. Unlike previous program examples, the STRINGS module does not run on its own. Instead, as later examples demonstrate, STRINGS requires a host program to use the subroutines in the module. To assemble STRINGS, use the command:

```
tasm strings
```

Or, if you plan to use Turbo Debugger to examine programs that use the string package, use the command:

```
tasm /zi strings
```

Be aware that using the */zi* option adds debugging information to the assembled code and, for this reason, can make the finished code file swell—often enormously. Use the former command (without the */zi* option) to reduce code-file size.

Whichever of the two commands you use, the result is a file named STRINGS.OBJ, containing the raw assembled code, ready to be linked into a host program. After the STRINGS.ASM listing are suggestions that describe how to do this. But, for the purposes of running other programs in this book, many of which require the STRINGS package, you need to store the STRINGS.OBJ code in a *library file*. Enter the following command, ignoring a probable warning that "STRINGS [was] not found in [the] library:"

```
tlib /E mta -+strings
```

Note: If you don't have a hard disk drive, you might want to store MTA.LIB on your Turbo Assembler diskette. If this diskette is in drive A:, use the name `a:mta` instead of `mta` here and from now on. You can then assemble other programs and modules that require the code in MTA.LIB without worrying whether the necessary .OBJ files are available.

The result of the `tlib` command is a file named MTA.LIB (for "Mastering Turbo Assembler Library") containing the STRINGS package. The */E* option stores an *extended dictionary* in the library file, which helps to speed linking by providing TLINK with additional information about the library's symbols. The `-+strings` command tells TLIB to replace any previous version of STRINGS with the new .OBJ code file. Later on, you'll add new object-code files to MTA.LIB, which will greatly reduce the complexity of assembling and linking programs that use routines in STRINGS and in other separately assembled modules. If you make any changes to the STRINGS.ASM listing, repeat the `tasm` and `tlib` commands to replace the old object code in the MTA.LIB file with the updated programming.

Program 5-1 *STRINGS.ASM*

```
 1:   %TITLE "String Procedures--Copyright 1989 by Tom Swan"
 2:
 3:           IDEAL
 4:           DOSSEG
 5:           MODEL   small
 6:
 7:           CODESEG
 8:
 9:           PUBLIC  MoveLeft, MoveRight, StrNull, StrLength
10:           PUBLIC  StrUpper, StrCompare, StrDelete, StrInsert
11:           PUBLIC  StrConcat, StrCopy, StrPos, StrRemove
12:
13:   ;-------------------------------------------------------------------
14:   ; Assemble with the command TASM STRINGS to create STRINGS.OBJ. To use
15:   ; the procedures, add EXTRN <procedure>:PROC statements where
16:   ; <procedure> is one of the following identifiers:
17:   ;
18:   ;       MoveLeft        -- memory move with increasing indexes
19:   ;       MoveRight       -- memory move with decreasing indexes
20:   ;       StrNull         -- erase all chars in string
21:   ;       StrLength       -- return number of chars in string
22:   ;       StrUpper        -- convert chars in string to uppercase
23:   ;       StrCompare      -- alphabetically compare two strings
24:   ;       StrDelete       -- delete chars from string
25:   ;       StrInsert       -- insert chars into string
26:   ;       StrConcat       -- attach one string to another
27:   ;       StrCopy         -- copy one string to another
28:   ;       StrPos          -- find position of substring in a string
29:   ;       StrRemove       -- remove substring from a string
30:   ;
31:   ; After assembling your program, link with STRINGS.OBJ. For example,
32:   ; if your program is named MYPROG, first assemble MYPROG to MYPROG.OBJ
33:   ; and link with the command TLINK MYPROG+STRINGS to create MYPROG.EXE.
34:   ;
35:   ; STRING VARIABLES:
36:   ; A string is a simple array of characters with one character per
37:   ; 8-bit byte. A null character (ASCII 0) must follow the last
38:   ; character in the string. An empty string contains a single null.
39:   ; Declare string variables this way:
40:   ;
41:   ;       STRING  DB      81 DUP (0)      ; 80-character string + null
42:   ;
43:   ; STRING CONSTANTS:
44:   ; Always allow one extra byte for the null terminator. Character
45:   ; constants (which may be used as variables) must be properly
46:   ; terminated. For example:
47:   ;
48:   ;       C1      db      'This is a test string.', 0
49:   ;
```

```
50:  ; SEGMENT REGISTERS:
51:  ; Routines in this package assume that ES and DS address the
52:  ; same segment. Set ES = DS before calling any of these routines.
53:  ;-----------------------------------------------------------------
54:
55:  ASCNull          EQU     0                    ; ASCII null character
56:
57:  %NEWPAGE
58:  ;-----------------------------------------------------------------
59:  ; MoveLeft       Move byte-block left (down) in memory
60:  ;-----------------------------------------------------------------
61:  ; Input:
62:  ;       si = address of source string (s1)
63:  ;       di = address of destination string (s2)
64:  ;       bx = index s1 (i1)
65:  ;       dx = index s2 (i2)
66:  ;       cx = number of bytes to move (count)
67:  ; Output:
68:  ;       count bytes from s1[i1] moved to the location
69:  ;       starting at s2[i2]
70:  ; Registers:
71:  ;       none
72:  ;-----------------------------------------------------------------
73:  PROC    MoveLeft
74:          jcxz    @@99            ; Exit if count = 0
75:          push    cx              ; Save modified registers
76:          push    si
77:          push    di
78:
79:          add     si, bx          ; Index into source string
80:          add     di, dx          ; Index into destination string
81:          cld                     ; Auto-increment si and di
82:          rep     movsb           ; Move while cx <> 0
83:
84:          pop     di              ; Restore registers
85:          pop     si
86:          pop     cx
87:  @@99:
88:          ret                     ; Return to caller
89:  ENDP    MoveLeft
90:  %NEWPAGE
91:  ;-----------------------------------------------------------------
92:  ; MoveRight      Move byte-block right (up) in memory
93:  ;-----------------------------------------------------------------
94:  ; Input:
95:  ;       (same as MoveLeft)
96:  ; Output:
97:  ;       (same as MoveLeft)
98:  ; Registers:
99:  ;       none
100: ;-----------------------------------------------------------------
```

```
101:    PROC    MoveRight
102:            jcxz    @@99            ; Exit if count = 0
103:            push    cx              ; Save modified registers
104:            push    di
105:            push    si
106:
107:            add     si, bx          ; Index into source string
108:            add     di, dx          ; Index into destination string
109:            add     si, cx          ; Adjust to last source byte
110:            dec     si
111:            add     di, cx          ; Adjust to last destination byte
112:            dec     di
113:            std                     ; Auto-decrement si and di
114:            rep     movsb           ; Move while cx <> 0
115:
116:            pop     si              ; Restore registers
117:            pop     di
118:            pop     cx
119:    @@99:
120:            ret                     ; Return to caller
121:    ENDP    MoveRight
122:    %NEWPAGE
123:    ;-----------------------------------------------------------------
124:    ; StrNull        Erase all characters in a string
125:    ;-----------------------------------------------------------------
126:    ; Input:
127:    ;       di = address of string (s)
128:    ; Output:
129:    ;       s[0] <- null character (ASCII 0)
130:    ; Registers:
131:    ;       none
132:    ;-----------------------------------------------------------------
133:    PROC    StrNull
134:            mov     [byte ptr di], ASCNull  ; Insert null at s[0]
135:            ret                     ; Return to caller
136:    ENDP    StrNull
137:    %NEWPAGE
138:    ;-----------------------------------------------------------------
139:    ; StrLength     Count non-null characters in a string
140:    ;-----------------------------------------------------------------
141:    ; Input:
142:    ;       di = address of string (s)
143:    ; Output:
144:    ;       cx = number of non-null characters in s
145:    ; Registers:
146:    ;       cx
147:    ;-----------------------------------------------------------------
148:    PROC    StrLength
149:            push    ax              ; Save modified registers
150:            push    di
151:
```

```
152:          xor     al, al          ; al <- search char (null)
153:          mov     cx, 0ffffh      ; cx <- maximum search depth
154:          cld                     ; Auto-increment di
155:          repnz   scasb           ; Scan for al while [di] <> null & cx <> 0
156:          not     cx              ; Ones complement of cx
157:          dec     cx              ;  minus 1 equals string length
158:
159:          pop     di              ; Restore registers
160:          pop     ax
161:          ret                     ; Return to caller
162: ENDP     StrLength
163: %NEWPAGE
164: ;-----------------------------------------------------------------
165: ; StrUpper       Convert chars in string to uppercase
166: ;-----------------------------------------------------------------
167: ; Input:
168: ;      di = address of string to convert (s)
169: ; Output:
170: ;      lowercase chars in string converted to uppercase
171: ; Registers:
172: ;      none
173: ;-----------------------------------------------------------------
174: PROC     StrUpper
175:          push    ax              ; Save modified registers
176:          push    cx
177:          push    di
178:          push    si
179:          call    StrLength       ; Set cx = length of string
180:          jcxz    @@99            ; Exit if length = 0
181:          cld                     ; Auto-increment si, di
182:          mov     si, di          ; Set si = di
183: @@10:
184:          lodsb                   ; al <- s[si]; si <- si + 1
185:          cmp     al, 'a'         ; Is al >= 'a'?
186:          jb      @@20            ; No, jump to continue scan
187:          cmp     al, 'z'         ; Is al <= 'z'?
188:          ja      @@20            ; No, jump to continue scan
189:          sub     al, 'a'-'A'     ; Convert lowercase to uppercase
190: @@20:
191:          stosb                   ; s[di] <- al; di <- di + 1
192:          loop    @@10            ; cx <- cx - 1; loop if cx <> 0
193: @@99:
194:          pop     si              ; Restore registers
195:          pop     di
196:          pop     cx
197:          pop     ax
198:          ret                     ; Return to caller
199: ENDP     StrUpper
```

```
200:    %NEWPAGE
201:    ;-----------------------------------------------------------
202:    ; StrCompare    Compare two strings
203:    ;-----------------------------------------------------------
204:    ; Input:
205:    ;       si = address of string 1 (s1)
206:    ;       di = address of string 2 (s2)
207:    ; Output:
208:    ;       flags set for conditional jump using jb, jbe,
209:    ;           je, ja, or jae.
210:    ; Registers:
211:    ;       none
212:    ;-----------------------------------------------------------
213:    PROC    StrCompare
214:            push    ax              ; Save modified registers
215:            push    di
216:            push    si
217:            cld                     ; Auto-increment si
218:    @@10:
219:            lodsb                   ; al <- [si], si <- si + 1
220:            scasb                   ; Compare al and [di]; di <- di + 1
221:            jne     @@20            ; Exit if nonequal chars found
222:            or      al, al          ; Is al=0? (i.e., at end of s1)
223:            jne     @@10            ; If no jump, else exit
224:    @@20:
225:            pop     si              ; Restore registers
226:            pop     di
227:            pop     ax
228:            ret                     ; Return flags to caller
229:    ENDP    StrCompare
230:    %NEWPAGE
231:    ;-----------------------------------------------------------
232:    ; StrDelete     Delete characters anywhere in a string
233:    ;-----------------------------------------------------------
234:    ; Input:
235:    ;       di = address of string (s)
236:    ;       dx = index (i) of first char to delete
237:    ;       cx = number of chars to delete (n)
238:    ; Output:
239:    ;       n characters deleted from string at s[i]
240:    ;       Note: prevents deleting past end of string
241:    ; Registers:
242:    ;       none
243:    ;-----------------------------------------------------------
244:    PROC    StrDelete
245:            push    bx              ; Save modified registers
246:            push    cx
247:            push    di
248:            push    si
249:
```

```
250:    ; bx = SourceIndex
251:    ; cx = Count / Len / CharsToMove
252:    ; dx = Index
253:
254:            mov     bx, dx          ; Assign string index to bx
255:            add     bx, cx          ; Source index <- index + count
256:            call    StrLength       ; cx <- length(s)
257:            cmp     cx, bx          ; Is length > index?
258:            ja      @@10            ; If yes, jump to delete chars
259:            add     di, dx          ;  else, calculate index to string end
260:            mov     [byte ptr di], ASCNull  ; and insert null
261:            jmp     short @@99       ; Jump to exit
262:    @@10:
263:            mov     si, di          ; Make source = destination
264:            sub     cx, bx          ; CharsToMove <- Len - SourceIndex
265:            inc     cx              ; Plus one for null at end of string
266:            call    MoveLeft        ; Move chars over deleted portion
267:    @@99:
268:            pop     si              ; Restore registers
269:            pop     di
270:            pop     cx
271:            pop     bx
272:            ret                     ; Return to caller
273:    ENDP    StrDelete
274:    %NEWPAGE
275:    ;-----------------------------------------------------------------
276:    ; StrInsert      Insert a string into another string
277:    ;-----------------------------------------------------------------
278:    ; Input:
279:    ;       si = address of string 1 (s1)
280:    ;       di = address of string 2 (s2)
281:    ;       dx = insertion index for s2 (i)
282:    ;       NOTE: s2 must be large enough to expand by length(s1)!
283:    ; Output:
284:    ;       chars from string s1 inserted at s2[i]
285:    ;       s1 not changed
286:    ; Registers:
287:    ;       none
288:    ;-----------------------------------------------------------------
289:    PROC    StrInsert
290:            push    ax              ; Save modified registers
291:            push    bx
292:            push    cx
293:
294:    ; ax = LenInsertion
295:    ; cx = CharsToMove
296:
297:            xchg    si, di          ; Exchange si and di
298:            call    StrLength       ;  and find length of s1
299:            xchg    si, di          ; Restore si and di
300:            mov     ax, cx          ; Save length(s1) in ax
301:
```

```
302:            call    StrLength       ; Find length of s2
303:            sub     cx, dx          ; cx <- length(s2) - i + 1
304:            inc     cx              ; cx = (CharsToMove)
305:
306:  ; bx = s1 index
307:
308:            push    dx              ; Save index (dx) and si
309:            push    si
310:            mov     si, di          ; Make si and di address s2
311:            mov     bx, dx          ; Set s1 index to dx (i)
312:            add     dx, ax          ; Set s2 index to i + LenInsertion
313:            call    MoveRight       ; Open a hole for the insertion
314:            pop     si              ; Restore index (dx) and si
315:            pop     dx
316:
317:            xor     bx, bx          ; Set s1 (source) index to 0
318:            mov     cx, ax          ; Set cx to LenInsertion
319:            call    MoveLeft        ; Insert s1 into hole in s2
320:
321:            pop     cx              ; Restore registers
322:            pop     bx
323:            pop     ax
324:            ret                     ; Return to caller
325:  ENDP    StrInsert
326:  %NEWPAGE
327:  ;-----------------------------------------------------------------
328:  ; StrConcat       Concatenate (join) two strings
329:  ;-----------------------------------------------------------------
330:  ; Input:
331:  ;       si = address of source string (s1)
332:  ;       di = address of destination string (s2)
333:  ;       Note: s2 must be large enough to expand by length (s1)!
334:  ; Output:
335:  ;       chars from s1 added to end of s2
336:  ; Registers:
337:  ;       none
338:  ;-----------------------------------------------------------------
339:  PROC    StrConcat
340:            push    bx              ; Save modified registers
341:            push    cx
342:            push    dx
343:
344:  ; dx = s2 destination
345:
346:            call    StrLength       ; Find length of destination (s2)
347:            mov     dx, cx          ; Set dx to index end of string
348:            xchg    si, di          ; Exchange si and di
349:            call    StrLength       ; Find length of source (s1)
```

```
350:            inc     cx              ; Plus 1 includes null terminator
351:            xchg    si, di          ; Restore si and di
352:            xor     bx, bx          ; Source index = 0
353:            call    MoveLeft        ; Copy source string to destination
354:
355:            pop     dx              ; Restore registers
356:            pop     cx
357:            pop     bx
358:            ret                     ; Return to caller
359:    ENDP    StrConcat
360:    %NEWPAGE
361:    ;-----------------------------------------------------------------
362:    ; StrCopy       Copy one string to another
363:    ;-----------------------------------------------------------------
364:    ; Input:
365:    ;       si = address of source string (s1)
366:    ;       di = address of destination string (s2)
367:    ; Output:
368:    ;       Chars in s1 copied to s2
369:    ;       Note: s2 must be at least Length(s1) + 1 bytes long
370:    ; Registers:
371:    ;       none
372:    ;-----------------------------------------------------------------
373:    PROC    StrCopy
374:            push    bx              ; Save modified registers
375:            push    cx
376:            push    dx
377:
378:            xchg    si, di          ; Swap si and di
379:            call    StrLength       ; Find length of source string (s1)
380:            inc     cx              ; Plus 1 includes null terminator
381:            xchg    si, di          ; Restore si and di
382:            xor     bx, bx          ; Source-string index = 0
383:            xor     dx, dx          ; Destination-string index = 0
384:            call    MoveLeft        ; Copy source to destination
385:
386:            pop     dx              ; Restore registers
387:            pop     cx
388:            pop     bx
389:            ret                     ; Return to caller
390:    ENDP    StrCopy
391:    %NEWPAGE
392:    ;-----------------------------------------------------------------
393:    ; StrPos        Search for position of a substring in a string
394:    ;-----------------------------------------------------------------
395:    ; Input:
396:    ;       si = address of substring to find
397:    ;       di = address of target string to scan
```

```
398:    ; Output:
399:    ;         if zf = 1 then dx = index of substring
400:    ;         if zf = 0 then substring was not found
401:    ;         Note: dx is meaningless if zf = 0
402:    ; Registers:
403:    ;         dx
404:    ;-------------------------------------------------------------
405:    PROC    StrPos
406:            push    ax                  ; Save modified registers
407:            push    bx
408:            push    cx
409:            push    di
410:
411:            call    StrLength           ; Find length of target string
412:            mov     ax, cx              ; Save length (s2) in ax
413:            xchg    si, di              ; Swap si and di
414:            call    StrLength           ; Find length of substring
415:            mov     bx, cx              ; Save length (s1) in bx
416:            xchg    si, di              ; Restore si and di
417:            sub     ax, bx              ; ax = last possible index
418:            jb      @@20                ; Exit if len target < len substring
419:            mov     dx, 0ffffh          ; Initialize dx to -1
420:    @@10:
421:            inc     dx                  ; For i = 0 to last possible index
422:            mov     cl, [byte bx + di]      ; Save char at s[bx] in cl
423:            mov     [byte bx + di], ASCNull ; Replace char with null
424:            call    StrCompare          ; Compare si to altered di
425:            mov     [byte bx + di], cl      ; Restore replaced char
426:            je      @@20                ; Jump if match found, dx = index, zf = 1
427:            inc     di                  ; Else advance target string index
428:            cmp     dx, ax              ; When equal, all positions checked
429:            jne     @@10                ; Continue search unless not found
430:
431:            xor     cx, cx              ; Substring not found. Reset zf = 0
432:            inc     cx                  ;   to indicate no match
433:    @@20:
434:            pop     di                  ; Restore registers
435:            pop     cx
436:            pop     bx
437:            pop     ax
438:            ret                         ; Return to caller
439:    ENDP    StrPos
440:    %NEWPAGE
441:    ;-------------------------------------------------------------
442:    ; StrRemove      Remove substring from a string
443:    ;-------------------------------------------------------------
444:    ; Input:
445:    ;         si = address of substring to delete
446:    ;         di = address of string to delete substring from
```

```
447:   ; Output:
448:   ;        if zf = 1 then substring removed
449:   ;        if zf = 0 then substring was not found
450:   ;        Note: string at si is not changed
451:   ;        Note: if zf = 0 then string at di is not changed
452:   ; Registers:
453:   ;        none
454:   ;-------------------------------------------------------------
455:   PROC    StrRemove
456:           push    cx              ; Save modified registers
457:           push    dx
458:
459:           call    StrPos          ; Find substring, setting dx=index
460:           jne     @@99            ; Exit if substring not found
461:           pushf                   ; Save zf flag
462:           xchg    si, di          ; Swap si and di
463:           call    StrLength       ; Find length of substring
464:           xchg    si, di          ; Restore si and di
465:           call    StrDelete       ; Delete cx chars at di[dx]
466:           popf                    ; Restore zf flag
467:   @@99:
468:           pop     dx              ; Restore registers
469:           pop     cx
470:           ret                     ; Return to caller
471:   ENDP    StrRemove
472:
473:
474:           END                     ; End of STRINGS.ASM module
```

Programming in Pieces

Before jumping into a description of the routines in the STRINGS module, you should know some of the ways that you can combine STRINGS with programs and with other object-code modules. Modules like STRINGS can declare subroutines, variables, and constants to be shared with programs and other modules. An object-code module is a self-contained package, assembled apart from other code, and then linked to a host program, creating the finished executable disk file.

Dividing large programs into modules is a great time saver. Instead of reassembling the identical code over and over, you can store that code in a separate module, assemble to disk, and then link with your program. When modifying existing programs, you have to reassemble only the modules that you modify. Modules also help simplify complex programs by letting you concentrate on smaller and easier to digest chunks of code. In addition, you can store object-code modules in library files, making your favorite subroutines instantly available to new programs.

In the source-code text, a separate module differs only slightly from the text of a main program. Referring to Program 5-1, you can see that the initial lines are the same as in previous listings (for example, see Program

4-7) but do not include a STACK directive. Only the main program can declare a stack segment—separate modules never need to do this.

Another difference is that separate modules lack the steps in a main program to initialize data-segment registers and to return control to DOS when the program ends. Instead, as you can see, Program 5-1 contains a series of procedures, marked by the PROC and ENDP directives. A final END directive ends the text but does not add an entry-point label to END as must be done in a main program file (for example, see line 46 in Program 4-7). Only the main program can specify an entry point.

Public Policy

Lines 9–11 in STRINGS declare several symbols in PUBLIC directives. These symbols are the same names used as labels in PROC procedure headers. (For example, see line 73.) Every symbol that you want a module to export to the outside world must be declared in a PUBLIC directive as shown here. You can use individual PUBLIC directives to declare symbols one at a time or string them together with commas as in this example. Symbols can be the names of numeric constants declared with equal signs (=), variables, or code labels. Constants declared with EQU cannot be exported.

> Note: In Ideal mode, EQU constants are treated during assembly as *text*, while equal sign (=) constants are treated as *values*. In MASM mode, some EQU constants are numeric and, therefore, can be exported. Other kinds of EQU constants must remain private. This does not mean that Ideal mode imposes additional limits on exporting symbols. It just means that, in Ideal mode, you always know which constants are exportable. In both modes, only the same types of numeric constants can be shared with the outside world.

All other symbols not declared PUBLIC (ASCNull at line 55, for instance) are private and cannot be used by other programs. Private symbols may be repeated by modules and programs without conflicting with the symbols declared private in other modules. Only symbols in PUBLIC directives are visible outside of the module. Notice that the symbols in the PUBLIC directive have no data-type identifiers—nothing to indicate what the symbols are. As later examples demonstrate, this is the responsibility of the program that imports the symbols.

> Note: Some programmers declare separate PUBLIC directives just above each PROC header. I prefer to collect all PUBLIC symbols into one place at the beginning of the file, where I can easily find and modify the list. Both methods are correct and have the same effects.

Assembling and Linking Separate Modules

Assembling separate modules is easy. Just type `tasm module` where *module* is the name of the text file to assemble. You do not have to specify the .ASM extension after the file name. To assemble the module for use with Turbo Debugger, use the command `tasm -zi module`, which adds extra information to the .OBJ file so that Turbo Debugger can locate variables and subroutines by name.

To assemble a program that uses the code in separate modules, use either of these same commands. You can assemble the main program and all its modules in any order, and none of the module's .OBJ files needs to be on disk during assembly of any other modules. After assembling all modules, you'll have a series of .OBJ files on disk. The next step is to link these separate pieces together to create the finished code. For example, if your main program is THEMEAT.ASM and your modules are LET-TUCE.ASM and MUSTARD.ASM, you would first assemble each module:

```
tasm lettuce
tasm themeat
tasm mustard
```

You can perform these steps in any order. Or, if these are the only .ASM files in the current directory, you can use the simpler command `tasm *.ASM` to assemble all three files. After assembling, you'll have THE-MEAT.OBJ, LETTUCE.OBJ, and MUSTARD.OBJ on disk. You then link these object-code files with the command:

```
tlink themeat lettuce mustard
```

The first name after `tlink` must refer to the main program. Subsequent names refer to the separate modules used in the program. Multiple module names may be listed in any order and are separated by spaces. (You can also use plus signs as in `tlink themeat+lettuce+mustard`.) The result of linking is a sandwich of all modules plus the main program in one finshed code file, in this example, THEMEAT.EXE. The name of the result is the same as the name of the first object file after TLINK but with the extension changed to .EXE. To specify a different name, SANDWICH.EXE for instance, add a comma and the new name after the object-file list:

```
tlink themeat lettuce mustard, sandwich
```

A comma must separate the object-file list from the new .EXE file name. During linking, TLINK creates a map file containing a report of the symbols and their addresses in the finished code. The map file has the same name as the default .EXE file but ends in .MAP, unless you specify a different name. This assembles the object files (represented here as <*obj-files*>), and creates both SANDWICH.EXE and SANDWICH.MAP:

```
tlink <obj-files>, sandwich, sandwich
```

If you don't want a map file, use the /x option before the object-file list. This saves disk space and speeds linking a tiny bit by reducing TLINK's work load. (Turbo Debugger does not require the map file, but some other debuggers and source-code utility products from other companies do. You may also want to save the map file as part of your program's documentation.) This command specifies no map file:

```
tlink /x <obj-files>
```

The final option you can specify with TLINK is the name of one or more library files, which contain separately assembled object modules in one disk file. Put spaces between multiple library file names. For example, if you have two libraries, BUTTER.LIB and BREAD.LIB, the complete linking command might be:

```
tlink <obj-files>,,, butter bread
```

You don't have to specify the .LIB extension. Notice the three commas after the object-file list. These commas tell Turbo Assembler to use the default names for the missing items. Without the commas, Turbo Linker can't know that BUTTER and BREAD are library files—it would mistake them for .OBJ files. You must add the commas to hold the places for optional items you don't specify. With square brackets representing optional items, the complete syntax for TLINK is:

```
tlink [options] obj-files[, [exe-file], [map-file], [lib-files]]
```

A String I/O Package

Although the **STRINGS** module can be used alone, another module is needed to display strings and to read new strings from the keyboard. This second module makes it easy to experiment with **STRINGS** and also serves as a useful module on its own. Assemble Program 5-2, STRIO.ASM, and add the object code to your MTA.LIB library file with the commands:

```
tasm /zi strio
tlib /E mta -+strio
```

For running host programs in Turbo Debugger, you must use the /zi option both here and when assembling STRINGS. To reduce code-file size, assemble with **tasm strio** and reinstall STRIO in the library. At the **tlib** command, ignore the probable warning that STRIO was not found in the library. You'll see this warning only the first time you add STRIO to MTA.LIB. At this point, you now have two modules in MTA.LIB: STRINGS and STRIO. To see a list of the symbols in the libary file, enter:

```
tlib mta, con
```

Or, replace **con** with **prn** to send output to the printer. You can also store tlib's output in a disk file with a command such as **tlib mta,temp.txt**. Be careful—TLIB won't warn you before erasing an existing file of the same name.

Program 5-2 *STRIO.ASM*

```
 1:   %TITLE "String Input/Output Routines"
 2:
 3:           IDEAL
 4:           DOSSEG
 5:           MODEL   small
 6:
 7:
 8:   ;-----  Equates
 9:
10:   BufSize        EQU     255            ; Maximum string size (<=255)
11:   ASCnull        EQU     0              ; ASCII null
12:   ASCcr          EQU     13             ; ASCII carriage return
13:   ASClf          EQU     10             ; ASCII line feed
14:
15:
16:   ;-----  String buffer structure for DOS function 0Ah
17:
18:   STRUC StrBuffer
19:     maxlen         db BufSize           ; Maximum buffer length
20:     strlen         db 0                 ; String length
21:     chars          db BufSize DUP (?)   ; Buffer for StrRead
22:   ENDS strBuffer
23:
24:
25:           DATASEG
26:
27:   buffer  StrBuffer <>                  ; Buffer variable for ReadStr
28:
29:
30:           CODESEG
31:
32:   ;-----  From: STRINGS.OBJ
33:
34:           EXTRN   StrLength:proc, StrCopy:proc
35:
36:           PUBLIC  StrRead, StrWrite, StrWrite2, NewLine
37:
38:   %NEWPAGE
39:   ;-------------------------------------------------------------
40:   ; StrRead                 Read string with editing keys
41:   ;-------------------------------------------------------------
42:   ; Input:
43:   ;       di = address of destination string
44:   ;       cl = maximum string length EXCLUDING null terminator
45:   ;       Note: if cl = 0, StrRead does nothing
46:   ;       Note: actual variable must be cl + 1 bytes long
47:   ;       Note: string length is limited to 255 characters
48:   ; Output:
49:   ;       String copied from standard input into your buffer
```

```
50:     ; Registers:
51:     ;          none
52:     ;-----------------------------------------------------------
53:     PROC    StrRead
54:             or      cl, cl              ; Is cl = 0?
55:             jz      @@99               ; If yes, jump to exit
56:
57:             push    ax                 ; Save modified registers
58:             push    bx
59:             push    dx
60:             push    si
61:
62:             mov     [buffer.maxlen], cl    ; Set maxlen byte
63:             mov     ah, 0ah            ; DOS Buffered-Input function
64:             mov     dx, OFFSET buffer.maxlen   ; Address struc with ds:dx
65:             int     21h                ; Call DOS to read string
66:             xor     bh, bh             ; Zero high byte of bx
67:             mov     bl, [buffer.strlen]    ; bx = # chars in buffer
68:             mov     [bx + buffer.chars], ASCnull  ; Change cr to null
69:             mov     si, OFFSET buffer.chars ; Address buffer with si
70:             call    StrCopy            ; Copy chars to user string
71:
72:             pop     si                         ; Restore registers
73:             pop     dx
74:             pop     bx
75:             pop     ax
76:     @@99:
77:             ret                        ; Return to caller
78:     ENDP    StrRead
79:     %NEWPAGE
80:     ;-----------------------------------------------------------
81:     ; StrWrite/StrWrite2    Write string to standard output
82:     ;-----------------------------------------------------------
83:     ; Input:
84:     ;       di = address of string (s)
85:     ;       cx = number of chars to write (StrWrite2 only)
86:     ; Output:
87:     ;       string s copied to standard output
88:     ;
89:     ; Registers:
90:     ;       cx (StrWrite only)
91:     ;-----------------------------------------------------------
92:     PROC    StrWrite
93:             call    StrLength          ; Set cx = length of string
94:
95:     PROC    StrWrite2                  ; Alternate entry point
96:             push    ax                 ; Save modified registers
97:             push    bx
98:             push    dx
99:
```

```
100:            mov     bx, 1           ; Standard output handle
101:            mov     dx, di          ; ds:dx address string
102:            mov     ah, 40h         ; DOS write to file or device
103:            int     21h             ; Call DOS (on ret ax = # chars written)
104:
105:            pop     dx              ; Restore registers
106:            pop     bx
107:            pop     ax
108:            ret                     ; Return to caller
109: ENDP       StrWrite2               ; End of alternate procedure
110: ENDP       StrWrite                ; End of normal procedure
111:
112: %NEWPAGE
113: ;-----------------------------------------------------------------
114: ; NewLine        Start new line on standard output file
115: ;-----------------------------------------------------------------
116: ; Input:
117: ;        none
118: ; Output:
119: ;        carriage return, line feed sent to standard output
120: ; Registers:
121: ;        ah, dl
122: ;-----------------------------------------------------------------
123: PROC       NewLine
124:            mov     ah, 2           ; DOS write-char routine
125:            mov     dl, ASCcr       ; Load carriage return into dl
126:            int     21h             ; Write carriage return
127:            mov     dl, ASClf       ; Load line feed into dl
128:            int     21h             ; Write line feed
129:            ret                     ; Return to caller
130: ENDP       NewLine
131:
132:
133:            END                     ; End of STRIO module
```

Procedures in STRIO

There are three procedures in the STRIO module, which many programs in this book use. The three routines are:

► StrRead—Read an ASCIIZ string

► StrWrite—Write an ASCIIZ string

► NewLine—Start a new output line

The first two procedures require strings in ASCIIZ form—the same form used by the STRINGS module. All three routines use the standard DOS input and output files—usually the keyboard and display. As future programs demonstrate, there are faster ways to display text on screen than StrWrite. But even so, this small module comes in handy for reading and writing string data.

Using the STRIO Module

The three procedures in STRIO.ASM (Program 5-2) should be easy for you to understand. Except for a data structure at lines 18–22, you already met most of the elements in this listing elsewhere. This section explains how to use STRIO's routines in your own programs to read and write ASCIIZ strings to the standard input and output files, normally the keyboard (input) and display (output). (We'll return to this program again in chapter 6, which explains complex data structures.)

StrRead (39–78)

Assign to es:di the address of any ASCIIZ variable, which can be from 1 to 255 characters long plus 1 byte for the null terminator. Normally, ASCIIZ strings can be just about any length. But, due to limitations of DOS, you can read strings up to a maximum of only 255 characters. Also set cl to the maximum number of characters you want people to be able to enter. If cl equals 0, StrRead does nothing. Here's how you might use StrRead to prompt for some data to be entered at the keyboard:

```
DATASEG
response  db    81 dup (0)        ; 80-character string + null
CODESEG
mov  di, OFFSET response          ; Address response with es:di
mov  cl, 80                       ; Allow 0 to 80 characters
call StrRead                      ; Read string
```

Notice that cl is set to 80 even though the string variable is 81 bytes long. This allows 1 byte for the null terminator at the end of the string. Don't forget this all important rule—you must leave room for StrRead to insert the string-terminator byte. StrRead calls DOS function 0Ah at line 65, which requires the string structure defined at lines 18–22 (further explained in chapter 6).

StrWrite (80–110)

To pass an ASCIIZ string to the standard output (usually the display), call StrWrite with es:di addressing the string. If you already know the string length, you can assign the length value to cx and call StrWrite2 instead—an example of a *nested procedure.* Notice how the procedure at lines 95–109 nests inside the outer procedure at lines 92–110. The difference between the two procedures is that, after calling StrWrite2, cx is not changed. After calling StrWrite, cx equals the string length. The nested procedure defines an *alternate entry point* into the subroutine.

Note: You don't have to define alternate entry points as nested procedures—you can simply add a new label and call or jump to that address. Using nested procedures makes the intention of the program perfectly clear—always a good plan, even when other strategies are available.

A typical use for StrWrite is to display a program's welcome message:

```
cr   EQU   13   ; ASCII carriage return
lf   EQU   10   ; ASCII line feed
DATASEG
welcome   db   cr, lf, 'Welcome to Noware Land'
          db   cr, lf, '(C) 1988 by Nobody, Inc.',cr,lf,lf,0
CODESEG
mov  ax, @data
mov  ds, ax                ; Initialize ds
mov  es, ax                ; Initialize es = ds
mov  di, OFFSET welcome    ; Address string with di
call StrWrite              ; Display string
```

There are several interesting points here that deserve a closer look. First, two equates assign the ASCII values of a carriage return and line feed to symbols cr and lf. In the data segment, a string variable is then created, adding cr and lf as needed. In assembly language, the flexible db operator lets you easily add control characters this way directly to strings. Also, because variables are stored consecutively in memory, really only one string variable is here—despite the fact that the string is declared in two separate db directives. Only one null terminator is at the end of the second line; therefore, this is one string, not two. Notice also how the string ends with a carriage return and two line feeds. The first carriage return sends the cursor to the far left of the display. After that, successive line feeds send the cursor down (or scroll the display up) twice. There's no need to add another carriage return. The ability to handle such flexible data structures is one of assembly language's most welcome features.

In the code segment of this sample, the first three instructions initialize ds and es to address the program's data segment. Always perform these steps in programs that use the STRIO module (as well as other modules in this book). After this, a mov instruction assigns the address of string welcome to di. A single call to StrWrite then displays the two-line string.

The code for the StrWrite in STRIO is fairly simple. Lines 102–103 call DOS function 40h with cx equal to the string length, bx equal to 1 (representing DOS's standard output file), and ds:dx equal to the string address. The other instructions save and restore modified registers (except for cx when calling the StrWrite entry point).

NewLine (113–130)
The final procedure in STRIO is NewLine. Call this procedure to start a new line on the display. The procedure works by passing carriage-return and line-feed control codes in register dl to DOS function 2, which writes single characters to the standard output. Note that the procedure changes ah and dl.

Linking Modules into a Program

You should now have the STRINGS and STRIO modules assembled and stored in MTA.LIB on disk. The good news is: You now possess two useful packages to manipulate, read, and write ASCIIZ strings—routines that other programs in this book use heavily and that you'll find many uses for in your own code. The bad new is: You have to enter one more program to demonstrate how to use routines in separate modules. For this purpose, assemble and link Program 5-3, ECHOSTR.ASM, creating ECHOSTR.EXE, with the command:

```
tasm /zi echostr
tlink echostr,,, mta
```

As described earlier, the three commas hold the places of missing items in the `tlink` command, telling Turbo Linker that `mta` is the name of a library file. Also, you need to use the `/zi` option only if you want to run ECHOSTR in Turbo Debugger. To run the program from DOS, just type `echostr`. Then, type any string of characters and press Enter. You should see the same string repeated below your typing—proof that the STRIO module is working. Admittedly, this is a very simple example. But, as you will soon see, there's much more that you can do with STRINGS and STRIO.

Program 5-3 *ECHOSTR.ASM*

```
 1:    %TITLE "String Read Test"
 2:
 3:            IDEAL
 4:            DOSSEG
 5:            MODEL   small
 6:            STACK   256
 7:
 8:    MaxLen  EQU     128       ; 128-character string
 9:    cr      EQU     13        ; ASCII carriage return
10:    lf      EQU     10        ; ASCII line feed
11:
12:
13:            DATASEG
14:
15:    exitCode    db      0
16:    welcome     db      'Welcome to Echo-String', cr, lf
17:                db      'Type any string and press Enter', cr,lf,lf, 0
18:    testString  db      MaxLen DUP (0), 0        ; MaxLen chars + null
19:
20:
21:            CODESEG
22:
23:    ;----- From STRIO.OBJ:
24:
25:            EXTRN   StrRead:proc, StrWrite:proc, NewLine:proc
26:
```

```
27:   Start:
28:            mov      ax, @data          ; Initialize ds to address
29:            mov      ds, ax             ;   of data segment
30:            mov      es, ax             ; Make ds = es
31:
32:            mov      di, OFFSET welcome ; Display welcome message
33:            call     StrWrite
34:
35:            mov      di, OFFSET testString ; di = address of testString
36:            mov      cx, MaxLen         ; cx = maximum len
37:            call     StrRead            ; Read string from keyboard
38:            call     NewLine            ; Start a new display line
39:            call     StrWrite           ; Echo string to display
40:
41:   Exit:
42:            mov      ah, 04Ch           ; DOS function: Exit program
43:            mov      al, [exitCode]     ; Return exit code value
44:            int      21h                ; Call DOS. Terminate program
45:
46:            END      Start       ; End of program / entry point
```

**New Features in
ECHOSTR.ASM**

The STRINGS and STRIO packages require ds and es to address the same data segment. Line 30 in ECHOSTR satisfies this requirement by assigning the same value to es as assigned to ds in the previous line. You might want to add this line now to EXESHELL.ASM (Program 2-3) to prevent forgetting this important step.

Line 25 in ECHOSTR shows how to import symbols that are declared in another module's PUBLIC directives. The EXTRN directive tells Turbo Assembler that various symbols are *external* to this program and that the actual addresses and values for these items will be supplied later when the program and all its modules are linked together. There are several things to keep in mind when using EXTRN:

▶ Every symbol in an EXTRN directive must eventually be resolved to a like symbol declared in a PUBLIC directive in a module linked to the program. Otherwise, you'll receive an error from Turbo Linker.

▶ EXTRN directives must specify the *type* of the symbol. In line 25, all three symbols are type proc, which tells the assembler that these are subroutine labels and, therefore, can be used as targets in call and jmp instructions. You can also declare code labels as near and far, forcing the assembler to generate either inter-segment or intrasegment subroutine calls. (It's still your responsibility to ensure that the correct ret instructions are used in the external routines.)

▶ When declaring external variables, allowable types are: byte, word, dword, fword, pword, dataptr, qword, and tbyte, corresponding to the data directives in Table 5-3. You must insert EXTRN directives for variables in the proper data segment, usually just after DATASEG. If you accidentally declare external variables inside the `CODESEG`, the linker will be unable to calculate the correct addresses for your external data.

▶ External numeric equates are always type `abs` (for absolute value). A good place for these `EXTRN` symbols is before the `DATASEG` directive.

▶ Object-code modules can declare `EXTRN` directives, too. For example, see line 34 in STRIO.ASM (Program 5-2), which imports two procedures from the STRINGS module. Any module can export its own symbols in `PUBLIC` directives and import external symbols from any other module in `EXTRN` directives.

▶ When multiple modules (including the main host program) refer to the same `EXTRN` symbols, only one copy of the object-code module containing those symbols is linked into the finished code file.

▶ You need to declare only the symbols your program uses. You don't have to declare all of the symbols that are declared `PUBLIC` in a module. Despite this, Turbo Linker always links entire modules into the finished code, even if you use only one or two procedures (or other declarations) in that module.

▶ To create a complete code file, you must link all modules containing the symbols that are declared in `EXTRN` directives among all the program's modules. Storing object code in library files makes linking easier by allowing Turbo Linker to pick out only the object-code modules it needs. The entire library is *not* linked into your code—only the necessary modules stored in the library.

A Simplified External Example

A few quick examples will help clarify the preceding details about exporting and importing equates, variables, and procedure labels. (You don't have to enter and run these samples, although you can if you want to.) Here's the object-code module:

```
          IDEAL
          DOSSEG
          MODEL    small
          PUBLIC   Maximum
Maximum =          100h
          DATASEG
          PUBLIC   counter
counter db         0Fh
          CODESEG
          PUBLIC   subroutine
PROC      subroutine
          ret
ENDP      subroutine
          END
```

After switching to Ideal mode, selecting standard segment ordering (`DOSSEG`), and specifying the small memory model, the module declares numeric equate `Maximum` public. In the data segment, another symbol—the byte variable `counter`—is also declared public. In the code segment, a third symbol, subroutine, a procedure label, is exported. Notice that the PUBLIC directives are placed in sensible places. A host program can import these symbols this way:

```
        IDEAL
        DOSSEG
        MODEL    small
        STACK    256
EXTRN   Maximum:abs
        DATASEG
EXTRN   counter:byte
        CODESEG
EXTRN   Subroutine:proc
Start:  mov      ax, @data            ; Initialize ds to address
        mov      ds, ax               ;  of data segment
        mov      ax, Maximum          ; Set ax = Maximum
        mov      cl, [counter]        ; Get value of counter
        mov      bx, OFFSET counter   ; Get address of counter
        call     Subroutine           ; Call external subroutine
Exit:
        mov      ax, 04C00h           ; DOS function: Exit program
        int      21h                  ; Call DOS. Terminate program
        END      Start        ; End of program / entry point
```

Look carefully at the placement of the EXTRN directives, especially for counter and Subroutine. These symbols are placed in the data and code segments so the linker will be able to resolve their addresses correctly. The type of the numeric equate is abs. The type of the db variable is byte. If the variable had been declared in the other module with dw, the type would be word. The Subroutine label is given the type proc. In the main program code, these symbols are used exactly as though they were declared directly in the program. If you want to assemble and run the finished program in Turbo Debugger, assuming you name the module MODULE.ASM and the main program MAIN.ASM, use these commands:

```
tasm /zi module
tasm /zi main
tlink /v main module
td main
```

Exploring the Strings Module

Now that you know how to write, assemble, and link separate modules, you're ready to explore the 12 procedures in Program 5-1, STRINGS. All the procedures in STRINGS operate on ASCIIZ strings—sequences of characters ending in a zero byte. You can also use the two routines MoveLeft and MoveRight on unterminated byte strings. In the interests of speed—and, therefore, in the spirit of blue-blooded assembly language programming—most routines in STRINGS do little error checking. For example, when copying one string to another, it's your responsibility to ensure that the destination is large enough to hold the copied characters.

The following sections describe each of the routines in STRINGS. Line numbers refer to those in Program 5-1.

> Note: The STRINGS and STRIO modules assume that segment registers **ds** and **es** address the same data segment in memory. Serious bugs are likely to occur if you fail to set **ds** = **es** before calling any of the routines in these modules.

MoveLeft (58–89)
MoveRight (91–121)

These two routines move bytes in memory from one location to another. Other string routines call `MoveLeft` and `MoveRight` to copy strings, attach one string to another, and insert characters into a string. You can also use these routines to fill buffers and to copy blocks of memory from place to place.

Both `MoveLeft` and `MoveRight` use a repeated string instruction, `movsb` at lines 82 and 114. The other instructions save and restore register values and prepare `si`, `di`, and flag `df` for the memory-block move. Notice how the `jcxz` instruction at line 74 prevents accidentally moving 65,536 bytes if `cx` is 0, jumping in this event to local label `@@99:` at line 87. A similar instruction at line 102 jumps to line 119 for the same reason. (Remember, local labels extend only up or down to the next nonlocal label; therefore, `@@99:` can be reused without conflict at lines 193, 267, and 467.)

> Note: When viewing a repeated string instruction such as `rep movsb` in Turbo Debugger, press F8 to execute the instruction to completion. Press F7 to execute one iteration at a time.

The comments to `MoveLeft` and `MoveRight` at lines 58–72 and 91–100 list required registers and explain the effects of calling each routine. `MoveRight` requires the same input parameters as `MoveLeft`. When using these or any other procedures in STRINGS, always be sure to check the "Registers" section in the procedure header, which lists any potentially modified registers. In this case, `MoveLeft` and `MoveRight` are friendly—they return all original register values intact. This isn't true for all procedures. By the way, the `%NEWPAGE` directives that begin each procedure in the STRINGS listing cause form-feed control characters to be written to the listing file, if you create one with Turbo Assembler's /l command. This makes listings neater by starting new procedures at the tops of fresh pages.

Call `MoveLeft` with `si` addressing the source string and `di` addressing the *destination*—the place to where you want to copy bytes. Assign to `bx` and `dx` index values for copying bytes somewhere other than the start of the strings. For example, to copy a 20-byte variable `v1` to the middle of a 40-byte variable `v2`, you could write:

```
DATASEG
v1        db        '12345678901234567890', 0  ; 20-byte string
v2        db        40 dup (0)                  ; 40-byte string
CODESEG
mov   si, OFFSET v1           ; Assign source address of v1
mov   di, OFFSET v2           ; Assign destination address of v2
mov   bx, 0                   ; Set source index (v1[0])
mov   dx, 10                  ; Set destination index (v2[10])
mov   cx, 20                  ; Specify the number of bytes to move
call MoveLeft                 ; Move bytes from v1[0] to v2[10]
```

MoveLeft copies bytes from left (low addresses) to right (high addresses). When the source and destination addresses overlap—as they may, for example, when moving bytes inside the same string variable—the direction of the move can have important consequences. An example explains this action:

```
mov   [buffer], 0            ; set first byte of buffer to 0
mov   si, OFFSET buffer      ; address start of buffer with si
mov   di, si                 ; address same buffer with di
xor   bx, bx                 ; set source index to 0
mov   dx, 1                  ; destination index to second byte
mov   cx, (LENGTH buffer) - 1 ; set count = length of buffer - 1
call MoveLeft                ; fill buffer with 0s
```

The first mov sets the first byte in buffer to 0. Registers si and di are assigned the same offset address of this variable. After this, source index bx is set to 0 (the first byte in buffer), and dx is set to 1 (the second byte in buffer). Then, using the LENGTH operator—which returns the number of bytes in a variable—cx is set to 1 less than the length of buffer. Calling MoveLeft with these parameters copies the byte at buffer[0] to buffer[1], then from buffer[1] to buffer[2], and so on, filling the entire buffer with the value originally at index 0.

> Note: A better way to fill a buffer with a byte value is to use a repeated stosb or stosw. MoveLeft is fast, but not as fast as a single string instruction!

When the source and destination addresses overlap and you don't want to replicate the source bytes in the destination, you must begin the move at the opposite end of the variables. MoveRight accomplishes this by adding cx-1 to si and di (see lines 109–112). Next, std prepares to decrement si and di automatically while the repeated string instruction at line 114 executes. This prevents the source bytes from shifting into the destination, which is especially useful for moving bytes to higher addresses in a variable—for example, to perform an insertion in a large text buffer. Here are a few more hints that will help you get the most from MoveRight and MoveLeft:

▸ When the source and destination addresses overlap, if the source is lower than the destination, call MoveRight to prevent accidentally replicating source data into the destination.

▷ When the source and destination addresses overlap, if the source is higher than the destination, call `MoveLeft` to prevent accidentally replicating source data into the destination.

▷ When the source and destination addresses do not overlap, always call `MoveLeft`. This routine runs a tiny bit faster because it does not have to adjust `si` and `di` by `cx-1`.

StrNull (123–136)

Call `StrNull` to erase the characters in a string addressed by `di`. `StrNull` operates by storing a zero byte at the start of the string (line 134). Examine the phrase in brackets, duplicated here for reference:

```
mov  [byte ptr di], ASCNull
```

The `byte ptr` operators tell Turbo Assembler that `di` addresses an 8-bit byte. You'd replace `byte` with `word` if `di` addresses a 16-bit word. The `ptr` is optional, and you could revise this line to read:

```
mov  [byte di], ASCNull
```

To use `StrNull`, assign the address of a string variable to `di` and call the procedure. For example, you might use `StrNull` to set the length of an uninitialized string variable to 0:

```
UDATASEG
string    db   81 dup (?)      ; Uninitialized 80-character string
CODESEG
mov  di, OFFSET string          ; Address string with di
call StrNull                    ; Set string length to 0
```

Because a zero-length ASCIIZ string has a null terminator as its first character, `StrNull` doesn't need to know the maximum string size and, therefore, works with any length string variables.

StrLength (138–162)

`StrLength` calculates how many characters are stored in an ASCIIZ string addressed by `di`. `StrLength` returns this value in `cx`, which can then be passed to other routines that need to know the length of a string. (Notice that line 146 tells you that `cx` is subject to change. If you are using `cx` for other purposes and need to call `StrLength`, you'll have to save `cx` somewhere—probably on the stack—and then restore the original value later.)

Suppose you want to jump to the end of the program if, after prompting for some input, the length of the string is 0. You could write:

```
DATASEG
string    db   'Sample user response string', 0
CODESEG
mov  di, OFFSET string    ; Address string with di
call StrLength            ; Set cx to string length
or   cx, cx              ; Is cx = 0?
jz   Exit               ; Jump to Exit if cx = 0
```

StrLength demonstrates how to use the scasb string instruction, introduced in chapter 4. Use scasb to scan byte strings for a specific value; use scasw to scan word strings. The value to search for must be in al for byte searches or in ax for word searches. Assign the starting address for the scan to es:di and set cx to the maximum number of bytes to scan. Both scasb and scasw compare the byte in al or the word in ax with the data at es:di, effectively performing a cmp. With these instructions, you can devise loops to search for byte and word values:

```
cld                     ; Prepare to auto-increment di
mov  di, buffer         ; Address buffer with es:di
mov  cx, lenbuffer      ; Set cx = length of buffer
mov  al, searchval      ; Set al = value to find
repne scasb             ; Repeat while bytes not equal
je   Match              ; Match found
jmp  NoMatch            ; Match not found
```

In this code, the repne prefix executes scasb repeatedly, while al and the byte at es:di are "not equal (ne)," decrementing cx and stopping if this makes cx = 0. After the scan, two jumps test whether the search ended at a matching byte, jumping to appropriate labels (not shown). Because scas sets the same flags as cmp, you can follow the scan with conditional jumps as shown here.

The effect of the repeated scan at line 155 in procedure StrLength is to scan an ASCIIZ string, stopping when the byte at es:di is 0 or when cx decrements to 0, thus preventing a runaway condition that might occur if you accidentally pass an uninitialized string to the procedure and if no zero bytes are in the data segment—unlikely, but possible.

Repeated-Loop Calculations

Lines 156–157 in StrLength use an obscure technique to calculate the number of times that a repeated string operation executes. The method requires cx to be initialized to 0FFFFh (−1 in two's complement notation) as done here at line 153. After the repeated scan (line 155), a simple logical operation calculates the number of times the previous scan had repeated. To understand how this works, first consider the classic method for calculating the repeated string instruction count:

```
mov  cx, -1     ; Initialize cx to -1
repnz scasb     ; Repeat while [di] <> al and cx <> 0
not  cx         ; Form one's complement of cx
```

The one's complement of cx equals the number of times the repnz scasb loop executed. Why this works is easier to fathom by thinking through the effect of a single iteration. Because cx initially equals −1, if the scasb stops after one repetition, then cx will equal −2, or FFFE hexadecimal. (The repnz prefix subtracts 1 from cx for each repetition of scasb.) The absolute value (two's complement) of −2 is, of course, 2—which is 1 too many. You could subtract 1 from the absolute value to get the correct answer (2 − 1 = 1 iteration), but recalling from chapter 3 that the two's complement of a value equals the one's complement plus 1, you may as well just take the one's complement as the final result! By the way, this works for positive values, too. If cx equals 32,766 after the scan, then 32,769 loops had been executed. Work out in binary the one's complement of 32,766 (7FFEh) to prove to yourself that this is so.

For StrLength's purposes, the classic method's result is 1 too many because the value counts the null terminator at the end of the string. For this reason, line 157 decrements cx to give the final answer.

StrUpper (164–199)

StrUpper converts lowercase letters in a string to uppercase without changing other nonalphabetic characters. Assign the string address to di and call the procedure this way:

```
DATASEG
lc    db    'abcdefghijklmnopqrstuvwxyz', 0
CODESEG
mov  di, OFFSET lc        ; Address string with es:di
call StrUpper             ; Convert chars to uppercase
```

The procedure demonstrates two popular string instructions lodsb and stosb, introduced in chapter 4, along with a new instruction, loop (see line 192). The loop instruction subtracts 1 from cx and, if cx is not yet 0, jumps to the specified target address. In StrUpper, the target address is the local label, @@10: at line 183. Loop effectively performs in one step the same job as these instructions:

```
dec  cx                   ; cx <- cx - 1
jnz  Target               ; Jump to Target if cx <> 0
```

Two other variations of loop are loopne/loopnz and loope/loopz. The mnemonic pairs are just different names for the identical instructions for the same reasons that other instructions such as repne/repnz and jnz/jne have double names. Loopne and loopnz also jump to a target label if, after decrementing cx, this register is not yet 0. At the same time, a test is made of zf, presumably set or cleared by a previous comparison. For example, to scan a buffer from back to front searching for a byte equal to 0FFh, you might use code such as:

```
     mov  cx, LENGTH buffer
     mov  bx, OFFSET buffer + LENGTH buffer
@@20:
     dec  bx
     cmp  [BYTE bx], 0FFh
     loopne  @@20
     je   Match
```

Register cx is set to the maximum number of bytes to scan; bx is set to the address just past the end of the buffer. The three instructions after @@20: then decrement the index pointer bx, comparing each byte at this address with 0FFh. The loopne instruction subtracts 1 from cx and jumps to @@20: only if cx is not 0 and if the cmp did not detect an 0FFh byte. After the search is completed, a je instruction jumps to label Match (not shown) only if the 0FFh value was found in the buffer. You can use loope similarly to locate bytes or words that don't match a certain value.

As you can see, loop, loope, and loopne are handy instructions for writing search loops. Returning to the STRINGS module, in StrUpper, after initializing cx to the string length, exiting immediately if the length is 0 (see lines 175–182), the instructions at lines 183–192 use lodsb, stosb, and loop to scan the string, examining each character with two cmp instructions. If a lowercase letter is found, line 189 adjusts the ASCII value to uppercase. Notice how the expression in sub al,'a'-'A' subtracts from al the numeric difference between ASCII lowercase and uppercase letters. Characters in assembly language are just numbers and, as this demonstrates, you can use them directly in numeric expressions. (BASIC and Pascal programmers may find this a bit strange. C programmers are no doubt right at home.) Remember that Turbo Assembler evaluates this and other constant expressions during assembly, not at run time. You could write sub al,32 to do the same thing, but then the purpose of the instruction would be less clear.

StrCompare (201–229)

Comparing two strings alphabetically is a surprisingly simple job, as you can see in the StrCompare procedure. To use StrCompare, assign the addresses of two strings to si and di and call the procedure. After that, use one of the unsigned conditional jump instructions jb, jbe, je, ja, or jae to test the result of the comparison. For example, to compare strings s1 and s2 and then jump to label StringsLess if s1 < s2, you can write:

```
DATASEG
s1   db   80 dup (0)      ; ASCIIZ string variables, presumably
s2   db   40 dup (0)      ;  assigned characters elsewhere
CODESEG
mov  si, OFFSET s1        ; Address first string with si
mov  di, OFFSET s2        ; Address second string with di
call StrCompare           ; Compare s1 and s2
jb   StringsLess          ; Jump if s1 < s2
jg   StringsGreater       ; Jump if s1 > s2
                          ; If here, s1 = s2!
```

You can use multiple jumps as shown here without calling StrCompare a second time. The string variables do not have to be the same size, and the string lengths can be 0. Both strings *must* end with 0 bytes, or StrCompare will start behaving strangely.

The code works by using lodsb and scasb at lines 219–220, loading a single character into al and comparing the ASCII value with the character at [es:di]. These two instructions also advance si and di by 1 (because of the previous cld instruction at line 217). The jne at line 221 exits the loop if the comparison fails. Obviously, if any characters are different, so are the strings, and the alphabetic result is known at the first such difference found. The or instruction at line 222 checks whether al is 0, indicating that the end of the first string at ds:si was found before reaching the end of the second string at es:di. If the end is not found, the jne at line 223 continues the comparison; otherwise, the loop ends.

You might be wondering what happens if the second string at `es:di` is shorter than the first at `ds:si`. In this event, assuming that all characters are equal up to the end of the shorter string, the `scasb` at line 220 compares a character from the first string at `ds:si` with the null terminator at the end of the second string at `es:di`. Obviously, this comparison fails; therefore, the result indicates that the longer string is alphabetically greater than the shorter. In other words, this comparison actually involves the null terminator, which is not a character in the string. However, the result is correct.

It may take a little effort to understand all this by simply reading the text and program. For a better picture of how `StrCompare` works, try running a small test program in Turbo Debugger and compare different strings. Watch in particular the `cf` and `zf` flags during the loop at lines 218–223.

StrDelete (231–273)

`StrDelete` deletes one or more characters starting at any position in a string and prevents you from deleting more characters than exist in the string, making it easy to perform jobs such as stripping the extension from the end of a file name or limiting responses to a certain number of characters. Assign to `di` the address of any ASCIIZ string variable, set `dx` to the index of the first character to delete (starting with 0 for the first character in the string), and assign to `cx` the number of characters to delete. For example, this deletes the phrase "and tigers" plus one space from a string:

```
DATASEG
string     db     'Lions and tigers and bears, oh my!', 0
CODESEG
mov  di, OFFSET string   ; Address string with es:di
mov  dx, 6               ; Index to the "a" in and
mov  cx, 11              ; Number of chars in "and tigers"
call StrDelete           ; Delete 11 chars at string[6]
```

Note: Although `StrDelete` prevents deleting more characters than exist in the string, `dx` must address a character in the string or point to the null terminator. In other words, `dx` must be less than or equal to the string length. Ignoring this rule might damage other variables and code in memory.

`StrDelete` works in two stages. Lines 259–261 handle the condition where you try to delete more characters than are in the string. In this case, the `mov` at line 260 inserts a null at the end of the new string and exits. Lines 263–266 delete characters by calling `MoveLeft` with both `si` and `di` addressing the same string. This moves the end of the string (including the null terminator) over top of the deleted characters. Notice the `short` operator (line 261) added to the `jmp` target address, telling Turbo Assembler that label `@@99:` is no more than about 127 bytes distant. This helps the assembler generate a more efficient form of `jmp` than is required to jump farther away.

StrInsert (275–325)

Call `StrInsert` to insert characters from one string into another at any position. Assign to `si` the address of the source string (the one to insert into the other) and to `di` the address of the destination string (the one to receive the insertion). Assign to `dx` the index into the destination string where you want to begin the insertion. Remember that the first character is at index 0. The source string is not changed. This example inserts the string "tab-A" into another string:

```
DATASEG
destination     db     'Insert into slot-B          ', 0
source          db     'tab-A ', 0
CODESEG
mov  si, OFFSET source          ; Address source string with ds:si
mov  di, OFFSET destination     ; Address destination with es:di
mov  dx, 7                      ; dx = index of "i" in destination
call StrInsert                  ; Insert source into destination
```

> Note: The destination string must be large enough to hold the inserted source string to prevent overwriting other variables and code in memory. It's up to you to prevent this condition when using `StrInsert`.

By this time, you should be able to understand the instructions for `StrInsert` from the comments in the listing. Hint: The `call` to `MoveRight` at line 313 punches a hole in the destination string just large enough to hold the insertion. Then the `call` to `MoveLeft` at line 319 copies the source-string characters into the hole. The other instructions initialize registers to prepare for these two block moves.

StrConcat (327–359)

`StrConcat` concatenates (joins) one string to another. The destination string at `es:di` must be large enough to hold the characters it now has plus the characters from the source string at `ds:si`. The source string is not changed. The following changes "This is" to "This is the end!":

```
DATASEG
source          db     'the end!', 0
destination     db     'This is                ', 0
CODESEG
mov  si, OFFSET source          ; Address source with ds:si
mov  di, OFFSET destination     ; Address destination with es:di
call StrConcat                  ; Attach source to destination
```

`StrConcat` calls `StrLength` at lines 346 and 349, once to find the end of the destination string and again to find the length of the source string. Notice how the `xchg` instructions at 348 and 351 temporarily swap `si` and `di` for these subroutine calls. After these steps, a call to `MoveLeft` at line 384 performs the attachment.

StrCopy (361–390)

StrCopy copies one string variable to another, which must be at least as long as the length of the original string plus 1 byte for the null terminator. The procedure is easy to use. Just assign the address of the source string to si and the destination to di. Then call StrCopy. Any characters in the destination string are subject to permanent erasure. For example, to copy the characters in one string to an uninitialized string variable, you could write:

```
DATASEG
s1       db       'Original string', 0
s2       db       80 dup (?)  ; Uninitialized string variable
CODESEG
mov      si, OFFSET s1  ; Address source string with si
mov      di, OFFSET s2  ; Address destination string with di
call     StrCopy        ; Copy string s1 to s2
```

The code to StrCopy isn't difficult to understand. An xchg instruction at line 378 swaps si and di so that StrLength, which uses di, can return the length of the source string. A second xchg (line 381) then restores the original register values. The other instructions in the procedure prepare registers for the call to MoveLeft, which performs the actual copy, moving the bytes of s1 into s2.

StrPos (392–439)

StrPos is the most complex in the STRINGS module, although the individual instructions should all be familiar to you. Call StrPos to determine if and where a substring at ds:si exists inside a target string at es:di. After StrPos returns, if zf equals 1, then dx equals the index in the target string where the substring begins. If zf is 0, then the substring was not found in the target and the value in dx is meaningless. An example shows how to use StrPos to determine if the extension .ASM is in a file-name string:

```
DATASEG
extension       db       '.ASM', 0
filename        db       'MYTEST.ASM', 0
CODESEG
mov  si, OFFSET extension   ; Address substring with ds:si
mov  di, OFFSET filename    ; Address target string with es:di
call StrPos                 ; Search for substring in target
jz   foundExtension         ; Jump if substring found at dx
jmp  notFound               ; Jump if substring not found
```

After checking that the substring length is less than or equal to the target string's length—otherwise, there's no sense continuing the search—lines 421–429 call StrCompare repeatedly until finding the substring or reaching the end of the target. The mov instructions at lines 422, 423, and 425 temporarily replace characters in the target with nulls, using the powerful base-indexed addressing mode, indexing the string at bx with register di. Repeating this operation and advancing a character at a time in the target eventually examines all possible positions where the substring might be located.

StrRemove (441–471)

Calling three other subroutines in the STRINGS module, StrRemove is handy for removing substrings from strings. It's simple to use, too. Assign to ds:si the address of the substring to delete. Assign to es:di the address of a target string. Then call StrRemove. If the substring is found in the target, the characters are removed; otherwise, no changes to the target are made. The substring is never changed. As in StrPos, the zf flag indicates the result of the removal: 1 if the substring was found and removed or 0 if not. Here's an example that deletes an area code from a phone number string:

```
DATASEG
phoneNumber     db      '(800)-555-1212', 0     ; Target string
areaCode        db      '(800)-', 0             ; String to delete
CODESEG
mov  si, OFFSET areaCode          ; Address substring to delete
mov  di, OFFSET phoneNumber       ; Address target string
call StrRemove                    ; Delete substring from target
```

Of interest in StrRemove are the pushf and popf instructions at lines 461 and 466, which save and restore the flag registers on the stack. This allows the procedure to return the zf flag result of the call to StrPos at line 459—necessary because the calls to StrLength and StrDelete change the flags.

Summary

All references to data take one of three forms: immediate, register, and memory. Immediate data is stored directly in machine-code instructions. Register data refers to values held in registers such as ax and ch. Memory references allow five variations: direct, register-indirect, base, indexed, and base-indexed. Despite the many different addressing methods available, the goal of all memory-addressing modes is to help the processor to form the effective address, a 16-bit unsigned offset from the start of a memory segment addressed by one of the four segment registers.

Expressions are reduced during assembly to constant values, which programs can use. Unlike a high-level language's expressions, expressions in assembly language are not evaluated at run time. Expressions can employ a variety of operators to combine labels, addresses, and other values in many different ways.

Simple variables are created by reserving space in a data segment with directives such as db and dw. The DUP operator can be added to these directives to reserve blocks of space. Initialized data is stored in the program's code file on disk. Uninitialized data is allocated at run time and is not preset to any specific values. The db directive can be used to allocate string variables delimited by single or double quotes.

The scope of local labels extends only to the next nonlocal label above or below. A local label is similar to a global label but begins with the symbol @@. Local labels help conserve memory by letting the assembler reuse RAM for other local labels. They also reduce the need to think up new label names for temporary use.

Modular programming divides large jobs into easy-to-manage pieces. Individual modules are assembled separately and then linked to a host program to create the finished code. Modules can export code, numeric constants, and variable labels in **PUBLIC** directives for other modules and programs to share. Programs and modules import symbols from other modules in **EXTRN** directives. The TLIB utility program stores object-code modules in library files, which can simplify linking multiple modules.

Exercises

5-1. Give examples of instructions that use immediate, register, and memory data.

5-2. Give examples of instructions that use each of the five memory-addressing modes.

5-3. Construct a data segment with byte, word, string, and one 1,024-byte buffer variables. Put the buffer into the uninitialized data-segment area.

5-4. Write a subroutine to initialize your buffer in exercise #5-3 to contain sequential byte values ranging from 0 to 255.

5-5. Insert your subroutine from exercise #5-4 into an object-code module. Then write a host program to call your subroutine. What steps are required to assemble and link your module and program?

5-6. What are some of the advantages of storing object-code modules in library files.

5-7. What does a **PUBLIC** directive do? What does **EXTRN** do?

5-8. To which local label does the following `jmp` refer?

```
@@40:
     inc  ax
Repeat:
     jmp  @@40
     cmp  ax, 0
     jl   Repeat
     lodsb
     je   @@Exit
@@40:
     xor  cx, cx
@@Exit:
     mov  ax, 04Ch
     int  21h
```

5-9. Which of the following equates can be exported in a **PUBLIC** directive? What EXTRN directive is needed to import these symbols into a program?

```
IDEAL
MaxCount   = 1000
cr           EQU  13
lf           EQU  10
YesAnswer  = 'Y'
MaxSize      EQU 4
BufferSize = MaxCount * MaxSize
```

5-10. Show three ways to declare a 20-character string variable.

5-11. Suppose you have the modules GETDATA, PRINTER, READ-TEXT, and the library file MTA.LIB. What instructions do you need to use to assemble and link a main program that uses the three modules plus the STRIO and STRINGS modules in the library?

5-12. What TLIB commands can you use to install the three modules in exercise #5-11?

5-13. Suppose there is a byte variable named Flag stored in the code segment. What instruction or instructions do you need to use to load this byte into register dh?

5-14. Declare the following string using a db directive.

```
"This 'string' can't have 'too' many quotes," she said.
```

Projects

5-1. Write improved versions of the MoveLeft and MoveRight procedures in the STRINGS module by moving 16-bit words at a time with movsw when the cx byte count is even.

5-2. Write a series of test procedures to put the STRINGS and STRIO modules through their paces.

5-3. Rewrite StrConcat so that it calls StrInsert instead of MoveLeft. Verify that your procedure operates identically to the original.

5-4. Write a module to send ASCIIZ strings to the printer.

5-5. Write a program to use your printer module from project #5-4 to initialize various print options on your printer.

5-6. [Advanced] Write a new STRINGS module to operate on byte-length strings. A byte-length string stores the length of the string in the first byte. The second and subsequent bytes store the characters of the string. There is no null terminator, and string lengths are limited to 255 characters. Your STRINGS module should use the same procedure names as the ASCIIZ STRINGS module in this chapter.

6 Complex Data Structures

183

Chapter **6 Complex Data Structures**

In This Chapter

Using STRUC to create multifield structures; viewing structures with Turbo Debugger; reading and writing structure field values; how to use RADIX to change the default number base; floating point numbers; binary coded decimals; working with arrays; using the LABEL and UNION directives; difference between unions and structures; bit fields and the RECORD directive; extracting and recombining packed bit-field values; using Turbo Assembler's predefined equates; programming a binary to ASCII library module; plus equipment determination and binary-hex-decimal conversion programs

Structures

A structure is a named variable that contains other variables, called *fields*. The keyword STRUC begins the structure, followed on the same line by any name you want, for example, MyStruct. A matching keyword ENDS follows the last field in the structure. You can attach a copy of the structure's name after ENDS or leave the name out—similar to the way you can repeat a procedure name after ENDP. For example, this structure contains three fields representing the date:

```
STRUC    Date
  day      db    1       ; Day field--default value = 1
  month    db    ?       ; Month field--no default value
  year     dw    1991    ; Year field--default value = 1991
ENDS     Date            ; "Date" is optional here
```

You can insert fields of any type inside a structure, using the same methods that you use to declare plain variables. This example has three fields: day, month, and year. The first two fields are single bytes, with the first of these values initialized to 1. The second byte field is uninitialized. The third field is a word, initialized to 1991. The indentation of each field is purely for show. When defining structures such as this, remember these important points:

template

▶ A structure is not a variable. A structure is a schematic for a variable.

▶ Structures may be declared anywhere. The STRUC directive does not have to be placed in the program's data segment, although it certainly can be.

▶ A structure tells Turbo Assembler about the design of variables that you plan to declare later on or that already exist elsewhere in memory.

▶ Even though you use directives such as db and dw to define the types of a structure's fields, the structure does not reserve space in the data segment or cause any bytes to be written to the finished program.

Declaring Structured Variables

To use a structure design, you must reserve space in memory for the structure's fields. The result is a variable that has the design of the structure. Start each such variable declaration with a label, followed by the structure name, and ending with a list of default values in angle brackets <>. Leave the brackets empty to use the defaults (if any) defined earlier in the structure definition. Returning to the example Date structure again, the program's data segment might declare several date variables:

```
DATASEG
birthDay       Date        <>              ; 1-0-1991
```

A label birthDay starts the variable declaration. Next comes the structure name Date at the same place you would normally use simple directives like dw. The empty angle brackets cause this date's fields to assume the default values declared in the structure. Uninitialized default field values—as in the month field here—are set to 0 unless all fields in the structure are uninitialized, and the variable is declared in the program's uninitialized data segment area. In that case, the actual field values are undefined. Here are a few more examples:

```
DATASEG
today          Date        <5,10>          ; 5-10-1991
dayInDayOut    Date        <11,12,1912>    ; 11-12-1912
monthOfSundays Date        <,8,>           ; 1-8-1991
```

The today date variable replaces the first two default values—day and month—with 5 and 10. The missing third field value assumes the default from the structure design, here 1991. The second variable dayInDayOut replaces all three default values. The third variable monthOfSundays specifies a new month value while using the defaults for others, here changing month to 8. The first comma is needed to "get to" the second structure field. The second comma is not needed, and you could also write:

```
monthOfSundays Date       <,8>
```

A Structured Demo
A good way to learn more about structures is to examine a few sample structured variables with Turbo Debugger. To experiment, enter Program 6-1, STRUC.ASM. Then refer to the numbered experiments following the listing after you assemble, link, and load the program into Turbo Debugger with the commands:

```
tasm /zi struc
tlink /v struc
td struc
```

Program 6-1 *STRUC.ASM*

```
 1:   %TITLE "Structure Demonstration for Turbo Debugger"
 2:
 3:           IDEAL
 4:           DOSSEG
 5:           MODEL   small
 6:           STACK   256
 7:
 8:   STRUC   Date
 9:   day     db      1         ; Day--default value = 1
10:   month   db      ?         ; Month--no default value
11:   year    dw      1991      ; Year--default value = 1991
12:   ENDS    Date
13:
14:   STRUC   CityState
15:   city    db      '####################', 0        ; 20 or so chars
16:   state   db      '##', 0                          ; 2 chars
17:   ENDS    CityState
18:
19:
20:           DATASEG
21:
22:   exitCode        db      0
23:
24:   today           Date            <>
25:   birthDay        Date            <8,8,1988>
26:   earthDay        Date            <1,1,2001>
27:   newYear         Date            <,,1990>
28:
29:   address         CityState       <>
30:   glitterTown     CityState       <'Hollywood','CA'>
31:   pennState       CityState       <'Pennstate','PA'>
32:   hotSpot         CityState       <'Brownsville', 'TX'>
33:   defaultState    CityState       <,'NH'>
34:   defaultCity     CityState       <'New York City'>
35:
36:
```

```
37:          CODESEG
38:
39:  Start:
40:          mov      ax, @data              ; Initialize ds to address
41:          mov      ds, ax                 ;  of data segment
42:
43:  ; Note: run in Turbo Debugger--program doesn't do anything
44:
45:  Exit:
46:          mov      ah, 04Ch               ; DOS function: Exit program
47:          mov      al, [exitCode]         ; Return exit code value
48:          int      21h                    ; Call DOS. Terminate program
49:
50:          END      Start         ; End of program / entry point
```

Running the STRUC Demo

You should have assembled STRUC and loaded the code into Turbo Debugger. Follow these suggested experiments to see how structured variables are stored in memory:

1. Press the Alt-V and V keys to select the View:Variables command. A window will pop into view, listing all the program's variables by name (in the window's right half).

2. Press Tab to move the selection bar into the variable list, and then press the down arrow key to move the bar to "today." Notice the field values listed in braces to the right of the field names, giving you a quick glance of the data stored in the structured variables.

3. Press Ctrl-I to inspect the today variable. (You can also press F5 at this point to zoom the small window to full screen for a less constricted view.) Turbo Debugger lists each field on a separate line, using the names from the STRUC definition and showing you the actual values stored in memory. Because db can reserve space for both ASCII characters and bytes, the debugger shows these values both ways. Just ignore the characters for noncharacter byte fields. Integer values are shown in decimal and hexadecimal in parentheses.

4. Press F3 to close the inspection window. (Hint: You can also press Esc, but F3 is the "close window" key and is normally used to get rid of windows you no longer need.) Move the selector bar down to the next variable (birthDay) and press Enter—a shorthand method to display an inspection window. Compare the listed field values with those in the program at line 25. Press F3 (or Esc) and repeat these same steps for the remaining two dates at lines 26–27.

5. Lines 14–17 declare another structure CityState, with two string fields city and state. So that you can see the default values in Turbo Debugger, these strings are preinitialized to hatch marks. Normally, you'd initialize string values with less obtrusive symbols such as blanks or nulls. Starting again from the Variables window, move the selector bar to address and press Enter.

6. The two default fields are now displayed in the inspection window. The bottom of this window tells you the type and size of the structure and individual fields. Use the cursor keys to move the selector bar to one field (watch how the bottom line changes) and press Enter again. This opens up a new inspection window, allowing you to view the individual bytes in a field variable. Move the selector bar down to any single byte and press Enter one more time to open yet another inspection window, this time showing the address of an individual byte. Being able to step down into the byte values of a structured variable is one of Turbo Debugger's best features for assembly language programming, where finding data structures in memory can sometimes be extremely frustrating.

7. Press Esc several times until only the Variables window is again active (with double-line borders). Move the selector bar down to the next variable pennState, and press Enter. Zoom to full screen with F5. Compare the displayed strings with the defaults at line 31. Notice that only the leading portion of the string field is replaced by the text in the angle brackets. The rest of the string is *padded* (filled) with the default characters from the STRUC definition.

8. Lines 15 and 16 declare this structure's fields as ASCIIZ strings, ending in null characters. But, on your display, the nulls appear to be missing. The reason for this discrepancy is that Turbo Debugger displays only the initial field value. To prove that the nulls are still where they should be, move the selector bar to city and press Enter. Then press the PgDn key until the bar rests on the final byte of this field (at line 19). Press Enter again and note the address (6C89:0060 for me). Press Esc twice, then select the state field. Press Enter. The address on my screen is 6C89:0062—indicating that there is an invisible byte at 6C89:0061. We've found the null!

9. To see the nulls in the string variables, press Esc several times to return to the Variables window. Press Alt-V and D to select the View:Dump commands. Press Ctrl-G and enter the string address from step 8—6C89h:0060h for me. You *must* type the small *h* letters after the segment and offset address values. Press F5 to zoom. You are now looking at the structured variable values as stored in the program's data segment. Try to pick out the nulls, which separate the individual string fields.

10. There's no need to run this program—it doesn't do anything beyond showing you how structures are assembled. When you're done experimenting, press Alt-X to return to DOS.

As you can see from these notes, string fields in structures are fixed-length items. The hatch marks (#) in the default values at lines 15–16 are replaced by new values assigned in the angle brackets at lines 29–34. Turbo Assembler in Ideal mode fills the rest of the string with the default characters in the structure definition. (In MASM mode, any remaining characters are magically changed to spaces—even if this isn't what you want.

Ideal-mode structures are much easier to use.) In Turbo Debugger, you can normally see only the first of a list of values declared in db and dw directives. To see each value, you could modify the CityState structure definition at lines 14–17, placing each field value on separate lines:

```
STRUC   CityState
 city   db      '####################'
 cnull  db      0
 state  db      '##'
 snull  db      0
ENDS    CityState
```

Because of the additional fields that now reserve bytes for the string null terminators, you also have to modify the variable declarations at lines 29–34, adding new values for each field. If you don't do this, you'll receive an "override" error during assembly, which happens when you try to override a default value such as a single byte with a multiple-byte string. Change lines 29–34 as follows, reassemble, and inspect the new variables with Turbo Debugger:

```
address         CityState       <>
glitterTown     CityState       <'Hollywood',0,'CA',0>
pennState       CityState       <'Pennstate',0,'PA',0>
hotSpot         CityState       <'Brownsville',0,'TX',0>
defaultState    CityState       <,,'NH'>
defaultCity     CityState       <'New York City'>
```

Using Structured Variables

Using the fields in a structured variable is only a little more difficult than using simple variables, as explained in chapter 5. All of the same addressing modes are available. Because field names are contained by the structure definition, to refer to an individual field, you must write both the structure and the field names, separating the two with a period. Refer back to Program 6-1. To assign a new value to the day field in today, you can assign an immediate value to a field in memory with:

```
mov  [today.day], 5     ; Change day to 5
```

You can also load field values into registers as in this instruction, which reads the year into ax:

```
mov  ax, [today.year]    ; Get year into ax
```

Other variations are possible. You can add, subtract, read, write, and logically combine fields and registers. Remember that in all cases, you have to give both the structure and variable names so the assembler can generate the correct address to your fields. Here are a few more examples:

```
inc  [earthDay.day]     ; Add 1 to day field
add  [newYear.year], cx ; Add cx to year field
cmp  [today.month],8    ; Is month = 8?
```

Note: In Turbo Assembler's Ideal mode, field names are local and unique to the structure in which the fields are defined. This means you can create multiple **STRUC** definitions with the same field names. For example, you might have two different structures each of which contains **day, month,** and **year** fields. You can't do the same in the more restrictive MASM mode, where all field names are global—meaning that one name can appear in only one structure definition throughout a program. For this reason, in MASM mode, you can't have two structures such as **Customer** and **Personal** with **Name** fields—you instead have to invent unique field names such as **CName** and **PName**. In Ideal mode, structures are much easier to use, although, because field names might be nonunique, you must write both the structure and field names separated by periods for all references.

STRIO Structures

Chapter 5 promised to explain the **StrBuffer** structure at lines 18–22 in STRIO.ASM, Program 5-2. For reference, this data structure is repeated here:

```
BufSize          EQU      255         ; Maximum string size
STRUC StrBuffer
 maxlen          db BufSize           ; Maximum buffer length
 strlen          db 0                 ; String length
 chars           db BufSize DUP (?)   ; Buffer for StrRead
ENDS strBuffer
```

BufSize is an equate equal to 255, the maximum-length string that DOS can read. The **StrBuffer** structure uses this value to declare three fields in the form required by DOS function 0Ah that reads strings from the standard input file (usually the keyboard). **StrRead** calls this routine to let you enter strings into variables. (See lines 39–78 in Program 5-2.) This raw input is then converted to ASCIIZ format for use with routines in STRINGS, STRIO, and other modules in this book.

Line 27 in Program 5-2 declares a variable **buffer** of the **StrBuffer** structure, using the default values in the structure definition. **StrRead** passes the address of this variable to DOS, which handles all the keyboard-processing details, limiting the result to the maximum length specified in field **maxlen**, storing the actual string length in field **strlen**, and inserting characters (if any) into field **chars**.

Note: Because **StrRead** calls DOS for input, you can edit your typing with the same function keys you are accustomed to using at the DOS prompt.

When you are done typing, pressing Enter causes DOS to set field **strlen** to the number of characters you typed. DOS also adds an ASCII carriage return to the end of the string. Because this is the wrong terminator for the ASCIIZ format, lines 66–68 in **StrRead** replace the carriage return with an ASCII null before copying the string to the program's variable (lines 69–70).

Notice how the program refers to string fields at lines 62, 64, 67, 68, and 69, using both direct- and base-addressing modes. In each case, the structure name is followed by a period and a field name. Line 62 stores the value of cl into the maxlen field of buffer. Line 64 shows how to find the offset address of a specific field maxlen. Line 68 adds the value of register bx to the start of the chars field, locating the address of the carriage return stored in chars.

More About Numeric Variables

In assembly language programs, you can represent values in hexadecimal, binary, or decimal. But, because the three number systems share the same digit symbols, you have to tell the assembler which number system you mean. To the end of your numbers, add a *b* for binary and an *h* for hexadecimal. Add nothing or *d* for decimal, the usual default for all numbers. For example, these variables represent the same values in the three number bases:

```
v1    dw    0100111101011100b    ; Binary
v2    dw    04F5Ch               ; Hexadecimal
v3    dw    20316                ; Decimal (default)
v4    dw    20316d               ; Decimal
```

Notice that the hex value (04F5Ch) begins with a leading 0. This 0 is required only if the first digit is A–F as in the value 0FACEh. Even so, it's not a bad idea to include the 0 anyway—if only to be consistent. Hex values must begin with *decimal* digits because the assembler can't know whether FaceH is a label or a value. As a result, you must observe one strict rule when writing numeric values: The first digit of all values in any base must be a digit—0 or 1 for binary; 0 to 9 for decimal and hex. Adding a leading 0 to hex values satisfies this rule.

Using RADIX Unless you end a number with *b* or *h*, Turbo Assembler assumes the value is decimal. To change this default behavior, use the **RADIX** directive. (*Radix* means "number base.") For example, to make hexadecimal the default radix, use the command:

```
RADIX 16      ; Default radix is hexadecimal
```

For most purposes, it's probably best to stick with the assembler's default decimal radix and use *h* and *b* to specify your hexadecimal and binary values. If you forget to change the **RADIX** to hexadecimal in a new program, you could easily mistake 100 for 256 decimal. There's just no mistaking 0100h as a hexadecimal value.

Note: The value following **RADIX** is always expressed in decimal and must be 2 (binary), 8 (octal), 10 (decimal), or 16 (hexadecimal), regardless of the current radix in effect. Also, if you change the default radix, remember to end *every* decimal value with *d*.

Signed and Unsigned Integers

When declaring values with **db** and **dw**, be aware of the differences between signed and unsigned values, as explained in chapter 3. Unlike high-level languages, assembly language enforces no limits on signed number ranges; therefore, as long as the value you specify fits within the space you allocate, the assembler accepts your every wish and command. For example, you can write:

```
v1    dw    32768        ; 08000h
v2    dw    -32768       ; 08000h !
v3    dw    -1           ; 0FFFFh
v4    dw    65535        ; 0FFFFh !
```

When Turbo Assembler stores these values in memory, the results may not be what you expect. Variable **v1** is stored as the unsigned value 32,768 or 08000h. (Note: Commas are used in numbers here to make them easier to read. You can't add commas to numbers in programs.) Notice that this value is identical to the signed value −32,768—at least it is in the world of fixed-length binary values in computer memory. Similarly, −1 and 65,535 both assemble to the identical value 0FFFFh. As this demonstrates, even though the allowable range of values is −32,768 to +65,535, values from −32,768 to −1 and from 32,768 to 65,535 are represented identically in binary. A thorough understanding of binary representations and two's complement notation is the best way to avoid confusion with these idiosyncracies of assembly language programming.

Floating Point Numbers

You can also declare floating point numbers with the **dt** directive, which reserves 10 bytes of memory, much the same as **dw** reserves 2 bytes. The result of **dt** with a floating point value is a binary 10-byte real number in standard IEEE (Institute for Electrical and Electronic Engineers) format. These values are compatible with the format used by 8087, 80287, and 80387 numeric coprocessors. You can also exchange floating point values in your assembly language programs with most high-level languages to process floating point expressions. Without a subroutine package to display and process floating point values in assembly language, floating point values are difficult to use. To declare a floating point number, use **dt** this way:

```
fp    dt    3.14159         ; 4000C90FCF80DC33721Dh
```

Binary Coded Decimals

Another use for **dt** is to declare packed binary-coded-decimal (BCD) numbers. These values are useful especially in business calculations where large numbers are frequently required but where the round-off errors possible with floating point values are unacceptable. BCD values take more room (10 bytes each) and require more time to process than byte and word integers, so you won't use this format except in special cases. (Chapter 11 describes BCD numbers in detail.) To declare a packed BCD value, use the same **dt** directive as for floating point values, but don't use a decimal point. For example:

```
bcd1    dt    1234
bcd2    dt    9876543210
bcd3    dt    250000
```

Each of these declarations reserves 10 bytes of memory, storing the initialized values with 2 *digits* per byte. In other words, a BCD value can have up to 20 digits. Values are stored in reverse order, so that the previous examples appear in memory with each digit assigned to a 4-bit *nybble* in the byte:

```
nnnn:0000   34 12 00 00 00 00 00 00 00 00
nnnn:0000   10 32 54 76 98 00 00 00 00 00
nnnn:0000   00 00 25 00 00 00 00 00 00 00
```

Arrays in Assembly Language

There are no native commands, structures, or methods for declaring and using arrays in assembly language programs. In high-level languages such as Pascal and C, you can declare arrays and then refer to array items with an index variable. For example, a Pascal program might declare an array of ten integers, indexed from 0 to 9:

```
VAR  intArray : ARRAY[ 0 .. 9 ] OF Integer;
```

In the program, statements can then refer to the array, perhaps using an index variable and a **FOR** loop to assign values to each array position:

```
FOR i := 0 TO 9 DO
   intArray[ i ] := i;
```

For those who are not familiar with Pascal, this statement assigns the values 0 through 9 to the ten arrayed integers. C and BASIC programmers have similar ways to create and use arrays. In assembly language, managing arrays is a little more difficult, but also more flexible because it is up to you to write the code to access array values. One way to create an integer array, for example, is to use the **DUP** operator:

```
anArray    db    10 DUP (?)      ; Array of 10 integers
```

You can also define ten values in sequence, declaring and initializing the array in a single step:

```
anArray    db    0, 1, 2, 3, 4, 5, 6, 7, 8, 9
```

Arrays of other structures such as strings and **STRUC** variables take more effort. For instance, suppose you need an array of four 20-byte strings. Because this array is so small, you may as well use four separate variables:

```
anArray    db    20 DUP (?), 0      ; anArray[0]
           db    20 DUP (?), 0      ; anArray[1]
           db    20 DUP (?), 0      ; anArray[2]
           db    20 DUP (?), 0      ; anArray[3]
```

The four variables are stored consecutively in memory; therefore, the same four 20-byte strings (plus 1 byte for the string terminator) can be accessed as individual variables or as a structure of four arrayed strings. Unless you love typing long programs, this approach may be impractical for creating large arrays. Consider how you might create space for one hundred 20-byte strings. Using two new directives LABEL and REPT, you can write:

in the Dataseg:

```
LABEL     anArray   Byte
REPT      100
 db  20 DUP (?), 0
ENDM
```

The first line declares the label anArray of type Byte. Other type names you can use here are Word, DWord, FWord, PWord, DataPtr, QWord, and TByte. Or you can use a structure name. The LABEL directive tells the assembler how to address the data that follows—it doesn't reserve any memory space. In this example, the data that follow are strings, which are always addressed as single bytes. The REPT (Repeat) command repeats any assembly language statement for a certain number of times, here 100. Everything between REPT and ENDM (End Macro) is repeated as though you had typed this line so many times. (The ENDM command also ends *macro definitions,* a subject for chapter 8.)

One useful trick is to change the declaration each time in the definition. For example, to create an array of ten integers and assign the values 0 through 9 to each array position, you can use this declaration:

```
value = 0
LABEL     anArray   Word
REPT      10
 dw  value
 value = value + 1
ENDM
```

The result is an array of Word integers with the values 0, 1, 2, 3, 4, 5, 6, 7, 8, and 9. The numeric value equate is initialized to 0. As you recall from chapter 5, symbols defined with equal signs can be redefined later—the key to this method. Inside the REPT definition, a dw directive defines one word of memory equal to value. After this, value is increased by 1 for the next pass. Remember that expressions such as value = value + 1 are evaluated at assembly time and that all the actions just described take place during assembly— not when the program runs. The result is an array of ten words initialized to successive values. No code is generated by these commands.

Note: Turbo Debugger's Variables window is unable to show all elements of arrays declared with REPT directives as demonstrated here. To see the array, use the View:Dump commands to view memory starting at the array's address.

Changing Types with LABEL

The LABEL directive is used most often to assign two or more labels of different types to the same data in memory. With this technique, you can read and write variables as bytes in some instructions but as words (or other types) elsewhere. The directive has three parts:

LABEL *identifier type*

The *identifier* is treated the same as any other label. The *type* can be near, far, proc, byte, word, dword, fword, pword, dataptr, qword, or tbyte. The *type* can also be the name of a STRUC data structure. Using LABEL, you can declare a value as two bytes, but view the value as a 16-bit word:

```
LABEL ByteValue byte
WordValue  dw    01234h
```

The hexadecimal value 01234h is labeled as WordValue and declared as a 16-bit word with dw. But the preceding LABEL creates a second byte label ByteValue, which addresses the same value in memory. This lets you write instructions such as:

```
mov   ax, [WordValue]         ; Get full 16-bit value
mov   bl, [ByteValue]         ; Get 8-bit LSB
mov   bh, [ByteValue + 1]     ; Get 8-bit MSB
```

The first mov loads the full 16-bit value, setting ax to 01234h. The second mov loads only the first 8 bits of this same value, setting bl to 034h. The third mov loads the second 8 bits, setting bh to 012h. Thus, the final two instructions set bx to the same value as ax. (Remember that words are stored in byte-swapped order—the value 01234h is stored in memory as the two bytes 034h and 012h.)

Using LABEL to assign labels of different types to variables is even more useful for addressing structures as collections of typed fields, but also as streams of 16-bit words. Using the Date structure from the beginning of this chapter, you could write:

```
LABEL    DayMonth      word
OneDay   Date          <>
```

OneDay is a single structured variable of type Date. The label DayMonth addresses this same memory but considers the data to be of type word. In the program's code, you can refer to the first two fields in OneDay normally as OneDay.day and OneDay.month. Or, because of the additional label, you can load these two byte fields directly into one 16-bit register:

```
mov   ax, [DayMonth]          ; Load day and month into ax
mov   al, [OneDay.day]        ; Load day into ah
mov   ah, [OneDay.month]      ; Load month into al
```

The first mov performs the identical function as the last two mov instructions. Sometimes, as this shows, using LABEL can help cut out an instruction or two, and, if that instruction is repeated often, this will also improve program performance.

Indexing Arrays   Now that you know how to declare arrays, the next step is to investigate ways to read and write arrayed values. For example, how do you refer to item number 5? The key to the answer is in realizing that array indexes in assembly language are simply addresses—as are all references to variables; therefore, regardless of the type of data stored in an array, the goal of indexing individual values reduces to these two steps:

▶ Multiply the size of the array elements by the array index *i*.

▶ Add the result to the array's base address.

For example, in a simple array of bytes, if *i* is 0, then *i* × *2* (0) plus the address of *array* locates the first value at *array[0]*. The second value (*array[1]*) is located at the base address of *array* plus 1, and so on. As Figure 6-1 shows, the goal is to convert array index values such as these to addresses in memory. Index 0 is equivalent to the address, 000D—the same as the base address of the entire array. Index 1 corresponds to 000E; index 2, to 000F; on down to index 9, which locates the value at offset 0016. A real-life example will help make this process clear. Byte arrays are the easiest to manage, so let's take those first. To load into **al** the 64th element of a 100-byte array, you can write:

```
DATASEG
anArray     db    100 DUP (0)
CODESEG
mov   al, [anArray + 63]
```

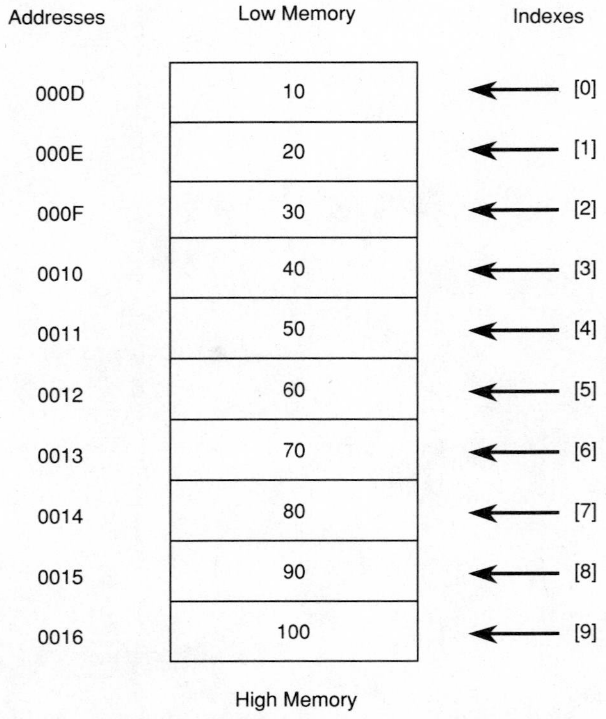

Addresses	Low Memory	Indexes
000D	10	← [0]
000E	20	← [1]
000F	30	← [2]
0010	40	← [3]
0011	50	← [4]
0012	60	← [5]
0013	70	← [6]
0014	80	← [7]
0015	90	← [8]
0016	100	← [9]

High Memory

Figure 6-1 *A simple array of bytes as they might appear in memory.*

The 63 in this example is correct because the first array element is at offset 0. An index of 64 would incorrectly locate the 65th item in the array, not the 64th. When calculating array indexes, you'll avoid much confusion and frustration if you always remember that the index range for an array of 100 items is 0 to 99, not 1 to 100.

Adding literal values like 63 as in the previous example doesn't allow for much flexibility. In most situations, you'll use a register or memory variable to hold the array index. Using the base-addressing mode introduced in chapter 5, you might store an array index value in register bx. For example, suppose you have a variable named index and you want to load the value of anArray[index] into a register. You can write:

```
DATASEG
index      dw     ?
anArray    db     100 DUP (?)
CODESEG
mov   bx, [index]          ; Get index value
mov   al, [bx + anArray]   ; al <- anArray[index]
```

The two data declarations reserve space for a 16-bit index and a 100-byte uninitialized array. In the code segment, the first mov loads the current value of index into bx. The second mov adds bx to the base address of the array, locating the correct byte and loading the arrayed value into al. You can also use registers si and di to do the same:

```
mov   si, [index]          ; Get index value
mov   al, [si + anArray] ; al <- anArray[index]
mov   di, [index]          ; Get index value
mov   al, [di + anArray] ; al <- anArray[index]
```

The top two lines perform the same function as the bottom two. Technically, this is the *indexed-* not *base*-addressing mode, although, as you can see, there's not much practical difference between the two methods.

Note: You can also use register bp to address arrays, but remember that this register's default segment is ss, not ds, which is the default for bx, si, and di in the base- and indexed-addressing modes.

Multibyte Array Values

Array addressing becomes trickier when arrayed values occupy more than 1 byte. Because of the computer's binary nature, calculating the addresses of multibyte array elements is simplest when the element sizes are powers of 2. In this case, you can use fast shift instructions to perform the initial multiplication of the index times the value byte size. Adding the result of this multiplication to the array's base address locates any arrayed value, as the following fragment demonstrates:

```
DATASEG
index      dw    ?
anArray    dw    100 DUP (?)
CODESEG
mov  bx, [index]          ; Get index value
shl  bx, 1                ; bx <- index * element-size (2)
mov  ax, [bx + anArray]   ; ax <- anArray[index]
```

In this example, the element size is 2 bytes; therefore, the easy (and fastest) way to multiply the index value by 2 is to shift the value left 1 bit. Compare Figure 6-2 with Figure 6-1. As you can see, addresses to the left increase by 2. To calculate the address of the fifth 2-byte array value (at index 4), you first multiply 4 × 2 and add the result to the base address of the array to get the final offset value of 0018h.

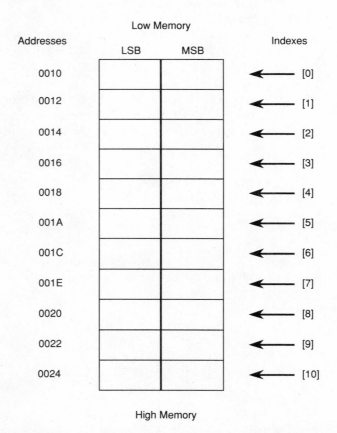

Figure 6-2 *When arrayed element sizes are powers of 2, translating indexes to offset addresses is relatively simple.*

Calculating index addresses when element sizes are not powers of 2 requires some fancy footwork to keep the code running as fast as possible. Of course, you can always use mul to perform the initial multiplication. Consider an array of elements, each occupying 5 bytes. To set bx to the offset address of the element at index requires several steps:

```
mov   ax, [index]            ; Get index value into ax
mov   bx, 5                  ; Set bx = element-size
mul   bx                     ; dx:ax <- index * element-size
mov   bx, ax                 ; move result to bx (ignoring dx)
add   bx, OFFSET anArray     ; Set bx <- address of element
```

Only the LSB of the multiplication is important—the high 16 bits in dx of the full 32-bit result are ignored. (Presumably another part of this program checks to be sure that index values are within bounds.) The problem with this approach is the mul instruction, which can take as many as 118 machine cycles to execute. For this reason, it pays to factor out the powers of 2 and use a combination of shifts and other faster instructions to calculate the address of arrayed values:

```
mov   bx, [index]            ; Get index value into bx
mov   ax, bx                 ; Save value in ax
shl   bx, 1                  ; bx <- bx * 2
shl   bx, 1                  ; bx <- bx * 4 (total)
add   bx, ax                 ; bx <- bx * 5 (total)
add   bx, OFFSET anArray     ; Set bx <- address of element
```

The comments in this fragment show the running total in **bx**. First, two left shifts multiply **bx** by 4. Adding this result to the original **index** value completes the full multiply-by-5. Obviously, 5 of any value equals 4 of that value plus 1 of that same value. Because 4 is a power of 2, the program can perform the first part of the multiplication with fast shift instructions before completing the result with a simple addition. This entire sequence of instructions runs *many* times faster than a single mul instruction.

Such tricks as these aren't always possible. But, in general, when you can use left shifts instead of multiplication, the results will be faster. The best approach is to pick array element sizes that are powers of 2. When that is impossible, try to find a combination of shifts and other instructions that will give you the result.

Unions

Defined with a **UNION** directive, a *union* has the identical form as a **STRUC** structure. Like structures, unions contain named fields, often of different data types. The difference between a union and a structure is that union fields overlay each other within the variable. A union with three byte fields, in other words, actually occupies only a single byte. As the next example shows, you can use this feature to construct variables that the assembler can reference as containing more than one type of data, similar to the way you learned how to use **LABEL** earlier:

```
UNION    ByteWord
  aByte    db   ?
  aWord    dw   ?
ENDS     ByteWord
```

An ENDS directive ends the union. In this example, aByte overlays the first byte of aWord. If this were a structure, then aByte and aWord would be stored in consecutive locations. Because this is a union, however, aByte and aWord are stored at the *same* location in memory. Therefore, inserting a value into aByte also changes the LSB of aWord:

```
mov   [aByte], bh    ; Store bh at aByte and aWord's LSB
```

When combined with structures, unions give you powerful ways to process variables. For example, Figure 6-3 lists a useful structure and union combination that you can use to refer to variables as 16-bit words and as 8-bit bytes.

```
STRUC   TwoBytes
  loByte            db        ?
  hiByte            db        ?
ENDS    TwoBytes


UNION   ByteWord
  asBytes           TwoBytes            <>
  asWord            dw                  ?
ENDS    ByteWord
```

Figure 6-3 *Union with nested structure.*

The TwoBytes structure defines two byte fields, loByte and hiByte. The union ByteWord also defines two fields. First is asBytes, of the previously defined TwoBytes structure. Next is asWord, a single 16-bit word. Variables of type ByteWord make it easy to refer to locations as both word and double-byte values without the danger of forgetting that words are stored in byte reversed order—a problem with the LABEL method. To use the nested union, first declare a variable, in this case assigned the value 0FF00h.

```
DATASEG
data    ByteWord            <,0FF00h>
```

You can now refer to data as a TwoBytes structure or as a 16-bit word. A short example demonstrates how to load the same memory locations into either byte or word registers. Because the TwoBytes structure is nested inside the union, two periods are required to "get to" the byte fields. Notice how the field names reduce the danger of accidentally loading the wrong byte of a word into an 8-bit register:

```
CODESEG
mov   al, [data.asBytes.loByte]  ; Load LSB into al
mov   ah, [data.asBytes.hiByte]  ; Load MSB into ah
mov   ax, [data.asWord]          ; Same result
```

Bit Fields Many times in assembly language programming you'll need to examine and change one or more bits in a byte or word value. You've already learned several ways to accomplish this with logical instructions such as `or`, `and`, and `xor` to set and clear individual bits without disturbing others. For example, to set bit number 2 in a byte register, you can use the instruction:

```
or    al, 00000100b
```

When doing this, it's often helpful to write out the values in binary—just remember the final *b*. As you also learned earlier, `and` can mask values, setting one or more bits to 0:

```
and   al, 11110000b
```

Even though writing the values in binary helps to clarify exactly which bits are affected by the instructions, you still have to count bits and take time to visualize the results of your logic. In complex programs, it's very easy to set or reset the wrong bit—a most difficult bug to find. To make processing bits easier, Turbo Assembler offers two devices—the `RECORD` and the `MASK`.

Declaring RECORD Types

`RECORD` is a directive that lets you give names to bit fields in bytes and words. You simply specify the width of each field—in other words, the number of bits the field occupies. Turbo Assembler then calculates the position of the field for you. For example, this `RECORD` defines `signedByte` as an 8-bit value with two fields:

```
RECORD   signedByte   sign:1, value:7
```

After the `RECORD` directive comes the record's name, followed by a series of named fields. Each field name ends with a colon and the width of the field in bits. The `sign` field in this example is 1 bit long. The `value` field is 7 bits long. Separate multiple fields with commas. If the total number of bits is less or equal to 8, Turbo Assembler assumes the record is a byte; otherwise, it assumes the record is a word. You can't construct records larger than a word, although you can create multifield structures containing multiple bit fields, which would accomplish the same thing. You don't have to specify exactly 8 or 16 bits, although most programmers do, inserting dummy fields to flesh out a bit record to account for every bit, whether used or not.

Creating variables of a `RECORD` type is similar to creating variables of structures and unions. In fact, the three forms appear identical, leading to much confusion over the differences between structures and records. A few samples will clear the air:

```
DATASEG
v1    signedByte    <>          ; default values
v2    signedByte    <1>         ; sign = 1, value = default
v3    signedByte    <,5>        ; sign = default, value = 5
v4    signedByte    <1,127>     ; sign = 1, value = 127
v5    signedByte    <3,300>     ; sign = 1, value = 44
```

A record variable declaration has three parts: a label, the `RECORD` name, and two angle brackets, with optional values inside. The first sample declares `v1` as a variable of type `signedByte`. Because no values are specified in brackets, the default values for all bit fields are used. (In this case, the defaults are 0. In a moment, you'll see how to set other defaults.) The second sample sets the sign bit of v2 to 1, leaving the value field equal to the default. The third line sets value to 5, letting the sign field assume the default value. The fourth line assigns values to both fields in the variable, setting sign to 1 and value to 127. The fifth line shows what happens when you try to use out-of-range values such as 3 and 300. In this case, the actual values inserted into the record equal the attempted values modulo (division remainder) 2^n, where n equals the number of bits in the field.

Setting Default Bit-Field Values

Normally, the default field values in RECORD variables are 0. To change this, add to the field width an equal sign and the default value you want. For example, to create a RECORD with an MSD default of 1 and a second field defaulting to 5, you can write:

```
RECORD   minusByte  msign:1 = 1, mvalue:7 = 5
```

Declaring a variable of this type with empty angle brackets sets the msign field to 1 and the mvalue field to 5. Specifying replacement values in brackets as explained before overrides these new defaults. Notice that different field names are used here. Even though the names are contained in the RECORD definition, Turbo Assembler considers these names to be global—active at all places in the program or module. Therefore, you must use unique field names among all your RECORD definitions in one module.

> Note: Unlike RECORD field names, STRUC and UNION field names are not global. You can reuse structure and union field names for other purposes, but not record field names, which must be unique throughout the program. Perhaps a future release of Turbo Assembler will remove this inconsistency and make RECORD field names local to the record. At present, this is not the case.

Using RECORD Variables

After declaring a RECORD type and a few variables of that type, you can use several different methods to read and write bit-field values in those variables. To demonstrate how to do this, we first need a new RECORD type:

```
RECORD   person  sex:1,married:1,children:4,xxx:1,age:7,school:2
```

RECORDs like this one can pack a lot of information into a small space. In this example, only 16 bits are needed to store five facts about a person—with field sex equal to 0 for male and 1 for female, married equal to 0 if false or 1 if true, children ranging from 0 to 15, a 1-bit dummy field xxx reserved for future use, an age field ranging from 0 to 127, and school from 0 to 3, representing four levels of a person's schooling. Figure 6-4 illustrates how these fields are packed into one 16-bit word. As with all 16-bit values, the two 8-bit bytes of this variable are stored in memory in reverse order, with bits 0–7 (LSB) at a lower address than bits 8–15 (MSB).

What's in a Field Name?

Turbo Assembler converts bit-field names into the number of right shifts required to move the field to the rightmost position in the byte or word.

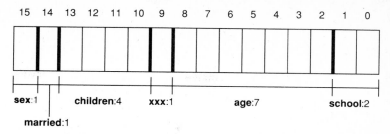

Figure 6-4 *A record packed with six bit fields stores a lot of information in a small space.*

The value is equal to the byte or word bit position of the least significant digit for this field. Referring to the person record, then, sex = 15, married = 14, children = 10, xxx = 9, age = 2, and school = 0. (See Figure 6-4.) You can use these field name constants as simple EQU equates. Normally, though, you'll use the values to shift bit fields into the rightmost position in a register, making it easy to process individual field values. The process works in reverse, too. If the children bit-field value is already in the rightmost position of ax, shifting ax left by the value of children moves the bit-field value into its proper position, ready to be packed into the record.

Using field names instead of manually counting bits saves time and helps prevent bugs. For example, to increment the age field, you can shift the appropriate bit-field value to the rightmost position in a word register, increment the register, and then shift the result back into position. Before doing this, however, you must strip out other bits from the variable. To help with this step, Turbo Assembler provides an operator called MASK, which takes the name of a bit field and generates an appropriate and mask with bits equal to 1 in all positions for this field. A good way to organize your masks is to use names similar to the associated fields:

```
maskSex       =     MASK sex
maskMarried   =     MASK married
maskChildren  =     MASK children
maskAge       =     MASK age
maskSchool    =     MASK school
```

Each new identifier—for example, maskSex and maskMarried—is assigned a mask for each bit field (except for xxx, which we'll just ignore). The names make the purpose of the various symbols easy to remember, although you can use whatever names you like. You don't have to preface the identifiers with "mask." With the bit-field names and masks, it's easy to isolate and process bit-field information without having to calculate the positions of fields in records. An example explains how this works. First, declare a variable named subject of type person:

```
DATASEG
subject   person   <>
```

Then, to set single bit fields to 1, use or to combine the mask with the record's current value:

```
CODESEG
or   [subject], maskSex        ; Set sex field = 1
or   [subject], maskMarried    ; Set married field = 1
```

To reset single-bit fields to 0, use the **NOT** operator along with the bit mask, toggling all bits in the mask. The following shows two ways to proceed:

```
and  [subject], NOT maskSex       ; Change sex field to 0
mov  ax, [subject]                ; Load subject into ax
and  ax, NOT maskMarried          ; Change married field to 0
mov  [subject], ax                ; Store result back in memory
```

Extracting Bit Fields

For bit fields of more than 1 bit, the process is similar but requires additional steps to isolate the values. There are several possible methods you could use, but these steps always work:

1. Copy the original variable into a register
2. AND the register with the field mask
3. Shift the register right by the field-name constant

After copying the variable into a register (either 8 or 16 bits wide, depending on the variable's size), step 2 isolates the field's bits, stripping other fields out of the record, thus setting all other bits but those in the desired field to 0. Step 3 then shifts the isolated field bits to the rightmost position in the register. To add a new member to our **subject's** family, use these steps:

```
mov  ax, [subject]        ; Step 1--copy the variable
and  ax, maskChildren     ; Step 2--isolate the bit field
mov  cl, children         ; Prepare shift count
shr  ax, cl               ; Step 3--shift field to right
inc  ax                   ; Add 1 to number of children
```

The mov and and instructions copy the **subject** variable into **ax** and strip other fields out of the value, leaving only the bits that apply to **children**. After loading the shift count into **cl**, the **shr** instruction shifts the **children** field to the far right of **ax**, preparing for **inc** to increment this value. If the **children** field was already rightmost in the variable—making the shift count equal to 0—the shift instructions can be skipped. For example, you could write:

```
        mov  cl, children    ; Move shift count into cl
        or   cl, cl          ; Is count = 0?
        jz   @@10            ; Jump if yes, cl = 0
        shr  ax, cl          ; Else shift ax, cl times
@@10:
        inc  ax              ; Add 1 to number of children
```

A better approach is to use a conditional **IF** directive, which chapter 8 explains in more detail. This lets the assembler, rather than the program, decide whether shifting is required. After completing steps 1 and 2 to copy and mask the record variable, the following instructions shift the result right only if the `children` constant is greater than 0:

```
IF children GT 0
     mov   cl, children    ; Move nonzero count into cl
     shr   ax, cl          ; Shift ax, cl times
ENDIF
     inc   ax              ; Add 1 to number of children
```

Conditional Assembly

If the expression in the conditional **IF** is true, then Turbo Assembler assembles the code up to the next **ENDIF** directive. If the expression is false, then the code is ignored. This method eliminates the unnecessary comparison, jump, and shift instructions of the previous technique.

Recombining Bit Fields

After extracting a bit field and processing its value, you now need a way to insert the result back into a record variable. Assuming the result is rightmost in a register, follow these four steps:

1. Shift the register left by field-name constant
2. AND the register with the field mask
3. AND the original value with NOT field mask
4. OR the register into the original value

Step 1 shifts the value into its correct position, again using the field name as the shift count but this time shifting left instead of right. Step 2 is an optional safety valve, which limits the new value to the field's width in bits. If you are positive that the new field value is within the proper range, you can skip this step. But any out-of-range values—accidentally giving our subject the burden of 45 children, for example—can change the values of other fields. For this reason, it's a good idea to mask the new value this way before combining that value back into the original variable. Step 3 complements step 2 by setting all bits of the field in the original value to 0—in a sense, punching a hole in the original value like a cookie cutter punching out a circle in dough. Step 4 then ORs the new value into this punched-out hole, completing the process.

To demonstrate these four steps in assembly language, the following code fragment moves the children field (now rightmost in register **ax**) back into the **subject** variable:

```
mov   cl, children                    ; Move shift count into cl
shl   ax, cl                          ; Step 1--shift into position
and   ax, maskChildren                ; Step 2--limit value
and   [subject], NOT maskChildren     ; Step 3--punch a hole, clear entire field
or    [subject], ax                   ; Step 4--drop value into hole
```

Skip if pure value is OK! →

As with the previous steps that extract a bit field, you can use a conditional **IF** directive to skip the shift if `children = 0`, indicating that this field is already rightmost in the variable. Also, you can eliminate the first **and** if the result cannot possibly be larger than 15—the maximum value that the 4-bit `children` field can express.

Putting the extraction and recombination steps together, here's another example that adds 10 to our subject's age field:

```
mov  ax, [subject]          ; Copy the variable into ax
and  ax, maskAge            ; Isolate the age field
mov  cl, age                ; Prepare shift count
shr  ax, cl                 ; Shift age field to right
add  ax, 10                 ; Add 10 to subject's age
shl  ax, cl                 ; Shift age back into position
and  ax, maskAge            ; Limit age to maximum range
and  [subject], NOT maskAge ; Punch a hole in (zero) age field
or   [subject], ax          ; Drop new age value into hole
```

Many programmers avoid using RECORD bit fields, probably because they do not understand the techniques. This fact is evident from the many assembly language programs that declare fixed constants for shift values and masks, making the code much more difficult to modify. If you take the time to learn how to use RECORD and MASK, defining your packed records as described here, you'll be able to write programs that automatically adjust for new situations—a change to the number of bits in the school field or a newly found use for the reserved xxx single-bit field. You can also change the default values assigned to fields without having to hunt through a lot of cryptic statements, making changes to programs that don't need fixing! Just change your RECORD definitions, and you're done. The same advantages apply to STRUC and UNION, which help take much of the complexity out of working with complex data structures.

Using Predefined Equates

Turbo Assembler knows a few predefined equates that you can use as default values for program variables. Table 6-1 lists these equates, all of which begin with two question marks.

Program 6-2, VERSION.ASM, demonstrates how to use these equates to create a version-number string automatically when the program is assembled. Assemble, link, and run the program with the commands:

```
tasm version
tlink version,,, mta
version
```

Table 6-1 *Predefined Equates*

Symbol	Meaning
??Date	Today's date in the DOS country-code style
??Filename	The module or program's disk-file name
??Time	The current time in the DOS country-code style
??Version	Turbo Assembler version number

VERSION uses the STRIO and STRINGS modules from chapter 5; therefore, the tlink command assumes that the assembled code for these modules is stored in MTA.LIB. If you want to examine the program in Turbo Debugger, add the /zi option to tasm and the /v option to tlink— as you probably know by now.

Program 6-2 *VERSION.ASM*

```
 1:   %TITLE "Automatic Program Version Demonstration"
 2:
 3:           IDEAL
 4:           DOSSEG
 5:           MODEL   small
 6:           STACK   256
 7:
 8:   cr      EQU     13          ; ASCII carriage return
 9:   lf      EQU     10          ; ASCII line feed
10:
11:
12:           DATASEG
13:
14:   exitCode        db      0
15:
16:   ident   db      cr, lf, ??FileName, ' ', ??Date, ' ', ??Time
17:           db      cr, lf, 0
18:
19:
20:           CODESEG
21:
22:   ;----- From STRIO.OBJ
23:
24:           EXTRN   StrWrite:proc
25:
26:   Start:
27:           mov     ax, @data           ; Initialize ds to address
28:           mov     ds, ax              ;   of data segment
29:           mov     es, ax              ; Make es = ds
30:
31:           mov     di, OFFSET ident    ; Address program id string
32:           call    StrWrite            ; Display string
33:
34:   Exit:
35:           mov     ah, 04Ch            ; DOS function: Exit program
36:           mov     al, [exitCode]      ; Return exit code value
37:           int     21h                 ; Call DOS. Terminate program
38:
39:           END     Start       ; End of program / entry point
```

Running VERSION   Lines 16–17 create an ASCIIZ string, starting and ending with a carriage return and line feed plus a null terminator. Inside the string, the predefined equates ??FileName, ??Date, and ??Time are used in a db directive to create a string with these three values, separated by a few spaces. Running the program displays a line similar to:

```
VERSION   12-20-88   16:56:22
```

The nice feature about building the automatic string is that merely reassembling the program automatically changes the version date and time. This simple device is very useful for keeping track of program updates.

Converting Numbers and Strings

In high-level languages, you can read and write numeric values directly. For example, to let someone enter a number and then display the result, assuming n is an integer, you might use these Pascal statements:

```
Write( 'Enter a value: ' );
Readln( n );
Writeln( 'Value is: ', n );
```

Native assembly language lacks similar abilities. Instead, you have to read and write strings and then convert those strings to and from binary values for processing, storing on disk, and so on. Of course, high-level languages must do this internally, too!

Program 6-3, BINASC.ASM, is a module that you can use to make this process easier to program. The module has routines that can convert 16-bit values to and from signed and unsigned decimal, hexadecimal, and binary ASCIIZ strings. Assemble to BINASC.OBJ and store this code in your MTA.LIB file with the commands:

```
tasm /zi binasc
tlib /E mta -+binasc
```

As with the modules in chapter 5, ignore the warning that BINASC is not in the library. It won't be until you install it the first time. Also, be aware that BINASC uses two procedures from STRINGS; therefore, you won't be able to link programs to BINASC until at least both of these modules are installed in MTA.LIB.

Program 6-3 *BINASC.ASM*

```
 1: %TITLE "Binary to/from ASCII Conversion Routines"
 2:
 3:        IDEAL
 4:        DOSSEG
 5:        MODEL   small
 6:
 7: ;----- Equates
 8:
 9: ASCnull        EQU     0              ; ASCII null character
10:
```

```
11:            DATASEG
12:
13:            CODESEG
14:
15:   ;----- From STRINGS.OBJ
16:
17:            EXTRN   StrLength:proc, StrUpper:proc
18:
19:            PUBLIC  HexDigit, ValCh, NumToASCII
20:            PUBLIC  BinToAscHex, SBinToAscDec, BinToAscDec, BinToAscBin
21:            PUBLIC  AscToBin
22:
23:   %NEWPAGE
24:   ;---------------------------------------------------------------
25:   ; HexDigit        Convert 4-bit value to ASCII digit
26:   ;---------------------------------------------------------------
27:   ; Input:
28:   ;       dl = value limited to range 0...15
29:   ; Output:
30:   ;       dl = ASCII hex digit equivalent
31:   ; Registers:
32:   ;       dl
33:   ;---------------------------------------------------------------
34:   PROC    HexDigit
35:            cmp     dl, 10          ; Is dl < 10 (i.e., hex 'A')?
36:            jb      @@10            ; If yes, jump
37:            add     dl, 'A'-10      ; Else convert to A, B, C, D, E, or F
38:            ret                     ; Return to caller
39:   @@10:
40:            or      dl, '0'         ; Convert digits 0 to 9
41:            ret                     ; Return to caller
42:   ENDP    HexDigit
43:   %NEWPAGE
44:   ;---------------------------------------------------------------
45:   ; ValCh           Convert ASCII digit char to binary value
46:   ;---------------------------------------------------------------
47:   ; Input:
48:   ;       dl = ASCII digit '0'..'9'; 'A'..'F'
49:   ;       bx = base (2 = binary, 10 = decimal, 16 = hexadecimal)
50:   ; Output:
51:   ;       cf = 0: dx = equivalent binary value
52:   ;       cf = 1: bad char for this number base (dx is meaningless)
53:   ; Registers:
54:   ;       dx
55:   ;---------------------------------------------------------------
56:   PROC    ValCh
57:            cmp     dl, '9'         ; Check for possible hex digit
58:            jbe     @@10            ; Probably '0'..'9', jump
59:            sub     dl, 7           ; Adjust hex digit to 3A..3F range
```

```
60:     @@10:
61:             sub     dl, '0'         ; Convert ASCII to decimal
62:             test    dl, 0f0h        ; Check 4 msbs (sets cf = 0)
63:             jnz     @@99            ; Jump  if error (not digit or A-F)
64:
65:             xor     dh, dh          ; Convert byte in dl to word in dx
66:             cmp     dx, bx          ; Compare to number base (cf = 1 if ok)
67:     @@99:
68:             cmc                     ; Complement cf to set/reset err flag
69:             ret                     ; Return to caller
70:     ENDP    ValCh
71:     %NEWPAGE
72:     ;-------------------------------------------------------------
73:     ; NumToASCII     Convert unsigned binary value to ASCII
74:     ;-------------------------------------------------------------
75:     ; Input:
76:     ;       ax = 16-bit value to convert
77:     ;       bx = base for result (2 = binary, 10 = decimal, 16 = hex)
78:     ;       cx = minimum number of digits to output
79:     ;       di = address of string to hold result
80:     ;       Note: assumes string is large enough to hold result
81:     ;       Note: creates full result if cx is less than the number
82:     ;             of digits required to specify the result or cx = 0
83:     ;       Note: if cx = 0 and ax = 0 then length of string will be 0
84:     ;             set cx = 1 if you want string to = '0' if ax = 0
85:     ;       Note: assumes (2 <= bx <= 16)
86:     ; Output:
87:     ;       none
88:     ; Registers:
89:     ;       ax, cx
90:     ;-------------------------------------------------------------
91:     PROC    NumToASCII              ; Normal entry point
92:             push    dx              ; Save some modified registers
93:             push    di
94:             push    si
95:
96:     ; si = count of digits on stack
97:
98:             xor     si, si          ; Set digit-count to 0
99:             jcxz    @@20            ; If cx = 0, jump to set cx = 1
100:    @@10:
101:            xor     dx, dx          ; Extend ax to 32-bit dxax
102:            div     bx              ; ax <- axdx div bx; dx <- remainder
103:            call    HexDigit        ; Convert dl to ASCII digit
104:            push    dx              ; Save digit on stack
105:            inc     si              ; Count digits on stack
106:            loop    @@10            ; Loop on minimum digit count
```

```
107:    @@20:
108:            inc     cx              ; Set cx = 1 in case not done
109:            or      ax, ax          ; Is ax = 0? (all digits done)
110:            jnz     @@10            ; If ax <> 0, continue conversion
111:            mov     cx, si          ; Set cx to stack char count
112:            jcxz    @@40            ; Skip next loop if cx = 0000
113:            cld                     ; Auto-increment di for stosb
114:    @@30:
115:            pop     ax              ; Pop next digit into al
116:            stosb                   ; Store digit in string; advance di
117:            loop    @@30            ; Loop for cx digits
118:    @@40:
119:            mov     [byte di], ASCnull      ; Store null at end of string
120:            pop     si              ; Restore saved registers
121:            pop     di
122:            pop     dx
123:
124:            ret                     ; Return to caller
125:    ENDP    NumToASCII
126:    %NEWPAGE
127:    ;-------------------------------------------------------------
128:    ; BinToAscHex   Convert binary values to ASCII hex strings
129:    ;-------------------------------------------------------------
130:    ; Input:
131:    ;       ax = 16-bit value to convert
132:    ;       cx = minimum number of digits to output
133:    ;       di = address of string to hold result
134:    ;       Note: assumes string is large enough to hold result
135:    ;       Note: outputs full result if cx is less than the number
136:    ;             of digits required to specify the result
137:    ; Output:
138:    ;       none
139:    ; Registers:
140:    ;       ax, cx
141:    ;-------------------------------------------------------------
142:    PROC    BinToAscHex
143:            push    bx              ; Save bx on stack
144:            mov     bx, 16          ; Set base = 16 (hex)
145:            call    NumToAscii      ; Convert ax to ASCII
146:            pop     bx              ; Restore bx
147:            ret                     ; Return to caller
148:    ENDP    BinToAscHex
149:    %NEWPAGE
150:    ;-------------------------------------------------------------
151:    ; BinToAscDec   Convert binary values to ASCII decimal strings
152:    ;-------------------------------------------------------------
153:    ; Input:
154:    ;       Same as BinToAscHex
155:    ; Output:
156:    ;       none
```

```
157:   ; Registers:
158:   ;        ax, cx (indirectly)
159:   ;----------------------------------------------------------------
160:   PROC    BinToAscDec
161:           push    bx              ; Save bx on stack
162:           mov     bx, 10          ; Set base = 10 (decimal)
163:           call    NumToAscii      ; Convert ax to ASCII
164:           pop     bx              ; Restore bx
165:           ret                     ; Return to caller
166:   ENDP    BinToAscDec
167:   %NEWPAGE
168:   ;----------------------------------------------------------------
169:   ; SBinToAscDec  Convert signed binary to ASCII decimal strings
170:   ;----------------------------------------------------------------
171:   ; Input:
172:   ;        Same as BinToAscHex (ax = signed 16-bit value)
173:   ; Output:
174:   ;        none
175:   ; Registers:
176:   ;        ax, cx
177:   ;----------------------------------------------------------------
178:   PROC    SBinToAscDec
179:           push    bx                      ; Save bx and di
180:           push    di
181:           cmp     ax, 0                   ; Is signed ax < 0?
182:           jge     @@10                    ; Jump if ax >= 0
183:           neg     ax                      ; Form two's complement of ax
184:           mov     [byte di], '-'          ; Insert '-' in string
185:           inc     di                      ; Advance string pointer
186:   @@10:
187:           mov     bx, 10                  ; Set base = 10 (decimal)
188:           call    NumToAscii              ; Convert ax to ASCII
189:           pop     di                      ; Restore bx and di
190:           pop     bx
191:           ret                             ; Return to caller
192:   ENDP    SBinToAscDec
193:   %NEWPAGE
194:   ;----------------------------------------------------------------
195:   ; BinToAscBin   Convert binary values to ASCII binary strings
196:   ;----------------------------------------------------------------
197:   ; Input:
198:   ;        Same as BinToAscHex
199:   ; Output:
200:   ;        none
201:   ; Registers:
202:   ;        ax, cx (indirectly)
203:   ;----------------------------------------------------------------
204:   PROC    BinToAscBin
205:           push    bx              ; Save bx on stack
206:           mov     bx, 2           ; Set base = 2 (binary)
```

```
207:          call    NumToAscii    ; Convert ax to ASCII
208:          pop     bx            ; Restore bx
209:          ret                   ; Return to caller
210: ENDP     BinToAscBin
211: %NEWPAGE
212: ;----------------------------------------------------------------
213: ; ChToBase       Return number base for string
214: ;----------------------------------------------------------------
215: ; Note:
216: ;        Private subroutine for AscToBin. Don't call directly.
217: ; Input:
218: ;        si = pointer to null terminator at end of string
219: ;        Note: assumes length of string >= 1
220: ; Output:
221: ;        bx = 2(binary), 10(decimal/default), 16(hexadecimal)
222: ;        si = address of last probable digit character in string
223: ; Registers:
224: ;        bx, dl, si
225: ;----------------------------------------------------------------
226: PROC     ChToBase
227:          mov     dl, [byte si - 1] ; Get last char of string
228:          mov     bx, 16          ; Preset base to 16 (hexadecimal)
229:          cmp     dl, 'H'         ; Is it a hex string?
230:          je      @@10            ; Jump if hex
231:          mov     bx, 2           ; Preset base to 2 (binary)
232:          cmp     dl, 'B'         ; Is it a binary string?
233:          je      @@10            ; Jump if binary
234:          mov     bx, 10          ; Preset base to 10 (decimal)
235:          cmp     dl, 'D'         ; Is it a decimal string?
236:          jne     @@20            ; Jump if NOT decimal
237: @@10:
238:          dec     si              ; Adjust si to last probable digit
239: @@20:
240:          ret                     ; Return to caller
241: ENDP     ChToBase
242: %NEWPAGE
243: ;----------------------------------------------------------------
244: ; AscToNum       Convert ASCII characters to binary
245: ;----------------------------------------------------------------
246: ; Note:
247: ;        Private subroutine for AscToBin. Don't call directly.
248: ; Input:
249: ;        ax = initial value (0)
250: ;        bx = number base (2 = binary, 10 = decimal, 16 = hexadecimal)
251: ;        di = address of unsigned string (any format)
252: ;        si = address of last probable digit char in string
253: ; Output:
254: ;        cf = 0 : ax = unsigned value
255: ;        cf = 1 : bad character in string (ax is meaningless)
```

```
256: ; Registers:
257: ;       ax, cx, dx, si
258: ;-----------------------------------------------------------
259: PROC    AscToNum
260:         mov     cx, 1           ; Initialize multiplier
261: @@10:
262:         cmp     si, di          ; At front of string?
263:         je      @@99            ; Exit if at front (cf = 0)
264:         dec     si              ; Do next char to left
265:         mov     dl, [byte si]   ; Load char into dl
266:         call    ValCh           ; Convert dl to value in dx
267:         jc      @@99            ; Exit if error (bad char)
268:         push    cx              ; Save cx on stack
269:         xchg    ax, cx          ; ax = multiplier; cx = partial value
270:         mul     dx              ; dxax <- digit value * multiplier
271:         add     cx, ax          ; cx <- cx + ax (new partial value)
272:         pop     ax              ; Restore multiplier to ax
273:         mul     bx              ; dxax <- multiplier * base
274:         xchg    ax, cx          ; ax=partial value; cx=new multiplier
275:         jmp     @@10            ; do next digit
276: @@99:
277:         ret                     ; Return to caller
278: ENDP    AscToNum
279: %NEWPAGE
280: ;-----------------------------------------------------------
281: ; AscToBin       Convert ASCII strings to binary values
282: ;-----------------------------------------------------------
283: ; Input:
284: ;       di = ASCIIZ string to convert to binary
285: ;           'H' at end of string = hexadecimal
286: ;           'B' at end of string = binary
287: ;           'D' or digit at end of string = decimal
288: ;           '-' at s[0] indicates negative number
289: ;       Note: no blanks allowed in string
290: ; Output:
291: ;       cf = 1 : bad character in string (ax undefined)
292: ;       cf = 0 : ax = value of string
293: ;       Note: chars in string converted to uppercase
294: ;       Note: null strings set ax to 0
295: ; Registers:
296: ;       ax
297: ;-----------------------------------------------------------
298: PROC    AscToBin
299:         push    bx              ; Save modified registers
300:         push    cx              ; (some of these are changed
301:         push    dx              ;  in subroutines called by
302:         push    si              ;  this procedure)
303:
```

```
304:          call     StrUpper       ; Convert string to uppercase
305:          call     StrLength      ; Set cx to length of string at di
306:          xor      ax, ax         ; Initialize result to 0 (cf = 0)
307:          jcxz     @@99           ; Exit if length = 0. ax = 0, cf = 0
308:          mov      si, di         ; Address string at di with si
309:          add      si, cx         ; Advance si to null at end of string
310:          cmp      [byte di], '-' ; Check for minus sign
311:          pushf                   ; Save result of compare
312:          jne      @@10           ; Jump if minus sign not found
313:          inc      di             ; Advance di past minus sign
314: @@10:
315:          call     ChToBase       ; Set bx = number base; si to last digit
316:          call     AscToNum       ; Convert ASCII (base bx) to number
317:          rcl      bx, 1          ; Preserve cf by shifting into bx
318:          popf                    ; Restore flags from minus-sign check
319:          jne      @@20           ; Jump if minus sign was not found
320:          neg      ax             ;  else form two's complement of ax
321:          dec      di             ;  and restore di to head of string
322: @@20:
323:          rcr      bx, 1          ; Restore cf result from AscToNum
324: @@99:
325:          pop      si             ; Restore registers
326:          pop      dx
327:          pop      cx
328:          pop      bx
329:          ret                     ; Return to caller
330: ENDP     AscToBin
331:
332:
333:          END                     ; End of module
```

Using the BINASC Module

There are eight subroutines in BINASC that you can call from your own programs. (See lines 19–21.) Two other subroutines are called by the routines in the module. The following notes describe each subroutine and list several sample program fragments. After this section are two full programs that also demonstrate how to use the routines described here.

HexDigit (24–42)

HexDigit converts a 4-bit value in register dl to the equivalent ASCII hex digit. You probably won't need to call this routine, although you certainly can if you find a purpose for it. Other routines in the module call HexDigit as part of their algorithms to convert longer binary values to ASCII.

ASCII digits 0 through 9 have the hexadecimal values 030h through 039h. As a result of this clever design, adding hex 30h converts any single digit to ASCII. The value 04h is 34h in ASCII, 08h is 038h, and so on. Also, to convert an ASCII digit character to its equivalent binary value is a simple matter of reversing the process, subtracting 30h.

Unfortunately, this neat plan fails to accommodate the 16 hexadecimal symbols 0–9 and A–F, requiring HexDigit to check at line 35 if dl is less than 10 decimal. If not, line 37 performs the conversion, changing the values 0Ah, 0Bh, 0Ch, 0Dh, 0Eh, and 0Fh into the correct ASCII character, A–F. Otherwise, the `or` instruction at line 40 inserts 30h into the value, converting the decimal digits 0–9 to ASCII.

> Note: `HexDigit` assumes that the most significant four bits are 0. In other words, `dl` must be limited to the range 0 to 15 or the results with not be correct.

ValCh (44–70)

`ValCh` reverses what `HexDigit` does, converting ASCII digit characters 0–9 and A–F into equivalent binary values. Because this routine is used to convert strings in various number bases, the code checks for characters that do not belong to the specified base in `bx`. To use `ValCh`, assign a digit character to `dl` and the number base to `bx`—2 for binary, 10 for decimal, or 16 for hexadecimal:

```
mov  dl, 'A'   ; Character to convert
mov  bx, 16    ; Number base = hex
call ValCh     ; Convert dl to binary in dx
```

`ValCh` returns the converted value in register `dx`. If a bad character is detected, flag `cf` is set to 1, in which case the value in `dx` should not be trusted. Usually, you should follow `ValCh` with a conditional jump that tests for this:

```
call ValCh     ; Convert char in dl to value in dx
jc   Error     ; Jump if bad digit detected
```

The procedure uses a few methods that may not be obvious on a casual reading. Lines 57–59 check for a hex character A–F, converting these digits to the ASCII characters with values 03Ah through 03Fh. (You might call these values pseudo-hex characters.) After this step, `dl` holds either an illegal character or a value in the range 030h through 03Fh, simplifying the upcoming conversion.

The next step is to convert the value in `dl` to binary by removing 030h (line 61). As explained in the comments to `HexDigit`, subtracting 030h converts characters to binary. In this case, the subtraction works also for the pseudo-hex characters from the previous steps.

The instructions at lines 65–66 complete the conversion by zeroing the upper half of `dx`—using the typical 8086 `xor` method. After this, `dx` is compared to the number base in `bx`. As long as the result is less than the base, the value is within range; otherwise, the original character must have been illegal. Unfortunately, this comparison leaves error flag `cf` in the opposite state that's needed, a problem easily fixed by the `cmc` instruction at line 68, which complements the carry flag, toggling it from 1 to 0 or from 0 to 1. This is also required if the test at line 62 detects an ASCII character value not in the range 030h through 03Fh.

NumToASCII (72–125)

NumToASCII is a general-purpose binary number to ASCII converter that you can use to convert values to ASCII strings in any number base from 2 to 16. Because NumToASCII requires considerable effort and planning to use correctly, you might want to call other routines such as BinToASCHex and BinToAscDec, which call NumToASCII to perform their conversions. I'll explain these routines in a moment. You should at least study NumToASCII's code, if only to understand how the programming operates.

Lines 76–85 list NumToASCII's register requirements along with a few important notes. The procedure assumes that register ax holds the value to convert, bx equals the number base (as explained for ValCh), cx equals the minimum number of digit characters to insert in the string, and es:di addresses a string variable large enough to hold the result. A few hints about these requirements will help you to understand the programming:

- For safety, make sure your string variable is at least 5 bytes long for hex values, 6 bytes for decimal values, and 17 bytes for binary values. These lengths ensure that the result will fit and include 1 extra byte for the all-important string terminator.

- Set cx to 1 if you want a zero value to be converted to '0' and not a blank string. If cx and the value to convert are both 0, the result is a zero-length string.

- The base in bx is not limited to 2, 10, and 16. You can convert binary values to octal by setting bx to 8, or to other bases as well. Register bx must be in the range 2–16.

- The usual numeric qualifying characters *b, d,* and *h* that end values like 0FA9Ch, 01110010b, and 12345d are not inserted into the string. You must add these characters if you need them.

- NumToASCII can't convert negative (two's complement) values to strings. To do this, call SBinToAscDec, which is designed to handle signed integers.

Although longer than most subroutines in this book, NumToASCII uses a simple method to convert values to ASCII. The div instruction at line 102 repeatedly divides the subject number by the base, calling HexDigit to convert the remainder in dx to ASCII. Each of these characters is pushed onto the stack (line 104). This action repeats until register cx becomes 0 at the loop instruction (line 106). When this happens, the code at lines 108–110 checks whether ax is 0, indicating that the value has been completely converted. If ax is not 0, then cx did not specify enough digits to hold the full result, and the jump at line 110 loops back to local label @@10 for another division until this condition is satisfied. The result is to push onto the stack at least the minumum number of digits required to represent the converted number, or as many digits as cx specifies, whichever is greater.

Line 105 counts in si the number of divisions performed, a value checked at lines 111–112. If si = 0, there aren't any digits. (Both cx and ax must have been 0.) If this condition is not detected, the code at lines 113–117 pops each digit from the stack—in the reverse order that the digits were pushed—and stores the digit characters in the string variable (line 116). The final step is to insert the null terminator (line 119) before ending the procedure.

BinToAscHex (127–148)
BinToAscDec (150–166)
SBinToAscDec (168–192)
BinToAscBin (194–210)

These four routines require the same parameters; therefore, I'll describe them together. BinToAscHex converts 16-bit unsigned values to hexadecimal strings. BinToAscDec converts 16-bit unsigned values to decimal strings. SBinToAscDec converts 16-bit signed values in two's complement notation to decimal strings. And BinToAscBin converts 16-bit values to binary.

> Note: Always be sure to allocate enough string space to hold the result of converting numbers to ASCII. Be conscious that binary values might be 16 digits long. *Remember to leave an extra byte for the null terminator.* Leave extra room to be safe. To keep your code running fast, these routines do not prevent accidentally overwriting other variables in memory.

To use one of these converters, assign to **ax** an appropriate value. Set **cx** to the minimum number of digits you want in the result—at least 1 if you need zeros to come out as "0." Set **es:di** to the address of your string variable, which may be uninitialized. For example, to load a value from memory and convert to a string, you can write:

```
DATASEG
value      dw    1234          ; A 16-bit decimal value
string     db    20 DUP (?)    ; More than enough space
CODESEG
mov   ax, @data
mov   ds, ax                   ; Initialize ds and es to
mov   es, ax                   ;  address program's data segment
mov   ax, [value]              ; Get value to convert
mov   cx, 1                    ; At least one digit, please
mov   di, OFFSET string        ; Address the string variable
call  BinToAscDec              ; Convert ax to decimal string
```

You can replace the call to BinToAscDec with any of the other three routines—the rest of the steps remain the same. As a reminder, this example includes the steps to initialize **ds** and **es**. BINASC calls routines in STRINGS, which requires **es** to equal **ds**.

The conversion routines are not difficult to understand. Three of the four routines are extremely simple, merely saving **bx**, setting **bx** to the appropriate base, and calling NumToASCII to perform the actual conversion. You can, of course, call NumToASCII directly if you want.

SBinToAscDec is more complex than the other three routines because it has to deal with possible negative values in two's complement notation. Line 181 checks for negative values by comparing **ax** with 0. If **ax** is positive (MSD = 0), then the procedure performs a straight conversion, identical to BinToAscDec. If **ax** is negative, then line 183 uses **neg** to calculate the absolute value. The next line then inserts a minus sign into the string. Line 185 increments the string pointer **di** to skip the minus sign, causing the subsequent call to NumToASCII to start inserting digits at this new position. Register di is then restored at line 189. (Line 180 pushed di onto the stack for this reason.)

> Note: When calling SBinToAscDec, be sure to leave one extra character for the minus sign. The minimum string length is 7—that is, as long as the minimum number of digits requested in cx is less than or equal to 6.

ChToBase (212–241)
AscToNum (243–278)

These two routines are private to the BINASC module, and you'll probably find few direct uses for them. (You may want to examine the code, though.) ChToBase returns a value in bx equal to the probable number base for a string ending in D or 0–9 for decimal, H for hexadecimal, and B for binary. (The letters must be capitals—lowercase d, h, and b will not work here.) Register si addresses the string's null terminator on entry to ChToBase and probably addresses the last significant character in the string that follows. Other than these points, the code is self explanatory.

AscToNum performs a raw conversion from ASCII to binary, calling ValCh in a loop at lines 261–275. For each character loaded at line 265 into dl, ValCh returns the equivalent value or indicates an error by setting cf. The code at lines 268–274 multiplies the temporary result by the multiplier (initialized at line 260), which is in turn multiplied by the number base (line 273). Repeating these steps increases the multiplier by the power of each successive column, multiplying that result by the value of the digit character in each column until done. Most of the instructions in this section are here to perform some fancy footwork so that the correct values appear in the necessary registers at the right times. For a better understanding of how this works, execute this section in Turbo Debugger and pay close attention to the register values.

AscToBin (280–330)

Call AscToBin to convert strings to binary values. The string format must be ASCIIZ and may end in d or a digit for decimal values, h for hexadecimal, or b for binary. Set es:di to the address of the string to convert. After AscToBin finishes, the carry flag cf indicates if the result in ax is valid (cf = 0) or if an illegal character was detected in the string (cf = 1). No blanks are allowed in the string, which is converted to uppercase. (Use StrCopy in STRINGS to copy the original string if you don't want this to happen.) Zero-length strings set ax to 0. The following illustrates the various string formats accepted by AscToBin:

```
DATASEG
s1    db    '12345', 0      ; Decimal string (default)
s2    db    '54321d', 0     ; Decimal string ending in d
s3    db    '-9876', 0      ; Negative decimal string
s4    db    'F19Ch', 0      ; Hexadecimal string
s5    db    '1010b', 0      ; Binary string
CODESEG
mov   di, OFFSET s1         ; Address string s1 (or s2-s5)
call  AscToBin              ; Convert string to value in ax
jc    Error                 ; Jump if error, else continue
```

As you can see from these samples, hexadecimal numbers do not require a leading digit as they do in assembly language programs. Signed integer values can range from −32,768 to +32,767. Unsigned integers can range from 0 to 65,535. Unusual values in the range −65,535 to −32,769 are illegal but do not cause errors. These values and others outside the allowable ranges "wrap around" to equivalent binary values.

The procedure operates by calling StrUpper and StrLength in STRINGS to convert the string to uppercase and to set cx to the string length. If cx is 0, the procedure ends (see line 307) with ax equal to 0. If the string length is not 0, lines 308–313 check if the first character is a minus sign, saving the result of the comparison at line 310 on the stack with a pushf instruction. ChToBase (line 315) then sets bx to the appropriate number base by testing the end of the string for a D, H, or B character. Then AscToNum performs the actual conversion to binary. After this, the flags from the minus-sign comparison are restored (line 318) and the value in ax is negated to two's complement notation (line 320) if a minus sign had been found. Notice how this plan allows converting both unsigned and signed integer ranges with the same code—65,535 and −1 are both correctly converted to the same binary value.

Two rotate instructions demonstrate one way to preserve the carry flag, which indicates AscToBin's success or failure. Line 317 rotates bx once to the left, shifting the carry flag into bx's LSD. This must be done because the very next instruction (popf) could change cf, the result of calling AscToNum. Later at line 323, the saved carry flag is rotated back into cf with rcr—a neat trick that works, if you can spare a register.

Putting BINASC to Work

Two example programs demonstrate how you can use BINASC to convert values to strings. Program 6-4, EQUIP.ASM, also defines a RECORD variable (line 20) to extract bit fields from a system variable that indicates the kind of equipment attached to your computer. The program uses routines from BINASC and STRIO and indirectly from STRINGS, which must be installed in MTA.LIB. Assemble and link the program with the commands:

```
tasm equip
tlink equip,,, mta
equip
```

Note: Type line 20 all on one line. Due to space limitations, line 20 is printed in this book as two lines.

Program 6-4 *EQUIP.ASM*

```
1:  %TITLE "Display PC Equipment Information"
2:
3:          IDEAL
4:          DOSSEG
5:          MODEL   small
6:          STACK   256
7:
8:
```

```
 9:   ;-----    Equates
10:
11:   EOS       EQU     0         ; End of string terminator
12:   cr        EQU     13        ; ASCII carriage return
13:   lf        EQU     10        ; ASCII line feed
14:
15:
16:   ;-----    Define byte records with fields for equipment information
17:
18:   ; !! NOTE : Type line 20 on ONE line !!
19:
20:   RECORD Equip printers:2, x:1, game:1, ports:3, y:1, drives:2, mode:2,
--:   ram:2, z:1, disk:1
21:
22:
23:   ;-----    Define masks for isolating individual bit fields
24:
25:   ;------------------------------------------
26:   ; AND Mask                    Field
27:   ;------------------------------------------
28:   maskPrinters    =      MASK    printers
29:   maskGame        =      MASK    game
30:   maskPorts       =      MASK    ports
31:   maskDrives      =      MASK    drives
32:   maskMode        =      MASK    mode
33:   maskDisk        =      MASK    disk
34:
35:
36:           DATASEG
37:
38:   exitCode        db      0
39:
40:   welcome         db      cr,lf,'Equipment determination'
41:                   db      cr,lf,'(C) 1989 by Tom Swan',cr,lf,lf,EOS
42:
43:   strPrinters     db      'Number of printers ........ ', EOS
44:   strGame         db      'Game I/O port ............. ', EOS
45:   strPorts        db      'Number of RS232 ports ..... ', EOS
46:   strDrives       db      'Disk drives (minus 1) ..... ', EOS
47:   strMode         db      'Initial video mode ........ ', EOS
48:   strDisk         db      'Has disk drive (1 = yes) .. ', EOS
49:
50:   string          db      40 DUP (?)       ; Work string
51:
52:
53:           CODESEG
54:
55:   ;-----    From STRIO.OBJ and BINASC.OBJ
56:
57:           EXTRN   BinToAscDec:proc, StrWrite:proc, NewLine:proc
58:
```

```
59:   Start:
60:           mov     ax, @data       ; Initialize ds to address
61:           mov     ds, ax          ;  of data segment
62:           mov     es, ax          ; Make es = ds
63:
64:           mov     di, OFFSET welcome      ; Address welcome message
65:           call    StrWrite                ; Display message
66:           int     11h                     ; BIOS equipment determination
67:           mov     bx, ax                  ; Save information in bx
68:
69:           mov     di, OFFSET strPrinters  ; Address item label
70:           mov     dx, maskPrinters        ; Assign AND mask
71:           mov     cl, printers            ; Assign shift count
72:           call    ShowInfo                ; Display label and info
73:
74:           mov     di, OFFSET strGame      ; Next item
75:           mov     dx, maskGame
76:           mov     cl, game
77:           call    ShowInfo
78:
79:           mov     di, OFFSET strPorts     ; Next item
80:           mov     dx, maskPorts
81:           mov     cl, ports
82:           call    ShowInfo
83:
84:           mov     di, OFFSET strDrives    ; Next item
85:           mov     dx, maskDrives
86:           mov     cl, drives
87:           call    ShowInfo
88:
89:           mov     di, OFFSET strMode      ; Next item
90:           mov     dx, maskMode
91:           mov     cl, mode
92:           call    ShowInfo
93:
94:           mov     di, OFFSET strDisk      ; Next item
95:           mov     dx, maskDisk
96:           mov     cl, disk
97:           call    ShowInfo
98:
99:   Exit:
100:          mov     ah, 04Ch                ; DOS function: Exit program
101:          mov     al, [exitCode]          ; Return exit code value
102:          int     21h                     ; Call DOS. Terminate program
103:  %NEWPAGE
104:  ;-----------------------------------------------------------------
105:  ; ShowInfo        Display label and equipment value
106:  ;-----------------------------------------------------------------
107:  ; Input:
108:  ;       bx = Equipment data from int 11h
109:  ;       cl = Bit field shift count
```

```
110:    ;          dx = Bit field AND mask
111:    ;          di = Address of label string
112:    ; Output:
113:    ;          label and data value displayed
114:    ; Registers:
115:    ;          ax, cx
116:    ;--------------------------------------------------------------
117:    PROC    ShowInfo
118:            mov      ax, bx              ; Assign equipment value to ax
119:            and      ax, dx              ; Isolate bit field in ax
120:            shr      ax, cl              ; Shift field far right in ax
121:            call     StrWrite            ; Display label at di
122:            mov      di, OFFSET string   ; Address work string
123:            mov      cx, 1               ; Request at least 1 digit
124:            call     BinToAscDec         ; Convert ax to ASCIIZ string
125:            call     StrWrite            ; Display string
126:            call     NewLine             ; Start a new line
127:            ret                          ; Return to caller
128:    ENDP    ShowInfo
129:
130:            END      Start       ; End of program / entry point
```

How EQUIP Works   The mask constants at lines 28–33 are used to extract each of the Equip RECORD's fields as defined at line 20. The ShowInfo subroutine at lines 104–128 does the work, using dx as the mask value. Most of the program is concerned with making calls to this routine (see lines 69–97). Line 66 calls a BIOS (Basic Input/Output System) ROM routine via interrupt 11h, which all PCs support, to load the system configuration into register ax.

   The ShowInfo subroutine calls BinToAscDec to convert the masked and shifted value in ax to a string for displaying with a call to StrWrite (line 125). Figure 6-5 shows a sample run of the program.

```
Equipment determination
(C) 1989 by Tom Swan

Number of printers ........ 1
Game I/O port ............. 0
Number of RS232 ports ..... 2
Disk drives (minus 1) ..... 0
Initial video mode ........ 2
Has disk drive (1 = yes) .. 1
```

Figure 6-5 *Sample run of Program 6-4, EQUIP.ASM.*

Programming a Number Base Converter

Putting together many of the ideas in this chapter, Program 6-5, CON-VERT.ASM, is a useful utility that you can use to convert values among binary, decimal, and hexadecimal number bases. The program demonstrates how to use many of the procedures in the BINASC module. Figure 6-6 shows a sample CONVERT session.

```
Convert binary, hexadecimal, decimal values
(c) 1989 by Tom Swan
Press Enter to quit.

Value to convert? 745

Binary ............. : 0000001011101001
Hexadecimal ........ : 02E9
Unsigned decimal ... : 745
Signed decimal ..... : 745

Value to convert? face

**ERROR: Illegal character in string

Value to convert? faceh

Binary ............. : 1111101011001110
Hexadecimal ........ : FACE
Unsigned decimal ... : 64206
Signed decimal ..... : -1330
```

Figure 6-6 *Sample run of Program 6-5, CONVERT.ASM.*

Because most of the groundwork is done by the STRINGS, STRIO, and BINASC modules, which should be in your MTA.LIB file, the CONVERT program is mostly a series of call instructions to the appropriate subroutines. Just about every other instruction is a mov to prepare registers for these calls. As a result, you should have little trouble reading the program and, by studying the comments, understanding what each line does. Assemble, link, and run CONVERT with the commands:

```
tasm convert
tlink convert,,, mta
convert
```

Program 6-5 *CONVERT.ASM*

```
1:  %TITLE "Convert Binary, Hexadecimal, Decimal Numbers"
2:
3:          IDEAL
4:          DOSSEG
5:          MODEL   small
6:          STACK   256
7:
```

```
 8:  ;-----   Equates
 9:
10:  EOS     EQU     0               ; End of string
11:  cr      EQU     13              ; ASCII carriage return
12:  lf      EQU     10              ; ASCII line feed
13:  maxLen  EQU     40              ; Maximum entry string length
14:
15:
16:          DATASEG
17:
18:  exitCode        db      0       ; DOS error code
19:
20:  welcome db      cr,lf,'Convert binary, hexadecimal, decimal values'
21:          db      cr,lf,'(c) 1989 by Tom Swan',cr,lf
22:          db      cr,lf,'Press Enter to quit.',cr,lf,EOS
23:  prompt  db      cr,lf,lf,'Value to convert? ', EOS
24:  error   db      cr,lf,'**ERROR: Illegal character in string',EOS
25:  binary  db      cr,lf,'Binary ............. : ',EOS
26:  hex     db      cr,lf,'Hexadecimal ........ : ',EOS
27:  decimal db      cr,lf,'Unsigned decimal ... : ',EOS
28:  sdecimal db     cr,lf,'Signed decimal ..... : ',EOS
29:
30:  value   dw      ?                       ; Result of AscToBin
31:  response db     maxLen + 1 DUP (?)      ; String for user response
32:
33:
34:          CODESEG
35:
36:  ;-----   From STRINGS.OBJ & STRIO.OBJ
37:
38:          EXTRN   StrLength:proc, StrRead:proc
39:          EXTRN   StrWrite:proc, NewLine:proc
40:
41:  ;-----   From BINASC.OBJ
42:
43:          EXTRN   BinToAscHex:proc, SBinToAscDec:proc, BinToAscDec:proc
44:          EXTRN   BinToAscBin:proc, AscToBin:proc
45:
46:  Start:
47:          mov     ax, @data               ; Initialize ds to address
48:          mov     ds, ax                  ;  of data segment
49:          mov     es, ax                  ; Make es = ds
50:
51:          mov     di, OFFSET welcome      ; Display welcome message
52:          call    StrWrite
53:
54:  ;-----   Prompt for value to convert
55:
```

```
 56:   Again:
 57:           mov     di, OFFSET prompt        ; Display prompt string
 58:           call    StrWrite
 59:           mov     di, OFFSET response      ; Get user response
 60:           mov     cx, maxLen               ; Maximum string length
 61:           call    StrRead
 62:           call    NewLine                  ; Start new display line
 63:           call    StrLength                ; Did user press Enter?
 64:           jcxz    Exit                     ; Exit if yes (cx = 0)
 65:
 66:   ;-----  Convert entered chars to binary
 67:
 68:           call    AscToBin                 ; Convert string to ax
 69:           mov     [value], ax              ; Save result in variable
 70:           jnc     Continue                 ; Jump if cf is 0--no error
 71:           mov     di, OFFSET error         ; Else display error message
 72:           call    StrWrite
 73:           jmp     Again                    ; Let user try again
 74:
 75:   ;-----  Convert binary value to various string number formats
 76:
 77:   Continue:
 78:           mov     di, OFFSET binary        ; Display binary label
 79:           call    StrWrite
 80:           mov     ax, [value]              ; Get value to convert
 81:           mov     cx, 16                   ; Minimum number of digits
 82:           mov     di, OFFSET response      ; Use same string for result
 83:           call    BinToAscBin              ; Convert to binary digits
 84:           call    StrWrite                 ; Display result
 85:
 86:           mov     di, OFFSET hex           ; Display hex label
 87:           call    StrWrite
 88:           mov     ax, [value]              ; Get value to convert
 89:           mov     cx, 4                    ; Minimum number of digits
 90:           mov     di, OFFSET response      ; Use same string for result
 91:           call    BinToAscHex              ; Convert to hex digits
 92:           call    StrWrite                 ; Display result
 93:
 94:           mov     di, OFFSET decimal       ; Display decimal label
 95:           call    StrWrite
 96:           mov     ax, [value]              ; Get value to convert
 97:           mov     cx, 1                    ; Minimum number of digits
 98:           mov     di, OFFSET response      ; Use same string for result
 99:           call    BinToAscDec              ; Convert to decimal digits
100:           call    StrWrite                 ; Display result
101:
102:           mov     di, OFFSET sdecimal      ; Display signed decimal label
103:           call    StrWrite
104:           mov     ax, [value]              ; Get value to convert
105:           mov     cx, 1                    ; Minimum number of digits
```

```
106:          mov     di, OFFSET response    ; Use same string for result
107:          call    SBinToAscDec           ; Convert to signed decimal
108:          call    StrWrite               ; Display result
109:          jmp     Again                  ; Repeat until done
110:  Exit:
111:          mov     ah, 04Ch               ; DOS function: Exit program
112:          mov     al, [exitCode]         ; Return exit code value
113:          int     21h                    ; Call DOS. Terminate program
114:
115:          END     Start       ; End of program / entry point
```

Summary

Structures are not variables; they're schematics that you can use to create multifield variables. A structure definition begins with **STRUC** and ends with **ENDS**. Default field values in the definition can optionally be overridden in a variable of the structure's design. To refer to the fields of a structure, write the structure variable's name, a period, and the field name. String fields in Ideal mode are padded with the default characters defined in the structure definition.

Decimal is the normal radix (number base) in assembly language programs. Hex values must begin with one decimal digit and end with b. Binary values end with b. Decimal values end with nothing or d. You can change the radix with the **RADIX** directive.

Turbo Assembler lets you specify signed integers in the range $-32,678$ to $65,535$, but values in the ranges $-32,768$ to -1 and $32,768$ to $65,535$ are represented identically in binary. You can declare floating point numbers in IEEE format with the **dt** directive, although using floating point values in assembly language is difficult. The same directive can create binary-coded-decimal (BCD) numbers, which pack two digits into single bytes for numbers up to 20 digits long. BCD numbers are useful in business calculations because they avoid round-off errors that can occur in the results of floating point expressions.

Although assembly language lacks built-in array mechanisms, the base- and indexed-addressing modes can be used to read and write individual array elements. There are many ways to create arrays in memory and, with the **LABEL** and **REPT** directives, you can even build arrays with automatically assigned values. The goal of array indexing is to calculate the address of an individual arrayed value. This is easiest to do when array element sizes are 1 byte or a power of 2.

Unions appear to be identical to structures but are declared with the **UNION** directive. A union's fields overlay each other in the union variable, differing from a structure where fields are distinct. Combinations of structures and unions make it possible to create complex data structures in assembly language.

The **RECORD** directive declares packed bit-field bytes and words. Field names in a record are constants that represent the number of shifts required to move field values to the rightmost position in a register or variable. The **MASK** operator converts a bit-field constant to a binary mask that can be used with logical instructions such as **and** and **or** to extract and combine bit-field values.

Turbo Assembler's predefined equates can be used, among other things, to create an automatic version stamp every time a program is assembled.

The BINASC module in this chapter converts signed and unsigned binary values to ASCIIZ strings and also converts ASCIIZ strings in three number bases to binary values. The routines are particularly useful for converting numeric input entered in ASCII at the keyboard into binary values for processing.

Exercises

6-1. Create a structure named **time** with fields for **hours**, **minutes**, and **seconds**.

6-2. Declare variables with predefined 24-hour-clock values for 10:30:45, 14:00:00, 16:30, and midnight.

6-3. Create a variable named **theTime** of type **time** from exercise #6-1 and write the assembly language instructions: to set the time to 15:45:12; to increment the hour; to reset the time to 00:00:00; and to copy **theTime** to a second variable **oldTime**.

6-4. Assume the default radix has been changed to 16. What are the decimal values of: 00001011, 10000000b, 1234, 4321d, FACE, and 00FF?

6-5. Create variables for the floating point values 2.5, 88.999, and 0.141. Create binary-coded-decimal values for 125,000 and 1,250,500. What is the largest possible BCD value you can create?

6-6. Create arrays of 45 two-byte words; 100 four-byte (doubleword) values; 1024 bytes; and 75 binary-coded-decimal values. How many bytes do each of your arrays occupy in memory?

6-7. Create a word index variable and, using this value, write instructions to load **bx** with the address of any element for the four arrays in exercise #6-6.

6-8. Define a union similar to Figure 6-3's **ByteWord**, but with fields that allow accessing values as bytes, words, and doublewords. Show example instructions for accessing variables as any of the three types.

6-9. Design a packed record named **inventory** with four bit fields (width in bits shown in parentheses): location (3), status (1), quantity (5), and vendor (4). How many bytes does a variable with this design occupy in memory? What are the range of values each field can represent?

6-10. Write instructions to perform these operations on your **inventory** record from question #9: create a variable named **inv** of type **inventory**, set **location** to 3, set **status** to 1, add 6 to **quantity**, load **vendor** field into dh, toggle the **status** field, and zero all fields in the record. Hint: Use the MASK operator to create AND masks.

6-11. Write a program ADDHEX.ASM to display the sum of two hexadecimal values entered at the keyboard. Use routines as needed from the BINASC, STRINGS, and STRIO modules in your answer.

6-12. Add an automatic version stamp to your answer in exercise #6-11.

Projects

6-1. Write routines to pack and unpack BCD numbers, converting a standard dt 2-digit-per-byte format to a 20-byte variable containing 1 digit per byte.

6-2. Write a logical calculator to display the results of performing AND, OR, XOR, NOT, NEG, SHL, and SHR operations on binary values. Users should be able to enter values and instructions at the keyboard.

6-3. [Advanced] Write a new version of BINASC named BINASC32 to handle 32-bit decimal integers.

6-4. Write a program to create an array of string records. Then write subroutines to let people enter and display field values in each record. (Note: Don't be concerned with saving your data on disk, a subject covered in chapter 9.)

6-5. Construct general-purpose subroutines to pack and unpack bit fields in record variable words. Your code should work with both word and byte values.

6-6. Write a general-purpose array index address calculator that returns the offset address for any array value of any byte size.

7 Input and Output

In This Chapter

Reading from the DOS standard input file; writing to the DOS standard output file; redirecting I/O; filtering Ctrl-C and other control codes; detecting key presses; reading function keys; how to flush (empty) the type-ahead buffer; standard I/O and DOS handles; writing a filter shell program; using the location counter symbol; printing text and selecting special printer features; speeding display output with direct-video memory techniques; how characters and attributes are formatted and stored in video memory buffers; positioning the cursor; eliminating CGA snow; introducing I/O ports; plus direct-video display and keyboard object-code modules

Standard Input and Output

If you want your programs to run on as many different DOS systems as possible, not only IBM PCs, you must use standard methods for reading input from the keyboard and for writing output to the display—not to mention communicating with other devices such as printers and plotters.

DOS provides several standard I/O functions, the simplest of which read and write one character at a time. For example, you can read a character from the standard input device into register al with two simple instructions:

```
mov  ah, 1       ; Specify DOS "Character Input" function
int  21h         ; Call DOS. Character returned in al
```

If the standard output device is the main console, as it usually is, reading input this way echoes each key press to the display. Because DOS I/O is redirectable, however, there's no guarantee that the input data will come from the keyboard. Unknown to the program, the person using the computer may have executed a command to tell DOS to change the standard input file from the keyboard to a disk file:

```
program <afile.txt
```

The advantage of using DOS functions to read data from the standard input file is that your program does not have to perform any special actions to permit someone changing from where input comes or to where output goes. For most purposes, the program is blissfully unaware of physical I/O device details. If someone wants to print a program's output instead of seeing it on screen, that's fine with DOS and the program. Similarly, to write a single character to the standard output device takes only a few simple commands:

```
mov   ah, 2          ; Specify DOS "Character Output" function
mov   dl, [thechar]  ; Move character into dl
int   21h            ; Call DOS
```

The character for output is loaded into dl from a byte variable theChar (not shown). Once again, because output for DOS function 2 may be redirected, there's no guarantee that this code will write a character to the display. For example, someone could execute a command such as the following to send your program's output to a serial output port, which might be attached to any sort of device:

```
program >com1
```

Taking a Break DOS functions 1 and 2 check whether Ctrl-C—the break command—was typed some time earlier. If so, DOS executes interrupt 23h, which halts the program. (Chapter 10 explains interrupts in more detail. As used here, an interrupt is similar to a subroutine call.) To avoid unexpectedly breaking out of a program when someone presses Ctrl-C, you have three choices:

▶ Use a different DOS function

▶ Replace the code for interrupt 23h with your own Ctrl-C handler

▶ Tell the device driver to ignore Ctrl-C key presses

Usually, the first choice is the best—other input methods are available that pass Ctrl-C back to your program just like any other key press. Writing your own interrupt handler is probably more work than necessary. The third choice takes more work (as I'll explain later in this section) but may be useful in some cases. A *device driver* is a program in a highly specialized form that interfaces with physical devices such as keyboards, printers, and displays. Many good DOS references explain this format.

Always remember that both of the standard input *and output* character functions 1 and 2 check for Ctrl-C key presses. When this happens due to a call to the DOS input function 1, your program never receives the Ctrl-C. When a Ctrl-C is detected during a call to DOS output function 2, the character in dl is passed to the standard output file *before* the Ctrl-C check takes place.

These checks for special characters are called *filters* because of the way they filter out certain key presses and characters for special action. In addition to filtering Ctrl-C, input and output functions 1 and 2 also filter other control codes, performing the actions listed in Table 7-1. Except for Ctrl-C, Ctrl-P, and Ctrl-S, which apply only to output, these actions occur for both input and output functions 1 and 2.

Unfiltered Input When you don't want to filter Ctrl-C and other control codes, you can use one of two functions:

- ▶ DOS function 6: Direct console I/O
- ▶ DOS function 7: Unfiltered input without echo

Function 6 is included in DOS mostly to accommodate programs converted from CP/M, which has a similar function for direct console I/O. Because there are other, and probably better, ways to access input and output devices directly in DOS, there's rarely any good reason to use function 6. Instead, it's usually best to employ function 7 to read characters quietly—that is, without echoing key presses to the standard output device and without filtering Ctrl-C. Except for the function number, the code is identical to the code for function 1:

```
mov  ah, 7        ; Specify DOS "Input without echo"
int  21h          ; Call DOS. Character returned in al
```

This method does not check for Ctrl-C or Ctrl-Break key presses and, therefore, prevents people from ending programs prematurely. Other control codes in Table 7-1 are returned to your program as normal key presses. To add filtering to input without echoing characters to the standard output device, use function 8, which generates the interrupt 23h break signal to end the program if DOS detects a Ctrl-C or Ctrl-Break key press. Except for this action, function 8 is identical to function 7.

Table 7-1 *Standard I/O Control Codes*

Ctrl Key	ASCII Code	Action
Ctrl-C	03	Generate interrupt 23h (break)
Ctrl-G	07	Ring the bell
Ctrl-H	08	Nondestructive backspace
Ctrl-I	09	Tab forward
Ctrl-J	10	Line feed (with possible scroll)
Ctrl-M	13	Carriage return
Ctrl-P	16	Toggle PRN device on/off
Ctrl-S	19	Stop output until next key press

Unfiltered Output As explained earlier, you can write ASCII$ strings with DOS function 9. Besides requiring the strange ASCII$ dollar-sign string format, function 9 (as function 2) detects Ctrl-C and responds to the other control codes in Table 7-1. If you must use these functions, prevent people from breaking out of a running program by calling DOS function 44h, "Device-driver control" or IOCTL—available beginning with DOS version 2. This function lets you reprogram the output device driver to ignore Ctrl-C and Ctrl-Break key presses. First, call function 44h with al equal to 0, reading the current device control bits from the device driver:

```
mov   ax, 4400h      ; DOS function 44h, item 00: get device info
mov   bx, 1          ; Specify standard output
int   21h            ; Call DOS. Returns data in dx
```

The device driver's bit settings are now in register dx. Bit 5 of the device driver settings tells the driver whether to process all data (bit = 1), or whether to filter characters for Ctrl-C and Ctrl-Break (bit = 0). Setting bit 5 turns off filtering:

```
mov   ax, 4401h      ; DOS function 44h, item 01: set device info
xor   dh, dh         ; dh must be 0 for this function call
or    dl, 20h        ; Set bit 5--process binary data
int   21h            ; Call DOS with data in dx
```

This technique disables Ctrl-C, Ctrl-S, and Ctrl-P filtering, not only for your program but also for any other programs including DOS itself that call functions 2 and 9 to pass data to the standard output device. For instance, after reprogramming the device driver, you will not be able to press Ctrl-C to interrupt a long directory started with the DIR command. So, as the video stores say, "Be kind: Rewind"—that is, before your program ends, clear bit 5 with the identical seven previous instructions but replace or dl, 20h with and dl, 0DFh to restore Ctrl-C checking.

Waiting Around— and Around

A program that reads input via DOS functions 1, 7, and 8 can become trapped in an endless cycle, waiting for key presses until the cows come home. (As far as I can tell, they always do. But, never mind.) Many times, you'll want a program to respond to key presses when they occur but to continue other operations if no input is ready. For example, a word processor could perform a lengthy search-and-replace operation, ending early if you press the Esc key. Or a simulation could update the display, taking various actions in real time as you type commands. There are two ways to achieve these goals:

- Interrupt-driven, buffered input
- Polling

In the first method, incoming data forces the CPU to execute special code designed to store input in memory buffers for later processing. (Chapter 11 explains this method in detail.) In the second method, a program periodically polls the input device, reading input only after detecting waiting data. If no input is available, the program continues with other operations.

With polling, you must read input often enough to avoid losing characters. For example, if someone presses two keys before you check the keyboard for new input, the first key press might be lost. Fortunately, routines in the IBM PC's ROM BIOS automatically respond to key presses, storing ASCII codes in a *type-ahead buffer*. When DOS reads data from the keyboard, it actually removes characters from this buffer. As a result, the only danger is that the buffer can fill before the program requests input. Even this danger is minimized by an automatic bell that sounds, warning a speedy typist to slow down.

> Note: Remember that the type-ahead buffer stores only keyboard input. When input and output are redirected to other devices, characters are probably not buffered, and you must poll the input device often enough to avoid losing data. This is an especially exasperating problem with serial I/O, which DOS calls *auxiliary I/O*. When communicating with a remote computer, perhaps via modem, your program will almost certainly lose incoming data if it does not check for new input often enough. Even the time required for a simple disk write can cause several characters to slip by unnoticed. Consequently, it's best to use other methods for serial I/O on DOS systems and especially on IBM PCs, as explained in chapter 11's discussion of interrupt processing.

Key Press Checking

To check whether incoming data is waiting to be read, use DOS function 11, "Get Input Status," which returns al equal to 0 if no input data is ready or to 0FFh if a character is waiting to be read. (Zero and 0FFh are the only two values returned by function 11; therefore, just checking whether al equals 0 is adequate.) With this method, you can write a simple loop to call a subroutine repeatedly, processing new characters only as they become available:

```
@@10:
  call OtherStuff      ; Code to execute until char is ready
  mov  ah, 11          ; DOS function "Get Input Status"
  int  21h             ; Call DOS. Result in al
  or   al, al          ; Is al = 0?
  je   @@10            ; Jump if al = 0. No input is waiting
  mov  ah, 7           ; Else read character with no echo
  int  21h             ; Call DOS. Character returned in al
  call ProcessChar     ; Process new input data in al
  jmp  @@10            ; Play it again, Sam
```

This fragment repeatedly calls OtherStuff (not shown) until function 11 indicates that a character is ready. When a new character becomes available—probably as a result of somebody pressing a key—function 7 reads the character. It then calls ProcessChar (also not shown) to take appropriate actions, which might include ending the program on detecting the Esc or another key. In fact, this simple example could be used as the entire "main loop" of any program that needs to continue processing while responding to key presses as they become available. Unfortunately, there's a fly in the ointment: Function 11 also detects Ctrl-C and Ctrl-Break, ending the program via interrupt 23h if those keys are pressed. This effectively destroys the advantage of using function 7 to read unfiltered input. Even reprogramming the device driver as described earlier is of no help this time.

The answer is to call BIOS routine 16h instead of DOS to test whether a key press is available. When ah equals 1, this routine returns the zero flag zf equal to 1 if the type-ahead buffer is empty or to 0 if at least one character is in the buffer. In addition, if a character is waiting to be read, the BIOS routine returns the character in al and its scan code (keyboard key number) in ah. When ah initially equals 0, the same function removes and returns in ax one character from the type-ahead buffer. These routines give you the means to program completely unfiltered, quiet I/O. The previous code now becomes:

```
@@10:
  call  OtherStuff    ; Code to execute until char is ready
  mov   ah, 1         ; Select "Input Status" routine
  int   16h           ; Call BIOS keyboard I/O function
  jz    @@10          ; Jump if zf = 1. No input is waiting
  xor   ah, ah        ; Select "Read Character" routine
  int   16h           ; Call BIOS Keyboard I/O function
  call  ProcessChar   ; Process new input data in al
  jmp   @@10          ; Once more, from the top
```

With this technique, no sequence of key presses can end the program prematurely. Having solved the problem for input, another BIOS function also lets you display characters with no Ctrl-C or Ctrl-Break filtering. With this function, you can program a procedure ProcessChar to display characters read by the previous sample code:

```
PROC ProcessChar
       cmp   al, 27     ; Is al = Escape key?
       je    Exit       ; If yes, exit program
       mov   bl, 15     ; Foreground color for graphics displays
       mov   ah, 14     ; Select "Write TTY" routine
       int   10h        ; Call BIOS Video I/O function
       ret              ; Return to caller
ENDP ProcessChar
```

First, al is compared with the ASCII code for Esc (27), jumping to the Exit label (not shown) if you press the Esc key. (Providing a way to end the program is essential when not relying on DOS to end the program upon sensing Ctrl-C or Ctrl-Break.) If Esc is not detected, bl is assigned a foreground color, required only for graphics displays. Then ah is set to 14 decimal, selecting the BIOS "Write TTY" routine—so called because its simple character output resembles that of a Teletype machine, in other words, lacking facilities for positioning the cursor, changing character colors and attributes, clearing to ends of lines, and so on. Still, interrupt 10h is useful for reasonably fast output, especially when you want the program to have total control over I/O.

> Note: The BIOS Write TTY routine of interrupt 10h filters Ctrl-G (bell), Ctrl-H (backspace), Ctrl-J (line feed), and Ctrl-M as described in Table 7-1. Other control codes in Table 7-1 are displayed as graphics characters.

As with most good things in life, you pay a price by calling the ROM BIOS I/O routines. As you can see from the last several samples, the program has eliminated all calls to DOS. Consequently, the program will now run only on IBM PCs and 100% compatibles that contain the proper ROM BIOS routines. The code may not execute on plain DOS systems or under other operating systems that run pseudo-versions of DOS. Because there are so many millions of PCs installed in offices throughout the world, this may not be as severe a problem as it has been in times past. However, when using these techniques, you should at least include a warning along with your program not to attempt execution on noncompatible systems.

A more nagging problem is the loss of I/O redirection, one of DOS's most appealing goodies. Calling BIOS routines to give programs total control over character I/O means that your program users will no longer be able to redirect input to come from a text file or to send output to the printer. Many programmers consider such loss an advantage, giving their programs complete control over what is printed, what appears on display, and so forth. But, for small programs and utilities, I/O redirection is a helpful feature to have, and you may want to consider using standard DOS function calls in such cases.

Reading Function Keys

The ASCII character set directly represents only 32 control codes with values from 0 to 31, 95 symbols with values from 32 to 126, plus a delete character with the value 127 (alias, *rubout*). Including uppercase and lowercase letters, punctuation, and various Ctrl, Shift, and Alt combinations, there simply aren't enough codes to cover all the key combinations offered by even a small 83- or 84-key PC keyboard.

> Note: Although the PC extends the usual set of 128 ASCII codes with values ranging from 128 to 255, these values are reserved for graphics characters, which you can use to draw boxes, display mathematical symbols, greek letters, and arrows, among other symbols. Enter these codes by pressing and holding the Alt key, and then typing on the numeric keypad the ASCII value of the symbol you want.

To handle the special keys, the DOS input methods discussed in the previous section return two codes representing a function key. The first code, always 0, is called the *lead-in character*. When any keyboard input routine returns a 0, the next character indicates which function key was pressed. This scheme leads to code such as:

```
mov   ah, 1          ; Specify DOS "Character Input" function
int   21h            ; Call DOS. Character returned in al
or    al, al         ; Check for lead-in from keyboard
jnz   NormalChar     ; Jump to process a normal character
int   21h            ; Call DOS for next character
jnz   FunctionKey    ; Jump to process a function key
```

As this shows, two DOS calls to function 1 are required to detect and read function keys, including special keys such as Ins, Del, PgUp, PgDn, the cursor keys, and the numbered function keys F1–F10 found on all PC keyboards. Normal characters are processed by jumping to `NormalChar` (not shown); function keys by jumping to `FunctionKey` (also not shown).

> Note: The previous sample sets `ah` to 1 for only the first call to DOS with `int 21h`. There's no need to set `ah` to 1 a second time because DOS preserves all registers except those specifically returned by various functions; therefore, it's safe to assume that unused registers remain unchanged between calls to DOS. When using this trick, take care that you don't inadvertently change the function number in `ah`, or disaster is sure to strike.

Many programmers use the double-DOS-call method, but I find this to be cumbersome in practice. Even though you can detect function keys, there's still no simple way to represent these keys as plain characters, as you can other keys like A and Q. For this reason, I *map* (that is, translate) function key values to single codes, a method described later in this chapter along with the listing for a keyboard input module you can add to your library.

Flushing the Type-Ahead Buffer

When prompting for a yes or no response to a dangerous operation—formatting a disk or erasing an important disk file—it's a good idea to flush (empty) the type-ahead buffer before reading the keyboard, thereby forcing people to consider carefully their answers to your program's more serious questions. There are two ways to flush the type-ahead buffer. The first is rather obvious—simply keep reading and throwing away key presses until none is available:

```
@@10:
  mov  ah, 1       ; Select "Input Status" routine
  int  16h         ; Call BIOS keyboard I/O function
  jz   @@20        ; Jump if zf = 1. No input is waiting
  xor  ah, ah      ; Select "Read Character" routine
  int  16h         ; Read and throw away one character
  jmp  @@10        ; Jump to repeat loop
@@20:              ; Type-ahead buffer is now empty
```

This code is similar to previous samples, calling BIOS interrupt 16h with `ah` equal to 1 to test whether input is available. If there is (as indicated by `zf = 0`), `ah` is set to 0, and interrupt 16h is again called to read one character from the type-ahead buffer, repeating these steps until no more characters are available.

> Note: You can also call one of the DOS character input functions, numbers 7 or 8 usually, to flush the type-ahead buffer. Be aware that this doesn't work if input has been redirected.

Another possibility is to call a special DOS function that clears the type-ahead buffer and then executes another character-input command. If your program must run on all DOS systems, this is the method to use. First, load ah with the function number 0Ch. Then load the number of another input command into al: either 1, 6, 7, 8, or 0Ah. If using 0Ah, the "Get String" command, also set ds:dx to the address of the buffer to use for string input. Call DOS with int 21h, which flushes the type-ahead buffer and then executes the function specified in al. For example:

```
mov   ah, 0Ch          ; Select "Reset input buffer & execute"
mov   al, 7            ; 1, 6, 7, 8, or 0Ah allowed
int   21h             ; Call DOS to flush buffer and
                      ;   execute the command in al
```

Some assembly language programmers employ yet another technique to empty the type-ahead buffer, fiddling with two pointers (addresses) that keep track of the buffer's head and tail. These pointers address the beginning (head) and end (tail) of the type-ahead buffer somewhere in memory. A third pointer locates the start of the buffer. By definition, when the head and tail pointers are equal, the buffer is empty. All three pointers are located in the BIOS data segment at 0040h, an area reserved for system variables. As the following fragment demonstrates, you can use this information to empty the type-ahead buffer by setting the head and tail pointers equal to the buffer's starting address:

```
bufferStart EQU 0080h      ; Buffer-start pointer
head        EQU 001Ah      ; Head pointer
tail        EQU 001Ch      ; Tail pointer

mov   ax, 0040h            ; Address BIOS data segment
mov   ds, ax               ;  with ds register
mov   ax, [bufferStart]    ; Get buffer starting address
cli                        ; Prevent interrupts from occurring
mov   [head], ax           ; Assign address to head pointer
mov   [tail], ax           ; Head = tail, emptying the buffer
sti                        ; Allow interrupts again
```

First, segment register ds is set to the BIOS data segment beginning at 0040h. Then ax is loaded with the value stored at [bufferStart], which holds the offset address of the type-ahead buffer. Inserting this value into both the head and tail pointers empties the buffer. The cli (clear interrupt) instruction prevents a keyboard interrupt from occurring during the time that the two pointers are being adjusted. The sti again allows interrupts after the buffer is cleared.

Note: The "keyboard interrupt" referred to here is known as a *hardware interrupt*. Every time you press a key, this interrupt causes a routine in the ROM BIOS to run, reading and storing key presses in the type-ahead buffer, as previously explained. This action can happen at just about any time, independently of whatever other code is running. Because of this, interrupts are temporarily disabled while clearing the type-ahead buffer to prevent the unlikely but possible event of your pressing a key before the erasure is completed.

Introducing DOS Handles

Another useful way to move data in and out of programs is to read and write files, identified by numbers called *handles*. The word "file" refers to disk files, as well as also to devices such as the display, keyboard, and printer. Instead of writing code to access such different devices directly, you can instead read from and write to logical files assigned to the devices, employing a single set of DOS function calls to communicate with a wide variety of hardware. (We'll return to the subject of handles in chapter 9, which covers how to use handles to read and write disk files.)

When DOS loads and runs a program, it initializes several standard files. Table 7-2 lists the five handles associated with these files, showing the values that assembly language programs can use to communicate with the display, keyboard, printer, and one serial I/O channel.

When you issue a DOS command to redirect I/O, using the redirection character < to specify a new input device or file and > to specify a new output device or file, DOS closes handles 0 and 1 and then reopens these defaults to the new devices, thus switching I/O away from the usual CON device, that is, the display and keyboard. This happens before your program begins running; therefore, all you have to do is read from handle 0 and write to handle 1 to give people complete control over your program's I/O.

Handle 2 is most often used for displaying error messages. Because I/O redirection affects only handles 0 and 1 and because handle 2 normally refers to the console, when redirecting output to another device, writing to handle 2 still goes to the display. This lets you display progress and error messages without worrying whether the messages will interfere with other output. (You can write anything you want to handle 2; you don't have to use this handle for only error messages.)

Handle 3 is assigned to the first serial port, also known as COM1. But, because DOS handles serial I/O so poorly, you should probably not try to use this handle for communicating with remote systems via modems and high-speed RS-232 interfaces.

Handle 4 is associated with the printer, which may be plugged into the computer's parallel or serial ports. Some assembly language programmers use the ROM BIOS printer routine, interrupt 17h, which works only for parallel printers. While this is the normal configuration for most PC systems, many people have serial printers. Writing to the standard print device is the best way to accommodate all possible printer setups.

Table 7-2 *Standard DOS Handles*

Handle	Device Name	Device Description
0	CON	Standard input device
1	CON	Standard output device
2	CON	Standard error output device
3	AUX	Auxiliary (serial I/O) device
4	PRN	Standard listing device (printer)

Writing DOS Filters

Using standard DOS I/O file-handling techniques, you can write *filter programs* that read the standard input file, perform some operation on incoming data, and then write the modified data to the standard output file. Multiple filter programs can be combined with a special character called a *pipe*, represented by a vertical bar (|). A pipe routes the output of one filter to the input of the next filter, which can route its output to a third filter, and so on. Combining multiple filters, each with a simple purpose—for instance, sorting text lines and extracting data based on various criteria—lets you build complex on-the-spot commands to solve problems that might otherwise require custom programming.

Along with its other utility programs, DOS provides three standard filter programs: FIND, MORE, and SORT. (Refer to your DOS manuals for information on using these programs.) You can also add your own filters to this basic set. To help you get started, Program 7-1, FILTER.ASM, is a shell that handles most of the low-level details involved with filter programming. FILTER is a complete filter, reading from the standard input device and writing to the standard output device. Because the program is only a shell, it doesn't perform any useful function. After the listing, I'll explain how to modify the shell to do something worthwhile. Just so you know whether you entered the program correctly, you can assemble FILTER with the command, `tasm filter`.

> Note: If you try to run FILTER without supplying input and output files, the computer will appear to "hang." Press Ctrl-Z (the DOS "end-of-file" key) and Enter to recover.

Program 7-1 *FILTER.ASM*

```
1:  %TITLE "Filter Shell"
2:
3:          IDEAL
4:          DOSSEG
5:          MODEL   small
6:          STACK   256
7:
8:
9:  ;----- Equates
10:
11: InputHandle    EQU    0           ; Standard input handle
12: OutputHandle   EQU    1           ; Standard output handle
13: ErrOutHandle   EQU    2           ; Standard error-out handle
14: bell           EQU    07          ; ASCII bell
15: cr             EQU    13          ; ASCII carriage return
16: lf             EQU    10          ; ASCII line feed
17: eof            EQU    26          ; DOS end-of-file char (^Z)
18:
19:
```

```
20:             DATASEG
21:
22:     exitCode        DB      0                   ; I/O error code
23:
24:
25:     ;-----   Error messages
26:
27:     errMessage      DB      bell, cr, lf, 'FILTER ERROR: '
28:     lenErrMessage   =       $-errMessage
29:
30:     codeAccess      EQU     5
31:     errAccess       DB      'access denied', cr, lf
32:     lenErrAccess    =       $-errAccess
33:
34:     codeNotOpen     EQU     6
35:     errNotOpen      DB      'bad handle or file not open', cr, lf
36:     lenErrNotOpen   =       $-errNotOpen
37:
38:     codeDiskFull    EQU     29
39:     errDiskFull     DB      'disk full', cr, lf
40:     lenErrDiskFull  =       $-errDiskFull
41:
42:     errGeneral      DB      'unknown cause', cr, lf  ; Code = ?
43:     lenErrGeneral   =       $-errGeneral
44:
45:
46:     ;-----   Input buffer
47:
48:     oneChar         DB      ?           ; Holds one input character
49:
50:
51:             CODESEG
52:
53:     Start:
54:         mov     ax, @data               ; Initialize ds to address
55:         mov     ds, ax                  ;   of data segment
56:         mov     es, ax                  ; Make es = ds (optional)
57:
58:     Repeat:
59:         call    ReadChar                ; Read next character
60:         jz      Done                    ; End loop if at end-of-file
61:
62:     ;-----   Process [oneChar] here
63:
64:         call    WriteChar               ; Write processed character
65:         jnz     Repeat                  ; Repeat unless disk is full
66:         mov     [exitCode], codeDiskFull  ; Set error code
67:         jmp     Exit                    ;   and skip eof write
```

```
68:  Done:
69:          mov     [oneChar], eof        ; Write end-of-file character
70:          call    WriteChar             ;  to standard output. Do NOT
71:                                        ;  check for disk full here!
72:  Exit:
73:          cmp     [exitCode], 0         ; Check for possible error
74:          jz      @@99                  ; Jump if no error detected
75:          call    DisplayError          ;  else display error message
76:  @@99:
77:          mov     ah, 04Ch              ; DOS function: Exit program
78:          mov     al, [exitCode]        ; Return exit code value
79:          int     21h                   ; Call DOS. Terminate program
80:
81:  %NEWPAGE
82:  ;-------------------------------------------------------------------
83:  ; ReadChar      Read one character from standard input
84:  ;-------------------------------------------------------------------
85:  ; Input:
86:  ;       none
87:  ; Output:
88:  ;       zf = 0 : al = next input character (0..255)
89:  ;       zf = 1 : no more input available
90:  ; Registers:
91:  ;       ax
92:  ;-------------------------------------------------------------------
93:  PROC    ReadChar
94:          push    bx                    ; Save modified registers
95:          push    cx
96:          push    dx
97:
98:          mov     ah, 03Fh              ; Read device function number
99:          mov     bx, InputHandle       ; Specify input handle
100:         mov     cx, 1                 ; Number of chars to read
101:         mov     dx, offset oneChar    ; Store input at ds:dx
102:         int     21h                   ; Call DOS. Get input
103:         jnc     @@10                  ; Jump if no error indicated
104:         mov     [exitCode], al        ;  else save error code
105:         jmp     Exit                  ;  and exit program early
106: @@10:
107:         or      ax, ax                ; Set/clear zero flag (zf)
108:
109:         pop     dx                    ; Restore registers
110:         pop     cx
111:         pop     bx
112:         ret                           ; Return to caller
113: ENDP    ReadChar
114: %NEWPAGE
115: ;-------------------------------------------------------------------
116: ; WriteChar     Write one character to standard output
117: ;-------------------------------------------------------------------
118: ; Input:
119: ;       [oneChar] = character to write
```

```
120:  ; Output:
121:  ;          zf = 0 : character written to standard output file
122:  ;          zf = 1 : output device is full (disk output only)
123:  ; Registers:
124:  ;          ax
125:  ;-------------------------------------------------------------
126:  PROC    WriteChar
127:          push    bx                      ; Save modified registers
128:          push    cx
129:          push    dx
130:
131:          mov     ah, 040h                ; Write device function number
132:          mov     bx, OutputHandle        ; Specify output handle
133:          mov     cx, 1                   ; Number of chars to write
134:          mov     dx, offset oneChar      ; Take input from ds:dx
135:          int     21h                     ; Call DOS. Write output
136:          jnc     @@10                    ; Jump if no error detected
137:          mov     [exitCode], al          ;  else save error code
138:          jmp     Exit                    ;  and exit program early
139:  @@10:
140:          or      ax, ax                  ; Set/clear zero flag (zf)
141:
142:          pop     dx                      ; Restore registers
143:          pop     cx
144:          pop     bx
145:          ret                             ; Return to caller
146:  ENDP    WriteChar
147:  %NEWPAGE
148:  ;-------------------------------------------------------------
149:  ; DisplayError          Display error message
150:  ;-------------------------------------------------------------
151:  ; Input:
152:  ;          [exitCode] = nonzero error code
153:  ; Output:
154:  ;          none: error message sent to standard error-output device
155:  ; Registers:
156:  ;          ax, bx, cx, dx
157:  ;-------------------------------------------------------------
158:  PROC    DisplayError
159:          mov     cx, lenErrMessage       ; Length of common string
160:          mov     dx, offset errMessage   ; Address of common string
161:          call    DisplayString           ; Display first part message
162:
163:          cmp     [exitCode], codeAccess  ; Test for codeAccess err
164:          jne     @@10                    ; Jump if not this code
165:          mov     cx, lenErrAccess        ; Set string length
166:          mov     dx, offset errAccess    ; Set string address
167:          jmp     DisplayString           ; Display string
```

```
168:    @@10:
169:            cmp     [exitCode], codeNotOpen
170:            jne     @@20
171:            mov     cx, lenErrNotOpen
172:            mov     dx, offset errNotOpen
173:            jmp     DisplayString
174:    @@20:
175:            cmp     [exitCode], codeDiskFull
176:            jne     @@30
177:            mov     cx, lenErrDiskFull
178:            mov     dx, offset errDiskFull
179:            jmp     DisplayString
180:    @@30:
181:            mov     cx, lenErrGeneral       ; Other error values
182:            mov     dx, offset errGeneral
183:
184:    DisplayString:
185:            mov     ah, 040h                ; Write device function number
186:            mov     bx, ErrOutHandle        ; Specify error output handle
187:            int     21h                     ; Call DOS. Write output
188:            ret                             ; Return to caller
189:
190:    ENDP    DisplayError
191:
192:            END     Start                   ; End of program / entry point
```

How FILTER Works   FILTER uses DOS handles to read and write characters to the standard input and output devices. The program also correctly handles error conditions—including a tricky disk-full condition that many similar programs fail to detect—and illustrates a few other goodies that you can put into operation in your own code.

The three equates at lines 11–13 are assigned the values of three standard DOS handles. (See Table 7-2.) Later on, these equates are passed to appropriate DOS functions to read and write characters. Lines 27–43 illustrate a different way to declare character strings. In place of the ASCII\$ and ASCIIZ methods described before, these strings are unterminated. The first string, errMessage at line 27, creates a string preceded by bell, carriage return, and line-feed control characters. Writing this string rings the bell and starts a new display line, as well as writing the visible characters, "FILTER ERROR:." Line 28 shows how to assemble a numeric equate equal to the length of the string. Here's a similar example:

```
DATASEG
dumbJoke        db      "My Texas fleas have dogs."
lenString       =       $ - dumbJoke
```

The dollar sign (\$) is called the *location counter*. Turbo Assembler replaces \$ with the current offset address at this place in the program—in this case, relative to the data segment, although you can use this symbol in any other segment, too. Because an offset address is just a number, as is the label dumbJoke, subtracting dumbJoke from the location counter *after* the string calculates the string length. You can use the same trick with any other label to calculate structure and array sizes or even to find the number of bytes of code between two points in the code segment.

> Note: In MASM mode, you can use either an EQU directive or an equal sign to equate symbols and expressions involving the location counter $. In Ideal mode, you *must* use an equal sign—EQU will not work. The reason for this is that Ideal mode stores EQU assignments as text, evaluating expressions only later when you use the equated symbol. Equal-sign equates are evaluated at the declaration point. For the $ symbol to have the correct value, therefore, the expression must be evaluated where it is declared, not later when the symbol is used!

In FILTER, the series of strings and string lengths at lines 27–43 are error messages, associated with values assigned by EQU directives. For example, codeAccess is the error code for the string errAccess, which has the length lenErrAccess. By the way, using similar names this way is a good technique for keeping programs organized, especially when you have more than just a few symbols to track.

Lines 58–67 perform FILTER's input and output duties, repeatedly calling two subroutines ReadChar and WriteChar, reading one character from the standard input device, and storing that character in a variable oneChar (line 48). At line 62, you can insert your own programming to process this character before the call to WriteChar at line 64 sends oneChar on its way to the standard output.

Lines 68–70 add an end-of-file control character, ASCII 26 (Ctrl-Z), to the end of the output file. (Some programs require this character; others do not. It's probably best to write the marker just to be safe.)

FILTER.ASM ends by first inspecting the exitCode variable, which hasn't been used up until now. In this program, an error code may be stored in exitCode by either ReadChar or WriteChar. In that event, a third subroutine DisplayError sends an appropriate message to the standard error-output device handle number 2. After this, the program ends via DOS function 04Ch, passing the exitCode value back in al (lines 77–79).

The code at lines 58–75 is carefully constructed to respond to all possible I/O errors. If ReadChar returns the zf flag set, then there is no more input to process, and line 60 jumps to the Done label, where the end-of-file marker is written. If WriteChar returns the zf flag set, then the output file must be a disk text file and the disk is full, a condition that DOS strangely does not report as an error. Many programs skip this all-important step of checking for a disk-full condition as at lines 64–67 here.

The rest of the FILTER shell is composed of three subroutines that you can call in your own programs. The next sections describe how to do this.

ReadChar (82–113)

ReadChar demonstrates how to read one character from the standard input device (handle 0). DOS function 03Fh, "Read from file or device," requires bx to hold the handle number, cx to hold the maximum number of characters to read, and ds:dx to hold a pointer to the location where DOS should store the input data. This routine returns cf set if an error is detected, in which case the error code (either 5 or 6) is stored in exitCode at line 104 followed by a jump to the Exit label, ending the program immediately if an error occurs. The or instruction at line 107 sets or clears zf. If ax is 0, then no more data is available from the input file; otherwise, ax equals the number of characters actually read, which may be fewer than the maximum specified in cx.

WriteChar (115–146)

WriteChar calls DOS function 040h, "Write to file or device," to write one character to the standard output device (handle 1). Again, bx equals the handle number; cx, the number of characters; and ds:dx, the address of the data to be written. If cf is set on return from DOS function 040h, lines 137–138 store the error code in al in variable exitCode and jump to the Exit label. Line 140 sets or clears zf as described before.

DisplayError (148–190)

DisplayError demonstrates how to display error (and other) messages in filter programs, using the same DOS function (040h) used in WriteChar. In this case, however, bx is assigned the standard error-output handle at line 186, with cx equal to the string length and ds:dx addressing the string variable. Because handle 2 is used, even if the standard output is redirected, error messages are still written to the display.

Customizing FILTER

Because FILTER reads characters from the standard input device and writes characters to the standard output device, you can use I/O redirection characters (< and >) and a pipe (|) to execute the program. To modify the program to do something useful, first copy FILTER.ASM to LC.ASM and replace line 62 in the copy with the code in Figure 7-1.

After adding the new lines, assemble and link with the commands:

```
tasm lc
tlink lc
```

You now have a new filter program LC to convert text files to all lowercase. One good use for LC is to convert to lowercase public domain assembly language listings, many of which are in all uppercase, which I find difficult to read. Before processing your valuable files, try the program

```
        mov     al, [oneChar]    ; Load al with input char
        cmp     al, 'A'          ; Test if > 'A'
        jb      @@10             ; Jump if al < 'A'
        cmp     al, 'Z'          ; Test if < 'Z'
        ja      @@10             ; Jump if al > 'Z'
        add     al, 'a'-'A'      ; Convert A-Z to a-z
        mov     [oneChar], al    ; Save converted character
@@10:
```

**Figure 7-1 *Code to replace line 62 in Program 7-1,
converting the FILTER.ASM shell to LC.ASM.***

on a *copy* of any text file. If your file is named OLDFILE.TXT, issue the command:

```
lc <oldfile.txt >newfile.txt
```

to convert the text in OLDFILE.TXT to lowercase and write the result to a new file named NEWFILE.TXT. No changes are made to OLDFILE.TXT.

> Note: One danger with redirected I/O and filter programs is that you receive no warning that an existing file is about to be overwritten by the new output. Be careful not to erase an important file when typing the output file name after the output redirection character >. Always keep backup copies of your files!

Another way to use a filter program like LC is to pipe the output of one filter into the input of another. For example, to display a sorted disk directory in all lowercase, use the command:

```
dir|lc|sort|more
```

DIR is, of course, a DOS command; LC is the filter from this chapter; MORE is a standard DOS filter program that inserts pauses at every screen full of lines; and SORT is another standard filter that sorts text lines. Because the display is the standard output file, there's no need to redirect output in this case. When you do want to redirect piped output, for example to print a directory in lowercase, use a command like this:

```
dir|lc >prn
```

Printing Text

The printer is just another output device; therefore, the easiest way to print text is to write to the standard list-device handle, number 4. (See Table 7-2.) For example, you can print a string with code such as in this fragment:

```
DATASEG
string     DB    'This string is printed'
lenString =      $ - string
CODESEG
mov   ah, 040h              ; DOS function "Write to File or Device"
mov   bx, 4                 ; Standard list device handle number
mov   cx, lenString         ; Assign length of string
mov   dx, offset string     ; Assign string address to ds:dx
int   21h                   ; Call DOS to print string
```

After this code executes, register ax equals the number of characters printed, unless cf is set, in which case ax equals an error code, probably

5 (access denied) or 6 (bad handle or file not open). If cf is not set, it's also possible, although unlikely, for ax to be less than cx, indicating that only some of the characters were successfully printed. You can deal with this situation if you want, but for most printing jobs, it's not necessary, continuing instead with:

```
        jnc   Continue        ; No error--continue
        mov   [errorCode], ax ; Else store error code
        jmp   Error           ; Exit program
Continue:
```

An easy way to print single characters is to use DOS function 5, which sends the character in dl to the standard list device associated with handle 4:

```
mov   ah, 5              ; DOS printer output
mov   dl, [anyChar]      ; Place character in dl
int   21h               ; Call DOS to print one character
```

Both this and the previous methods ensure portability and will work with just about any printer/interface combination your program is likely to meet. As mentioned earlier, you can also print a character by calling the ROM BIOS interrupt 17h, although this method won't work with serial printers:

```
mov   ah, 0              ; Select print routine of interrupt 17h
mov   al, [anyChar]      ; Place character in al
mov   dx, 0              ; Printer number 0, 1, or 2
int   17h               ; Call ROM BIOS to print one character
```

After this code, if ah equals 1, then the character was not printed—probably because the printer is either off line, or, perhaps, there is no printer. Use this method only if you are sure that your program will drive a printer attached to the computer's parallel interface, and you are sure the system has an IBM-compatible BIOS.

Selecting Printer Features

All modern printers understand a variety of control codes to select various features, switch on underlines, print in bold face, and so on. To select a feature is a simple matter of "printing" the correct control-code sequence. When the printer receives such a sequence, it interprets the values as instructions instead of ASCII codes to print. For example, to switch to compressed text on most IBM-type (Epson) printers, you can write:

```
mov   ah, 5              ; DOS printer output
mov   dl, 14             ; Compressed-text control code
int   21h               ; "Print" the command
```

Some commands require two or more successive codes, usually starting with an escape character (ASCII 27). Probably, the best way to handle such codes is to write a small subroutine to print one character:

```
PROC PrintChar
        mov  ah, 5          ; DOS printer output
        int  21h            ; Print character
        ret                 ; Return to caller
ENDP PrintChar
```

Then place the value to print in dl and call PrintChar. To turn on underlining, you can write:

```
mov  dl, 27
call PrintChar
mov  dl, 45
call PrintChar
mov  dl, 1
call PrintChar
```

This sends the sequence 27, 45, 1, which tells the printer to begin to underline subsequent text. (Change the 1 to 0 to cancel underlining.) Table 7-3 lists a subset of the more popular control sequences understood by most IBM printers. Consult your printer manual for other codes.

Table 7-3 *Typical Printer Control Sequences*

ASCII Code	Decimal Values	Action
BELL	7	Ring printer's bell
HT	9	Horizontal tab (forward)
LF	10	Line feed
VT	11	Vertical tab
FF	12	Form feed
CR	13	Carriage return
SO	14	Double width text on*
SI	15	Compressed text on
DC2	18	Compressed text off
DC4	20	Double width text off
CAN	24	Clear printer buffer
ESC,−,NUL	27,45,0	Underlining off
ESC,−,SOH	27,45,1	Underlining on
ESC,E	27,69	Emphasized text on
ESC,F	27,70	Emphasized text off
ESC,W,NUL	27,87,0	Double width text off
ESC,W,SOH	27,87,1	Double width text on

*Cancelled by CR, LF, or DC4.

Memory-Mapped Video

To paraphrase a well-known writer whose name is similar to mine (but ends with a big bad Wolfe instead of a beautiful Swan), assembly language programmers like to power their code to the edge of the envelope. To achieve the best possible output speed in PC programming, there's only one way to fly—write characters directly to the PC's memory-mapped video.

Although there are several different kinds of video adapters and systems available for IBM PCs and compatibles, all use one of two special memory areas that other circuits read to display text on screen. These areas, called video or *regen* buffers, begin at segment address 0B000h for monochrome and Hercules displays and at 0B800h for graphics systems, including CGA, EGA, and VGA standards. Each word in the buffer specifies an extended ASCII character value from 0 to 255 plus a second byte that selects attributes such as bold face and underlining on monochrome systems or background and foreground colors on color monitors. Although there are many different modes and features of these display standards that you can use, when it comes to displaying text by directly writing to the video buffers, the process is relatively straightforward.

The reason for having two video buffers, by the way, is that the original IBM PC allowed both monochrome and color graphics adapters to be used simultaneously. Although most people use a single CRT and adapter card today, obviously, such dual use requires two buffers to hold screen data. The first job, then, is to discover whether the system has a monochrome or color adapter—or which of the two is active in systems with both setups. Do this by calling the ROM BIOS interrupt 10h with ah equal to 15 decimal:

```
DATASEG
vBASE   dw      ?           ; Video buffer base address
CODESEG
 mov  [vBASE], 0B800h       ; Initialize default segment address
 mov  ah, 15                ; ROM BIOS "Get video state" number
 int  10h                   ; Call BIOS video I/O service
 cmp  al, 7                 ; Is result monochrome?
 jne  @@10                  ; Jump if not monochrome
 mov  [vBASE], 0B000h       ; Else change default segment address
@@10:
```

These instructions call the BIOS video routine with int 10h and check the result returned in al. If al is 7, this is a monochrome system (including those with the popular Hercules adapter); otherwise, the system has a graphics card of some kind. Accordingly, the word variable vBASE is set to the proper segment address for other routines to use.

After this step, writing a character to the display is a simple matter of poking an ASCII value and an 8-bit attribute code into a memory location, offset from the segment specified by vBASE. There are several ways to proceed, but the method I have found easiest to use is to load es with the segment address and di with the offset:

```
mov  es, [vBASE]           ; Address video buffer segment with es
mov  di, 0                 ; Assign offset address to di
```

After this, load an ASCII value into al and the attribute or color value into ah and execute stosw to display the character:

```
mov  al, [anyChar]        ; Load character to display into al
mov  ah, [attribute]      ; Load attribute into ah
stosw                     ; Store ax at es:di
```

If you are going to store successive characters and attributes with this method, execute a `cld` instruction before the first `stosw` to prepare for auto-incrementing `di`. When displaying only one character, it doesn't matter whether `di` increases or decreases, so you can leave this step out.

Figure 7-2 illustrates that characters in monochrome and color video memory buffers are composed of character and attribute bytes. Figure 7-3 shows the format of a character attribute byte, which is identical for both color and monochrome adapters. Of course, you see colors only on color displays. On monochrome systems, "colors" are shown as underlines, bold face, and reversed (black on bright) video.

In the video buffer memory, character bytes are stored at even addresses; attribute bytes, at odd addresses. When reading and writing the character value and attribute together into a 16-bit register, remember that the 8086 stores word values in byte-swapped order. Consequently, assuming the value of `di` is even, executing either of the following two instructions loads the character value into `al` and the attribute into `ah`:

```
lodsw                     ; al <- character; ah <- attribute
mov  ax, [es:di]          ; Same, but di is not changed
```

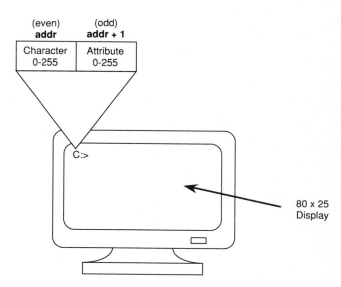

Figure 7-2 *Screen positions and video buffers.*

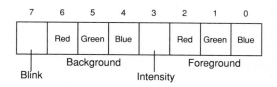

Figure 7-3 *Monochrome and color attribute byte.*

Cursor Coordinates

To position the cursor to a specific location, call BIOS interrupt 10h with ah equal to 2, dh equal to the row number, and dl equal to the column. Location (0,0) is at the upper left corner; therefore, the maximum column is 79 and the maximum row 24 for a typical 80 × 25 character display. Because some video systems can display multiple pages, you must also assign a page number to bh. Usually, you can get away with specifying the default page 0, positioning the cursor with:

```
xor  bh, bh            ; Select page 0 (default)
mov  ah, 2             ; Specify set-cursor routine number
mov  dh, [row]         ; Load row into dh
mov  dl, [column]      ; Load column into dl
int  10h              ; Call BIOS video I/O service
```

If your program uses other page numbers, or if you change pages with:

```
mov  ah, 5             ; Specify change-page routine number
mov  al, 1             ; Specify page number 1 (second page)
int  10h              ; Call BIOS video I/O service
```

then you should request the current page number before changing the cursor location. Do this by calling interrupt 10h with ah equal to 15 decimal:

```
mov  ah, 15            ; Specify get-video-state routine number
int  10h              ; Call BIOS video I/O service
```

This loads the current display page number into bh, sets ah to the display width (usually 80) and, as described earlier, also sets al to the current display mode. With the page number in bh, you can then position the cursor without worrying that you may be doing this on the wrong page—an error that even some commercial programs make. (If you've ever used a program where the cursor sometimes disappears or behaves strangely, you're probably seeing this problem in action.)

> Note: If you change text display pages, be sure to switch back to page 0 before your program ends.

Snow Code

Snow is beautiful stuff, but not when it "drifts" onto a computer display. Unfortunately, by writing directly to video display memory in CGA text mode, you can introduce snow by interferring with the timing of circuits responsible for updating, or *refreshing*, the screen. (The same problem does not occur with monochrome, Hercules, and newer EGA and VGA display adapters.) This refreshing action is performed automatically about 60 times a second creating the illusion of stability when the truth is anything but.

The trick to eliminating snow is to access video memory only during the time when display circuits are not likely to read data at the same addresses. The most reliable time to do this is during the *vertical retrace* period when the CRT beam moves invisibly from the bottom to the top of the display after finishing one full refresh cycle. Writing to video buffer memory during this time is guaranteed not to interfere with the CGA's own timing requirements. Detecting the vertical retrace period requires reading a register in the Motorola 6845 CRT Controller with an **in** instruction, which, along with its sister instruction **out**, have the general forms:

in   *accumulator, port*
out   *port, accumulator*

The *accumulator* may be either **al** (to input a byte) or **ax** (to input a word). The *port* specifies the physical address of the device being read and must be a number from 0 to 255 or a value in **dx** from 0 to 65,535. An **in** instruction reads a byte or word from a port. An **out** instruction writes a byte or word to a port. For some ports, simply reading or writing the correct address causes an action to occur and, in this case, the data transfer is meaningless.

To eliminate snow, an **in** instruction reads the 6845 controller's status register byte at address 03DAh. If bit 3 of the result in **al** is 1, then a vertical retrace operation is in progress, and it's safe to poke a character quickly into memory. The code to accomplish this is:

```
M6845 EQU 03DAh      ; Address of CGA 6845 CRT Controller

      mov  dx, M6845     ; Set dx to input port address
@@10:
      in   al, dx        ; Read 6845 status
      test al, 08h       ; Test if bit 3 = 1
      je   @@10          ; Repeat if bit 3 = 0
```

Immediately after this, it's safe to store a character and attribute into the video regen buffer. You can use any of the addressing methods described in this book, but the fastest way is to employ a string **stosw** instruction. Assuming that **es:di** addresses the video buffer and that **cx** holds the character in **cl** and attribute in **ch**, you can follow the previous code with:

```
mov  ax, cx        ; Move character/attribute into ax
stosw              ; Store ax at es:di
```

Unfortunately, all this effort to prevent snow on CGA text screens negates most of the speed gained from writing directly to video buffers in the first place. Worse, because the program now has to check whether "snow control" is required before writing every character, output to other display types goes more slowly, too. For these reasons, you may want to consider writing two library modules, one with snow control and the other without. Also, be aware that some users are willing to put up with snow to achieve faster displays, so you should always make snow removal optional. Unfortunately, some reviewers and computer journalists have decided that snow is totally unacceptable, failing in many cases to point out that the trade-off is a severe loss of output speed. Many people welcome the extra speed even if they have to watch an occasional snowfall.

More About I/O Ports

As the previous section suggests, reading and writing ports with in and out instructions are among the lowest of low-level, hardware-specific programming jobs you can perform. Port addresses are hard wired into computer and interface circuits, and you can't change the addresses in a program. (Some interfaces allow you to select port addresses by flipping switches or installing a jumper wire. Also, it's possible to design interface cards that have programmable port addresses but, in practice, this is highly unusual. Most port addresses are fixed.)

Because port addresses can differ from computer to computer, directly accessing I/O ports can limit programs to running only on a specific computer model. Some addresses such as serial I/O ports (discussed in chapter 10) are always set to one value or another. Others are added by manufacturers to control special features. For example, the following instructions switch my system (an ALR 386/2) between slow and fast speeds:

```
; Switch to slow speed
mov  al, 0EAh          ; Assign value to al
out  64h, al           ; Output al to port 64h
; Switch to fast speed
mov  al, 0E5h          ; Assign value to al
out  64h, al           ; Output al to port 64h
```

Undoubtedly, these same instructions will fail on a different system, so don't try them unless you're using the same computer. If you do write such hardware-dependent code, you should give users the ability to change the port address assignments, to select alternate code (perhaps to call a DOS routine for systems without a certain feature), or to bypass the hardware-specific instructions altogether.

A Memory-Mapped Video Module

Program 7-2, SCREEN.ASM, includes several procedures that implement the memory-mapped video ideas in this chapter. As with STRINGS, STRIO, and BINASC, the program is in the form of a library module and, therefore, requires linking to a host program before running. (A full example follows this section.) There are several new techniques in SCREEN.ASM, described later in the section "Using the SCREEN Module." But all the 8086 instructions in the listing have been introduced in this and in earlier chapters, and you should have little trouble understanding most of the code. Assemble and store SCREEN in your MTA.LIB library file with the commands:

```
tasm /zi screen
tlib /E mta -+screen
```

Repeat these instructions if you later modify SCREEN. (As explained for other modules, ignore a possible warning that SCREEN is not in the library.) You can remove the /zi switch to reduce code-file size if you don't plan to run assembled programs in Turbo Debugger.

Program 7-2 *SCREEN.ASM*

```
 1:        %TITLE "Memory-Mapped Video Screen Output Routines"
 2:
 3:
 4:    ;----- NOTE: You must call ScInit before calling other routines
 5:    ;                in this package!
 6:
 7:
 8:              IDEAL
 9:              DOSSEG
10:              MODEL    small
11:
12:    MaxRow         EQU      25      ; Maximum number of display rows
13:    MaxCol         EQU      80      ; Maximum number of display columns
14:    MonoBASE       EQU      0b000h  ; Monochrome RAM segment address
15:    DefaultBASE    EQU      0b800h  ; Other mode RAM segment address
16:
17:
18:    ;----- Character attribute byte & AND masks
19:
20:    RECORD attrByte Blink:1, Background:3, Intensity:1, Foreground:3
21:
22:    BlinkMask      EQU      MASK     Blink
23:    BackMask       EQU      MASK     Background
24:    IntensityMask  EQU      MASK     Intensity
25:    ForeMask       EQU      MASK     Foreground
26:
27:
28:
29:              DATASEG
30:                                    〈0,0,7〉
31:    attribute      attrByte <0,0,7>          ; Attribute, default values
32:    vBASE          DW       DefaultBASE      ; Video RAM buffer address
33:
34:
35:    ;----- ScRow: Array of offsets (from vBASE) in video RAM buffer
36:
37:    BytesPerRow = MaxCol * 2
38:    row = 0
39:    LABEL  ScRow   Word
40:    REPT   MaxRow
41:     dw ( row * BytesPerRow )
42:     row = row + 1
43:    ENDM
44:
45:              CODESEG
46:
47:              PUBLIC  ScGotoXY, ScReadXY, ScPokeChar, ScPokeStr, ScClrRect
48:              PUBLIC  ScSetBack, ScSetFore, ScBright, ScDim, ScBlink
49:              PUBLIC  ScNoBlink, ScGetAttribute, ScSetAttribute, ScInit
50:
```

```
51:  %NEWPAGE
52:  ;-------------------------------------------------------------
53:  ; SetVidAddr     Prepare video-RAM address
54:  ;-------------------------------------------------------------
55:  ; Note:
56:  ;        Private subroutine for ScPokeChar and ScPokeStr
57:  ; Input:
58:  ;        dh = row (0 is top line)
59:  ;        dl = column (0 is at far left)
60:  ; Output:
61:  ;        es:di = video RAM buffer address for (row, column)
62:  ;        Note: dh and dl are not checked!!
63:  ; Registers:
64:  ;        bx, dx, di, es changed
65:  ;-------------------------------------------------------------
66:  PROC    SetVidAddr
67:          mov     es, [vBASE]     ; Set es to video segment address
68:          xor     bh, bh          ; Zero upper half of bx
69:          mov     bl, dh          ; Assign row to bl
70:          shl     bx, 1           ; Multiply row (bx) times 2
71:          mov     di, [scRow + bx] ; Set di to video buffer row address
72:          xor     dh, dh          ; Convert column to 16-bit word
73:          shl     dx, 1           ; Multiply column (dx) times 2
74:          add     di, dx          ; Add column offset to row address
75:          ret                     ; Return to caller
76:  ENDP    SetVidAddr
77:  %NEWPAGE
78:  ;-------------------------------------------------------------
79:  ; ScGotoXY       Set cursor position
80:  ;-------------------------------------------------------------
81:  ; Input:
82:  ;        dh = row (0 is top line)
83:  ;        dl = column (0 is at far left)
84:  ; Output:
85:  ;        Cursor in current page repositioned to (row, column)
86:  ; Registers:
87:  ;        none
88:  ;-------------------------------------------------------------
89:  PROC    ScGotoXY
90:          push    ax              ; Save modified registers
91:          push    bx
92:          mov     ah, 15          ; Get display page number into bh
93:          int     10h             ; Call BIOS video service
94:          mov     ah, 2           ; BIOS function number
95:          int     10h             ; Call BIOS--set cursor position
96:          pop     bx              ; Restore registers
97:          pop     ax
98:          ret                     ; Return to caller
99:  ENDP    ScGotoXY
```

```
100:    %NEWPAGE
101:    ;----------------------------------------------------------------
102:    ; ScReadXY       Get cursor position
103:    ;----------------------------------------------------------------
104:    ; Input:
105:    ;        none
106:    ; Output:
107:    ;        dh = row (0 is top line)
108:    ;        dl = column (0 is at far left)
109:    ; Registers:
110:    ;        dx changed
111:    ;----------------------------------------------------------------
112:    PROC    ScReadXY
113:            push    ax              ; Save modified registers
114:            push    bx
115:            push    cx
116:            mov     ah, 15          ; Get display page number into bh
117:            int     10h             ; Call BIOS video service
118:            mov     ah, 3           ; BIOS function number
119:            int     10h             ; Call BIOS--get cursor position
120:            pop     cx              ; Restore registers
121:            pop     bx
122:            pop     ax
123:            ret                     ; Return to caller
124:    ENDP    ScReadXY
125:    %NEWPAGE
126:    ;----------------------------------------------------------------
127:    ; ScPokeChar     Poke a character into the display
128:    ;----------------------------------------------------------------
129:    ; Input:
130:    ;        al = ASCII character code
131:    ;        dh = row (0 is top line) *
132:    ;        dl = column (0 is at far left) *
133:    ; Output:
134:    ;        Character in al displayed at position (row, column)
135:    ;        * Note: Row and Column values not checked!!
136:    ; Registers:
137:    ;        ax, bx, dx, di changed
138:    ;----------------------------------------------------------------
139:    PROC    ScPokeChar
140:            push    es              ; Save es segment register
141:            call    SetVidAddr      ; Prepare es:di
142:            mov     ah, [attribute] ; Assign attribute to ah
143:            stosw                   ; Display attribute and char
144:            pop     es              ; Restore es register
145:            ret                     ; Return to caller
146:    ENDP    ScPokeChar
```

```
147:    %NEWPAGE
148:    ;----------------------------------------------------------------
149:    ; ScPokeStr       Poke a string into the display
150:    ;----------------------------------------------------------------
151:    ; Input:
152:    ;       cx = number of characters to write
153:    ;       dh = row (0 is top line) *
154:    ;       dl = column (0 is at far left) *
155:    ;       ds:si = address of ASCII string (any format)
156:    ; Output:
157:    ;     * Note: Row and Column values not checked!!
158:    ;       Note: Any string terminator is ignored
159:    ; Registers:
160:    ;       ax, bx, cx, dx, di, si changed
161:    ;----------------------------------------------------------------
162:    PROC    ScPokeStr
163:            push    es              ; Save es segment address
164:            call    SetVidAddr      ; Prepare es:di
165:            mov     ah, [attribute] ; Assign attribute to ah
166:            cld                     ; Auto-increment si, di
167:    @@10:
168:            lodsb                   ; Get next char into al
169:            stosw                   ; Display attribute and char
170:            loop    @@10            ; Loop on cx
171:            pop     es              ; Restore es segment address
172:            ret                     ; Return to caller
173:    ENDP    ScPokeStr
174:    %NEWPAGE
175:    ;----------------------------------------------------------------
176:    ; ScClrRect       Clear rectangular area on display
177:    ;----------------------------------------------------------------
178:    ; Input:
179:    ;       ch, cl = row & column of upper left corner
180:    ;       dh, dl = row & column of lower left corner
181:    ; Output:
182:    ;       Rectangle defined by ch,cl & dh,dl cleared
183:    ;        to current attributes
184:    ; Registers:
185:    ;       ax
186:    ;----------------------------------------------------------------
187:    PROC    ScClrRect
188:            mov     ah, 6           ; Select BIOS scroll routine
189:            mov     al, 0           ; Tells routine to clear area
190:            mov     bh, [attribute] ; Get attribute to use
191:            int     10h             ; Call BIOS video service
192:            ret                     ; Return to caller
193:    ENDP    ScClrRect
```

```
194:    %NEWPAGE
195:    ;------------------------------------------------------------
196:    ; ScSetBack      Set background color (attribute)
197:    ;------------------------------------------------------------
198:    ; Input:
199:    ;       al = background color
200:    ; Output:
201:    ;       Background color set for ScPokeChar and ScPokeStr
202:    ; Registers:
203:    ;       al
204:    ;------------------------------------------------------------
205:    PROC    ScSetBack
206:    IF Background GT 0
207:            push    cx                      ; If background not in lsbs
208:            mov     cl, Background          ;   then shift bits into
209:            shl     al, cl                  ;   position for ORing into
210:            pop     cx                      ;   attribute byte
211:    ENDIF
212:            and     al,BackMask             ; Isolate bits in al
213:            and     [attribute], NOT BackMask ; Zero background bits
214:            or      [attribute], al         ; Add background to attribute
215:            ret                             ; Return to caller
216:    ENDP    ScSetBack
217:    %NEWPAGE
218:    ;------------------------------------------------------------
219:    ; ScSetFore      Set foreground color
220:    ;------------------------------------------------------------
221:    ; Input:
222:    ;       al = foreground color
223:    ; Output:
224:    ;       Foreground color set for ScPokeChar and ScPokeStr
225:    ; Registers:
226:    ;       al
227:    ;------------------------------------------------------------
228:    PROC    ScSetFore
229:    IF Foreground GT 0
230:            push    cx                      ; If foreground not in lsbs
231:            mov     cl, Foreground          ;   then shift bits into
232:            shl     al, cl                  ;   position for ORing into
233:            pop     cx                      ;   attribute byte
234:    ENDIF
235:            and     al, ForeMask            ; Isolate bits in al
236:            and     [attribute], NOT ForeMask ; Zero foreground bits
237:            or      [attribute], al         ; Add foreground to attribute
238:            ret                             ; Return to caller
239:    ENDP    ScSetFore
240:    %NEWPAGE
241:    ;------------------------------------------------------------
242:    ; ScBright       Turn on intensity bit
243:    ; ScDim          Turn off intensity bit
```

```
244: ; ScBlink        Turn on blink bit
245: ; ScNoBlink      Turn off blink bit
246: ;------------------------------------------------------------------
247: ; Input:
248: ;        none
249: ; Output:
250: ;        Attribute's intensity & blink bits modified
251: ; Registers:
252: ;        none
253: ;------------------------------------------------------------------
254: PROC    ScBright
255:         or      [attribute], IntensityMask
256:         ret
257: ENDP    ScBright
258:
259: PROC    ScDim
260:         and     [attribute], NOT IntensityMask
261:         ret
262: ENDP    ScDim
263:
264: PROC    ScBlink
265:         or      [attribute], BlinkMask
266:         ret
267: ENDP    ScBlink
268:
269: PROC    ScNoBlink
270:         and     [attribute], NOT BlinkMask
271:         ret
272: ENDP    ScNoBlink
273: %NEWPAGE
274: ;------------------------------------------------------------------
275: ; ScGetAttribute       Get current attribute value
276: ;------------------------------------------------------------------
277: ; Input:
278: ;        none
279: ; Output:
280: ;        dl = current attribute value
281: ; Registers:
282: ;        dl
283: ;------------------------------------------------------------------
284: PROC    ScGetAttribute
285:         mov     dl, [attribute]      ; Get attribute byte
286:         ret                          ; Return to caller
287: ENDP    ScGetAttribute
288: %NEWPAGE
289: ;------------------------------------------------------------------
290: ; ScSetAttribute       Change attribute value
291: ;------------------------------------------------------------------
292: ; Input:
293: ;        al = new attribute value
```

```
294:  ; Output:
295:  ;       none: attribute stored for later use
296:  ; Registers:
297:  ;       none
298:  ;---------------------------------------------------------------
299:  PROC    ScSetAttribute
300:          mov     [attribute], al         ; Set attribute byte
301:          ret                             ; Return to caller
302:  ENDP    ScSetAttribute
303:  %NEWPAGE
304:  ;---------------------------------------------------------------
305:  ; ScInit        Initialize SCREEN package
306:  ;---------------------------------------------------------------
307:  ; Input:
308:  ;       none
309:  ; Output:
310:  ;       vBASE initialized
311:  ; Registers:
312:  ;       none
313:  ;---------------------------------------------------------------
314:  PROC    ScInit
315:          push    ax                      ; Save modified registers
316:          push    bx
317:          mov     ah, 15                  ; BIOS function number
318:          int     10h                     ; Get video mode in al
319:          cmp     al, 7                   ; Is mode monochrome?
320:          jne     @@10                    ; If no, jump
321:          mov     [vBASE], MonoBASE       ; Assign monochrome address
322:  @@10:
323:          pop     bx                      ; Restore registers
324:          pop     ax
325:          ret                             ; Return to caller
326:  ENDP    ScInit
327:
328:          END                     ; End of module
```

A SCREEN Demonstration   To give you a model program for experimenting with the new SCREEN module while you read the later procedure descriptions, here's a quick demonstration. Program 7-3, CHARS.ASM, displays a chart of your system's video display attributes and colors. The program also shows how to combine the STRIO module from chapter 5 with the memory-mapped video routines in SCREEN without conflict, even though both of these modules have similar subroutines. Assemble, link, and run CHARS with the commands:

```
tasm /zi chars
tlink /v chars,,, mta
chars
```

Program 7-3 *CHARS.ASM*

```
1:  %TITLE "Display Character/Attribute Reference"
2:
3:          IDEAL
4:          DOSSEG
5:          MODEL   small
6:          STACK   256
7:
8:
9:  cr          EQU     13          ; ASCII carriage return
10: lf          EQU     10          ; ASCII line feed
11: ChartRow    EQU     7           ; Row for attribute chart
12:
13:
14:         DATASEG
15:
16: exitCode    DB      0
17: welcome     DB      'Character attributes -- by Tom Swan',cr,lf
18:             DB      'Rows = background, Columns = foreground',cr,lf
19:             DB      'First char is dim, second char is bright',0
20: template    DB      '   00  01  02  03  04  05  06  07',cr,lf
21:             DB      '00',cr,lf,'01',cr,lf,'02',cr,lf,'03',cr,lf
22:             DB      '04',cr,lf,'05',cr,lf,'06',cr,lf,'07',0
23: blinkString DB      'This line should be blinking.', 0
24:
25:
26:         CODESEG
27:
28: ;----- From STRINGS.OBJ, STRIO.OBJ
29:         EXTRN   StrLength:proc, StrWrite:proc
30:
31: ;----- From SCREEN.OBJ
32:         EXTRN   ScInit:proc, ScGotoXY:proc, ScClrRect:proc
33:         EXTRN   ScPokeChar:proc, ScSetBack:proc, ScSetFore:proc
34:         EXTRN   ScPokeStr:proc, ScDim:proc, ScBright:proc
35:         EXTRN   ScBlink:proc, ScNoBlink:proc
36:
37: Start:
38:         mov     ax, @data           ; Initialize ds to address
39:         mov     ds, ax              ;  of data segment
40:         mov     es, ax              ; Make es = ds
41:
42:         call    ScInit              ; Initialize SCREEN package
43:         call    Setup               ; Set up display
44:         call    Attributes          ; Display attribute chart
45:         call    Blinking            ; Display blinking chars
46:
47:         mov     dh, 23              ; Position cursor on next to
48:         mov     dl, 0               ;  last display line before
49:         call    ScGotoXY            ;  ending program
50:
```

```
51:   Exit:
52:            mov      ah, 04Ch              ; DOS function: Exit program
53:            mov      al, [exitCode]        ; Return exit code value
54:            int      21h                   ; Call DOS. Terminate program
55:
56:
57:   ;-----   SETUP: Initialize display
58:
59:   PROC     SetUp
60:            mov      ch, 0                 ; Clear screen
61:            mov      cl, 0
62:            mov      dh, 24
63:            mov      dl, 79
64:            call     ScClrRect
65:            mov      dh, 1                 ; Display welcome message
66:            mov      dl, 0
67:            call     ScGotoXY
68:            mov      di, offset welcome
69:            call     StrWrite
70:            mov      dh, ChartRow          ; Display chart template
71:            mov      dl, 0
72:            call     ScGotoXY
73:            mov      di, offset template
74:            call     StrWrite
75:            ret
76:   ENDP     Setup
77:
78:
79:   ;-----   ATTRIBUTES: Display attribute chart
80:
81:   UDATASEG
82:   row              DB       ?          ; Uninitialized variables
83:   column           DB       ?
84:   background       DB       ?
85:   foreground       DB       ?
86:
87:   CODESEG
88:   PROC     Attributes
89:            mov      [row], ChartRow       ; Initialize row
90:            mov      [background], 0       ; Initialize background
91:   @@10:
92:            inc      [row]                 ; Next row
93:            mov      al, [background]      ; Set background attribute
94:            call     ScSetBack
95:            mov      [column], 1           ; Initialize column
96:            mov      [foreground], 0       ; Initialize foreground
97:   @@20:
98:            add      [column], 3           ; Move to next column
99:            mov      al, [foreground]      ; Set foreground attribute
100:           call     ScSetFore
```

```
101:            call    ScDim               ; First char is dim
102:            call    OneChar
103:            inc     [column]
104:            call    ScBright            ; Next char is bright
105:            call    OneChar
106:            inc     [foreground]        ; Repeat for all foregrounds
107:            cmp     [foreground], 7
108:            jbe     @@20
109:
110:            inc     [background]        ; Repeat for all backgrounds
111:            cmp     [background], 7
112:            jbe     @@10
113:
114:            ret
115: ENDP     Attributes
116:
117:
118: ;-----   ONECHAR: Local subroutine for ATTRIBUTES
119:
120: PROC     OneChar
121:            mov     dh, [row]           ; Get row number
122:            mov     dl, [column]        ; Get column number
123:            mov     al, 'A'             ; Character to display
124:            call    ScPokeChar          ; Display char
125:            ret
126: ENDP     OneChar
127:
128:
129: ;-----   BLINKING: Display blinking/nonblinking text
130:
131: PROC     Blinking
132:            mov     al, 0
133:            call    ScSetBack           ; Set background to black
134:            mov     al, 7
135:            call    ScSetFore           ; Set foreground to white
136:            call    ScBright            ; Make it whiter than white
137:            call    ScBlink             ; Turn on blinking
138:            mov     di, offset blinkString ; Address string with di
139:            call    StrLength           ; Set cx to string length
140:            mov     dh, 19              ; Assign location to dh, dl
141:            mov     dl, 0
142:            mov     si, offset blinkString ; Address string with si
143:            call    ScPokeStr           ; Display the string
144:            call    ScNoBlink           ; Turn off blinking
145:            ret
146: ENDP     Blinking
147:            END     Start        ; End of program / entry point
```

Using the SCREEN Module

There are 14 public procedures in SCREEN plus one private subroutine used internally. You can call any of the public procedures from your own programs. This section describes how each of these routines operates and also points out interesting techniques that you can put to work in your own projects. Refer to the CHARS.ASM listing (Program 7-3) for real-life examples while you read these descriptions. Unless specifically noted otherwise, all line numbers here refer to those in SCREEN.ASM, Program 7-2.

> Note: The most important rule to remember is to call `ScInit` before using any of the SCREEN routines described next. This step initializes `vBASE` to address the correct video buffer segment. If you forget to call `ScInit`, your programs will not run correctly on systems with monochrome display adapters.

SetVidAddr (52–76)

`SetVidAddr` is called privately by other SCREEN procedures; therefore, you'll probably never need to use this procedure directly. The methods employed in the subroutine are applicable to a wide range of programming problems, and you may want to take time to understand how `SetVidAddr` works. The procedure takes a row and column number in `dh` and `dl` and returns `es:di` to the correct segment and offset address for the corresponding character and attribute bytes at any screen position.

Line 67 initializes `es` by loading the value of `vBASE`. Lines 68–74 then calculate the offset into the video buffer for the row and column values in `dh` and `dl`. In the interest of speed, no checks are performed on these values. As a result, if you try to write to out-of-bounds locations, you could overwrite values elsewhere in memory. Obviously, you'll want to prevent such disasters by checking `dh` and `dl` before calling SCREEN routines unless you are positive that the values are in range.

There are several well-known methods for calculating a video buffer's offset address for specific row and column screen positions. Usually, a complex formula is used, similar to the methods for locating values in arrays as described in chapter 6. (A video buffer is, after all, just an array of characters and attribute values.) But, there's a better way, using a data structure called a *lookup table*, created at lines 37–43 and duplicated here for reference:

```
BytesPerRow = MaxCol * 2
row = 0
LABEL   ScRow   Word
REPT    MaxRow
 dw ( row * BytesPerRow )
 row = row + 1
ENDM
```

The result of this construction is similar to the auto-initialized arrays introduced in chapter 6, but with a few new twists. The `LABEL` directive assigns to label `ScRow` of type `Word` the starting address of the array. The `REPT...ENDM` section repeats for the number of times specified by `MaxRow` (defined at line 12). On each pass through the repeated loop, a `dw` directive initializes a word value equal to the `row` number times the number of bytes in one buffer row, using the `BytesPerRow` numeric equate, calculated earlier.

The number of bytes in one buffer row equals the number of display columns (`MaxCol`) times 2—because each displayed character, as you recall, is composed of one character and one attribute byte. After each word is stored in memory, `row` is incremented for the next cycle.

Assembling the repeated loop creates a table of words corresponding to the offset addresses of the leftmost character on each display line— (0,0), (0,1), (0,2), . . . , (0,79). `SetVidAddr` picks up the correct row address from this table by first multiplying the row number by 2 (lines 68–70) and then loading the address from the table into `di` (line 71). At this point, `di` addresses the row containing the character and attribute at the position specified by `dh` and `dl`. The final step is to add the column number times 2 to `di`, thus advancing the pointer to the exact display address for this row. Lines 72–74 accomplish this with two logical instructions (`xor` and `shl`) followed by an `add`. The multiplication by 2 accounts for the character and attribute bytes at each position.

By using logical instructions and a lookup table to avoid repeated calculations, `SetVidAddr` runs very fast. In your own programs, whenever you need to calculate values from parameters that are mostly within known ranges (as the row and column numbers are here), consider precalculating and storing the values in a lookup table instead. This can greatly increase program speed—especially for routines like `SetVidAddr` that will be called thousands of times during a typical program run.

ScGotoXY (78–99)
ScReadXY (101–124)

Because these two routines complement each other, it's appropriate to describe them together. `ScGotoXY` positions the cursor to the location specified in `dh` (row) and `dl` (column), calling the BIOS 10h routine as described earlier in this chapter. `ScReadXY` returns the cursor's current location in these same registers. Both routines also set `bh` to the current display page number (lines 92–93 and 116–117)—an important step that many programs ignore in their cursor-positioning routines. (The page number is not returned in `bh` to your program.)

One way to use `ScGotoXY` is demonstrated in procedure `SetUp` in CHARS.ASM, Program 7-3, at lines 59–76, which position the cursor before calling STRIO's `StrWrite`. This works because `StrWrite` calls DOS function 040h, which writes text to the current cursor position when the standard output file is the console. The same method does *not* work, however, with the output routines in `SCREEN`, which display text at locations independent of where the cursor is. Instead, you must call `ScReadXY` to find out where the cursor is and then pass this location to one of the other routines (described later) that display text:

```
call   ScReadXY        ; Get cursor location
push   dx              ; Save row and column
mov    al, '@'         ; Character to display
call   ScPokeChar      ; Display character at (dl,dh)
pop    dx              ; Restore row and column values
inc    dl              ; Increment column
call   ScGotoXY        ; Position cursor
```

In practice, you also have to check whether incrementing the column number in dl would move the cursor beyond the right screen edge, but at least this sample shows the general strategy. When adding memory-mapped video routines to your own code, remember that it's always your responsibility to control the cursor and to decide where text is to appear.

ScPokeChar (126–146)
ScPokeStr (148–173)

These two routines are short and very fast. ScPokeChar displays the character in al, which may be any extended ASCII code from 0 to 255, at the row and column specified by dh and dl. If there's any chance that these values might be out of range, precede calls to ScPokeChar and ScPokeStr with code such as:

```
        cmp   dh, 24        ; Is dh (row) <= 24?
        jbe   @@10          ; Jump if dh <= 24
        mov   dh, 24        ; Else set dh = 24
@@10:
        cmp   dl, 79        ; Is dl (column) <= 79?
        jbe   @@20          ; Jump if dl <= 79
        mov   dl, 79        ; Else set dl = 79
@@20:
```

You can then safely call ScPokeChar to display a single character, without worry that this will accidentally overwrite other memory locations. Of course, for top speed, you can leave such checks out if you are sure that row and column numbers are within range. For example, the following code places a plus sign at the end of every display row:

```
        mov   dh, 24        ; Initialize dh to maximum row
        mov   dl, 79        ; Initialize dl to maximum column
@@10:
        mov   al, '+'       ; Character to display
        push  dx            ; Save dx--changed by ScPokeChar
        call  ScPokeChar    ; Display one character
        pop   dx            ; Restore dx
        dec   dh            ; Subtract one from row number
        jns   @@10          ; Jump if dh >= 0
```

Note how this code fragment decrements the row number in dh, looping to @@10: as long as the result is positive or 0. When dh is decremented below 0, the sign flag sf is set to 1, causing the jns instruction not to jump.

To keep these routines running fast, they do not include the snow control checking instructions described earlier. If you are using a CGA text display and are having problems with snow, you may want to modify both procedures to write to the video buffer only during the vertical retrace period.

Both ScPokeChar and ScPokeStr display text using the current attribute setting, which other routines in SCREEN can modify. (For example, see ScSetBack and ScSetFore.) The CHARS.ASM program offers a good example of how to display characters in all possible variations. Also, both routines call SetVidAddr to initialize es:di to the correct address in the video buffer corresponding to the requested row and column.

ScPokeStr displays an entire string, which may or may not be in ASCIIZ format. To use this routine, you must set cx to the number of characters to display, dh and dl to the row and column number where you want the first character to appear, and ds:si to the address of the first character in the string. If your string is in ASCIIZ format, you can call the STRINGS StrLength routine to initialize cx prior to calling ScPokeStr, as in this sample, which displays a string at the top of the display:

```
DATASEG
string    DB    'My Program. Version 1.00.', 0
CODESEG
mov  ax, @data          ; Initialize segment registers
mov  ds, ax             ;  ds and es to address the program's
mov  es, ax             ;  data segment
mov  di, offset string  ; Address string with di
call StrLength          ; Set cx to string length
xor  dx, dx             ; Position at (0,0)
mov  si, di             ; Address string with si
call ScPokeStr          ; Display string
```

Note: Displaying text with ScPokeChar and ScPokeStr never causes the display to scroll. This means you can poke a character to the lower right corner at position (79,24) without disturbing any text on display. Also, these two routines display a symbol for every extended ASCII code from 0 to 255 including carriage returns, line feeds, bells, and other control codes.

ScClrRect (175–193)

ScClrRect clears a rectangle defined by registers ch and cl (top left row and column) and dh and dl (bottom right row and column). Be sure these registers are within range before calling ScClrRect, which does not check for out-of-bounds values. The procedure calls ROM BIOS interrupt 10h with ah equal to 6 (the number of the video service routine's scroll-up command). When al equals 0, this routine clears the defined display area using the attribute specified in bh (see line 190).

Some programmers devise their own super-fast clear screen routines, which you certainly can do using methods described earlier for writing to the video buffer. For example, you might simply erase the entire video buffer, using a repeated stosw command to set every character to a blank (ASCII 20h) and every attribute to a certain background color (0 for black, probably). For most uses, however, the standard method used in ScClrRect is more than adequate.

ScSetBack (195–216)
ScSetFore (218–239)

Use these routines to change the foreground and background attribute settings for subsequent calls to ScPokeChar, ScPokeStr, and ScClrRect. Call

ScSetBack with al equal to a new background color with values from 0 to 7. Call ScSetFore with al equal to a new foreground color with values also from 0 to 7. Table 7-4 lists the color values for CGA, EGA, and VGA displays. (To obtain the foreground colors in the intensified column, you must call ScBright and ScDim, described next. Background colors can't be intensified.) Table 7-5 lists equivalent values and associated effects for monochrome displays. You can also call ScBright, ScDim, ScBlink, and ScNoBlink for additional variations. Also, other foreground and background values in the range 0–7 are allowed but produce the same visible effects as the values in the table.

ScSetBack and ScSetFore use the packed bit-field methods described in chapter 5 to modify individual values in attribute bytes, defining an attrByte record at line 20 corresponding to Figure 7-3. Notice how the IF/ENDIF conditional statements at lines 206–211 and 229–234 prevent unnecessary code from being assembled if the Foreground or Background fields are already far right in the byte. In this case, because the attribute byte format is unlikely to change, the extra IF/ENDIF statements are probably unnecessary. Even so, the instructions demonstrate how to write routines to allow for possible changes to other less stable RECORD designs.

Table 7-4 *Foreground and Background Color Values*

Value	Color	Intensified (foreground only)
0	Black	Dark gray
1	Blue	Light blue
2	Green	Light green
3	Cyan	Light cyan
4	Red	Light red
5	Magenta	Light magenta
6	Brown	Yellow
7	White	Bright white

Table 7-5 *Monochrome Attribute Values*

Background	Foreground	Effect
0	0	No display
0	1	Underline
0	7	Normal text
7	0	Reversed text

ScBright (241–257)
ScDim (259–262)
ScBlink (264–267)
ScNoBlink (269–272)

These four routines modify the Blink and Intensity bits in the attribute variable declared at line 31. The instructions use and and or masks to set and clear these bits, further modifying the values assigned by ScSetFore and `ScSetBack` for future calls to `ScPokeChar`, `ScPokeStr`, and `ScClrRect`. The names and purposes of the routines should be obvious.

> Note: Due to hardware limitations, you can blink only foreground colors. Background colors don't blink. Also, on color displays, some "dim" colors actually appear brighter than their "intensified" partners. I find it helpful to think of "intense" colors as being mixed with white paint—rather than being "brighter."

ScGetAttribute (274–287)
ScSetAttribute (289–302)

Instead of calling `ScSetFore`, `ScSetBack`, `ScBright`, `ScDim`, `ScBlink`, and `ScNoBlink`, you can call `ScSetAttribute` with any 8-bit attribute value. Subsequent calls to `ScPokeChar`, `ScPokeStr`, and `ScClrRect` will then use the new value for all displayed text. In most cases, this is faster than calling multiple combinations of other routines to select various colors and attributes. Along with `ScGetAttribute`, the routines also allow you to save and restore the current attribute at times when you want to make a temporary color change. For example, to display a flashing error message in red, you might use code such as:

```
call ScGetAttribute     ; Load current attribute into dl
push dx                 ; Save value on stack
mov  al, 4              ; Assign red color to al
call ScSetFore          ; Change foreground to red
call ScBright           ; Intensify color
call ScBlink            ; Set foreground blinking
;
;----- display error message here with new attributes
;
pop  ax                 ; Pop saved attribute off stack
call ScSetAttribute     ; Reset attribute to previous value
```

Another useful technique is to build attribute values by calling `ScSetFore` and `ScSetBack` (among others) and then store the result in a variable for later use. For example, you might do this in a setup utility that lets people adjust the colors of the main program:

```
DATASEG
customColor     db      0
CODESEG
mov  al, 6              ; Assign yellow color to al
call ScSetFore          ; Change foreground to yellow
call ScBright           ; Intensify color
mov  al, 1              ; Assign blue color to al
call ScSetBack          ; Change background to blue
call ScGetAttribute     ; Get composite attribute
mov  [customColor], dl  ; Save attribute for later
```

To use the attribute, all you have to do is load [customColor] into al and call ScSetAttribute. You don't have to repeat any of the other steps.

ScInit (304–326)

The final routine in the SCREEN module is ScInit, which you must remember to call at the beginning of your program before using ScPokeChar or ScPokeStr to display text. Because vBASE is preinitialized to the color display segment address (see line 32), if you forget to call ScInit, your program will not operate on systems with monochrome (including Hercules) display adapters.

A Module for Keyboard Control

Most of the time, the methods described at the beginning of this chapter provide adequate keyboard input abilities for assembly language programming. But, there are also times when standard DOS function calls are inadequate. For one, you may not want people to be able to redirect input. And, for another, DOS makes special- and function-key handling difficult by requiring two DOS-function calls to read single keystrokes.

To answer these challenges, Program 7-4, KEYBOARD.ASM, contains two routines that I've found helpful. All key presses including ASCII characters, control keys, and function keys can be read with a single subroutine call. Following the listing is an example that explains how this works. Assemble KEYBOARD and install in the MTA.LIB library file with the commands:

```
tasm /zi keyboard
tlib /E mta -+keyboard
```

As always, ignore the possible warning that KEYBOARD is not in the library and leave out the /zi option to reduce code-file size if you don't plan to run host programs in Turbo Debugger.

Program 7-4 *KEYBOARD.ASM*

```
 1:  %TITLE "Keyboard Input Routines"
 2:
 3:        IDEAL
 4:        DOSSEG
 5:        MODEL   small
 6:
 7:
 8:        CODESEG
 9:
10:        PUBLIC  KeyWaiting, GetCh
11:
```

```
12:    %NEWPAGE
13:    ;-----------------------------------------------------------------
14:    ; KeyWaiting    Test if a key press is available
15:    ;-----------------------------------------------------------------
16:    ; Input:
17:    ;        none
18:    ; Output:
19:    ;        zf = 0 : (JNZ) Character is waiting to be read
20:    ;        zf = 1 : (JZ)  No character is waiting
21:    ; Registers:
22:    ;        none (flags only)
23:    ;-----------------------------------------------------------------
24:    PROC    KeyWaiting
25:            push    ax              ; Save modified register
26:            mov     ah, 1           ; BIOS check buffer function
27:            int     16h             ; Call BIOS keyboard service
28:            pop     ax              ; Restore register
29:            ret                     ; Return to caller
30:    ENDP    KeyWaiting
31:    %NEWPAGE
32:    ;-----------------------------------------------------------------
33:    ; GetCh         Return ASCII, control, or function key value
34:    ;-----------------------------------------------------------------
35:    ; Input:
36:    ;        none
37:    ; Output:
38:    ;        zf = 0 (ah = 1) : (JNZ) al = ASCII character
39:    ;        zf = 1 (ah = 0) : (JZ) al = ASCII control or function
40:    ; Registers:
41:    ;        ax
42:    ;-----------------------------------------------------------------
43:    PROC    GetCh
44:            xor     ah, ah          ; BIOS read-key function
45:            int     16h             ; Call BIOS keyboard service
46:            or      al, al          ; Is ASCII code = 0?
47:            jnz     @@10            ; If no, jump (not a special key)
48:            xchg    ah, al          ; Else set ah <- 0, al <- scan code
49:            add     al, 32          ; Adjust scan code to >= 32
50:            jmp     short @@20      ; Jump to exit
51:    @@10:
52:            xor     ah, ah          ; Initialize ah to 0
53:            cmp     al, 32          ; Is ASCII code < 32 (i.e., a Ctrl)?
54:            jb      @@20            ; If yes, jump (al = control key)
55:            inc     ah              ; Else set ah = 1 (al = ASCII char)
56:    @@20:
57:            or      ah, ah          ; Set or clear zf result flag
58:            ret                     ; Return to caller
59:    ENDP    GetCh
60:
61:            END                     ; End of module
```

A KEYBOARD Demonstration

Program 7-5, KEYS.ASM, demonstrates how to use the KEYBOARD module. When you run the program, press any key to see the key type and numeric value. (Note: You may find that function-key values are different than in many other programs. The reason for this discrepancy is explained later.) Press Esc to end the program. Assuming you have assembled and installed the other modules in this and previous chapters, assemble, link, and run KEYS with the commands:

```
tasm /zi keys
tlink /v keys,,, mta
keys
```

Program 7-5 *KEYS.ASM*

```
 1:   %TITLE "Display Key Values"
 2:
 3:           IDEAL
 4:           DOSSEG
 5:           MODEL   small
 6:           STACK   256
 7:
 8:   cr      EQU     13          ; ASCII carriage return
 9:   lf      EQU     10          ; ASCII line feed
10:
11:
12:           DATASEG
13:
14:   exitCode        DB      0
15:   charKey         DB      'Character key : ', 0
16:   funcKey         DB      'Function key  : ', 0
17:   numString       DB      7 DUP (0)
18:   welcome         DB      cr,lf,'Display Key Values--by Tom Swan'
19:                   DB      cr,lf,'Press any key, or press Esc to quit'
20:                   DB      cr,lf,lf,0
21:
22:
23:           CODESEG
24:
25:   ;----- From BINASC.OBJ
26:           EXTRN   BinToAscDec:proc
27:
28:   ;----- From STRIO.OBJ
29:           EXTRN   StrWrite:proc, NewLine:proc
30:
31:   ;----- From KEYBOARD.OBJ
32:           EXTRN   Keywaiting:proc, Getch:proc
33:
34:   Start:
35:           mov     ax, @data           ; Initialize ds to address
36:           mov     ds, ax              ;  of data segment
37:           mov     es, ax              ; Make es = ds
38:
```

```
39:         mov     di, offset welcome      ; Display welcome message
40:         call    StrWrite
41:
42: Repeat:
43:         call    KeyWaiting              ; Wait for any key press
44:         jz      Repeat                  ; Repeat until key waiting
45:         call    GetCh                   ; Read key press
46:         mov     di, offset charKey      ; Address charKey string
47:         jnz     @@10                    ; Jump if key is a character
48:         cmp     al, 27                  ; Was Escape key pressed?
49:         je      Exit                    ; If yes, jump to exit
50:         mov     di, offset funcKey      ; Address funcKey string
51: @@10:
52:         call    StrWrite                ; Display key-type label
53:         xor     ah, ah                  ; Convert al to 16 bits
54:         mov     cx, 1                   ; Minimum number of digits
55:         mov     di, offset numString    ; Address number string
56:         call    BinToAscDec             ; Convert number to string
57:         call    StrWrite                ; Display key value
58:         call    NewLine                 ; Start new display line
59:         jmp     Repeat                  ; Get next key press
60:
61: Exit:
62:         mov     ah, 04Ch                ; DOS function: Exit program
63:         mov     al, [exitCode]          ; Return exit code value
64:         int     21h                     ; Call DOS. Terminate program
65:
66:         END     Start          ; End of program / entry point
```

Using the KEYBOARD Module	Note: Line numbers in the following descriptions refer to those in Program 7-4 unless otherwise noted.

KeyWaiting (13–30)

KeyWaiting returns the zf flag cleared (equal to 0) if a character is waiting to be read from the keyboard type-ahead buffer. If the zf flag is set (equal to 1), then no character is waiting. Use KeyWaiting in loops such as:

```
@@10:
    call AnyProcedure   ; Code to execute while waiting
    call KeyWaiting     ; Check for a key press
    jz   @@10           ; Jump if no key was pressed
    call GetCh          ; Read character from keyboard
```

GetCh (32–59)

GetCh is my personal answer to the dilemma of reading PC function keys. The "normal" method is to call a DOS input routine twice—once to read the lead-in null character (ASCII 0) and a second time to read the function-key value. Because of this scheme, all programs must detect function keys to avoid displaying these special values as text. (You have probably seen programs that forget to do this, writing Ks and other strange letters when you press an arrow or other function key.)

With GetCh, zero flag zf indicates whether the value returned in ah is a plain ASCII character (zf = 0) or is a function or control key (zf = 1). ASCII character values range from 32 to 255. Function- and control-key values range from 0 to 255. A single call to GetCh is all you need to process any keystroke. Table 7-6 lists the function- and control-key values returned by GetCh for zf = 1. Table 7-7 lists additional values for keys with normal ASCII values in the first two columns (zf = 0) and various Ctrl, Alt, and a few Shift+Ctrl combinations for those same keys in the other columns (zf = 1). Values that are not available are marked with dashes. Key combinations that return the same values as other combinations are in parentheses. All values in both tables are in decimal.

Using GetCh is easy. Just call the subroutine and then inspect the state of zf to distinguish between plain ASCII and function or control keys:

```
call GetCh        ; Get a character from keyboard
jz   FunctionKey  ; Call routine for function/control keys
jnz  ASCIIKey     ; Call routine for normal ASCII keys
```

The code in GetCh works by calling ROM BIOS interrupt 16h with ah equal to 0, reading the next key press, or taking a key-press value from

Table 7-6 *GetCh Function- and Control-Key Values*

Key	Normal	+Shift	+Ctrl	+Alt
F1	91	116	126	136
F2	92	117	127	137
F3	93	118	128	138
F4	94	119	129	139
F5	95	120	130	140
F6	96	121	131	141
F7	97	122	132	142
F8	98	123	133	143
F9	99	124	134	144
F10	100	125	135	145
Ins	114	(114)	—	—
Del	115	(115)	—	—
Home	103	(103)	151	—
PgUp	105	(105)	164	—
PgDn	113	(113)	150	—
Up	104	(104)	—	—
Down	112	(112)	—	—
Left	107	(107)	147	—
Right	109	(109)	148	—
End	111	(111)	149	—
Esc	27	(27)	(27)	—

Table 7-7 *Additional GetCh Key Values*

Key	Normal	+Shift	+Ctrl	+Alt
A	97	65	1	62
B	98	66	2	80
C	99	67	3	78
D	100	68	4	64
E	101	69	5	50
F	102	70	6	65
G	103	71	7	66
H	104	72	8	67
I	105	73	9	55
J	106	74	10	68
K	107	75	11	69
L	108	76	12	70
M	109	77	13	82
N	110	78	14	81
O	111	79	15	56
P	112	80	16	57
Q	113	81	17	48
R	114	82	18	51
S	115	83	19	63
T	116	84	20	52
U	117	85	21	54
V	118	86	22	79
W	119	87	23	49
X	120	88	24	77
Y	121	89	25	53
Z	122	90	26	76
0	48	41	—	161
1	49	33	—	152
2	50	64	35	153
3	51	35	—	154
4	52	36	—	155
5	53	37	—	156
6	54	94	30	157
7	55	38	—	158
8	56	42	—	159
9	57	40	—	160
]	93	125	29	—
[	91	123	27	—
—	45	95	31	162

the type-ahead buffer. The BIOS interrupt routine returns the keyboard scan code (a number representing the key's position) in ah and the ASCII value in al. If al is 0, then ah represents a function key; otherwise, the key is a plain ASCII character. The code at lines 48–50 adds 32 to function-key values to prevent conflicts with control codes in the range 0–31. For this reason, the values returned by GetCh do not match similar functions in most high-level languages. Use the KEYS program along with Tables 7-6 and 7-7 to determine which keys produce which values. The other instructions in GetCh set ah to 1 for ASCII characters or to 0 for function and control keys. Line 57 then ORs ah with itself to set zf to 1 only if ah is 0.

Summary

Standard DOS I/O methods may not be glamorous, but they allow programs to run on as wide a variety of systems as possible. One advantage of using standard DOS I/O is to give computer operators the ability to redirect input and output without the program's (or your) advance knowledge.

The type-ahead buffer fills with keystrokes independently of other program actions. Every key press causes an interrupt routine to capture the key value and store it in memory. When the keyboard is the standard input device, as it usually is, calls to DOS input functions remove key values from the type-ahead buffer. Erasing the keyboard buffer is a simple matter of resetting two pointers that mark the first and last character in the buffer.

Handles are numbers that refer to logical files, which provide a common interface between programs and various peripheral devices. DOS initializes five handles, which programs can use to write to the display, read the keyboard, display error messages, access a communications port, and print text. One good use for handles is to write simple filter programs that can have their input and output piped together with other filters to perform complex operations.

The dollar sign ($) is Turbo Assembler's location counter, equal to the current address at any place in a program. This symbol is particularly useful to determine the sizes of variables, especially strings. In Ideal mode, equated expressions involving the location counter must be assigned with the equal-sign operator.

Printing text is most easily accomplished by writing to the DOS standard list device, using one of the preassigned handles. Calling the ROM BIOS to print text is not a good idea because this routine does not work with printers attached to a serial port.

There's no faster way to display text than to write characters directly to memory-mapped video buffers. The memory buffers store characters along with attribute values, which select colors and features such as underlining and reverse video on monochrome systems. Using memory-mapped video techniques on older CGA text displays can produce snow. This problem can be eliminated by synchronizing the program with the display's vertical retrace signal, but the trade-off is a serious loss of output speed.

Exercises

7-1. What are three DOS functions that programs can use to input single characters? Write the assembly language instructions to call these functions.

7-2. Write a program to read single characters from the keyboard, convert the characters to uppercase (regardless of whether the Caps Lock or shift keys are pressed), and write the modified characters to the standard output file. Pressing Esc should end your program.

7-3. Write a subroutine that returns the zero flag set (zf = 1) if the Esc key has been pressed. The subroutine should return the zero flag cleared (zf = 0) if: a) there is no key press waiting to be read, or b) there is a key press waiting and the value of that key is not Esc. The subroutine should return zf = 1 *only* if a key is waiting and that key is Esc. The subroutine should *not* pause for input and should preserve all registers. (ASCII Esc equals 27 decimal.)

7-4. Revise your answer in exercise #7-3 to return zf = 1 if function key F1 is pressed. Write your solution without using GetCh in the KEYBOARD module. (Hint: DOS returns a null [0] followed by 03Bh for key F1.)

7-5. What is a handle? How are handles used? How many handles are preassigned by DOS?

7-6. Why are filter programs useful? Name at least one filter supplied with DOS.

7-7. Create an equate that automatically is assigned the length of the string "I hate meeses to pieces."

7-8. Write a subroutine to fill the screen with any single character passed as a parameter in register al. Use the SCREEN module in your answer.

7-9. Display the string "ERROR: Dumb mistake detected" with bright white flashing letters on a red background on color displays. Use the SCREEN module in your answer. (Note: On monochrome displays, a red background appears black.)

7-10. What routine must you call in the SCREEN module to ensure correct operation on monochrome displays?

7-11. Write a subroutine to return the zero flag set (zf = 1) if an operator presses the Y key. The zero flag should be cleared (zf = 0) if any other key is pressed. Preserve all registers. Use the KEYBOARD module in your answer.

Projects

7-1. Develop an object-code module with CRT terminal functions such as clear screen, clear to end of line, clear to end of screen, position cursor, and ring the bell. The module should use standard DOS function calls.

7-2. Write a subroutine to insert a sequence of characters (preferably an ASCIIZ string) into the keyboard type-ahead buffer. How might you use such a routine?

7-3. Write a filter to convert tab control characters in a text file to blanks. Write another filter to convert blanks to tabs.

7-4. Write a program to select all (or most of) your printer's special print modes. Make the program easy to modify for other printer models.

7-5. Modify the SCREEN module to eliminate snow on CGA text displays.

7-6. [Advanced] Write an object-code module to scroll the display up, down, left, and right without calling BIOS routines to perform these actions.

Chapter *8* **Macros and Conditional Assembly**

8 **Macros and Conditional Assembly**

In This Chapter

How to write macros; advantages and disadvantages of using macros; purging old macro definitions; adding parameters to macro definitions; formal and actual parameters; symbolic parameters; numeric parameters; string parameters; creating new data types with macros; creating variables with macros; using repetitive macros; code macros; preserving register values in macros; using the INCLUDE directive; conditional compilation techniques; conditional directives and constant expression operators; plus a sample macro library, DOSMACS.ASM

What Are Macros?

As you gain experience in assembly language programming, you'll undoubtedly repeat yourself many times, retyping the same instruction sequences over and over. To reduce the amount of repetition in a program, you can store one or more instructions in a named *macro definition* and then use the simpler macro name whenever you need that same code. When Turbo Assembler assembles a macro name, it replaces the name with the instruction sequence from the macro definition. In addition, you can pass parameters to macros, changing the assembled instructions to handle new requirements. With macros, you invent new commands to customize Turbo Assembler to operate according to your tastes.

In addition to a wide selection of macro operators and directives, Turbo Assembler provides a set of *conditional assembly directives* that are often used inside macro definitions. These directives let you write programs that assemble differently based on various conditions usually listed at the beginning of a module or program. For example, you can write programs that assemble special code for debugging, but then remove that code from the final version.

Macro Advantages and Disadvantages

Some programmers never use macros. Others create extensive libraries of complex macro definitions, extending assembly language to the point of having more macro identifiers in their programs than common assembly language mnemonics. Used this way, macros tend to be personal, letting programmers mold their individuality into Turbo Assembler.

For team programming projects, macros can help to ensure consistent coding techniques. For example, a software company might develop a macro library of common routines, reducing the frequency of bugs introduced by simple carelessness. Macros could be written to drive special hardware such as a custom CRT controller or a plotter. Team members would then be required to use the macros for all I/O to the device, ensuring that correct instruction sequences for specific operations are assembled.

Macros can also help clarify program logic by replacing cryptic assembly language mnemonics with macro names such as `GetValue` and `RingBell`. A good set of macro names can make assembly language programs look almost like Pascal or C.

But, despite these and other advantages, macros do have a few drawbacks. Unlike separate object-code modules that you can stuff into a library file for linking directly into programs, macros are stored in text form and, therefore, must be reassembled for each separate module. For this reason, an extensive macro library can increase assembly time, especially if only a few of the many macros in a library are actually used. Also, while helping to customize and clarify assembly language, macro definitions can easily hide the effects of individual instructions. A good example of this is a macro instruction that changes a register value—a fact that will not be obvious by simply reading the listing. Like subroutines, macros require careful documentation detailing the use of registers, flags, and variables.

Constructing Macros

You can define a macro anywhere in a program, but the most common (and probably the best) location for macro definitions is in the beginning of a file, near other equates, records, and structures. The simplest macro starts with the keyword MACRO and a name, followed by one or more instructions, and ends with ENDM:

```
MACRO   Terminate
        mov     ah, 04Ch        ;; "Exit program" function
        mov     al, [exitCode]  ;; Load exitCode into al
        int     21h             ;; Call DOS. Terminate program
ENDM    Terminate
```

You probably recognize these instructions—they're the same as those used in most of this book's programs to transfer control back to COMMAND.COM when the program is finished. If you insert this macro definition into a program—preferably above the DATASEG directive—you can then end the program by simply writing `Terminate`. During assembly, Turbo Assembler replaces the macro name with the instructions from the definition, a process called *macro expansion*. Of course, if you use the `Terminate` macro only once, it's hardly worth the effort to store the instructions in a macro. Even so, there's little doubt what `Terminate` means, and the additional clarity added to the program is itself an important benefit.

Notice that comments in this macro begin with double semicolons. As you know, comments normally begin with single semicolons. Both kinds of comments are allowed in macros, but those with single semicolons are written to the listing text file if you request one with the /l option when assembling. If the program uses the same macro dozens or more times, the repetitive comments are unsightly and might lengthen printing time. In that case, you can eliminate the comments from the macro expansions by preceding the text with double semicolons. (The comments are still listed along with the macro definition.)

Purging Macro Definitions

After reading a macro definition, Turbo Assembler remembers the macro name and instruction sequences throughout the program. When assembling large programs with extensive macro libraries, the assembler could run out of room for new symbols if your system has limited memory capacity. If this happens and you receive an out-of-memory error during assembly, you can purge the macro definitions you don't need, releasing additional memory for other uses. To purge a macro, use the `PURGE` keyword along with the macro name:

```
PURGE Terminate
```

After purging `Terminate`, Turbo Assembler no longer recognizes the macro name. Another reason to purge a macro definition is to replace a macro temporarily in a library with a new instruction sequence. This can be useful when you need to test a revision to a macro that you'll later add to the full macro library. For example, to change `Terminate` into a code sequence that restarts the program, you can write:

```
PURGE   Terminate
MACRO   Terminate
        jmp     Start
ENDM    Terminate
```

The `PURGE` directive removes `Terminate`'s old definition, after which a new macro of the same name is created. If you do this at the beginning of the program, every place that `Terminate` formerly ended the program will now jump to the beginning of the code at label `Start:` (not shown). You might do this to create a presentation version of your code, which runs normally but "never" ends.

Note: Turbo Debugger normally treats macro instructions as though they were native assembly language commands. Pressing F7 or F8 when the cursor is at a macro name executes all instructions associated with the macro. To execute a macro's individual instructions one by one, view the CPU window and press Ctrl-M to select the display style you prefer. Pressing F7 or F8 will then move separately through the macro's instructions.

Parameter Substitution

Adding parameters to macro definitions lets you change the way the macro expands at assembly time. Macro definitions can have three types of parameters:

▶ Symbolic parameters

▶ Numeric parameters

▶ String parameters

Symbolic parameters refer to register names, instruction mnemonics, and other assembly language keywords and identifiers. *Numeric parameters* are signed and unsigned integers or expressions. *String parameters* are plain unterminated character strings. The use of a parameter determines the parameter's type and, for this reason, some parameters can represent more than one type of data. Name your parameters the same way you name other identifiers, listing the names on the first line of the macro definition:

```
MACRO   Swap16  v1, v2
        push    [word v1]
        push    [word v2]
        pop     [word v1]
        pop     [word v2]
ENDM    Swap16
```

This macro, named `Swap16`, defines two parameters `v1` and `v2`, called *dummy parameters* or, more correctly, *formal parameters*. There are no actual variables named `v1` and `v2` in the program—the two identifiers belong strictly to the macro definition. Multiple parameters are separated by commas. The code inside the `Swap16` macro uses the parameter names in `push` and `pop` instructions, first pushing the two words `v1` and `v2` onto the stack, and then immediately popping the same two parameters off the stack in the opposite order. The effect is to exchange the values of two variables in memory.

To use a macro with parameters, write the macro name followed by the actual items to process. For example, if you declare two word variables `countA` and `countB`, you can use the previous macro to swap their values:

```
DATASEG
countA   dw        100
countB   dw        200
CODESEG
swap16   countA, countB
```

CountA and countB are called *actual parameters* because they represent the actual values to process. When expanding the macro, Turbo Assembler replaces the dummy (formal) parameters v1 and v2 with the actual parameters countA and countB, assembling the swap16 macro as though you had written:

becomes

```
push     [word countA]
push     [word countB]
pop      [word countA]
pop      [word countB]
```

You can also pass register names to Swap16, representing pointers to data to swap. If bx addresses countB, then you could write:

```
swap16   bx, countA       ; swaps word at [bx] with [countA]
```

As an alternative, you can separate multiple parameters with blanks instead of commas. For example, this is identical to the previous instruction:

```
swap16   bx countA        ; separate parameters with commas or blanks
```

Because the dummy parameters can be replaced by symbols such as bx or by labels such as countA (which represent offset address values), in this example, v1 and v2 are numeric as well as symbolic parameters. The actual type depends on how the parameters are eventually used.

As these samples illustrate, parameters let you create general-purpose macros that you can reprogram to meet new demands. Understanding how to declare and use parameters is crucial to writing effective macros that do more than simply repeat common instruction sequences. The next section examines each of the three kinds of macro parameters in detail.

Note: Parameter names such as v1 and v2 in the previous sample macros are local to the macro definitions. You can use the same names elsewhere as labels in other parts of the program without conflict.

Symbolic Parameters

Symbolic formal parameters can be replaced by any actual symbols, mnemonics, directives, and keywords normally used in assembly language programming. One use for symbolic parameters is to define new names for instructions. For example, you can give the 8086 a spelling lesson, replacing mov with Move:

```
MACRO    Move      aSym, bSym
         mov       aSym, bSym
ENDM     Move
```

In this example, `aSym` and `bSym` are the symbolic dummy parameters that are replaced by the names of registers or other text when the macro is used:

```
Move    ax, bx          ; Assembles to mov ax, bx
Move    [value], cx     ; Assembles to mov [value], cx
mov     cx, dx          ; Assembles normally
```

You can now use `mov` or `Move` with identical results. (Touch typists may find this macro helpful, especially if, like me, you're constantly typing *move* with an *e* by mistake instead of *mov*.) You can also create symbolic dummy parameters that become new global labels when the macro is expanded. To demonstrate how this works, here's how to write a macro to reserve space for a word variable, the name of which is passed to the macro as a parameter:

```
MACRO   DeclareWord     vName, vValue
vName   dw      vValue
ENDM    DeclareWord
```

The `DeclareWord` macro expands to a `dw` directive, reserving one word of memory labeled `vName` and initialized to `vValue`. To create a word variable with the initial value of 100, you can write:

```
DeclareWord TheCount, 100
```

Of course, it's just as easy to use `dw` directly. A similar but more practical example illustrates how to write macros that automatically label variables according to their initial values. To accomplish this requires using the *substitute operator* &, which tells Turbo Assembler that the text after & is the name of a dummy parameter and not something else. The reason for this is easier to see in an example:

```
MACRO   AWord   vNum
Word&vNum       dw      vNum
ENDM    AWord
```

The `AWord` macro declares one formal parameter `vNum`. At the `dw` directive, the label `Word&vNum` tells Turbo Assembler that `vNum` refers to the formal parameter of this name. Without the &, the assembler would not be able to know that `vNum` in `WordvNum` refers to the formal parameter. Using the `AWord` macro automatically labels word variables:

```
AWord   1
AWord   2
AWord   3
```

These macro calls must be done in the Dataseg.

The effect is to create three 16-bit variables named `Word1`, `Word2`, and `Word3`, as though you had written:

```
Word1    dw       1
Word2    dw       2
Word3    dw       3
```

becomes

Notice that with the macro, a single change modifies both the value and the label. For example, changing the 3 to 8 creates a word variable Word8 initialized to 8. Without the macro, you'd have to change two numbers to do the same.

Numeric Parameters

As you can see in some of the previous examples, symbolic parameters are sometimes treated as numbers. For example, vNum in the AWord macro is a symbol when used as part of a label and a number when used to initialize a word variable. The context of the parameter's use determines the data type. A parameter is numeric only when a later instruction requires a number at this place. Let's examine another macro that uses both symbolic and numeric parameters:

```
MACRO    ShiftLeft        destination, count
         push     cx
         mov      cl, count
         shl      destination, cl
         pop      cx
ENDM     ShiftLeft
```

The ShiftLeft macro defines two parameters—destination, representing the register or memory location to shift, and count, representing the number of times to shift the target value left. You could write similar macros for other shift and rotate instructions, too. The instructions in the macro save cx on the stack, assign the numeric count parameter to cl, shift the destination left that many times, and then restore cl. To use the macro, write commands such as:

```
ShiftLeft        ax, 5
ShiftLeft        [value], 3
ShiftLeft        <[word bx]>, 2
```

The first line shifts the value of ax left five times. The second line shifts variable value (not shown) left three times. The third line demonstrates a problem with parameters that have blanks. If you try to write:

```
ShiftLeft        [word bx], 2
```

you receive an error that the operand types do not match the macro definition. This occurs because blanks or commas separate multiple actual parameters. (Multiple formal parameters in the macro definition must be separated with commas.) To solve this dilemma, use < and > to surround parameters that contain blanks, as in:

```
ShiftLeft        <[byte si]>, 4
ShiftLeft        <[word bx + di]> 2
```

When passing expressions to macro numeric parameters, you must decide when you want the expression to be evaluated. Normally, parameters are passed to the macro in text form with expressions such as `My-Size * MyCount` being evaluated inside the macro. To force evaluation to occur before the macro is expanded, preface the expression with a percent sign %, the "Expression evaluate operator." For example:

```
ShiftLeft        ax, MySize * MyCount
```

⤺ multiply directive!

This points out a particularly troublesome aspect of macros and numeric parameters. Unfortunately, Turbo Assembler ignores the "`* My-Count`" portion of the expression, thinking that these symbols are merely extra parameters. To pass the expression to the macro, you have to use angle brackets as explained previously:

```
ShiftLeft        ax, <MySize * MyCount>
```

This solution is less than perfect, however, because the expression `MySize * MyCount` is passed as text to the macro. To evaluate and pass the expression *result*, use a leading percent sign like this:

```
ShiftLeft        ax, %MySize * MyCount
```

The percent sign forces the assembler to evaluate the expression and pass the final result to the macro. This can be useful if the macro's formal parameter (`count` in this example) is used more than once. If you pass an expression as text, the assembler has to evaluate the expression each time it is used. If you pass the result of an expression, though, evaluation occurs only once.

String Parameters

As in the previous samples, you must surround string parameters with `<` and `>`, which tell the assembler that the enclosed text is literal, including blanks and punctuation normally used to separate individual identifiers. A useful macro employs this technique to declare ASCIIZ-format character string variables:

```
MACRO    ASCIIZ  name, chars
name        db      '&chars', 0     ;; String + null terminator
name&len    dw      $ - name - 1    ;; Length of chars
ENDM     ASCIIZ
```

The `ASCIIZ` macro defines two parameters—`name`, which is used to create two labels, and `chars`, the characters that make up the string. Inside the macro, the `db` directive creates a null-terminated string, using `name` as the label. The & operator tells Turbo Assembler that `chars` is the name of a parameter. This is necessary to prevent the assembler from creating a string of the five characters: 'c', 'h', 'a', 'r', and 's', which it would do if the literal quotes were not used in the macro. The `dw` directive stores the length of the string (minus the null terminator) as a word variable that follows the string. Although not part of the standard ASCIIZ format, this length value gives programs a quick way to read the length of a string—

at least for string constants that don't change length. Notice how another & operator creates a label beginning with name and ending in "len." For example, if name is MyString, the length word would be labeled MyStringLen. To use the ASCIIZ macro, surround the characters for the string in angle brackets:

```
ASCIIZ  s1, <Any old string will do>
ASCIIZ  s2, <Commas, and periods, work too.>
```

When Turbo Assembler processes these lines, it creates two strings, one at label s1 and another at s2. In addition, the assembler stores the lengths of the strings at s1len and s2len. As a result, you can use the StrLength procedure in the STRINGS module to calculate string lengths or to load the lengths directly, as these examples illustrate:

```
mov     di, offset s1   ; Address string s1 with di
call    StrLength       ; Calculate cx = string length
mov     cx, [s1len]     ; Same as above two instructions
```

If the string length changes, you could call StrLength and then store the result at s1len. Assuming cx equals the new string length, you could write:

```
mov     [s1len], cx     ; Save new string length
```

> Note: Use Turbo Debugger's View:Variables window to examine the labels and values created by the ASCIIZ macro.

To create strings with characters interpreted specially in a macro, use an exclamation point (!), the "Quoted character operator." For example, to include an angle bracket as a character in a string, you can use the line:

```
ASCIIZ s3, <Couldn''t locate --!> >
```

The effect is to create a variable s3 equal to the string "Couldn't locate —>," which you would probably follow with a second string, perhaps a file name that couldn't be found on disk. The quoted character operator inserts the angle bracket (>) as a character. Notice also the double apostrophes, needed here to insert a single apostrophe because the ASCIIZ macro uses this same character as string delimiters.

Macros and Variables

A good use for macros is to add custom data types such as the ASCIIZ macro to assembly language. Any combination of directives such as dw and db, as described in previous chapters, can be used in macro definitions. Along with the DUP operator, this makes it easy to write macros to create arrays:

```
MACRO    WordArray aName, aSize, aValue
aName&count     dw       aSize
aName           dw       aSize DUP (aValue)
ENDM     WordArray
```

WordArray has three parameters: a label identifier (aName), the number of words in the array (aSize), and the initial value to assign to each word (aValue). In the macro's body, the first dw directive creates a variable equal to the number of words in the array, labeling this variable by the array name plus "count." The second dw directive declares the array values, using the DUP operator to reserve space for aSize values initialized to aValue. Two examples show how to use the macro:

```
WordArray       a1, 10, 0
WordArray       a2, 100, ?
```

Expanding these macro commands creates two arrays, the first at label a1 with ten words initialized to 0 and the second at label a2 with 100 uninitialized words. Two variables a1count and a2count are also created and initialized to the number of words in each array. Programs can read these variables to find out how many values the arrays hold:

```
mov     cx, [a1count]   ; Set cx = number of words in array a1
mov     cx, [a2count]   ; Set cx = number of words in array a2
```

Definitions That Repeat

These are all Macro calls, not defns!

Three directives—IRP, IRPC, and REPT—can be used to construct macros that repeat instructions, usually with different parameters on each repetition. The directives can be used alone or inside macros to create powerful new commands. As with plain macro definitions, end your repeating definitions with ENDM. Earlier, you learned how to use the REPT directive to create automatically initialized arrays. (For example, see lines 37–43 in Program 7-2, SCREEN.ASM.) IRP operates similarly, but takes arguments listed inside angle brackets and separated by commas:

```
IRP     register, <ax, bx, cx, dx>
        inc     register
ENDM
```

; These macros are expanded
; where they are defined!

When expanded during assembly, the effect is to create four inc instructions, one for each of the four registers listed in brackets:

```
inc     ax
inc     bx
inc     cx
inc     dx
```

The IRPC directive operates similarly to IRP but, instead of using arguments in brackets, it repeats the instructions for each letter in a string.

(The C in IRPC stands for Character.) As the next example demonstrates, you can use IRPC to create strings where each character is stored in a word instead of a byte, as db normally does:

```
LABEL    chars   WORD
IRPC     nextChar, ABCDEFG
         dw      ' &nextChar'
ENDM
```

The LABEL directive is necessary in this case because the assembler doesn't allow a label to preface an IRPC construction directly. The dummy parameter nextChar takes successive characters from the string ABCDEFG, which does not require surrounding quotes. On each repetition, a dw directive creates a two-character variable consisting of a space and the ASCII value in this loop's nextChar. Notice how & identifies nextChar as a parameter name. The effect of this example is the same as writing:

```
chars   dw      ' A'
        dw      ' B'
        dw      ' C'
        dw      ' D'
        dw      ' E'
```

Note: To see these characters in Turbo Debugger, use the View:Variables commands, press Tab and arrow keys to position the cursor to chars, and call up the View:Dump window.

You can use IRP, IRPC, and REPT inside macros, too, which lets you give names to repeated constructions. A typical example uses IRP to push registers onto the stack at the start of a procedure:

```
MACRO   PushReg registers
 IRP    reg, <registers>
        push    reg
 ENDM
ENDM
```

Notice that two ENDM directives are required—one to end the IRP command and the other to end the macro. A corresponding macro pops the registers from the stack, presumably at the end of a procedure:

```
MACRO   PopReg registers
 IRP    reg, <registers>
        pop     reg
 ENDM
ENDM
```

In each macro, a dummy parameter named registers passes the register list to IRP. The reg parameter in the IRP loop takes successive values from this list, assembling one push or pop instruction for each reg value until the list is empty. Together, PushReg and PopReg simplify procedure design by making it unnecessary to write instruction sequences such as:

```
push    ax
push    bx
push    cx
push    dx
```

becomes

Instead, to push these same four registers, you can simply write:

```
PushReg <ax, bx, cx, dx>
```

The four registers listed inside angle brackets expand to four push instructions, one for each register. At the end of the procedure, you would then use PopReg to restore these registers in the reverse order. With the two macros, you can write your procedures in this general form:

```
PROC    Subroutine
        PushReg <ax, bx, cx, dx, si, di>
;
;-----  Subroutine's instructions
;
        PopReg  <di, si, dx, cx, bx, ax>
        ret
ENDP    Subroutine
```

Could use pusha popa instead

Must have directive .286 (MASM) P286 (Ideal) in src file

Note: Before I'm accused of not practicing what I preach, I'd better explain that, to avoid using techniques before they are introduced and because macros are always optional, program listings in this book do not employ macros in procedures as suggested here to save and restore registers. You can certainly modify the listings to use **PushReg** and **PopReg**, which can save typing and can also help to eliminate bugs by forcing you to list pushed and popped registers on easy-to-compare single lines.

Macros and Code

As mentioned earlier, macros let you invent new commands that expand to individual assembly language instructions. Used this way, a macro is a kind of subroutine that is inserted directly in line with other instructions instead of requiring a call to activate. In fact, one way to optimize programs for top speed is to replace subroutine calls with macros that perform the same jobs. This can improve the program's performance by eliminating call and ret instructions. For example, suppose you have the procedure:

```
PROC    DecReg
        dec     ax
        dec     bx
        dec     cx
        dec     dx
        ret
ENDP    DecReg
```

After debugging the program, you decide to *unroll* the subroutine's instructions—that is, inserting the instructions directly where they are needed. The easiest way to do this is to create a macro:

```
MACRO   DecReg registers
 IRP    reg, <registers>
        dec     reg
 ENDM
ENDM
```

becomes *def'n*

There are simpler ways to write this macro, of course, but while going to the trouble of putting macros into the code, you may as well make the macro as versatile as possible. After designing `DecReg`, you can then use your text editor's global search and replace (or a utility program) to translate all the `call DecReg` instructions to:

```
DecReg  <ax, bx, cx, dx>
```

If `DecReg` is called often in the program, perhaps from inside a critical loop, the unrolled code runs faster by eliminating multiple executions of `call` and `ret` instructions. In addition, `DecReg` is even more useful as a macro than a subroutine because the macro allows you to decrement any combination of registers, which the procedure cannot do.

> Note: Macros can also nest; that is, you can use a macro name inside another macro definition. Such macros can be powerful, but they can also expand to many lines of code.

Register Preservation

A potential danger lurks when a macro changes the value of one or more registers. Because the register names do not appear in the source code, you can easily miss this fact and expect a register to retain an important value. Some programmers write macros that preserve all registers with `push` and `pop` instructions:

```
MACRO   DispChar ch
        push    ax              ;; Save ax
        push    dx              ;; Save dx
        mov     ah, 2           ;; Load function number into ah
```

```
        mov     dl, '&ch'       ;; Load character to display
        int     21h             ;; Call DOS--display character ch
        pop     dx              ;; Restore saved dx
        pop     ax              ;; Restore saved ax
ENDM    DispChar
```

The `DispChar` macro defines a single parameter `ch`, which is assigned to register `dl`, again using the & operator to tell the assembler that `ch` is a parameter name and not the two characters *c* and *h* in quotes. Next, the number of the DOS standard output routine (2) is assigned to `ah`, after which `int 21h` calls DOS to write the character in `dl` to the standard output file. Two pairs of `push` and `pop` instructions save and restore the values of the registers used by the macro. In the program, you might use this macro to display a character:

```
DispChar <Q>
```

If the `DispChar` macro does not preserve the registers it uses, you might easily forget that calling `DispChar` changes the values in `ah` and `dl`. Of course, the downside of this is that multiple uses of `DispChar` push and pop the same registers over and over, even when unnecessary. It's impossible to say whether you should or shouldn't preserve registers in your macros—the choice is up to you. If you don't, be careful to document the registers used by your macros—or get settled for some nice, long sessions with Turbo Debugger while you try to figure out why your programs aren't working.

Using the Include Directive

Although you can declare individual macros at the start of your program, a better plan is to store macro definitions in a separate text file and then load that file during assembly. To do this, insert an **INCLUDE** directive such as:

```
INCLUDE "MACROS.ASM"    ; Read library of macro definitions
```

> Note: You must use quotes around file names when assembling **INCLUDE** directives in Ideal mode. In MASM mode, the quotes are not required, but then, you also can't end the line with a comment as shown here because the assembler would consider the comment to be part of the file name.

You can also include files containing other assembly language text—you don't have to use **INCLUDE** to load only macro definitions. The text in the included file is inserted into the program and assembled, as though the two files were one. Many programmers store a program's equates in separate files to be included as needed in one or more modules. An **INCLUDE** directive can appear anywhere inside the program text and can be used to load equates, macros, variables, and assembly language instructions. You can also nest multiple **INCLUDE** directives, having an included file include some more text, which includes still another file, and so forth.

In practice, it's probably best not to use INCLUDE to insert variables and instructions into programs. A better idea is to write separate object-code modules for these items and then link the code to your program, using the techniques explained for modules such as SCREEN and STRINGS in this book. Remember that included text is assembled over and over along with the other instructions in a program, while separately assembled object-code modules are immediately ready for linking.

Conditional Compilation

Conditional compilation directives form a kind of minilanguage built into Turbo Assembler. With conditional directives, you can change the way a program assembles based on various conditions, normally defined at the start of a program module (or stored in a separate INCLUDE file) and assigned to identifiers called *conditional symbols*. For example, you could define a conditional symbol named DisplayType to indicate which kind of display adapter the computer has. To modify the program for new display hardware, you simply change DisplayType to the correct value and reassemble. Some software companies build hundreds of such symbols into programs, letting programmers quickly generate custom applications for customers by simply tweaking a few symbols here and there.

Table 8-1 lists Turbo Assembler's conditional compilation directives, none of which directly generates any machine code. Pass-dependent directives such as ERRIF1 and ERRIF2 are included for compatibility with MASM, which processes assembly language programs in two passes. Because Turbo Assembler is a one-pass assembler, these directives should not be used. (Nor should they ever be needed.)

Defining
Conditional
Symbols

Define conditional symbols just as you do other equates, assigning a value, which must be numeric, to a named identifier. For example, to define a conditional symbol named DisplayType, you could write:

```
DisplayType    =    1
```

You can also use EQU to define conditional symbols, but normally you should use an equal sign, which creates a numeric symbol. Because the "1" in this example isn't very meaningful, you'll probably define other equates for assigning to your conditional symbols. For example, you might set up four symbols representing various common display types:

```
CGAAdapter     =    0
MonoAdapter    =    1
EGAAdapter     =    2
VGAAdapter     =    3
```

The actual values don't matter in this example—it's the names we're after, which lend extra readability to programs, as in the perfectly clear assignment:

```
DisplayType    =    EGAAdapter
```

Table 8-1 *Conditional Compilation Directives*

Directive	Meaning
ELSE	Assemble next lines if previous IF is false
ELSEIF	End of ELSE directive. Begin new IF
ENDIF	End of IF directive
ERR	Force assembler to display error message
ERRIF	Error if an expression is true
ERRIF1	Error if on pass 1*
ERRIF2	Error if on pass 2*
ERRIFB	Error if an argument is blank
ERRIFDEF	Error if an argument is defined
ERRIFDIF	Error if arguments differ
ERRIFDIFI	Error if arguments differ (ignoring case)
ERRIFE	Error if an expression is false (equal to 0)
ERRIFIDN	Error if arguments are identical
ERRIFIDNI	Error if arguments are identical (ignoring case)
ERRIFNB	Error if an argument is not blank
ERRIFNDEF	Error if an argument is not defined
IF	Assemble if expression is true
IF1	Assemble if on pass 1*
IF2	Assemble if on pass 2*
IFB	Assemble if an argument is blank
IFDEF	Assemble if a symbol is defined
IFDIF	Assemble if arguments differ
IFDIFI	Assemble if arguments differ (ignoring case)
IFE	Assemble if an expression is false (equal to 0)
IFIDN	Assemble if arguments are identical
IFIDNI	Assemble if arguments are identical (ignoring case)
IFNB	Assemble if argument is not blank
IFNDEF	Assemble if argument is not defined

*Note: Pass 1 and 2 conditional directives, included for compatibility with MASM, should not be used in Turbo Assembler.

At this point in the program, the symbol `DisplayType` is said to be *defined* regardless of the value the symbol has. A symbol is defined as soon as you equate any value to that symbol. A symbol is *undefined* if the symbol is never assigned a value. Be sure to understand the difference between the value of a symbol and the fact that a symbol is or is not defined. These hints further explain the distinction:

▶ A symbol is defined when you equate any value to that symbol. The actual value is unimportant.

▶ A symbol is undefined if you never equate a value to that symbol.

▶ Testing whether a symbol is defined is not the same as testing whether a symbol has a specific value.

▶ For best results, use the equal sign to define conditional symbols, which should be numeric. This also allows you to later redefine the same symbols if necessary.

When creating conditional symbols, remember that symbol names represent simple values. This is important because conditional directives such as IF and IFE work only with expressions and arguments that evaluate to integer values.

Using Conditional Symbols

The most common use for conditional symbols is to select which of two or more sections of code is actually assembled. For example, suppose you need two versions of a program—one for debugging purposes and another for the final production model. The debugging version might include special instructions to display stack usage, dump important variables to the printer, and so forth. Naturally, you don't want to include such features in the production model. Conditional compilation directives make it easy to assemble either version by simply defining a few conditional symbols at the top of the program module:

```
False        =      0      ; Value meaning false
True         =      1      ; Value meaning true
Debugging    =      True   ; False for production
```

You now have a way to tell the assembler which version to create, depending on the setting of Debugging. This lets you change variables, insert code, call debugging procedures, and modify other program features, all by setting Debugging to True or False. In the data segment, you could test Debugging in a conditional directive to change the program's indentifying string:

```
DATASEG
IF Debugging
programID       db        'Chess v1.0 (TEST MODEL)', 0
ELSE
programID       db        'Chess v1.0', 0
ENDIF
```

When Turbo Assembler processes this directive, if Debugging is True (equal to any nonzero value), the "TEST MODEL" string is assembled; otherwise, the production string is assembled. Only one string is ever included in the final code, even though the program text appears to repeat "Chess v1.0" wastefully. There's no such waste because, if Debugging is False, the first db directive *is completely skipped during assembly*. Remember that conditional directives are commands to Turbo Assembler— the IF, ELSE, and ENDIF directives generate no code and are not instructions that execute at run time.

Another test of Debugging might be used later on in the program's code segment. For example, perhaps the program must call a special subroutine to initialize values required only during debugging. This does the job:

```
IF Debugging EQ True
        call    DebugInit       ; Initialize for debugging
ENDIF
```

If `Debugging` equals `True`, then the `call` instruction to `DebugInit` is assembled. Otherwise, the assembler completely skips the `call`. Another section of the program could then insert the debugging procedure only if `Debugging` is `True`:

```
IF Debugging
PROC    DebugInit
;
; ----- Debugging initialization subroutine
;
        ret     ; Return to caller
ENDP    DebugInit
ENDIF
```

Both the `call` to the subroutine and the procedure itself are added to the finished product only if `Debugging` is `True`. If `Debugging` is `False`, the program is assembled as though these items didn't exist.

You may have noticed in these samples that one `IF` directive used the expression `IF Debugging EQ True`, while the other simply states `IF Debugging`. Both forms are correct and have the same effect—as long as you follow the convention that any nonzero value (usually 1 or −1) represents `True` and that 0 represents `False`. The `EQ` operator in the first conditional directive is one of several listed in Table 8-2 that you can use in similar conditional expressions.

`IF` directives must be followed (eventually) by `ENDIF`, marking the end of the conditional section. In between, you can insert an optional `ELSE` clause, selecting alternate instructions that assemble if the expression evaluates to false. This lets you use `IF` alone:

Table 8-2 *Constant Expression Operators*

Operator	Meaning
AND	Logical AND
EQ	Equal
GE	Greater or equal
GT	Greater than
LE	Less or equal
LT	Less than
MOD	Modulus (integer division remainder)
NE	Not equal
NOT	One's complement (bit toggle)
OR	Logical OR
SHL	Shift left
SHR	Shift right
XOR	Logical exclusive OR

```
IF Debugging
; code for debugging = True
ENDIF
```

or, with **ELSE** to select alternate instructions:

```
IF Debugging
; code for debugging = True
ELSE
; code for debugging = False
ENDIF
```

To Define or Not to Define

Instead of using **IF** to test if an expression evaluates to true (not 0) or **IFE** to test for false (equal to 0), you can use the **IFDEF** and **IFNDEF** directives to test if a symbol is defined or not defined. As you recall from earlier, a symbol is defined as soon as you give it a value. In a program, if you write:

```
IFDEF Debugging
call  DebugInit
ENDIF
```

the **call** is assembled only if **Debugging** was assigned a value, no matter what that value is. To define **Debugging**, you might add to the beginning of the program the line:

```
Debugging     =     1        ; Define Debugging
```

To undefine the symbol, just remove this line or insert a semicolon at far left, converting the line into a comment. You can also test if symbols are not defined with statements such as:

```
IFNDEF Debugging
welcome         db        'Production version 5.01', 0
ENDIF
```

IFDEF and **IFNDEF** are most useful when used along with Turbo Assembler's **/d** option, which you can use to define symbols at the DOS command line. To assemble a program named Banana with debugging features, you could issue the command:

```
tasm /dDebugging=1 Banana
```

The **/dDebugging=1** defines the **Debugging** symbol when you assemble the program—there's no need to add a **Debugging** equate to the program source text. (The value assigned to the symbol is unimportant.) Notice that there is no space between the **/d** and the symbol name. Later, after debugging is no longer needed, assembling normally undefines **Debugging**, stripping the test code from the finished version:

```
tasm Banana
```

Handling Conditional Errors
You can create multiple conditionals with IF, ELSE, and ELSEIF, ending the whole shebang with ENDIF. For example, to define a string according to the display types listed earlier, you can write:

```
DATASEG
IF DisplayType EQ CGAAdapter
displayID        db        'CGA Adapter', 0
ELSEIF DisplayType EQ MonoAdapter
displayID        db        'Monochrome Adapter', 0
ELSEIF DisplayType EQ EGAAdapter
displayID        db        'EGA Adapter', 0
ELSEIF DisplayType EQ VGAAdapter
displayID        db        'VGA Adapter', 0
ENDIF
```

Only one string is defined in the final code, depending upon the DisplayType setting. However, this example is incomplete because it does not allow for the possibility that DisplayType could specify an unknown value. To handle this condition, you could replace ENDIF with:

```
ELSE
displayID        db        'Unknown adapter type', 0
ENDIF
```

Or, to prevent the program from assembling with an unknown condition, you can force an error to occur by replacing the original ENDIF with:

```
ELSE
ERR
DISPLAY "**Error** Unknown DisplayType value"
ENDIF
```

When this is assembled, if the DisplayType is unknown, the ERR directive forces Turbo Assembler to display a "user generated" error message. The DISPLAY directive also displays a quoted string, in this example, telling you that something is wrong with DisplayType. Assembling the program generates this text on screen:

```
Assembling file:   TEST.ASM
**Error** Unknown DisplayType value
**Error** TEST.ASM(102) User generated error
Error messages:    1
Warning messages:  None
Remaining memory:  331k
```

Starting a DOS Macro Library

Many assembly language programs spend a great deal of time calling DOS routines, all of which have special requirements, for example, expecting values to be in certain registers. The DOS macros in this section can help make writing programs easier in two ways: by reducing to single names the common sequences for calling DOS routines and by helping to document register assignments and other requirements.

Do not assemble the macros in Program 8-1, DOSMACS.ASM. Instead, store the text file on disk and add the macros to your programs by including this line somewhere in the beginning of your program (preferably just before the DATASEG directive):

```
INCLUDE "DOSMACS.ASM"
```

Program 8-1 *DOSMACS.ASM*

```
 1:   %NOLIST
 2:
 3:   ; Subset of DOS Macros for Turbo Assembler (Ideal mode)
 4:
 5:   ;-------------------------------------------------------------
 6:   ; MS_DOS              Call any DOS function
 7:   ;-------------------------------------------------------------
 8:   ; Input:
 9:   ;      functionNumber = DOS function number
10:   ; Output:
11:   ;      depends upon specific function
12:   ; Registers:
13:   ;      depends upon specific function
14:   ;-------------------------------------------------------------
15:   MACRO   MS_DOS   functionNumber
16:           mov      ah, functionNumber      ;; Assign function number
17:           int      21h                     ;; Call DOS
18:   ENDM    MS_DOS   functionNumber
19:
20:   ;-------------------------------------------------------------
21:   ; (01h) DOS_GetChar      Get character with echo
22:   ;-------------------------------------------------------------
23:   ; Input:
24:   ;      none
25:   ; Output:
26:   ;      al = next character from standard input
27:   ; Registers:
28:   ;      ax
29:   ;-------------------------------------------------------------
30:   MACRO   DOS_GetChar
31:           mov      ah, 1              ;; Assign DOS function number
32:           int      21h                ;; Call DOS
33:   ENDM    DOS_GetChar
34:
35:   ;-------------------------------------------------------------
36:   ; (02h) DOS_PutChar      Write character to standard output
37:   ;-------------------------------------------------------------
38:   ; Input:
39:   ;      dl = ASCII character (0-255)
```

```
40:  ; Output:
41:  ;        none
42:  ; Registers:
43:  ;        ah
44:  ;------------------------------------------------------------
45:  MACRO   DOS_PutChar
46:          mov    ah, 2          ;; Assign DOS function number
47:          int    21h            ;; Call DOS
48:  ENDM    DOS_PutChar
49:
50:  ;------------------------------------------------------------
51:  ; (05h) DOS_PrintChar    Send character to standard list device
52:  ;------------------------------------------------------------
53:  ; Input:
54:  ;        dl = ASCII character (0-255)
55:  ; Output:
56:  ;        none
57:  ; Registers:
58:  ;        ah
59:  ;------------------------------------------------------------
60:  MACRO   DOS_PrintChar
61:          mov    ah, 5          ;; Assign DOS functon number
62:          int    21h            ;; Call DOS
63:  ENDM    DOS_PrintChar
64:
65:  ;------------------------------------------------------------
66:  ; (07h) DOS_GetRawChar  Get unfiltered char with no echo
67:  ;------------------------------------------------------------
68:  ; Input:
69:  ;        none
70:  ; Output:
71:  ;        al = next character from standard input
72:  ; Registers:
73:  ;        ax
74:  ;------------------------------------------------------------
75:  MACRO   DOS_GetRawChar
76:          mov    ah, 7          ;; Assign DOS function number
77:          int    21h            ;; Call DOS
78:  ENDM    DOS_GetRawChar
79:
80:  ;------------------------------------------------------------
81:  ; (08h) DOS_GetCharNoEcho        Get filtered char with no echo
82:  ;------------------------------------------------------------
83:  ; Input:
84:  ;        none
85:  ; Output:
86:  ;        al = next character from standard input
87:  ; Registers:
88:  ;        ax
89:  ;------------------------------------------------------------
```

```
 90:   MACRO   DOS_GetCharNoEcho
 91:           mov     ah, 8           ;; Assign DOS function number
 92:           int     21h             ;; Call DOS
 93:   ENDM    DOS_GetCharNoEcho
 94:
 95:   ;-------------------------------------------------------------------
 96:   ; (09h) DOS_PutString   Write ASCII$ string to standard output
 97:   ;-------------------------------------------------------------------
 98:   ; Input:
 99:   ;       string = label of ASCII$ variable
100:   ; Output:
101:   ;       none
102:   ; Registers:
103:   ;       ah, dx
104:   ;-------------------------------------------------------------------
105:   MACRO   DOS_PutString   string
106:           mov     ah, 9           ;; Assign DOS function number
107:           mov     dx, offset string ;; Address string with ds:dx
108:           int     21h             ;; Call DOS
109:   ENDM    DOS_PutString
110:
111:   ;-------------------------------------------------------------------
112:   ; (OBh) DOS_Keypressed  Check if a keyboard character is waiting
113:   ;-------------------------------------------------------------------
114:   ; Input:
115:   ;       none
116:   ; Output:
117:   ;       zf = 0 : (jnz) A character is waiting to be read
118:   ;       zf = 1 : (jz) No character is waiting
119:   ; Registers:
120:   ;       ax
121:   ;-------------------------------------------------------------------
122:   MACRO   DOS_Keypressed
123:           mov     ah, OBh         ;; Assign DOS function number
124:           int     21h             ;; Call DOS
125:           or      al, al          ;; Set/clear zf
126:   ENDM    DOS_Keypressed
127:
128:   ;-------------------------------------------------------------------
129:   ; (OEh) DOS_SetDrive    Change current drive
130:   ;-------------------------------------------------------------------
131:   ; Input:
132:   ;       dl = drive number (0 = A:, 1 = B:, 2 = C:, ..., 25 = Z:)
133:   ;       Note: F: to Z: requires LASTDRIVE=Z in CONFIG.SYS file
134:   ; Output:
135:   ;       al = total number of drives available
136:   ; Registers:
137:   ;       ax
138:   ;-------------------------------------------------------------------
```

```
139:    MACRO   DOS_SetDrive
140:            mov     ah, OEh         ;; Assign DOS function number
141:            int     21h             ;; Call DOS
142:    ENDM    DOS_SetDrive
143:
144:    ;-----------------------------------------------------------------
145:    ; (19h) DOS_GetDrive    Get current drive number
146:    ;-----------------------------------------------------------------
147:    ; Input:
148:    ;       none
149:    ; Output:
150:    ;       al = drive number (0 = A:, 1 = B:, 2 = C:, ..., 25 = Z:)
151:    ; Registers:
152:    ;       ax
153:    ;-----------------------------------------------------------------
154:    MACRO   DOS_GetDrive
155:            mov     ah, 19h         ;; Assign DOS function number
156:            int     21h             ;; Call DOS
157:    ENDM    DOS_GetDrive
158:
159:    ;-----------------------------------------------------------------
160:    ; (25h) DOS_SetVector   Set interrupt vector
161:    ;-----------------------------------------------------------------
162:    ; Input:
163:    ;       interrupt = interrupt number (0-255)
164:    ;       address   = label at start of interrupt routine
165:    ; Output:
166:    ;       none
167:    ; Registers:
168:    ;       ax, dx
169:    ;-----------------------------------------------------------------
170:    MACRO   DOS_SetVector   interrupt, address
171:            push    ds              ;; Save current ds register
172:            mov     ax, SEG address ;; Assign segment address of
173:            mov     ds, ax          ;;  interrupt service to ds
174:            mov     dx, OFFSET address ;; Assign offset address to dx
175:            mov     ah, 025h        ;; Assign DOS function number
176:            mov     al, interrupt   ;; Assign interrupt number to al
177:            int     21h             ;; Call DOS
178:            pop     ds              ;; Restore ds segment register
179:    ENDM    DOS_SetVector
180:
181:    ;-----------------------------------------------------------------
182:    ; (35h) DOS_GetVector   Get interrupt vector
183:    ;-----------------------------------------------------------------
184:    ; Input:
185:    ;       interrupt = interrupt number
186:    ; Output:
187:    ;       es:bx = segment:offset address of interrupt
```

```
188:   ; Registers:
189:   ;        ax, bx, es
190:   ;-----------------------------------------------------------------
191:   MACRO   DOS_GetVector   interrupt
192:           mov     al, interrupt    ;; Assign interrupt number to al
193:           mov     ah, 35h          ;; Assign DOS function number
194:           int     21h              ;; Call DOS
195:   ENDM    DOS_GetVector
196:
197:   ;-----------------------------------------------------------------
198:   ; (3Bh) DOS_ChDir        Change current directory
199:   ;-----------------------------------------------------------------
200:   ; Input:
201:   ;        dirName = label of ASCIIZ string in ds data segment
202:   ; Output:
203:   ;        cf = 0 : (jnc) Change was successful
204:   ;
205:   ;        cf = 1 : (jc) Change was not successful
206:   ;        ax = error code (3 = directory not found)
207:   ; Registers:
208:   ;        ax, dx
209:   ;-----------------------------------------------------------------
210:   MACRO   DOS_ChDir   dirName
211:           mov     ah, 3Bh           ;; Assign DOS function number
212:           mov     dx, OFFSET dirName ;; Assign string address to ds:dx
213:           int     21h               ;; Call DOS
214:   ENDM    DOS_ChDir
215:
216:   ;-----------------------------------------------------------------
217:   ; (3Ch) DOS_CreateFile  Create new file
218:   ;-----------------------------------------------------------------
219:   ; Input:
220:   ;        fileName = label of ASCIIZ string in ds data segment
221:   ;        cx = attribute to use in directory
222:   ;            00 = normal file
223:   ;            01 = read-only (access denied for read/write)
224:   ;            02 = hidden (DIR does not show name)
225:   ;            04 = system file
226:   ; Output:
227:   ;        cf = 0 : (jnc) File created
228:   ;        ax = file handle for future operations
229:   ;
230:   ;        cf = 1 : (jc) File not created
231:   ;        ax = error code
232:   ;            3 = path not found
233:   ;            4 = no more handles available
234:   ;            5 = access denied
235:   ; Registers:
236:   ;        ax, dx
237:   ;-----------------------------------------------------------------
```

```
238:   MACRO   DOS_CreateFile  fileName
239:           mov     ah, 3Ch         ;; Assign DOS function number
240:           mov     dx, OFFSET fileName ;; Assign name address to ds:dx
241:           int     21h             ;; Call DOS
242:   ENDM    DOS_CreateFile
243:
244:   ;--------------------------------------------------------------
245:   ; (3Dh) DOS_OpenFile    Open file for I/O
246:   ;--------------------------------------------------------------
247:   ; Input:
248:   ;       fileName = label of ASCIIZ string in ds data segment
249:   ; Output:
250:   ;       cf = 0 : (jnc) File opened
251:   ;       ax = file handle for future operations
252:   ;
253:   ;       cf = 1 : (jc) File not opened
254:   ;       ax = error code
255:   ;           2 = file not found
256:   ;           3 = path not found
257:   ;           4 = no more handles available
258:   ;           5 = access denied
259:   ; Registers:
260:   ;       ax, dx
261:   ;--------------------------------------------------------------
262:   MACRO   DOS_OpenFile  fileName
263:           mov     ah, 3Dh         ;; Assign DOS function number
264:           mov     al, 02          ;; Open for read/write access
265:           mov     dx, OFFSET fileName  ;; Assign name address to ds:dx
266:           int     21h             ;; Call DOS
267:   ENDM    DOS_OpenFile
268:
269:   ;--------------------------------------------------------------
270:   ; (3Eh) DOS_CloseFile   Close a previously opened file
271:   ;--------------------------------------------------------------
272:   ; Input:
273:   ;       bx = file handle from DOS_CreateFile or DOS_OpenFile
274:   ; Output:
275:   ;       cf = 0 : (jnc) File closed
276:   ;
277:   ;       cf = 1 : (jc) File not closed
278:   ;       ax = error code
279:   ;           6 = bad handle or file was not open
280:   ; Registers:
281:   ;       ax
282:   ;--------------------------------------------------------------
283:   MACRO   DOS_CloseFile
284:           mov     ah, 3Eh         ;; Assign DOS function number
285:           int     21h             ;; Call DOS
```

```
286:  ENDM    DOS_CloseFile
287:
288:  ;------------------------------------------------------------
289:  ; (3Fh) DOS_ReadFile    Read from file or device
290:  ;------------------------------------------------------------
291:  ; Input:
292:  ;        bx = file handle from DOS_CreateFile or DOS_OpenFile
293:  ;        cx = number of bytes requested to read
294:  ;        buffer = label of destination buffer in ds data segment
295:  ;        Note: buffer must be at least cx bytes long!
296:  ; Output:
297:  ;        cf = 0 : (jnc) Read was successful
298:  ;        ax = actual number of bytes read (0 = at end of file)
299:  ;
300:  ;        cf = 1 : (jc) Read was not successful
301:  ;        ax = error code
302:  ;            5 = access denied
303:  ;            6 = bad handle or file was not open
304:  ; Registers:
305:  ;        ax, dx
306:  ;------------------------------------------------------------
307:  MACRO   DOS_ReadFile  buffer
308:          mov    ah, 3Fh          ;; Assign DOS function number
309:          mov    dx, OFFSET buffer ;; Address buffer with ds:dx
310:          int    21h              ;; Call DOS
311:  ENDM    DOS_ReadFile
312:
313:  ;------------------------------------------------------------
314:  ; (40h) DOS_WriteFile   Write to file or device
315:  ;------------------------------------------------------------
316:  ; Input:
317:  ;        bx = file handle from DOS_CreateFile or DOS_OpenFile
318:  ;        cx = number of bytes requested to write
319:  ;        buffer = label of source buffer in ds data segment
320:  ; Output:
321:  ;        cf = 0 : (jnc) Write was successful
322:  ;        ax = actual number of bytes written (0 = disk is full)
323:  ;
324:  ;        cf = 1 : (jc) Write was not successful
325:  ;        ax = error code
326:  ;            5 = access denied
327:  ;            6 = bad handle or file was not open
328:  ; Registers:
329:  ;        ax, dx
330:  ;------------------------------------------------------------
331:  MACRO   DOS_WriteFile  buffer
332:          mov    ah, 40h          ;; Assign DOS function number
333:          mov    dx, OFFSET buffer ;; Address buffer with ds:dx
334:          int    21h              ;; Call DOS
```

```
335:   ENDM    DOS_WriteFile
336:
337:   ;------------------------------------------------------------
338:   ; (42h) DOS_Seek          Change location for next read/write
339:   ;------------------------------------------------------------
340:   ; Input:
341:   ;       bx = file handle from DOS_CreateFile or DOS_OpenFile
342:   ;       cx = high word of 32-bit byte offset
343:   ;       dx = low word of 32-bit byte offset
344:   ; Output:
345:   ;       cf = 0 : (jnc) Seek was successful
346:   ;       dx = high word of 32-bit offset position after seek
347:   ;       ax = low word of 32-bit offset position after seek
348:   ;
349:   ;       cf = 1 : (jc) Seek was not successful
350:   ;       ax = error code
351:   ;            6 = bad handle or file was not open
352:   ; Registers:
353:   ;       ax
354:   ;------------------------------------------------------------
355:   MACRO   DOS_Seek
356:           mov     ah, 42h         ;; Assign DOS function number
357:           xor     al, al          ;; Seeks to absolute position in cx,dx
358:           int     21h             ;; Call DOS
359:   ENDM    DOS_Seek
360:
361:   ;------------------------------------------------------------
362:   ; (47h) DOS_GetDir        Get name of current directory
363:   ;------------------------------------------------------------
364:   ; Input:
365:   ;       string = address of 64-byte (minimum) variable
366:   ; Output:
367:   ;       directory name inserted into string in ASCIIZ format
368:   ; Registers:
369:   ;       ax, dl, si
370:   ;------------------------------------------------------------
371:   MACRO   DOS_GetDir  string
372:           mov     ah, 47h         ;; Assign DOS function number
373:           xor     dl, dl          ;; 0 specifies current drive
374:           mov     si, OFFSET string ;; Address string with ds:si
375:           int     21h             ;; Call DOS
376:   ENDM    DOS_GetDir
377:
378:   ;------------------------------------------------------------
379:   ; (4Ch) DOS_Terminate    End program
380:   ;------------------------------------------------------------
381:   ; Input:
382:   ;       code = [label] or value to pass to DOS or parent process
383:   ; Output:
384:   ;       none
```

```
385:  ; Registers:
386:  ;       ax
387:  ;-----------------------------------------------------------------
388:  MACRO   DOS_Terminate code
389:          mov     ah, 4Ch          ;; Assign DOS function number
390:          mov     al, code         ;; Assign return code
391:          int     21h              ;; Call DOS
392:  ENDM    DOS_Terminate
393:
394:  %LIST
```

Using DOSMACS.ASM

Most of the macros in DOSMACS should be self-explanatory—just read the comments preceding each macro for a list of all requirements, output, and modified registers. The DOSMACS.ASM file begins with a **%NOLIST** command to prevent listing the macro definitions even if you specify the **/L** listing option during assembly. This reduces the length of your program listings by not repeating the same text for all modules that include the macros. For reference, Table 8-3 lists each macro along with the associated function number in hexadecimal.

Table 8-3 *DOSMACS Macros*

No.	MACRO Name and Parameters
—	MS_DOS *functionNumber*
01h	DOS_GetChar
02h	DOS_PutChar
05h	DOS_PrintChar
07h	DOS_GetRawChar
08h	DOS_GetCharNoEcho
09h	DOS_PutString *string*
0Bh	DOS_Keypressed
0Eh	DOS_SetDrive
19h	DOS_GetDrive
25h	DOS_SetVector *interrupt, address*
35h	DOS_GetVector *interrupt*
3Bh	DOS_ChDir *dirName*
3Ch	DOS_CreateFile *fileName*
3Dh	DOS_OpenFile *fileName*
3Eh	DOS_CloseFile
3Fh	DOS_ReadFile *buffer*
40h	DOS_WriteFile *buffer*
42h	DOS_Seek
47h	DOS_GetDir *string*
4Ch	DOS_Terminate *code*

> Note: DOSMACS contains only a subset of DOS functions. A good project would be to expand DOSMACS to the full DOS set; be aware that this will also increase the time it takes to assemble programs that include the macros.

The macros are easy to use. Just load any required registers and specify any needed variables and then write the macro name plus the necessary parameters. For example, to read a character from the standard input file, write:

```
DOS_GetChar      ; al = next char from standard input
```

You can also call DOS functions by number, using the MS_DOS macro instead of loading ah and executing int 21h. Remember that this changes ah. To display a character loaded into dl, you could write:

```
mov     dl, 'A'          ; Character to display
MS_DOS  2                ; Call DOS output-character function
```

To use a macro that specifies parameters, read the comments, load a register, or allocate space for a variable and use the label identifier as the parameter. For writing ASCII$ strings to the standard output file, use instructions such as:

```
DATASEG
Welcome         db       'Welcome to my program', '$'
CODESEG
DOS_PutString Welcome    ; Display welcome message
```

Some macros return results in registers and flags. For instance, to check whether a character is available from the keyboard, you can write:

```
@@10:   DOS_Keypressed       ; Is a keypress waiting?
        jz      Continue     ; Jump if not
        DOS_GetRawChar       ; Else get the char (no echo)
        Call ProcessChar     ; Call routine to process char
Continue:
```

If DOS_Keypressed sets the zf flag, then no character is waiting to be read, and the program continues at label Continue:. If zf is reset, then a second macro DOS_GetRawChar reads the character and calls a subroutine ProcessChar (not shown) to handle the keystroke. The macros help document the program by converting DOS function numbers into understandable names.

Note: If you receive a strange error such as an "Undefined symbol" when using known keywords such as OFFSET, check that you have specified all required parameters. Also, try surrounding parameters with angle brackets as in <OFFSET CodeLabel>. If you still can't determine what's causing an error, insert %MACS at the start of the program and assemble with the /L option to create a listing showing your macro calls along with the expanded instructions. You should be able to figure out what is going wrong by reading this listing.

Summary

By storing common instruction sequences in macro definitions, you add custom commands to Turbo Assembler. Macros can clarify assembly language, reduce the size of the program text, and help to ensure consistent programming methods, especially in team projects. Macros have a few drawbacks, requiring modules to reassemble the macro library repeatedly and hiding effects on register values.

A macro definition begins with MACRO and ends with ENDM. Purging a macro with PURGE removes the macro definition from memory, conserving RAM and letting you replace individual macros, perhaps for testing revisions.

There are three types of macro parameters: symbolic, numeric, and string. Formal parameters are listed in the macro definition. Actual parameters are listed when the macro is used. In the program, when Turbo Assembler encounters a macro name, it expands the macro, replacing the macro name with the instructions from the macro definition and inserting the actual parameters for the formal parameter names. Parameters let you write programmable macros that change according to new requirements.

Macros can be used to define new data types, using common directives like db and dw. Code macros can be used to unroll subroutines, replacing call instructions with in-line code, an important optimization technique that can increase program speed. Repetitive macros can generate multiple instructions for lists of register values and characters.

Conditional symbols and directives let you write programs that assemble differently based on conditions defined at the beginning of the program. A conditional symbol is a numeric equate. By definition, a symbol is defined when you assign a value to the symbol. A symbol is not defined if it is never given a value. Various directives such as IF and IFE can test the value of symbols and expressions involving symbols. Other directives such as IFDEF and IFNDEF test if symbols are defined.

Multiple macros are often stored in text files and then loaded into modules with an INCLUDE directive. This chapter includes a sample macro library, DOSMACS.ASM, with several macros for calling common DOS functions.

Exercises

8-1. What are some of the advantages and disadvantages of using macros?

8-2. Write a macro named `Startup` to initialize registers `es` and `ds` at the start of a program.

8-3. What value or values should the conditions *true* and *false* have? What value or values are typically used to represent *true*?

8-4. What do double semicolons ;; do?

8-5. How do you throw away a macro definition?

8-6. How do you specify a parameter's type in a macro definition?

8-7. Write macros `stz` and `clz` to set and clear the zero flag `zf`. The macros should not affect any other flags and should preserve all register values.

8-8. Write a macro to assign a literal value to any segment register. Show how to use your macro to set `es` to the address of the color video buffer 0B800h.

8-9. What instruction or instructions would you use to add the hypothetical macro library files FLOAT.MAX, BIOSMAC.TXT, and CUSTOM.MAX to a program?

8-10. Create a conditional symbol named `HasFastCrt` set to true or false at the beginning of a program, indicating whether the system has a memory-mapped video display, as do all PCs, or a slower "dumb" terminal, such as might be found on plain MS-DOS systems. Use your symbol in a subroutine that displays a character, appropriately selecting the SCREEN module's `Sc-PokeChar` routine (see chapter 7) or a similar DOS output function. The procedure should operate identically in all respects regardless of the selected hardware. You may use DOS-MACS.ASM in your answer.

Projects

8-1. Apply the same idea expressed in exercise #8-10 to all procedures in the SCREEN module, creating a module that you can assemble for PCs with memory-mapped video or for plain MS-DOS systems using a slower dumb terminal as the main console.

8-2. Write a module to select features for a variety of printers, conditionally selecting code to switch on bold face printing, underlining, and other options. Construct your code to allow printing text on plain printers lacking such features.

8-3. Create a BIOSMACS.ASM library of macros similar to DOS-MACS.ASM in this chapter. Your routines should make it easy to call ROM BIOS functions, as listed in a PC reference book (see Bibliography).

8-4. Locate a public domain assembly language listing (or take one of the listings from this book) that makes repeated subroutine calls. Replace the subroutines with macros, injecting code directly in line with other instructions. Test the effects this has on program speed and code-file size.

8-5. Create a library of macro files and object-code modules that make it easy to add standard debugging features to programs. Include routines to display (or print) stack usage by procedures, to list values of key variables, and to verify other values, for example, the range of an array index.

8-6. Write macros that use conditional directives to create variables in ASCIIZ and ASCII$ formats, with and without automatic length variables.

Chapter **9 Disk-File Processing**

▶ Getting a Handle on Files, *318*

▶ Disk-File Concepts, *319*

▶ Maximum Files, *319*

▶ Opening and Closing Files, *320*

▶ Flushing File Buffers, *321*

▶ Closing Files, *321*

▶ Dealing with Disk Errors, *322*

▶ Creating New Files, *326*

▶ Reading the DOS Command Line, *326*

▶ Reading and Writing Text Files, *335*

▶ Reading and Writing Data Files, *341*

▶ Reading the Disk Directory, *343*

▶ Summary, *347*

▶ Exercises, *348*

▶ Projects, *349*

Chapter *9 Disk-File Processing*

In This Chapter

Using file handles to read and write disk files; concepts of file handling; maximum files allowed by DOS; how to open and close existing files; how to create new files; DOS file buffers; handling disk file I/O errors; getting extended error information from DOS; reading parameters from the DOS command line; processing text files; processing multibyte records in data files; seeking records by number; options for seek operations; reading disk directories; plus several modules and example programs

Getting a Handle on Files

The concept of a file handle was introduced beginning with DOS version 2.0. As explained in chapter 7, handles are nothing mysterious. They're just simple 16-bit unsigned integers that DOS and programs use to refer to logical files attached to devices such as printers and keyboards. This chapter expands on that theme, showing how to use handles in assembly language programs to process data stored in disk files—including files on floppy diskettes, hard disk drives, and similar devices.

Before DOS 2.0, disk file I/O was accomplished by maintaining data structures called *file-control blocks* (FCB). Various fields in an FCB keep track of the location affected by subsequent read or write operations, the size of records in a file, plus other facts, many of which are required by DOS but seldom (if ever) of direct use in a program. File handles simplify disk file I/O by eliminating the need to create and keep track of FCBs, but without sacrificing any operational abilities. After creating a new file or opening an existing file on disk, a single file handle is all you need to activate even the most sophisticated file operations. For these reasons and because Microsoft discourages using older FCB function calls, this chapter concentrates exclusively on the newer file-handle methods.

Disk-File Concepts

Before writing programs to read and write data in disk files, it's important to understand a few universal concepts associated with disk file I/O. Later in this chapter, you'll learn how to put these important concepts into practice:

▶ You must open a file before you can read data from the file or write new data to disk. Opening existing files preserves information previously stored in the file.

▶ Creating a new file also opens the file for I/O but erases any information stored in an existing file of the same name, if one exists.

▶ DOS temporarily stores in memory buffers the data you write to disk files. Never assume that a disk write operation actually transfers any data to disk.

▶ Closing a file writes any buffered data to disk, ensuring that all data previously written is saved.

▶ Closing a file also updates the file's entry in the disk directory and releases the file handle for future use.

▶ The *current location* is a pointer to the place in the file where the next read or write operation will begin. DOS keeps this pointer for you. You can move the current location around at will to access data at different locations in a file, but there is only one such pointer associated with each open file.

Maximum Files

Every program can simultaneously have open a maximum of 20 files, up to a grand total of 255 files for all active programs. When one program runs another by calling the DOS Exec function 04Bh, DOS allocates to the new program a maximum of 20 file handles, as long as this does not exceed the total of 255 file handles permitted for all executing programs. Ending a program with DOS function 04Ch closes all active file handles, releasing the handles for use by other programs. Out of the 20 available file handles available to each active program, DOS reserves the five handles 0 through 4 for standard I/O devices (see chapter 7); therefore, programs are normally limited to opening 15 files. To increase this limit, you can close one or more of the standard handles. For example, programs that don't call DOS functions to drive the printer and serial I/O ports can gain two more files by executing:

```
mov     ah, 03Eh        ; DOS Close-File function number
mov     bx, 3           ; Set bx to AUX file-handle number (3)
int     21h             ; Call DOS to close file
inc     bx              ; Set bx to PRN file-handle number (4)
int     21h             ; Call DOS to close file
```

Opening and Closing Files

Opening a file for reading and writing is like opening a door before carrying furniture in and out. After opening a file, you may read and write data in the file as often as you wish—provided, of course, no errors occur. To open a disk file in assembly language, pass the address of the file name in ASCIIZ string format to DOS function 03Dh as in this sample:

```
DATASEG
fileName        DB          'C:\TASM\TEST.ASM', 0
CODESEG
mov     ax, @data               ; Initialize ds to address
mov     ds, ax                  ;  of data segment
mov     dx, offset fileName     ; Address file name with ds:dx
mov     ah, 03Dh                ; DOS Open-File function number
mov     al, 0                   ; 0 = Read-only access
int     21h                     ; Call DOS to open file
jc      Error                   ; Call routine to handle errors
```

The file name may specify a disk drive letter and subdirectory path names as in this sample. After initializing segment register ds (as you must do in all programs), use ds:dx to address the file name for function call 03Dh. In addition, register al is set to 0, telling DOS to allow only read operations on this file. Under DOS 2.0 and later versions, al can be one of three values:

▶ al = 0 = Read-only operations

▶ al = 1 = Write-only operations

▶ al = 2 = Read and write operations

Under DOS 3.0 and (presumably) later versions, additional values for shared files in a networked system are available. (See Bibliography for DOS references that describe these values.) After calling DOS to open a file, the carry flag cf indicates whether the operation was successful. As the previous sample code shows, this lets you use conditional jumps such as jc to jump to an error routine if the operation fails, probably because the requested file was not found. In this case, ax holds one of the error codes listed in Table 9-1. If no error occurred, then ax holds the file handle,

Table 9-1 *Open-File Error Codes*

Error Code	Meaning
01	File sharing not enabled
02	File does not exist
03	Path or file does not exist
04	No more handles available
05	Access denied (wrong file attribute)
0Ch	Bad access value in register al

which you can use for subsequent operations. Usually, it's a good idea to store this handle immediately in a variable, freeing **ax** for other uses:

```
DATASEG
handle   DW      ?                     ; Word variable for file handle
CODESEG
;
; open file with DOS function 03Dh
;
mov      [handle], ax                  ; Save file handle for later
```

Flushing File Buffers

A *file buffer* is an area of memory that serves as a kind of way station for data traveling to and from disk. Your program may also create private file buffers for storing data. Be aware that DOS has its own file buffers, controlled by the **BUFFERS** = n command in your CONFIG.SYS file. Most authorities recommend setting *n* to 20 to ensure at least one buffer for each of the maximum number of files a program might use.

When you write data to a file, the data is probably stored temporarily in a file buffer instead of being written directly to disk. Later, when the program reads other data from the file, opens a new file, or performs other file operations, DOS may flush the modified buffers to disk to make room in memory for the new data. Always be aware of this delayed action—the data you write to disk may not be permanently stored until later. To force any buffered data to be written to disk, duplicate the file handle with DOS function 45h and then close the duplicate, leaving the original file handle open:

```
mov      ah, 45h          ; Duplicate-handle function number
mov      bx, [handle]     ; Handle to duplicate
int      21h              ; Call DOS
jc       Error            ; Jump if error occurs (cf = 1)
mov      bx, ax           ; Assign duplicate handle to bx
mov      ah, 3Eh          ; Close-file function number
int      21h              ; Call DOS
jc       Error            ; Jump if error occurs (cf = 1)
```

Closing Files

Closing a file is simple—just pass in register **bx** the handle of any open file to function 03Eh. Closing a file instructs DOS to write to disk any data held in memory buffers and to update the directory entry for the file, recording the file size, date, and time. Assuming that you opened the file as described previously and saved the file handle, close the file with:

```
mov     bx, [handle]        ; Assign handle to bx
mov     ah, 03Eh            ; DOS Close-File function number
int     21h                 ; Call DOS to close the file
jc      Error               ; Jump if error detected
```

After calling DOS function 03Eh, check the carry flag as suggested here with a jc instruction. If cf = 1, then ax holds an error code, probably 6, indicating that the handle is bad (maybe you didn't assign the correct handle to bx) or the file was not open.

Closing files releases their handles for future use. Although it's good programming practice to close all open files before ending a program, DOS function 04Ch, which almost all example programs in this book use to transfer back to DOS, also closes all open file handles as one of its clean-up chores. This means that you can open several files, read and write data, and just end your program with confidence that DOS will save to disk any modified data in memory.

Dealing with Disk Errors

When processing files, you must be careful to detect and deal with all possible error conditions. This is especially important in assembly language programming, which lacks the built-in error mechanisms typically found in Pascal and BASIC. It's your responsibility to detect errors, to display appropriate warnings and messages, and to take appropriate actions when the disk is full and when other problems occur.

In all cases, the carry flag indicates the success (cf = 0) or failure (cf = 1) of a file operation; therefore, you should always check the carry flag after every file function call. What you do after this is up to you. On the simplest level, you can simply end the program whenever an error occurs. (Remember that this closes all open files.) Or you might return to a known place—the main menu, for example—allowing users to retry the failed operation. For more details, you can also call function 059h, which interrogates DOS for additional error information. (You can do this after any int 21h call, by the way. The function is not just for file operations.)

Program 9-1, DISKERR.ASM, uses this method in a subroutine to obtain extended error information from DOS and to display an appropriate message. The program is written as a library module, which you can link to your own programs (and to others in this chapter) as part of your error-control logic. Assemble the module and add the object code to your MTA.LIB library file with the commands:

```
tasm /zi diskerr
tlib /E mta -+diskerr
```

Repeat these steps if you later modify DISKERR.ASM, and ignore the usual warning that DISKERR is not in the library the first time you execute the tlib command. To reduce code-file size, leave out the /zi option, required only for running programs in Turbo Debugger.

Program 9-1 *DISKERR.ASM*

```
 1:   %TITLE "Disk-Error Handler"
 2:
 3:           IDEAL
 4:           DOSSEG
 5:           MODEL   small
 6:
 7:           DATASEG
 8:
 9:   errString      DB        '** ERROR: ', 0
10:
11:   err00   DB      'Unknown cause', 0
12:   err01   DB      'Bad function number', 0
13:   err02   DB      'File not found', 0
14:   err03   DB      'Path not found', 0
15:   err04   DB      'Too many open files', 0
16:   err05   DB      'Access denied', 0
17:   err06   DB      'File handle invalid', 0
18:   err07   DB      'Memory control blocks destroyed', 0
19:   err08   DB      'Not enough memory for operation', 0
20:   err09   DB      'Bad memory block address', 0
21:   err0A   DB      'Bad environment', 0
22:   err0B   DB      'Bad format', 0
23:   err0C   DB      'Bad access code', 0
24:   err0D   DB      'Bad data', 0
25:   err0E   DB      'Unknown cause', 0
26:   err0F   DB      'Bad disk drive letter', 0
27:   err10   DB      'Removing current directory is not allowed', 0
28:   err11   DB      'Device is not the same', 0
29:   err12   DB      'No more files available', 0
30:   err13   DB      'Disk is write-protected', 0
31:   err14   DB      'Unknown unit', 0
32:   err15   DB      'Disk drive is not ready', 0
33:   err16   DB      'Unknown command', 0
34:   err17   DB      'Data (CRC) error', 0
35:   err18   DB      'Bad structure length', 0
36:   err19   DB      'Seek error', 0
37:   err1A   DB      'Unknown type of medium', 0
38:   err1B   DB      'Sector not found', 0
39:   err1C   DB      'Printer is out of paper', 0
40:   err1D   DB      'Disk write error', 0
41:   err1E   DB      'Disk read error', 0
42:   err1F   DB      'General failure', 0
43:
```

```
44:   errors   DW      err10, err11, err12, err13, err14, err15, err16, err17
45:            DW      err08, err09, err0A, err0B, err0C, err0D, err0E, err0F
46:            DW      err10, err01, err12, err13, err04, err15, err06, err17
47:            DW      err18, err19, err1A, err1B, err1C, err1D, err1E, err1F
48:
49:            CODESEG
50:
51:   ;-----  From STRIO.OBJ
52:            EXTRN   NewLine:proc, StrWrite:proc
53:
54:            PUBLIC  DiskErr
55:
56:   %NEWPAGE
57:   ;-------------------------------------------------------------------
58:   ; DiskErr       Write disk error message to standard output
59:   ;-------------------------------------------------------------------
60:   ; Input:
61:   ;       none (cf = 1 following a DOS file operation)
62:   ; Output:
63:   ;       none (error message displayed)
64:   ; Registers:
65:   ;       ax, bp, bx, cx, dx, di, si changed
66:   ;-------------------------------------------------------------------
67:   PROC    DiskErr
68:            push    ds                      ; Save segment registers
69:            push    es                      ;  modified by DOS fn 59h
70:            mov     ah, 59h                 ; DOS Extended err fn num
71:            xor     bx, bx                  ; Must be 0
72:            int     21h                     ; Get extended error info
73:            pop     es                      ; Restore segment registers
74:            pop     ds
75:
76:            cmp     ax, 1Fh                 ; Is ax > 1Fh?
77:            jbe     @@10                    ; Jump if ax <= 1Fh
78:            xor     ax, ax                  ; Use "Unknown Cause" message
79:   @@10:
80:            shl     ax, 1                   ; Multiply ax by 2
81:            mov     bx, ax                  ; Copy ax to bx
82:            mov     di, [errors + bx]       ; Get address of string
83:            push    di                      ; Save di temporarily
84:            call    NewLine                 ; Start new display line
85:            mov     di, offset errString    ; Address first part of message
86:            call    StrWrite                ; Write ERROR message
87:            pop     di                      ; Restore address of message
88:            call    StrWrite                ; Write message to std out
89:            call    NewLine                 ; Start a new display line
90:            ret                             ; Return to caller
91:   ENDP    DiskErr
92:
93:            END                     ; End of module
```

Using DiskErr   To use the DISKERR module, add an `EXTRN DiskErr:Proc` command to your program. Then, assuming your program is named MYSTUFF.ASM, assemble and link to your library file with the commands:

```
tasm mystuff
tlink mystuff,,, mta
```

In your program code, after detecting an error from a file or disk directory DOS function, call `DiskErr` to display an appropriate message on screen. After this, you must take evasive action, ending the program or repeating a menu as suggested earlier. `DiskErr` doesn't do anything to solve the cause of an error—it just calls DOS for additional information and displays a message. Later in this chapter, you'll see examples of `DiskErr` at work. (For example, peek ahead to Program 9-4, line 156.)

How DiskErr Works   In addition to performing a useful operation, the `DiskErr` procedure demonstrates an interesting assembly language technique for selecting elements from an array of variable-length items, in this case, an array of ASCIIZ strings. First, the strings are declared at lines 11–42, giving each string a unique label, `err01`, `err02`, etc. Then, a second array at lines 44–47 is created using each string label. Remember that labels are addresses; therefore, the `errors` array is simply a list of the 16-bit offset addresses of each variable-length character string.

Each entry in the `errors` array points to the error string associated with an error code value (0–1Fh), used as index values into `errors`. (See Figure 9-1.) After obtaining the extended error information from DOS (lines 68–74), the error code value is multiplied by 2 (because each `errors` entry is a 2-byte word), after which line 82 loads `di` with the address of the correct string. The rest of the procedure displays the string, prefacing the text with "** ERROR:."

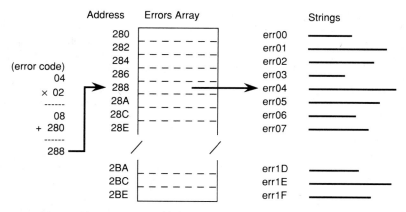

Figure 9-1 *An array of offset addresses (center) locates indexed elements (left) from an array of variable-length strings (right). Program 9-1 uses this technique in the DiskErr procedure to select individual strings from an ASCIIZ string array.*

Creating New Files

As far as the program instructions are concerned, creating a new file is similar to opening an existing file. Assign the address of an ASCIIZ string containing the file's name and set cx to one of the values listed in Table 9-2. This value is placed in the file's attribute byte in the disk directory, affecting future operations on the file. Most of the time, set cx to 0. After completing these initialization steps, call function 03Ch to create the file:

```
DATASEG
fileName      DB       'C:\NEWFILE.TXT', 0
handle        DW       ?
CODESEG
mov    ax, @data              ; Initialize ds to address
mov    ds, ax                 ;  of data segment
mov    dx, offset fileName    ; Address file name with ds:dx
mov    ah, 03Ch               ; DOS Create-File function number
xor    cx, cx                 ; Specify normal file attributes
int    21h                    ; Call DOS to create the file
jc     Error                  ; Jump if an error is detected
mov    [handle], ax           ; Save handle for later
```

As usual, the carry flag indicates the success or failure of function 03Ch. If cf = 1, then ax holds an error code—3, 4, or 5, as listed in Table 9-1—otherwise, ax holds the file handle, saved by this example in a global variable handle.

Note: One danger with creating new files is that DOS does not check whether a file of the same name exists. If you create a file of an existing name, the old file's contents are erased or *truncated*, as some DOS references say. For this reason, it's wise to test if a file already exists *before* calling DOS function 03Ch to create a new file and possibly erasing existing data. Later in this chapter are examples of how to do this in assembly language.

Table 9-2 *Create-File Attributes*

Value	Meaning
00	Normal file (most data files)
01	Read-only (write operations fail)
02	Hidden (invisible to DIR directory)
04	System file (better to use Hidden instead)

Reading the DOS Command Line

The traditional DOS program lets you enter one or more file names, options, and other data on the command line. In other words, you want people to be able to type commands such as:

```
C>textsort /d file1.txt file2.txt
```

Presumably, this hypothetical command runs a text sorting program, which operates on file1.txt, writes the finished output to file2.txt, and uses an option /d to select a descending sort. Most high-level languages provide methods for reading parameters like these separated by spaces after the file name. But in assembly language there are no similar built-in mechanisms, and reading the DOS command-line parameters is more difficult. In this section, you'll assemble a program that adds this essential feature to your assembly language programs.

When COMMAND.COM loads an .EXE code file, it prepares a 256-byte block of memory called the *Program Segment Prefix* (PSP), which contains among other items any text entered on the DOS command line after the program name. These characters are called the *command tail*. Upon starting an .EXE program, both **ds** and **es** address the PSP, of which 128 bytes are devoted to storing the command tail. Unfortunately, this same area—from offset 80h to FFh—also serves as a temporary disk buffer for some DOS functions; therefore, the first job is to copy the text out of the PSP into a variable for safe keeping.

The actual number of characters in the command tail is stored at offset 0080h in the PSP. The first character (if there is one) is at 0081h. The last character is always a carriage return (0Dh). Program 9-2, PARAMS.ASM, uses these facts to extract the command-line parameters from the PSP, saving the individual parameters as uppercase ASCIIZ strings in a 128-byte buffer in the program's data segment. Like other modules in this book, PARAMS requires a host program before it will run. In a moment, I'll list a sample host. For now, assemble PARAMS and install the object code in your MTA.LIB library file with the commands:

```
tasm /zi params
tlib /E mta -+params
```

As always, ignore the error that PARAMS isn't in the library, which it won't be until you install it the first time. Repeat these commands if you later modify the listing. Remove the /zi option to conserve disk space, unless you plan to run programs with Turbo Debugger.

Program 9-2 *PARAMS.ASM*

```
 1:  %TITLE "Parse DOS Command-Line Parameters"
 2:
 3:          IDEAL
 4:          DOSSEG
 5:          MODEL   small
 6:
 7:
 8:  TailLen       EQU    0080h        ; Offset of param len byte
 9:  CommandTail   EQU    0081h        ; Offset of parameters
10:
11:
```

```
12:          DATASEG
13:
14: numParams       DW      ?              ; Number of parameters
15: params          DB      128 DUP (?)    ; 128-byte block for strings
16:
17:
18:          CODESEG
19:
20:          PUBLIC  ParamCount, GetParams, GetOneParam
21:
22: %NEWPAGE
23: ;------------------------------------------------------------------
24: ; Separators    Private routine to check for blanks, tabs, and crs
25: ;------------------------------------------------------------------
26: ; Input:
27: ;        ds:si addresses character to check
28: ; Output:
29: ;        zf = 1 (je)  = character is a blank, tab, or cr
30: ;        zf = 0 (jne) = character is not a separator
31: ; Registers:
32: ;        al
33: ;------------------------------------------------------------------
34: PROC    Separators
35:          mov     al, [si]              ; Get character at ds:si
36:          cmp     al, 020h              ; Is char a blank?
37:          je      @@10                  ; Jump if yes
38:          cmp     al, 009h              ; Is char a tab?
39:          je      @@10                  ; Jump if yes
40:          cmp     al, 00Dh              ; Is char a cr?
41: @@10:
42:          ret                           ; Return to caller
43: ENDP    Separators
44: %NEWPAGE
45: ;------------------------------------------------------------------
46: ; ParamCount    Return number of parameters
47: ;------------------------------------------------------------------
48: ; Input:
49: ;        none
50: ; Output:
51: ;        dx = number of command-line parameters
52: ;        Note: When calling GetOneParam, cx should be less
53: ;         than the value returned in dx by ParamCount
54: ; Registers:
55: ;        dx
56: ;------------------------------------------------------------------
57: PROC    ParamCount
58:          mov     dx, [numParams]       ; Get value from variable
59:          ret                           ; Return to caller
60: ENDP    ParamCount
```

```
61:    %NEWPAGE
62:    ;----------------------------------------------------------------
63:    ; GetParams      Get DOS Command-Line Parameters
64:    ;----------------------------------------------------------------
65:    ; Input:
66:    ;         ds = Program Segment Prefix (PSP)
67:    ;         es = Program's data segment
68:    ;         Note: until you change it, ds addresses the PSP
69:    ;          when all .EXE programs begin
70:    ; Output:
71:    ;         global params filled with ASCIIZ strings
72:    ;         [numParams] = number of parameters
73:    ;         ds = Program's data segment (es not changed)
74:    ; Registers:
75:    ;         al, bx, dx, si, di, ds
76:    ;----------------------------------------------------------------
77:    PROC    GetParams
78:
79:    ;----- Initialize counter (cx) and index registers (si,di)
80:
81:            xor     ch, ch              ; Zero upper half of cx
82:            mov     cl, [ds:TailLen]    ; cx = length of parameters
83:            inc     cx                  ; Include cr at end
84:            mov     si, CommandTail     ; Address parameters with si
85:            mov     di, offset params   ; Address destination with di
86:
87:    ;----- Skip leading blanks and tabs
88:
89:    @@10:
90:            call    Separators          ; Skip leading blanks & tabs
91:            jne     @@20                ; Jump if not a blank or tab
92:            inc     si                  ; Skip this character
93:            loop    @@10                ; Loop until done or cx = 0
94:
95:    ;----- Copy parameter strings to global params variable
96:
97:    @@20:
98:            push    cx                  ; Save cx for later
99:            jcxz    @@30                ; Skip movsb if count = 0
100:           cld                         ; Auto-increment si and di
101:           rep     movsb               ; copy cx bytes from ds:si to es:di
102:
103:    ;----- Convert blanks to nulls and set numParams
104:
105:    @@30:
106:           push    es                  ; Push es onto stack
107:           pop     ds                  ; Make ds = es
108:           pop     cx                  ; Restore length to cx
109:           xor     bx, bx              ; Initialize parameter count
110:           jcxz    @@60                ; Skip loop if length = 0
111:           mov     si, offset params   ; Address parameters with si
```

```
112:   @@40:
113:           call    Separators              ; Check for blank, tab, or cr
114:           jne     @@50                    ; Jump if not a separator
115:           mov     [byte ptr si], 0        ; Change separator to null
116:           inc     bx                      ; Count number of parameters
117:   @@50:
118:           inc     si                      ; Point to next character
119:           loop    @@40                    ; Loop until cx equals 0
120:   @@60:
121:           mov     [numParams], bx         ; Save number of parameters
122:           ret                             ; Return to caller
123:   ENDP    GetParams
124:   %NEWPAGE
125:   ;-----------------------------------------------------------------
126:   ; GetOneParam    Get one parameter address by number
127:   ;-----------------------------------------------------------------
128:   ; Input:
129:   ;       cx = parameter number (0 = first)
130:   ;       Note: cx should always be less than the value
131:   ;         returned in dx by ParamCount
132:   ; Output:
133:   ;       di = offset of ASCIIZ string for this parameter
134:   ; Registers:
135:   ;       al, cx, di
136:   ;-----------------------------------------------------------------
137:   PROC    GetOneParam
138:           xor     al, al                  ; Init search value to 0
139:           mov     di, offset params       ; Address parameter strings
140:           jcxz    @@99                    ; If number = 0, jump to exit
141:           cmp     cx, [numParams]         ; Compare number with max
142:           jae     @@99                    ; Exit if > maximum number
143:           cld                             ; Auto-increment di
144:   @@10:
145:           scasb                           ; Scan for null terminator
146:           jnz     @@10                    ; Repeat until found
147:           loop    @@10                    ; Repeat for count in cx
148:   @@99:
149:           ret                             ; Return to caller
150:   ENDP    GetOneParam
151:
152:           END                     ; End of module
```

Running a PARAMS Demonstration

To understand how the PARAMS module works, it will help to assemble and run a test program. After this are details about how to use PARAMS in your own code. Save Program 9-3 as SHOWPARM.ASM and assemble, link, and run with the commands:

```
tasm /zi showparm
tlink /v showparm,,, mta
showparm param1 param2 param3
```

Note: The `tlink` command assumes that object-code modules PARAMS, BIN-ASC, STRINGS, and STRIO from this and previous chapters are installed in MTA.LIB.

Program 9-3 *SHOWPARM.ASM*

```
 1:     %TITLE "Display DOS Command-Line Parameters"
 2:
 3:             IDEAL
 4:             DOSSEG
 5:             MODEL   small
 6:             STACK   256
 7:
 8:             DATASEG
 9:
10:    exitCode       DB      0
11:    string         DB      20 DUP (0)
12:    s1             DB      'Number of parameters = ', 0
13:
14:            CODESEG
15:
16:    ;-----  From PARAMS.OBJ
17:            EXTRN   ParamCount:Proc, GetParams:Proc, GetOneParam:Proc
18:
19:    ;-----  From BINASC.OBJ, STRINGS.OBJ, STRIO.OBJ
20:            EXTRN   BinToAscDec:Proc, NewLine:Proc, StrWrite:Proc
21:            EXTRN   BinToAscHex:Proc, StrUpper:Proc
22:
23:    Start:
24:            mov     ax, @data        ; Set ax to data segment
25:            mov     es, ax           ; Set es to data segment
26:            call    GetParams        ; Get parameters with ds = PSP
27:                                     ; Note: ds now equals es
28:
29:    ;-----  Display number of parameters
30:
31:            call    NewLine          ; Start new display line
32:            mov     di, offset s1    ; Address string
33:            call    StrWrite         ; Display string
34:            call    ParamCount       ; Get number of parameters
35:            mov     ax, dx           ; Assign count to ax
36:            mov     cx, 1            ; Specify at least one digit
37:            mov     di, offset string ; Address work string
38:            call    BinToAscDec      ; Convert ax to decimal digits
39:            call    StrWrite         ; Display number
40:            call    NewLine          ; Start a new display line
41:
42:            xor     cx, cx           ; Initialize count to 0
```

```
43:  @@10:
44:          call    ParamCount          ; Get number of parameters
45:          cmp     cx, dx              ; Compare counter to number
46:          je      Exit               ; Exit when cx = dx
47:          push    cx                 ; Save cx on stack
48:          call    GetOneParam         ; Get address of one parameter
49:          call    StrUpper            ; Convert to uppercase
50:          call    StrWrite            ; Display parameter string
51:          call    NewLine             ; Start a new display line
52:          pop     cx                 ; Restore saved cx value
53:          inc     cx                 ; Advance to next parameter
54:          jmp     @@10               ; Repeat until done
55:  Exit:
56:          mov     ah, 04Ch            ; DOS function: Exit program
57:          mov     al, [exitCode]      ; Return exit code value
58:          int     21h                ; Call DOS. Terminate program
59:
60:          END     Start              ; End of program / entry point
```

Using PARAMS   The PARAMS module contains three procedures—ParamCount (45–60), GetParams (62–123), and GetOneParam (125–150)—that you can call to extract command-line parameters. As shown in SHOWPARM at lines 24–26, start your program by setting es to the program's data segment and then immediately call GetParams:

```
mov     ax, @data      ; Set ax to data segment
mov     es, ax         ; Set es to data segment
call    GetParams      ; Get parameters with ds = PSP
```

Notice that this differs from the usual start-up sequence by *not* initializing ds. Because ds addresses the PSP when the program begins, you must not change ds before calling GetParams; otherwise, the procedure won't be able to find the command-tail characters. As an added benefit, GetParams assigns the value of es to ds, so there's no need to initialize ds after calling the procedure.

> Note: Because of the effect that GetParams has on ds, you should never call this procedure more than once at the start of a program.

After these initializing steps, the individual parameters are available as ASCIIZ strings. Call ParamCount to set dx to the number of strings in memory. Because the first parameter is number 0, the maximum parameter number is always one less than the value ParamCount returns in dx—that is, unless dx is 0, in which case there aren't any parameters. To use an individual parameter string, assign the parameter number to cx and call GetOneParam as SHOWPARM demonstrates (line 48). This assigns the offset address of the ASCIIZ string for this parameter to di, which you can then pass to any procedure that operates on ASCIIZ strings. For example, to open a file entered as the first parameter, you can start your code segment with:

```
mov     ax, @data              ; Set ax to data segment
mov     es, ax                 ; Set es to data segment
call    GetParams              ; Get parameters with ds = PSP
call    ParamCount             ; Get number of parameters (dx)
or      dx, dx                 ; Does number = 0?
jz      Exit                   ; Exit if no parameters entered
```

At this point, the program ends if no parameters are entered. (A better program might also display a message, telling the user what to do next time.) If there is at least one parameter, the program continues, first locating the address of parameter string number 0, passing this address to DOS function 03Dh to open the file, and jumping to an error handler if an error is detected:

```
xor     cx, cx                 ; Specify parameter number 0
call    GetOneParam            ; Get address of parameter
mov     dx, di                 ; Address ASCIIZ string with ds:dx
mov     ah, 03Dh               ; Select DOS function 03Dh
int     21h                    ; Call DOS to open the file
jc      Error                  ; Jump if error detected
mov     [handle], ax           ; Else, save handle for later
```

You can also call GetOneParam to locate a parameter string and pass the address to any of the ASCIIZ string procedures in the STRINGS and STRIO modules. For example, to convert all parameters to uppercase, execute this code:

```
        call    ParamCount     ; Get number of parameters
@@10:
        or      dx, dx         ; Does number = 0?
        jz      @@20           ; Jump if yes
        dec     dx             ; Else subtract 1 from number
        mov     cx, dx         ; Assign param number to cx
        call    GetOneParam    ; Get address of parameter string
        call    StrUpper       ; Convert string to uppercase
        jmp     @@10           ; Repeat until finished
@@20:
```

If you don't do this, parameters are stored in mixed uppercase and lowercase, exactly as typed on the DOS command line. You might take advantage of this fact by programming case-sensitive option letters. For example, the lowercase option /s could have a different effect from the uppercase /S.

How PARAMS Works

GetParams in the PARAMS module (Program 9-2, lines 62–123) copies the command-tail characters into a global variable params, declared at line 15. Before doing this, the procedure skips any leading blanks or tabs (lines 89–93) entered after the file name. At this point, register cx equals the count of the number of characters in the parameter block. If this count is 0, line 99 skips the copy operation, carried out by the repeated string command at line 101. The rest of the procedure scans the copied characters looking for parameter separators—blanks, tabs, and carriage returns—converting these characters to nulls and consequently also converting the parameters to ASCIIZ strings.

> Note: Because `GetParams` converts two adjacent blanks, tabs, and carriage returns to nulls, it's possible to introduce zero-length parameters accidentally by typing several spaces between parameters on the DOS command line. This does no harm—just ignore any null parameter strings returned by `GetOneParam`.

`GetOneParam` (125–150) scans the parameter block, looking for ASCII nulls and setting register `di` to the address of the requested string. The first part of the procedure checks that the parameter number in `cx` is in range, limiting the scan to the number of strings in memory. (If you specify a parameter number that is out of range, the procedure returns the address of the first parameter if there is one.) The code at lines 143–147 demonstrates an important assembly language technique for scanning a list of variable-length items. For reference, the code is repeated here:

```
        cld                 ; Auto-increment di
@@10:
        scasb               ; Scan for null terminator
        jnz     @@10        ; Repeat until found
        loop    @@10        ; Repeat for count in cx
```

First, `df` is cleared by `cld` so that `scasb` increments `di` automatically on each pass through the loop. (The code assumes that register `di` addresses the first parameter string to be scanned.) The `scasb` instruction compares the byte at `[es:di]` to the value in `al`, previously initialized to 0 (line 138). The result of `scasb` is to set the zero flag `zf` if the compared bytes match. If no match is found, the `jnz` instruction repeats the `scasb`; otherwise, the program continues to the `loop` instruction. At this point, `cx` equals the number of strings remaining to be scanned in the parameter block. The `loop` instruction subtracts 1 from `cx` and, if this does not make `cx` equal to 0, jumps to label `@@10:`, starting another scan of the next string. When `cx` becomes 0, `di` addresses the first character of the requested string.

Returning to the PARAMS module, `ParamCount` (Program 9-2, lines 45–60) simply returns the value of the global variable `numParams`. Another way to accomplish the same task is to declare the `ParamCount` variable public, adding the label to PUBLIC directive inside the data segment (line 20). If you make this change to PARAMS.ASM, you can remove the `ParamCount` procedure and use an EXTRN directive to refer to the external variable:

```
EXTRN numParams:Word
```

This tells the assembler that `numParams` addresses a Word variable in an external module to which you plan to link the host code. You can then read and write values to [numParams] just as though you had declared this variable in the main module. As you can see from the listings in this book, I generally prefer to declare only procedures public, returning values via subroutines rather than allowing other modules to access global variables directly. This helps avoid possible conflicts that might occur if two procedures change the same value. But there's no technical reason to prevent modules from sharing data this way.

Reading and Writing Text Files

When learning how to process file data in any new language, a good place to start is with a simple program that copies one file character by character (or byte by byte) to a new file. With this basic shell available, it's a simple matter to insert code to modify characters on their way through the program. You can use this same design to write programs to convert characters to uppercase or lowercase letters, to count the number of words in a file, to encrypt data with a password, and to perform other useful operations.

Program 9-4, KOPY.ASM, expects you to enter two file names on the DOS command line. The program opens and reads the first file, creates a new file of the second file name, and copies every byte of the first file to the second. If a file of the second name already exists, the program asks for permission to remove the old file. If you don't enter exactly two parameters, the program displays instructions. These features represent the bare minimum design that programs of this nature probably should follow. Assemble and link KOPY with the commands:

```
tasm /zi kopy
tlink /v kopy,,, mta
```

Omit the /zi and /v options unless you want to test KOPY in Turbo Debugger. From the DOS command line, type kopy and press Enter to display instructions. Or supply two file names for KOPY to process. For example, to copy the file ORIGINAL.TXT to a new file named NEW-TEXT.TXT, enter:

```
kopy original.txt newtext.txt
```

Program 9-4 *KOPY.ASM*

```
 1:   %TITLE "Copy Input to Output"
 2:
 3:           IDEAL
 4:           DOSSEG
 5:           MODEL   small
 6:           STACK   256
 7:
 8:   cr      EQU     13              ; ASCII carriage return
 9:   lf      EQU     10              ; ASCII line feed
10:
11:
```

```
12:           DATASEG
13:
14: exitCode      DB      0
15:
16: inFile        DW      0           ; Input file handle
17: outFile       DW      0           ; Output file handle
18: oneByte       DB      0           ; Byte I/O variable
19:
20: prompt        DB      cr,lf,'Erase this file? (y/n) ', 0
21: diskFull      DB      cr,lf,'**ERROR: Disk is full', 0
22:
23: notes   DB      cr,lf,'KOPY copies all bytes from one file to a new file'
24:         DB      cr,lf,'as a demonstration of file read and write methods'
25:         DB      cr,lf,'in assembly language. The program can be modified'
26:         DB      cr,lf,'to process data on its way to the output file,'
27:         DB      cr,lf,'although this version makes no changes to the'
28:         DB      cr,lf,'information in the input file. Use the program by'
29:         DB      cr,lf,'supplying two file names: the first name is the'
30:         DB      cr,lf,'file you want to read; the second is the new file'
31:         DB      cr,lf,'you want KOPY to create:',cr,lf
32:         DB      cr,lf,'KOPY <input file> <output file>',cr,lf, 0
33:
34:
35:           CODESEG
36:
37: ;----- From STRIO.OBJ
38:           EXTRN StrWrite:Proc, NewLine:Proc
39:
40: ;----- From DISKERR.OBJ
41:           EXTRN DiskErr:Proc
42:
43: ;----- From PARAMS.OBJ
44:           EXTRN GetParams:Proc, ParamCount:Proc, GetOneParam:Proc
45:
46: Start:
47:
48: ;----- Initialize and display notes if no parameters entered
49:
50:           mov     ax, @data           ; Set ax to data segment
51:           mov     es, ax              ; Set es to data segment
52:           call    GetParams           ; Get parameters with ds = PSP
53:           call    ParamCount          ; Get number of parameters (dx)
54:           cmp     dx, 2               ; Does count = 2?
55:           je      @@10                ; Continue if param count = 2
56:           mov     di, offset notes    ; Address text with di
57:           call    StrWrite            ; Display notes
58:           jmp     Exit                ; Exit program
59:
60: ;----- Attempt to open the input file
61:
```

```
62:    @@10:
63:            xor     cx, cx              ; Specify parameter number 0
64:            call    GetOneParam         ; Get address of parameter string
65:            mov     dx, di              ; Address file name with ds:dx
66:            xor     al, al              ; Specify read-only access
67:            mov     ah, 3Dh             ; DOS Open-file function
68:            int     21h                 ; Open the input file
69:            jnc     @@20                ; Continue if no error
70:            jmp     Errors              ; Else jump to error handler
71:
72:    ;-----  Check whether the output file already exists
73:
74:    @@20:
75:            mov     [inFile], ax        ; Save input file handle
76:            mov     cx, 1               ; Specify parameter number 1
77:            call    GetOneParam         ; Get address of parameter string
78:            mov     dx, di              ; Address file name with ds:dx
79:            call    FileExists          ; Does output file exist?
80:            jc      @@30                ; Jump if file does not exist
81:            call    StrWrite            ; Display file name
82:            call    Confirm             ; Else confirm file removal
83:            je      @@30                ; Continue if permission given
84:            jmp     Exit                ; Else exit program
85:
86:    ;-----  Attempt to create the output file
87:
88:    @@30:
89:            mov     cx, 1               ; Specify parameter number 1
90:            call    GetOneParam         ; Get address of parameter string
91:            mov     dx, di              ; Address file name with ds:dx
92:            xor     cx, cx              ; Specify normal attributes
93:            mov     ah, 3Ch             ; DOS Create-file function
94:            int     21h                 ; Create the output file
95:            jnc     @@40                ; Continue if no error
96:            jmp     Errors              ; Else jump to error handler
97:    @@40:
98:            mov     [outFile], ax       ; Save output file handle
99:
100:   ;-----  At this point, the input and output files are open and
101:   ;       their handles are stored at inFile and outFile. The next
102:   ;       step is to read from the input file and write each byte
103:   ;       to the output.
104:
105:   @@50:
106:           mov     ah, 3Fh             ; DOS Read-file function
107:           mov     bx, [inFile]        ; Set bx to input file handle
108:           mov     cx, 1               ; Specify one byte to read
109:           mov     dx, offset oneByte  ; Address variable with ds:dx
110:           int     21h                 ; Call DOS to read from file
111:           jnc     @@60                ; Jump if no error detected
112:           jmp     Errors              ; Else jump to error handler
```

```
113:  @@60:
114:          or      ax, ax                  ; Check for end of input file
115:          jz      @@80                    ; ax = 0 = end of file; jump
116:          mov     ah, 40h                 ; DOS Write-file function
117:          mov     bx, [outFile]           ; Set bx to output file handle
118:          mov     cx, 1                   ; Specify one byte to write
119:          mov     dx, offset oneByte      ; Address variable with ds:dx
120:          int     21h                     ; Call DOS to write to file
121:          jnc     @@70                    ; Jump if no error detected
122:          jmp     Errors                  ; Else jump to error handler
123:  @@70:
124:          or      ax, ax                  ; Check for disk-full condition
125:          jnz     @@50                    ; Repeat for next byte
126:
127:  ;----- Handle special case of disk-full condition
128:
129:          mov     di, offset diskFull     ; Address disk-full message
130:          call    StrWrite                ; Display message
131:
132:  ;----- Close the input and output files. This is not strictly
133:  ;      required as ending the program via function 04Ch also closes
134:  ;      all open files. Note: Errors are handled only when closing
135:  ;      the output file because no changes are made to the input.
136:
137:  @@80:
138:          mov     bx, [inFile]            ; Get input file handle
139:          mov     ah, 3Eh                 ; DOS Close-file function
140:          int     21h                     ; Close input file
141:          mov     bx, [outFile]           ; Get output file handle
142:          mov     ah, 3Eh                 ; DOS Close-file function
143:          int     21h                     ; Close output file
144:          jnc     Exit                    ; Exit if no errors detected
145:          jmp     Errors                  ; Else jump to error handler
146:  Exit:
147:          mov     ah, 04Ch                ; DOS function: Exit program
148:          mov     al, [exitCode]          ; Return exit code value
149:          int     21h                     ; Call DOS. Terminate program
150:
151:  ;----- Instructions jump to here to handle any I/O errors, which
152:  ;      cause the program to end after displaying a message.
153:
154:  Errors:
155:          mov     [exitCode], al          ; Save error code
156:          call    DiskErr                 ; Display error message
157:          jmp     Exit                    ; Exit program
158:
159:  %NEWPAGE
160:  ;---------------------------------------------------------------
161:  ; FileExists              Test whether a file already exists
162:  ;---------------------------------------------------------------
163:  ; Input:
164:  ;       ds:dx = address of ASCIIZ file name
```

```
165:   ; Output:
166:   ;         cf = 0 (jnc) = File of this name exists
167:   ;         cf = 1 (jc)  = File of this name does not exist
168:   ; Registers: ax, bx
169:   ;-------------------------------------------------------------
170:   PROC     FileExists
171:            xor     al, al          ; Specify read-only access
172:            mov     ah, 3Dh         ; DOS Open-file function
173:            int     21h             ; Call DOS to open the file
174:            jc      @@99            ; Exit--file doesn't exist
175:            mov     bx, ax          ; Copy handle to bx
176:            mov     ah, 3Eh         ; DOS Close-file function
177:            int     21h             ; Close the file
178:            clc                     ; Clear carry flag (file exists)
179:   @@99:
180:            ret                     ; Return to caller
181:   ENDP     FileExists
182:   %NEWPAGE
183:   ;-------------------------------------------------------------
184:   ; Confirm            Get Yes/No confirmation from user
185:   ;-------------------------------------------------------------
186:   ; Input:
187:   ;         none
188:   ; Output:
189:   ;         zf = 0 (jnz) = user typed N or n
190:   ;         zf = 1 (jz)  = user typed Y or y
191:   ; Registers: ax, cx (indirectly), di
192:   ;-------------------------------------------------------------
193:   PROC     Confirm
194:            mov     di, offset Prompt   ; Address prompt string
195:            call    StrWrite            ; Display message
196:            mov     ah, 1               ; DOS GetChar function
197:            int     21h                 ; Get user response
198:            cmp     al, 'Y'             ; Compare with Y
199:            je      @@99                ; Exit if char = Y
200:            cmp     al, 'y'             ; Compare with y
201:            je      @@99                ; Exit if char = y
202:            cmp     al, 'N'             ; Compare with N
203:            je      @@20                ; Handle No response
204:            cmp     al, 'n'             ; Compare with n
205:            jne     Confirm             ; Repeat if not Y, y, N, n
206:   @@20:
207:            cmp     al, '@'             ; Reset zero flag (zf = 0)
208:   @@99:
209:            ret                         ; Return to caller
210:   ENDP     Confirm
211:
212:            END     Start       ; End of program / entry point
```

How KOPY.ASM Works KOPY.ASM demonstrates how to process files one character at a time, copying the contents of one disk file to another. Because this requires numerous calls to DOS, the program runs more slowly than the DOS COPY and XCOPY commands, which perform similar duties. Although you can certainly use KOPY as a utility, the program is more useful as a shell for writing new programs that process all the characters in a file. For example, make a copy of KOPY.ASM to a new file named UPCASE.ASM and insert code between lines 115 and 116 to modify the value stored in variable oneByte:

```
        mov     al, [oneByte]       ; Get input byte
        cmp     al, 'a'             ; Is byte >= 'a'?
        jb      @@Continue          ; Jump if byte < 'a'
        cmp     al, 'z'             ; Is byte <= 'z'?
        ja      @@Continue          ; Jump if byte > 'z'
        sub     al, 32              ; Convert lower- to uppercase
        mov     [oneByte], al       ; Store char back in variable
@@Continue:
```

You'll probably also want to revise the instructions at label notes (lines 23–32). After making these changes, assemble and link the program with the commands:

```
tasm upcase
tlink upcase,,, mta
```

Lines 74–84 demonstrate how to check whether a file already exists, preventing a disaster that can easily occur if you accidentally specify the wrong output file name. Subroutine FileExists (lines 160–181) tries to open the file, returning the carry flag cleared if no errors are detected. Otherwise, the carry flag is set, indicating that this file can't be found. The procedure is careful to close the file if the open operation succeeds (lines 176–177). If the code didn't do this, repeated calls to FileExists could eventually cause DOS to run out of handles.

Another subroutine, Confirm (lines 183–210), displays a message and waits for you to answer Y for Yes or N for No, confirming whether you want to erase an existing file.

After the preliminary steps of getting the file-name parameters, checking for an existing file, and asking your permission to erase any old data—steps that occupy most of the program—lines 105–125 perform the actual copying, calling DOS function 03Fh to read from the input file and function 040h to write to the output file. Carefully study this section to see how errors are handled, calling DiskErr (line 156) in the DISKERR module. Also observe how lines 124–130 deal with the onerous disk-full error condition.

To read from an open file, pass to DOS function 03Fh the file handle in bx and the number of bytes to read in cx. Also assign to ds:dx the address of a variable at least cx bytes long. DOS reads from the file, deposits the data at the address you specify, and returns the carry flag cleared if no errors are detected. In this case, ax equals the number of bytes actually read, which may be less than the number you request. If the carry flag is set, then ax equals the error code. If no errors occur and ax equals 0, then there is no more data in the input file to read.

To write to a file, pass to DOS function 0040h the file handle in `bx` and the number of bytes to write in `cx`. Also assign the address of the source data to `ds:dx`. DOS writes up to `cx` bytes from `ds:dx`, returning the carry flag cleared if no errors occur. If the carry flag is set, then `ax` equals the error code. If no errors occur, then `ax` equals the number of bytes actually written. But, if `ax` is 0, then the disk is full, requiring special action.

Reading and Writing Data Files

Of course, text files are just a special case of a data file, which might contain any kind of information—name and address records, statistics, raw data from bar code readers, and so on. In assembly language programming, the contents of a file are unspecified, and it's up to you to write programs that choose correct methods for reading and writing data in various formats. Even so, you can use the same DOS functions discussed previously to process all files, regardless of the type of data they contain.

However, there is a big difference between reading and writing files one byte or character at a time and processing files that contain multibyte records. In most cases, programs need the ability to read and write such records in arbitrary order, for example, to allow editing record number 1,068 out of the 3,277 records stored on disk—without requiring the entire file to be copied to a new location. In general, doing this requires two new file I/O concepts, adding to the list at the beginning of this chapter:

▶ A seek operation positions the internal location pointer to the first byte of a record in the file

▶ Reading or writing a specified number of bytes after a seek operation affect only one file record, leaving other data unchanged.

The concept of seeking in a file simply means to position DOS's internal file pointer, which tells DOS where to read or write data in each open file. The important rule to remember in assembly language file processing is that DOS always seeks to a byte position, no matter how many bytes each file record occupies. Therefore, to position the file pointer to the beginning of a multibyte record, the first job is to multiply the size of the record by the record number. (The first record in a file is number 0.) Assuming that the record size is stored in a variable named `recSize` and the record number is in `ax`, begin with:

```
mov     cx, [recSize]           ; cx = record size in bytes
mul     cx                      ; ax:dx <- ax * cx
```

The `mul` instruction multiplies the record number in `ax` by the record size in `cx`, storing the 32-bit result in `ax` (lower half) and `dx` (upper half). These values must then be transferred to `cx` (upper half) and `dx` (lower half) to accommodate the requirements of the DOS seek function 042h:

```
mov     cx, dx              ; cx <- MSW of result
mov     dx, ax              ; dx <- LSW of result
mov     ah, 042h            ; DOS Seek-file function
mov     al, 0               ; Seek from beginning of file
mov     bx, [handle]        ; Assign file handle to bx
int     21h                 ; Position file pointer
jc      Error               ; Handle error
```

After performing these steps, the next read or write to the file occurs at the new position. To read a record into a variable named **Buffer**, you can execute:

```
mov     ah, 03Fh            ; DOS Read-file function
mov     bx, [handle]        ; Assign file handle to bx
mov     cx, [recSize]       ; cx = number of bytes to read
mov     dx, offset Buffer   ; ds:dx = destination address
int     21h                 ; Read cx bytes from file
jc      Error               ; Handle error
```

Because reading (and writing) also advances the file pointer to the next record, you do not have to perform another seek if you want to read multiple records starting from a certain position. Writing an individual record is identical to the previous sample, but it calls function 040h instead of 03Fh. Also, some of the steps shown here for the sake of completeness may be unnecessary in practice. For example, **bx** already equals the file handle from the seek operation, so there's no need to reload the register.

You can also change the way the DOS seek function 042h operates. If **al** = 0, as it did in a previous sample, then the byte position value in **cx:dx** is considered to be absolute—in other words, relative to the beginning of the file. If **al** = 1, then the position value represents an offset relative to the current location. You can use this feature to advance to the next record:

```
xor     cx, cx              ; Zero upper half of value
mov     dx, [recSize]       ; cx:dx = size of record in bytes
mov     ah, 042h            ; DOS Seek-file function
mov     al, 1               ; Seek from current position
mov     bx, [handle]        ; Assign file handle to bx
int     21h                 ; Position file pointer
jc      Error               ; Handle error
```

If **al** = 2, the seek is performed backwards from the end of the file. This suggests a handy way to position the file pointer to the end of the file, perhaps in preparation for attaching new data at the end:

```
xor     cx, cx              ; Zero upper half of value
xor     dx, dx              ; Zero lower half of value
mov     ah, 042h            ; DOS Seek-file function
mov     al, 2               ; Seek from end of file
mov     bx, [handle]        ; Assign file handle to bx
int     21h                 ; Position file pointer
jc      Error               ; Handle error
```

Reading the Disk Directory

Two DOS functions make reading directories easy. The basic plan is to call the first function to start scanning a directory and then repeatedly call the second function to scan the rest of the directory, finding all matches in the directory for *wild card strings* such as *.*, *.PAS, or MYFILE.???— identical to the file names and wild cards you can type in a DOS DIR command. In assembly language programs, these strings are conveniently stored in ASCIIZ format.

Program 9-5, DR.ASM, demonstrates how to read a disk directory, displaying a simple file listing similar in style to the result of the command dir /w. As with DIR, the program allows you to type an optional wild card string. For example, typing dr *.asm lists all the .ASM files in the current directory. Typing dr alone lists all files. Assemble and link DR.ASM with the commands:

```
tasm /zi dr
tlink /v dr,,, mta
```

The tlink command assumes that object-code modules PARAMS, STRINGS, and STRIO from this and previous chapters are stored in the MTA.LIB library file.

Program 9-5 *DR.ASM*

```
 1:  %TITLE "Display Disk Directory"
 2:
 3:          IDEAL
 4:          DOSSEG
 5:          MODEL    small
 6:          STACK    256
 7:
 8:  FileName      EQU    30      ; Offset to file name in dirData
 9:
10:
11:          DATASEG
12:
13:  exitCode      DB     0
14:
15:  defaultSpec   DB     '*.*', 0        ; Default ASCIIZ wild card
16:  DTAseg        DW     ?               ; Segment for DTA
17:  DTAofs        DW     ?               ; Offset for DTA
18:  dirData       DB     43 DUP (?)      ; Holds one directory entry
19:
20:
21:          CODESEG
22:
23:  ;----- From PARAMS.OBJ
24:          EXTRN   GetParams:Proc, GetOneParam:Proc, ParamCount:Proc
25:
```

```
26: ;----- From STRINGS.OBJ, STRIO.OBJ
27:         EXTRN   StrLength:Proc, StrWrite:Proc, NewLine:Proc
28:
29: Start:
30:         mov     ax, @data               ; Set ax to data segment
31:         mov     es, ax                  ; Set es to data segment
32:         call    GetParams               ; Get parameters with ds = PSP
33:         call    NewLine                 ; Start new display line
34:         call    ParamCount              ; Get number of parameters (dx)
35:         mov     di, offset defaultSpec  ; Address default search string
36:         or      dx, dx                  ; Does dx = 0?
37:         jz      @@10                    ; Jump if dx (num params) = 0
38:         xor     cx, cx                  ; Else specify param #0
39:         call    GetOneParam             ; Get address of parameter
40: @@10:
41:         mov     bx, offset Action       ; Address action subroutine
42:         call    DirEngine               ; Scan directory entries
43: Exit:
44:         call    NewLine                 ; Start new display line
45:         mov     ah, 04Ch                ; DOS function: Exit program
46:         mov     al, [exitCode]          ; Return exit code value
47:         int     21h                     ; Call DOS. Terminate program
48:
49: %NEWPAGE
50: ;--------------------------------------------------------------
51: ; DirEngine     Directory scan "engine"
52: ;--------------------------------------------------------------
53: ; Input:
54: ;       cs:bx = address of subroutine
55: ;       ds:di = address of ASCIIZ search string (e.g. *.ASM)
56: ; Output:
57: ;       routine at cs:bx called for each directory entry match
58: ; Registers:
59: ;       ax, cx, dx + any changed in action subroutine at cs:bx
60: ;--------------------------------------------------------------
61: PROC    DirEngine
62:
63: ;----- Get current Disk Transfer Address (DTA) and save
64:
65:         push    es                      ; Save registers modified
66:         push    bx                      ;  by DOS 2Fh function
67:         mov     ah, 2Fh                 ; DOS Get DTA function
68:         int     21h                     ; Get current DTA
69:         mov     [DTAseg], es            ; Save segment address
70:         mov     [DTAofs], bx            ; Save offset address
71:         pop     bx                      ; Restore registers
72:         pop     es
73:
```

```
74:   ;-----   Set new DTA to global 43-byte dirData variable
75:
76:           mov     dx, offset dirData      ; Address variable with ds:dx
77:           mov     ah, 1Ah                 ; DOS Set DTA function
78:           int     21h                     ; Set new DTA
79:
80:   ;-----   Scan directory for matches to string at ds:dx
81:
82:           mov     ah, 4Eh                 ; DOS Search-first function
83:           mov     cx, 10h                 ; Attribute--files + subdirs
84:           mov     dx, di                  ; Address string with ds:dx
85:           jmp     short @@20              ; Skip next assign to ah
86:   @@10:
87:           mov     ah, 4Fh                 ; DOS Search-next function
88:   @@20:
89:           int     21h                     ; Search first/next entry
90:           jc      @@99                    ; Exit on error or done
91:           call    bx                      ; Call Action subroutine
92:           jmp     @@10                    ; Repeat until done
93:
94:   ;-----   Restore original DTA address
95:
96:   @@99:
97:           push    ds                      ; Preserve current ds
98:           mov     ds, [DTAseg]            ; Assign old DTA address
99:           mov     dx, [DTAofs]            ;   to ds:dx
100:          mov     ah, 1Ah                 ; DOS Set-DTA function
101:          int     21h                     ; Reset to old DTA
102:          pop     ds                      ; Restore ds
103:          ret                             ; Return to caller
104:  ENDP    DirEngine
105:  %NEWPAGE
106:  ;------------------------------------------------------------------
107:  ; Action          Called for each directory entry "hit"
108:  ;------------------------------------------------------------------
109:  ; Input:
110:  ;       dirData = directory entry (as returned by DOS)
111:  ; Output:
112:  ;       one file/subdirectory name displayed
113:  ; Registers:
114:  ;       ah, dl, cx, di
115:  ;------------------------------------------------------------------
116:  PROC    Action
117:          mov     di, offset dirData + FileName
118:          call    StrWrite
119:          call    StrLength
120:          sub     cx, 16
121:          neg     cx
```

```
122:  @@10:
123:          mov     ah, 2
124:          mov     dl, ' '
125:          int     21h
126:          loop    @@10
127:          ret                         ; Return to caller
128:  ENDP    Action
129:
130:          END     Start           ; End of program / entry point
```

How DR Works

DR illustrates a couple of new assembly language techniques. Line 41 assigns the offset address of a subroutine to register bx, passing this value to DirEngine (lines 50–104). Then, at line 91, DirEngine calls this subroutine with the instruction:

```
call    bx              ; Call routine at cs:bx
```

There is no difference between this kind of a subroutine call and the more familiar variety where you specify the routine's label as an immediate value. But the bx method allows you to pass different subroutine addresses to another routine. In this program, the technique allows you to change the action taken for each directory match or "hit." As this demonstrates, writing routines to accept the address of another routine as an input parameter is a valuable technique.

Most of the DirEngine subroutine is concerned with preserving and setting the Disk Transfer Address (DTA), the memory location that DOS uses for some nonhandle file operations. When reading directories, DOS copies individual directory entries into a 43-byte DTA, which you must provide. Study the comments in DirEngine and be sure you understand how the code saves and preserves the current DTA—not strictly required in this example, as ending the program makes restoring the original DTA unnecessary. However, in a larger program, it's a good idea to preserve the DTA as shown here.

The Action subroutine (lines 106–128) displays one file name from the DTA filled in by DirEngine. Figure 9-2 illustrates the format of the directory fields in this 43-byte variable. Here, the program needs only the one field at offset 30 decimal, locating the first byte of an ASCIIZ string containing the entry's file name. Displaying this string requires setting di to the offset address inside the dirData DTA variable, calculated by adding the known offset to the file name (30) plus the offset address of dirData:

```
mov     di, offset dirData + FileName
```

Then, StrWrite (from STRIO.OBJ) displays the file name. To align the columns, three instructions then calculate how many blanks are required between the last character of each file name and the start of the next column:

```
call    StrLength       ; Find length of file name string
sub     cx, 16          ; Subtract length-16
neg     cx              ; Find absolute value (two's complement)
```

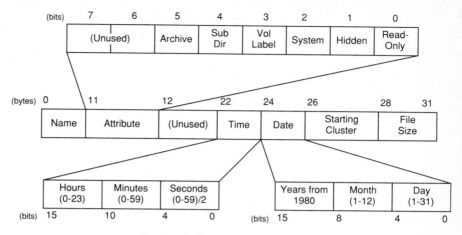

Figure 9-2 *Directory entry format.*

There are other ways to set `cx` to the number of blanks required to flesh out a variable-length column, but this trick usually works. First, subtract the length of the variable-length part (the file name's length in this case) from the fixed column width, 16 here. Assuming that the variable-length part is less than 16, this produces a negative number in two's complement form. Negate this result to find the absolute value—the number of blanks to write to align the cursor to the next column to the right. The reason for performing the subtraction this way is that you cannot write:

```
sub     16, cx              ; ???
```

which gives you an "Illegal Immediate" error. The 8086 `sub` instruction cannot subtract a register value from a literal number—it can only subtract literal numbers from registers and values stored in memory. Following `sub` with `neg` is one way to circumvent this restriction.

Summary

File handles first appeared in DOS version 2.0, replacing the older and no longer recommended FCB methods for disk file I/O. Handles simplify disk-file processing by eliminating the need to create and maintain FCB records, which contain information that is seldom of direct use to programs.

Files must be opened to make the data they contain available to programs. Creating new files erases any data stored in a file of the same name. Memory buffers store data on its way to and from disk—you should never assume that a disk write operation actually transfers bytes to disk. Closing a file flushes (writes) any buffered data to disk, updates the disk directory, and releases the file handle. The current location points to the place in a file where the next read or write operation will occur. These are important and universal file I/O concepts to learn.

Programs can open up to 20 files, as long as the total specified in a CONFIG.SYS *files=n* command is not exceeded, up to a maximum of 255 handles for all active programs. Because DOS reserves handles 0 to 4 for standard I/O, programs are normally limited to opening 15 files simultaneously. You can slightly increase this limit by closing one or more of the five standard handles.

Because data written to disk is buffered in memory, the only reliable method for ensuring that all information is saved on disk is to close the file. The DOS "flush buffer" command is inadequate for this task. Ending programs with DOS function 04Ch automatically closes all open files; therefore, programs may safely end with files left open.

Disk errors must be carefully handled in assembly language, which, unlike most high-level languages, has no built-in features to detect errors and take appropriate actions. When writing to disk, it's especially important to handle a disk-full condition, which DOS doesn't flag as an error. Extended error information is also available, either by using the DISKERR module in this chapter or by calling DOS directly. The DISKERR module also demonstrates how to create an array of variable-length items, such as character strings.

The traditional DOS program allows you to type parameters on the command line, passing options, file names, and other information to programs. You can use the PARAMS module in this chapter to convert parameters into easy-to-use ASCIIZ strings.

Processing text files one character at a time is a simple matter of calling DOS functions to read input and write output. You can also use the same functions to process multibyte records in other kinds of data files. With the help of the DOS seek function, you can operate on individual records without disturbing other data in the file.

Another pair of DOS functions let you read disk directories, matching file names with wild cards such as *.TXT. Each entry from the directory is loaded by DOS into a memory area called the DTA, from which you can extract directory information.

Exercises

9-1. What does closing a file do?

9-2. What does opening a file do?

9-3. Write a subroutine to prompt for a file name and, unless the user simply presses Enter, to open the file (if it exists).

9-4. Write a subroutine to flush any in-memory data to disk. The subroutine input should include the file name and a file handle.

9-5. Write a subroutine to read a record of *n* bytes by number from an open data file.

9-6. Write a subroutine to return the next record *past* the current record of *n* bytes from an open data file.

9-7. Write a subroutine to return the zero flag set if an option letter such as -d or /z is located among the parameters entered on the DOS command line.

9-8. Write a routine to separate a DOS file name from its extension, returning a single string exactly 12 characters long. (For examples of this format, type **DIR /w** at the DOS prompt.) Modify DR to use the new routine to display file names in this new format.

9-9. What instructions could you insert into the KOPY.ASM program shell to remove all the control codes (except for carriage returns and line feeds) from a text file? (As an alternative, you can replace control codes with blanks.)

9-10. Modify a copy of DR.ASM to list all the .COM and .EXE code files in the current disk directory.

Projects

9-1. Rewrite the PARAMS module to eliminate null parameter strings if any are detected in the command tail.

9-2. Write a new version of KOPY.ASM that reads *n* bytes from a file into a large program variable of a suitable size, for example, 256 or 512 bytes long. Then devise a subroutine to return characters from your buffer. What does this do to the speed of KOPY?

9-3. Describe how you might design a program to operate simultaneously on more than the maximum of 15 or so files allowed by DOS. What data structures and variables does the program need? What are the probable subroutines required?

9-4. Convert DR.ASM to a library module that any program can use.

9-5. Because command-line parameters are usually short, the 128-byte **params** buffer in Program 9-2, PARAMS.ASM, is rarely filled to the brim. Come up with a plan to limit the size of this buffer to only as much space as needed to store the command tail, reducing space currently wasted at the end of this buffer.

9-6. Write subroutines to read and write ASCIIZ strings a line at a time, recognizing the carriage-return and line-feed control codes as line separators in a text file.

10 Interrupt Handling

10 Interrupt Handling

In This Chapter

External and internal interrupts; writing interrupt service routines (ISR); differences between maskable and nonmaskable interrupts; understanding the 8259 interrupt controller; interrupt vectors; returning from an interrupt; using `hlt` to synchronize programs to external events; installing your own ISRs; hooking into the PC timer interrupt; writing reentrant ISRs; end-of-interrupt command; switching to a local stack inside an ISR; trapping divide fault exceptions; installing memory-resident programs; interrupt-driven asynchronous serial I/O; setting the trap flag; running programs in single-step mode; plus several example programs and modules

Interrupt This Program . . .

An interrupt is an event that temporarily halts a running program, executes a subroutine called an *interrupt service routine* (ISR), and then restarts the original program as though nothing had happened. This action resembles the interruption of a television program for an "important message," resuming the normal broadcast after an announcer reads the news.

In computer programming, interrupts help to eliminate *polling*—repeatedly examining peripheral devices such as keyboards, printers, and light pens to see whether they require input or whether they have output ready for processing. Instead, such devices may generate an interrupt signal, which automatically runs an appropriate ISR, servicing the device's needs upon demand. By this action, devices can use interrupts to run their own personal programs independently of other software actions. In 8086 programming, this classic definition of interrupts is extended with two kinds of interrupt signals:

> ▶ External interrupts
> ▶ Internal interrupts

External interrupts occur when a device attached to the processor generates an interrupt signal. *Internal interrupts* occur from within the processor in two ways: as the result of software `int` instructions and from certain conditions such as dividing by 0 with `div`, which generates a default interrupt signal (called an *exception*) for this error condition. In addition, internal `int` interrupts—also called *software interrupts*—can simulate the external kind, a useful technique for debugging external ISRs.

Writing Interrupt Service Routines

An ISR can do anything that other assembly language code can do. An ISR is nothing more than a special kind of subroutine, called by the interrupt actions just described. Putting aside a few of the more subtle issues for the moment, there are four basic rules to follow when coding your own interrupt service routines:

> ▶ Save all registers at the beginning of the routine
> ▶ Execute `sti` to process interrupts from within the ISR
> ▶ Restore all registers at the end of the routine
> ▶ Execute `iret` as the last instruction

External interrupts may occur at any time; therefore, it's vital that an external ISR makes no changes to any register values. There's no telling which registers might be in use when an external interrupt occurs; as a consequence, forgetting to save and restore a register changed inside the service routine is likely to have disastrous effects on other software. Internal ISRs may change register values because programs have more control over when this kind of interrupt can occur. (Internal ISRs operate similarly to subroutines.) Execute an `sti` instruction, setting the interrupt-enable flag (`if`), if you want other interrupts to be able to interrupt the current service routine. Otherwise, new interrupts will not be recognized until your routine executes an `iret` (Interrupt Return) instruction, which must be last in every interrupt service routine.

[handwritten margin note: sti, always do this in your ISR's for your pgms.]

Note: Although interrupts may occur at any time, they are recognized by the processor only *between* other instructions. In other words, if an interrupt occurs during a `mul` instruction, which might take as long as 139 machine cycles to complete, the `mul` will be completed before the interrupt is recognized. As a result of this potential delay, and because most instructions take differing numbers of cycles to execute, even the most regular interrupt signals are likely to be processed at irregular time intervals. Repeated string instructions such as `rep movsb` can be interrupted between repetitions.

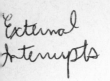
External Interrupts

Maskable vs Nonmaskable Interrupts

The 8086 processor chip has two input pins that can be attached to external interrupt-generating devices. These pins, or input lines, are:

▶ Maskable Interrupts (INTR)

▶ Nonmaskable Interrupts (NMI)

The INTR line is used by most interrupt-generating devices to signal the 8086 that the device needs servicing. The `cli` and `sti` instructions affect interrupts coming in on this line. Executing `cli` prevents—or *masks*—the processor from recognizing INTR interrupts. Executing `sti` allows the processor to again recognize INTR interrupt signals. Neither of these two instructions has any effect on the second interrupt line NMI, which cannot be disabled. Usually, NMI is reserved for disaster control, executing code when a power drop is detected, halting the system if a memory error occurs, and so forth. In the original IBM PC design, NMI handles memory parity errors, which occur if a bad memory bit is detected. Today, other devices share NMI, complicating NMI interrupt servicing.

The `sti` and `cli` instructions have no effect on software interrupts—those generated by an `int` instruction in a program or by the occurrence of a divide fault and similar conditions. Regardless of the setting of `if`, you can always execute `int` to force an interrupt service routine to run.

> Note: Some programmers are mistaken in their belief that NMI can be disabled. It can't. However, in the IBM PC, it's possible to disable other circuits that generate interrupt signals to the NMI line into the processor, thus preventing NMI from occurring. On the IBM XT and true compatibles, you might be able to mask NMI by writing 00h (disable) or 080h (enable) to output port 0A0h. This may not have the effect you want, however, because this does not prevent other programs from enabling NMI after you disable them. Also, be aware that some peripheral interface circuits use NMI for their own purposes.

Interrupt Vectors and the 8259 Chip

With only two interrupt lines INTR and NMI, you might think that the 8086's interrupt possibilities are severely limited. But, with the help of another chip, Intel's 8259 *Programmable Interrupt Controller* (PIC), IBM PCs can service up to eight interrupt-generating devices. (IBM ATs cascade a second PIC to service even more devices.) Each device is assigned one PIC level number from 0 to 7 (up to 15 on ATs) with lower numbers having higher priorities. This means that, if two interrupts occur simultaneously, the 8259 controller gives priority service to the device with the lowest number. Table 10-1 lists the devices associated with each PIC level. Level 2 serves as a channel between two cascaded 8259s on AT computers. Because NMI is also externally generated, it's listed in the table, although this line is not attached to an 8259 controller.

Table 10-1 *External Hardware Interrrupts*

PIC Level	Interrupt Number	Device
0	08h	Timer (software clock)
1	09h	Keyboard
2	0Ah	To slave 8259
3	0Bh	Secondary serial I/O (COM2)
4	0Ch	Primary serial I/O (COM1)
5	0Dh	Fixed (hard) disk
6	0Eh	Removable (floppy) disk
7	0Fh	Parallel printer
8	070h*	Hardware clock
9	071h*	To Master 8259 Level 2
10	072h*	—
11	073h*	—
12	074h*	—
13	075h*	Numeric coprocessor
14	076h*	Fixed (hard) disk
15	077h*	—
NMI	02h	Memory parity

*IBM AT and compatibles only.

As you can see from Table 10-1, each PIC level is associated with a second value called an *interrupt number*—also called an *interrupt type* or an *interrupt level*—ranging from 08h to 0Fh on PC-, PCjr-, and XT-type computers with an additional eight levels on ATs. This dual-numbering system for external interrupts confuses many people. Remember that the PIC level refers to the actual pin on the 8259 controller to which the device is attached. The interrupt number identifies the ISR that runs when this device requires servicing. In programming, you can ignore the PIC level and refer to interrupts by their interrupt numbers instead.

Table 10-2 lists the full range of interrupt numbers assigned in typical PC/XT-type computers. Except for the first eight external interrupts from Table 10-1, which are repeated in this table, most of the interrupts from this complete set are of the internal software variety. Regardless of the kind of interrupt, every interrupt number is associated with a unique *interrupt vector*, stored at the locations listed in the center of Table 10-2.

An interrupt vector is simply a pointer—a 32-bit (4-byte) address with segment and offset values—stored in the lowest addresses of memory, from 0000:0000 through 0000:03FF. Each vector locates the start of the interrupt service routine associated with one interrupt number, ranging from 00 to FFh, for a total of up to 256 software and hardware interrupts in a typical PC design. When an external interrupt signal is generated by one of the devices listed in Table 10-1, the 8259 controller activates the processor's INTR line, waits for an acknowledgment (which occurs automatically), and then sends the appropriate interrupt number to the processor. The processor uses this interrupt number to pick out the right vector from low memory and calls the ISR. A similar action occurs when a program calls

Table 10-2 *Software Interrupt Numbers and Vectors*

Interrupt Number	Vector Location	Purpose
000h	0000h	Divide faults
001h	0004h	Single step (trap)
002h	0008h	Nonmaskable interrupt (NMI)
003h	000Ch	Breakpoint
004h	0010h	Overflow
005h	0014h	Print screen
006h	0018h	*
007h	001Ch	*
008h	0020h	Timer (software clock)
009h	0024h	Keyboard
00Ah	0028h	*
00Bh	002Ch	Secondary serial I/O (COM2)
00Ch	0030h	Primary serial I/O (COM1)
00Dh	0034h	Fixed (hard) disk
00Eh	0038h	Removable (floppy) diskette
00Fh	003Ch	Parallel printer
010h	0040h	Video
011h	0044h	Equipment check
012h	0048h	Memory check
013h	004Ch	Disk
014h	0050h	RS-232 I/O
015h	0054h	Cassette (PC), Aux (AT)
016h	0058h	Keyboard
017h	005Ch	Printer
018h	0060h	BASIC in ROM
019h	0064h	Bootstrap
01Ah	0068h	Time of day
01Bh	006Ch	Keyboard Ctrl-Break
01Ch	0070h	User-installed timer routine
01Dh	0074h	Video initialization
01Eh	0078h	Disk parameters pointer†
01Fh	007Ch	Bit-mapped characters pointer†
020h–03Fh	0080h–00FCh	Reserved for DOS
040h–06Fh	0100h–01BCh	Various
070h	01C0h	Hardware clock
071h	01C4h	*
072h	01C8h	*
073h	01CCh	*
074h	01D0h	*
075h	01D4h	Numeric coprocessor
076h	01D8h	Fixed (hard) disk
077h	01DCh	*
078h–0FFh	01E0h–03FCh	Various

*Reserved or not used.
†Not an interrupt service routine.

[handwritten in left margin: all interrupts HW & SW.]

[handwritten right margin next to 01Ch row: automatically a TS]

a software interrupt with an `int` instruction or when an internal interrupt is generated as the result of a divide fault or similar condition. For both external and internal interrupts, several events occur after the processor receives the interrupt number:

▶ The flags are pushed onto the stack

▶ The `if` and `tf` flags are cleared   *No interrupts/traps during ISf*

▶ The `ip` and `cs` registers are pushed onto the stack

▶ The interrupt vector is copied to `cs:ip`

The last step of this process causes the interrupt service routine to begin running at the vector address stored in memory for the interrupt number, as listed in Table 10-2. By changing one or more of these vectors, you can insert your own interrupt service routines in place of the default code that services interrupts on your system. You can also chain your interrupt services to existing ISRs, a method that resident utilities such as Borland's SideKick and Lotus's Metro use to recognize certain key presses as their activation commands, allowing other key presses to pass through unchanged. When the ISR is finished servicing the interrupt, it executes an `iret` instruction, which causes these actions to occur:

▶ The `cs` and `ip` registers are popped from the stack

▶ The flags are popped from the stack

The first of these actions causes the interrupted program to continue running normally. The second step restores any flags that may have been changed by instructions inside the ISR. Because the flags are automatically saved and restored this way and because a hardware interrupt is serviced only if the `if` flag is set (via an `sti` instruction, for example), you never need to execute `sti` inside an ISR to allow future interrupts to be serviced after the ISR is finished—a common misconception. The original flags are pushed onto the stack before `if` and `tf` are cleared by the processor; therefore, if `if` is set beforehand, it will be set after `iret` executes. You need to execute `sti` in your service routine only if you want interrupts to be recognized *during* execution of the ISR.

When you want an ISR to return flag values—for example, as often done by the DOS function `int 21h` instruction—you have two choices: Change the flag values on the stack before executing `iret` or remove the flags from the stack and execute a plain `ret` instead. Remember that an interrupt service routine is just a special kind of subroutine; therefore, to pass back flags changed inside the routine, you can use code such as:

```
retf    2       ; Return and discard 2 stack bytes
```

This returns from the ISR and, after popping the code segment and instruction pointer registers from the stack, removes 2 bytes from the stack. Those 2 bytes hold the flag values that were pushed onto the stack when the ISR was activated. Do this only for internal ISRs, which programs call like subroutines. By discarding the flags saved on the stack by the processor after acknowledging an interrupt, you effectively convert the ISR to a plain subroutine, which can end in `ret`. You can then use `call` instructions to execute the same code, starting from a different entry point, of course.

Although you won't often use this trick, it's useful to understand that an ISR is just a special kind of subroutine, and it's up to you to decide what the code does and how it returns control to its callers.

Why hlt Doesn't Halt

Closely related to interrupt programming, the hlt instruction behaves differently than you might think. Upon executing hlt, the 8086 processor pauses, effectively stopping the program at this location. At this time, if interrupts are enabled, an interrupt signal to the processor's INTR line is recognized as usual, causing the interrupt service routine to execute and, thus, breaking out of the halted condition. When the ISR ends, processing continues with the instruction following the hlt. In other words, hlt doesn't really halt—it waits for an interrupt to occur. If interrupts are disabled, however, hlt can indeed lock up the computer system by preventing recognition of INTR signals. Therefore, to bring the 8086 to its knees, you might be able to execute:

Don't do this →

```
cli    ; Disable interrupts by clearing if
hlt    ; Halt until interrupt, which can't occur!
```

After these two instructions, only two events can unlock the processor: a RESET or an NMI, both of which ignore the setting of if. (RESET is an input line to the processor, which may not be connected to a reset button on your system. Most PCs do not have reset buttons.)

A more practical use for hlt is to synchronize programs to external events, pausing until an interrupt signal from a specific device occurs. The key to this idea is the sti instruction, which sets the if flag, enabling INTR interrupts to be recognized. However, this recognition occurs only after the *next* instruction following the sti; therefore, to synchronize a program with an external interrupt, you should never write:

Due to 2 stage pipeline! →

```
sti    ; Allow interrupts to occur
cli    ; Disable interrupts ???
```

Because interrupts are recognized only after the instruction following sti, if that instruction disables interrupts, then even the sneakiest interrupt signal will not have enough time to sneak through. The correct way to synchronize a program to an external event is with code such as:

only these 3 are necessary {

```
cli    ; Disable interrupts
sti    ; Enable interrupts following next instruction  the halt!
hlt    ; Pause for an INTR interrupt to occur
cli    ; Disable interrupts again (optional) ← !
```

If interrupts are already disabled, the first cli is not needed. The second cli is needed only if you want to prevent additional interrupts from occurring. By following sti with hlt, your program is assured of continuing only upon receipt of an external interrupt INTR signal, generated, for example, by a key press or a character received at a serial input port.

Servicing Interrupts

ISR code follows the same basic design for external and internal interrupts. This section demonstrates how to write ISRs to handle interrupts and also explores a few subtleties of interrupt handling in 8086 assembly language.

Program 10-1, SLOWMO.ASM, taps into the PC's free-running timer interrupt to add regular pauses to a program, slowing code execution to a crawl. This can be a useful device for debugging a fast program when the action speeding by is too chaotic to see. The program also demonstrates the correct way to handle interrupts that come in via the 8259 PIC chip. When the interrupt is from the PC timer interrupt, special care is required to avoid disrupting the system clock. SLOWMO serves as a platform for illustrating these subjects. Assemble and link SLOWMO with your MTA.LIB file using the commands:

```
tasm slowmo
tlink slowmo,,, mta
```

Program 10-1 *SLOWMO.ASM*

```
1:  %TITLE "Slow Motion Interrupt Generator"          Installs a HW intr.
2:
3:          IDEAL
4:          DOSSEG
5:          MODEL   small
6:          STACK   256
7:
8:  delay         EQU    0010h          ; Amount of delay
9:  cr            EQU    13             ; ASCII carriage return
10: lf            EQU    10             ; ASCII line feed
11: BIOSData      EQU    040h           ; BIOS data segment address
12: LowTimer      EQU    006Ch          ; Address of low timer word
13: PIC8259       EQU    0020h          ; 8259 PIC chip port address
14: EOI           EQU    0020h          ; End of interrupt value
15:
16:         DATASEG
17:
18: exitCode      DB     0
19: string        DB     'This is a test of the timer', cr, lf
20:               DB     ' slow-mo interrupt handler', cr, lf, 0
21: timerSeg      DW     ?                 ; Saved vector for original
22: timerOfs      DW     ?                 ;   Int 1Ch ISR
23:
24:
```

```
25:             CODESEG
26:
27:    ;-----  From STRIO.OBJ, KEYBOARD.OBJ
28:             EXTRN   StrWrite:proc, KeyWaiting:proc
29:
30:    Start:
31:             mov     ax, @data                ; Initialize ds to address
32:             mov     ds, ax                   ;  of data segment
33:             mov     es, ax                   ; Make es = ds
34:
35:             mov     [word cs:difference],delay  ; Set amount of delay
36:
37:             push    es                       ; Save es register
38:             mov     ax, 351Ch                ; Get interrupt 1C vector
39:             int     21h                      ; Call DOS for vector
40:             mov     [timerSeg], es           ; Save segment value
41:             mov     [timerOfs], bx           ; Save offset value
42:             pop     es                       ; Restore es
43:
44:             push    ds                       ; Save ds register
45:             mov     ax, 251Ch                ; Set interrupt 1C vector
46:             push    cs                       ; Make ds = cs to address
47:             pop     ds                       ;  the new ISR, placing full
48:             mov     dx, offset SlowMo        ;  address into ds:dx
49:             int     21h                      ; Set new interrupt vector
50:             pop     ds                       ; Restore ds
51:
52:             mov     di, offset string        ; Address test string
53:    @@10:
54:             call    StrWrite                 ; Display string
55:             call    KeyWaiting               ; Check for a key press
56:             jz      @@10                     ; Loop until any key press
57:
58:             push    ds                       ; Save ds, changed below
59:             mov     ax, 251Ch                ; Set interrupt 1C vector
60:             mov     dx, [timerOfs]           ; Get saved offset value
61:             mov     ds, [timerSeg]           ; Get saved segment value
62:             int     21h
63:             pop     ds                       ; Restore ds
64:    Exit:
65:             mov     ah, 04Ch                 ; DOS function: Exit program
66:             mov     al, [exitCode]           ; Return exit code value
67:             int     21h                      ; Call DOS. Terminate program
68:
69:    %NEWPAGE
70:    ;------------------------------------------------------------------
71:    ; SlowMo          Slow Motion Timer Interrupt Service Routine
72:    ;------------------------------------------------------------------
73:    ; Input:
74:    ;        none
```

Timer Interrupt installed → (line 49)

↑

these intrs must never allow further interrupt processing (which is default!)

↓

Timer Interrupt back to normal → (line 62)

```
75:    ; Output:
76:    ;        none (waits for time difference)
77:    ; Registers:
78:    ;        none
79:    ;-----------------------------------------------------------
80:
81:    ;-----  Variables declared inside the code segment, where they
82:    ;         will be easy to find during execution of the ISR
83:
84:    inProgress    DB      0       ; In-progress flag (0 = no, 1 = yes)
85:    difference    DW      0       ; Relative pause time
86:
87:    PROC    SlowMo
88:
89:    ;-----  Test the inProgress flag, which indicates if a previous
90:    ;         copy of SlowMo is already executing. This must be prevented
91:    ;         or the system will lock up.
92:
93:            cmp     [byte cs:inProgress], 0 ; Check in-progress flag
94:            jne     @@99                    ; Jump if SlowMo is running
95:            inc     [byte cs:inProgress]    ; Else, set flag = 1
96:
97:            sti                             ; Allow interrupts to occur
98:            push    ax                      ; Save modified registers
99:            push    ds
100:           push    dx
101:
102:           mov     al, EOI                 ; al = end-of-interrupt value
103:           out     PIC8259, al             ; Issue end of interrupt
104:
105:           mov     ax, BIOSData            ; Address BIOS data area
106:           mov     ds, ax                  ;   with ds
107:           mov     ax, [word LowTimer]     ; Get low word of timer value
108: @@10:
109:           mov     dx, [word LowTimer]     ; Get new timer value into dx
110:           sub     dx, ax                  ; Subtract new-old timer
111:           cmp     dx, [cs:difference]     ; Compare to difference
112:           jb      @@10                    ; Loop until difference passes
113:
114:   ;-----  Disable interrupts while we clean up and exit after the pause
115:
116:           cli                             ; Disable interrupts
117:           dec     [byte cs:inProgress]    ; Reset in-progress flag
118:           pop     dx                      ; Restore saved registers
119:           pop     ds
120:           pop     ax
121: @@99:
122:           iret                            ; Interrupt return
123:   ENDP    SlowMo
124:
125:           END     Start           ; End of program / entry point
```

Handwritten annotations:

- Next to lines 81–83: "or lines 61 & 63"
- Near line 82: "47"
- Line 83 (handwritten): "because a clk int can occur between lines 49 & 50."

Tapping into the PC Timer Interrupt

All IBM PCs—and even less than 100% compatibles—contain a hardware timer that generates an interrupt signal approximately 18.2 times or "ticks" per second. In the ROM BIOS, interrupt 08h services these interrupt signals, which are connected to the 8259 PIC's input line 0. (See Table 10-1.) This gives the timer interrupt the highest priority. As long as interrupts are enabled, the timer ISR will be the first to execute if more than one interrupt signal occurs simultaneously.

The ROM BIOS timer ISR performs two basic functions. First, the code increments a 32-bit value, thus counting the total number of timer ticks that have occurred since the system was switched on. (This value is zeroed every 24 hours—not necessarily at midnight.) Second, another counter that controls how long the diskette motor stays on is decremented. When this value becomes 0, the disk drive motor is turned off (if it was on), which leaves the disk drive turning long enough to improve floppy disk read and write speeds. (Every time the diskette starts, it takes a moment for the spindle to come up to speed. If the motor were turned off immediately after each read and write, these pauses would slow disk I/O unacceptably.) As you can see, the timer ISR is the PC's heartbeat and, like all hearts, arresting its duties for too long can lead to problems; therefore, it's usually wise never to turn off interrupts with cli for more than 1/18.2 (about 0.05) seconds before issuing sti to switch interrupts back on. *Don't miss timer interrupts!*

The timer ISR performs a third function that lets you hook into the PC's heartbeat. At every timer tick, this routine executes a software interrupt number 01Ch, which normally causes no action to occur. By installing your own 01Ch ISR, your code is executed about 18.2 times per second in addition to the timer's other duties. SLOWMO.ASM uses this feature to add pauses to a running program.

Timer Tick Tricks   The first step in hooking into the PC timer interrupt is to save the current interrupt 01Ch vector, as Program 10-1 does at lines 37–42, calling DOS function 035h to obtain the vector address in registers es:bx, which are saved in the variables timerSeg and timerOfs. Next, lines 44–50 call DOS function 025h with the address of the new interrupt vector—equal to the offset in the code segment of the SlowMo procedure starting at line 87. This replaces the original vector with the address of the new ISR. You could also switch off interrupts and insert the address directly into the appropriate low-memory slot, but calling the DOS routines written for this purpose is easier. Notice how register ds is set to the current code segment with:

```
push    cs              ; Push cs onto stack
pop     ds              ; Pop the cs value into ds
```

This is a useful trick to remember and avoids assigning a segment value to a third register (ax, for example) only to then assign that value to the destination. When installing your own ISRs, if you use code similar to lines 37–50 to replace existing vectors with the addresses of your own routines, be sure to save and restore segment registers es and ds as illustrated here.

> Note: Always restore any interrupt vectors you change in your program. When your program ends, your ISRs are subject to being overlayed by subsequent commands and programs. Therefore, leaving an ISR running after a program ends without also taking steps to protect the memory the ISR occupies is almost certain to cause a system crash. DOS does not restore vectors that your program changes.

Lines 52–56 display a test string and wait for you to press any key, ending the program. During this loop, the SlowMo ISR executes, seemingly on its own, but actually as a result of the ROM BIOS timer routine's call to interrupt 01Ch at the rate of 18.2 times per second. Although this may appear to make the loop at lines 52–56 and the ISR run concurrently, remember that interrupts cause the program to pause while the ISR runs—thus, the concurrency is only an illusion conjured by the magic of the PC's timer interrupt.

After you press a key, the program ends. Just before this, lines 58–63 call DOS function 025h once again, but this time with the vector saved earlier. This replaces the original interrupt 01Ch ISR (probably, but not necessarily, addressing a lone iret instruction) that was in effect before SLOWMO began.

Interrupts and Variables

Program 10-1's SlowMo ISR procedure (lines 70–123) executes when the ROM BIOS timer interrupt executes software interrupt 01Ch. Because this can happen at any time—in between an instruction in the main program, during a call to DOS, or even during a call to another ROM BIOS routine—the values of segment registers es and ds cannot be trusted to locate the program's data segment. Because of this, an ISR must be careful to initialize ds (and es if necessary) before loading or changing data segment variables. One way to do this is to save ds and then assign it the value of the data segment, as is usually done at the start of the program:

```
push    ds                  ; Save current ds
mov     ax, @data           ; Assign data segment address
mov     ds, ax              ;   to ds by way of ax
;
;----- Interrupt code goes here
;
pop     ds                  ; Restore ds
iret                        ; Return from interrupt
```

The ISR must do this at the start of its code every time it runs, saving the current ds value, which the interrupted code may be using to address its own variables. Another method, demonstrated at lines 84–85, is to declare ISR variables inside the code segment. This method requires using a cs: segment override to tell the assembler (and the CPU) to use cs as the base address for locating variables in memory. For example, to load the inProgress byte into al, you could execute:

```
mov     al, [byte cs:inProgress]
```

If you did not use the cs: override, the assembler would assume that ds addresses the current data segment, a common mistake that often leads to disaster. Because there's no way to predict the value of ds or any other register during an externally executed ISR, addressing variables without either reinitializing ds or without using a segment override to access data in the code segment could overwrite memory locations belonging to other programs.

Interrupting ISRs   As explained earlier, the timer interrupt is the PC's heartbeat. Because it's vital that the timer not be disabled for very long, interrupts must be turned on in the SlowMo ISR (line 97). This poses a tricky problem. If interrupts are on, it's very likely that the ISR could actually interrupt itself. In this case, the ISR code would pause, the flags, cs, and ip registers would be pushed onto the stack, and the timer interrupt would be serviced. If this happened repeatedly with no opportunity for the ISR invocations to unwind, the stack would eventually overflow, probably leading to a system crash.

When a routine is allowed to interrupt itself, it is said to be *reentrant*—in other words, a new instance of the code sequence can begin running from the top before a previous instance finishes. Such code must allocate fresh space for variables—global variables won't do. To understand why, consider the SlowMo ISR. Because there is only one each of the inProgress and difference variables at lines 84–85, the new invocation of the code will use these same variables, possibly changing their values, if the ISR is allowed to interrupt itself. Therefore, when this second execution of SlowMo ends, causing the original instance to pick up again, the variables may have changed—a side effect that must be prevented if the routine is to be truly reentrant.

> Note: You may have heard that DOS and the ROM BIOS are not reentrant. This means that the routines access global variables, similar to those in SlowMo. Such routines can't reenter themselves because there is only one set of variables. In reality, however, some DOS and BIOS routines are reentrant, despite their use of global variables. The timer interrupt is a prime example—it certainly may and does interrupt itself without conflict. In fact, to keep the system time correct, it must do so.

Obviously, because it uses only one set of global variables, our SlowMo routine is definitely not reentrant. But, to keep the system clock running during SlowMo's lengthy pause, interrupts *must* be enabled—even though this will cause subsequent timer interrupts to reexecute SlowMo, in effect "pausing the pause" and stopping the system dead in its tracks. We have a difficult problem to solve: The vital PC timer interrupt must be allowed to execute during a lengthy pause, while our own SlowMo ISR must be prevented from interrupting itself, which it will do anyway as a result of the timer ISR executing another 01Ch interrupt. Whew!

Luckily, there's a simple answer to this typical conflict, demonstrated here at lines 93–95. First, the `inProgress` byte is examined. If this byte is 0, the ISR is allowed to run normally. If the `inProgress` byte is not 0, the program assumes that a previous instance of the ISR has been interrupted. This must be so because only line 95 sets `inProgress` to 1 (via an `inc` instruction) and only line 117 resets `inProgress` to 0. If `inProgress` is not 0 at the start of `SlowMo`, then the instructions between line 98–116 must have been interrupted by a timer tick, causing `SlowMo` to be reentered. The simple `inProgress` flag detects this condition, allowing only one instance of the ISR to execute. As a result, the ROM BIOS timer ISR may continue to run during an execution of `SlowMo`, keeping the system clock on time.

> Note: The Print Screen function uses a similar trick to prevent you from pressing the PrtSc key more than once while a screen dump is in the process of printing. When you press the PrtSc key and printing begins, a second PrtSc key press actually restarts the Print Screen function. But a flag similar to `inProgress` indicates that a previous printing operation is executing, thus preventing multiple screen printouts when only one is wanted.

The End-of-Interrupt Command

Line 97 in SLOWMO.ASM turns on interrupts with `sti`, allowing the PC timer to continue running during `SlowMo`'s pause. Because timer interrupts come in via the 8259 PIC as described earlier, `sti` alone is not sufficient to allow future interrupts to be recognized. In addition to `sti`, you must also tell the 8259 PIC that you want fresh interrupts to be processed. Do this by issuing an *end-of-interrupt* (EOI) command to the 8259 port:

```
EOI     EQU     020h    ; End-of-interrupt value
PIC8259 EQU     020h    ; 8259 port address

sti                     ; Allow interrupts to occur
mov     al, EOI         ; al = end-of-interrupt value
out     PIC8259, al     ; Issue end of interrupt
```

Both `EOI` (the end-of-interrupt equate) and `PIC8259` (the port address equate) have the same value 020h, a meaningless coincidence. The `sti` instruction sets the `if` flag in the processor, which was reset automatically by the processor upon recognizing the interrupt signal that caused the ISR to begin running. Setting `if` allows the processor to again recognize external interrupt signals. Because those signals come from the 8259, the end-of-interrupt command also must tell the 8259 to pass the interrupts it receives along to the processor. Executing `sti` alone is not enough. When servicing interrupts generated via the 8259—and any interrupts called from inside the associated ISRs, as in the case of `SlowMo`—you must issue this same three-instruction sequence to allow future external interrupts to occur.

You are probably getting the idea by now that servicing interrupts—particularly those attached to the PC timer—requires you to be on your toes. Most of the work in writing ISRs is overhead—avoiding conflicts with global variables, dealing with reentrancy issues, making sure future interrupts can occur, saving and restoring register values, and so on. The actual guts of an ISR may be relatively simple, as they are in this example at lines 105–112. These instructions examine the low word of the timer tick value, which the ROM BIOS timer ISR increments as described earlier. When this value increases by the amount of the difference variable, the SlowMo ISR exits.

Notice that no instruction in the closed loop at lines 108–112 changes the LowTimer value directly. If you were to read this code out of context, the loop would seem to be incomplete, and you might assume that you had found a bug. If no instruction changes LowTimer, then the subtraction at line 110 will always be 0, causing the jb at line 112 to repeat endlessly. The fact that this does not happen proves that the ROM BIOS timer ISR is executing independently of the loop, incrementing the timer counter 18.2 times a second and eventually causing the jb to allow the program to continue.

Interrupts and Stacks

Because external interrupts can occur at any time, there's no way to predict the values of segment registers when an external ISR begins running. The only segment register you can depend upon is cs. Obviously, this register always equals the value of the current code segment containing the instructions that are now executing. But es, ds, and ss might point anywhere. As explained earlier, to reference local data, you must initialize ds and es, preserving their current values for restoring just before the ISR ends. Unfortunately, correct handling of the stack-segment register is not so simple.

In Program 10-1's ISR procedure SlowMo, three words are pushed onto the stack at lines 101–103. But which stack? DOS has its own stack space, as does the main program. In addition, there may be other ISRs in memory that have their own stacks. If any of these programs is interrupted, the value of ss will be the value assigned by that program. In other words, ISRs normally use whatever stack segment is current when the interrupt occurs. SlowMo simply assumes that at least three words of stack space are available—in addition to the three words required by the processor, which pushes onto the stack the flags and cs:ip registers before executing the ISR.

In most cases, it's probably safe to assume that a little stack space will always be available. But to many programmers, such an assumption is a painfully vague pill to swallow in the meticulous world of computer programming that demands exacting perfection from its practitioners. If relying on faith seems chancy—and especially if your ISR requires more than a few bytes of stack memory—you must switch to a local stack.

> Note: In your own programs, always add a few more bytes to your STACK directive than strictly required. Otherwise, you may cause problems for ISRs, ROM BIOS routines, DOS, and other resident code that assumes a few stack bytes will be available. Some DOS references recommend a minimum stack size of 2,048 bytes, although simple examples such as the programs in this book can usually get away with far less.

Changing stacks in an ISR is not difficult, but you must execute the instructions in the correct order. The reason for this is that the 8086 temporarily disables interrupts for exactly one instruction whenever you assign a value to a segment register. In other words, when you write the familiar initialization code,

```
mov     ax, @data
mov     ds, ax
mov     dx, offset string
```

interrupts are off for the `mov` to `dx`—a fact that's not evident from the source text. In this example, the effect on interrupts is unimportant. But consider what happens when changing the stack-segment register:

```
mov     ax, offset stackSpace
mov     ss, ax
mov     sp, offset endOfStack
```

Register `sp` is the stack pointer, locating the current top of the stack relative to the segment address in `ss`. Because two instructions are required to change both `ss` and `sp`, if an interrupt occurred between the assignment to `ss` and the assignment to `sp`, the old stack pointer would be used along with the new stack segment—a dangerous situation that can easily lead to a system crash. For this reason, interrupts are disabled for one instruction after the assignment to `ss`—just enough time to assign the `endOfStack` value to `sp`. Interrupts are also disabled for `pop` instructions involving a segment register. Remember, this effect lasts for only one instruction, and the `mov` to `sp` *must* immediately follow the `mov` to `ss`.

> Note: When assigning a value to `ss`, always follow immediately with an assignment to `sp`. Never reverse these two instructions and never insert an instruction between the two assignments. These steps are not optional!

In an ISR routine, to switch to a local stack, first declare some space in your program's code segment. There are many possible approaches, but this works:

```
ALIGN
myStack         DB      512 DUP (0)     ; Local 512-byte stack
endOfStack      =       $
```

The ALIGN directive ensures that the stack begins on a word boundary, in other words, at an even address. The stack begins at `myStack` and, in this sample, is 512 bytes long. A numeric equate `endOfStack` marks the bottom of the stack space. Next, save the current values of `ss` and `sp` in global variables, which you'll use later to restore the registers to their values at the start of the routine:

```
oldSS           DW      0           ; Hold stack segment
oldSP           DW      0           ; Hold stack offset


PROC    ISR
        mov     [cs:oldSS], ss      ; Save stack segment
        mov     [cs:oldSP], sp      ; Save stack pointer
```

Because the variables are declared in the code segment, a segment override `cs:` is needed to save `ss` and `sp` at the correct locations. After this, you're ready to switch to the local stack, assigning the current code-segment value to `ss` and the `endOfStack` offset to `sp`. Note that this still requires one word of stack space for pushing `cs`:

```
push    cs                      ; Push current code segment
pop     ss                      ; Pop cs value into ss
mov     sp, offset endOfStack   ; Interrupts disabled temporarily
```

To eliminate even this much stack usage requires using a third variable to save `ax` (or another register). Because you can't assign the value of one segment register to another, the current `cs` value is first assigned to `ax`, which is then assigned to `ss`:

```
oldAX   DW      0               ; Variable in code segment
mov     [cs:oldAX], ax          ; Save ax in variable
mov     [cs:oldSS], ss          ; Save stack segment
mov     [cs:oldSP], sp          ; Save stack pointer
mov     ax, cs                  ; Assign cs to ax
mov     ss, ax                  ; Assign ax to ss (ss = cs)
mov     sp, offset endOfStack   ; Interrupts disabled temporarily
```

Later, you can restore `ax` from the saved value at `cs:oldAX`. Usually, you don't have to go to such lengths—at least three words of stack space must have been available to execute the ISR in the first place, and it's reasonable to assume that at least one more word will be available.

Because the stack grows from high-memory addresses toward low-memory addresses, `sp` must be initialized to point to the end of the stack, not to the beginning. Also, because a `push` instruction decrements the stack pointer by 2 before transferring the pushed word to the location addressed by `ss:sp`, it's safe for `sp` to address the memory location just *after* the last byte allocated to the stack. But some programmers prefer to use an alternate instruction to load `sp`:

```
mov     sp, offset endOfStack-2
```

which points ss:sp to the last word in the stack, rather than to the byte beyond the bottom of the stack. This wastes one word of stack space but ensures that sp never points to anywhere but a legal stack location.

After switching to the local stack, you can push registers, refer to variables relative to bp, and so on. Remember, your new stack might be shared by any other interrupts that occur during this ISR's execution. After the ISR is done, restore the original stack with the instructions:

```
mov     ss, [cs:oldSS]          ; Restore stack segment register
mov     sp, [cs:oldSP]          ; Restore stack pointer register
```

Again, be sure to execute these instructions in this order without any other intervening instructions as interrupts will be temporarily disabled during the assignment to sp.

Note: Saving and restoring ss and sp from global variables brings up the old question of reentrancy again. In the previous examples, because the new stack space is a global variable, the ISR must be prevented from interrupting itself. Attempting to write a completely reentrant ISR that switches to a local stack will certainly put hair on your chest. You'll need fresh stack space and variables for each ISR invocation or, at the very least, an **inProgress** flag as in **SlowMo** to prevent a reentered ISR from corrupting a stack used by a previous call to the same routine.

Using int and into Instructions

As you know, DOS functions are called by the software interrupt instruction int 21h. True interrupts are generated externally and can occur at any time. Software interrupts called by int can occur only when a program executes this instruction. Therefore, software interrupts operate more like common subroutines than ISRs. Except for this difference, internal software and external hardware interrupts are identical, vectoring through values in low memory to the start of the ISR with the flags and cs:ip registers pushed on the stack. Software interrupts end with the same iret instruction, too.

One interesting fact is that int calls are not disabled by clearing if with cli. You can always call software interrupts even when external interrupts are disabled. You can even call an external ISR with an int instruction. For example, it's perfectly legal to "generate" your own timer tick with:

```
int     08h                     ; Force a timer tick
```
Don't do this!

There may not be any good reason for forcing the ROM BIOS timer ISR to run as the result of a software interrupt instruction, but there's nothing to prevent you from doing this—even though doing so frequently is likely to throw the system clock out of kilter. Also, be aware that some ISRs (the BIOS code for keyboard interrupt 09h, for example) assume that certain registers in various circuits have data to process. This might not be true if you force a hardware interrupt to occur via a software int instruction. But calling hardware interrupts with software int instructions is a useful technique for debugging external ISRs, letting you simulate the effects of hardware that, perhaps, doesn't yet exist.

In addition to int, you can also use the instruction into (interrupt on overflow) to force an interrupt type 4 if the overflow flag is set (of = 1) as the result of a previous arithmetic instruction. In practice, the into instruction is rarely used, and the interrupt vector for interrupt number 4 normally points to a plain iret instruction, thus having no effect even if a program does execute into. You can assign this vector (using DOS function 025h as described earlier) to your own ISR if you want to handle overflows with an ISR of your own design.

Trapping Divide-Fault Interrupts

The misnamed "divide-by-zero" interrupt is the source of much misinformation. A div or idiv instruction causes an automatic interrupt type 0 whenever the result of a division is larger than the maximum value that can be held in the destination (ax or al) and also when the divisor is 0. For example, this code causes an interrupt type 0:

```
mov     ax, 100h        ; Assign 100h to ax (low word)
xor     dx, dx          ; Zero dx (high word)
xor     bx, bx          ; Zero bx (divisor)
div     bx              ; Divide ax:dx by bx
```

Because the divisor (bx) is 0, the div fails, executing the ISR at the vector stored at 0000:0000—the first location in memory. What many people fail to realize is that the following code also generates a divide-by-zero interrupt:

```
mov     ax, 100h        ; Assign 100h to ax
mov     bl, 1           ; Set divisor (bl) to 1
div     bl              ; Interrupt type 0 generated!
```

The result of dividing 100h by 1 is, of course, 100h. But because this value is too large to fit within an 8-bit divide's destination register al, an interrupt type 0 is generated, even though the divisor is definitely not 0. For this reason, the divide-by-zero interrupt is better named the "divide-fault" interrupt, which you can't circumvent with code such as:

```
        or      bl, bl          ; Is divisor 0?
        jne     @@10            ; Jump if yes (bl = 0)
        call    Error           ; Call error handler
@@10:
        div     bl              ; ??
```

Despite appearances, this does not prevent an interrupt type 0 from occurring. Checking whether the divisor is 0 before executing div is a waste of time because an interrupt type 0 occurs whenever the result of a division exceeds the capacity of the destination register. When this happens, an ISR inside DOS executes, halting the program—an event that commercial programs must prevent. The solution is to install a custom divide-fault ISR to replace the DOS ISR for interrupt 0. As you will see, however, this is more difficult to do than you may suspect.

Fixing a Divide Fault

What should happen when a divide fault occurs? The answer depends on the application. A calculator program should probably display an error symbol. A spreadsheet program might insert an error message into a "cell" on screen. Another less critical program might simply ignore the condition—useful in some cases, as long as the program executing the division is aware of this possibility. A common approach is to write a simple ISR such as:

```
PROC    DivFault
        xor     ax, ax  ; Optionally set quotient to 0
        iret            ; Return from interrupt
ENDP    DivFault
```

Reassigning the interrupt 0 vector to DivFault causes an iret instruction to execute if a divide fault occurs, which would seem to be the easy way to ignore such an error. The quotient is optionally reset to 0—a reasonable (if not correct) answer in the event of a divide error. Unfortunately, this solution works only on systems with 8086/88 processors. On systems with 80286 and 80386 processors, the iret in this example actually returns to the same div or idiv that caused the interrupt to occur—effectively locking the system. The reason this happens is that an interrupt level 0 pushes the address of the *next* instruction for 8086/88 processors, but it pushes the address of the *current* instruction for 80286 and 80386 processors. This is an extremely nasty problem for programmers who have to write code to run on a wide range of PCs, XTs, and ATs.

Correctly handling this unusual condition requires some fancy footwork. The answer is to adjust the offset return address on the stack to skip the div or idiv instruction that caused the ISR to begin running. Some references recommend just adding 2 to the offset portion of the return address on the stack and then ending the ISR with iret. But this common plan fails to take into account that a div or idiv instruction can be 2 or 4 bytes long, depending on whether the divisor is a register (2 bytes) or a memory location (4 bytes). Dealing with this situation requires peeking back at the machine code of the div or idiv instruction. If the first two bits of the second byte equal 1, then the operand is a register; otherwise, the operand is a memory reference. Knowing this, the program can adjust the return address by 2 or 4, skipping the div or idiv on executing iret.

Note: Deciphering the bits that make up individual machine codes is painstaking work and, fortunately, is rarely necessary. See Bibliography for references that document the exact bit formats for other machine-code instructions.

Installing a Divide-Fault Handler

A good way to handle divide faults is to install a "memory-resident" program to trap type 0 interrupts if they occur. After doing this, all divide errors are routed through the new ISR, preventing DOS from halting a program unexpectedly. Program 10-2, DIV286.ASM, accomplishes this while also demonstrating how to write memory-resident assembly language programs. Assemble DIV286 and link with the commands:

memory resident ≡ TSR

```
tasm div286
tlink /t div286,,, mta
```

Don't run DIV286 just yet—you'll first want to execute a second program (described in a moment) to test the effects of the new interrupt handler. Notice the /t switch in the tlink command; it is necessary to create a .COM file instead of the usual .EXE format. "Memory resident" .EXE code files are more difficult to write, although they can be larger than resident .COM files, which are limited to about 64K. For our purposes, the .COM format is more than adequate.

Note: You must have an 80286 or 80386 processor to use DIV286.ASM. To create a similar program for 8086 and 8088 systems, replace lines 42–61 with the much simpler DivFault procedure listed earlier. You might want to name this program DIV86.ASM.

Program 10-2 *DIV286.ASM*

```
1:  %TITLE "80286/386 Divide-Fault ISR Installer"
2:
3:          IDEAL
4:          DOSSEG
5:          MODEL   tiny
6:
7:  cr      EQU     13
8:  lf      EQU     10
9:
10:
11:         DATASEG
12:
13: welcome DB      cr, lf, '80286/386 Divide-Fault Handler Installed'
14:         DB      cr, lf, 'Address = ', 0
15: string  DB      40 dup (?)
16:
17:
```

```
18:          CODESEG
19:
20:          ORG      100h                ; Standard .COM start address (origin)
21:
22:          EXTRN    StrWrite:proc, BinToAscHex:proc, NewLine:proc
23:
24: Start:
25:          jmp      Begin               ; Jump over resident ISR
26:
27: %NEWPAGE
28: ;------------------------------------------------------------------
29: ; DivFault              Divide-Fault handler ISR
30: ;------------------------------------------------------------------
31: ; Input:
32: ;        none  (called internally upon a DIV or IDIV fault)
33: ; Output:
34: ;        ax = 0 (al = 8-bit quotient, ax = 16-bit quotient)
35: ;
36: ;        Note: Program continues normally with the instruction
37: ;        following the DIV or IDIV that caused the fault.
38: ;
39: ; Registers:
40: ;        ax changed
41: ;------------------------------------------------------------------
42: PROC     DivFault
43:          sti                          ; Enable CPU interrupts
44:          push     bp                  ; Save current bp register
45:          mov      bp, sp              ; Address stack values with ss:bp
46:          push     si                  ; Save other modified registers
47:          push     ds
48:          lds      si, [bp + 2]        ; Address div or idiv with ds:si
49:          lodsw                        ; Get div plus second byte (in ah)
50:          and      ah, 0C0h            ; Isolate first two bits (MOD field)
51:          cmp      ah, 0C0h            ; Are bits = 1? (register based instr)
52:          je       @@10                ; Jump if yes--div is 2 bytes long
53:          add      [word bp + 2], 2    ; div is 4-bytes add 2 to offset
54: @@10:    add      [word bp + 2], 2    ; Add 2 (or 2 more) to offset
55:          xor      ax, ax              ; Set quotient to 0 (remainder also 0
56:                                       ;  for 8-bit divide only)
57:          pop      ds                  ; Restore saved registers
58:          pop      si
59:          pop      bp
60:          iret                         ; Return from interrupt
61: ENDP     DivFault
62:
63: Begin:
64:          mov      ax, 2500h           ; Set new vector for Divide
65:          mov      dx, offset DivFault
66:          int      21h
67:          mov      di, offset welcome  ; Display welcoming message
68:          call     StrWrite
```

```
69:            mov     ax, cs                      ; Display segment value
70:            call    ShowAX
71:            mov     dl, ':'                     ; Display a colon (:)
72:            mov     ah, 2
73:            int     21h
74:            mov     ax, offset DivFault         ; Display offset value
75:            call    ShowAX
76:            call    NewLine
77:
78: ;-----  Terminate and stay resident, keeping only the code up to
79: ;         the end of the new Divide-Fault ISR
80:
81: Exit:
82:            mov     dx, offset Begin            ; New free mem address
83:            int     27h                         ; Terminate, stay resident
84:
85: ;-----  Subroutine to display AX in hexadecimal
86:
87: PROC    ShowAX                                 ; Show value in AX
88:            mov     cx, 4                       ; Minimum number of chars
89:            mov     di, offset string           ; Address of string variable
90:            call    BinToAscHex                 ; Convert AX to hex
91:            call    StrWrite                    ; Display hex string
92:            ret                                 ; Return to caller
93: ENDP    ShowAX
94:
95:            END     Start          ; End of program / entry point
```

Testing DIV286   To test the before and after effects of DIV286, assemble Program 10-3, DIVFAULT.ASM, which forces a divide fault to occur. Assemble and link to MTA.LIB in the usual way:

```
tasm divfault
tlink divfault,,, mta
```

Run the test program by typing `divfault` and pressing Enter. This should generate the DOS message "Divide Overflow," halting the program prematurely. Depending on your version of DOS (and, perhaps, other resident programs loaded into memory), you may have to reboot by pressing Ctrl-Atl-Delete. Some DOS versions are known to become unstable following a divide-fault error.

Next, execute DIV286 to install the resident ISR. (On 8086 and 8088 systems, run the modified DIV86 program instead.) Then run DIVFAULT again. This time, you should see the message "Program continues," proving that DOS no longer halts the program upon receiving a divide-fault interrupt.

Note: Run DIV286 or DIV86 only one time or you'll needlessly install multiple copies of the divide-fault handler in memory.

Program 10-3 *DIVFAULT.ASM*

```
 1:   %TITLE "Divide-Fault Demonstration"
 2:
 3:           IDEAL
 4:           DOSSEG
 5:           MODEL   small
 6:           STACK   256
 7:
 8:   cr      EQU     13                  ; ASCII carriage return
 9:   lf      EQU     10                  ; ASCII line feed
10:
11:
12:           DATASEG
13:
14:   exitCode        DB      0
15:   message1        DB      cr,lf,'Forcing a divide by zero fault...',0
16:   message2        DB      cr,lf,'Program continued normally',cr,lf,0
17:
18:
19:           CODESEG
20:
21:   ;----- From STRIO.OBJ
22:           EXTRN   StrWrite:proc
23:
24:   Start:
25:           mov     ax, @data           ; Initialize ds to address
26:           mov     ds, ax              ;  of data segment
27:           mov     es, ax              ; Make es = ds
28:
29:           mov     di, offset message1 ; Address welcome message
30:           call    StrWrite
31:
32:           mov     ax, 100h            ; Assign value to ax
33:           xor     bx, bx              ; Zero divisor
34:           div     bx                  ; Force Divide-Fault Exception
35:
36:   Exit:
37:           mov     di, offset message2 ; Address "continued" message
38:           call    StrWrite            ; Display string
39:
40:           mov     ah,04Ch             ; DOS function: Exit program
41:           mov     al,[exitCode]       ; Return exit code value
42:           int     21h                 ; Call DOS. Terminate program
43:
44:           END     Start          ; End of program / entry point
```

How DIV286 Works DIV286 calls the DOS Terminate-and-Stay-Resident (TSR) software interrupt 27h at line 83, installing in memory a copy of the divide fault ISR at lines (28–61). Executing `int` 27h returns control to COMMAND.COM but tells DOS to retain all occupied memory up to the address in `cs:dx`. Line

82 sets dx to the offset address just below the last instruction to be kept in memory—in this example, the iret at line 60. There are other ways to install TSR code—for example, DOS function 031h—but when the size of the program is relatively small (less than about 64K), interrupt 27h is much easier to use.

Notice that a DATASEG directive is used to declare program variables at lines 11–15. Because this is a .COM program, the data and code segments are actually one and the same. The stack segment in a .COM program also shares the same 64K segment; consequently, the program does not specify a separate stack in a **STACK** directive.

> Note: By the way, variables declared after a **DATASEG** directive in a .COM program are stored above (at a higher address than) the executable code. As a result, these variables do not remain in memory after executing interrupt 27h. Variables that must remain resident after the program ends should be declared in the code segment at an offset below (at a lower address than) the address passed to interrupt 27h in **cs:dx**.

Installing TSR Code in Memory

The first instruction in a TSR program usually jumps over the code that is to remain in memory after the program ends (see line 25). The actual first instruction in the program is at the destination of this jump—in DIV286, at label **Begin:** (line 63). Here, the divide-fault interrupt vector is changed to the address of the new ISR—the resident portion of this program at lines 28–61.

Be sure you understand that DIV286 is really two programs in one convenient package. The code that runs when you execute DIV286 starts at line 25, jumps to line 63, and ends at line 93. The resident **DivFault** procedure does not execute at this time. Instead, this ISR remains in memory after DIV286 ends, ready to handle a divide error when it occurs. The sole purpose of the DIV286 program is to install the **DivFault** ISR and to display a message on screen that this has been done. To help you locate the code in memory (if you need to do this), DIV286 also displays the address where **DivFault** resides.

After DIV286 ends, leaving the **DivFault** ISR behind, a subsequent divide-fault interrupt executes the ISR, starting at line 43, which immediately executes sti, allowing other interrupts to be serviced while **DivFault** runs. At this point, the stack contains the system flags plus the address of the div or idiv instruction that caused the interrupt to occur. Borrowing a popular technique from high-level languages, **DivFault** locates the return address on the stack, first executing the instructions:

```
push    bp              ; Save current bp
mov     bp, sp          ; Address stack with bp
```

The order of these two instructions is important. First, the current value of register bp is saved on whatever stack space happens to be in use. Then the value of the stack pointer sp is assigned to bp, thus addressing the stack with ss:bp. (Addressing memory with the bp register defaults to the segment addressed by ss. You could use other registers to address data on the stack, but bp is the most convenient.)

Figure 10-1 illustrates how the stack appears during execution of the DivFault ISR. (The return address, flags, and other values on a stack make up what's known as a procedure's *stack frame*.) When addressing variables on the stack, it helps to draw a diagram of the stack frame. Disturbing the wrong data on the stack can have disastrous results, so there's precious little room for error. Figure 10-1 labels the stack pointer at different stages, while DivFault executes:

sp0: The stack pointer before the divide-fault interrupt occurs.

sp1: The stack pointer after the divide-fault interrupt signal is processed. The processor has pushed the flag, cs, and ip registers onto the stack.

sp2: The stack pointer after pushing the current value of bp

sp3: The stack pointer after pushing registers si and ds

The plan is to read the values of cs:ip from the stack, examine the div or idiv instruction, and increment the return address by either 2 or 4 bytes. To do this, register bp was assigned the value of sp2, thus addressing stack byte number 4. (The numbers in the diagram are there just for reference—they don't refer to real memory addresses.) Because each box in the figure represents a 2-byte word, the 16-bit ip register value is at [bp + 2]. The cs register value is at [bp + 4]. If you wanted to access the flags on the stack, you could use [bp + 6].

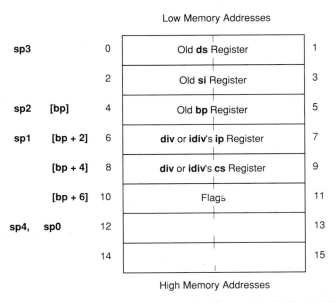

Figure 10-1 *The stack frame during execution of the DivFault ISR in DIV286.ASM.*

Line 48 of DIV286.ASM executes `lds` to load the `ds` and `si` registers with the address of the `div` or `idiv` instruction that caused the divide-fault interrupt. You could just as well use two `mov` instructions to load the words at `[bp + 2]` and `[bp + 4]`, but `lds` performs the same job and is shorter and a little faster. (You can use any 16-bit register as the destination for the offset portion of the address, not only `si`.)

After line 48, `ds:si` addresses the faulty `div` or `idiv`. Line 49 loads the first word of this instruction into `ax` for examination. If the first 2 bits are equal to 1, then this is a 2-byte instruction; otherwise, it's a 4-byte version. Lines 53–54 increment the offset portion of the return address on the stack accordingly by 2 or 4 bytes.

The net effect of these actions is to ignore the `div` or `idiv` that caused the interrupt type 0. Register `ax` is cleared (line 55), setting the 8-bit (`al`) or 16-bit (`ax`) quotient to 0. (Note: For 8-bit divides, this also sets the remainder in `ah` to 0.) Because the return address was incremented, when the interrupt ends at line 60, program execution continues with the instruction following the faulty divide.

Interrupt-Driven Serial Communications

DOS has its critics but even fans agree with detractors about one thing: Asynchronous serial I/O (also called auxiliary I/O) in DOS is about as useful as shoes for a mermaid. Although there are two DOS functions available for reading (function 3) and writing (function 4) characters to a serial I/O port, experts generally agree that programs using these functions are unreliable except, perhaps, at the slowest baud rates. There are at least three possible solutions to the problem:

1. Write a custom device driver for reading and writing to a serial port as a named file.
2. Call the BIOS asynchronous interrupt 14h directly for all serial communications.
3. Install interrupt-driven code to read and write characters independently of DOS and the BIOS.

Number 1 is a good idea, especially if you need to access special communications hardware—a multiport peripheral card, for example. However, writing custom device drivers is a subject that would require an entire chapter and, therefore, is an impractical solution to cover here. (Most good DOS references discuss this subject in detail.) Number 2 is also good. The ROM BIOS in all PCs handles asynchronous serial I/O with excellent results. But, even though number 3 requires direct access to hardware registers—thus making the program difficult to transfer to non-PCs—an interrupt-driven asynchronous serial I/O package makes writing communications programs so much easier than the other two methods that most programmers prefer this approach.

Program 10-4, ASYNCH.ASM, can serve as the basis for any communications program. The code implements a buffered, interrupt-driven, input channel for incoming data and uses a non-interrupt-driven method for output. After the listing is an example program that demonstrates how to use the ASYNCH module. Assemble, link, and install ASYNCH in MTA.LIB with the commands:

```
tasm /zi asynch
tlib /E mta -+asynch
```

As usual, ignore any warning about ASYNCH not being in the library. If you change any of ASYNCH.ASM, repeat these two steps. Take out the /zi option to reduce code-file size by stripping the information for Turbo Debugger.

> Note: Change the equate value at line 9 to 0 for COM1: or to 1 for COM2:.

Program 10-4 *ASYNCH.ASM*

```
 1:  %TITLE "Asynchronous Serial Communications Module"
 2:
 3:          IDEAL
 4:          DOSSEG
 5:          MODEL   small
 6:
 7:          PUBLIC  ComPort
 8:
 9:  ComPort = 0             ; 0 = COM1:, 1 = COM2:
10:
11:  IF ComPort EQ 0
12:          Port        EQU     03F8h   ; 8250 base address
13:          VectorNum   EQU     0Ch     ; Interrupt vector number
14:          EnableIRQ   EQU     0EFh    ; Mask to enable 8259 IRQ
15:          DisableIRQ  EQU     10h     ; Mask to disable 8259 IRQ
16:
17:  ELSEIF ComPort EQ 1
18:          Port        EQU     02F8h   ; same comments as above
19:          VectorNum   EQU     0Bh
20:          EnableIRQ   EQU     0F7h
21:          DisableIRQ  EQU     08h
22:  ELSE
23:          DISPLAY "ComPort must be 0 or 1"
24:          ERR
25:  ENDIF
26:
27:  ;----- Adapter register addresses
28:
29:  TxRegister    =       Port + 0      ; Transmit Register
30:  RxRegister    =       Port + 0      ; Receive Register
31:  IntEnable     =       Port + 1      ; Interrupt Enable Register
32:  IntIdent      =       Port + 2      ; Interrupt Identification
33:  LineControl   =       Port + 3      ; Line Control Register
```

```
34:     ModemControl    =        Port + 4        ; Modem Control Register
35:     LineStatus      =        Port + 5        ; Line Status Register
36:     ModemStatus     =        Port + 6        ; Modem Status Register
37:
38:     ;-----  Other equates
39:
40:     Ctrl8259_0      EQU      020h            ; 8259 port
41:     Ctrl8259_1      EQU      021h            ; 8259 port (masks)
42:     EOI             EQU      020h            ; 8259 end-of-interrupt
43:     BufSize         EQU      2048            ; Size of input buffer
44:
45:
46:             DATASEG
47:
48:     vectorSeg       DW       ?               ; Old vector segment
49:     vectorOfs       DW       ?               ; Old vector offset
50:     bufHead         DW       ?               ; Buffer head pointer
51:     bufTail         DW       ?               ; Buffer tail pointer
52:     buffer          DB       BufSize DUP (?) ; Input buffer
53:
54:
55:             CODESEG
56:
57:             PUBLIC  AsynchInit, AsynchStop, AsynchStat
58:             PUBLIC  AsynchOut, AsynchIn, AsynchInStat
59:
60:     %NEWPAGE
61:     ;----------------------------------------------------------------
62:     ; EmptyBuffer             Empty the input buffer
63:     ;----------------------------------------------------------------
64:     ; Note:
65:     ;       Private to module
66:     ; Input:
67:     ;       none
68:     ; Output:
69:     ;       none
70:     ; Registers:
71:     ;       none
72:     ;----------------------------------------------------------------
73:     PROC    EmptyBuffer
74:             cli                              ; Prevent interrupts
75:             push    ax                       ; Save ax
76:             mov     ax, offset buffer        ; Buffer is empty when
77:             mov     [bufHead], ax            ;   the head and tail pointers
78:             mov     [bufTail], ax            ;   are equal
79:             pop     ax                       ; Restore ax
80:             sti                              ; Enable interrupts
81:             ret                              ; Return to caller
82:     ENDP    EmptyBuffer
```

```
 83:   %NEWPAGE
 84:   ;------------------------------------------------------------
 85:   ; AsynchInit           Initialize serial port and install ISR
 86:   ;------------------------------------------------------------
 87:   ; Input:
 88:   ;       none
 89:   ; Output:
 90:   ;       none
 91:   ;
 92:   ;       NOTE: Precede (usually) with call to int 14h to
 93:   ;       set baud rate
 94:   ;
 95:   ;       NOTE: Interrupt-driven input begins immediately
 96:   ;       upon exit from this routine.
 97:   ;
 98:   ;       WARNING: You must call AsynchStop before your
 99:   ;       program ends to avoid a system crash!
100:   ;
101:   ; Registers:
102:   ;       ax, bx, dx
103:   ;------------------------------------------------------------
104:   PROC    AsynchInit
105:
106:           call    EmptyBuffer             ; Initialize buffer
107:
108:   ;-----  Save and reassign interrupt vector
109:
110:           push    ds                      ; Save segment registers
111:           push    es
112:           mov     ax, 3500h + VectorNum   ; Get vector address
113:           int     21h                     ; Call DOS
114:           mov     [vectorSeg], es         ; Save segment address
115:           mov     [vectorOfs], bx         ; Save offset address
116:           push    cs                      ; Address AsynchISR
117:           pop     ds                      ;  with ds:dx, and call
118:           mov     dx, offset AsynchISR    ;  DOS function 25h to
119:           mov     ax, 2500h + VectorNum   ;  set the new vector
120:           int     21h                     ;  address.
121:           pop     es                      ; Restore saved registers
122:           pop     ds
123:
124:   ;-----  Enable 8259 interrupt (IRQ) line for this asynch adapter
125:
126:           in      al, Ctrl8259_1          ; Read 8259 enable masks
127:           and     al, EnableIRQ           ; Clear masked bit
128:           out     Ctrl8259_1, al          ; Write new 8259 masks
129:
```

```
130:    ;----- Enable 8250 interrupt-on-data ready
131:
132:            mov     dx, LineControl         ; First, read the line control
133:            in      al, dx                  ;  register and clear bit
134:            and     al, 07Fh                ;  7, the Divisor Latch Access
135:            out     dx, al                  ;  Bit, or DLAB
136:            mov     dx, IntEnable           ; With DLAB = 0, set bit 0 of
137:            mov     al, 1                   ;  interrupt enable register
138:            out     dx, al                  ;  to 1, enabling interrupt
139:
140:    ;----- Clear 8250 status and data registers
141:
142:    @@10:
143:            mov     dx, RxRegister          ; Clear data register
144:            in      al, dx                  ;  by reading port
145:            mov     dx, LineStatus          ; Clear line status
146:            in      al, dx                  ;  by reading port
147:            mov     dx, ModemStatus         ; Clear modem status
148:            in      al, dx                  ;  by reading port
149:            mov     dx, IntIdent            ; Check interrupt ident
150:            in      al, dx                  ;  register
151:            test    al, 1                   ; Bit 1 should be 1
152:            jz      @@10                    ; Jump if interrupt pending
153:
154:    ;----- Set bit 3 of modem control register
155:
156:            mov     dx, ModemControl        ; Interrupts will be
157:            in      al, dx                  ;  acknowledged as soon as
158:            or      al, 08h                 ;  this bit is set to 1
159:            out     dx, al                  ; Done!
160:
161:    ;----- Empty input buffer again, just in case a stray character
162:    ;      managed to squeak in
163:
164:            call    EmptyBuffer             ; Empty buffer again
165:
166:            ret                             ; Return to caller
167:    ENDP    AsynchInit
168:    %NEWPAGE
169:    ;-------------------------------------------------------------
170:    ; AsynchStop              Uninstall Asynch ISR
171:    ;-------------------------------------------------------------
172:    ; Input:
173:    ;       none
174:    ; Output:
175:    ;       none
176:    ;
177:    ;       WARNING: Always call AsynchStop before your program
178:    ;       ends or a system crash is inevitable!
179:    ;
```

```
180:    ; Registers:
181:    ;       al, dx
182:    ;------------------------------------------------------------
183:    PROC    AsynchStop
184:
185:    ;-----   Mask (disable) 8259 IRQ interrupt
186:
187:            in      al, Ctrl8259_1      ; Read 8259 masks
188:            or      al, DisableIRQ      ; Mask IRQ bit
189:            out     Ctrl8259_1, al      ; Write new masks
190:
191:    ;-----   Disable 8250 interrupt
192:
193:            mov     dx, LineControl     ; First, read the line control
194:            in      al, dx              ;  register and clear bit
195:            and     al, 07Fh            ;  7, the Divisor Latch Access
196:            out     dx, al              ;  Bit, or DLAB
197:            mov     dx, IntEnable       ; With DLAB = 0, clear all bits
198:            xor     al, al              ;  to disable interrupts
199:            out     dx, al              ; Write new register value
200:
201:    ;-----   Set bit 3 in modem control register to 0
202:
203:            mov     dx, ModemControl    ; Assign port address
204:            in      al, dx              ; Get current register
205:            and     al, 0F7h            ; Clear bit 3
206:            out     dx, al              ; Output new register value
207:
208:    ;-----   Interrupts are disabled. Restore saved interrupt vector.
209:
210:            push    ds                  ; Save segment register
211:            mov     ax, 2500h + VectorNum ; Set interrupt vector
212:            mov     dx, [vectorOfs]     ; Get saved offset
213:            mov     ds, [vectorSeg]     ; Get saved segment
214:            int     21h                 ; Set interrupt vector
215:            pop     ds                  ; Restore saved register
216:
217:            ret                         ; Return to caller
218:    ENDP    AsynchStop
219:    %NEWPAGE
220:    ;------------------------------------------------------------
221:    ; AsynchStat          Get status for output
222:    ;------------------------------------------------------------
223:    ; Input:
224:    ;       none
225:    ; Output:
226:    ;       ah = line status
227:    ;       al = modem status
228:    ; Registers:
229:    ;       ax, dx
230:    ;------------------------------------------------------------
```

```
231:    PROC    AsynchStat
232:            mov     ah, 3                      ; Get-status function number
233:            mov     dx, ComPort                ; 0 = COM1:, 1 = COM2:
234:            int     14h                        ; Call BIOS RS232_IO service
235:            ret                                ; Return to caller
236:    ENDP    AsynchStat
237:    %NEWPAGE
238:    ;-----------------------------------------------------------------
239:    ; AsynchOut              Output a byte (to output port)
240:    ;-----------------------------------------------------------------
241:    ; Input:
242:    ;       al = character (or byte) to output
243:    ; Output:
244:    ;       none
245:    ; Registers:
246:    ;       none
247:    ;-----------------------------------------------------------------
248:    PROC    AsynchOut
249:            push    dx                         ; Save modified dx
250:            push    ax                         ; Save char in al
251:    @@10:
252:            mov     dx, LineStatus             ; Address Line Status Register
253:            in      al, dx                     ; Get line status
254:            and     al, 020h                   ; Isolate Trasmit Holding Reg.
255:            jz      @@10                       ; Jump if THRE is not empty
256:            pop     ax                         ; Restore character
257:            mov     dx, TxRegister             ; Address transmit register
258:            out     dx, al                     ; Output char in al
259:            pop     dx                         ; Restore saved dx
260:            ret                                ; Return to caller
261:    ENDP    AsynchOut
262:    %NEWPAGE
263:    ;-----------------------------------------------------------------
264:    ; AsynchIn               Input a byte (from buffer)
265:    ;-----------------------------------------------------------------
266:    ; Input:
267:    ;       none
268:    ; Output:
269:    ;       al = char from buffer
270:    ;
271:    ;       Note: If buffer is empty, al will be 0, with
272:    ;       no indication that this is not an input value.
273:    ;       Precede with call to AsynchInStat to avoid reads
274:    ;       from an empty buffer.
275:    ;
276:    ; Registers:
277:    ;       al, bx
278:    ;-----------------------------------------------------------------
```

```
279:  PROC    AsynchIn
280:          xor     al, al                    ; Preset result to null
281:          mov     bx, [bufTail]             ; Get tail pointer
282:          cmp     bx, [bufHead]             ; Test if buffer is empty
283:          je      @@99                      ; Exit if empty (al = 0)
284:          mov     al, [byte ptr bx]         ; Else read char from buffer
285:          inc     [bufTail]                 ; Advance tail pointer
286:          cmp     [word ptr bufTail], offset buffer + BufSize  ; At end?
287:          jb      @@99                      ; Jump if not so
288:          mov     [bufTail], offset buffer  ; Else reset tail pointer
289:  @@99:
290:          ret                               ; Return to caller
291:  ENDP    AsynchIn
292:  %NEWPAGE
293:  ;-----------------------------------------------------------------
294:  ; AsynchInStat        Get status of input buffer
295:  ;-----------------------------------------------------------------
296:  ; Input:
297:  ;       none
298:  ; Output:
299:  ;       dx = number of bytes (or chars) in buffer
300:  ; Registers:
301:  ;       dx
302:  ;-----------------------------------------------------------------
303:  PROC    AsynchInStat
304:          mov     dx, [bufHead]             ; Get head pointer
305:          sub     dx, [bufTail]             ; Subtract tail from head
306:          jge     @@99                      ; Jump if result >= 0
307:          add     dx, BufSize               ; Handle negative result
308:  @@99:
309:          ret                               ; Return to caller
310:  ENDP    AsynchInStat
311:  %NEWPAGE
312:  ;-----------------------------------------------------------------
313:  ; AsynchISR    Asynchronous input interrupt service routine
314:  ;-----------------------------------------------------------------
315:  ; Input:
316:  ;       none
317:  ; Output:
318:  ;       none (char read and deposited in buffer)
319:  ;
320:  ;       NOTE: This version ignores buffer overflows
321:  ;
322:  ; Registers:
323:  ;       none
324:  ;-----------------------------------------------------------------
325:  PROC    AsynchISR
326:          push    ax                        ; Save modified registers
327:          push    bx
328:          push    ds
329:          push    dx
330:
```

```
331:            mov     ax, @data               ; Address local data with ds
332:            mov     ds, ax
333:            mov     dx, RxRegister          ; dx = Receive Register
334:            in      al, dx                  ; Read byte from port
335:            mov     bx, [bufHead]           ; Get head pointer
336:            mov     [byte ptr bx], al       ; Store byte in buffer
337:            inc     bx                      ; Advance head pointer
338:            cmp     bx, offset buffer + BufSize  ; Is ptr at end?
339:            jb      @@10                    ; Jump if not
340:            mov     bx, offset buffer       ; Else reset to beginning
341: @@10:
342:            cmp     bx, [bufTail]           ; Check for overflow
343:            jne     @@20                    ; Jump if no overflow
344:            mov     bx, [bufHead]           ; Cancel pointer advance
345: @@20:
346:            mov     [bufHead], bx           ; Save new head pointer
347:            mov     al, EOI                 ; Issue end of interrupt to
348:            out     Ctrl8259_0, al          ;   8259 port
349:
350:            pop     dx                      ; Restore saved registers
351:            pop     ds
352:            pop     bx
353:            pop     ax
354:            iret                            ; Return from interrupt
355: ENDP       AsynchISR
356:
357:            END                             ; End of module
```

Running an ASYNCH Demonstration

Program 10-5, TRM.ASM, demonstrates how to use the ASYNCH package. Although not a complete terminal emulator, TRM is useful for debugging communications with a remote system. It's frequently helpful to be able to see not only normal ASCII text but also every control byte that goes in and out of a communications link. TRM displays normal text normally, but brackets control codes with their ASCII values. For example, a carriage return and line feed are displayed as [13][10]. Just seeing the sequence of control codes coming in from a remote source is often all that's needed to fix communications problems. Assemble and link TRM with the commands:

```
tasm /zi trm
tlink /v trm,,, mta
```

Note: If you have access to two PCs, connect them with a serial cable and execute TRM on both systems. Then type control codes and press Esc, Enter, and so on to see how TRM displays text and controls. If you don't have two PCs, you might be able to use TRM with a modem, but you'll have to either enter modem-initialization commands manually or use a full-blown terminal program to log on to a remote system before running TRM.

Program 10-5 *TRM.ASM*

```
 1:   %TITLE "Terminal Emulator with Control-Code Debugging"
 2:
 3:            IDEAL
 4:            DOSSEG
 5:            MODEL    small
 6:            STACK    1024
 7:
 8:   ;----- From ASYNCH.OBJ
 9:            EXTRN    ComPort:abs
10:
11:   cr              EQU      13        ; ASCII carriage return
12:   lf              EQU      10        ; ASCII line feed
13:   bd9600          EQU      0e3h      ; 9600 baud, no parity, 1 stop, 8 bits
14:   ExitKey         EQU      100       ; GetCh value for F10
15:
16:
17:            DATASEG
18:
19:   exitCode        DB       0
20:
21:   welcome         DB       cr, lf, 'Terminal Emulator by Tom Swan', cr, lf
22:                   DB       cr, lf, 'Configured for 9600 baud. Displays'
23:                   DB       cr, lf, 'control codes in brackets for debugging'
24:                   DB       cr, lf, 'an RS232 serial line. Press F10'
25:                   DB       cr, lf, 'to exit.', cr, lf, lf, 0
26:
27:   string          DB       80 DUP (?)       ; Miscellaneous string
28:
29:
30:            CODESEG
31:
32:   ;----- From ASYNCH.OBJ
33:            EXTRN    AsynchInit:proc, AsynchStop:proc, AsynchStat:proc
34:            EXTRN    AsynchOut:proc, AsynchIn:proc, AsynchInStat:proc
35:
36:   ;----- From KEYBOARD.OBJ
37:            EXTRN    KeyWaiting:proc, GetCh:proc
38:
39:   ;----- From BINASC.OBJ
40:            EXTRN    BinToAscDec:proc
41:
42:   ;----- From STRIO.OBJ
43:            EXTRN    StrWrite:proc
44:
45:   Start:
46:            mov      ax, @data                ; Initialize ds to address
47:            mov      ds, ax                   ;  of data segment
48:            mov      es, ax                   ; Make es = ds
49:
```

```
50:            mov      di, offset welcome      ; Display welcoming message
51:            call     StrWrite
52:
53:    ;-----  Initialize baud rate and Asynch package
54:
55:            mov      ah, 0                   ; BIOS RS232 init function
56:            mov      al, bd9600              ; configuration
57:            mov      dx, ComPort             ; Port number (0 or 1)
58:            int      14h                     ; Call RS232_IO service
59:            call     AsynchInit              ; Initialize asynch package
60:
61:    ;-----  Perform terminal I/O emulation
62:
63:    Emulate:
64:            call     AsynchInStat            ; Any chars come in yet?
65:            or       dx, dx                  ; Check if dx > 0
66:            jz       @@10                    ; dx = 0, check for key press
67:            call     AsynchIn                ; Read char from buffer
68:            call     DispChar                ; Display character locally
69:            jmp      Emulate                 ; Continue emulation
70:    @@10:
71:            call     KeyWaiting              ; Check if key was pressed
72:            jz       Emulate                 ; Loop if not
73:            call     GetCh                   ; Else get key press
74:            jnz      @@20                    ; Jump if not fn or ctrl key
75:            cmp      al, ExitKey             ; Program-exit key pressed?
76:            je       Exit                    ; Jump to Exit if yes
77:    @@20:
78:            call     AsynchOut               ; Else send char on its way
79:            jmp      Emulate                 ; Loop until done
80:
81:    ;-----  End of emulation. Deinitialize Asynch package and exit.
82:
83:    Exit:
84:            call     AsynchStop              ; Halt Asynch package
85:            mov      ah,04Ch                 ; DOS function: Exit program
86:            mov      al,[exitCode]           ; Return exit code value
87:            int      21h                     ; Call DOS. Terminate program
88:
89:    %NEWPAGE
90:    ;----------------------------------------------------------------
91:    ; DispChar/OneChar       Display any ASCII value
92:    ;----------------------------------------------------------------
93:    ; Input:
94:    ;        al = ASCII value (0...255)
95:    ; Output:
96:    ;        none
97:    ;
98:    ;        NOTE: Control codes are displayed as [13], [10], etc., for
99:    ;        debugging a serial I/O line.
```

```
100:    ; Registers:
101:    ;       ax, cx, dl, di
102:    ;--------------------------------------------------------------
103:    PROC    DispChar
104:            cmp     al, 32              ; Is character a control?
105:            jae     OneChar             ; Jump if not
106:
107:    ;-----   Display bracketed control codes
108:
109:            xor     ah, ah              ; Convert al to 16-bit value
110:            mov     cx, 1               ; Specify at least one char
111:            mov     di, offset string   ; Address string variable
112:            call    BinToAscDec         ; Convert to string
113:            mov     al, '['             ; Display [ char
114:            call    OneChar             ; Display char in al
115:            call    StrWrite            ; Display ctrl-code string
116:            mov     al, ']'             ; "Fall through" to OneChar
117:
118:    PROC    OneChar
119:            mov     dl, al              ; Assign char to dl
120:            mov     ah, 2               ; DOS output-char function
121:            int     21h                 ; Call DOS to display char
122:            ret                         ; Return to caller
123:    ENDP    OneChar
124:
125:    ENDP    DispChar
126:
127:            END     Start               ; End of program / entry point
```

How TRM Works   Program 10-5, TRM.ASM, demonstrates how to use the ASYNCH package routines, described in detail after this section. Lines 55–58 call BIOS function 14h to initialize the primary serial port, passing the baud rate and other parameters in register al. The default setting used here is 9600 baud, no parity, 1 stop bit, and 8 data bits (see line 13).

Table 10-3 lists the meanings of the bits in the 8-bit value passed in al with ah = 0 and dx set to the ComPort value to BIOS interrupt 14h. The top of the table lists the bit numbers and meanings for each field. Below

Table 10-3 *Interrupt 14h Configuration Bits*

7	6	5 (baud rate)	4	3 (parity)	2 (stop bits)	1	0 (data bits)
0	0	0 (110)	0	0 (none)	0 (1)	0	0 (???)
0	0	1 (150)	0	1 (odd)	1 (2)	1	0 (7)
0	1	0 (300)	1	1 (even)		1	1 (8)
0	1	1 (600)					
1	0	0 (1200)					
1	0	1 (2400)					
1	1	0 (4800)					
1	1	1 (9600)					

this are the bit settings you can use to select various configuration parameters.

Line 59 calls `AsynchInit` to install the `AsynchISR` interrupt handler. Be aware that incoming data will be stored in the input buffer as soon as `AsynchInit` finishes—so don't delay checking for incoming data too long after this step. The loop at lines 63–79 checks for input, reads characters from the input buffer, checks for local key presses, and exits when you press F10. (Pressing Esc to end is inappropriate in this program because you may want to pass an Esc character to a remote device.) Subroutine `DispChar` at lines 90–125 displays an ASCII value or control code.

`DispChar` demonstrates an assembly language trick that's worth learning. Examine the nested procedure `OneChar` at lines 118–123, which displays a single character by calling DOS function 2. Above this, line 114 (in the outer procedure) calls `OneChar`. But look closely at the entire `DispChar` procedure—there is only one return instruction at line 122, despite the fact that there are two subroutines here. This is not a mistake! After the `mov` at line 116, the program "falls through" to the `OneChar` subroutine, running this code as an extension of the outer procedure `DispChar`. Earlier, however, `DispChar` calls this inner portion of itself as a subroutine. When the `call` at line 112 executes, the `ret` at line 122 passes control back to line 113. When the program falls through into `OneChar` after line 116, this same `ret` instruction passes control back to the code that originally called `DispChar`. When using this trick, be sure to document your program carefully so that others will understand what's happening.

How to Use the ASYNCH Package

ASYNCH.ASM contains seven routines to read and write asynchronous serial data at any baud rates supported by your hardware. (Unless stated otherwise, line numbers in the following sections refer to Program 10-4.) The seven routines are:

1. AsynchInit   Initializes the ASYNCH package
2. AsynchStop   Deinitializes the ASYNCH package
3. AsynchStat   Returns the status of the serial port
4. AsynchOut   Writes 1 byte to the serial port
5. AsynchIn   Reads 1 buffered input byte
6. AsynchInStat   Returns status of input buffer
7. AsynchISR   Inputs interrupt service routine

Programs never directly call `AsynchISR`—this is the interrupt service routine that automatically handles input from a serial port. Most of the time, you'll use the other six routines in this order:

1. Call ROM BIOS interrupt 14h to set the baud rate. Because PCs already have this initialization code built in, ASYNCH does not duplicate this programming.

2. Call `AsynchInit` to initialize the ASYNCH package and install the `AsynchISR` code.

3. Use `AsynchStat` to determine the status of the serial port—for example, to see if the hardware is ready to accept a character for output.

4. Call `AsynchOut` to send characters to the remote system.

5. Call `AsynchInStat` to find out if any characters are stored in the input buffer.

6. If `AsynchInStat` reports at least one character in the buffer, call `AsynchIn` to extract a character from the buffer.

7. Call `AsynchStop` to detach the `AsynchISR` code and halt interrupt-driven input.

> Note: Be sure to call `AsynchStop` before your program ends, or a system crash is practically guaranteed. Leaving `AsynchISR` (or any other ISR) in memory after passing control back to COMMAND.COM is sure to cause serious problems.

ASYNCH Equates and Variables

ASYNCH.ASM assigns a series of equates for addressing two integrated circuits: an 8250 asynchronous I/O chip and the 8259 interrupt controller that you learned how to control earlier in this chapter. Line 9 determines whether the package accesses the primary (`ComPort = 0`) or secondary (`ComPort = 1`) serial ports available on most PCs. Line 7 declares this equate public. In your own programs, import the `ComPort` value by adding this line to your other equates:

```
EXTRN    ComPort:abs
```

Lines 11–25 assign values to four constants depending on the value of `ComPort`. Notice how errors are handled at lines 22–25. Try assembling the program with `ComPort` equal to 3 to see the effect of these statements. First, line 23 displays an error message with the DISPLAY directive. Then line 24 executes ERR, displaying Turbo Assembler's user error message and preventing the .OBJ file from being created.

Lines 29–36 assign additional equates for reading and writing registers located at various offsets from the base `Port` value, which is initialized at either line 12 or 18. The program uses these values to control the 8250 chip directly without calling DOS or BIOS routines. A few more equates at lines 40–43 reference the 8259 interrupt controller as explained before.

You can change `BufSize` (line 43) to increase or decrease the size of the input buffer. The best size depends on the type of communications program you're writing. A program that reads and writes lines of text might get away with a small buffer, perhaps no larger than 256 bytes. A terminal emulator should probably be able to store the equivalent of several text screens in memory. The default value 2048 is a reasonable compromise.

Ring Around the Asynch Buffer

The variables at lines 50–52 reserve space for the input buffer. Two pointers `bufHead` and `bufTail` address bytes in this buffer. When these variables point to the same address, the buffer is empty. New bytes are stored in the buffer at the location addressed by `bufHead`. Bytes are extracted from the buffer at the location addressed by `bufTail`. These two pointers are incremented until reaching the end of the buffer, when they are reset to the beginning of this variable. As data flows in and out, bufHead and bufTail chase each other around the buffer space, creating a structure called a *queue* in which the oldest data in the buffer is the first to leave. Study lines 280–346 to see how this structure is implemented in ASYNCH.

AsynchInit (84–167)

AsynchInit initializes communications by first emptying the input buffer with a call to a private subroutine EmptyBuffer at lines 61–82. Next, the current interrupt vector for the selected I/O port is saved in two variables vectorSeg and vectorOfs. (See lines 112–115.) Even though it's unlikely that another communications program would be running at the same time as yours, it's a good policy to save and restore all changed interrupt vectors. After this step, lines 116–120 install the new AsynchISR code.

The next instructions (lines 126–159) configure the 8250 and 8259 registers. As you can see, several steps are required to switch on interrupts and clear registers. These notes will help explain the programming in this section:

▶ The interrupt request line (IRQ) for the appropriate interrupt type must be enabled, allowing the 8259 PIC to pass this interrupt signal to the processor. (See lines 126–128 and Table 10-1.) Unless this is done, interrupts from the 8250 serial I/O chip would be blocked from the processor's INTR line.

▶ Next, the 8250 serial I/O chip must be told to generate an interrupt signal whenever a new byte of data comes in from the remote source. (See lines 132–138.) This signal is sent to the 8259 PIC, which, as the previous note explains, passes the interrupt request to the processor.

▶ Several 8250 registers are cleared (see lines 142–152) by reading them with in statements. When the interrupt identification register (IntIdent) reports that no interrupts are pending (bit 0 = 1), the program is allowed to continue.

▶ Bit 3 of the modem control register in the 8250 chip must be set to 1 at lines 156–159 before interrupts will be allowed to occur. (Some references name this bit "OUT2." Another bit "OUT1" can be used to reset an internal Hayes compatible modem.) This step—acting as a kind of communications ignition switch—allows the AsynchISR to begin receiving input as soon as the out at line 159 is executed.

▶ Just in case a stray character got into the input buffer during any of the previous steps, line 164 calls EmptyBuffer again to empty the input buffer.

After executing this intricate sequence, the next character to come into the 8250 will cause an interrupt signal to be sent to the 8259 PIC, which will pass the signal to the 8086 processor, which—after completing any in-progress instruction—will transfer control to the vector for the interrupt type also passed to the 8086 by the 8259 PIC. The net effect of these complex actions is to cause the AsynchISR code at lines 312–355 to read and deposit one character into the input buffer.

AsynchStop (169–218)

AsynchStop reverses what AsynchInit does. Always call AsynchStop before your program ends. First, lines 187–189 disable interrupts by resetting the IRQ bit in the 8259 interrupt controller. Although this step alone prohibits future 8250 interrupts from reaching the processor, to be on the safe side, lines 193–206 disable 8250 interrupts and reset bit 3 of the modem control register, putting these registers back to their normal noninterrupt states. The final instructions in this procedure restore the saved interrupt vector (lines 210–215), detaching the AsynchISR code.

AsynchStat (220–236)

AsynchStat returns the status of the 8250 chip. Instead of directly accessing 8250 registers, the procedure calls BIOS routine 14h. Table 10-4 lists the bits and their meanings in ah and al following a call to AsynchStat.

One way to use AsynchStat is to test ah bit 5 before writing characters. After calling AsynchStat, if this bit equals 0, then a previous character has not yet been sent on its way. You might call this procedure in a loop such as:

```
@@10:
        call    AsynchStat      ; Get line status
        test    ah, 020h        ; Is bit 5 = 1?
        jz      @@10            ; No, jump if bit 5 = 0
        call    OutputChar      ; Call output routine
```

Table 10-4 *AsynchStat Results*

Line Status Register		Modem Status Register	
ah	**bit = 1**	**al**	**bit = 1**
0	Data ready	0	Delta clear to send
1	Overrun error	1	Delta data set ready
2	Parity error	2	Trailing edge ring detect
3	Framing error	3	Delta RX line detect
4	Break interrupt	4	Clear to send
5	TX holding reg empty	5	Data set ready
6	TX shift reg empty	6	Ring indicator
7	Time out	7	RX line signal detect

Note: TX=Transmit, RX=Receive

AsynchOut (238–261)

AsynchOut could call AsynchStat for the line status, but lines 251–255 demonstrate another way to do the same thing, directly reading the line status port with an in instruction. Only when bit 5 is equal to 1, indicating that the transmit holding register is empty and ready to receive another character, is the out instruction at line 258 allowed to send the character in al to the output.

AsynchIn (263–291)

Call `AsynchIn` to read one character from the input buffer. Because the procedure has no effect if the buffer is empty, you should precede `AsynchIn` with a call to `AsynchInStat`, described next. Notice how lines 285–288 increment `bufTail`, wrapping the pointer around to the front of the buffer if necessary.

AsynchInStat (293–310)

`AsynchInStat` simply subtracts `bufTail` from `bufHead`, returning in `dx` the number of characters held in the input buffer. Normally, you'll just check if `dx` is 0 after calling `AsynchInStat`. If `dx` is not 0, call `AsynchIn` to read one character from the buffer. Remember always that characters may be coming into the buffer even as `AsynchInStat` is executing; therefore, the value returned in `dx` may not be exact by the time you examine the register.

The instruction at line 307 finds the correct positive value of a negative result from the subtraction at line 305. This is needed because the `bufTail` and `bufHead` pointers could be greater or less than each other at any time except when the buffer is empty.

AsynchISR (312–355)

You should be able to follow the programming in `AsynchISR` by reading the comments. Notice how the all important end-of-interrupt signal is given to the 8259 PIC (lines 347–348), allowing future interrupts to be processed. Line 334 reads a character by executing an `in` instruction on the 8250 receive-data register (`RxRegister`). The other instructions stuff the character into the input buffer, advancing `bufHead` unless the buffer is full.

> Note: Error handling in `AsynchISR` is minimal at best. If the input buffer overflows, subsequent characters are simply ignored. This means that your program must call `AsynchIn` often enough to prevent overflows. If this is not possible, you will have to modify `AsynchISR` to: a) set a flag indicating that an overflow has occurred and b) send a stop signal to the remote system to prevent new input. Normally, the stop signal must be sent several characters before overflow occurs to give the remote system's software a chance to detect the overflow condition. Of course, you then have to send a start signal to the remote system to begin receiving input again. There isn't room here to list the code for all of this—consult Bibliography for an excellent reference on the subject of serial communications.

Debugging with Interrupts

The breakpoint interrupt, type 3, is reserved for debugging. (See Table 10-2.) Although Turbo Debugger lets you press F2 to set a breakpoint, halting a program just before executing a particular instruction, you can also cause a temporary halt by inserting the line:

```
int     3       ; Set breakpoint
```

When you run a program with this instruction under control of Turbo Debugger (and most other debuggers), the program halts when int 3 executes. When running the program from DOS, the breakpoint has no effect because the vector for interrupt type 3 normally points to a plain iret instruction in DOS. You can insert as many int 3 instructions as you like into a program. When setting many breakpoints in a large program, you may find this easier to do than other methods provided by Turbo Debugger.

Single Stepping

Setting the trap flag (tf = 1) causes the processor to run in single-step mode. In this state, nearly every instruction is followed by a type 1 automatic interrupt signal, allowing an ISR to examine registers and memory, display values, and monitor other program effects. Installing your own ISR for this interrupt number gives you a way to gain control of an executing program after almost every instruction.

> Note: Turbo Debugger sets tf for its own single-step command, so don't use these techniques in programs that you want to run under control of the debugger. The same is true for other debuggers, too.

A few instructions do not cause type 1 interrupts to occur. These instructions include all prefixes such as rep, assignments via mov and pop to segment registers (which, as you recall, temporarily turns off interrupts, including type 1) and the wait instruction. But after other instructions execute with tf = 1, these three steps are taken:

1. The flags, cs, and ip registers are pushed onto the stack
2. The tf and if flags are cleared
3. The ISR at interrupt type 1's vector is executed

Because the second step clears both the trap and interrupt flags, the single-step ISR does not run in single-step mode; therefore, you do not have to be concerned that this ISR will attempt a self examination by interrupting itself, even if you allow interrupts to be recognized (as you probably should) by executing sti in the ISR. When the ISR finishes, the iret instruction restores the flag settings, throwing the processor back into single-step mode.

Setting and Clearing tf

Because there are no built-in instructions for setting and clearing tf, another method must be found. At first, you might be tempted to try using the lahf and sahf instructions, which transfer values between some processor flags and ah. But this doesn't work because lahf and sahf affect only the af, cf, pf, sf, and zf flags—of, df, if, and tf can't be changed with sahf.

One answer to the problem is to push the flags onto the stack with pushf, pop the flag values into ax, modify the tf bit, push the flags back onto the stack and execute popf, transferring the modified flag values back into the flag register:

```
pushf                   ; Push flags onto the stack
pop      ax             ; Transfer flags into ax
or       ax, 0100h      ; Set tf bit = 1
push     ax             ; Push modified flags onto the stack
popf                    ; Pop stack into flag register
```

To reset tf, disabling single stepping, change the or instruction to and ax, 0FEFFh. The only problem with this method is that the instructions to disable single stepping must execute in single-step mode. Although this probably won't cause any harm, there is a more elegant solution—enable and disable the trap flag inside the single-step ISR, which, as you recall, executes at full speed.

Program 10-6, SINGLE.ASM, demonstrates this method, placing the processor in single-step mode for a sample subroutine that counts to 100. During this time, if a local counter reaches 50, the single-step ISR pauses to display a message. Pressing any key continues the program. This simulates how to write a single-step ISR to examine variables in memory, which you might do to learn which sections of a buggy program are changing those variables. (Turbo Debugger has commands for performing similar operations, of course, but knowing how to install your own debugging code is still a useful technique.) Assemble and link SINGLE.ASM with the commands:

```
tasm single
tlink single,,, mta
```

Note: Do not execute SINGLE in Turbo Debugger (or in any other debugger). If the debugger throws the processor into single-step mode, a conflict may occur.

Program 10-6 *SINGLE.ASM*

```
1:  %TITLE "Single-Step (Trap) Demonstration"
2:
3:          IDEAL
4:          DOSSEG
5:          MODEL   small
6:          STACK   256
7:
```

```
 8:    cr            EQU      13              ; ASCII carriage return
 9:    lf            EQU      10              ; ASCII line feed
10:    Trapping      EQU      0               ; "Single stepping is enabled"
11:    TurnOnTrap    EQU      1               ; Code to enable single step
12:    TurnOffTrap   EQU      2               ; Code to disable single step
13:
14:
15:            DATASEG
16:
17:    exitCode      DB       0
18:
19:    spaces        DB       '    ', 0        ; String of 4 blank characters
20:
21:    offMsg        DB       cr, lf, 'Single-step trap is off', cr, lf, 0
22:    onMsg         DB       cr, lf, 'Single-step trap is on', cr, lf, 0
23:    pauseMsg      DB       'Press any key to continue...', 0
24:    countMsg      DB       cr, lf, lf, 'Count = 50!', cr, lf, 0
25:
26:    trapSwitch    DB       0               ; Trap enable/disable switch
27:    string        DB       40 DUP (?)      ; Miscellaneous string
28:    count         DW       ?               ; For Counter subroutine
29:    trapSeg       DW       ?               ; Old int type 1
30:    trapOfs       DW       ?               ;   vector address
31:
32:
33:            CODESEG
34:
35:    ;----- From STRIO.OBJ, BINASC.OBJ, KEYBOARD.OBJ
36:            EXTRN    StrWrite:proc, NewLine:proc, BinToAscDec:proc
37:            EXTRN    GetCh:proc
38:
39:    Start:
40:            mov      ax, @data            ; Initialize ds to address
41:            mov      ds, ax               ;   of data segment
42:            mov      es, ax               ; Make es = ds
43:
44:    ;----- Save int type 1 vector and reassign to Stepper ISR
45:
46:            mov      ax, 3501h            ; Get int type 1 vector
46.1:         int      21h                  ; Call DOS
47:            mov      [trapSeg], es        ; Save segment value
48:            mov      [trapOfs], bx        ; Save offset value
49:            push     ds                   ; Save current ds register
50:            mov      ax, 2501h            ; Set int type 1 vector
51:            push     cs                   ;   to the address of
52:            pop      ds                   ;   the Stepper ISR
53:            mov      dx, offset Stepper
54:            int      21h
55:            pop      ds                   ; Restore ds
56:            push     ds                   ; Reset es to ds's current value
56.1:         pop      es
```

```
57:  ;-----   Execute sample code at full speed
58:
59:          mov     di, offset offMsg      ; Display "Trapping is off"
60:          call    Counter                ; Call sample subroutine
61:
62:  ;-----   Execute sample code in single-step mode
63:
64:          mov     di, offset onMsg       ; Display "Trapping is on"
65:          mov     [trapSwitch], TurnOnTrap     ; Tell ISR to turn
66:          int     1                            ;   on trapping
67:          call    Counter                ; Call sample subroutine
68:          mov     [trapSwitch], TurnOffTrap    ; Tell ISR to turn
69:                                               ;   off trapping
70:  ;-----   Reexecute sample code at full speed
71:
72:          mov     di, offset offMsg      ; Display "Trapping is off"
73:          call    Counter                ; Call sample subroutine
74:
75:  Exit:
76:          push    ds                     ; Save current ds register
77:          mov     ax, 2501h              ; Reset int type 1 vector
78:          mov     ds, [trapSeg]          ;   to the address saved
79:          mov     dx, [trapOfs]          ;   at trapSeg and trapOfs
80:          int     21h
81:          pop     ds                     ; Restore ds
82:          mov     ah, 04Ch               ; DOS function: Exit program
83:          mov     al, [exitCode]         ; Return exit code value
84:          int     21h                    ; Call DOS. Terminate program
85:
86:
87:  ;-----   Subroutine: Displays string, pauses, and counts to 100
88:
89:  PROC    Counter
90:          call    StrWrite               ; Display id message
91:          call    Pause                  ; Wait for key press
92:          mov     [count], 0             ; Zero count
93:  @@10:
94:          inc     [count]                ; count <- count + 1
95:          mov     ax, [count]            ; Convert count to string
96:          mov     cx, 4                  ; Minimum string size
97:          mov     di, offset string
98:          call    BinToAscDec
99:          call    StrWrite               ; Display string
100:         mov     di, offset spaces      ; Display 4 blanks
101:         call    StrWrite
102:         cmp     [count], 100           ; Repeat until count = 100
103:         jb      @@10
104:         ret                            ; Return to caller
105: ENDP    Counter
106:
107:
```

```
108:    ;-----   Subroutine: Display message and wait for key press
109:
110:    PROC    Pause
111:            mov     di, offset pauseMsg     ; Display pause message
112:            call    StrWrite
113:            call    GetCh                   ; Wait for a key press
114:            call    NewLine                 ; Start new display line
115:            ret                             ; Return to caller
116:    ENDP    Pause
117:
118:
119:    %NEWPAGE
120:    ;----------------------------------------------------------------
121:    ; Stepper         Single-step trap ISR
122:    ;----------------------------------------------------------------
123:    ; Input:
124:    ;       [trapSwitch] = TurnOnTrap
125:    ;                   Single-step mode enabled
126:    ;       [trapSwitch] = TurnOffTrap
127:    ;                   Single-step mode disabled
128:    ;       [trapSwitch] = ???
129:    ;                   no action
130:    ; Output:
131:    ;       none
132:    ; Registers:
133:    ;       none
134:    ;----------------------------------------------------------------
135:    PROC    Stepper
136:            sti                             ; Allow interrupts
137:            push    bp                      ; Save current bp register
138:            mov     bp, sp                  ; Address stack with bp
139:            push    ax                      ; Save all registers
140:            push    bx
141:            push    cx
142:            push    dx
143:            push    di
144:            push    si
145:            push    ds
146:            push    es
147:
148:    ;-----   Address local data with ds, es
149:
150:            mov     ax, @data               ; Initialize ds to address
151:            mov     ds, ax                  ;  of data segment
152:            mov     es, ax                  ; Make es = ds
153:
```

```
154:    ;-----  Test trapSwitch to turn single-step mode on/off
155:
156:            cmp     [trapSwitch], TurnOnTrap
157:            jne     @@10
158:            or      [word bp + 6], 0100h    ; Set tf (enable trap)
159:            mov     [trapSwitch], Trapping  ; "Trapping is enabled"
160:            jmp     @@99                    ; Exit
161:    @@10:
162:            cmp     [trapSwitch], TurnOffTrap
163:            jne     @@20
164:            and     [word bp + 6], 0FEFFh   ; Reset tf (disable trap)
165:            jmp     @@99                    ; Exit
166:
167:    @@20:
168:
169:    ;-----  Insert single-stepping trap code here
170:
171:            cmp     [count], 50             ; Is count = 50
172:            jne     @@99                    ; If not, exit
173:            mov     di, offset countMsg     ; Else display count message
174:            call    StrWrite
175:            call    Pause                   ; And wait for keypress
176:            inc     [count]          ; To allow program to continue
177:            call    NewLine
178:
179:    @@99:
180:            pop     es                      ; Restore all registers
181:            pop     ds
182:            pop     si
183:            pop     di
184:            pop     dx
185:            pop     cx
186:            pop     bx
187:            pop     ax
188:            pop     bp
189:            iret                            ; Return from interrupt
190:    ENDP    Stepper
191:
192:            END     Start            ; End of program / entry point
```

How SINGLE Works

When you run SINGLE, you first receive a message that the single-step trap is off. Press Enter and the program then calls a subroutine to count from 1 to 100 at full speed. After this, single-step mode is turned on by setting tf. Pressing Enter again calls the counting subroutine, which as you can see, runs much more slowly because every instruction is interrupted, giving the custom ISR control. When this ISR detects a count of 50, it halts the counting and asks you to press any key. Press Enter to resume operation. To show that you can return from single stepping to full speed at any time, the program resets the trap flag. Press Enter a final time to count once again at top speed.

Three equates in SINGLE—`Trapping`, `TurnOnTrap`, and `TurnOffTrap` at lines 10–12—define three states recognized by the `Stepper` ISR (lines 120–190). Byte variable `trapSwitch` at line 26 holds one of these three values, which alter the way `Stepper` runs. If `trapSwitch` equals `TurnOnTrap`, then `Stepper` enables single stepping by setting the `tf` flag. If `trapSwitch` equals `TurnOffTrap`, then `Stepper` disables single stepping by resetting `tf`. If `trapSwitch` equals `Trapping`, then `Stepper` runs a small section of code that examines the global `count` variable (see line 28). When `count` equals 50, the program displays a message and asks you to press a key.

SINGLE begins by saving the current vector for interrupt type 1 and then changing this vector to address the custom `Stepper` ISR (lines 46–55). Next, the program calls the `Counter` subroutine (lines 89–105), which counts to 100, displaying columns of values on screen. After this first call to `Counter`, which runs at full speed, the `trapSwitch` is set to `TurnOnTrap` (lines 64–65). Line 66 then immediately forces a trap to interrupt type 1 with the software interrupt command:

```
int     1
```

This causes the `Stepper` ISR to begin running for the first time. When the ISR senses that the `trapSwitch` is set to `TurnOnTrap` (lines 156–160), an `or` instruction modifies the `tf` flag stored on the stack by the `int` instruction, using the `bp` register method for addressing stack variables. After setting the flag bit on the stack, the next `iret` instruction, which restores the actual flags from the saved values on the stack, throws the processor into single-step mode. To do this, line 160 changes the `trapSwitch` to `Trapping`, and the program jumps to exit the ISR, skipping the rest of the code.

As soon at the `iret` at line 189 executes, the program starts running in single-step mode. Interrupts of type 1 are now automatically generated by the processor after nearly every instruction, causing the `Stepper` ISR to run at this frequency. But this time, because the `trapSwitch` was set to `Trapping`, the jump at line 157 bypasses the code that sets `tf`, executing the main ISR body at lines 162–177. The first job is to test the `trapSwitch` again to see if the program is requesting single-step mode to be turned off. If so, the `and` instruction at line 164 modifies the flag bit on the stack (similar to the way this bit was set earlier) and jumps to exit the ISR. Upon executing the `iret` this time, `tf` remains off (it's off during the ISR, remember), causing the program to continue at full speed.

If the `trapSwitch` equals `Trapping`, then line 163 jumps to the instructions at lines 167–177, which examine the `count` variable and pause if this value equals 50. (To prevent pausing more than once, line 176 increments `count`.) By replacing only this section (lines 171–177), you can use the `Stepper` ISR in your own programs to examine whatever you want after almost every instruction executes. To do this, copy lines 10–12, 26, and the `Stepper` ISR at lines 120–190. Remove lines 171–177 and insert your own test instructions. Then, to enable single stepping, use the instructions:

```
mov     [trapSwitch], TurnOnTrap
int     1
```

To disable single stepping, returning the processor to full speed, execute:

```
mov     [trapSwitch], TurnOffTrap
```

Note: Before returning to DOS, you must disable single stepping in any program that sets the **tf** flag. Failure to follow this rule could hang the computer, forcing you to reboot. If the program ends unexpectedly, reboot as soon as possible—if you are able.

Summary

An interrupt is a signal that causes an executing program to pause, run a special subroutine called an interrupt service routine (ISR), and then resume normal execution. In the 8086 processor family, there are two kinds of interrupt signals: external and internal. External interrupts can occur at any time. Internal or software interrupts occur only when programs execute an **int** or **into** instruction or when certain conditions occur, such as a divide exception.

Because an external interrupt signal can occur at any time, external ISRs must preserve all registers. Flags are preserved automatically by the processor when it recognizes an interrupt signal. Internal ISRs may pass values in registers back to programs, similar to the way common subroutines operate. In either case, interrupts are never processed until the current instruction finishes.

Maskable interrupts can be temporarily disabled with **cli** and enabled with **sti** instructions. Nonmaskable interrupts can't be disabled. (You may be able to disable circuits that generate nonmaskable interrupts.) On PCs, externally generated interrupts are piped to an 8259 interrupt controller (PIC) chip, which resolves conflicts between multiple interrupts and passes interrupt signals to the processor's single INTR input line.

Interrupt vectors are stored in low memory at segment 0000, from offset 0000h to 03FFh. You can install your own ISR code by inserting the address of your routine into the correct vector location for the appropriate interrupt number. DOS contains functions to return interrupt vector values and to insert new values in the interrupt vector table. If you change any vectors, it's your responsibility to restore their original values before your program ends.

Divide errors occur when the divisor to **div** or **idiv** is 0, or when the result of the division is too large to fit in the 8- or 16-bit destination. A divide error causes an automatic interrupt type 0 to be generated, executing the ISR at the vector stored in location 0000:0000 and usually halting the program. This condition can be prevented by installing a custom ISR to trap the interrupt. But the job is complicated by subtle differences between 8086/88 and 80286/386 processors. Solving this problem is tricky, but it can be done as an example in this chapter demonstrates.

A good method to write programs to communicate with remote computers over a serial line or through a modem is to use interrupt-driven routines to capture data as it comes in, thus eliminating the problems that can occur when a program pauses for a disk write or another operation for too long, resulting in lost data. The ASYNCH package in this chapter demonstrates the techniques. An accompanying terminal program helps debug a serial interface line.

Although Turbo Debugger can run programs in single-step mode, it's useful to know how to install your own single stepper. The SINGLE program in this chapter illustrates how to do this and can serve as a shell for your own single-stepping debugging sessions.

Exercises

10-1. Why is it important to save register values in an external ISR?

10-2. What does `iret` do?

10-3. What instruction disables interrupts? What instruction enables interrupts? What do these instructions do? In an ISR, what are logical locations for these instructions?

10-4. Write code to install a new ISR named `NewISR` for interrupt number 01Ch. Write code to restore the original interrupt vector before the program ends.

10-5. Can an interrupt service routine be interrupted by another interrupt?

10-6. After processing an externally generated interrupt, what instructions must you execute to ensure that future interrupts are recognized?

10-7. The external Print Screen interrupt is number 5. Write a subroutine that prints the screen. It should not be necessary to press the PrtSc key!

10-8. What is the difference between a divide-fault interrupt on 8086/88 and 80286/386 processors?

10-9. What instruction can you use to insert breakpoints in programs?

10-10. Write instructions to set the trap flag, using a method different from the two that are described in this chapter.

Projects

10-1. Rewrite the TRM program, adding subroutines to emulate a full CRT terminal.

10-2. Improve the ASYNCH module by adding code to send a stop signal (usually ASCII 013h or Ctrl-S) before the input buffer overflows. Also add code to send a start signal (usually ASCII 011h or Ctrl-Q), allowing input to again be received.

10-3. Add interrupt-driven output routines to ASYNCH.ASM. (Note: You'll need additional references for the 8250 and 8259 chips to accomplish this project.)

10-4. Write a version of the divide-fault program (DIV286.ASM) that uses conditional compilation to create a program for all processor models.

10-5. Convert the SINGLE program to a library module for adding single-step debugging code to any program. (Hint: Use the `call bx` method from Program 9-5, DR.ASM, line 91, to call custom code from inside the single-step ISR.)

10-6. Write a program to print a report of all interrupt numbers and vector addresses.

11 Advanced Topics

11 *Advanced Topics*

In This Chapter

Packed and unpacked binary-coded-decimal formats; creating BCD varia-bles; "ASCII" BCD assembly language instructions; converting BCDs to and from ASCII; "Decimal" BCD assembly language instructions; a math pack-age for packed BCDs; using the `COMM`, `GLOBAL`, and `INCLUDELIB` directives; table processing with `xlat`; declaring segments with `SEGMENT`; what `ASSUME` does; using `GROUP` to collect multiple segments; a shell for declaring seg-ments "the hard way"; declaring phantom segments at fixed locations; adding far data segments to a simplified memory model; using 80286 in-structions; using 80386 instructions; 80386 extended registers and flags

Advancing Your Assembly Language Knowledge

In the preceding chapters, you learned how to use most of the 8086 in-struction set, and you entered and ran many examples illustrating various assembly language techniques. At this point, you're probably ready to begin writing your own programs—if you haven't done so already. But, we still have some fertile ground to cover, including a few new instructions for business mathematics and table processing, special instructions in 80286 and 80386 processors, and directives that simplify sharing data among multiple program modules.

Many of you may someday tackle a large assembly language project that requires special data-segment handling not provided by the simplified memory models used by most programs in this book. For this, you'll prob-ably want to specify segments "the hard way," telling Turbo Assembler and Turbo Linker the exact size and location of data and code segments. You may also want to attach a *far* data segment—a quick way to double your program's data capacity. This chapter covers these and other subjects, collected here in a kind of grab bag of tips, hints, and programs for advanced assembly language programming.

Binary Coded Decimals

Numbers in business application programming must be large and precise—two requirements that pose special problems for assembly language programmers accustomed to dealing with relatively small binary values. For example, representing dollar amounts with word integers ranging from −32,768 to +32,767 won't do—after adding an imagined decimal point, amounts are limited to the penny-pinching range, −$327.68 to +$327.67. 32-bit doubleword values ranging from −$21,474,836.48 to +$21,474,836.47 are better, but may still be too restrictive for businesses that need to keep running totals on inventory and payroll and for other accounting purposes. Also, converting such double-precision values to and from ASCII is time consuming. Floating point representations are even worse, introducing the possibility of round-off errors, which may be acceptable for scientific measurements that allow for such errors, but which are unacceptable in business.

One answer to these problems is to store numbers in binary coded decimal (BCD) form, which is easily converted to and from ASCII, and which can store very large numbers containing up to 20 digits for a maximum dollar amount of $999,999,999,999,999,999.99 (about a trillion trillion). There are two main variations of BCD numbers:

▶ *Packed BCD numbers* store 2 digits per byte, usually with individual digits in high-to-low order, but with the bytes in low-to-high order.

▶ *Unpacked BCD numbers* store 1 digit per byte, ordering the bytes in either low-to-high or high-to-low sequence.

Packed BCD numbers are probably the most common, storing 2 decimal digits in each byte—1 digit in the upper 4 bits and the other in the lower 4 bits. Although convenient, this format is inefficient compared with straight binary. Because 4 bits can represent binary values from 0 to 15, using 4 bits to represent numbers ranging from only 0 to 9 wastes a little space in each byte. (Another way to look at this is to consider that a packed BCD byte can store values from only 0 to 99 while a binary byte can normally represent values from 0 to 255.)

Unpacked BCD numbers are mostly used as an intermediate form for converting packed BCD numbers to and from ASCII characters. As you'll see in a moment, there is a nearly direct relationship between ASCII and unpacked BCDs. Unfortunately, this format is even more inefficient, able to represent values ranging from only 0 to 9 in a single byte.

BCDs in Memory You can create packed and unpacked BCD variables in memory with the dt and db directives. The dt directive creates a 10-byte, 20-digit, packed BCD value. For example:

```
packed    dt  81659247  ; Packed BCD number
```

This command always allocates 10 bytes, in this case, storing the value 00000000000081659247 at label `packed`. Ignoring leading zeros, Figure 11-1 shows how this value is stored in memory. The lower two digits (4 and 7) occupy the first byte, the next higher two digits (9 and 2) occupy the second byte, and so on. As you'll see in a moment, this semireversed ordering makes it easy to perform mathematics operations on two packed BCD numbers.

Turbo Assembler lacks directives for creating unpacked BCD numbers, although you can use `db` if you're careful. For example, here is the same value, 81,659,247, allocated as an unpacked 20-byte BCD number:

```
unpacked  db 7,4,2,9,5,6,1,8,0,0  ; Unpacked BCD number
          db 0,0,0,0,0,0,0,0,0,0
```

Figure 11-2 illustrates how this value appears in memory, again ignoring leading digits. Like the packed format (Figure 11-1), the digits are reversed, an arbitrary choice that depends only on how other software uses the unpacked values. You can just as easily store unpacked BCDs the other way around—as long as you're prepared to write the necessary code to handle this format.

Note: Turbo Debugger recognizes packed BCD numbers and can display their values in the Watch and Variables windows. The debugger does not recognize unpacked BCD numbers. Use the View:Dump commands to view the bytes of unpacked values.

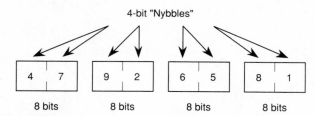

Figure 11-1 *The packed BCD value 81,659,247 as stored in memory.*

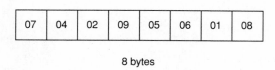

Figure 11-2 *The unpacked BCD value 81,659,247 as stored in memory.*

Unpacked BCD Instructions

Four 8086 instructions `aaa`, `aad`, `aam`, and `aas` convert unpacked BCD digits to and from binary values, making operations on BCD numbers easy to write. Let's take these one by one.

Use `aaa` (ASCII Adjust After Addition) after adding two single-digit BCD bytes with `add` or `adc`. The sum must be in `al`. If the sum is greater than 09, then ah is incremented, and al is adjusted to be within the range 0–9. For example, to add the two digits 04 and 08, you can write:

```
mov bl, 04h      ; First digit in bl
mov al, 08h      ; Second digit in al
add al, bl       ; Sum must be in al
xor ah, ah       ; Zero ah
aaa              ; Adjust to unpacked BCD
```

This adds the unpacked values 04 and 08, placing the sum in al. Because the addition is done in binary, al in this example now equals 0Ch. To convert this value back to unpacked BCD form, xor zeros ah, and aaa is executed. Because in this example the sum in al is greater than 9, ah is incremented, and al is adjusted. The result is ax = 0102—the answer (12) in unpacked BCD format.

A similar instruction aas (ASCII Adjust After Subtraction) adjusts the difference of two unpacked BCD digits after sub or sbb. If a borrow was required, then 1 is subtracted from ah, and al is adjusted to be within the range 0–9. For example, to subtract 08 from 0406, you can write:

```
mov ax, 0406h    ; Assign first value to ax
mov bl, 08h      ; Assign second value to bl
sub al, bl       ; Subtract 0406h - 08h
aas              ; Adjust to unpacked BCD
```

The binary subtraction leaves ax = 04FEh, which aas then converts to the unpacked BCD value 0308h, or 38 decimal—the result of subtracting 46 − 8.

Two other instructions aad (ASCII Adjust Before Division) and aam (ASCII Adjust After Multiplication) convert unpacked BCD values to and from binary, which you might do before and after BCD multiplication and division. But don't be taken in by the suggestive mnemonics—you can use these instructions at other times, too. You don't have to follow aad with a division or precede aam with a multiplication.

To convert two unpacked BCD numbers in ax to binary, use aad. Because the largest such number that ax can hold is 0909h, aad always zeros ah while setting al to the binary equivalent of the BCD digits. For example:

```
mov ax, 0406h    ; Assign unpacked BCD to ax
aad              ; Convert. ax = 002Eh (46 decimal)
```

The unpacked BCD value 0406h in ax is converted to the binary equivalent value 002Eh (46 decimal) by aad. To reverse the process, converting binary values to unpacked BCD, use aam as in this sample:

```
mov ax, 005Fh    ; Assign binary value to ax
aam              ; Convert. ax = 0905h (05F hexadecimal)
```

The binary value 005Fh (95 decimal) in ax is converted to the unpacked BCD equivalent 0905h by aam. The largest such value that aam can handle in ax is 0063h (99 decimal).

**Converting
Unpacked BCD
and ASCII**

Because the upper 4 bits of an unpacked BCD byte always equal 0 (see Figure 11-2), converting unpacked BCDs to and from ASCII easy. Recall that the ASCII digits 0–9 are encoded as the hexadecimal values 30h–39h; therefore, to convert unpacked BCD digits to ASCII is a simple matter of setting the upper 4 bits to 3:

```
mov ax, 0307h   ; Assign unpacked BCD to ax
or  ax, 3030h   ; Convert to ASCII (ax = 03337h)
```

ORing ax with 3030h sets the upper 4 bits in both ah and al to 3, changing 0307h to 3337h—the two ASCII encoded digits 33h (3) and 37h (7). Converting ASCII digits to unpacked BCD format is equally simple—just use and to strip the ASCII information from each digit:

```
mov ax, '81'    ; Assigns 03831h to ax
and ax, 0F0Fh   ; Convert to unpacked BCD (ax = 0801h)
```

After assigning the string '81' (equal to 03831h) to ax, a logical AND with the mask 0F0Fh sets the upper 4 bits of both ah and al to 0, thus converting the digits to unpacked BCD format.

> Note: The order of digits in the previous two samples is not reversed as shown in Figure 11-2. When converting unpacked BCDs to and from ASCII, you have to pay attention to such details.

**Packed BCD
Instructions**

Two "Decimal" instructions daa and das operate on packed BCD values, similar to the way the "ASCII" instructions aaa and aas work. Use daa after adding two packed BCD bytes containing two digits each as in:

```
xor ah, ah      ; Zero ah
mov al, 087h    ; Set al to packed BCD 87
mov bl, 035h    ; Set bl to packed BCD 35
add al, bl      ; Add al <- al + bl
daa             ; Convert. al = 22h, cf,af = 1
```

The xor zeros ah for reasons explained later. The two packed BCD values 87h and 35h are assigned to al and bl. An add instruction adds the values, placing the binary sum in al, which then equals 0BCh. Executing daa converts this binary value to packed BCD, setting al to 22h. But the correct answer is 122 (87 + 35), not 22, and the code must be completed by checking the carry flag for a possible overflow:

```
jnc @@10        ; Skip increment if cf = 0
inc ah          ; Add 1 to ah
@@10:
```

Technically, if daa detects an overflow when the packed BCD result after addition is greater than 99 (the maximum BCD value that 1 byte can store), both cf and af flags are set to 1; otherwise, both flags are cleared. In practice, you can just check cf to detect this condition. In this example, ah is incremented, setting ax to the correct answer 0122h. This is the reason that ah was zeroed earlier.

> Note: After daa, if af = 1 and cf = 0, then the result in al is within the range 10h to 99h—in other words, a carry was generated out of the lower 4 bits of the answer—a fact of little practical value.

The complement to daa is das, which adjusts packed BCD values after subtraction by sub or sbb. Because subtraction can generate negative numbers, using das requires a little extra care. First, let's look at a sample that produces a positive result:

```
mov al, 062h      ; Set al to packed BCD 62
mov bl, 036h      ; Set bl to packed BCD 36
sub al, bl        ; Subtract al <- al - bl
das               ; Convert. al = 026h
```

The packed BCD values 62h and 36h are assigned to al and bl. A sub instruction subtracts the values, depositing the binary difference (02Ch) in al. Executing das converts this binary value to packed BCD, changing al to 026h—the correct answer in decimal for the subtraction 62 − 36. After this, if cf equals 0, then no borrow was required; therefore, the answer in al can be used directly.

> Note: Technically, both cf and af must equal 0 to indicate no borrow. If cf = 0 but af = 1, then a borrow was required by the lower digits. If you run the previous sample in Turbo Debugger, you'll see this happen. Subtracting 62 − 36 requires a borrow for the lower two digits (2 and 6). Normally, you can ignore this special condition and just inspect cf to see if a borrow was required for the full subtraction.

When a subtraction generates a negative result, the process becomes more complicated. You must check the carry flag to detect a borrow from the subtraction, indicating that the result in al is a negative decimal complement, which can then be further manipulated to find the absolute value of the answer. An example helps clarify how to do this:

```
mov al, 036h      ; Set al to packed BCD 36
mov bl, 062h      ; Set bl to packed BCD 62
sub al, bl        ; Subtract al <- al - bl
das               ; Convert. al = 074h
jnc @@10          ; Jump if no borrow
neg al            ; Negate al (in binary)
das               ; Convert to packed BCD
@@10:
```

As before, al and bl are assigned the packed BCD values to be subtracted. A sub instruction subtracts bl from al, which in this sample creates a negative (two's complement) binary result in al equal to 0D4h. This value is converted to packed BCD format by das, changing al to 74h. But this is not the correct answer—62 − 36 = −26, not 74. A check of the carry flag by jnc detects this condition, indicating that al is a decimal complement, converted to an absolute value by subtracting 100. (74 − 100 = −26, the correct answer.) The easiest (though perhaps not most obvious) way to find the decimal complement is to execute neg, which subtracts its operand value (al in this case) from 0. Because this leaves the answer in al in binary, another das again converts the result back to packed BCD format, setting al at long last to the correct absolute value answer, 26.

A BCD Math Package

Performing math operations on *multiple-precision values*—those containing more bytes or words than can comfortably fit within registers and, therefore, requiring multiple operations to add, subtract, multiply, and divide—adds an additional level of difficulty to programming BCD procedures. To demonstrate some of the issues involved in writing such routines, and to give you a few useful procedures that you can use in your own code, Program 11-1, BCD.ASM, contains six subroutines to add and subtract packed BCD values and to convert BCD numbers among packed, unpacked, and ASCIIZ string formats. There's also a procedure that copies a packed BCD 10-byte value to another BCD variable. Assemble and store the module in MTA.LIB with the commands:

```
tasm /zi bcd
tlib /E mta -+bcd
```

As usual, ignore the warning that BCD is not in the library—it won't be until you install it the first time. If you make any changes to the programming, use these same commands to reassemble and install the new module. Instructions for using the BCD module follow the listing.

Program 11-1 *BCD.ASM*

```
 1:  %TITLE "Binary-Coded-Decimal (BCD) Routines"
 2:
 3:          IDEAL
 4:          DOSSEG
 5:          MODEL   small
 6:
 7:
 8:  ;----- Equates
 9:
10:  ASCIINull     EQU     0      ; ASCII end-of-string null character
11:  PackedSize    EQU     10     ; Bytes in a packed BCD value
12:  UnpackedSize  EQU     20     ; Bytes in an unpacked BCD value
13:
14:  ;----- note: PackedSize must be even!
15:
16:
```

```
17:          UDATASEG
18:
19: TempUPBCD      DT      ?, ?     ; Unpacked BCD word space (20 bytes)
20:
21:
22:          CODESEG
23:
24:          PUBLIC  BCDAdd, BCDSubtract, PackedToUnpacked
25:          PUBLIC  UnpackedToPacked, BCDToASCII, BCDCopy
26:
27: %NEWPAGE
28: ;------------------------------------------------------------
29: ; BCDAdd                  Add two packed BCD numbers
30: ;------------------------------------------------------------
31: ; Input:
32: ;      si = address of source BCD value (10 bytes)
33: ;      di = address of destination BCD value (10 bytes)
34: ; Output:
35: ;      destinationBCD <- destinationBCD + sourceBCD
36: ;      cf = 0 : No error
37: ;      cf = 1 : Overflow error occurred
38: ; Registers:
39: ;      none
40: ;------------------------------------------------------------
41: PROC   BCDAdd
42:        push   ax                   ; Save modified registers
43:        push   cx
44:        push   di
45:        push   si
46:
47:        cld                         ; Auto-increment si & di
48:        clc                         ; Clear carry for first adc
49:        mov    cx, PackedSize       ; Assign loop count to cx
50: @@10:
51:        lodsb                       ; Get 2 digits of source
52:        adc    al, [byte di]        ; Add 2 digits of dest + cf
53:        daa                         ; Adjust to packed BCD format
54:        stosb                       ; Store result in destination
55:        loop   @@10                 ; Loop until done (cx = 0)
56:
57:        pop    si                   ; Restore saved registers
58:        pop    di
59:        pop    cx
60:        pop    ax
61:        ret                         ; Return to caller
62: ENDP   BCDAdd
```

```
 63:    %NEWPAGE
 64:    ;----------------------------------------------------------------
 65:    ; BCDSubtract            Subtract two packed BCD numbers
 66:    ;----------------------------------------------------------------
 67:    ; Input:
 68:    ;       si = address of source BCD value (10 bytes)
 69:    ;       di = address of destination BCD value (10 bytes)
 70:    ; Output:
 71:    ;       destinationBCD <- destinationBCD - sourceBCD
 72:    ;       cf = 0 : No error
 73:    ;       cf = 1 : Underflow error occurred
 74:    ; Registers:
 75:    ;       none
 76:    ;----------------------------------------------------------------
 77:    PROC    BCDSubtract
 78:            push    ax                      ; Save modified registers
 79:            push    cx
 80:            push    di
 81:            push    si
 82:
 83:            cld                             ; Auto-increment si & di
 84:            clc                             ; Clear carry for first sbb
 85:            mov     cx, PackedSize          ; Assign loop count to cx
 86:    @@10:
 87:            lodsb                           ; Get two digits of source
 88:            sbb     [byte di], al           ; dest <- dest - source bytes
 89:            mov     al, [byte di]           ; Load binary result into al
 90:            das                             ; Adjust to packed BCD format
 91:            stosb                           ; Store result in destination
 92:            loop    @@10                    ; Loop until done (cx = 0)
 93:
 94:            pop     si                      ; Restore saved registers
 95:            pop     di
 96:            pop     cx
 97:            pop     ax
 98:            ret                             ; Return to caller
 99:    ENDP    BCDSubtract
100:    %NEWPAGE
101:    ;----------------------------------------------------------------
102:    ; PackedToUnpacked       Convert packed BCD to unpacked BCD
103:    ;----------------------------------------------------------------
104:    ; Input:
105:    ;       si = address of source packed BCD value (10 bytes)
106:    ;       di = address of destination unpacked BCD value (20 bytes)
107:    ; Output:
108:    ;       destinationBCD <- unpacked( sourceBCD )
109:    ; Registers:
110:    ;       none
111:    ;----------------------------------------------------------------
```

```
112:    PROC    PackedToUnpacked
113:            push    ax                      ; Save modified registers
114:            push    cx
115:            push    di
116:            push    si
117:
118:            cld                             ; Auto-increment si & di
119:            mov     cx, PackedSize          ; Assign loop count to cx
120:    @@10:
121:            lodsb                           ; Get 2 digits of source
122:            mov     ah, al                  ; Copy digits from al to ah
123:            shr     ah, 1                   ; Shift upper digit to
124:            shr     ah, 1                   ;   lower 4 bits of ah
125:            shr     ah, 1
126:            shr     ah, 1
127:            and     al, 0Fh                 ; Mask upper digit from al
128:            stosw                           ; Store ax to destination
129:            loop    @@10                    ; Loop until done (cx = 0)
130:
131:            pop     si                      ; Restore saved registers
132:            pop     di
133:            pop     cx
134:            pop     ax
135:            ret                             ; Return to caller
136:    ENDP    PackedToUnpacked
137:    %NEWPAGE
138:    ;-----------------------------------------------------------------
139:    ; UnpackedToPacked       Convert unpacked BCD to packed BCD
140:    ;-----------------------------------------------------------------
141:    ; Input:
142:    ;       si = address of source unpacked BCD value (20 bytes)
143:    ;       di = address of destination packed BCD value (10 bytes)
144:    ; Output:
145:    ;       destinationBCD <- packed( sourceBCD )
146:    ; Registers:
147:    ;-----------------------------------------------------------------
148:    PROC    UnpackedToPacked
149:            push    ax                      ; Save modified registers
150:            push    cx
151:            push    di
152:            push    si
153:
154:            cld                             ; Auto-increment si & di
155:            mov     cx, PackedSize          ; Assign loop count to cx
156:    @@10:
157:            lodsw                           ; Get 2 digits of source
158:            shl     ah, 1                   ; Shift digit to
159:            shl     ah, 1                   ;  upper 4 bits of ah
160:            shl     ah, 1
```

```
161:            shl     ah, 1
162:            or      al, ah              ; Pack 2 digits into al
163:            stosb                       ; Store al to destination
164:            loop    @@10                ; Loop until done (cx = 0)
165:
166:            pop     si                  ; Restore saved registers
167:            pop     di
168:            pop     cx
169:            pop     ax
170:            ret                         ; Return to caller
171:    ENDP    UnpackedToPacked
172:    %NEWPAGE
173:    ;-------------------------------------------------------------
174:    ; BCDToASCII            Convert packed BCD value to ASCII
175:    ;-------------------------------------------------------------
176:    ; Input:
177:    ;       si = address of source packed BCD value (10 bytes)
178:    ;       di = address of destination ASCIIZ string (21 bytes)
179:    ; Output:
180:    ;       ASCIIZ <- ASCII( sourceBCD) + null character
181:    ; Registers:
182:    ;       none
183:    ;-------------------------------------------------------------
184:    PROC    BCDToASCII
185:            push    ax                  ; Save modified registers
186:            push    cx
187:            push    di
188:            push    si
189:
190:            push    di                  ; Save destination address
191:            mov     di, offset TempUPBCD ; Use temporary work area
192:            call    PackedToUnpacked    ; Unpack source to temp
193:            pop     di                  ; Restore destination address
194:
195:    ;----- Address last word of temporary work space
196:            mov     si, offset TempUPBCD + UnpackedSize - 2
197:
198:            mov     cx, PackedSize      ; Assign loop count to cx
199:    @@10:
200:            std                         ; Auto-decrement si
201:            lodsw                       ; Get 2 digits into ax
202:            or      ax, 03030h          ; Convert to ASCII
203:            xchg    ah, al              ; Swap characters
204:            cld                         ; Auto-increment di
205:            stosw                       ; Store chars in destination
206:            loop    @@10                ; Loop until done (cx = 0)
207:            mov     [byte di], ASCIINull ; Store end-of-string marker
208:
```

```
209:            pop     si                      ; Restore saved registers
210:            pop     di
211:            pop     cx
212:            pop     ax
213:            ret                             ; Return to caller
214:   ENDP     BCDToASCII
215:   %NEWPAGE
216:   ;-------------------------------------------------------------
217:   ; BCDCopy              Copy a packed BCD value
218:   ;-------------------------------------------------------------
219:   ; Input:
220:   ;        si = address of source BCD value (10 bytes)
221:   ;        di = address of destination BCD value (10 bytes)
222:   ; Output:
223:   ;        destinationBCD <- sourceBCD
224:   ; Registers:
225:   ;        none
226:   ;-------------------------------------------------------------
227:   PROC     BCDCopy
228:            push    cx                      ; Save modified registers
229:            push    di
230:            push    si
231:
232:            cld                             ; Auto-increment si & di
233:            mov     cx, PackedSize/2        ; Assign loop count to cx
234:            rep     movsw                   ; Copy using word moves
235:
236:            pop     si                      ; Restore saved registers
237:            pop     di
238:            pop     cx
239:            ret                             ; Return to caller
240:   ENDP     BCDCopy
241:
242:            END                     ; End of BCD module
```

Using the BCD Module The six routines in the BCD module recognize the packed and unpacked BCD data formats described at the beginning of this chapter. (See Figures 11-1 and 11-2.) Packed BCD values must be 10 bytes long and may contain up to 20 digits. Unpacked BCD values must be 20 bytes long and may also contain up to 20 digits. It's your responsibility to ensure that variables are large enough to hold the results of various operations. Also, because string instructions are used by all subroutines, segment registers es and ds must address the same data segment. To use the package in a program, declare the subroutines you need in EXTRN statements usually just after a CODESEG directive as in:

```
CODESEG
EXTRN   BCDAdd:proc, BCDSubtract:proc, PackedToUnpacked:proc
EXTRN   UnpackedToPacked:proc, BCDToASCII:proc, BCDCopy:proc
```

You can then run any of the six routines with `call` instructions. The following notes explain each of the routines, listing line numbers from Program 11-1 in parentheses.

Note: All BCD values must be unsigned. To use these routines with negative numbers, you must keep track of the sign separately. Also, be aware that Turbo Assembler 1.0 contains a bug that prevents declaring negative BCD values correctly with the `dt` directive.

BCDAdd (28-62)

Assign the offset addresses of two packed BCD numbers to `si` and `di` and call `BCDAdd` to add the values, replacing the value addressed by `di` with the sum. (You can use `BCDCopy` as described later to preserve the modified value if necessary.) After `BCDAdd`, if `cf = 1`, an overflow occurred; otherwise, the answer is within the maximum BCD range. Here's an example of how to use `BCDAdd` to add two BCD values `v1` and `v2`:

```
DATASEG
v1      dt      81659247        ; BCD 81,659,247
v2      dt      74295618        ; BCD 74,295,618
CODESEG
mov     ax, @data       ; Initialize ds to address
mov     ds, ax          ;  of data segment
mov     es, ax          ; Make es = ds
mov     si, offset v1   ; Address v1 with si
mov     di, offset v2   ; Address v2 with di
call    BCDAdd          ; Add v2 <- v1 + v2
jc      Exit            ; Jump to Exit if overflow
```

As a reminder, the steps for initializing `ds` and `es` are shown here. (To save space, examples that follow leave these required steps out.) Registers `si` and `di` are assigned the offset addresses of two packed BCD values to add. Then `BCDAdd` adds `v1 + v2`, storing the result at `v2`. If this causes an overflow to occur, `jc` jumps to the `Exit` label (not shown).

Note: As with unsigned addition in binary, overflows cause a "wrap-around" effect in the answer. In other words, the result of adding 3 to 99999999999999999998 is 00000000000000000001. If this is acceptable to your program, you can ignore overflows.

The code to `BCDAdd` demonstrates one way to add two multiple-precision values. The direction flag is cleared with `cld` (line 47) so that the later string instructions increment `si` and `di`, thus advancing the pointers through the bytes of the BCD values. Remember that packed BCDs are stored in reverse byte order (see Figure 11-1); therefore, the `lodsb` and `adc` instructions at lines 51–52 first add the least significant digits, then the next higher digits, and so on until the loop count in `cx` decrements to 0 at line 55, ending the repeated loop. The daa at line 53 converts the result of each addition to packed BCD before stosb stores this value in the destination.

Notice how the clc at line 48 clears the carry flag. Because of this, the first adc performs an add (adding a 0 carry to the answer). This trick eliminates the need to use the add instruction to sum the low-order values, followed by subsequent adc instructions to add higher-order values with possible carries.

BCDSubtract (64–99)

BCDSubtract operates similarly to BCDAdd. In fact, only three instructions differ (compare lines 88–90 to lines 52–53). Assign the offset addresses of two packed BCD values to si and di and then call BCDSubtract to calculate the difference, storing the result in the variable addressed by di. If cf = 1 after BCDSubtract, then underflow occurred and, as with unsigned binary subtractions, the value at di "wraps around." In other words, subtracting BCD 03 from 01 produces 99999999999999999998 and sets cf to 1. Here's an example:

```
DATASEG
v1      dt      81659247        ; BCD 81,659,247
v2      dt      74295618        ; BCD 74,295,618
CODESEG
mov     si, offset v2   ; Address v2 with si
mov     di, offset v1   ; Address v1 with di
call    BCDSubtract     ; Subtract v2 <- v2 - v1
jc      Exit            ; Exit on underflow
```

Take care to assign the offset addresses in the correct order, remembering that the value at si is subtracted *from* the value at di, which is also replaced with the answer. You might want to call BCDCopy to preserve the original value addressed by di.

The two instructions at lines 88–89 subtract packed BCD bytes in the correct order (destination-source) and then load the answer into al for the subsequent conversion to packed BCD form with das at line 90. Other than these three instructions, the rest of the procedure operates as explained for BCDAdd.

PackedToUnpacked (101–136)
UnpackedToPacked (138–171)

Call PackedToUnpacked to convert a packed BCD value to unpacked format. Register si must address a 10-byte packed BCD variable. Register di must address a 20-byte space to hold the result. The value at si is not changed. Make sure that at least 20 bytes are available at di to prevent PackedTo-Unpacked from overwriting other data or code in memory. The packed BCD value must be in the format created by dt as illustrated in Figure 11-1—individual digit pairs are stored in high-to-low order, while the bytes in the BCD value are stored in reverse low-to-high order. PackedToUnpacked stores one BCD digit per byte (upper 4 bits cleared) in low-to-high order. (See Figure 11-2.)

Call `UnpackedToPacked` to reverse these steps, converting an unpacked BCD 20-byte value to a packed BCD 10-byte variable. Register `si` must address the unpacked 20-byte BCD value. Register `di` must address a 10-byte space to hold the result. The value at `si` is not changed. As with `PackedToUnpacked`, make sure that at least 10 bytes are available at `di` to prevent the procedure from overwriting other items in memory.

Both of these procedures use similar methods to load and convert values. Notice how both byte and word forms of string instructions (lines 121, 128, 157, and 163) are used along with the logical AND and OR and shift instructions to shuffle digits into the proper positions for the conversions. You should be able to follow these instructions by reading the comments, but, if you need a little help, run a test program in Turbo Debugger and watch the `ax` register as you pack and unpack various BCD variables.

BCDToASCII (173–214)

This routine converts a packed BCD value as created by `dt` to an ASCIIZ string, which must be at least 21 bytes long. Failure to observe this minimum length restriction could overwrite other values in memory. Along with the `StrWrite` routine from the STRIO package in chapter 5, you can use `BCDToASCII` to display (or print) BCD values. For example:

```
DATASEG
v1       dt        81659247        ; BCD 81,659,247
string   db        40 dup (0)      ; At least 21 bytes!
CODESEG
mov      si, offset v1             ; Address v1 with si
mov      di, offset string         ; Address string with di
call     BCDToASCII                ; Convert BCD to ASCIIZ
call     StrWrite                  ; Write string to output
call     NewLine                   ; Start a new output line
```

This code writes 00000000000081659247 to the standard output file, usually the display. As you can see, the string is unformatted, and you may want to add commas and a decimal point, strip leading zeros, and perhaps attach a dollar sign, possibly using some of the STRING module's procedures described in chapter 5.

The code at lines 190–207 may seem overly complex for what should be a simple conversion. The instructions are necessary (as you'll see if you work through them in Turbo Debugger) because of the format differences between packed and unpacked values and strings. The procedure calls `PackedToUnpacked` at line 192, first converting the packed BCD value to unpacked format. Then, after initializing `si` to address the end of the string (line 196), a loop at lines 199–206 converts digit pairs to ASCII (see line 202), swaps the digits with `xchg`, and stores the result in correct order into the string variable. A final `mov` at line 207 tags on a null terminator, required by the ASCIIZ string format.

BCDCopy (216–240)

Call `BCDCopy` to copy one packed BCD variable to another. Register `si` addresses the original value. Register `di` addresses the destination, which must be at least 10 bytes long. After `BCDCopy`, the value at `di` is replaced with the value from `si`. For example:

```
DATASEG
v1      dt      7295155         ; BCD 7,295,155
v2      dt      ?
CODESEG
mov     si, offset v1   ; Address v1 (source) with si
mov     di, offset v2   ; Address v2 (destination) with di
call    BCDCopy         ; Copy BCD at v1 to v2
call    BCDAdd          ; Add v2 <- v2 + v1 (i.e., v1 * 2)
```

In this sample, `BCDCopy` copies the value at `v1` to the uninitialized value at `v2`. After this, `BCDAdd` adds the two variables, setting `v2` to `v1` times 2.

Advanced Separate Assemblies

Turbo Assembler has three directives that can smooth some of the bumps associated with assembling large, multimodule programs. This section describes how to use the directives:

▶ COMM—Communal Variables

▶ GLOBAL—Global Variables

▶ INCLUDELIB—Include Library Module

Note: Turbo Linker 2.0 currently does not support the **COMM** directive discussed in this section, although Turbo Assembler 1.0 does. If you must use **COMM**, try linking your program with another linker such as LINK.EXE or replace **COMM** with the more capable **GLOBAL** directive discussed later in this chapter. Perhaps this deficiency in Turbo Linker will be fixed by the time you read these comments; therefore, I decided to include the following section about the way **COMM** *should* work.

Using Communal Variables

The `COMM` directive defines *communal variables*, which are similar to uninitialized variables and can be declared in multiple modules. For example, suppose several modules use a 100-byte array of bytes plus an index variable. You can declare these variables in `COMM` directives this way:

```
DATASEG
COMM near index:Word
COMM near array:Byte:100
```

Multiple definitions can be separated by commas in a single `COMM` statement, but separate lines as shown here are easier to read. The first item after `COMM` is optional and can be either `near` or `far`, indicating whether this variable is addressable in the current data segment or in another segment. When using a simplified memory model, it's not necessary to specify near or far—Turbo Assembler will check all references to communals, issuing an error if you try to address a variable in the wrong segment. The second item is the name of the variable followed by a colon and size, which can be byte, word, dword, fword, pword, qword, or tbyte. You can also specify a structure name. After this comes an optional colon and count value (:100 in the second line of the example), telling the assembler how many bytes to allocate for this item. If you don't specify a count, Turbo Linker allocates space for only one element of the specified size.

The actual storage space for communal variables is not allocated until you link the modules. Variables of the same names declared in multiple modules are overlayed in the result. This way, instead of declaring variables PUBLIC in the defining modules and EXTRN in the using modules, you can simply define all variables communal in all modules and let Turbo Linker reduce all such multiple references to single variables.

The price you pay for this convenience is the inability to initialize communal variables. Like all uninitialized variables, communal variables have no specific values when the program runs. There's also no guarantee about where or in what order the variables will appear in memory—so don't assume that two communal variables will be in consecutive locations when the program runs. To avoid these restrictions and still enjoy the benefits of not having to use PUBLIC and EXTRN, Turbo Assembler has a similar but more flexible directive GLOBAL, described next.

Using Global Variables

The GLOBAL directive is similar to COMM but allows you to assign initial values to variables that multiple modules share. Using the same two variables described in the previous section, one module might declare and initialize array and index variables with the statements:

```
DATASEG
GLOBAL index:Word
GLOBAL array:Byte:100
;
;
index    dw      0
array    db      100 dup (1)
```

Inside the current data segment, two GLOBAL directives declare a word index and a byte array. The data types after the colon may be the same as for COMM. The optional count (100) after the array declaration tells the assembler how many bytes this variable occupies. You have to specify a count only if the allocation directives (db, dw, etc.) declare multiple values or use the dup operator; otherwise, the assembler has no way of knowing that array in this example is not a single byte. The actual two variables are declared and initialized as usual, creating an index initialized to 0 with dw and an array of 100 bytes initialized to 1s with db.

To refer to these same variables in other modules, just repeat the GLOBAL directives. The actual variable allocations (using dw and db, for example) must appear in only one module. As these examples demonstrate, the variables are now accessible from all program modules without a single PUBLIC or EXTRN.

Including Global Variables

A good way to organize a large multimodule program is to keep global variables in a separate file and then include that file in all modules. This keeps the variables in one handy place and avoids nasty surprises and conflicts that can arise when using hundreds of PUBLIC and EXTRN directives. Also, in situations like this, you'll begin to appreciate the real power of the GLOBAL directive. A good approach is to declare your global variables in a text file, perhaps named GLOBALS.ASM:

```
; GLOBAL.ASM file
;
GLOBAL index:Word
GLOBAL array:Byte:100
;
; other globals
```

Then, in each module that needs to refer to one or more global variables, add this statement usually somewhere after a DATASEG directive:

```
; AMODULE.ASM (partial)
;
DATASEG
INCLUDE "GLOBAL.ASM"
;
; other local variables
```

You can still declare other local variables in this module—only the global variables are shared with other modules. The INCLUDE directive loads the global declarations from GLOBAL.ASM, making the definitions available to the module. In addition, you need an initialization module that actually declares the variables:

```
; INIT.ASM (partial)
DATASEG
INCLUDE "GLOBAL.ASM"
index   dw      0
array   db      100 dup (1)
```

INIT.ASM declares and initializes the variables. Again, GLOBAL.ASM is included, just as in other modules. (You can either assemble INIT.ASM just as you do other separate modules or include the text in your main program.) With GLOBAL, you avoid using PUBLIC and EXTRN, while you add the ability to store all global variables and initializations in one or two handy files. Also, you avoid the restriction of COMM, which does not allow initialization of variables.

Using the INCLUDELIB Directive

In most of the preceding chapters, instructions are given for adding module .OBJ files to the MTA.LIB library file. Turbo Linker commands then refer to this file to extract the modules containing procedures declared in

EXTRN directives in a program's (or other module's) code segment. To simplify the link command, you can insert an INCLUDELIB directive, which tells the linker to look in a named library file for modules. For example, you can add this line somewhere near the beginning of the main program:

```
INCLUDELIB "MTA"
```

If you don't add a file-name extension, the linker assumes the name ends with .LIB. The file name may also have path information as in "c:\library\MTA.LIB." You can now assemble and link the program with commands such as:

```
tasm myprog
tlink myprog
```

Because of the INCLUDELIB directive, the necessary modules are extracted from MTA.LIB automatically without referring to the library file explicitly in the tlink command. Put the INCLUDELIB directive only in the main module—don't use this directive to refer to the same library file in more than one module at a time.

Note: Even with an INCLUDELIB directive, you still have to use EXTRN directives to import procedures declared PUBLIC in library modules.

Processing Tables

As a general rule of thumb, if you can look up values in a table rather than calculate those same values with numeric expressions, your programs will gain speed. Usually, it takes only a couple of instructions to look up a value, while it takes several instructions to perform a calculation. If you can use the special 8086 table-processing instruction xlat (Translate From Table), you may be able to save even more time.

The xlat instruction requires ds:bx to address a table of bytes. An index value in al is added to this address, locating one of the bytes in the table. Executing xlat loads this byte into al, replacing the register's original value. In other words, the index value in al is *translated* to an associated byte from the table. A small example explains how this works. Assemble and link Program 11-2, TABLE.ASM, with the commands:

```
tasm /zi table
tlink /v table
```

Program 11-2 *TABLE.ASM*

```
1:        IDEAL
2:        DOSSEG
3:        MODEL    small
4:        STACK    256
5:
```

```
 6:            DATASEG
 7:
 8:    ;-------------------------------------------------
 9:    ;indexes       0, 1, 2, 3,  4,  5,  6,  7,  8,  9
10:    ;-------------------------------------------------
11:    table   db     0, 1, 4, 9, 16, 25, 36, 49, 64, 81
12:
13:            CODESEG
14:
15:    Start:
16:            mov    ax,@data            ; Initialize ds to address
17:            mov    ds,ax               ;  of data segment
18:
19:            mov    bx, offset table    ; Address table with ds:bx
20:            mov    cx, 9               ; Assign loop count to cx
21:    @@10:
22:            mov    al, cl              ; Copy index value to al
23:            xlat                       ; Translate from table
24:            loop   @@10                ; Loop on cx
25:
26:    Exit:
27:            mov    ax,04C00h           ; DOS function: Exit program
28:            int    21h                 ; Call DOS. Terminate program
29:
30:            END    Start       ; End of program / entry point
```

How TABLE.ASM Works

Load the assembled TABLE program into Turbo Debugger with the command `td table` and press Alt-V-C to switch to the CPU window. Press F5 to zoom the window to full screen and then follow these steps:

1. Press F7 twice, then once again to load `bx` with the offset address of the `table` variable at line 11. Press F7 again to load `cx` with the loop count (9).

2. The cursor should be on the `mov` instruction. Press F7 to copy `cl` to `al`. You should see the `al` register (upper right of the screen) change to 09.

3. Press F7 to execute the `xlat` instruction, translating the value in `al` to a value in the `table` addressed by `ds:bx`. On the first time through the loop, this changes `al` to 51h (81 decimal)—twice the original value in `al`.

4. Press F7 repeatedly to execute all passes through the loop, setting `al` to smaller and smaller index values, which are translated to other bytes from the `table`.

This experiment demonstrates how `xlat` works, translating index values in `al` to table bytes, although you could do the same job more easily by simply adding `al` to itself. A more useful example follows.

Practical xlat Uses

One of the most common uses for `xlat` is to translate ASCII characters to other characters, perhaps in a terminal emulator program that needs to pass certain values to a remote system when you press a control key. The easy way to program this is to create a table of values indexed by the original ASCII characters. As an example of how this works, Program 11-3, BOXCHAR.ASM, translates keys Alt-1, Alt-2, . . . , Alt-0 to ten extended ASCII characters commonly used on PCs to draw boxes. Assemble, link, and run the program with MTA.LIB on disk and the commands:

```
tasm boxchar
tlink boxchar,,, mta
boxchar
```

Press Alt and any digit key to display a box character. This illustrates how xlat can translate key codes to other ASCII values. Press F10 to end the demonstration.

Program 11-3 *BOXCHAR.ASM*

```
 1:             IDEAL
 2:             DOSSEG
 3:             MODEL   small
 4:             STACK   256
 5:
 6: cr          EQU     13      ; ASCII carriage return
 7: lf          EQU     10      ; ASCII line feed
 8: Fn10        EQU     100     ; GetCh value for F10
 9: LowIndex    EQU     152     ; GetCh value for Alt-1
10: HighIndex   EQU     161     ; GetCh value for Alt-0
11:
12:             DATASEG
13:
14: message db      cr, lf, 'Sample Character Table Translation'
15:         db      cr, lf, 'Press Alt-1 to Alt-0 to display characters'
16:         db      cr, lf, 'Press F10 to end', cr, lf, lf, 0
17:
18: table   db      179, 180, 191, 192, 193, 194, 195, 196, 217, 218
19:
20:             CODESEG
21:
22:             EXTRN   StrWrite:proc, GetCh:proc
23:
24: Start:
25:         mov     ax, @data           ; Initialize ds to address
26:         mov     ds, ax              ;  of data segment
27:         mov     es, ax              ; Make es = ds
28:
29:         mov     di, offset message  ; Display instructions
30:         call    StrWrite
31: @@10:
32:         call    GetCh               ; Get key press
33:         jnz     @@10                ; Repeat if not function key
34:         cmp     al, Fn10            ; Check for F10
35:         je      Exit                ; Exit if F10 pressed
```

```
36:            cmp     al, LowIndex        ; Verify that al is within
37:            jb      @@10                ;   range of LowIndex to
38:            cmp     al, HighIndex       ;   HighIndex
39:            ja      @@10
40:            sub     al, LowIndex        ; Convert al to 0..n
41:            mov     bx, offset table    ; Address table with ds:bx
42:            xlat                        ; Translate al from table
43:            mov     dl, al              ; Move new char in al to dl
44:            mov     ah, 2               ; DOS "display char" function
45:            int     21h                 ; Call DOS to display char
46:            jmp     @@10                ; Repeat until done
47:   Exit:
48:            mov     ax,04C00h           ; DOS function: Exit program
49:            int     21h                 ; Call DOS. Terminate program
50:
51:            END     Start       ; End of program / entry point
```

How BOXCHAR.ASM Works

The `table` variable at line 18 defines the extended ASCII characters for the keys Alt-1, Alt-2, . . . , Alt-0. The code at lines 31–39 calls `GetCh` in the KEYBOARD module (see chapter 7) for a key press, returned in `al`. The other instructions in this section check for F10, which ends the program, and check that `al` is within the range of `LowIndex` to `HighIndex`. After this, line 40 subtracts the value of `LowIndex` from `al`, thus reducing the key value range from 151–161 to 0–10. Then lines 41 and 42 translate this adjusted index value to one of the `table` values, displaying this character with a call to DOS function 2 (lines 43–45).

Using xlat with Multiple-Dimension Tables

On occasion, `xlat` comes in handy for translating values in `al` representing the column number in a two-dimensional matrix. Along with the `lea` (Load Effective Address) instruction, working with such complex arrays is not as difficult in assembly language as you may imagine. For example, suppose you have the following 4-row by 8-column matrix:

```
DATASEG
matrix db    00Fh, 04Bh, 087h, 0C3h, 00Fh, 04Bh, 01Eh, 05Ah
       db    096h, 0D2h, 01Eh, 05Ah, 02Dh, 069h, 0A5h, 0E1h
       db    02Dh, 069h, 03Ch, 078h, 0B4h, 0F0h, 03Ch, 078h
       db    09Dh, 0D2h, 04Fh, 067h, 003h, 079h, 099h, 000h
```

Next, suppose the program assigns a column number to `al` in the range 0–7 and a row number to `si` in the range 0–3. To load the byte at `matrix[row, column]` requires only a few instructions:

```
CODESEG
mov    al, 4            ; Load column number into al
mov    si, 2            ; Load row number into si
mov    cl, 3            ; Load shift count into cl
shl    si, cl           ; si <- si * 8
lea    bx, [matrix + si] ; ds:bx addresses table row
xlat                    ; al <- table[row, column]
```

Here, al equals 4 and si equals 2, the row and column index numbers. The third mov and shl instructions multiply the row number in si by the number of bytes in one row—8 in this example. Then lea loads bx with the offset address of this row. After loading bx, an xlat instruction translates the column index in al to the byte at the indexed column in this row of the table. The lea instruction has the same effect as the two instructions:

```
mov     bx, offset matrix
add     bx, si
```

Instead of doing this, always use lea—it's faster than computing a complex address reference manually by addition. You can use any of the addressing modes discussed in chapter 5 as the parameter to lea. You can also assign the result to any general-purpose register, although bx is commonly used with the instruction.

Other xlat Forms

The xlat instruction allows a few variations. You can supply a table variable as a parameter to xlat, letting Turbo Assembler verify that the variable is addressable by ds:bx, which you still must initialize. For example:

```
mov     bx, offset table    ; Address table with bx
mov     al, [index]         ; Load index value into al
xlat    [table]             ; Translate al from table (ds:bx)
```

With a parameter to xlat, Turbo Assembler verifies that table is in the segment addressed by ds. You can use a similar construction with a segment override to reference a table located in a segment addressed by es:

```
mov     bx, offset table    ; Address table with bx
mov     al, [index]         ; Load index value into al
xlat    [es:table]          ; Translate al from table (es:bx)
```

The segment override changes xlat's usual segment base register ds to es. You must specify a parameter in this case, but if you don't want to refer to the variable by name, you can also use bx this way:

```
mov     bx, offset table    ; Address table with bx
mov     al, [index]         ; Load index value into al
xlat    [es:bx]             ; Translate al from table (es:bx)
```

In addition, you can use the shorthand mnemonic xlatb in exactly the same way as xlat without a parameter:

```
mov     bx, offset table    ; Address table with bx
mov     al, [index]         ; Load index value into al
xlatb                       ; Translate al from table (ds:bx)
```

To be honest, it's not clear to me why the xlatb mnemonic even exists—you can just use xlat without a parameter to perform the identical task. The only significant difference between the two names is that the `xlatb` mnemonic may never have a parameter, while `xlat` may be used with or without a parameter.

Declaring Segments the Hard Way

Most of the programs in this book take advantage of Turbo Assembler's simplified memory models, using directives such as `CODESEG` and `DATASEG` to define the start of the program's code and data segments. For most purposes, this gives you all the control you need to separate code from data and to organize your program sensibly. On the rare occasions that you need more control over the names and sizes of segments, however, simplified memory models may be inadequate. At such times, you must declare segments "the hard way," using the `SEGMENT`, `ASSUME`, and `GROUP` directives.

The SEGMENT Directive

`SEGMENT` tells Turbo Assembler to collect whatever follows into one memory segment, which can store data, code, or the stack. A program can declare many segments, assigning various attributes and names that cause the data or code to be combined according to all sorts of rules and regulations. The full syntax for `SEGMENT` is:

SEGMENT *name [align] [combine] [use] [' class']*

The segment *name* is required and can be any identifier you like—similar to any other program label. The other four elements are optional (as indicated by the brackets). Each operand has its own rules and formats, explained in the following notes:

- ▶ *name*—Any identifier such as `MYDATA` or `SEGA45X`. You can repeat the same name in multiple `SEGMENT` declarations, even in multiple-program modules. Turbo Assembler combines all equally named segments into one large segment. You can locate this segment in memory by assigning the offset address of *name* to a segment register.

- ▶ *align*—Specifies a boundary restriction for the start of the segment. Table 11-1 lists the various symbols that you can use for *align*. During assembly, if the current location at the start of the segment does not satisfy the specified rule for this align type, the assembler's location counter is advanced by an appropriate amount, forcing the segment to begin farther down (at a higher address) and possibly wasting a few bytes. If you don't specify an alignment, segments are aligned to the next highest 16-byte paragraph.

Table 11-1 *SEGMENT align Symbols*

Symbol	Align Segment to the Next . . .
Byte	Byte address (current location)
Word	Word address (LSD of address = 0)
Dword	Doubleword address (2 LSDs of address = 0)
Para	16-byte paragraph (4 LSDs of address = 0)
Page	256-byte page (8 LDSs of address = 0)

Table 11-2 *SEGMENT combine Symbols*

Symbol	Meaning
At *expression*	Locate segment at the address specified by *expression*, which must be an absolute paragraph address such as 0F00h or 0040h. Use this option to refer to data already in memory such as ROM BIOS variables.
Common	Segments of the same name are overlayed. The size of the segment equals the size of the largest of all segments. Use this option to refer to common variables among multiple modules.
Memory	Identical to `Public`. Causes segments of the same names to be joined one after the other.
Private	The default setting. Causes segments of the same name to be treated as separate segments. You must initialize a segment register to address each segment before you can access variables in the segment.
Public	Causes all segments of the same name to be joined one after the other in memory, in the order declared in the program. The result is one large segment containing all data or code in all segments. You need to initialize a segment register to address only the first of all combined segments to access variables declared in the segments.
Stack	Use this option only to declare stack space, usually in the main program module. All .EXE programs must declare a stack segment. The linker inserts information in the .EXE file that DOS uses to load registers `ss` and `sp` automatically at run time. You don't have to load these registers in your program. Multiple segments of the same name with the *combine*-type STACK are joined one after the other to form one large stack segment. This allows separate modules to declare as much space as needed for the stack. (Remember to add extra room for DOS, BIOS, and interrupt handlers.)

▶ *combine*—Specifies rules for organizing segments and for combining multiple segments in memory. Table 11-2 lists the symbols that you can use for *combine*. The default *combine* rule is `Private`.

▶ *use*—Applies only to 80386 programs using the P386 or P386N directives to enable this processor's special instructions and extended registers. Table 11-3 lists the symbols that you can use for *use*. Most programs do not need this operand.

▶ *'class'*—Serves as a kind of category specification. All segments with identical *'class'* names—even those with different *name*

Table 11-3 *SEGMENT use Symbols*

Symbol	Meaning
Use16	The default setting. Enables 16-bit segment displacement (offset) addressing and limits segment size to 64K.
Use32	Enables 32-bit segment displacement (offset) addressing and allows a maximum segment size of 4GB (gigabytes or billions of bytes).

names—are physically loaded together in memory when the program runs.

Using SEGMENT   A few examples will help explain how to set up segments in your own programs. Suppose you need three word variables in a data segment. You can declare them this way:

```
SEGMENT Dseg Para Public 'DATA'
v1      dw      0
v2      dw      1
v3      dw      2
ENDS    Dseg
```

The ENDS directive marks the end of the segment and must be included. You may add the same name Dseg here after ENDS or leave the space to the right blank. The segment is aligned to the next highest 16-byte paragraph in memory Para and, because of the Public *combine* type, is added to all other segments that are either named Dseg or that have the same *'class'* name 'DATA'. To find the variables in this segment, you must initialize an appropriate segment register, usually ds. For example, to load dx with the value of variable v2 requires these steps:

```
mov     ax, Dseg
mov     ds, ax
ASSUME  ds:Dseg
mov     dx, [v2]
```

We'll get to ASSUME in a moment, but, for now, be aware that you must initialize a segment register to refer to variables in segments. In most cases, you can do this by assigning the value of the segment name—Dseg in this example. The problem is: These instructions are floating in space—they too must go in a segment. A typical code segment for a main program module might be:

```
SEGMENT Cseg Para Public 'CODE'
Start:
        mov     ax, Dseg        ; Assign segment address
        mov     ds, ax          ;   to ds
        mov     es, ax          ;   and to es
```

```
ASSUME  ds:Dseg, es:Dseg
;
; other instructions go here
;
ENDS    Cseg              ; End of code segment
END     Start             ; End of text
```

The code segment is named Cseg, is aligned to the next highest paragraph boundary, and is combined with other Csegs in other modules or with segments of different names but with 'CODE' class designations. Notice how END specifies a start address, which the linker uses to insert information in the .EXE file for DOS to load the code segment (or segments) properly into memory, initialize cs, and jump to the first program instruction.

In addition to code and data segments, a STACK segment is required, or Turbo Linker will warn you that the program has no stack—a serious error unless the program is of the .COM variety. A typical stack segment is:

```
SEGMENT Sseg Word Stack 'STACK'
theStack         db       128 dup ('**Stack*')
ENDS
```

Because of the *combine*-type Stack, the ss:sp registers are automatically initialized to this stack space, which is aligned to the next highest word address. The class name 'STACK' causes multiple stack segments of the same class to be combined, just as for other segments. Don't confuse these two items, which are usually spelled the same; only the *combine* type tells the linker that this is a stack segment. The stack space is allocated in this sample by a db directive, storing 128 copies of the string '**Stack*' in 1,024 bytes. During debugging, this makes finding the stack in memory easy—just hunt for the '**Stack*' strings. Also, after the program is finished, you can examine the declared stack and see how much stack space was used by looking for where the strings are obliterated. (Remember to add extra room for interrupt handlers—never pare your stack space down to the bare minimum.)

Note: One problem with this method is that stack data is stored in the .EXE code file on disk. In the finished version, you may want to convert your stack to a simplified memory-model STACK directive or declare uninitialized stack space using the question mark operator (?) instead of literal strings. This will reduce the code-file size.

These three elements—a data, code, and stack segment—are usually the minimum requirements in a program that declares stacks "the hard way." Before using these ideas to write a full program, you also need to understand what ASSUME does.

The ASSUME Directive

To understand the ASSUME directive, think of your program as existing in two time dimensions. The first dimension is *assembly time*—the actions that occur when Turbo Assembler assembles the program text. The second dimension is *run time*—the actions that occur when COMMAND.COM loads your program into memory and executes the first instruction.

The ASSUME directive belongs strictly to the assembly time dimension—it has no effect on the program at run time. Use ASSUME to tell Turbo Assembler that segment registers such and such address segments so and so. For example, given the previous data-segment declaration for Dseg, to initialize the es register to address the segment in memory, you can write:

```
mov      ax, Dseg        ; Assign address of Dseg
mov      es, ax          ;  to es via ax
ASSUME   es:Dseg         ; Tell Turbo Assembler where es points
```

At run time, the two mov instructions load es with the address of the Dseg data segment. At assembly time, the ASSUME directive tells Turbo Assembler where es currently points. The reason both steps are necessary is that Turbo Assembler assembles but doesn't "understand" assembly language code; therefore, you must tell the assembler to where es points, even though the previous instructions loaded es to that very same segment. ASSUME takes the general form:

ASSUME *segReg:segName* | *NOTHING, . . . , segReg:segName* | *NOTHING*

The *segReg* may be cs, ds, es, or ss. 80386 programs can also specify the fs and gs registers, which are not available on the 8086 and 80286. The *segName* must refer to the name of a segment as declared in a SEGMENT directive. (As you'll see in a moment, *segName* can also refer to a segment group.) Instead of a *segName*, you can use the word NOTHING, which tells the assembler that the specified register addresses no specific segment at the moment.

By using ASSUME, you give Turbo Assembler the ability to perform two actions:

▶ Verify addressability of variables in data segments

▶ Add segment overrides automatically as needed

The second of these advantages is most important. By using ASSUME, Turbo Assembler can insert an es: segment override instruction. For example, suppose the previous Dseg segment is addressed only by es. This instruction:

```
ASSUME   es:Dseg
mov      dx, [v1]
```

is actually assembled as:

```
mov      dx, [es:v1]
```

You can still specify the segment override, but you don't have to. ASSUME lets Turbo Assembler decide whether an override is needed. This is particularly handy when using string instructions and when referring to multiple segments with both ds and es. By using ASSUME after every assignment to a segment register, you ensure that Turbo Assembler will do everything possible to verify that memory references at least make sense and that variables are actually in the segments addressed by segment registers.

You can also specify multiple assumptions separated by commas. For example, using the segment declarations from the previous discussion for SEGMENT, a typical ASSUME directive might be:

ASSUME cs:CSeg, ds:DSeg, es:NOTHING, ss:Sseg

The GROUP Directive

Now that you have the tools you need to declare segments "the hard way," you'll probably want to use a GROUP directive to simplify references to multiple segments. GROUP has the form:

GROUP *name segName [, . . . , segName]*

The *name* and GROUP elements are reversed when assembling in MASM mode. The *name* can be any unused identifier such as dgroup or stacksegs. After the *name* comes one or more *segName*s, which must be the names used in other SEGMENT declarations.

> Note: The GROUP *segName* can also be an expression beginning with SEG as in GROUP newgroup SEG myLabel, although this use is rare. Usually, it's better to define named segments with SEGMENT and use the names in a GROUP directive.

Use GROUP when you have multiple segments of different names that you want to address with a single segment register. The segments may not have the same class names. In fact, if both the segment and class names are different, a GROUP directive is the only way to ensure that multiple segments are combined in memory. For example, if three modules declare data segments named DSeg, LocalSeg, and OtherSeg, you could use this GROUP directive:

GROUP DataGroup DSeg, LocalSeg, OtherSeg

Despite whether these segments are of the same class, they will be joined into one large segment in memory. You can now refer to all variables in the three segments by initializing ds (or es) and telling Turbo Assembler where ds now points:

```
mov     ax, DataGroup    ; Assign address of DataGroup
mov     ds, ax           ;  to ds via ax
ASSUME  ds:DataGroup     ; Tell Turbo Assembler where ds points
```

Instead of loading ds with the offset of an individual segment, you now can load the offset to the group name, in this case **DataGroup**. The same group name is also used in an ASSUME directive, telling Turbo Assembler to where ds points.

After grouping multiple segments this way, offsets to individual variables in all joined segments are automatically computed. As long as the ds or es segment registers address the group name, you can be confident that all your variables are directly addressable. The only restriction is that all grouped segments can occupy no more than 64K.

Using Segments in Programs

When not using simplified memory models, declaring segments requires careful planning. Most of the time, a simplified model will do the job, but there is one little-known restriction on all such models. In your Turbo Assembler Reference Guide, in the discussion of the .MODEL directive (in Ideal mode, it is spelled MODEL with no period), several tables list the segment names used by various simplified models. For reference, Table 11-4 lists these names for the small memory model, but showing the Ideal-mode directives used to declare each segment type.

> Note: Most of the other memory models use names that are similar to those in Table 11-4. If you need to know what these names are, refer to the Turbo Assembler Reference Guide or assemble a program with the command tasm /l filename. You'll find the segment names near the end of the .LST listing file.

Table 11-4 reveals a disturbing feature of simplified memory models. The data, uninitialized data, constant, and stack segments are combined

Table 11-4 *Simplified Small Memory Model Segments*

Directive*	Name	Align	Combine	Class	Group
CODESEG	_TEXT	Word	Public	'CODE'	
FARDATA	FAR_DATA	Para	Private	'FAR_DATA'	
UFARDATA	FAR_BSS	Para	Private	'FAR_BSS'	
DATASEG	_DATA	Word	Public	'DATA'	DGROUP
CONST	CONST	Word	Public	'CONST'	DGROUP
UDATASEG	_BSS	Word	Public	'BSS'	DGROUP
STACK	STACK	Para	Stack	'STACK'	DGROUP

*Note: Ideal mode only.

under the group name DGROUP. This means that the *total* size of these segments is limited to 64K! In other words, the more stack space you declare, the less room you have for data. This is not true just for the small memory model. *All* simplified memory models group the stack and data segments together in DGROUP.

By declaring your own segments, you can eliminate this restriction, as demonstrated in Program 11-4, HARDSHEL.ASM—a "hard-way" version of the EXESHELL.ASM program from chapter 2. Use HARDSHEL.ASM as a template for your own programs when you want full control over segments. The shell allows space for two 64K data segments, one 64K stack segment, and a 64K code segment for a total potential program size of about 256K. To assemble the shell (which doesn't do anything, although it does run) and to print copies of the listing and map files, enter the commands:

```
tasm /l hardshel
tlink hardshel
type hardshel.lst >prn
type hardshel.map >prn
```

Program 11-4 *HARDSHEL.ASM*

```
 1:  %TITLE "Shell for .EXE Code Files with Unsimplified Segments"
 2:
 3:          IDEAL
 4:          DOSSEG
 5:
 6:  ;----- Insert EQU and = equates here
 7:
 8:
 9:  SEGMENT SSeg Para Stack 'STACK'
10:
11:  ;       db      1024 dup ('**Stack*')    ; 8K debugging stack
12:          db      8192 dup (?)             ; 8K uninitialized stack
13:
14:  ENDS    SSeg
15:
16:
17:  SEGMENT DSeg Word Public 'DATA'
18:
19:  exitCode        DB      0
20:
21:  ;----- Declare other variables with DB, DW, etc., here
22:
23:  ;----- Specify any EXTRN variables here
24:
25:  ENDS    DSeg
26:
27:
```

```
28:    SEGMENT ESeg Word Public 'EDATA'
29:
30:    ;-----  Alternate (far) data segment
31:
32:    ENDS    ESeg
33:
34:
35:    SEGMENT CSeg Word Public 'CODE'
36:
37:    ;-----  Specify any EXTRN procedures here
38:
39:    Start:
40:           ASSUME  ds:DSeg
41:           mov     ax, DSeg              ; Initialize ds to address
42:           mov     ds, ax               ;   of data segment
43:           ASSUME  es:ESeg
44:           mov     ax, ESeg              ; Initialize es to address
45:           mov     es, ax               ;   of extra data segment
46:
47:    ;-----  Insert program, subroutine calls, etc., here
48:
49:    Exit:
50:           mov     ah, 04Ch             ; DOS function: Exit program
51:           mov     al, [exitCode]       ; Return exit code value
52:           int     21h                  ; Call DOS. Terminate program
53:
54:    ENDS    CSeg                 ; End of code segment
55:
56:           END     Start         ; End of program / entry point
```

Using HARDSHEL.ASM

A few notes will help you to use the HARDSHEL.ASM template. First, notice that line 4 specifies the DOSSEG directive, normally used with simplified memory models. You can remove this line if you want even more control over the ordering of segments in memory. But DOSSEG is added here to ensure that the stack segment is loaded last. Because line 12 declares 8K of uninitialized stack space, this keeps the .EXE code-file size to a minimum. (If you take out line 4, assemble, and link the shell, the code file grows by 8K!)

Line 11 is commented out. Remove the semicolon and turn line 12 into a comment to add 8K of **Stack** strings to the code file. When debugging, you can then examine the stack memory to see how much stack space the program actually uses.

Two segments DSeg and ESeg are declared at lines 17–32. These segments are not grouped together, although they could be if you want. (Of course, grouping multiple data segments also limits the total size of the combined segments to 64K.) Examine how the code at lines 40–45 initializes the **es** and **ds** segment registers to address the two separate segments.

Note: Most of the modules in this book assume that **es** and **ds** address the *same* data segment. When using HARDSHEL.ASM, you may have to modify these modules or temporarily reassign **es** to **ds** before calling module subroutines.

The code segment at lines 35–54 may contain up to 64K. If you need more space than this, you can declare additional code segments and make far subroutine calls to routines in those modules. If you do this, be sure to end the subroutines with `retf`, not `ret`.

Where It's At Table 11-2 lists the *combine* types that you can use in a **SEGMENT** directive. One of these types is *At*, which locates a segment at a specific address in memory. Such a segment is a *phantom*—a means to overlay variables declared in the program but already existing in memory as the result of other processes. This technique is especially useful for referring to variables that belong to DOS and the ROM BIOS. Obviously, such variables are not created by your own code but are initialized when you switch on the computer's power. There are two ways to locate BIOS data. You can simply equate a symbol to an address in memory and read or write values to that address. (Consult a hardware technical reference for these addresses.) For improved clarity, which can help to avoid bugs caused by writing to the wrong places, it's a good idea to declare an *At* segment, as demonstrated by Program 11-5, COLDBOOT.ASM. Assemble and link the program with the commands:

```
tasm coldboot
tlink coldboot
```

Note: Running COLDBOOT reboots your system, erasing any data in memory. Don't run the program unless that's what you want to do.

Program 11-5 *COLDBOOT.ASM*

```
 1:   %TITLE "Perform ReBoot"
 2:
 3:           IDEAL
 4:           DOSSEG
 5:           MODEL   small
 6:           STACK   256
 7:
 8:
 9:   WarmBoot        EQU     1234h   ; Skips cold boot tests
10:   ColdBoot        EQU     1234d   ; Or any value <> 1234h
11:
12:
13:   ;----- Tell assembler where the ResetFlag word is located
14:
```

```
15:     SEGMENT BIOSData at 0040h
16:             ORG     0072h
17:     LABEL   ResetFlag Word
18:     ENDS
19:
20:
21:     ;----- Tell assembler where the Reset routine is located
22:
23:     SEGMENT BIOS para at 0F000h
24:             ORG     0E05Bh
25:     LABEL   Reset   FAR
26:     ENDS
27:
28:
29:             CODESEG
30:
31:     Start:
32:             mov     ax, BIOSData            ; Address BIOSData segment
33:             mov     ds, ax                  ;   with ds
34:
35:     ASSUME  DS:BIOSData
36:             mov     [ResetFlag], ColdBoot   ; Set ResetFlag
37:             jmp     far Reset               ; Jump to reset routine
38:
39:             END     Start          ; End of program / entry point
```

**How
COLDBOOT.ASM
Works**

The COLDBOOT program declares two "hard-way" segments, even though it also uses a simplified memory model. There's nothing wrong with this—you can combine memory models and custom segments at will. In this program, two segments are declared at specific addresses. The first segment is declared to exist at the absolute address 0040h, which happens to be the start of the ROM BIOS data segment:

```
SEGMENT BIOSData at 0040h
```

When the program runs, this segment is not actually loaded into memory; therefore, you can't insert initialized variables into BIOSData. That would be a bad idea anyway—you'd be changing values that belong to the ROM BIOS. Usually, you'll refer to variables that already exist, as demonstrated by lines 16–17. First, an ORG directive sets the origin to 0072h, the address of a variable representing the BIOS reset flag. After this, a LABEL directive assigns a word label ResetFlag to this address so that later instructions have a way to refer to the data at this spot. The reason for using ORG is to avoid duplicating other variables at lower addresses, which the program doesn't need. There's no reason to duplicate the entire BIOS data segment just to refer to a single variable.

Similar directives specify an absolute segment at 0F000h, the start of the BIOS code segment. A far label named Reset is associated with offset address 0E05Bh.

With these details out of the way, the program is ready to access data and code in the *At* segments. Lines 32–35 perform the crucial steps of loading ds with the address of BIOSData and using an ASSUME directive to tell Turbo Assembler where ds now points. After this, a mov assigns to ResetFlag the value of ColdBoot, declared at line 10. Then line 37 executes a far jmp to the Reset label in the BIOS code segment. The result is to restart the computer as though you had just switched on power.

Line 9 shows the value to assign to ResetFlag if you want to perform a warm boot—the same effect as pressing Ctrl-Alt-Delete. Using this value in place of ColdBoot at line 36 still restarts the system but bypasses memory and other hardware tests, thus saving a little time.

Far Data Segments

When you need extra data space but you still want to use simplified memory models, you can use the FARDATA directive to create as many additional data segments as you need. There's only one rule to remember—it's up to you to initialize segment registers to access data in far segments. Other than this minor complication, using far data segments is easy. For example, suppose you want to put all your program strings in a separate segment, thus leaving room in the default data segment for other variables. First, declare the segment with a FARDATA directive:

```
FARDATA
s1      db      'Welcome to TurboCalc', 0
s2      db      'Copyright 1999 by PC Universe', 0
s3      db      'Support hot line: 800-555-1212', 0
```

That's all you have to do to create a far data segment. Because such segments are not included in DGROUP (see Table 11-4), they are not combined with other segments. Consequently, to access variables in a far data segment, you must initialize one or more segment registers in your program code. For example, if you want to display the strings in this sample using routines in the STRIO module, you'll have to initialize both es and ds with:

```
CODESEG
mov     ax, @farData    ; Load address of far data segment
mov     ds, ax                      ; Assign to ds
mov     es, ax                      ; Assign also to es
ASSUME  ds:@farData, es:@farData  ; Tell Turbo Assembler!
```

First, es and ds are initialized to the address of the far data segment, using the predefined @farData symbol. The required ASSUME directive tells Turbo Assembler about this change to ds. You can then import routines in other modules such as STRIO and display strings with code such as:

```
EXTRN   StrWrite:proc, NewLine:proc
mov     di, offset s1
call    StrWrite
call    NewLine
```

To again restore es and ds to the default data segment, execute the usual instructions:

```
mov     ax, @data           ; Initialize ds to address
mov     ds, ax              ;  of data segment
mov     es, ax              ; Make es = ds
ASSUME  ds:@data, es:@data  ; Tell Turbo Assembler!
```

Don't forget the ASSUME directive. Remember, it's a good idea (and in this case required) always to tell Turbo Assembler about your assignments to segment registers. Another possibility is to push and pop segment registers to switch temporarily to a far data segment. For instance, suppose you want to load dx with a variable v1 allocated in a FARDATA segment:

```
FARDATA
v1      dw      99          ; Variable in far data segment
CODESEG
;
push    ds                  ; Save current ds on stack
mov     ax, @farData        ; Assign address of far data
mov     ds, ax              ;  segment to ds
ASSUME  ds:@farData         ; Tell Turbo Assembler where ds points
mov     dx, [v1]            ; Load value from far segment into dx
pop     ds                  ; Restore original data segment register
ASSUME  ds:@data            ; Tell Turbo Assembler where ds points
```

Again, ASSUME directives keep Turbo Assembler informed about the changes to ds. Don't forget the ASSUME after the pop ds instruction. Even though this restores ds to its original value, this action occurs at run time. You still have to tell Turbo Assembler what's going on during assembly time.

Multiple Far Data Segments

Normally, if you insert multiple FARDATA directives in various modules, all far data segments are combined into one segment up to 64K long. By adding an optional name to the directives, you can declare as many separate far data segments as you need. Let's assume you need two such segments. Here's how you might begin:

```
FARDATA FarOut
v1      dw      1
v2      dw      2

FARDATA FartherOut
v3      dw      3
v4      dw      4
```

The program now has two distinct far data segments FarOut and FartherOut. Each of these segments can be as large as 64K, increasing the program's total data space to 192K (including the default data segment less stack space and other items in DGROUP). The names after FARDATA prevent the segments from being combined.

Note: If you repeat the same names after multiple FARDATA directives, the segments are combined as though the optional names did not exist.

To locate your data in various far data segments, load a segment register with the name you assigned to FARDATA. Use an ASSUME directive to tell Turbo Assembler to where the segment registers point. For example, suppose you want to load cx with the value of v1 (in the FarOut segment) and dx with the value of v3 (in the FartherOut segment).

```
mov     ax, FarOut        ; Initialize ds to
mov     ds, ax            ;  address FarOut segment
ASSUME  ds:FarOut         ; Tell Turbo Assembler
mov     ax, FartherOut    ; Initialize es to
mov     es, ax            ;  address FartherOut segment
ASSUME  es:FartherOut     ; Tell Turbo Assembler
mov     cx, [v1]          ; Load FarOut's v1 into cx
mov     dx, [v3]          ; Load FartherOut's v3 into dx
```

Because the ASSUME directives always keep Turbo Assembler informed about where ds and es point, the final two mov instructions simply load the variables by name. The assembler checks that v1 and v3 are addressable with these instructions and, in the case of the mov to dx from [v3], inserts an es: segment override, required because es addresses the segment in which v3 is declared. You can see this if you examine the machine code to this program fragment with Turbo Debugger. Look for hexadecimal 26h, the machine-code value for the es: segment override prefix.

Uninitialized Far Data Segments

Another directive UFARDATA begins an uninitialized far data segment, similar to an uninitialized regular data segment declared with UDATASEG. Because the far segment is not part of a DGROUP, it becomes a distinct segment just like a FARDATA segment, but with variables containing no predetermined values. Always use the question mark ? when declaring variables in UFARDATA segments. For example:

```
UFARDATA
index   dw      ?
array   db      1024 dup (?)
```

As long as you do not specify any initial values, the variables exist only at run time. To locate variables in the uninitialized data area, use the symbol @FarData? this way:

```
mov     ax, @FarData?
mov     ds, ax
ASSUME  ds:@FarData?
```

This assigns the address of the far segment to ds. When declaring multiple far data segments with UFARDATA, add a name as previously explained for FARDATA and assign the value of that name to a segment register and also in an ASSUME directive. For example, here are two distinct unin-itialized far data segments, each with the capacity to hold 64K of data:

```
UFARDATA BlackHole
space           dw        ?
moreSpace       dw        ?


UFARDATA BlackerHole
deepSpace       dw        ?
deeperSpace     dw        ?
```

To initialize ds to address BlackHole and es to address BlackerHole, execute the code:

```
CODESEG
mov     ax, BlackHole
mov     ds, ax
mov     ax, BlackerHole
mov     es, ax
ASSUME  ds:BlackHole, es:BlackerHole
```

Note: Unfortunately, tests indicate that uninitialized far data segments are allocated by Turbo Linker 2.0 in the .EXE code file on disk, even though they shouldn't be. Perhaps a future release of the linker will be able to remove this dead wood from disk files. I hope so!

Programming the 80286

If you are certain that your program will run on a system with an 80286 processor (or one with the fully compatible 80386), you can use special 80286 instructions. If you do this, be aware that your program will not run on systems with 8086 and 8088 processors. To enable the special instruc-tions, use one of the two commands:

▶ P286—Enable all 80286 instructions

▶ P286N—Enable only 80286 non-protected-mode instructions

Most of the time you'll use P286N—protected-mode instructions en-abled by P286 are strictly for writing multitasking operating software and are rarely (if ever) useful in applications programming, on which this book concentrates. Chapter 14 lists the protected-mode instructions. For more information about writing operating systems, see the Intel and other ref-erences listed in the Bibliography.

Because 80286 flags and registers are identical to those in 8086 pro-cessors, you can begin programming the 80286 immediately. (Actually, there are a few new flags, but these are used only by protected-mode instructions that don't concern us here.) In addition, the 80286 under-stands all 8086 instructions as described in this and previous chapters.

Table 11-5 lists the new instructions available only on 80286 (and 80386) systems.

Also refer to chapter 14 for more details on all of the instructions in Table 11-5. The two string instructions, which can read to and write strings from hardware ports, each have shorthand forms, listed separately here even though the mnemonics represent the identical instructions. The `ins`, `insb`, and `insw` mnemonics represent one instruction, as do the `outs`, `outsb`, and `outsw` mnemonics.

Three instructions `bound`, `enter`, and `leave` were added to the 80286 specifically for use by high-level language compilers, although you can certainly use these instructions in pure assembly code, too, as explained next.

Using the bound Instruction

The `bound` instruction verifies that an index is within a specified range—sometimes called *range checking* in a high-level language. Because most such languages make subroutine calls to check array index values, using the `bound` instruction can increase program speed while retaining the safety of using range checks, which many programmers disable to gain speed.

The `bound` instruction requires two operands. The first operand must be a 16-bit register such as `dx` or `bx` containing an index value to be verified by `bound`. The second operand is the address of a 32-bit doubleword variable in memory containing the low and high ranges allowed for the index value. If the value of the first operand is outside of the specified range, the processor issues an interrupt type 5. Obviously, you also have to install an appropriate interrupt service routine to handle this interrupt.

Note: Interrupt type 5 happens to service the "Print Screen" function in ATs and compatibles, resulting in a classic conflict that began with the release of the 8086 and 8088 chips. At that time, Intel reserved interrupt 5 for its own use—a restriction that IBM ignored when it designed the original PC. Later on, when releasing the 80286, Intel claimed its due rights and programmed interrupts into the `bound` instruction. (Of course, the company must have known that this would conflict with the PC's PrtSc key.) So now, if you use `bound` to check array indexes and an index is found to be outside of the allowable range, unless you disable the PrtSc key, the error also prints the display contents. Worse, this happens over and over until you reboot. A funny story, but nobody's laughing.

As an example of how to install a `bound` interrupt handler, Program 11-6 simulates an index range-checking error. Assemble, link, and run the program with the commands:

```
tasm bound286
tlink bound286,,, mta
bound286
```

Table 11-5 *80286 Instructions (Non-Protected-Mode)*

Mnemonic/Operands	Description
bound *destination, source*	Check array bounds
enter *immediate, immediate*	Make a procedure stack frame
ins *destination, dx*	Input string from port
insb	Input string bytes from port
insw	Input string words from port
leave	Leave procedure (after enter)
outs *dx, source*	Output string to port
outsb	Output string bytes to port
outsw	Output string words to port
popa	Pop all general registers
pusha	Push all general registers

Note: Run the following program *only* on systems with an 80286 or 80386 processor.

Program 11-6 *BOUND286.ASM*

```
1:   %TITLE "Bound Test--80286/386 Only!"
2:
3:          P286N
4:          IDEAL
5:          DOSSEG
6:          MODEL   small
7:          STACK   256
8:
9:          DATASEG
10:
11:  exitCode        DB      0
12:
13:  errorMsg        db      '**Error: array index out of bounds', 0
14:  normalMsg       db      'Program ending with no errors', 0
15:
16:  lowRange        DW      100     ; Lowest index range
17:  highRange       DW      199     ; Highest index range
18:  oldSeg          DW      ?       ; Saves interrupt 5 segment
19:  oldOfs          DW      ?       ; Saves interrupt 5 offset
20:
21:          CODESEG
22:
23:  ;----- From    STRIO.OBJ
24:          EXTRN   StrWrite:proc, NewLine:proc
25:
```

```
26:     Start:
27:             mov     ax, @data               ; Initialize ds to address
28:             mov     ds, ax                  ;  of data segment
29:             mov     es, ax                  ; Make es = ds
30:
31:             push    es                      ; Save es
32:             mov     ax, 03505h              ; Get interrupt 5 vector
33:             int     21h                     ; Call DOS
34:             mov     [oldSeg], es            ; Save segment address
35:             mov     [oldOfs], bx            ; Save offset address
36:             pop     es                      ; Restore es
37:
38:             push    ds                      ; Save ds
39:             mov     ax, 02505h              ; Set new interrupt 5 vector
40:             mov     dx, offset Int5ISR      ; To this offset address
41:             push    cs                      ; And to this code
42:             pop     ds                      ;  segment address
43:             int     21h                     ; Call DOS
44:             pop     ds                      ; Restore ds
45:
46:             mov     bx, 2                   ; Assign index value to bx
47:             bound   bx, [lowRange]          ; Test index range
48:
49:             mov     di, offset normalMsg    ; Display "no errors"
50:             call    StrWrite                ;  message
51:             call    NewLine
52:
53:     Exit:
54:             push    ds                      ; Save ds on stack
55:             mov     ax, 02505h              ; Set interrupt 5 vector
56:             mov     dx, [oldOfs]            ; To this offset and
57:             mov     ds, [oldSeg]            ; This segment
58:             int     21h                     ; Call DOS
59:             pop     ds                      ; Restore ds
60:
61:             mov     ah, 04Ch                ; DOS function: Exit program
62:             mov     al, [exitCode]          ; Return exit code value
63:             int     21h                     ; Call DOS. Terminate program
64:
65:     ;----- Interrupt 5 service routine: Abort program
66:
67:     PROC    Int5ISR
68:             mov     ax, @data               ; Reset ds and es just
69:             mov     ds, ax                  ; to be safe
70:             mov     es, ax
71:             mov     di, offset errorMsg     ; Address error message
72:             call    StrWrite                ; Display message
73:             call    NewLine
74:             jmp     Exit                    ; Exit program
```

```
75:     ENDP    Int5ISR
76:
77:             END     Start           ; End of program / entry point
```

How BOUND286.ASM Works

Most of BOUND286.ASM is concerned with changing and restoring the vector to interrupt 5, a subject covered in chapter 10. The ISR at lines 67–75 is a little different from normal. Instead of preserving and restoring registers as is usually required, the code simply initializes ds and es (unnecessary, perhaps, but a good idea anyway) and, after displaying an error message, jumps to the program's Exit label, halting execution if bound detects an error.

Lines 46–47 demonstrate bound. Register bx is loaded with the index value to check. Change the 2 to 150 (or any other legal index in the range 100–199). When you run the program, you'll receive a different message, proving that the ISR for interrupt 5 was not activated.

Lines 16–17 store the low and high index range values tested by bound. These two values must be together in memory and in the order shown here. Although line 47 uses simple direct addressing to locate these values, you can also use other addressing modes with bound (see chapter 4).

Using enter and leave

The enter and leave instructions are useful for preparing procedure stack frames, allocating and reclaiming stack space for local variables in subroutines. Such variables are dynamic—existing only for as long as the procedure runs. These methods are usually employed by high-level languages as part of their procedure and function implementation methods, but you can use the instructions in pure assembly code if you want. (See chapters 12 and 13 for more information on addressing local stack variables.)

Use enter as the first instruction in a procedure. Enter takes two operands, both of which must be literal numbers. (The operands can be expressions or equates as long as the result is a literal number.) The first operand represents the number of bytes to reserve on the stack. The second operand represents the procedure's nesting level. If three procedures nest inside each other, the innermost procedure is at level 2, the middle procedure is at level 1, and the outer procedure is at level 0. Nesting levels are provided mostly to handle languages such as Pascal, which allow nested (child) procedures to access local variables declared in outer (parent) procedures.

When enter executes, it performs the work of three 8086 instructions:

```
push    bp              ; Save current bp
mov     bp, sp          ; Assign stack pointer to bp
sub     sp, n           ; Allocate stack space for variables
```

First, bp is pushed onto the stack, preserving its current value. Then the stack pointer sp is assigned to bp, allowing instructions to use this register to address the procedure's local variables. Space for the variables is then allocated by subtracting the value of enter's first parameter n from the stack pointer.

In any procedure that uses enter, execute leave just before ret to reclaim the stack space allocated by enter and to restore sp and bp. The leave instruction performs the same jobs as these two 8086 instructions:

```
mov     sp, bp          ; Restore stack pointer from bp
pop     bp              ; Restore saved bp
```

Copying bp to sp reclaims any space allocated on the stack before restoring the saved value of bp, which may be used by other procedures to address their own local variables. As an example of a complete procedure that uses enter and leave, here's a sample subroutine that allocates space for four word variables on the stack:

```
PROC AnyProc
        enter   8, 0            ; Reserve 8 bytes on stack
        mov     [word bp - 0], 4 ; Assign 4 to v1
        mov     [word bp - 2], 3 ; Assign 3 to v2
        mov     [word bp - 4], 2 ; Assign 2 to v3
        mov     [word bp - 6], 1 ; Assign 1 to v4
        leave                   ; Reclaim reserved stack space
        ret                     ; Return to caller
ENDP AnyProc
```

The enter instruction reserves 8 bytes of stack space—room for four word variables. The instruction also prepares bp to address the variables, as illustrated by several mov instructions. The first word is at [bp − 0], the second is at [bp − 2], and so on. In place of word, you can specify byte, dword, and other qualifiers to address data of different sizes. The leave instruction reclaims the stack space used by the local variables (also destroying their values in the process) and restores sp and bp, preparing for the ret instruction.

Using pusha and popa

Two instructions push and pop all general-purpose registers, usually at the beginning and end of an interrupt service routine, although you might use the instructions in procedures, too. Execute pusha to push registers ax, cx, dx, bx, sp, bp, si, and di in that order. Notice that the stack pointer is also pushed. But the value copied to the stack for sp equals the value of sp *before* executing pusha.

The complementary instruction popa removes all general-purpose registers from the stack. Executing popa (usually after a previous pusha) pops registers di, si, bp, sp, bx, dx, cx, and ax in that order. Technically, the value for sp is discarded because, if popa actually restored sp before popping the remaining di, si, and bp, these registers would receive the wrong values and the stack would shrink by three words too many. The effect of popa is just what you probably expect: All general-purpose registers are restored to the values they had before the most recent pusha.

Note: Segment registers are not saved and restored by **pusha** and **popa**.

Reading and Writing Port Strings

The two 80286 string instructions ins and outs read and write strings at hardware ports specified by dx. These instructions and their shorthand forms (see Table 11-5) operate similarly to other string instructions. In the case of ins, registers es:di address an area where the string data is to be stored. Executing `ins` reads one byte or word from the specified port, storing the data at `es:di`. If `df = 0`, then `di` is incremented by 1 for bytes or by 2 for words. If `df = 1`, then `di` is decremented by like amounts. Usually, `ins` is prefaced by the `rep` prefix and a count in `cx` to load multiple bytes and words with code such as:

```
DATASEG
string   db  80 dup (?)
strlen   =   $ - string
CODESEG
P286N
mov      dx, port number        ; Assign port number to dx
mov      ax, SEG string         ; Address segment containing
mov      es, ax                 ;  string with es
ASSUME   es:SEG string          ; Tell tasm where es points
mov      di, offset string      ; Address string with es:di
mov      cx, strlen             ; Assign repeat count to cx
cld                             ; Auto-increment di
rep      insb                   ; Load string bytes from port
```

To complete this example, you must load an actual port number into `dx`. Even then you may not be able to run this code unless your system has a port from which you can read strings. (Most PCs don't.) Still, this demonstrates how to use `insb` for peripherals or custom systems with the appropriate hardware.

You can use similar code to write strings to output ports. With the `outs` instruction, the port number is in `dx`, and `ds:si` addresses the source string data. Or you can use an override to address strings with `es` as in:

```
cld
rep      outs    dx, [byte es:si]        ; Output string to port
```

Usually, `outs` is used as in this sample with a repeat prefix and a count in `cx` to send multiple bytes and words to hardware ports. If `df = 0`, then `si` is incremented by 1 for bytes or by 2 for words. If `df = 1`, then `si` is decremented by like amounts.

Immediate Shift and Rotate Values

A subtle improvement in 80286 instructions is the ability to specify immediate shift and rotate values greater than 1. This means that the 8086 instructions:

```
mov      cl, 4           ; Assign shift count to cl
shl      ax, cl          ; Shift ax left four times
```

can be simplified to:

```
shl      ax, 4
```

This same change applies to all 8086 shift and rotate instructions. You can still specify a shift count in `cl` if necessary.

Programming the 80386

If your system has an 80386 processor, you have all of the 8086 and 80286 instructions at your disposal—plus the advantage of extra speedy processing, as you no doubt already know. As with the 80286, the 80386 has protected- and non-protected-mode instructions. With few exceptions, the protected-mode instructions are identical to those in the 80286. (See Table 14-1.) In addition to running in protected and non-protected modes, the 80386 includes a third mode for running programs in a *virtual 8086 machine*. Such advanced programming techniques are the realm of multi-tasking software such as Xenix and, perhaps someday, OS/2. As mentioned earlier, Turbo Debugger can run programs in this mode for better control over system crashes, accesses to restricted memory locations, and so on. There isn't room here to describe how to write operating system software, but the good news is that if you stick to 8086 instructions, no matter what mode the 80386 is in, your programs will run.

If you are certain your program will be executed on an 80386, you can take advantage of several additional instructions listed in Table 11-6.

Starting to Program the 80386   Figure 11-3 (page 452) illustrates the 80386 32-bit registers and flags. Notice that all the 8086 registers are available but are extended to a full 32-bit width. Segment registers are identical, although there are two more (fs and gs). You can use the extended registers with most 8086-type instructions. For example, to clear the 32-bit accumulator, write:

```
P386N
xor     eax, eax
```

To enable 80386 instructions, use the P386N (non-protected mode) or P386 (all modes) directives. You can do this on any system—you don't have to have an 80386 to assemble and link your program. Of course, you must have an 80386 to run the resulting code.

Many of the instructions in Table 11-6 are 32-bit variations of the similar 8086 instructions you already know how to use. For example, cmpsd works identically to cmps (Compare Strings) but adds the ability to compare doubleword values in addition to the usual bytes and words. Similarly, insd, lodsd, movsd, outsd, scasd, and stosd add doubleword abilities to the 8086 string instructions lods, movs, and scas plus the 80286 instructions ins and outs. Other instructions use 32-bit extended registers to perform operations similar to those available on the 8086 and 80286. There are also a few newcomers, as described in the following sections.

> Note: For more details on all the instructions in Table 11-6, please refer to chapter 14.

Scanning and Setting Bits   Use the bsf (Bit Scan Forward) and bsr (Bit Scan Reverse) to load a register with the position number of the first 1 bit found in a byte, word, or doubleword. Forward scans go from the LSD (bit 0) to the MSD; reverse scans

Table 11-6 *80386 Instructions (Non-Protected-Mode)*

Mnemonic/Operands	Description
bsf *destination, source*	Bit scan forward
bsr *destination, source*	Bit scan reverse
bt *destination, source*	Bit test
btc *destination, source*	Bit test and complement
btr *destination, source*	Bit test and reset
bts *destination, source*	Bit test and set
cdq	Convert doubleword to quadword
cmpsd	Compare string doublewords
cwde	Convert word to extended doubleword
insd	Input string doublewords
lfs *destination, source*	Load pointer and fs
lgs *destination, source*	Load pointer and gs
lss *destination, source*	Load pointer and ss
lodsd	Load string doublewords
movsd	Move string doublewords
movsx *destination, source*	Move and extend sign
movzx *destination, source*	Move and extend zero sign
outsd	Output string doublewords
popad	Pop all 32-bit registers
popfd	Pop all 32-bit flags
pushad	Push all 32-bit registers
pushfd	Push all 32-bit flags
scasd	Scan string doublewords
set *condition*	Set byte conditionally
shld *destination, source, count*	Double-precision shift left
shrd *destination, source, count*	Double-precision shift right
stosd	Store string doublewords

go the other way, from the MSD to the LSD. If no 1 bits are found, zf is set to 0. One way to use the instructions is to set cl to the number of bits required to shift a single bit to the LSD position. For example:

```
P386N
mov bx, 00100000b        ; Set bit 5 to 1
xor cl, cl               ; Zero cl in case all bits = 0
bsf cx, bx               ; Scan from bit 0 to 15
shr bx, cl               ; Shift bit into LSD position
@@10:
```

In this sample, the value to test is in bx, shown here in binary for clarity. Bit number 5 in the value equals 1; therefore, the bsf instruction sets cx to 5. After this, shr shifts bx to move the single bit to the LSD position. In this case, both bsf and bsr produce the identical results. But consider the case where more than one bit equals 1:

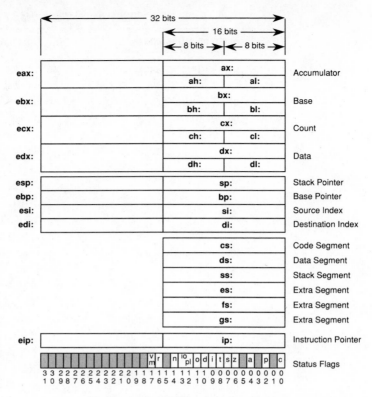

Figure 11-3 *80386 registers and flags.*

```
P386N
mov bx, 00010110b      ; Set bits 1, 2, and 4
bsf cx, bx             ; Sets cx to 1
bsr cx, bx             ; Sets cx to 4
```

The `bsf` instruction locates the first 1 bit starting from bit 0, thus setting `cx` to 1. The `bsr` instruction scans in the other direction, setting `cx` to 4—the position of the first 1 bit from the MSD in `bx`.

Testing Bits   The `bt`, `btc`, `btr`, and `bts` instructions all do similar but slightly different jobs. Each instruction takes two operands. The operands may each be a 16- or 32-bit register; the second operand may also be an immediate value. Whatever its form, the second operand represents the bit number to copy from the first operand to the carry flag. For example, this sets `cf` to 1:

```
mov dx, 00100000b      ; Set bit 5 to 1
bt  dx, 5              ; Copy bit 5 to cf
```

The other three instructions work exactly the same way but have different effects on the bit in the original value after copying the bit to `cf`. The `btc` instruction complements (toggles) the original bit; `btr` resets the original bit to 0; and `bts` sets the bit to 1. A few examples help make this clear:

```
mov dx, 01010011b            ; Assign initial value to dx
btc dx, 7                    ; cf = 0; dx = 11010011 (bit 7 <- 0)
btr dx, 0                    ; cf = 1; dx = 11010010 (bit 1 <- 0)
bts dx, 3                    ; cf = 0; dx = 11011010 (bit 3 <- 1)
```

The btc instruction in this sample copies bit 7 of dx to cf and complements the original bit in dx. The btr instruction copies bit 0 to cf and then resets that bit to 0. The bts instruction copies bit 3 to cf and then sets that bit to 1.

More Conversions

In addition to cbw, which converts bytes to words, and cwd, which converts words to doublewords, you can use cdq to convert 32-bit doublewords to 64-bit quadwords and cwde to convert words to doublewords in the extended accumulator eax. These instructions are useful when working with signed integers of different sizes. A simple example explains how to use the new 80386 additions:

```
mov     ax, -3 ; Set ax to -3 (ax = 0FFFDh)
cwde           ; Sets eax to -3 (eax = 0FFFF FFFDh)
cdq            ; Sets edx:eax to -3 (edx = 0FFFF FFFFh;
               ;                     eax = 0FFFF FFFDh)
```

The 16-bit value in ax (−3) is converted to the full 32-bit width of the extended accumulator eax by cwde. This value is then further extended into two registers edx and eax. In all cases, register assignments are fixed as shown here—you can only extend values in ax to eax and edx. You can't extend values in other general-purpose registers.

Other 80386 Instructions

You can load pointers into general-purpose registers plus the two additional segment registers fs and gs with lfs and lgs. A third instruction lss lets you initialize ss and sp. These operate identically to les and lds but load segment values into the specified segment registers. For example:

```
DATASEG
ptr48     dw      1, 2, 3
CODESEG
P386N
lfs     ebx, [pword ptr48]      ; Loads ptr48 into fs:ebx
lgs     edi, [pword ptr48]      ; Loads ptr48 into gs:edi
;lss    esp, [pword ptr48]      ; Loads ptr48 into ss:esp
```

Notice the pword qualifier to the memory reference in the second operand of each instruction. This tells Turbo Assembler that the variable, declared here with a multipart dw directive, is really a 48-bit pointer (16-bit segment and 32-bit offset). The lfs instruction sets ebx to 00020001h and fs to 0003h, picking up these values at label ptr48 in the data segment. Similarly, the lgs instruction sets edi to 00020001h and gs to 0003h. The lss instruction sets ss and esp to similar values but probably also crashes the system. For this reason, the lss instruction is shown here as a comment. You must exercise great care when using lss to change the stack segment and pointer.

Other useful 80386 instructions include two move commands `movsx` and `movzx`. Use these to assign signed and unsigned values from small registers or memory variables to larger registers. With both instructions, the first operand must be a 16- or 32-bit extended register. The second operand may be an 8- or 16-bit register or memory reference. For example, if you have a signed 8-bit value in `bl`, you can transfer the value to a 16-bit register `dx` with:

```
mov     bl, -7          ; Initialize bl to -7 (8 bits)
movsx   dx, bl          ; Sets dx to -7 (16 bits)
```

Or you can copy a 16-bit value to a 32-bit register with:

```
mov     dx, -8          ; Initialize dx to -8 (16 bits)
movsx   eax, dx         ; Sets eax to -8 (32 bits)
```

Use `movzx` to do the same, but with unsigned values. For example:

```
mov     bl, 255         ; Initialize bl to 255 (8 bits)
movzx   ax, bl          ; Set ax to 255 (16 bits)
mov     bx, 25890       ; Initialize bx to 25,890 (16 bits)
movzx   eax, bx         ; Set eax to 25,890 (32 bits)
```

Similar to the 80286 `pusha` and `popa` instructions, use `pushad` and `popad` to push and pop all 80386 general-purpose extended (doubleword) registers. Execute `pushad` to push registers `eax, ecx, edx, ebx, esp, ebp, esi,` and `edi` in that order. The value pushed for `esp` equals the value of the stack pointer *before* executing `pushad`. Execute `popad` to remove these same registers from the stack in this order: `edi, esi, ebp, esp, ebx, edx, ecx,` and `eax`. The value for `esp` is discarded, although `esp` is still restored to the same value it had prior to `pushad`.

One other instruction `set-condition` is similar to a conditional jump. The effect, however, is to set a byte register or memory value to 1 or 0 depending on whether the specified condition is satisfied. For instance:

```
cmp     ax, 1
sete    bh
```

sets `bh` to 1 only if `ax` equals 1. The endings to `set` are the same as for the conditional jump instructions: `setb, seta, setz, setnle,` and so on. See `set-condition` in chapter 14 for a complete list of mnemonics and flag settings tested by this instruction.

Double-Precision Shifts

The last two 80386 instructions to cover are `shld` and `shrd`, which take an unusual three operands. In most cases, when you need to shift 32-bit registers, you can just use the 8086 shift and rotate instructions such as `shr` and `rcr`, specifying an extended register as in:

```
mov     eax, 4          ; Initialize eax to 4 (32 bits)
shl     eax, 3          ; Multiply eax by 8
```

The doubleword shift instructions operate a bit differently. The first operand to `shld` and `shrd` specifies the destination and may be a word or doubleword register or memory reference. The second operand, which must be a word or doubleword register, holds the bits to be shifted into the first operand. The third operand represents the number of bits to be shifted in the indicated direction (right for `shrd` and left for `shld`). This operand may be an immediate value 0 to 31 or the register `cl`. For example:

```
shld    eax, ebx, 4      ; Shift first 4 bits of ebx -> eax
```

shifts 4 bits from `ebx` into `eax`. The value in `ebx` does not change. Loops with `shld` or `shrd` instructions are especially useful for performing multiple-precision shifts on very large values. For a more complete example of how this works, see the sample code in chapter 14 for `shld`.

Summary

Binary-coded-decimal values store 20-digit numbers in a format that's easy to convert to and from ASCII characters. Packed BCDs store 2 digits per byte. Unpacked BCDs store 1 digit per byte. The `dt` directive creates 20-digit packed BCD variables. Although there is no similar directive to create unpacked BCD variables, `db` is an adequate substitute.

The `aaa` and `aas` instructions adjust binary results after adding and subtracting unpacked BCD values back to unpacked BCD format. The `aad` and `aam` instructions convert between binary and unpacked BCD values. Despite the suggestive names of these two instructions, they don't have to be used in conjunction with division and multiplication. Converting unpacked BCDs to and from ASCII takes only a simple `and` or `or` instruction because of the ASCII encoding scheme used for digits 0–9. The `daa` and `das` instructions adjust binary results after adding and subtracting packed BCD values back to packed BCD format.

Communal variables, which can't be assigned initial values, are declared with the `COMM` directive. Unfortunately, Turbo Linker can't link programs with communal variables—at least not yet. Similar to communal variables, global variables declared with the `GLOBAL` directive can have initial values and can be shared among multiple modules. `GLOBAL` eliminates the need to declare variables `PUBLIC` in one module and `EXTRN` in others—just put all your global declarations in one or two files and assemble and link your application using `INCLUDE` directives to load global definitions into individual modules. In large projects, you may also want to specify a default library file with the `INCLUDELIB` directive, which simplifies linking.

Use `xlat` to translate byte index values to bytes stored in table form in memory. This can save time because looking up values in memory is usually faster than performing complex calculations. A typical use for `xlat` is to translate ASCII codes to other symbols. The instruction can also be used (often along with `lea`) to select values from two-dimensional matrixes.

Simplified memory models take care of many details that you must specify yourself when declaring segments "the hard way" with the `SEGMENT` directive. A typical .EXE program needs at least three such segments—one for data, one for code, and one for the stack. Various rules and naming conventions change the way Turbo Assembler and Linker organize your program and load segments into memory, combining some segments into units and leaving others separate.

When declaring your own segments, you must initialize segment registers, remembering always that such assignments occur at run time. Use the ASSUME directive, which operates at assembly time, to tell Turbo Assembler about the segment register assignments your program makes. Another related directive GROUP collects multiple segments of different names and, perhaps, different classes into one large segment up to 64K long.

By declaring segments with a *combine* type equal to *At*, you create a phantom segment that's overlayed on variables or code already existing in memory when your program runs. This gives you a way to read and write variables—and call or jump to procedures—that belong to other processes such as the ROM BIOS.

When you need additional space for variables, you can attach one or more far data segments to a simpified memory model. Far data segments can be initialized or uninitialized and, with an optional name after the FARDATA and UFARDATA directives, can reserve multiple chunks of 64K memory for use by even "small" memory-model programs.

The 80286 processor adds several new instructions to the basic 8086 set of mnemonics. The 80386 adds even more instructions plus extended 32-bit registers, flags, and two more segment registers. Although Turbo Assembler can assemble code for these processors on any system, the results run only on computers with the appropriate hardware.

Exercises

11-1. How many digits would there be in a hypothetical packed 4-byte BCD value? How many digits would there be in a hypothetical unpacked 6-byte BCD value? How many BCD digits does the dt directive allow you to specify in a value?

11-2. Write code to convert a packed BCD byte in register al to binary in register ax.

11-3. What GLOBAL directives do you need to share the following variables among multiple modules?

```
string   db      'This is an ASCIIZ string,' 0
count    dw      0
BCD      dt      123456789
```

11-4. Using xlat, write code to translate a value in cl to the following values (equal to the cubes of 0–6):

```
cl        cl*cl*cl
--------------------
0         0
1         1
2         8
3         27
4         64
5         125
6         216
```

11-5. What does ASSUME do?

11-6. Declare a data segment named MoreData aligned to the next highest 256-byte page and combined with other segments of the class 'DATA'. Store a word variable named MyWord in your segment and show the necessary code required to load ax with the value of MyWord.

11-7. What does GROUP do? How would you use GROUP to refer to the four segments SomeData, MoreData, TableSeg, and StringSeg.

11-8. The PC KbFlag (keyboard flag) byte is stored at offset 017h in the BIOS data segment at 040h. Bit 6 of this value indicates whether the CapsLock key is on (1) or off (0). Write a program to display the current setting of this key. Use an absolute *At* data segment in your answer.

11-9. Write an 80286 interrupt service routine shell that saves and restores all general-purpose registers.

11-10. Write the equivalent 8086 code to duplicate the following 80386 instructions:

```
bt       dx, 3
btc      dx, 12
btr      dx, 8
bts      dx, 1
```

Projects

11-1. Add multiplication and division procedures to BCD.ASM. Hint: Unpack packed BCD variables and use aad and aam to convert values to and from binary.

11-2. Write ASCIIZ string-formatting commands to add decimal points and dollar signs and (optionally) to strip leading zeros from packed BCD values. Hint: Use the BCDToASCII procedure in BCD.ASM to perform the raw conversion from BCD to ASCII digits, then use STRINGS procedures to insert and delete characters.

11-3. Using a PC technical reference (see Bibliography), write an include file that defines an absolute (*At*) data segment for all or most ROM BIOS variables.

11-4. Develop a set of macros to assemble programs with 8086, 80286, and 80386 instructions based on a conditional symbol assigned at the beginning of a module. Duplicate as many special 80286 and 80386 instructions as you can, using only 8086 instructions.

11-5. Hunt for program examples in this book that might be improved by assembling with special 80286 and 80386 instructions. Use your macros from project #11-4 to reassemble the code and run time trials to test your assumptions.

11-6. Write a module that allows you to program various function key presses into other key strokes with the xlat command. Design the module so that you can reprogram the command keys in a program.

II Multilanguage Programming

12 Optimizing Pascal with Assembly Language

12 Optimizing Pascal with Assembly Language

In This Chapter

Why even fast compilers like Turbo Pascal can benefit from a little assembly language; how to organize your disks to compile and assemble programs; when and when not to convert Pascal to assembly language; identifying the critical code; three ways to add assembly language to Pascal programs; writing external procedures and functions; Pascal memory model; static variables; calling external routines from Pascal; calling Pascal routines from assembly language; examples of most data- and code-sharing problems; storing initialized data in the code segment; function results; addressing Pascal variables; parameter passing; the TPASCAL memory model; using the ARG directive; external string functions; plus optimizing a sample Pascal program with assembly language

Room for Improvement

In an ideal programming world, high-level language compilers would generate the fastest, smallest, and best machine code for any program design. If that were possible, there would be no need for this chapter—perhaps no need for this book. But it's not possible. Despite many improvements in compiler design, no high-level language is yet able to duplicate the tight, fast, clever code written by an experienced assembly language expert.

Why should this be? A probable answer is: because compilers generalize the tasks they perform. There's only one way to write a FOR loop in Pascal, but there are dozens of ways to implement that same FOR loop in assembly language. For a compiler to choose the ideal implementation method in every situation—and consider every consequence on other sections of the program—the compiler would need the intellect of a genius, the understanding of an artist, and the intuition of a fortune teller. Today's high-level language compilers are smart, but they aren't that smart.

Of all the Pascal compilers available, Turbo Pascal comes the closest to reaching the ideal. Turbo's compiled machine code runs fast, takes up little disk space, and can be used without modification in many cases. However, as good as Turbo Pascal is, there's still room for improvement, and a little assembly language sprinkled here and there can remarkably improve program speed and reduce code-file size. Also, adding assembly language to Pascal can make it easier to access hardware registers and perform other low-level tasks such as writing characters directly to video memory.

Note: This chapter assumes that you have some familiarity with Turbo Pascal and that you know how to run the Pascal compiler.

Suggested Disk Organization

The first step in adding assembly language to Pascal is to organize your disk for easy access to the files and subdirectories required by both Turbo Assembler and Turbo Pascal. If you have a hard disk, this is simple—just install the two languages in separate subdirectories, probably C:\TPAS and C:\TASM. If you have floppy disk drives, it's probably best to create separate disks for Pascal and assembly language. With this setup, you'll have to compile and assemble pieces of programs separately and then link the pieces manually. With a hard disk drive, you can use the MAKE utility program to automate these steps.

Note: The identical MAKE.EXE program is supplied on the Turbo Pascal and Assembler disks. Because Borland might update this program in future versions, however, you should use the copy of MAKE with the most recent file date and time.

The next step is to add the subdirectory file names to a PATH command in your AUTOEXEC.BAT file. This lets you change to a directory containing Pascal and assembly language program source files but still be able to run the compiler and assembler. Assuming you also have a common directory named DOS for miscellaneous utilities, you could insert this line into AUTOEXEC.BAT:

```
PATH=C:\DOS;C:\TASM;C:\TPAS;C:\TDEBUG
```

After rebooting, you can then change to another directory with the CD command and run Turbo Assembler, Turbo Pascal, and Turbo Debugger as though these programs were all in the same directory. As a result, MAKE can assemble .ASM files and compile .PAS files automatically. All you have to do is tell MAKE which code files depend on which other files that if changed require reassembling, relinking, or recompiling. Later in this chapter are examples of how to create such MAKE files.

**To Assemble or
Not to Assemble**

Even more important than knowing how to add assembly language to Pascal is knowing when to do so—and when not. Always keep in mind that, by writing a portion of a program in assembly language, you'll have to rewrite that same code from scratch if you later need to transfer the program to a non-8086 computer. To reduce future headaches, it helps to follow a few simple guidelines:

▶ Convert only critical code to assembly language

▶ Leave noncritical sections in pure Pascal

▶ Write procedures in Pascal first, then recode in assembly language

Critical code refers to those sections of a program that bear more than their fair share of the total execution time. In most programs, a few procedures, functions, and loops always execute more frequently than others. Because these critical procedures account for the major share of a program's running time, rewriting the instructions in assembly language can dramatically improve a program's performance. In fact, many experts agree that most programs spend about 90% of their total operating time executing about 10% of the instructions in the entire program; therefore, a small improvement in the critical-code sections can have a major impact on program speed.

Conversely, recoding the other 90% of the instructions into assembly language may produce less dramatic results. In fact, the amount of actual improvement can be zero. For example, you probably shouldn't rewrite a simple prompt that lets someone type in a file name. People can type only so fast and, even if the code runs more efficiently, the perceived benefit will be nil. Don't waste your time rewriting sections of a program that already operate as quickly as necessary.

Identifying Critical Code

Identifying the critical 10% of a program is not always easy. In some cases, your experience with the program will tell you which sections need to be redone. For instance, you may know that a certain display is not coming on screen with the snap, crackle, and pop that you know the computer is capable of producing. In other cases, your experience with Pascal will tell you that certain operations—for example, direct access to hardware ports—will probably run faster in assembly language.

At other times the choices are not as obvious, and you may need to purchase a *profiler* program to help locate the critical code areas. The profiler monitors a running program and builds tables of statistics that identify the instructions that execute more frequently than others. After profiling a program, you can then begin recoding these sections in assembly language, leaving the other less critical code in Pascal. This approach to program optimization helps reduce programming time and promises dramatic improvements in performance.

Even with the help of a profiler, it's easy to lose sight of your objective and end up revising far too much code. Remember that your aim is to identify the critical sections and then convert these sections to assembly language. While doing this, you should also be continually testing and retesting the program, observing the results of your work. You'll find the going easier if you:

- ▶ Don't profile programs that use overlays
- ▶ Do use a variety of sampling rates
- ▶ Don't optimize large programs in pieces

In large programs that use overlays to conserve memory by loading independent code sections into the same areas of RAM, it's probably best to optimize the overlays as though they were individual programs. Most programmers develop large systems by first writing the overlays as stand-alone programs rather than waste time compiling and linking other sections already completed. The final program code is constructed as one of the last steps before production. Following this approach makes optimization easier. You can simply profile the individual overlays before they are combined into the finished program. You many want to consider using this method for your next large program.

The *sample rate* refers to how frequently the profiler monitors a running program. The IBM PC's internal clock, ticking away at 18.2 times per second, is too slow to produce a useful profile because too many instructions are likely to execute in 1/18 second—practically an eon to a computer. For this reason, some profilers reprogram the internal clock to achieve sampling rates of between 40 and 30,000 samples per second. Finding the correct sampling rate can be tough; therefore, it's a good idea to profile the same program using at least three rates such as 500, 1,000, and 2,000.

Never attempt to profile and optimize a large program all at once. If your Pascal program is larger than about 10,000 lines, you'll need to devise a plan for optimizing the program one section at a time. One possibility is to profile the overlays separately. Or your profiler may allow you to insert commands into your source code to limit monitoring to specific areas.

Converting Pascal to Assembly Language

After locating the critical code in a Pascal program, you're ready to begin converting the Pascal statements to assembly language. At this point, you have three methods at your disposal:

- ▶ InLine statements
- ▶ InLine procedures and functions
- ▶ External procedures and functions

InLine statements are actually commands to the Pascal compiler to inject machine language instructions directly into the code that the compiler normally generates. Suppose, for example, that you want to disable interrupts. Because there's no Pascal statement to do this directly, an InLine statement inserts the code for the 8086 cli instruction into the compiled output:

```
InLine( $FA );              { cli -- disable interrupts }
:
{ statements to execute with interrupts disabled }
:
InLine( $FB );              { sti -- enable interrupts again }
```

Usually, InLine statements are most useful for inserting a limited number of machine-code instructions. Because you have to use machine-code values, InLine statements are inconvenient for converting larger Pascal sections into assembly language.

> Note: A good way to obtain the machine-code binary values for various instructions is to write a small assembly language program and then execute the assembled code in Turbo Debugger. Use the View/CPU command and copy the bytes to InLine statements, perhaps using a pop-up utility such as Borland's SideKick to cut the hex values out of Turbo Debugger's display, transferring that text directly to your Pascal program.

The second method is to use an InLine procedure or function. These devices operate much like assembly language macros, inserting machine code into a program where the name of the procedure or function appears. Early in the Pascal program, you declare such procedures like this:

```
PROCEDURE ClrInt; InLine( $FA );
PROCEDURE SetInt; InLine( $FB );
```

Functions are declared similarly. The effect is to associate the machine-code bytes in the InLine statements with the procedure identifiers ClrInt and SetInt. Later on, when you use these identifiers, the Pascal compiler inserts the machine code directly into the compiled code. You might, for example, use statements such as:

```
ClrInt;
Writeln( 'Interrupts are off' );
SetInt;
Writeln( 'Interrupts are on' );
```

The advantage of this method is the machine language is hidden. Although it appears as if procedure calls are made to ClrInt and SetInt, the compiler actually inserts machine language directly into the code stream. This improves the program's portability by isolating the machine language to one place in the program source code. For another system, you can easily convert the code by replacing the InLine procedures with real Pascal procedures. This is far preferable than having to hunt through a program to locate all the InLine statements sprinkled throughout.

> Note: The previous InLine examples are similar to those in chapter 14 of my book, *Mastering Turbo Pascal*, which includes more details on using these Pascal assembly language tools.

External Procedures and Functions

Although it requires more organizational effort, writing external assembly language procedures and functions that you assemble separately from the Pascal source code is usually the best method. There are several reasons why this is so:

▶ The Pascal program retains a higher degree of portability

▶ External routines can be debugged separately

▶ External routines can be used with other languages

If you write your programs purely in Pascal and then selectively convert individual procedures and functions, you will improve your program's portability. After optimizing, if you need to transfer a program to another computer—for example, a Macintosh with a 68000 processor—it's relatively simple to replace the optimized assembly language modules with the original Pascal code that you wisely saved on disk. Then, after the program is working correctly on the new computer, you would start optimizing sections of the code in that computer's native tongue.

Another advantage of using external assembly language routines is to simplify debugging. In most cases, you can write simple test programs (either in Pascal or in assembly language) to put your code through its paces. The same code might also be usable with other languages such as C or BASIC. Many programmers build a library of such routines, ready to insert into their high-level programs.

> Note: Subroutine-calling conventions and memory models differ among languages; therefore, you can't always use the same external routines without making some changes. Even so, external assembly language code is easier to revise for this purpose than direct **InLine** injections.

Calling External Routines from Pascal

To add external assembly language procedures to Pascal, you'll need to perform these steps:

▶ Write a **NEAR** or **FAR** assembly language **PROC**

▶ Declare the **PROC PUBLIC**, exporting the external procedure's label to Pascal

▶ Use the {**$L** <file>} Pascal compiler command to load the assembled .OBJ module from disk during compilation

▶ Declare the procedure **EXTERNAL** in Pascal

The assembly language procedure has the same format as in other stand-alone object-code modules in this book. Be careful to declare the procedure as **NEAR** or **FAR** so that Pascal knows whether to make a long (other segment) or short (same segment) call to the procedure code. (Procedures are **NEAR** by default.) Also, so that Pascal can locate the start of the procedure code in the .OBJ module, you must place the procedure name in a **PUBLIC** statement. The general format is:

```
PUBLIC  ProcName
PROC    ProcName NEAR
:
;----- Code in procedure
:
        ret             ; Return to caller
ENDP    ProcName
```

Change NEAR to FAR for a far (other segment) procedure. In the Pascal program, use the {$L <file>} compiler command to load the assembled object code during compilation. Also, declare the procedure in a Pascal EXTERNAL declaration, which tells the compiler the name of the procedure plus the names, numbers, and types of any parameters. In Pascal, assuming the module is named MYCODE.OBJ, you would use these lines:

```
{$L MYCODE.OBJ}
PROCEDURE ProcName; EXTERNAL;
```

In this example, ProcName has no parameters. If it did, you would declare them here. (I'll cover parameter passing later in this chapter.) After completing these steps, you're ready to call the external procedure. To do this, just use the procedure name (ProcName here) as a statement—exactly the way you call other Pascal procedures. You can also declare external functions, as later examples demonstrate. Upon reading the {$L} directive, Turbo Pascal automatically combines the external code in the .OBJ file into the final .EXE file on disk (or into memory if you are using the integrated Turbo Pascal compiler version). All you have to do is compile the program—there are no extra linking steps to perform.

The Pascal Memory Model

Although the foregoing describes the necessary elements to write an external assembly language procedure for a Pascal program, one important element is missing: the format of the assembly language source text. Unfortunately, the format used in most programs in this book won't work because Pascal has its own way of organizing memory. Instead, you must use one of two different models for the Pascal compiler to be able to combine the assembled object-code file with the compiled Pascal statements.

Program 12-1, PASSHELL.ASM, is a do-nothing shell that you can fill in with real code and data for your own Pascal external modules. As you can see, the shell declares data and code segments the hard way instead of using the simplified memory models of most other examples in this book. Following the listing, I'll explain why this is necessary.

Program 12-1 *PASSHELL.ASM*

```
 1:  %TITLE "Shell for Turbo Pascal .OBJ Modules"
 2:
 3:          IDEAL
 4:
 5:  SEGMENT DATA word public
 6:
 7:  ;-----  Insert EXTRN data declarations here
 8:
 9:  ;-----  Insert static (uninitialized) variables here
10:
11:  ENDS    DATA
12:
13:
14:  SEGMENT CODE byte public
15:
16:  ASSUME  cs:CODE, ds:DATA
17:
18:  ;-----  Insert PUBLIC code declarations here
19:
20:  ;-----  Insert EXTRN code declarations here
21:
22:
23:  %NEWPAGE
24:  ;----------------------------------------------------------------
25:  ; PROCEDURE ProcName( <parameters> );
26:  ;----------------------------------------------------------------
27:  PROC    ProcName        NEAR
28:          ret                     ; Return to caller
29:  ENDP    ProcName
30:
31:  %NEWPAGE
32:  ;----------------------------------------------------------------
33:  ; FUNCTION FuncName( <parameters> ) : <type>;
34:  ;----------------------------------------------------------------
35:  PROC    FuncName        NEAR
36:          ret                     ; Return to caller
37:  ENDP    FuncName
38:
39:  ENDS    CODE
40:
41:          END                     ; End of module
```

PASSHELL's DATA Segment

The PASSHELL listing declares data and code segments "the hard way," using SEGMENT directives instead of selecting a simplified memory model in a MODEL directive. Lines 5–11 declare a public data segment—aligned to even word addresses—so that Pascal can find the segment's beginning and end.

Note: Aligning the data segment on even addresses can improve access speed to 16-bit data. Specifying word alignment in the **SEGMENT** directive forces the first variable in the segment to be aligned at an even address, skipping a byte if necessary to make this happen. If you declare any byte variables in the data segment, however, you can throw the word alignment out of whack for subsequent variables. To avoid this, follow single-byte **db** directives with your own dummy-byte values, ensuring word alignment for all variables. This is necessary only in super time-critical code, however. For most programs, you can ignore the subtleties of segment alignment.

Inside the data segment, you can declare variables just as you can in any other assembly language module. There is one important difference: All variables must be *uninitialized*. In other words, these declarations will not work:

```
astring        db        15, 'A sample string'
counter        dw        100h
asciiEsc       db        27
```

Turbo Assembler accepts these declarations, but Turbo Pascal does not recognize the initialized data. This happens because the global data segment is a phantom in a compiled Pascal program, existing only when the program is executed; therefore, you can't declare preinitialized variables in the external module. Instead, you must use declarations such as:

```
astring        db        16 DUP (?)
counter        dw        ?
asciiEsc       db        ?
```

These commands allocate space for a 16-character string, a word, and a byte. When the program runs, the variables have no specific values, and it's up to you to figure out how to initialize them. Also, such variables are strictly for use in the assembly language module—you cannot export variable labels to Pascal. The reason for this restriction is that Pascal lacks an **EXTERNAL** directive that can be applied to variables. The **EXTERNAL** keyword in Pascal works only with procedures and functions. (There is a way to circumvent this problem, using a technique explained later in this chapter.)

Using Static Variables

You can get static, preinitialized variables into an assembly language module, but the method requires a little help from the Pascal compiler. Instead of using **db** and **dw** directives in the assembly language text, declare the variables in the Pascal program as *variable constants*. (Turbo Pascal's manual calls these *typed constants*.) For example, the Pascal program might include the lines:

```
CONST   astring : string[15] = 'A sample string';
        counter : integer = $100;
        asciiEsc: byte = 27;
```

Over in the assembly language data segment, you can import these Pascal constants in an `EXTRN` directive, telling Turbo Assembler that the actual addresses of the real data will be supplied later during compilation:

```
SEGMENT DATA word public
        EXTRN astring : BYTE, counter : WORD, asciiEsc : BYTE
ENDS    DATA
```

You can now use `astring`, `counter`, and `asciiEsc` as though these variables were declared directly in the assembly language module. Notice that a string in Pascal is a byte pointer in assembly language. It's still up to you to figure out ways to use variables of Pascal data types such as strings, records, and sets.

PASSHELL's CODE Segment

Lines 14–39 in PASSHELL declare the module's CODE segment, aligned to any address (`byte`) and made `PUBLIC` for the Pascal compiler. Line 16 uses an `ASSUME` directive to inform Turbo Assembler about the relation between segment registers `cs` and `ds` and the module's segments. Pascal places no restrictions on register `es`; therefore, no declaration for this register is needed. If you plan to address the data segment with `es`, you can change line 16 to:

```
ASSUME  cs:CODE, ds:DATA, es:DATA
```

Remember that the `ASSUME` directive merely tells the assembler about the module's organization—it does not generate any code or ensure that segment registers actually address specific segments. In particular, you must be careful to initialize `es`, which is not preserved between calls to internal Pascal routines. Pascal initializes `ds` to address the global data segment, of which there can be only one, up to 64K long. Consequently, you do not have to initialize `ds` in your module's code.

> Note: Pascal takes care of allocating space for the stack. Never declare stack space or reassign `ss` in your external modules.

Calling Pascal Procedures

Line 18 shows where to insert `PUBLIC` declarations. After the keyword `PUBLIC`, insert the names of all the procedures in the module that you want to export to Pascal. You don't have to list every procedure. For example, a module can have local subroutines for the private use of other procedures inside the module. But every name in the `PUBLIC` declaration must have a corresponding `EXTERNAL` procedure or function declaration in the Pascal text. Also, remember that only code, not data, can be declared public.

Line 20 shows where to insert `EXTRN` declarations. These refer to Pascal procedures and functions that you want to call from within your assembly language code. For example, suppose you have a Pascal routine named Pause, which displays a message and waits for you to press the Enter key:

```
PROCEDURE Pause;
BEGIN
   Writeln;
   Write( 'Press <Enter> to continue...' );
   Readln
END; { Pause }
```

To export Pause from Pascal to an assembly language module, you must be sure that the Pascal compiler knows the name of the procedure before it loads the assembled object code. One way to do this is to declare Pause FORWARD *before* the {$L <file>} directive that loads the file from disk. If the assembly language module is named ANYCODE.OBJ, you could use these Pascal statements near the beginning of the program:

```
PROCEDURE Pause; FORWARD;
{$L ANYCODE.OBJ}
```

To call Pause from within the external assembly language module, construct the CODE segment something like this:

```
SEGMENT CODE byte public
ASSUME  cs:CODE, ds:DATA
EXTRN   Pause:NEAR
PROC    MyProc  NEAR
        call    Pause           ; Call Pascal procedure
        ret
ENDP    MyProc
ENDS
```

The EXTRN directive tells Turbo Assembler that Pause is a near procedure (in the same code segment). If this is not so—for example, if in the Pascal text you used the {$F+} directive to turn on far-code generation or if the procedure is listed in the interface section of a unit—then you must declare Pause as FAR. The actual call to Pause is no different than calls to other assembly language subroutines. In this example, however, there are no parameters. If there were, you'd also have to pass the parameters in the exact way expected by the Pascal code—a subject we'll tackle in a moment.

The Code-Segment Body
Lines 24–37 in PASSHELL list empty shells for external procedures and functions. The only difference between a procedure and a function is that a function returns a value—a procedure does not. (In Pascal, functions are used in expressions, while procedures are called by name in statements.)

The final section in PASSHELL appears at lines 39–41. Because a simplified memory model is not used, the CODE segment must be terminated with an ENDS directive (line 39). The END at line 41 tells the assembler that this is the last line of the source text. You may not specify an entry point label after END, as you do for stand-alone assembly language .EXE programs.

A (Somewhat) Crazy Example

Program 12-2, PASDEMO.ASM, and Program 12-3, PASDEMO.PAS, will help answer many questions about how to pass code and data back and forth among Pascal and assembly language modules. The example is a little "crazy"—it doesn't perform any useful actions other than to demonstrate various subjects (discussed after the listings). Except for parameter passing, the program illustrates almost every combination of sharing code and data and will serve as a useful guide for your own projects. To assemble and compile the test, use these commands:

```
tasm /zi pasdemo
tpc /v pasdemo
```

The options /zi and /v add debugging information to PASDEMO.EXE so that Turbo Debugger can show you both the Pascal and assembly language source-code lines along with the assembled and compiled machine code. Another choice is to create a file named MAKEFILE containing these lines:

```
pasdemo.exe: pasdemo.obj pasdemo.pas
    tpc /v pasdemo

pasdemo.obj: pasdemo.asm
    tasm /zi pasdemo
```

With this text stored on disk in a file named MAKEFILE, type make to create PASDEMO.EXE. (If you name MAKEFILE something else, PASDEMO.MAK for example, type make -fpasdemo to create PASDEMO.EXE.) The MAKEFILE statements declare that PASDEMO.EXE depends on (is created from) PASDEMO.OBJ and PASDEMO.PAS. If either of these two files changes, then the tpc command compiles the Pascal program, combining this code with the assembled object code. The second part of MAKEFILE says that PASDEMO.OBJ depends on PASDEMO.ASM. If this file changes, then Turbo Assembler assembles PASDEMO.ASM, creating PASDEMO.OBJ (which also causes PASDEMO.PAS to be recompiled).

Program 12-2 *PASDEMO.ASM*

```
1:    %TITLE "Test Pascal External .OBJ Module"
2:
3:            IDEAL
4:
5:    ;----- Data segment combines with Pascal's global data segment
6:
```

```
 7:   SEGMENT DATA word public
 8:
 9:   ;----- Import typed constants and variables from Pascal
10:           EXTRN   value : WORD, cr : BYTE, lf : BYTE
11:
12:   asmCount        dw       ?          ; Static variable
13:
14:   ENDS    DATA
15:
16:
17:   ;----- Code segment combines with Pascal's main program
18:
19:   SEGMENT CODE byte public
20:
21:   ASSUME  cs:CODE, ds:DATA         ; Explain memory model to assembler
22:
23:   ;----- Export public procedures to Pascal
24:           PUBLIC  AsmProc, CountPtr
25:
26:   ;----- Import procedures and functions from Pascal
27:           EXTRN   PasProc : NEAR, PasFunc : NEAR
28:
29:
30:   ;--------------------------------------------------------------
31:   ; PROCEDURE asmProc;
32:   ;--------------------------------------------------------------
33:
34:   ;----- Preinitialized variables must go in the code segment
35:   testString      db       'asmProc: Should be a "hatch mark" --> ', '$'
36:
37:   PROC    AsmProc NEAR
38:
39:   ;----- Call a Pascal procedure
40:
41:           call    PasProc                  ; pasProc is in PASDEMO.PAS
42:
43:   ;----- Use local data stored in the code segment
44:
45:           push    ds                       ; Save Pascal's ds register
46:           push    cs                       ; Address code segment with
47:           pop     ds                       ;  register ds
48:   ASSUME  ds : CODE                        ; Inform assembler
49:           mov     dx, offset testString    ; Address the test string
50:           mov     ah, 09h                  ; Display the test string by
51:           int     21h                      ;  calling DOS function 9
52:           pop     ds                       ; Restore Pascal's ds register
53:   ASSUME  ds : DATA                        ; Inform assembler
54:
55:
```

```
56:    ;-----   Get typed-constants from Pascal and use local static variables
57:
58:            mov     ax, [value]              ; Get value from Pascal
59:            mov     [asmCount], ax           ; Initialize static variable
60:
61:
62:    ;-----   Call a Pascal function for a character value
63:
64:            call    PasFunc                  ; Get test char from Pascal
65:            mov     dl, al                   ; Assign char to dl
66:            mov     ah, 2                    ; Display char with DOS
67:            int     21h                      ;  function 2
68:
69:
70:    ;-----   Get variables from Pascal
71:
72:            mov     ah, 2                    ; DOS display-char function
73:            mov     dl, [cr]                 ; Get cr from Pascal
74:            int     21h                      ; Perform carriage return
75:            mov     dl, [lf]                 ; Get lf from Pascal
76:            int     21h                      ; Perform line feed
77:            ret                              ; Return to caller
78:
79:    ENDP    AsmProc
80:
81:
82:    %NEWPAGE
83:    ;-----------------------------------------------------------------
84:    ; FUNCTION CountPtr : intPtr;
85:    ;-----------------------------------------------------------------
86:    PROC    CountPtr        NEAR
87:            mov     dx, SEG asmCount         ; Pass segment address in dx
88:            mov     ax, OFFSET asmCount      ; Pass offset address in ax
89:            ret                              ; Return to caller
90:    ENDP    CountPtr
91:
92:    ENDS    CODE                     ; End of code segment
93:
94:            END                      ; End of module
```

Program 12-3 *PASDEMO.PAS*

```
1:    PROGRAM PasDemo;
2:
3:    { Test program, to be linked to externals in PASDEMO.OBJ }
4:
5:    {$D+}     { Include debugging information }
6:
7:    CONST   value : Integer = 1234;      { Typed-constant declaration }
8:
```

```
 9:   TYPE    IntPtr = ^Integer;              { Pointer to integer type }
10:
11:   VAR     cr, lf : Char;                  { Global variables }
12:
13:   PROCEDURE PasProc; FORWARD;             { Must come before $L directive }
14:   FUNCTION PasFunc: Char; FORWARD;
15:
16:   {$L PASDEMO.OBJ}        { Tell Pascal to load the assembled object code }
17:
18:   { External declarations, telling Pascal the format of the
19:   external routines in PASDEMO.ASM. }
20:
21:   PROCEDURE AsmProc; EXTERNAL;
22:   FUNCTION CountPtr: IntPtr; EXTERNAL;
23:
24:   PROCEDURE PasProc;
25:   VAR     i : Integer;                    { Can't be exported to ASM module }
26:   BEGIN
27:      Writeln( 'PasProc: Inside the Pascal procedure' )
28:   END; { PasProc }
29:
30:   FUNCTION PasFunc: Char;
31:   BEGIN
32:      PasFunc := '#'                       { Pass a character to ASM module }
33:   END; { PasFunc }
34:
35:   BEGIN
36:      cr := chr( 13 );
37:      lf := chr( 10 );
38:      AsmProc;
39:      Writeln( 'Main: asmCount = ', countPtr^ )
40:   END.
```

Note: In the following notes, line numbers prefaced with "p" refer to PAS-DEMO.PAS, while those prefaced with "a" refer to PASDEMO.ASM.

Understanding PASDEMO

Lines a7–14 declare the assembly language module's data segment. An EXTRN directive imports one variable constant value and two variables cr and lf from the Pascal code (see lines p7, p11). Notice that the Pascal program does not have to export variables and variable constants but that the assembly language module must import these items to make the names available to assembly language instructions.

Line a12 declares a static uninitialized variable. The question mark must be used here because initialized variables are not permitted in external code.

The PUBLIC directive at line a24 exports asmProc and countPtr assembly language modules (see lines a30–90) to Pascal. Lines p21–22 correspondingly declare these two routines EXTERNAL, allowing calls to this code from within the Pascal program. Notice how line p22 specifies the function result type, which is declared as a Pascal data type (a pointer to an integer) back at line p9.

Another EXTRN directive, this time in the code segment at line a27, imports a Pascal procedure PasProc and a function PasFunc into the assembly language module. This code is called at lines a41 and a64, illustrating how to call Pascal routines from external assembly language modules. The NEAR qualifiers in the EXTRN directive (line a27) tell the assembler that this code is in the same segment. FAR qualifiers would be necessary if the Pascal routines were compiled with the {$F+} directive or if they appear in the interface section of a unit. In the Pascal text, PasProc and PasFunc are declared FORWARD (see lines p13–14), making these identifiers known to the compiler before the {$L} command at line p16, which loads the assembled object code from disk. The Pascal code for these routines appears at lines p24–33.

Addressing Code-Segment Data

Although you can't declare initialized variables in the data segment of an assembly language module to be linked to Pascal, you can insert data into the code segment as shown at line a35 in PASDEMO.ASM. Be careful to separate code and data, preferably placing the variables outside of your PROC directives.

> Note: The main code segment in a compiled Pascal program is limited to 64K and includes the main program body plus all global procedures and functions, so it's best to keep the number and size of initialized variables here to a minimum.

Addressing variables in the code segment requires using a code-segment override (cs:) in the memory reference. More difficult is passing the address of such variables to other routines, especially to DOS function calls, demonstrated here at lines a45–53. First, the current ds register is saved on the stack. This is vital. Pascal requires ds to point to the global data segment at all times. If you change ds in the assembly language module and forget to restore the register's original value before returning to Pascal, the program will almost surely suffer a horrendous crash.

> Note: Despite this dire warning about changing ds, you may change es at any time. Pascal makes no assumptions about the segment addressed by es. However, you should not assume that es will retain its value between calls to external procedures.

Lines a46–47 set ds equal to cs, addressing the code segment with the data-segment register. Because of this, it's a good idea to use an ASSUME directive (line a48) to tell Turbo Assembler about the change to ds. After these steps, lines a49–51 call DOS function 9 to display an ASCII$ string. Then, line a52 restores Pascal's ds segment register value, requiring another ASSUME (line a53) to inform Turbo Assembler that ds again addresses the DATA segment.

Addressing Variable Constants

Lines a58–59 in PASDEMO.ASM initialize the global asmCount variable, declared at line a12. First, the variable constant value (see line p7 in the Pascal text) is moved into register ax (line a58). Turbo Assembler knows that value addresses a 16-bit word because of the EXTRN declaration at line a10. As this illustrates, it's up to you to ensure that your EXTRN directives specify the correct data types for variables declared in Pascal. If you declared value to be type byte, Turbo Assembler has no way of knowing that this is wrong.

Line a59 assigns the value in ax to the asmCount uninitialized static variable stored in the data segment. As you can see from this example, there's no indication in the program (lines a58–59) about where the variables are declared. You can read and write variables (and variable constants) the same way whether they are declared in the assembly language module or in the Pascal text.

Note: Unlike variables and variable constants, you can't export CONST and TYPE declarations from Pascal to assembly language. Plain constants and data-type identifiers can be used only in the Pascal program.

Calling Pascal Functions

Calling Pascal functions from within an assembly language module is no different than calling Pascal procedures. After calling PasFunc (line a64), the value returned in ax by the function is assigned to register dl. Because PasFunc returns a character, only the low half of ax is needed. This character is then displayed using DOS function 2.

Note: It's your responsibility to use function values appropriately in the assembly language module and to know which registers are affected by calling Pascal functions. Table 12-1 (copied in part from *Mastering Turbo Pascal*) lists function result sizes and the registers used to return values of these types.

Table 12-1 *Pascal Function Types and Sizes*

Function Type	Size in Bytes	Register(s)
Boolean	1	al
Char	1	al
Enumerated (8-bit)	1	al
Enumerated (16-bit)	2	ax
ShortInt	1	al
Byte	1	al
Integer	2	ax
Word	2	ax
LongInt	4	dx = high, ax = low words
Single	See note 1	
Double	See note 1	
Real	6	dx = high, bx = mid, ax = low words
Extended	See note 1	
Comp	See note 1	
Pointer	4	dx = segment, ax = offset
String	See note 2	

Note 1. These function types are returned in the math coprocessor top-of-stack register.
Note 2. String functions receive a pointer to a temporary work space created by the caller to the function. The function stores characters at this address, returning the pointer undisturbed on the stack.

Addressing Pascal Variables

Lines a72–76 execute a carriage return and line feed, passing to DOS function 2 the values of two Pascal variables cr and lf, which are declared at line p11 and initialized in Pascal at lines p36–37. (If you think this is an odd way to start a new display line, you're right. Even so, the code illustrates how to pass data from Pascal to an external module.) Notice that these variables are imported into the assembly language module as bytes in the EXTRN declaration at line a10. The variables (and variable constants) are stored in Pascal's global data segment and, therefore, are easily accessed as shown here.

> Note: Variables local to Pascal procedures and functions—for example, the integer variable i at line p25—cannot be accessed from inside an assembly language module. Local variables in Pascal exist only while the declaring procedures or functions are active; therefore, you cannot tell Turbo Assembler where these variables will be in memory until the program runs. To get around this restriction, you must pass local variables by value or by address as parameters to external procedures and functions.

Calling External Functions

Lines a83–90 implement a small external function that demonstrates several additional concerns. The function name is made public (line a24) and declared as an EXTERNAL function in the Pascal text (line p22). The data type for this function is a pointer to type integer, defined as IntPtr in the Pascal program at line p9. The assembly language module can't use this data type directly, and the program has to return values in the proper registers expected by Pascal for this and other function types. Turbo Assembler can't check the correctness of external function results.

In this case, because the type is a pointer, Pascal expects dx to hold the segment and ax the offset values of the address (see Table 12-1 and lines a87–88). In the Pascal code, line p39 uses this address by dereferencing the function identifier, displaying an integer value in a writeln statement. But what is this value? Looking again at the assembly language code, you can see that lines a87–88 assign the address of the asmCount uninitialized variable, declared in the data segment at line a12. The SEG operator returns the segment value of the label's address. The OFFSET operator returns the offset value. Together, the two values exactly locate asmCount in memory, displaying the value of this variable in the writeln statement. This demonstrates how to pass external variables to Pascal. Remember, a PUBLIC declaration for data labels is accepted by Turbo Assembler but rejected by Turbo Pascal because, except for variable constants, the Pascal data segment doesn't exist until the program runs. Passing the address of a variable to Pascal is required to transfer variables from external modules to Pascal programs.

> Note: You can also pass pointers as procedure and function parameters, as the next section explains. However, using pointer functions to locate variables declared in assembly language modules is usually the best approach because of the additional programming required to manipulate procedure and function parameters.

Passing Parameters

External assembly language routines become more complicated when variable and value parameters are added. There are many issues involved: whether the parameters are passed by value or by reference; how to handle special cases such as strings and arrays; how to ensure that the stack is correctly configured for return to Pascal; and how to perform all of this in reverse—that is, when passing parameters from inside the assembly language module to Pascal procedures and functions.

The best way through this thicket of details is to have a thorough understanding of Pascal programming and to have a good grasp on how the Pascal compiler implements procedures and functions in machine code. Don't forget that you have one of the world's best teachers at your disposal—Turbo Debugger. Examining test Pascal programs at the machine-code level with the View:CPU command is a great way to learn how Pascal implements statements in machine code.

Value Parameters   Value parameters are passed as simple variables on the stack. For example, to pass an integer parameter, Pascal pushes the value of the parameter onto the stack before calling the procedure that requires that value. A Pascal procedure such as:

```
PROCEDURE Count( i : Integer );
```

would be called in machine language with instructions similar to:

```
mov     ax, [i]         ; Get value of i
push    ax              ; Push i's value onto the stack
call    Count           ; Call procedure
```

The compiled code for the `Count` procedure has to retrieve the value of i from the stack. In Pascal, procedures and functions do this by referencing the stack with register `bp`. Consequently, compiled procedures and functions normally begin with:

```
push    bp              ; Save current bp value
mov     bp, sp          ; Address stack with bp
```

Figure 12-1 illustrates the stack at the start of `Count` after these two instructions execute. The value of i is under the 2-byte return address, which is in turn under the saved value of `bp`. (Each numbered box in this diagram represents one byte. The numbers do not represent real addresses in memory, though.)

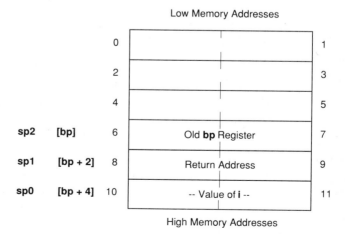

Figure 12-1 *Stack showing one Pascal value parameter.*

Counting from `bp` to the start of i, you can see that adding 4 to `bp` finds the start of i. Therefore, to load `ax` with the value stored at this location on the stack, you can write:

```
mov     ax, [word bp + 4]        ; Assign i's value to ax
```

You can also refer to values directly with instructions such as:

```
inc     [word bp + 4]            ; i := i + 1
```

One complication with this arises in FAR procedures. In these routines, the return address is 4 bytes long, having both segment and offset parts. (See Figure 12-2.) Therefore, to load the value of i, use the correct offset 6, instead of 4:

```
mov     ax, [word bp + 6]        ; Load i into ax (FAR routine)
```

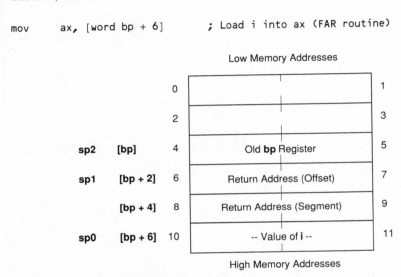

Low Memory Addresses

	0		1
	2		3
sp2 [bp]	4	Old **bp** Register	5
sp1 [bp + 2]	6	Return Address (Offset)	7
[bp + 4]	8	Return Address (Segment)	9
sp0 [bp + 6]	10	-- Value of **i** --	11

High Memory Addresses

Figure 12-2 *Stack after calling a FAR procedure with one value parameter.*

Returning from External Code

When the external assembly language routine ends, it must use a special form of the ret instruction to remove the parameter bytes from the stack in addition to ret's normal duty of popping the return address and continuing the program after the call that activated the routine. In this case, there are two parameter bytes on the stack; therefore, the routine would end with:

```
ret     2                        ; Return and pop 2 bytes from stack
```

The optional immediate value following ret is added to the stack pointer *after* popping the return address into ip (and cs in the case of an intersegment FAR call). Remember that the intermediate value represents the number of *bytes* of all parameters passed on the stack. Because Pascal never pushes a value less than 2 bytes long—even single-byte characters are passed as 2-byte words—the optional ret value in Pascal external routines should always be an even number.

Variable Parameters

Variable parameters—those prefaced with VAR in the Pascal procedure or function parameter list—are passed by reference, that is, by address. The 4-byte address of each such variable is passed on the stack and referenced just like any other value. The assembly language code can use the address as a pointer to the actual value somewhere else in memory. This is easier to see with a few examples. Suppose the previous procedure declares a variable parameter:

```
PROCEDURE Count( VAR i : Integer );
```

In the compiled code, the caller to the `Count` procedure pushes the address of i onto the stack. Assuming i is stored in the program's data segment, the compiled instructions might be similar to:

```
mov     di, offset i          ; Get offset of variable i
push    ds                    ; Push segment address of i
push    di                    ; Push offset address of i
call    Count                 ; Call Count procedure
```

At the start of `Count`, after saving and assigning to `bp` the stack-pointer register, the stack appears as in Figure 12-3. With the stack configured as in this figure, you can get the value of i into the assembly language module in several ways. One possibility is to load `es` and another register (`di` is a good choice as is `bx`) from the stack:

```
mov     es, [word bp + 6]     ; Get segment value
mov     di, [word bp + 4]     ; Get offset value
```

After doing this, `es:di` addresses the value of i in memory. Be aware that this location could be anywhere—in a data segment or, perhaps, in a stack segment if, for example, i is a local variable declared in a Pascal procedure or function. Another way to accomplish the same result is to use the `les` instruction:

```
les     di, [bp + 4]          ; Load es:di with address of i
mov     ax, [word es:di]      ; Load value of i into ax
```

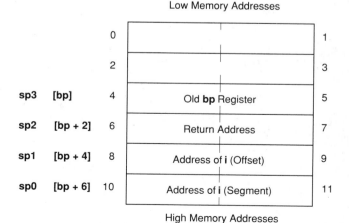

Figure 12-3 *Stack with one variable parameter.*

The les instruction loads both es and di (or another general purpose register) with the address stored at the specified location, here 4 bytes in advance of where ss:bp points. The second instruction then addresses this location to load the value of the variable parameter into ax. A similar instruction lds can be used to load the segment portion of an address into ds. Because Pascal needs ds to address the global data segment, if you use lds, be sure to save and restore the original value of ds before your external routine ends.

Using the TPASCAL Memory Model

One way to simplify addressing variables on the stack is to use a special Turbo Assembler memory model TPASCAL, designed for use with Turbo Pascal. The advantages of this method are:

▶ You can use simplified CODESEG and DATASEG directives instead of declaring named segments manually.

▶ Turbo Assembler automatically prepares and restores the bp register for you.

▶ Parameter addresses on the stack are precalculated, allowing you to address parameters by name rather than computing stack offsets, for example, as in [bp + 8].

▶ The correct immediate value is added automatically to the ret instruction to remove parameter bytes from the stack.

A disadvantage of the TPASCAL memory model is the inability to prevent Turbo Assembler from generating instructions to prepare bp for addressing stack variables. Even in procedures that have no parameters, these instructions are blindly inserted. One of the reasons for adding assembly language to Pascal in the first place is to strip every unnecessary instruction, honing your code to a fine edge. Using TPASCAL is convenient in some cases—as in the following examples. But, for the ultimate in low-level control, you must declare SEGMENT directives manually as in PASSHELL.ASM.

Using the ARG Directive

With the TPASCAL memory model in effect, you can use an ARG directive to simplify parameter addressing. ARG tells Turbo Assembler the names and sizes of parameters passed to external PROCs on the stack. The assembler uses this information to calculate the offset values relative to ss:bp where the parameter values are stored.

> Note: **ARG** works with other memory models and with nonsimplified segments, too. However, there is a difference. With the **TPASCAL** memory model, parameters must appear in **ARG** directives in the same order they appear in Pascal procedure and function declarations. When not using **TPASCAL**, you must list parameters in the *reverse* order.

ARG requires a series of elements separated by commas, with each element describing one parameter. For example, this Pascal procedure declaration:

```
PROCEDURE StoreNum( MyNumber : Integer );
```

has the corresponding **PROC** declaration:

```
PROC    StoreNum        NEAR
        ARG MyNumber:WORD
```

After executing this, move the value of `MyNumber` into a register using assembly language instructions such as:

```
mov     ax, [MyNumber]          ; Load ax with value of MyNumber
```

Contrast this with the usual method of addressing stack variables relative to `bp`:

```
mov     ax, [word bp + 4]
```

If you later change the number of parameters passed to the procedure—or if you change the procedure type from **NEAR** to **FAR**—reassemble the external object-code module to adjust the location of `MyNumber` on the stack. Without an **ARG** directive, you must recalculate and change the literal 4 manually, greatly increasing the chances of introducing a bug if you make a mistake.

Deallocating Stacked Parameters

If you follow an **ARG** parameter list with an equal sign = and a temporary name, Turbo Assembler calculates the number of bytes occupied by all parameters and assigns this value to the name you supply. For example, the following sets `ArgSize` to the number of bytes occupied by the two parameters, `his` and `hers`:

```
PROC    Share           NEAR
        ARG his:WORD, hers:WORD =ArgSize
```

When not using the **TPASCAL** memory model, you can use `ArgSize` with `ret` to remove parameter bytes from the stack:

```
ret     ArgSize         ; Return and deallocate stack parameters
```

Don't do this when using the **TPASCAL** memory model, in which case Turbo Assembler automatically adds the correct value to `ret` (assuming you specified the correct number and sizes of parameters in an ARG directive). When using the TPASCAL memory model, always end your external PROCs with a plain ret instruction. (You can still add =ArgSize to the ARG directive and use the value equated to ArgSize in other ways.)

Writing External String Functions

A third option lets you specify parameters that are not to be removed from the stack when your external routine ends. To do this, follow the element list (plus an optional =ArgSize command) with RETURNS, in turn followed by a list of parameters that should remain on the stack when the PROC ends.

In Pascal, the only time you'll probably need RETURNS is when writing external string functions. When Pascal calls a string function, it first pushes the function result—a 4-byte pointer—onto the stack before pushing other parameters (if there are any) passed to the function. The function result pointer addresses a temporary area where your external code can store the characters of the string returned by the function. When the external routine ends, Pascal expects the string function pointer to remain on the stack. (Instructions following the subroutine call later remove these bytes or just pass the address to another procedure or function that uses the function's string result.) Because of this special action, if you declare the function result in the ARG's main parameter list, the procedure will not work because Turbo Assembler deallocates the parameter bytes plus the function result pointer at the ret instruction.

Program 12-4, FILLSTR.ASM, demonstrates the correct way to write an external Pascal string function. Program 12-5, FILLSTR.PAS, shows how to link the external module to a Pascal program. Assemble, compile, and run the Pascal test with the commands:

```
tasm fillstr
tpc fillstr
fillstr
```

Program 12-4 *FILLSTR.ASM*

```
 1:  %TITLE "External Pascal String-Filler Function"
 2:
 3:          IDEAL
 4:          MODEL   TPASCAL
 5:
 6:          CODESEG
 7:
 8:          PUBLIC FillString
 9:
10:  %NEWPAGE
11:  ;-----------------------------------------------------------
12:  ; FUNCTION FillString( n : Byte; ch : Char ) : String;
13:  ;-----------------------------------------------------------
```

```
14:  PROC    FillString      NEAR
15:          ARG n:BYTE:2, c:BYTE:2 RETURNS string:dword
16:
17:          les     di, [string]           ; es:di addresses fn result
18:          mov     al, [n]                ; Load n into al
19:          cld                            ; Auto-increment di
20:          stosb                          ; Initialize string length
21:          xor     ch, ch                 ; Zero upper half of cx
22:          mov     cl, al                 ; cx = requested string len
23:          mov     al, [c]                ; al = fill character
24:          jcxz    @@99                   ; Exit if length = 0
25:          repnz   stosb                  ; Store cx chars in string
26:  @@99:
27:          ret                            ; Return to caller
28:  ENDP    FillString
29:
30:          END                     ; End of module
```

Program 12-5 *FILLSTR.PAS*

```
 1:  PROGRAM FillStr;
 2:
 3:  { Test using the FillString external function }
 4:
 5:  VAR     s : String;
 6:
 7:  FUNCTION FillString( n : Byte; ch : Char ) : String; EXTERNAL;
 8:  {$L FILLSTR.OBJ}
 9:
10:  BEGIN
11:      s := FillString( 45, '@' );
12:      Writeln( 'After filling: ', s )
13:  END.
```

How FILLSTR Works   Line 15 in FILLSTR.ASM constructs an **ARG** declaration to return a parameter on the stack. For reference, this line is repeated below:

```
ARG n:BYTE:2, c:BYTE:2 RETURNS string:dword
```

First come the two parameters n and c, each of which are single bytes. Notice that the ch:char parameter from the Pascal text is renamed c here because ch in assembly language refers to the high byte of register cx and can't be used for an identifier. (I purposely contrived this conflict to illustrate that, in the ARG declaration, parameter names can be anything you like—they don't have to mirror their Pascal counterparts.)

Because Pascal always pushes values onto the stack in multiples of 2 bytes, an additional qualifier :2 is added to the two parameters, telling Turbo Assembler that, even though it should address n and c as bytes, it should consider these variables to occupy 2 bytes of stack space. If you don't include the :2, Turbo Assembler will miscalculate the number of bytes occupied by the parameters and will not correctly fix up the stack when the external routine ends.

Note: The symptom of an incorrect stack deallocation is a "Stack Overflow" error. If you receive this error, check that all single-byte parameters have a :2 specification in your ARG lists.

Following the two parameters is the phrase RETURNS string:dword. The name string can be any identifier, which simply gives you a way to refer to the function result inside the external code. The ":dword" part of this directive tells Turbo Assembler that string addresses a 4-byte value on the stack. (A string function actually returns a pointer in Turbo Pascal, and pointers are always 4 bytes.)

You can address the string function result in various ways. The easiest method is to load es:di or ds:si with the address of the area reserved for the result:

```
les     di, [string]    ; es:di addresses function result
```

After this, the string's length byte is located at es:di. The first character of the string is at es:di + 1, and so on. Storing characters at es:di passes those characters back as the string function result. You don't have to perform any other steps to return the string to the caller to the external function. In FILLSTR.ASM, a repeated stosb instruction uses these methods to return a string filled with n characters of any ASCII value.

Declaring Parameters Without ARG

There's another way to declare parameters that doesn't use ARG—just place the parameter list after the PROC and NEAR or FAR directive. For example, you can replace lines 14–15 in FILLSTR.ASM with:

```
PROC FillString NEAR n:BYTE:2, c:BYTE:2 RETURNS string:dword
```

In other words, if you write everything on one line, you don't need an ARG directive. But because long PROC declarations such as this can be confusing to read, I prefer to list arguments in a separate ARG directive. The results are identical, however, and you can use whichever method you like.

Note: The Turbo Assembler Reference Guide (version 1.0) incorrectly lists the syntax for PROC argument lists, which actually have the identical syntax as ARG and can include an =ArgSize specification before the optional RETURNS.

Going for Speed

Let's face it. There's only one reason to spend time optimizing Pascal or any other language with system-dependent assembly language: to achieve the blinding speed that, when used well, only assembly language promises. In this section, you'll write a Pascal program, take apart the machine code generated by Turbo Pascal, and write highly optimized replacement external code in assembly language. As you'll see, the results are worth the effort.

The Pascal Program

First, we need a Pascal program. Program 12-6, STR.PAS, contains two useful procedures, `ASCIIZtoStr` and `StrToASCIIZ`, which convert Pascal strings to and from the ASCIIZ format used by many assembly language programs in this book. To save space here, the optimized version of the Pascal code is listed. For test purposes, therefore, after you enter this program, copy STR.PAS to another file named STRSLOW.PAS.

Next, load STRSLOW.PAS into your editor and delete lines 12, 18–19, 30, 36–37, and 45. This converts the listing to pure Pascal, eliminating the references to the external routines that you'll add back later. After making the modifications, compile STRSLOW with the command:

```
tpc /v strslow
```

Program 12-6 *STR.PAS*

```
 1:  PROGRAM StringConversion;
 2:
 3:  { Convert ASCIIZ strings and Pascal strings }
 4:
 5:  TYPE  ASCIIZString    = ARRAY[ 0 ... 255 ] OF Char;
 6:        ASCIIZptr       = ^ASCIIZString;
 7:
 8:  VAR   a : ASCIIZString;
 9:        s : String;
10:
11:
12:  {$L STR.OBJ}
13:
14:
15:  { Convert an ASCIIZ string (a) to a Pascal string (s) }
16:
17:  PROCEDURE ASCIIZtoStr( a : ASCIIZString; VAR s : String );
18:     EXTERNAL;
19:  (*
20:  VAR   len : Integer;
21:  BEGIN
22:     len := 0;
23:     WHILE ( len < 255 ) AND ( a[ len ] <> Chr( 0 ) ) DO
24:     BEGIN
25:        len := len + 1;
26:        s[ len ] := a[ len - 1 ]
27:     END; { while }
28:     s[ 0 ] := Chr( len )
29:  END; { ASCIIZtoStr }
30:  *)
31:
32:
```

```
33:  { Convert a Pascal string (s) to an ASCIIZ string (a) }
34:
35:  PROCEDURE StrToASCIIZ( s : String; VAR a : ASCIIZString );
36:     EXTERNAL;
37:  (*
38:  VAR   len, i : Integer;
39:  BEGIN
40:     len := Length( s );
41:     FOR i := 1 TO len DO
42:        a[ i - 1 ] := s[ i ];
43:     a[ len ] := Chr( 0 )
44:  END; { StrToASCIIZ }
45:  *)
46:
47:
48:  { Display an ASCIIZ string }
49:
50:  PROCEDURE ShowASCIIZ( a : ASCIIZString );
51:  VAR   i : Integer;
52:  BEGIN
53:     i := 0;
54:     WHILE ( i < 255 ) AND ( a[ i ] <> Chr(0) ) DO
55:     BEGIN
56:        Write( a[ i ] );
57:        i := i + 1
58:     END { while }
59:  END; { ShowASCIIZ }
60:
61:
62:  BEGIN
63:     s := 'This is a test';
64:     StrtoASCIIZ( s, a );
65:     ShowASCIIZ( a );
66:     Writeln;
67:     s := '';
68:     ASCIIZtoStr( a, s );
69:     Writeln( s )
70:  END.
```

Examining STRSLOW's Code

After compiling STRSLOW, to see the machine code produced by Turbo Pascal, run the program under control of Turbo Debugger with the command:

```
td strslow
```

Then, press F7 repeatedly to step through the program. When you get inside the StrToASCIIZ and ASCIIZtoStr procedures, use the View/CPU commands to look at the machine code that Turbo Pascal generates for these routines. You may be amazed at the lengths to which the Pascal compiler goes to convert apparently simple high-level statements into machine code. In many cases, Turbo Pascal generates very tight and fast-executing code. But, obviously, this is not one of those cases. With a little assembly language, we can do much better.

Figure 12-4 lists the disassembled assembly language that corresponds with the Pascal procedure StrToASCIIZ (lines 35–44 in STR.PAS). The comments should help you to understand most of what's happening here. (Calls to undocumented Turbo Pascal runtime routines are marked "(internal sub)" and are not explained. When viewing this code in Turbo Debugger, some of the instructions will have slightly different formats.)

Lines 7–18 in Figure 12-4 point out one reason that even superb high-level language compilers like Turbo Pascal can sometimes generate slowly executing code. This procedure happens to have a string parameter s passed by value; therefore, the compiler correctly assumes that string s might be changed inside the procedure. As a result, and because strings and other arrays are *always* passed internally by address, the code at lines 7–18 blindly copies the entire string to a temporary work space on the stack—a process that repeats every time you call the procedure. However, as you can see in the Pascal code, the string is not changed, and all this code is unnecessary, a fact that the compiler just isn't smart enough to discern.

There are other places in this code (and in the other procedure, ASCIIToStr) that could stand improvements, too. For example, line 28 apparently isn't needed as ax must already have the value stored at [bp – 0102h] due to the earlier instruction at line 24. These observations seem to suggest that pure assembly language routines will save space and run more quickly.

```
1:  ; PROCEDURE StrToASCIIZ( s : String; VAR a : ASCIIZString );
2:
3:  PROC     StrToASCIIZ      NEAR
4:
5:           push    bp                         ; Save bp on stack
6:           mov     bp, sp                     ; Address params with bp
7:           mov     ax, 0106h                  ; Check if 106h stack bytes
8:           call    far ptr (internal sub)     ;   are available
9:           sub     sp, 0106h                  ; Reserve stack space for s
10:          les     di, [dword ptr bp + 8]     ; es:di = address of s
11:          push    es                         ; Push source address (seg
12:          push    di                         ;   and offset)
13:          lea     di, [bp - 0100h]           ; ss:di = address of s copy
14:          push    ss                         ; Push destination address
15:          push    di                         ;   (seg and offset)
16:          mov     ax, 00FFh                  ; Number of bytes to copy
17:          push    ax                         ; Push count
18:          call    far ptr (internal sub)     ; Copy string to temp variable
19:
```

Continued

Figure 12-4 *Commented assembly language for the StrToASCIIZ procedure in STR.PAS (modified, nonoptimized version, renamed STRSLOW.PAS).*

```
20:     ; len := Length( s )
21:
22:             mov     al, [bp - 0100h]            ; Get length of s
23:             xor     ah, ah                     ; Zero upper half of ax
24:             mov     [bp - 0102h], ax           ; Initialize len variable
25:
26:     ; FOR i := 1 TO len DO
27:
28:             mov     ax, [bp - 0102h]           ; Assign len to ax
29:             mov     [bp - 0106h], ax           ; Assign len to stop value
30:             mov     ax, 0001h                  ; Assign start value to ax
31:             cmp     ax, [bp - 0106h]           ; Is start > stop value?
32:             jg      @@09                       ; If yes, skip FOR loop
33:             mov     [bp - 0104h], ax           ; Else initialize i
34:             jmp     short @@08                 ; Jump into loop
35:     @@07:
36:             inc     [word bp - 0104h]          ; Increment control var (i)
37:
38:     ; a[ i - 1 ] := s[ i ]
39:
40:     @@08:
41:             mov     di, [word bp - 0104h]      ; Assign i to di
42:             mov     dl, [byte bp+di-0100h]     ; Get char at s[ i ]
43:             mov     ax, [word bp - 0104h]      ; Set ax to i
44:             dec     ax                         ; Adjust ax to i - 1
45:             les     di, [dword bp + 04]        ; es:di addresses a
46:             add     di, ax                     ; advance di to a[ i - 1 ]
47:             mov     [byte es:di], dl           ; Store char from s[ i ]
48:             mov     ax, [word bp - 0104h]      ; Set ax to control var (i)
49:             cmp     ax, [word bp - 0106h]      ; Compare with stop value
50:             jne     @@07                       ; Jump if ax <> stop value
51:
52:     ; a[ len ] := Chr( 0 )
53:
54:     @@09:
55:             mov     ax, [word bp - 0102h]      ; Set ax to len
56:             les     di, [word bp + 04]         ; es:di addresses a
57:             add     di, ax                     ; es:di addresses a[ len ]
58:             mov     [byte es:di], 0            ; Store 0 at a[ len ]
59:
60:     ; END; { StrToASCII }
61:
62:             mov     sp, bp                     ; Restore stack pointer
63:             pop     bp                         ; Restore saved bp register
64:             retn    8                          ; Return and deallocate params
65:
66:     ENDP    StrToASCIIZ
```

Figure 12-4 *Continued*

Optimizing STR.PAS

Program 12-7, STR.ASM, replaces the ASCIIZtoStr and StrToASCIIZ procedures in STR.PAS with assembly language external routines. (If you've been following along, you copied STR.PAS to STRSLOW.PAS earlier. Be sure you have the original copy of STR.PAS on disk for the next steps.) Assemble, compile, and run the test with the commands:

```
tasm str
tpc str
str
```

Program 12-7 *STR.ASM*

```
 1:   %TITLE "ASCIIZ and Pascal String Conversions"
 2:
 3:           IDEAL
 4:           MODEL   TPASCAL
 5:
 6:           CODESEG
 7:
 8:           PUBLIC  ASCIIZtoStr, StrToASCIIZ
 9:
10:   %NEWPAGE
11:   ;-------------------------------------------------------------
12:   ; PROCEDURE ASCIIZtoStr( a : ASCIIZString; VAR s : String );
13:   ;-------------------------------------------------------------
14:   PROC    ASCIIZtoStr     NEAR
15:           ARG a:dword, s:dword = ArgSize
16:           push    ds                  ; Save Pascal's ds register
17:           les     di, [s]             ; Address s with es:di
18:           push    di                  ; Save address for later
19:           inc     di                  ; Address s[1] with es:di
20:           lds     si, [a]             ; Address a with ds:si
21:           cld                         ; Auto-increment si, di
22:           xor     cl, cl              ; Set len (cl) to 0
23:   @@10:
24:           cmp     cl, 255             ; Is len = 255 yet?
25:           je      @@20                ; If yes, exit
26:           lodsb                       ; Get char (al <- a[i])
27:           or      al, al              ; Is al = 0 (ASCII null)?
28:           jz      @@20                ; If char = null, exit
29:           inc     cl                  ; len := len + 1
30:           stosb                       ; s[ len ] := a[ len - 1 ]
31:           jmp     @@10                ; Loop until done
32:   @@20:
33:           pop     di                  ; es:di again addresses s[0]
34:           mov     [byte es:di], cl    ; s[ 0 ] := Chr( len )
35:           pop     ds                  ; Restore Pascal's ds register
36:           ret                         ; Return to caller
37:   ENDP    ASCIIZtoStr
38:
```

```
39:    %NEWPAGE
40:    ;----------------------------------------------------------------
41:    ; PROCEDURE StrToASCIIZ( s : String; VAR a : ASCIIZString );
42:    ;----------------------------------------------------------------
43:    PROC    StrToASCIIZ      NEAR
44:            ARG s:dword, a:dword = ArgSize
45:            push    ds                      ; Save Pascal's ds register
46:            les     di, [a]                 ; Address a with es:di
47:            lds     si, [s]                 ; Address s with ds:si
48:            cld                             ; Auto-increment si, di
49:            xor     ch, ch                  ; Zero upper half of cx
50:            lodsb                           ; al := Length( s )
51:            mov     cl, al                  ; cx = string length
52:            jcxz    @@10                    ; Exit if length = 0
53:            repnz   movsb                   ; Transfer s to a
54:    @@10:
55:            mov     [byte es:di], cl        ; a[ len ] := Chr( 0 )
56:            pop     ds                      ; Restore Pascal's ds register
57:            ret                             ; Return to caller
58:    ENDP    StrToASCIIZ
59:
60:            END                     ; End of module
```

How STR.ASM Works

You've seen all the instructions, commands, and other items in STR.ASM and, therefore, should have little trouble understanding how the code works. Notice how ARG is used to make addressing the parameters on the stack easy, without requiring confusing and error-prone specifications like [word bp + 4]. Also, the TPASCAL memory model lets Turbo Assembler initialize and restore bp automatically and add the proper immediate value to the ret instructions, removing parameters from the stack as necessary.

Pay special attention to lines 17, 20, and 46–47, which load es:di and ds:si with the addresses of the a and s parameters. Because this potentially changes ds—the variables may not be in the Pascal program's data segment—the procedures carefully preserve ds.

Another optimization technique demonstrated here takes advantage of the fact that, even though a is a value parameter to ASCIIZtoStr and that s is a value parameter to StrToASCIIZ, Turbo Pascal always passes strings and arrays by address. Therefore, because these variables aren't changed, the optimized external code skips the steps of copying the values as done in the code generated by the compiler.

Note: In this example, variables a and s are stored in the data segment and, if you run the test in Turbo Debugger, you may observe that ds doesn't actually change at lines 20 and 47. But another program could pass parameters to these procedures that are not stored in the data segment. In which case, ds probably would change. Such details are the source of many bugs, and the best prevention is a thorough knowledge of how Pascal works on the machine-code level. Don't assume that, just because you don't see a register value changing one time, that it won't change at another.

The speed gains in STR.ASM are mostly due to the use of fast 8086 string instructions at lines 26, 30, and 53. Contrast these instructions to the laborious methods employed in the pure Pascal output. (See Figure 12-4.) There's just no substitute for keeping values in fast general-purpose registers, using string indexes si and di, and taking advantage of powerful string instructions such as lodsb and movsb. As you can see, a little assembly language added to Pascal can go a long way toward improving program performance.

In Turbo Pascal's favor, I am forced to admit here that STR.PAS could be written to run quite a lot faster by using unique Turbo Pascal instructions such as Move. Even though I could be accused of "cooking the books" to create a good example of assembly language optimization, there are times when you may want to avoid Turbo's unique commands—even if this results in slower code. By restricting your programs to standard Pascal commands—as defined by Jensen and Wirth (see Bibliography)—your code will be easier to transfer to other systems. In fact, I sometimes write three versions of a program: one in standard Pascal, another optimized in Turbo Pascal, and a third optimized in assembly language, replacing procedures and functions from either of the first two versions. This takes extra work, of course, but also greatly improves the prospects that the code will run with minimum modifications on a variety of hardware.

Summary

Compilers are smarter today than ever before, but they're still no match for a clever assembly language programmer. Even programs compiled to super-fast code by Turbo Pascal can often be improved. But knowing how to add assembly language to Pascal is only half the story. Knowing when to do so is equally if not more important. Usually, it's best to convert only critical code, leaving noncritical sections in Pascal. To maintain a program's portability to other systems, it's also wise to write the Pascal statements first before converting critical sections to assembly language.

Finding the critical code is not always easy, but most experts agree that programs generally spend about 90% of their time executing about 10% of their instructions. Optimizing that critical 10% can greatly increase performance. Optimizing the other 90% may be a waste of time. A profiler can help identify critical sections by keeping statistical data about an executing program.

Turbo Pascal allows you to use InLine statements, InLine procedures and functions, and external procedures and functions to add assembly language to Pascal. The last of these is usually best because it improves the chances of porting the program to another system. External routines also can be assembled and debugged separately and might be usable with other languages, too.

Pascal's unusual memory model requires special handling, requiring you to declare data and code segments the hard way for the most flexible results. As an alternative, the TPASCAL memory model can be used, although this has the disadvantage of adding startup instructions to every procedure, whether needed or not.

You can call external procedures and functions from Pascal, and you can call Pascal procedures and functions from assembly language. You must be careful to know which procedures are NEAR and which are FAR. You can also import data from Pascal into external modules, but because Pascal lacks an EXTERNAL directive for variables, you can't export data from assembly language to Pascal. (You can pass the addresses of external data to Pascal and, with this method, gain access to external variables.)

Writing Pascal functions requires extra care to be sure that proper values are passed back to callers in the correct registers. Parameters further complicate the job of writing external code, requiring assembly language modules to address variables on the stack. Using the ARG directive can help (especially when used with the TPASCAL memory model) by letting external code address parameters by name instead of error-prone expressions such as [bp + 8].

Of course, the ultimate goal of adding assembly language to Pascal is to add speed to programs. As an example in this chapter demonstrates, the results of optimizing can save memory, reduce code-file size, and greatly enhance performance.

Exercises

12-1. What is "critical code"?

12-2. What does a profiler do?

12-3. The clc instruction's machine code is 0F8h. The stc instruction's machine code is 0F9h. Write InLine statements and procedures using these instructions to set and clear the carry flag.

12-4. What is the correct way to code the following Pascal procedure declaration in an external assembly language module:

```
{$F+}
PROCEDURE PlayBall;
```

12-5. Suppose you have an external assembly language module named NEWSTUFF.ASM, assembled to NEWSTUFF.OBJ. In it are one procedure OldStuff and an integer function OlderStuff. What Pascal statements are required to compile and link the Pascal and assembly language files?

12-6. Why is the TPASCAL memory model potentially disadvantageous? What are the advantages and alternatives?

12-7. Given the following Pascal declarations, write the directive or directives required to import the values into an assembly language module. Which (if any) of these declarations can't be imported into the external module?

```
TYPE    Months = (Jan, Feb, Mar, Apr, May,
                Jun, Jul, Aug, Sep, Oct, Nov, Dec );

CONST   MaxLevel = 17;
        AreaCode : Integer = 555;
        Esc = #27;

VAR     YourName : String;
        Score : Integer;
        SalesPerMonth : Array[ Months ] OF Integer;
```

12-8. Given the following Pascal procedure, write the necessary instructions to call the routine from inside an assembly language module named ASCII.OBJ:

```
PROCEDURE WriteASCII( ch : Char );
BEGIN
   Writeln( 'ASCII value = ', Ord(ch) )
END;
```

12-9. Suppose you have a global variable declared with **dd** named **LongValue**. What assembly language instructions do you need to use to pass this value back to Pascal as a function result type?

12-10. [Advanced.] Using an **ARG** directive and assuming the **TPASCAL** memory model is being used, write the assembly language code required to replace the Pascal **LotsOfParams** procedure shown here with an external module that loads parameter **a** into **cx** and **b** into **dx**, adds 5 to **number**, and loads **al** with **ch**. Write a Pascal program to test your code. (Hint: Write a Pascal version first, examine the code in Turbo Debugger, and *then* write the assembly language module.)

```
PROCEDURE LotsOfParams( a, b : Integer; VAR number : Integer;
    VAR ch : char );
```

Projects

12-1. Convert the STRINGS module from chapter 5 to external procedures that can be linked to Pascal programs, adding ASCIIZ string abilities to Turbo Pascal.

12-2. Write a terminal emulator in Pascal, using external procedures from chapter 10's ASYNCH module to initialize and drive the serial I/O port.

12-3. Identify the critical code as best you can in a sizable Pascal program, preferably one of about 1,000 lines. (Most public domain libraries have suitable candidates.) Optimize key procedures and functions in the program and document the improvements.

12-4. Pascal's **Write** and **Writeln** have to handle multiple parameters, integers, real numbers, and strings. They're handy, but they can also produce needlessly lengthy machine-code instruction sequences. Write simplified string I/O procedures for writing Pascal string variables to the standard output.

12-5. Develop a fast direct-video package in assembly language for displaying strings at high speed on PCs.

12-6. Use Turbo Debugger to examine the machine code for Turbo Pascal's standard CRT unit, supplied on Turbo's master disks. Identify and comment as many of the instructions as you can. (Doing this is a good way to learn how Pascal compiles programs, but don't worry if you can't figure out every instruction.)

Chapter *13* **Optimizing C with Assembly Language**

13 *Optimizing C with Assembly Language*

In This Chapter

The two ways to add assembly language to Turbo C programs; organizing your disk for multilanguage programming; Turbo C and Turbo Assembler version numbers; finding a program's critical code; register use in assembly language modules; using in-line asm statements; how to compile and assemble programs with in-line statements; declaring in-line code and data; sharing code and data between C and assembly language; using C structures; writing external assembly language modules; simplified memory models and external code; calling assembly language functions from C; calling C functions from assembly language; several ways to assemble, compile, and link multimodule C and assembly language programs; debugging C programs with assembly language; function result types; plus local variables

Adding Assembly Language to C

The reasons for adding assembly language to Turbo C programs are the same as the reasons discussed in chapter 12 for optimizing Turbo Pascal—speed and access to the lowest reaches of the hardware. But the pitfalls are identical, too—reduced program portability and an increased likelihood of bugs. For most programs, Turbo C generates tight fast code that's hard to beat. Still, no compiler, not even Turbo C, is as clever as a crack assembly language expert, and, many times, the only way to add real zip to a program is to drop a little machine code into your deep and true blue "C" using one of two methods:

▶ In-line statements

▶ External functions

In-line statements inject assembly language directly into Turbo C source code. This technique is quick and easy but does have a few drawbacks, as I'll explain later. *External functions*, while more difficult to manage than in-line statements, have the advantage of giving you full access to all of Turbo Assembler's features. This chapter examines both methods, listing many examples that you can use as templates for your own projects. First, however, you need to organize your disk so that both Turbo C and Turbo Assembler can work together.

> Note: This chapter assumes that you have some familiarity with Turbo C. Also, as you read the following sections, if you experience a little *déjà vu*, don't be alarmed. A few paragraphs from chapter 12 are intentionally duplicated here.

Suggested Disk Organization

The first step in adding assembly language to C is to organize your disk for easy access to the files and subdirectories required by both Turbo Assembler and Turbo C. If you have a hard disk, this is simple—just install the two languages in separate subdirectories, probably C:\TC and C:\TASM. If you have floppy disk drives, it's probably best to create separate disks for C and assembly language. With this setup, you'll have to compile and assemble pieces of programs separately and then link the pieces manually. But if you're careful, you might be able to shoehorn Turbo Assembler into your Turbo C directory so that the compiler can call the assembler directly. With a hard disk drive, you can let Turbo C automate these steps.

> Note: The identical TLINK.EXE program is supplied on the Turbo C and Assembler disks. Because Borland might update this program in future releases, you should use the copy of TLINK.EXE with the most recent file date and time.

The next step is to add the subdirectory file names to a PATH command in your AUTOEXEC.BAT file. This lets you change to a directory containing C and assembly language program source files but still be able to run the compiler and assembler. Assuming you also have a common directory named DOS for miscellaneous utilities, you could insert this line into AUTOEXEC.BAT:

```
PATH=C:\DOS;C:\TASM;C:\TC;C:\TDEBUG
```

After rebooting, you can then change to another directory with the CD command and run Turbo Assembler, Turbo C, and Turbo Debugger as though these programs were all in the same directory. Also, this arrangement allows Turbo C to run Turbo Assembler automatically. Or you can use MAKE to automate compiling and assembling large programs with many related files. We'll see many examples of these methods for compiling programs that contain optimized assembly language.

Version Numbers This chapter assumes that you are using Turbo Assembler 1.0 and Turbo C 2.0 or later versions. Earlier Turbo C releases are designed to call the Microsoft Macro Assembler; therefore, if you must use an early Turbo C version, you'll have to rename TASM.EXE to MASM.EXE. (You may also experience difficulties with a few in-line assembly language features, but this trick should at least get you started until you can upgrade your compiler.)

Identifying Critical Code

As explained in chapter 12, a program's critical code usually amounts to about 10% of the instructions, which often can share as much as 90% of the processing burden. Rewriting this critical 10% in fast assembly language should produce remarkable speed improvements, while optimizing the other 90% may be a waste of time. For this reason, the primary mixed-language rule to remember is: Don't rewrite C statements that already run as fast as necessary.

Locating a program's critical code is not always easy. Sometimes, your familiarity with the program will tell you which sections could stand a little extra juice. At other times, you'll need the help of a commercial profiler to monitor a program and create a statistical report, listing heavily traveled routines.

A good battle plan is to write your program entirely in C and then, after debugging your code, convert selected areas to assembly language. Keep track of the results as you go along and try to keep the amount of assembly language to the minimum. That may seem to be strange advice to find in an assembly language book, but one of the main reasons for writing a program in C or any other high-level language is to improve the chances for transferring the code to another computer. To keep these chances alive, it's probably best to use as little assembly language as possible. (Besides, a little machine code goes a long way.)

Using Registers

You can use all processor registers in your assembly language routines. To prevent mishaps in other Turbo C functions, you must restore bp, cs, ds, sp, and ss to the values they had at the start of your routine. You can safely assume that calls to other functions will not change these registers.

Registers ax, bx, cx, dx, di, si, and es are free for the taking, and you do not have to preserve the values of these registers before your routine ends. This freedom applies to other functions, too, so be aware that these same registers can change if you call Turbo C functions from your assembly language routines.

Because Turbo C uses di and si for register variables, if you use either of these two registers in in-line assembly language statements, the compiler turns off register variable optimizations, avoiding a possible conflict with your code. Unfortunately, this can also slow down the very C code you're trying to revise for extra speed. For this reason, it's usually best to avoid using di and si unless absolutely necessary. When linking external assembly language modules to C, it's up to you to preserve si and di for other functions that use register variables.

In-Line Assemblies

An in-line assembly language statement in Turbo C begins with the word asm and is followed by an assembly language mnemonic plus any operands required by the instruction. For example, to synchronize a program with an external interrupt signal, you can write:

```
/* wait for an interrupt */
asm sti
asm hlt
printf("Interrupt received\n");
```

When Turbo C compiles a program with embedded asm commands, it first creates an assembly language text file for the *entire* program, inserting your assembly language instructions along with the compiled code for other C statements into the text. The compiler then calls Turbo Assembler and Linker to assemble and link the program into the final code file. The complete syntax for asm is:

asm *[label] mnemonic/directive operands[;] [/* C comment */]*

The optional *label* is allowed only for data directives. You can't label instruction mnemonics. For example, to create a word variable named ForWord, you can write:

```
asm ForWord dw ?
```

To label an instruction in a function, you must use a *C label*—an identifier followed by a colon:

```
ThisLocation:
asm inc ax
:
:
asm or  ax, ax
asm jz ThisLocation
```

The *mnemonic/directive* may be any legal assembly language instruction or Turbo Assembler directive. The *operands* to the mnemonic or directive are the same as those used in "pure" assembly code. For example, you can increment an integer variable named Level with the command:

```
int Level;
asm inc [word Level];
```

Notice that the word qualifier is necessary to tell the assembler the size of Level. You have to add word, byte, tbyte, and other qualifiers only if the size of a variable is ambiguous. In unambiguous cases, you can leave the qualifier out:

```
int Bevel;
asm mov ax, [Bevel];
```

This moves the value of Bevel into ax. Because ax is a word register, Turbo Assembler assumes that Bevel is the same size. Also, as demonstrated here, you don't have to be concerned with *where* variables are located—the same assembly language constructions work for variables on the stack or variables in the data segment—just use the variable names as in these samples.

The semicolon at the end of an asm statement is optional. Don't confuse the semicolon with an assembly language comment character—Turbo C removes the semicolon before assembly. For this reason, to comment an assembly language statement, you must use C-style comments as in:

```
int Swivel;
int Drivel;
asm mov cx, [Swivel];    /* Load cx with value of Swivel */
asm shl ax, cl           /* Shift ax left by value in cl */
asm mov [Drivel], ax;    /* Save shifted ax in Drivel */
```

The semicolons at the ends of the asm lines and the C comments between /* and */ are stripped from the text before assembly. (I prefer to leave out the semicolons as in the middle asm statement in the example.)

Compiling and Assembling In-Line Code

There are four ways to compile C programs with embedded asm instructions. To demonstrate the differences between these methods, save Program 13-1 as TALLY.C. The notes after the listing explain how to compile the program.

Program 13-1 *TALLY.C*

```
1:  /* TALLY.C -- A Short In-Line Assembly Language Example */
2:
3:  #include <stdio.h>
4:
5:  main()
6:  {
7:      int votes;
8:      int tally;
9:
```

```
10:        votes = 100;
11:        tally = 500;
12:        printf("Tally : %d\n", tally);
13:        asm mov ax, [votes]
14:        asm add [tally], ax
15:        printf("Tally : %d\n", tally);
16:    }
```

How to Compile   TALLY.C uses two embedded `asm` statements to add the value of an integer
TALLY.C   variable `votes` to another variable `tally`, having the same effect as the C
statement:

```
tally = tally + votes;
```

Assuming you have prepared your disk directories as suggested earlier, to compile, assemble, and link the program, use the command:

```
tcc tally
```

You must use the DOS command-line compiler TCC.EXE for this.
You can't use the integrated editor and compiler program TC.EXE to compile programs containing in-line `asm` statements. During compilation, when
Turbo C reaches the first `asm` statement, it displays "Warning 13" and restarts compiling the program from the beginning. Normally, Turbo C compiles directly to .OBJ code files and then calls Turbo Linker to join the
program's object and library modules to create the final .EXE code file.
Because of the embedded `asm` statements, Turbo C instead compiles to an
.ASM text file, in this case creating the file TALLY.ASM. This file contains
the entire C program in assembly language form along with the `asm` statements. Next, Turbo C calls Turbo Assembler to assemble TALLY.ASM to
TALLY.OBJ. Then, after removing TALLY.ASM from disk, the compiler calls
Turbo Linker to link TALLY.OBJ with an appropriate Turbo C library and
other files, creating the finished TALLY.EXE code file—lots of action for
such a short command.

The problem with this method is the time wasted by compiling the
program up to the first `asm` statement, when Turbo C finally realizes it has
to generate an assembly language text file instead. You can avoid this by
specifying the **-B** option on the command line. (The B must be in uppercase.) For example:

```
tcc -B tally
```

compiles TALLY.C to TALLY.ASM, assembles TALLY.ASM to TALLY.OBJ,
and links TALLY.OBJ with a library file to create TALLY.EXE. TALLY.ASM
is erased from disk. To save the assembly language text file, use the **-S**
option (which also must be in uppercase):

```
tcc -S tally
```

This compiles TALLY.C to TALLY.ASM but does not assemble or link
the result. Use this command when you want to examine the assembly

language generated by Turbo C, giving you a close look at the instructions used to implement commands such as for loops and function calls. After examining the assembly language text, repeat the compilation with a –B command to create the finished program. (You can also assemble TALLY.ASM separately, but then you'll have to run Turbo Linker to join TALLY.OBJ with an appropriate Turbo C run-time library as explained in the Turbo C User's Guide and later in this chapter.)

Pragmatic Assemblies

Another method to compile programs such as TALLY.C with embedded asm commands is to insert the line:

```
#pragma inline
```

at the beginning of the module. To try this, add #pragma inline to TALLY.C between lines 1 and 2 (or as the first line) and compile with the command:

```
tcc tally
```

As you can see, the #pragma directive—an ANSI C standard method for activating a compiler's custom features—does the same job as the –B command-line option, avoiding the time that's otherwise wasted restarting the compiler after reaching the first asm statement.

Locations for Data and Code Statements

Every line of C code is either inside or outside a function, and you can insert asm statements in both places. The exact location of an asm statement affects where the code or directive is assembled. When an asm statement appears outside a function, it's assembled into the program's data segment. When an asm statement appears inside a function, it's assembled into the program's code segment. Usually, to create variables, you'll insert asm statements outside functions; to create code, you'll insert them inside functions. Here's a sample of both uses:

```
asm count db ?
main()
{
    asm shl [count], 1          /* multiply count by 4 */
    asm shl [count], 1
}
```

The variable count is declared in the program's data segment (relative to ds). The statements inside function main multiply count by 4, using fast shift instructions instead of mul. If you declare variables inside a function, the data is assembled into the code segment, requiring special handling:

```
main()
{
    asm jmp OverThere
    asm count db ?
OverThere:
    asm shl [count], 1          /* multiply count by 4 */
    asm shl [count], 1
}
```

Because the variable count is now in the code segment, a jmp instruction is required to avoid accidentally executing the value of count as machine code. Notice that the shl references to count are unchanged—Turbo C automatically inserts segment overrides (in this case, cs:) as needed to refer to variables in their proper segments.

Enabling 80286/ 386 Instructions

You can enable 80286 and 80386 instructions by inserting appropriate Turbo Assembler directives into the code. For example, to switch on nonprotected 80286 instructions, use the command:

```
asm .286C
```

Remember to use the MASM format instead of the Ideal-mode equivalent P286N, unless you also switch to Ideal mode. If you do this, remember to switch back to MASM mode, which is used for Turbo C's own assembly language output:

```
asm Ideal       /* switch on Ideal mode */
asm P286N       /* enable 80286 non-protected instructions */
asm MASM        /* switch back to MASM mode */
```

Sharing Data

In-line asm statements have ready access to C variables and structures—one of the most attractive advantages of the in-line method over the traditional external module approach (described later in this chapter). Table 13-1 lists Turbo C's data types, showing the assembly language qualifiers to use in ambiguous references, the number of bytes occupied by variables of each type, and the equivalent Turbo Assembler directive to create variables of the same size. Note that dq can be used to create initialized double floating point variables in assembly language but that there is no Turbo Assembler directive to create C float variables directly.

In asm statements, you can refer to named C variables of the types in Table 13-1 with code such as:

```
unsigned char initial;

initial = 'T';
asm mov dl, [initial]     /* load character into dl */
asm mov ah, 2             /* send character to DOS */
asm int 21h               /*  standard output function */
```

Table 13-1 *Turbo C Data Types*

Data Type	Qualifier	Bytes	Directive
unsigned char	Byte ptr	1	db
char	Byte ptr	1	db
enum	Word ptr	2	dw
unsigned short	Word ptr	2	dw
short	Word ptr	2	dw
unsigned int	Word ptr	2	dw
int	Word ptr	2	dw
unsigned long	Dword ptr	4	dd
long	Dword ptr	4	dd
float	Dword ptr	4	—
double	Qword ptr	8	dq
long double	Tbyte ptr	10	dt
near *	Word ptr	2	dw
far *	DWord ptr	4	dd

The unsigned character variable `initial` is loaded into `dl` by an `asm` statement. From Table 13-1, because `dl` and the `unsigned char` data type are both bytes, there's no need to use a `Byte` qualifier in the reference, although doing so is harmless:

```
asm mov dl, [Byte ptr initial]
```

The brackets, which are normally used to indicate a reference to memory rather than the value (that is, the address) of a label, result in the assembly language statement:

```
mov dl, [[Byte ptr initial]]
```

The double brackets cause no trouble, so don't worry about them. (Unless you're compiling with the **-s** option, you won't see these brackets anyway.) You can avoid this odd double-bracket behavior by not using brackets in the `asm` statement:

```
asm mov dl, initial
```

although now, the program is less clear. (Does `initial` refer to the address or the value of this variable?)

Declaring Assembly Language Data You can also declare variables for use only by your assembly language statements. For example, to create a 16-bit word named `TwoBytes` and load the variable's value into `cx`, you can write:

```
asm TwoBytes  db  1, 2
main()
{
    asm mov cx, [Word ptr TwoBytes]
}
```

The `TwoBytes` variable is declared in the program's data segment (outside a function), using the `db` directive to store 2 bytes (1 and 2) in memory. An assembly language statement then loads the value of `TwoBytes` into `cx`, setting `cl` to 1 and `ch` to 2. The `Word ptr` qualifier is necessary to refer to `TwoBytes` as a 16-bit word.

Because `TwoBytes` is declared in an `asm` statement, you can't refer to the variable with C code. For this reason, unless you need private variables for your assembly language instructions, you'll usually declare C variables and refer to them from assembly language.

C Structures

Member (field) names in C structures are internally stored as offset values from the beginning of the structure. For example, the structure:

```
struct PersonRec {
    char Name[50];
    char Address[60];
    char CityStZip[60];
    char AgeInYears;
} Person;
```

assigns offset values to `Name`, `Address`, and `CityStZip` representing the positions of these fields in the `PersonRec` structure. Keeping this fact in mind, you have to use both the variable and member identifiers separated by a period to refer to structure fields in an assembly language statement:

```
asm mov si, offset Person.Address
```

which assembles to:

```
mov si, 0038h
```

The 0038h (which might be a different value on your system if you view this in Turbo Debugger) represents the offset from the beginning of the data segment to the `Address` field—that is, `Person + Address`. Contrast this with the instruction:

```
asm mov al, Byte ptr Person.AgeInYears
```

which assembles to:

```
mov al, Byte ptr DGROUP:_Person + 170
```

In this case, the *value* of the `AgeInYears` field is loaded into `al`. The 170 represents the offset value of this field from the start of the `Person` record. (Turbo C adds underscores to variable names—but more about that later.)

Many times, you'll want to refer to structures with pointers, usually loaded into bx. For example, to initialize bx to the address of the Person record, use the statement:

```
asm mov bx, offset Person
```

With ds:bx addressing Person, you can now load the values or addresses of other fields relative to the pointer:

```
asm mov dl, [bx.AgeInYears]
```

No size qualifier such as Byte ptr is needed because both the field and register are the same size.

When two or more structures have identical field names, you must resolve ambiguous pointer references by adding the structure name in parentheses before field names. For example, suppose there is another record type named Customers with a field CityStZip—the same field name as in the PersonRec structure. To load si with the offset address of the CityStZip field from a variable TheBakery of type Customers addressed by bx, you can write:

```
asm mov bx, offset TheBakery
asm lea si, [bx.(struct Customers) CityStZip]
```

The first asm command loads bx with the offset address of TheBakery. The second command loads si with the effective address of the CityStZip field relative to bx. The structure name in parentheses lets Turbo C resolve the ambiguous field name reference to CityStZip.

Note: The Turbo Assembler 1.0 User's Guide suggests that resolving ambiguous field name references is *always* necessary. This is not true. When specifying structures by name, Turbo C already has all the information it needs to know to which structure a field refers. You have to specify the structure name only when using pointers as in this example to address structures containing duplicate field names.

Sharing Code

In-line assembly language statements can call C functions, and C statements can call functions written entirely in assembly language. Let's start with the easier of these two techniques, showing how to write a complete function in assembly language and call that function with C statements. Enter Program 13-2, UPDOWN.C, and compile, assemble, and link with the command:

```
tcc -v updown
```

You need to use the -v option only if you want to examine the source code while running the program in Turbo Debugger. If you want to examine the assembly language output, enter the following command and use your text editor to view the UPDOWN.ASM file:

```
tcc -S updown
```

Program 13-2 *UPDOWN.C*

```
 1:  /* In-Line Assembly Language Function Demonstration */
 2:
 3:  #pragma inline
 4:  #include <stdio.h>
 5:
 6:  extern void BumpStrUp( unsigned char far * TheString,
 7:      int StringLength );
 8:
 9:  extern void BumpStrDown( unsigned char far * TheString,
10:      int StringLength );
11:
12:  char *MixedUp = "UppER aNd LOwEr CaSE";
13:
14:  main()
15:  {
16:      printf("Before BumpStrUp: %s\n", MixedUp);
17:      BumpStrUp( MixedUp, strlen(MixedUp) );
18:      printf("After BumpStrUp:   %s\n", MixedUp);
19:      BumpStrDown( MixedUp, strlen(MixedUp) );
20:      printf("After BumpStrDown: %s\n", MixedUp);
21:  }
22:
23:  void BumpStrUp( unsigned char far * TheString,
24:      int StringLength )
25:  {
26:      asm les di, TheString          /* Address string with es:di */
27:      asm mov cx, StringLength       /* Load string length into cx */
28:      asm jcxz Exit                  /* Exit if length = 0 */
29:      asm cld                        /* Auto-increment di */
30:  NextChar:
31:      asm mov al, [Byte ptr es:di]   /* Load next character */
32:      asm cmp al, 'a'                /* Skip conversion if */
33:      asm jb NotLower                /*   character is not */
34:      asm cmp al, 'z'                /*   lowercase */
35:      asm ja NotLower
36:      asm sub al, 32                 /* Convert to uppercase */
37:  NotLower:
38:      asm stosb                      /* Store character in string */
39:      asm loop NextChar              /* Loop until done */
40:  Exit:;
41:  }
42:
```

```
43:    void BumpStrDown( unsigned char far * TheString,
44:        int StringLength )
45:    {
46:        asm les di, TheString          /* Address string with es:di */
47:        asm mov cx, StringLength       /* Load string length into cx */
48:        asm jcxz Exit                  /* Exit if length = 0 */
49:        asm cld                        /* Auto-increment di */
50:    NextChar:
51:        asm mov al, [Byte ptr es:di]   /* Load next character */
52:        asm cmp al, 'A'                /* Skip conversion if */
53:        asm jb NotUpper                /*   character is not */
54:        asm cmp al, 'Z'                /*   uppercase */
55:        asm ja NotUpper
56:        asm add al, 32                 /* Convert to lowercase */
57:    NotUpper:
58:        asm stosb                      /* Store character in string */
59:        asm loop NextChar              /* Loop until done */
60:    Exit:;
61:    }
```

How UPDOWN.C Works

Lines 6–10 declare two external functions `BumpStrUp` and `BumpStrDown`, which convert strings to all uppercase or to all lowercase. For convenience, the functions are listed together with the main program, but they could be in separate modules if you're prepared to handle all the details of linking yourself.

The main function (lines 14–21) calls the external functions, displaying the effect on a string variable (line 12) addressed by a far pointer. Function `BumpStrUp` (23–41) lists two parameters, a `far char` pointer and an integer representing the string length. The first assembly language instruction (line 26) uses `les` to load the `es:di` registers with the full 32-bit address of the string. You should be able to understand the purpose of the other instructions from the comments to the right of most lines.

Line 40 illustrates an idiosyncracy of labels in Turbo C. The emerging ANSI standard for the C language specifies that a label must be followed by a statement. Because the assembly language code needs a method to jump to the end of the function, this poses a problem—solved here by an extra semicolon after the `Exit:` label.

The `BumpStrDown` function (lines 43–61) is nearly the same as `BumpStrUp` except for lines 52–56, which convert uppercase letters to lowercase.

Behind the Scenes

UPDOWN.C has a few backstage surprises that are not evident from the program listing. As you'll discover if you examine the assembly language output, both `BumpStrUp` and `BumpStrDown` begin with the instructions:

```
push   bp              ; Save bp on stack
mov    bp, sp          ; Address stack with bp
push   si              ; Save si
push   di              ; Save di
```

The first and second instructions save `bp` before equating this same register with `sp`, preparing to address parameters on the stack. The second and third instructions save the values of si and di. This is done because the functions use di; therefore, Turbo C takes the safe route and saves both si and di to avoid all possibility of a conflict with any register variables used by other routines that may call this one. Later on, both functions end with:

```
pop     di          ; Restore saved di
pop     si          ; Restore saved si
pop     bp          ; Restore saved bp
ret                 ; Return to caller
```

This restores di, si, and bp to their original values before returning to the instruction following the call that activated the function.

As you can see from this, when using embedded asm statements, Turbo C takes care of the details associated with addressing parameters, saving and restoring register variables, keeping the stack "right," and manipulating bp. While this is certainly helpful, there are disadvantages to having so much help. For one thing, neither custom function uses si; therefore, saving and restoring this register is a waste of time. Also, in this case, there isn't any need to save and restore di either because the main program, which calls the custom functions, has no register variables, and no conflict is possible by changing di.

For better control over such details—and to avoid having to preface each assembly language statement with asm—you can write external assembly language modules to link to Turbo C programs. This takes more work, but the results are often worth the trouble, as the next section explains.

External Assemblies

Because both Turbo Assembler and Turbo C can create the same .OBJ code-file format, you can write portions of a program in C and other parts in assembly language and then use Turbo Linker to join the object-code files into the finished .EXE program. Turbo C is also able to run the assembler and linker directly, simplifying compilation, at least for relatively small programs. Despite adding complexity to a programming project, external assembly language methods offer several advantages over in-line asm statements:

▶ Reduced compilation time

▶ Assembly language modules can use Ideal mode

▶ No "hidden" instructions are added

▶ The C program retains a higher degree of portability

▶ External routines can be debugged separately

▶ External routines can be used with other languages

Compilation times are reduced because Turbo C no longer has to generate an assembly language text file, required for assembling embedded in-line asm statements. You can use the preferred Ideal mode in your assembly language modules, which also helps Turbo Assembler to run fast. No extra instructions, stack manipulations, or `push` and `pop` instructions are added—these are items that Turbo C inserts into in-line `asm` functions whether needed or not.

If you write your programs purely in C and then selectively convert individual functions to assembly language, you will improve your program's portability. After optimizing, if you need to transfer a program to another computer—for example, a Macintosh with a 68000 processor—it's relatively simple to replace the optimized assembly language modules with the original C code that you wisely saved on disk. Then, after the program is working correctly on the new computer, you would start optimizing sections of the code in that computer's native tongue.

External assembly language routines can also simplify debugging. You can assemble and debug external routines apart from the main progam—a far easier task than hunting for small monsters in the jungle of an 80K code file. You might also be able to use your external routines with other languages. Despite these many advantages, there are a few drawbacks to be aware of when using external routines:

▶ You can no longer mix C and assembly language statements as you can with `asm` statements. You must code entire functions in assembly language.

▶ You must have a good understanding of segments and segment registers, addressing modes, simplified memory models, and related directives. (Of course, you've carefully read every word in this book, so these details won't give you any problems.)

▶ The steps to compile and link a program may be more complex, although Turbo C can help by running the assembler and linker directly.

Simplified Memory Models

The good news about external routines is that "hard-way" SEGMENT directives are completely unnecessary. Segment names, classes, and other segment options are identical for Turbo C and Turbo Assembler memory models. This means you can use simplified memory-model directives such as `DATASEG, CODESEG, FARDATA,` and `CONST` to organize your assembly language module's data and code segments. If you really must declare segments manually, you can certainly do so—as long as you're careful to follow the various conventions expected by Turbo C and Turbo Linker. I can hardly imagine a situation where this is necessary, however, so I won't waste space discussing the details here. Consult your Turbo C User's and Reference Guides for more information.

Program 13-3, CSHELL.ASM, shows one of the many possible ways to organize an external assembly language module. You can use CSHELL as a template for your own designs, inserting various items where shown by comments in the listing. There's no reason to assemble this program—it doesn't do anything useful, but if you want to be sure you didn't make any typing mistakes, assemble with:

```
tasm /ml cshell
```

The /ml option tells Turbo Assembler to switch on case sensitivity. This matches the way Turbo C works, considering names such as MyFunction and myfunCTion to be *different* identifiers.

Program 13-3 *CSHELL.ASM*

```
 1:  %TITLE "Shell for Turbo C .OBJ Modules"
 2:
 3:          IDEAL
 4:          MODEL   small
 5:
 6:  DATASEG
 7:
 8:  ;-----  Insert PUBLIC data declarations here
 9:
10:  ;-----  Insert EXTRN data declarations here
11:
12:  ;-----  Insert initialized variables here
13:
14:
15:  FARDATA
16:
17:  ;-----  Insert far-data-segment variables here
18:
19:
20:  CODESEG
21:
22:  ;-----  Insert PUBLIC code declarations here
23:
24:  ;-----  Insert EXTRN code declarations here
25:
26:
27:  %NEWPAGE
28:  ;--------------------------------------------------------------
29:  ; <type> funcname( <parameters> )
30:  ;--------------------------------------------------------------
31:  PROC    funcname        NEAR
32:          push    bp
33:          mov     bp, sp
34:
35:  ;       sub     sp, n           ; Optional: reserve space for locals
36:  ;       push    di              ; Optional: save register var di
37:  ;       push    si              ; Optional: restore register var si
38:
39:  ;-----    Insert instructions here
40:
41:  ;       pop     si              ; Optional: restore si
42:  ;       pop     di              ; Optional: restore di
43:  ;       mov     sp, bp          ; Optional: restore sp
44:
```

```
45:             pop      bp              ; Restore old bp pointer
46:             ret                      ; Return to caller
47:   ENDP      funcname
48:
49:             END                      ; End of module
```

> Note: If your assembly language module declares no near or far variables,
> you may remove the **DATASEG** and **FARDATA** directives from CSHELL.ASM.

Using CSHELL.ASM   CHSELL begins by selecting Ideal mode and specifying Turbo C's default small memory model. Change `small` to `tiny`, `medium`, `compact`, `large`, or `huge`, matching the memory model used by your C program. Notice the absence of `DOSSEG` and `STACK` directives. This allows Turbo C and Turbo Linker to arrange segments as needed by C run-time library routines and to specify the stack size, usually 4K unless you change it (see `_stklen` in the Turbo C Reference Guide).

The shell has three segments: two for data (**DATASEG** and **FARDATA**) and one for code (**CODESEG**). As the comments in the listing indicate, you can declare variables and code PUBLIC, thus sharing items in the assembly module with other modules. For example, to create a word integer and export the variable to C, you could insert these lines after **DATASEG**:

```
; In the assembly language module:
PUBLIC  _AsmValue
_AsmValue        dw         100
```

The `_AsmValue` label is exported by **PUBLIC** to other modules, including those written in C. A corresponding declaration in the main program tells Turbo C about the external variable:

```
/* In the C program: */
extern int AsmValue;
```

Likewise, a variable in the C program can be imported by the assembly language module. All symbols are public in C; therefore, the C text just declares a variable normally:

```
/* In the C program: */
int NewValue;
main()
{
    NewValue = 500;
}
```

Then, in the assembly language module, to import `NewValue`, insert an **EXTRN** directive inside the data segment:

```
DATASEG
EXTRN   _NewValue:Word
```

You can now use _NewValue in assembly language statements. For example, to copy the value of the imported C variable _NewValue to the word variable _AsmValue declared in the assembly language module, you could use these commands in the code segment:

```
CODESEG
mov     ax, [_NewValue]         ; Load C variable into ax
mov     [_AsmValue], ax         ; Copy to assembly module variable
```

The code segment (lines 20–49) includes a shell for an external function. Line 31 declares the function name, which should be made public with the line:

```
PUBLIC funcname
```

The shell function is declared NEAR (line 31), indicating that the code will be stored in the same segment as the call instructions to the function. You can take out or change NEAR to FAR if you plan to call the function from another segment.

Lines 32–33 and 45 prepare, save, and restore bp for addressing function parameters on the stack, using methods explained in a moment. The instructions at lines 35–37 and 41–43 are optional. You need to save and restore si and di only if these registers are used in the function. Also, you can subtract a value from sp to create space for temporary (local) variables (see line 35), later reclaiming this space by assigning bp to sp (see line 43).

About Underscores As several of the previous examples show, you must preface all PUBLIC and EXTRN symbols with underscores. You need to do this only in the assembly language module (not in the C source) because Turbo C adds an underscore to all global symbols unless you are using the -u option to compile programs. (Don't use this option unless you're also prepared to recompile the entire Turbo C run-time library, which expects global symbols to be underscored.) If you receive "undefined symbol" errors during linking, the cause may be a missing underscore in an assembly language module.

Using Far Data If you declare variables in a far data segment after the FARDATA keyword, you must prepare a segment register to locate the variables in memory. (See chapter 11 for a more complete discussion on this subject.) First, declare your variables after a FARDATA directive:

```
FARDATA
_OuterLimits    dw      ?
```

Next, in the code segment, you must prepare a segment register before using the variable. One approach is to use the SEG operator to load the address of the far data segment:

```
mov     ax, SEG _OuterLimits    ; Address far data segment
mov     es, ax                  ; with es
mov     [es:_OuterLimits], dx   ; Store dx to variable
```

Or, you can use the predefined @fardata symbol:

```
mov     ax, @fardata              ; Address far data segment
mov     es, ax                    ;  with es
mov     [es:_OuterLimits], dx     ; Store dx to variable
```

Sharing Code Calling assembly language functions is identical to calling C functions. As an example, Program 13-4, CFILLSTR.C, declares an external function to fill strings with characters. The example also demonstrates how to replace C functions with assembly language. I'll list commands for compiling and assembling CFILLSTR later—as you'll see, there are many ways to proceed.

Program 13-4 *CFILLSTR.C*

```
 1:  /* Test CFILL External Module */
 2:
 3:  #include <stdio.h>
 4:
 5:  extern void fillstring( unsigned char far * thestring,
 6:      int stringlength, char fillchar );
 7:
 8:  char *test = "Filled to the brim";
 9:
10:  main()
11:  {
12:      printf("Before fillstring:  %s\n", test);
13:      fillstring( test, strlen(test), '@' );
14:      printf("After fillstring:   %s\n", test);
15:  }
16:
17:  /*
18:  void fillstring( unsigned char far * thestring,
19:      int stringlength, char fillchar )
20:  {
21:      int i;
22:
23:      for (i = 0; i < stringlength; i++)
24:          thestring[ i ] = fillchar;
25:  }
26:  */
```

Compiling Just to be sure that you typed CFILLSTR correctly, temporarily delete lines
CFILLSTR.C 17 and 26, activating the function at lines 18–25. Later, you'll replace this "pure C" version of the fillstring function with an optimized assembly language module. But first, compile and run the program with the commands:

```
tcc -v cfillstr
cfillstr
```

Use the -v option only if you want to examine the code with Turbo Debugger. If you do that, you may also want to use the View:CPU commands to examine the machine code for fillstring. As Figure 13-1 shows, Turbo C's output is impressively tight, but we can still do better. Notice that, unlike in-line asm statements, only si and not di is saved and restored, a small improvement. Even so, instructions such as les inside the for loop are inefficient. The compiler apparently isn't smart enough to realize that es isn't changed anywhere else in the loop; therefore, reinitializing the register on each pass is unnecessary.

Calling Assembly Language Functions from C

Replace the comment brackets /* and */ at lines 17 and 26 in CFILLSTR.C if you removed these lines. Then, save Program 13-5, CFILL.ASM, which contains an assembly language version of the fillstring function. Instructions for assembling the modules into a finished program follow the listing.

```
_fillstring: void fillstring( unsigned char far * thestring,
      cs:022C 55             push   bp
      cs:022D 8BEC            mov    bp,sp
      cs:022F 56             push   si
CFILLSTR#37:  for (i = 0; i < stringlength; i++)
      cs:0230 33F6            xor    si,si
      cs:0232 EB0A            jmp    023E
CFILLSTR#38:  thestring[ i ] = fillchar;
      cs:0234 8A460A          mov    al,[bp + 0A]
      cs:0237 C45E04          les    bx,[bp + 04]
      cs:023A 268800          mov    es:[bx + si],al
      cs:023D 46             inc    si
      cs:023E 3B7608          cmp    si,[bp + 08]
      cs:0241 7CF1            jl     CFILLSTR#38 (0234)
CFILLSTR#39: }
      cs:0243 5E             pop    si
      cs:0244 5D             pop    bp
      cs:0245 C3             ret
```

Figure 13-1 *The fillstring function from CFILLSTR.C as disassembled by Turbo Debugger.*

Program 13-5 *CFILL.ASM*

```
1:  %TITLE "Fill C Strings--External Module Demonstration"
2:
3:         IDEAL
4:         MODEL   small
5:
6:         CODESEG
7:
8:         PUBLIC  _fillstring
9:
```

```
10:    ;--------------------------------------------------------------
11:    ; void fillstring( unsigned char far * thestring,
12:    ;     int stringlength, char fillchar )
13:    ;--------------------------------------------------------------
14:    PROC    _fillstring      NEAR
15:
16:            ARG thestring:Dword, stringlength:Word, fillchar:Byte
17:
18:            push    bp                      ; Save old bp pointer
19:            mov     bp, sp                  ; Address parameters
20:            mov     cx, [stringlength]      ; Assign string len to cx
21:            jcxz    @@99                    ; Exit if length = 0
22:            push    di                      ; Save di
23:            les     di, [thestring]         ; Address string with es:di
24:            mov     al, [fillchar]          ; Assign fill char to al
25:            repnz   stosb                   ; Store characters in string
26:            pop     di                      ; Restore saved di
27:    @@99:
28:            pop     bp                      ; Restore saved bp
29:            ret                             ; Return to caller
30:    ENDP    _fillstring
31:
32:            END                     ; End of module
```

Assembling and Linking External Modules

You should now have two files on disk, CFILLSTR.C (with the fillstring function converted to a comment) and CFILL.ASM, containing the assembly language replacement for this same function. There are several methods you can use to assemble, compile, and link the separate modules (and similar multiple-file programs) to create the finished .EXE program. The simplest technique is to let Turbo C do all the work:

```
tcc cfillstr cfill.asm
```

Because .C is the default file-name extension for Turbo C, this command first compiles CFILLSTR.C to CFILLSTR.OBJ. Then, recognizing the .ASM file-name extension as an assembly language module, Turbo C calls Turbo Assembler to assemble CFILL.ASM to CFILL.OBJ. Finally, the compiler calls Turbo Linker to join the object-code modules into CFILLSTR.EXE. When you have only a few modules to compile and assemble, this one-step method is the easiest to use.

Note: I purposely did not name the assembly language module in this example CFILLSTR.ASM. If the C program (CFILLSTR.C) has any in-line **asm** statements, Turbo C outputs the entire program in assembly language to CFILLSTR.ASM, thus erasing the assembly language text file with no prior warning. For safety, always use different names for your C and assembly language modules. In other words, if your main program file is KERMIT.C, *don't* save your external routines in KERMIT.ASM.

Assembling and Linking Separately

When you have many modules, you'll save time by assembling and linking separately. The first step is to assemble all your .ASM files. Because the `fillstring` example has only one such file, a single command does the job:

```
tasm /ml cfill
```

The `/ml` option turns on case sensitivity, meaning that symbols such as `UpAndDown` and `upanddown` are considered to be different, as they normally are in C programs. (Turbo Assembler usually ignores case sensitivity, so the `/ml` option is necessary to avoid errors during linking.) After assembling all external modules, compile the main C program. Again, this example has only one .C file, so only one command is needed:

```
tcc -c cfillstr
```

The `-c` option tells Turbo C to "compile only," generating CFILLSTR.OBJ but not linking the program into a finished code file. To include all modules, you have to complete this step yourself, calling Turbo Linker to join the object-code files along with the appropriate Turbo C run-time library routines to create CFILLSTR.EXE. There are two ways to accomplish this task: the long way and the not-so-long way. Let's cover the more difficult long way first:

```
tlink c:\tc\lib\c0s cfillstr cfill, cfillstr,, c:\tc\lib\cs
```

The first item after `tlink` specifies an object-code file in the C:TC\LIB directory for the appropriate memory model, in this case C0S.OBJ. (The 0 is a zero; *not* the letter O.) The second and third items list the .OBJ code files to link—any order for these files is okay. A comma separates the list of .OBJ files from the name to use for the finished code file, in this case, CFILLSTR.EXE. Two commas then follow, holding a place for an optional map file, not created in this example. Finally, the run-time library is specified, also in the C:TC\LIB directory.

The C0S object-code file and CS library file names must match the memory model used by the program. The final letter of these two file names represents one of the models listed in Table 13-2.

Easier Linking

An easier (but slightly less quick) method for linking separate modules is to use Turbo C as a "front end" to Turbo Linker. In other words, by giving Turbo C various commands, you can skip compiling and go straight

Table 13-2 *C Run-Time Library File Names*

Memory Model	Object File	Library File	TCC Option
Tiny	C0T.OBJ	CS.LIB	-mt
Small	C0S.OBJ	CS.LIB	-ms
Medium	C0M.OBJ	CM.LIB	-mm
Compact	C0C.OBJ	CC.LIB	-mc
Large	C0L.OBJ	CL.LIB	-ml
Huge	C0H.OBJ	CH.LIB	-mh

to linking. Doing this eliminates the need to specify run-time library file names and, therefore, simplifies the link command. For example, to assemble, compile, and link the CFILLSTR demo takes three commands:

```
tasm /ml cfill
tcc -c cfillstr
tcc -ms cfillstr.obj cfill.obj
```

The first two commands are the same as described before. The third command calls Turbo C a second time, using the **-ms** option to specify a memory model, in this case *small*. (See Table 13-2 for other memory-model option letters.) After the memory-model option are the object-code files to link. Although you must include the .OBJ file-name extension with each file, this not-so-long linking method simplifies most of the dirty work of running Turbo Linker directly.

Debugging Multilanguage Programs

There are two approaches to debugging programs that mix C and assembly language. The first method adds debugging information only for C statements. To do this, compile with the one-step command:

```
tcc -v cfillstr cfill.asm
```

This is the same command listed earlier but with a **-v** option added to include debugging information in CFILLSTR.EXE. You can then debug the code with:

```
td cfillstr
```

The problem is, this command does not allow you to see your assembly language source code—only C source lines are listed in the main window. To also see assembly language, you must assemble and link separately, using the more complex methods discussed in the previous section. Using the CFILL.ASM and CFILLSTR.C examples, the complete steps are:

```
tasm /ml /zi cfill
tcc -c -v cfillstr
tcc -ms -lv cfillstr.obj cfill.obj
```

First, CFILL.ASM is assembled, using the /ml option to switch on case sensitivity and /zi to include debugging information in CFILL.OBJ. Next, Turbo C compiles CFILLSTR.C, specifying compilation only (-c) and adding more debugging information to CFILLSTR.OBJ (-v). Finally, Turbo C is called into service as a front end for Turbo Linker. The -ms option selects an appropriate memory model. The -lv option passes an option letter, in this case v, to Turbo Linker so that all of the debugging information in both CFILLSTR.OBJ and CFILL.OBJ is transferred to the finished code file CFILLSTR.EXE. The result can then be loaded into Turbo Debugger with:

```
td cfillstr
```

If you try this, press F7 repeatedly to step through the program. When you get to the call to fillstring, Turbo Debugger switches to the assembly language source, letting you step through the individual instructions in the external module. When the assembly language module finishes, you again see the Turbo C source code. (Of course, for this to work, both CFILLSTR.C and CFILL.ASM must be in the current directory.)

How CFILLSTR.C and CFILL.ASM Work

Now that you know how to assemble, compile, and link multiple modules in assembly language and C, let's take a closer look at how the two files work together. First, examine CFILLSTR.C (Program 13-4) lines 5–6, which declare function fillstring external, using the extern directive. This allows Turbo C to know that the code for the call to fillstring at line 13 will be supplied later. (If it isn't, Turbo Linker displays an error.)

Program 13-5, CFILL.ASM, replaces the fillstring function with an assembly language module. Line 8 declares _fillstring to be public, adding an underscore to conform with Turbo C's rule for all global symbols. Inside the function, an ARG directive (line 16) simplifies addressing parameters passed on the stack. Without ARG, you'd have to calculate offsets from bp and use instructions such as:

```
mov     cx, [bp + 6]
```

assuming, that is, that the parameter you want is 6 bytes ahead of where ss:bp points. Instead of using this error-prone method, ARG lets you list the function parameters in the same order that the identifiers appear in the function prototype (see lines 11–12). For each parameter separated by commas, list the name and size, using one of the size qualifiers from Table 13-1, but without the ptr suffix. Using ARG this way allows lines 20 and 23–24 to refer to parameters by name. Of course, you still have to be careful to specify the correct sizes for your variables.

After loading the appropriate registers, line 25 uses a repeated string instruction to store the requested number of characters into the string. No checks are made on this length—so be careful, or you'll overwrite other items in memory. Compare this with the compiled code in Figure 13-1 for the pure C version of fillstring. It doesn't take much detective work to know that a single string instruction runs faster than the C `for` loop, which takes eight assembly language instructions.

The assembly language `fillstring` also preserves register `di` just in case a register variable is being used by another function that calls `fillstring`. But notice how lines 22 and 26 postpone saving and restoring `di` until after the previous code checks the string length and exits if the length is 0 (lines 20–21). Although this may be a minor improvement, it could reduce running times if `fillstring` is called frequently with zero-length strings.

Calling C Functions from Assembly Language

So far, you've learned how to share variables between C and assembly language and how to call external assembly language functions from a C program. Going the other direction—that is, calling a C function from an assembly language module—is also possible, but it requires care to accomplish properly.

If the function has no parameters, the process is simple. Just declare the C function in an `EXTRN` directive and use a `call` instruction:

```
CODESEG
EXTRN _cfunction:proc
;
;
call _cfunction
```

This assumes that a function named `cfunction` exists in the C program to be linked with the assembly language module. Once again, an underscore is added in the assembly language declaration (but not in the C text).

When functions require parameters, the process becomes more difficult. Simple parameters such as characters and integers are often passed directly on the stack. Complex variables such as strings, structures, and arrays are passed by reference, that is, by address. Also, many functions return results in specific registers. When calling C functions from assembly language, it's your responsibility to take care of these details.

First, let's look at the simplest case: calling a C function with one integer parameter:

```
void showscore( int thescore )
{
    printf("\nThe score is: %d\n", thescore );
}
```

From inside an assembly language module, to call the `showscore` routine, passing the value of a word variable as `thescore`, you can write:

```
CODESEG
EXTRN     _showscore:proc
mov       ax, 76          ; Assign score to a register
push      ax              ; Pass parameter on stack
call      _showscore      ; Call the C function
pop       ax              ; Fix the stack
```

First, a sample score is assigned to ax (any other register would do as well), which is then pushed onto the stack before calling _showscore. After returning from the function, a word is popped from the stack. This is required because in C it is the caller's responsibility to remove parameters from the stack. (If you read chapter 12, you'll recall that, in Pascal, procedures and functions take care of removing stacked parameters before returning. It's possible, but not usually recommended, to do the same in C. Normally, C requires the caller to remove parameters.) When you have several parameters, it may be better just to add the total number of bytes to sp. For example, to call a function that takes four 16-bit parameters, you might use:

```
push      [v1]            ; Push four word variables (not shown)
push      [v2]            ;   onto the stack
push      [v3]
push      [v4]
call      _aCfunction     ; Call a C function
add       sp, 8           ; Remove parameters
```

Push multiple parameters in the *reverse* order in which they are declared in the C function. Assuming the fillstring function is defined as:

```
void fillstring( unsigned char far * thestring,
    int stringlength, char fillchar )
```

to call this function from assembly language and fill a string variable with blanks, requires several steps. First, the assembly language module declares a string variable:

```
DATASEG
PUBLIC    _astring
_astring          db        80 dup (0)
```

Then, the same module declares _fillstring in an EXTRN directive and calls the function to fill the string variable with blanks:

```
CODESEG
EXTRN     _fillstring:proc
;
;
xor       ah, ah          ; Zero upper half of ax
mov       al, ' '         ; Assign blank char to al
push      ax              ; Push fillchar parameter
mov       ax, 79          ; Assign string length to ax
push      ax              ; Push stringlength parameter
```

```
push    ds              ; Push segment of string address
mov     ax, offset _astring     ; Assign offset address to ax
push    ax              ; Push offset of string address
call    _fillstring     ; Call the function
add     sp, 8           ; Remove parameters from stack
```

Each parameter—the fill character, string length, and 32-bit pointer to the string variable—is pushed onto the stack in the reverse order as listed in the function definition. In the case of the pointer, the segment address ds is pushed before the offset. After the call to _fillstring, 8 bytes are added to the stack pointer sp, removing the parameters from the stack.

Even though in this example the _fillstring function is actually written in assembly language, calling pure C functions is no different. When you are not sure about exactly how to call a library routine (the ubiquitous printf(), for example), run a test C program in Turbo Debugger and examine the compiled machine code. This will tell you what parameters are required and will also give you many new insights into how compilers convert C statements to assembly language—knowledge that you can use for your own external modules.

Function Results

Many C functions return values in registers or, in the case of float, double, and long double values, in the math coprocessor top of stack (st(0)). Table 13-3 lists the registers used to return various Turbo C data types. All 8-bit types are returned in al; 16-bit types, in ax; and 32-bit types, in dx:ax, with the low-order portion of the value (for example, the offset of a pointer) in ax.

Table 13-3 *Turbo C Function Result Types*

Data Type	Bytes	Register(s)
Unsigned char	1	al
Char	1	al
Enum	2	ax
Unsigned short	2	ax
Short	2	ax
Unsigned int	2	ax
Int	2	ax
Unsigned long	4	dx:ax
Long	4	dx:ax
Float	4	st(0) (8087 stack)
Double	8	st(0) (8087 stack)
Long double	10	st(0) (8087 stack)
Near *	2	ax
Far *	4	dx:ax

LOCAL Variables

In addition to variables declared in the data segment or shared with a C program, you can also use local variables on the stack in your assembly language modules. A local variable exists only while the function runs. Stack space is created for the variable at the start of the function and is then reclaimed before the function ends. This way, other functions can share the same memory for their own local variables, cutting down on the program's total memory requirements. You probably know how to declare local variables in C functions, for example, as control variables in a **for** loop:

```
void countup()
{
    int i;

    for (i = 0; i < 10; i++)
        printf( "%d ", i );
}
```

Integer variable i is allocated on the stack at the start of the **countup** function and exists only while the function runs. You can do the same in an assembly language module with a **LOCAL** directive. Here's an example of a complete function:

```
PROC    _cfunction      NEAR
        LOCAL i:Word =stacksize
        push    bp
        mov     bp, sp
        sub     sp, stacksize
        mov     [i], 0
@@10:
        inc     [i]
;
;-----  Code to use local variable [i]
;
        cmp     [i], 10
        jne     @@10
        mov     sp, bp
        pop     bp
        ret                     ; Return to caller
ENDP    _cfunction
```

The **LOCAL** directive in this example prepares a variable i of type **Word**. The =stacksize is assigned the total number of bytes occupied by all local variables—in this case, 2 bytes. This value is subtracted from **sp** after preparing to address variables on the stack. Then, to refer to i, use instructions such as **mov**, **inc**, and **cmp**. Because of the **LOCAL** directive, references such as [i] are translated into:

```
mov     [bp - 2], 0
inc     [bp - 2]
```

and so on. With LOCAL, you don't have to calculate the negative offsets from bp to locate variables on the stack—you can just use the variable names.

Notice the mov sp, bp instruction just before this sample function restores bp. Because bp doesn't change during the function, you can reset sp from bp, removing the local variable space from the stack, or you can add stacksize to sp with:

```
add     sp, stacksize
```

Either method works, but restoring sp from bp is faster. You can also declare multiple local variables with statements such as:

```
LOCAL i:Word; j:Word; c:Byte =stacksize
```

You can then use the three local variables i, j, and c, after subtracting stacksize from the stack pointer to reserve space on the stack. (You must always do this. LOCAL simplifies addressing local variables; it doesn't create space for the variables in memory.)

> Note: I included local variables in this section because you should know how to use them. But remember that one of the reasons compiled C programs can run slowly is that addressing local variables takes time. The same is true for Pascal and other languages. One of the motives behind adding assembly language to high-level language code is to squeeze as much speed as possible into a program. And, one way to do that is to store variables in fast processor registers instead of on the stack. The morale is: Don't use techniques that seem interesting; go for the techniques that give you the speed gains you're after.

Summary

The main reasons for adding assembly language to C programs are to add speed to your code and to provide low-level access to the hardware. Turbo C has two methods for injecting assembly language into programs: in-line asm statements and external functions. In-line statements are easy to use but aren't as versatile as external functions.

Because most programs spend 90% of the time running about 10% of the instructions, finding and optimizing a program's critical 10% often produces remarkable speed increases. Rewriting the other 90% may be a waste of time. Don't rewrite C statements that already run as fast as necessary.

Registers bp, cs, ds, sp, and ss must be restored before an assembly language module ends. Registers ax, bx, cx, dx, di, si, and es may be used freely. Because Turbo C uses di and si for register variables, it's a good idea to preserve these two registers.

Inserting in-line `asm` statements causes Turbo C to generate an assembly language text version of the entire program. This file can then be assembled and linked to create the finished program. You can save time by using the **-B** option to compile programs to assembly language from the start, or you can insert an equivalent `#pragma inline` statement. Another option **-S** lets you examine the assembly language text file, which is normally removed.

In-line `asm` statements inside functions go in the program's code segment. In-line `asm` statements outside functions go in the program's data segment. You can share code and data with C, and you can access C structures in assembly language statements.

Writing external assembly language functions takes more work than injecting `asm` statements directly into a C program, but the results are often worth the effort. External modules save compilation time by letting you develop programs in pieces—and there's no need to compile the program to assembly language text. You can also use Ideal mode in assembly language modules. Best of all, simplified memory models make writing external functions easier than if you had to declare segments "the hard way," which you still can do if you want. Assembling, compiling, and linking multimodule programs is tricky, but using Turbo C as a "front end" to Turbo Linker can save time and hassle.

Calling assembly language functions from C is identical to calling other C functions. Going the other way—calling C functions from assembly language—requires you to push function parameters onto the stack and then, after the function returns, to remove those parameters. You can also declare local variables in functions, although programs may run faster if you can use a register to hold temporary values.

Exercises

13-1. What are the two ways of adding assembly language to C programs? How does compilation differ between the two methods?

13-2. When is it necessary to save and restore registers `si` and `di` in an assembly language function? When is it not necessary to do this?

13-3. Write an in-line assembly language function to display the values of the 8086 flags. The only C statement you may use is a call to `printf` to display the results—the rest of the instructions should be `asm` statements. Hint: See Figure 4-2 for flag bit positions.

13-4. Suppose you have a C structure named `Things` and a variable of this structure named `MyThings`. What in-line `asm` statement can you use to load the *address* of a structure field named `OneThing`?

13-5. What command-line option can you use to compile a program to assembly language text? What is the danger of doing this?

13-6. Suppose you have two external functions named FUNC1.ASM and FUNC2.ASM. What commands are required to assemble, compile, and link the external modules to a main C program named MAIN.C, creating a finished program named MAIN.EXE? Assume the program uses the small memory model.

13-7. What **ARG** directive can you use to address the parameters of the following function prototype?

```
extern void copystring( unsigned char far * source,
    unsigned char far * destination,
    int sourcelen );
```

13-8. What C statements are needed to call the external function as defined in question number #13-7?

13-9. Write an external module to finish the `copystring` function listed in questions #13-7 and #13-8. The module should copy `sourcelen` characters from a `source` string to the `destination` string.

13-10. Given the external function in question #13-9, what assembly language statements do you need to call the function to pass the addresses and length of two strings `string1` and `string2`, declared in an external data segment?

Projects

13-1. Compile various C programs (perhaps from a public domain library) with the **-S** option, creating .ASM files that you can examine. Hunt for C statements where in-line `asm` code would improve running times. Recompile, run-time trials, and keep track of the results of your optimizations.

13-2. Convert the procedures in ASYNCH.ASM module from chapter 10 (or another module if you prefer) to external C functions.

13-3. The standard C `printf` function is certainly versatile—able to write all sorts of string, character, and numeric data to the standard output. But programming such versatility takes time. Write a set of simplified output functions for writing strings and integers.

13-4. Develop a fast direct-video library of external C functions for displaying text on the PC's memory-mapped video screen.

13-5. Write a C program to convert all the text in a file to lowercase, perhaps also capitalizing sentences. After debugging your program, selectively convert sections to assembly language to improve running times.

13-6. Use Turbo Debugger to trace function calls to various routines in Turbo C's run-time library. Document as much of the code as you can. (This is a useful exercise for learning how standard functions are implemented in assembly language. You may also want to consider purchasing the library source code from Borland, but be aware that this Turbo C add-on product is expensive.)

III Reference

Chapter **14 8086/88, 80286, 80386 Reference Guide**

14 8086/88, 80286, 80386 Reference Guide

In This Chapter

How to use this reference; the 8086, 8088, 80286, and 808386 instruction set listing applicable processor(s), flags, purpose, syntax, examples, sample code, description, and a cross reference for each instruction mnemonic

About the Reference

This chapter lists all 8086, 8088, 80286, and 80386 non-protected-mode mnemonics in alphabetic order, showing the affected flags, listing the syntax for all instruction forms, and giving examples and descriptions that explain how the instructions work. The material here supplements the information in the preceding chapters; therefore, to get the most from this reference, you may also want to consult the Subject Index to locate more details about specific instructions. Read the next sections for hints on using this chapter and for the meanings of various terms.

Protected-Mode Instructions

Protected-mode 80286 and 80386 instructions are not included in this reference. These instructions are typically used only for writing operating system code that needs to juggle multiple processes apparently running at the same time but in fact executing in sequence. The protected-mode-programming's main purpose is to switch among such processes rapidly enough to give the illusion of simultaneous execution.

Some people may criticize the omission of protected-mode instructions in this reference but, after much thought about the subject, I decided that to list the instructions without also including the necessary background material required to write multitasking operating system software would be nothing more than a waste of space. For application programming, protected-mode instructions are not needed. Even so, this book would be incomplete if it did not at least mention the protected-mode instruction set. (See Table 14-1.) For a list of books that contain more information about using these instructions and about writing multitasking operating systems, see the Bibliography.

> Note: Special 80286 and 80386 non-protected-mode instructions such as **bound, enter, leave,** and the conditional **set** instructions *are* covered here in detail along with syntax descriptions for 80386 extended 32-bit registers. Also, instructions restricted to specific processors are clearly marked.

Going to the Source

At least five sources were used to confirm the instruction formats and flag settings in this chapter. When any of these references did not exactly agree (which was often the case), the documentation printed here was confirmed by experiment. This extensive cross checking turned up a surprising number of mistakes in various Intel and Microsoft references. Naturally, all of these errors are corrected here.

Table 14-1 *Protected-Mode 80286, 80386 Instructions*

Mnemonic	Description
arpl	Adjust RPL Field of Selector
clts	Clear Task-Switched Flag in CR0
lar	Load Access Rights Byte
lgdt	Load Global Descriptor Table Register
lidt	Load Interrupt Descriptor Table Register
lldt	Load Local Descriptor Table Register
lmsw	Load Machine Status Word
lsl	Load Segment Limit
ltr	Load Task Register
mov (386)	Move To/From Special Registers*
sgdt	Store Global Descriptor Table Register
sidt	Store Interrupt Descriptor Table Register
sldt	Store Local Descriptor Table Register
smsw	Store Machine Status Word
str	Store Task Register
verr	Verify Segment for Reading
verw	Verify Segment for Writing

*80386 only.

Instruction Timings and Binary Encodings

Because this book is primarily a practical guide to programming applications in assembly language, instruction timings and binary encodings for machine codes generated by the assembler are not listed. If you need to, you can find this data in the Intel references listed in the Bibliography.

The timing values, which many references blindly copy but which, I suspect, few programmers actually use, are omitted here for good reasons. Formulas that calculate theoretical timings for specific instructions tend to be inaccurate in practice. Factors such as the on-chip instruction cache, which preloads a certain amount of machine code for faster execution, plus the existence of multiple interrupt signals and memory wait states in real-life computer systems are likely to throw monkey wrenches into even the most carefully constructed timing formulas. A stopwatch and a good profiler will do you more good than hours spent calculating instruction loop timings. In general, your programs will run as fast as possible if you simply adhere to a few suggestions for selecting among various instruction formats:

▶ Instructions that refer to the accumulator—`al`, `ax`, or `eax` (80386 only)—may run faster than all other forms. (The instructions may also occupy fewer bytes of machine code.) Because of this, any such instructions are always listed first in this chapter's *Syntax/Example* sections. For instance, see the first two lines of the syntax for `adc` plus the first line of the 80386 syntax forms.

▶ Instructions that use only registers for all operands usually run faster than when these same instructions refer to data stored in memory. This is especially so when an 8086 instruction refers to data located at odd addresses because the 8086 can load data from even addresses a tiny bit more quickly. In other words, if you have a choice between using a register and a memory variable, use the register—your program may run faster.

▶ Arithmetic instructions `imul`, `mul`, `div`, and `idiv` are notoriously slow. Always use shifts and rotates to multiply and divide by powers of 2 or use a math coprocessor if possible.

Binary-machine-code formats for instructions are also not listed. In fact, the complicated bit formats and binary operation codes for individual instructions are rarely mentioned anywhere in this book. After all, one reason for using an assembler is to avoid having to worry about such details. On the very rare occasion that you need to know the exact bits generated for a specific instruction, you can just as easily write a test program and examine the assembled code with Turbo Debugger.

That about sums up what's not here. Now, lets take a look at what the reference does contain.

How to Use the Reference

The reference that follows describes each mnemonic separately except for conditional jump and set (80386 only) instructions, which are listed in tables for easier lookup. (See entries for j-*condition* and set-*condition*.) A few mnemonics that generate the same machine codes such as cmps, cmpsb, cmpsw, and cmpsd are listed together, but only when this does not disrupt the reference's alphabetic order. For example, sal and shl are listed separately, even though these two mnemonics represent the identical instruction.

The data for each mnemonic are divided into sections, each with a specific purpose. The divisions are:

▶ *Header*—Lists the mnemonic, name, processors on which the instruction is available, and effects on flag settings.

▶ *Purpose*—Gives a brief description of the instruction. Read these parts for quick reference and while browsing.

▶ *Syntax/Example*—Shows the various forms that the instruction may take and lists allowable register and memory operands. This section also shows a typical program example for each instruction form. When the instruction is available on multiple processors, any unique syntax forms for 80286 and 80386 processors are listed separately.

▶ *Sample Code*—Places the instruction in a brief programming sample, giving a practical example of the way this instruction might be used in a typical program.

▶ *Description*—Fully explains how the instruction operates and frequently refers to the *Sample Code* section to explain further how to apply the instruction. Also, any unusual uses of flags and register assignments are described here.

▶ *See Also*—Refers to other instructions related in some way to this one.

More About the Headers

As a sample of the reference headers, Figure 14-1 duplicates the header for the and instruction. The mnemonic and is listed in lowercase, telling you exactly how to spell the instruction in a program. The name of the instruction is printed directly across from the mnemonic. Under these two items is a list of processors and flags. The 80186 processor, which is not used in any PC computers, is not listed here. The functionally equivalent 8086 and 8088 processors are listed jointly as 8086/88. The filled-in triangles under the processor numbers indicate which processors support this instruction. In this sample, the header indicates that and is available on all four processors.

The flags are listed to the right of the processor numbers. (See Figure 14-1.) Under each flag are one or more symbols that indicate how this instruction affects the flag bits. A digit 0 or 1 indicates that the instruction

and   Logical AND

Processor:	8086/88	80286	80386	*Flags:*	of	df	if	tf	sf	zf	af	pf	cf
	▲	▲	▲		0	—	—	—	▲	▲	u	▲	0

Figure 14-1 *Sample header for the and instruction.*

resets or sets the flag to this value. A lowercase *u* indicates that, after the instruction executes, the value of this flag is undefined. A dash (−) indicates that the instruction does not change the setting of this flag. A filled-in triangle (▲) tells you that the flag value is subject to change according to the rules listed in Table 14-2. When other rules and conditions apply or, in a few cases where more than one symbol is listed (see sal, for example), the flag settings are discussed in the instruction's *Description*.

More About the
Syntax/Example
Sections

Table 14-3 lists the symbols used in the *Syntax/Example* sections. Along with this table, the syntax references tell you exactly what forms of each

Table 14-2 *Standard Flag Usage*

Flag	Name	Set to 1 if . . . , else reset to 0
of	Overflow	Positive value is too large, or negative value is too small.
sf	Sign	MSD of value = 1.
zf	Zero	Full-width result = 0.
af	Auxiliary	Carry out of or borrow to four LSDs of al occurred.
pf	Parity	Eight LSDs of result have an even number of ones (even parity).
cf	Carry	Carry out of or borrow to full-width result occurred.

Table 14-3 *Symbols Used in the Reference*

Symbols	Meaning
|	Either or
&	And
[ ]	Items in brackets are optional
farTarget	Address reference in foreign segment
nearTarget	Address reference within current segment
shortTarget	Address reference within −128 to 127 bytes
imm6	A 6-bit value (esc instruction only)
immB	Any 8-bit immediate value
immW	Any 16-bit immediate value
immDW	Any 32-bit immediate value
memB	Any 8-bit-byte memory reference
memW	Any 16-bit-word memory reference
memDW	Any 32-bit-doubleword memory reference
memFW	Any 48-bit-farword memory reference
memQW	Any 64-bit-quadword memory reference
memALL	Any B, W, DW, FW, or QW memory reference
regB	Any 8-bit-byte general register
regW	Any 16-bit-word general register
regDW	Any 80386 32-bit-doubleword general register
no operands	Requires no operands

instruction are allowed. For example, one of the syntax and example lines for shl is:

shl *regW | memW, cl*   shl [aword + bx], cl

Referring to Table 14-3 reveals that this form of shl requires two operands: a word (16-bit) general-purpose register or a word memory reference and the register cl. The example to the right of the syntax shows how an instruction of this form might appear in a program. Remember that this example is only one of many possible combinations of registers and memory references.

> Note: Unless otherwise mentioned, memory references include all addressing modes described in chapter 5.

More About the Examples and Samples

All examples and sample code sections were assembled and tested directly from this text. You can be sure that every scrap of code listed here represents actual instructions as they might appear in programs. To conserve space, however, I did not use complete programs for the sample code sections. To run the code, you'll need to insert the instructions into a copy of EXESHELL.ASM from chapter 2. You'll also have to initialize the ds and es segment registers appropriately.

> Note: If you do run any of the samples, be careful with instructions that read and write to hardware ports. Because of the system-dependent nature of instructions such as in, out, ins, and outs, the samples for these mnemonics may assemble but may not perform any useful function. They may even cause a system crash. Such samples are clearly marked with a comment warning you not to run the code.

aaa

ASCII Adjust After Addition

				Flags:	of	df	if	tf	sf	zf	af	pf	cf
Processor:	8086/88	80286	80386		u	–	–	–	u	u	▲	u	▲
	▲	▲	▲										

Purpose   Adjusts numeric sum of two unpacked BCD digits to unpacked BCD format, which is easily converted to ASCII.

Syntax/Example   aaa *no operands*   aaa

Sample Code
```
mov ah, 07      ; First digit = 07
mov al, 08      ; Second digit = 08
add al, ah      ; Sum in al = 0Fh (15 decimal)
sub ah, ah      ; Clear ah to 00
aaa             ; Adjust: ah = 01, al = 05
or  ax, 3030h   ; Convert digits to ASCII
```

Description   After adding two unpacked BCD digits and storing the 8-bit result in al, aaa converts al back to unpacked BCD format. If the previous add generated a carry or if al is greater than 9, then ah is incremented, and both cf and af are set to 1; otherwise, cf and af are set to 0. The four MSDs (upper half) of al are always zeroed. As the example shows, after aaa, you can OR either or both ah and al with 030h to convert the BCD result to ASCII.

See Also   aad, aam, aas, daa, das

aad

ASCII Adjust Before Division

				Flags:	of	df	if	tf	sf	zf	af	pf	cf
Processor:	8086/88	80286	80386		u	–	–	–	▲	▲	u	▲	u
	▲	▲	▲										

Purpose   Converts two unpacked BCD digits in ax to binary.

Syntax/Example   aad *no operands*   aad

Sample Code
```
mov ah, '7'     ; Set ah to ASCII '7'
mov al, '6'     ; Set al to ASCII '6'
and ax, 0F0Fh   ; Convert ASCII to BCD (ax = 0706h)
aad             ; Convert to binary (ax = 004Ch)
```

Description   Assign two unpacked BCD values to ah (most significant digit) and al (least significant digit), then execute aad to convert the digits to a 16-bit binary value in ax. Despite the instruction's name, aad can be used at any time—it doesn't have to precede a division. The largest possible value that aad can convert is 0909, equal to hexadecimal 063h, or 99 in decimal.

Consequently, after using aad on unpacked BCD values from 0000 to 0909, register ah always equals 0.

See Also   aaa, aam, aas, daa, das

ASCII Adjust After Multiplication   **aam**

Processor:	8086/88	80286	80386	Flags:	of	df	if	tf	sf	zf	af	pf	cf
	▲	▲	▲		u	–	–	–	▲	▲	u	▲	u

Purpose   Converts 16-bit binary values from 0 to 99 decimal in ax to unpacked BCD digits, which are easily converted to ASCII.

Syntax/Example   aam *no operands*   aam

Sample Code
```
mov ax, 04Ch    ; Set ax to 76 decimal
aam             ; Convert to BCD (ax = 0706h)
or  ax, 3030h   ; Convert ax to ASCII (ax = 3736h)
```

Description   Use aam to convert a value in ax less or equal to hexadecimal 063h (99 decimal) from binary to unpacked BCD format, with the most significant digit in ah and the least significant digit in al. This operation reverses what aad does. Despite aam's name, you do not have to precede the instruction with a multiplication.

See Also   aaa, aad, aas, daa, das

ASCII Adjust After Subtraction   **aas**

Processor:	8086/88	80286	80386	Flags:	of	df	if	tf	sf	zf	af	pf	cf
	▲	▲	▲		u	–	–	–	u	u	▲	u	▲

Purpose   Adjusts numeric difference of two unpacked BCD digits to unpacked BCD format, which is easily converted to ASCII.

Syntax/Example   aas *no operands*   aas

Sample Code
```
mov ah, 01     ; Set ah to BCD 01
mov al, 04     ; Set al to BCD 04
mov bl, 07     ; Set bl to BCD 07
sub al, bl     ; al <- al - bl (14 - 7)
aas            ; Adjust to BCD (ax = 0007)
or  ax, 3030h  ; Convert ax to ASCII (ax = 3037h)
```

aas

Description   Subtract two BCD digits, place the result in al, and execute aas to convert the numeric difference to BCD format, which can then be converted to ASCII. If the previous sub required a borrow, then aas also subtracts 1 from ah and sets af and cf to 1; otherwise, ah is unchanged, and the two flags are set to 0. The example subtracts 07 (in bl) from 0104 (14 decimal in unpacked BCD format in ax), giving the BCD answer in ax—0007.

See Also   aaa, aad, aam, daa, das

adc   Add With Carry

Processor:	8086/88	80286	80386		Flags:	of	df	if	tf	sf	zf	af	pf	cf
	▲	▲	▲			▲	–	–	–	▲	▲	▲	▲	▲

Purpose   Adds bytes, words, and doublewords (80386 only) plus the current value (1 or 0) of the carry flag.

Syntax/Example

adc *al, immB*	adc al, 2
adc *ax, immW*	adc ax, 1024
adc *regB	memB, immB*	adc bl, 2
adc *regW	memW, immW*	adc [word bx], 1024
adc *regW	memW, immB*	adc cx, 2
adc *regB	memB, regB*	adc [byte bx], dl
adc *regW	memW, regW*	adc dx, bx
adc *regB, regB	memB*	adc bl, bh
adc *regW, regW	memW*	adc dx, [word bx]

80386 only:

adc *eax, immDW*	adc eax, 65537
adc *regDW	memDW, immDW*	adc edx, 65537
adc *regDW	memDW, immB*	adc [dword bx], 2
adc *regDW	memDW, regDW*	adc edx, ecx
adc *regDW, regDW	memDW*	adc ecx, [dword bx]

Sample Code

```
DATASEG
var dd 01FFFEh   ; 131070 decimal
CODESEG
mov ax, 5                  ; Value to add
mov bx, offset var         ; Address var
add [word bx], ax          ; Add low-order word
adc [word bx + 2], 0       ; Add in carry (var = 131075)
```

Description   When adding multibyte or multiword values, use adc after the initial add of the low-order values to add in possible carries to the higher-order bytes and words. The example demonstrates how this works, adding 5 to the doubleword value stored at label `var`. The `adc` adds a possible carry generated by the initial `add` of the low-order word and the immediate value 5.

See Also add, sbb, sub

Add Without Carry   add

Processor:	8086/88	80286	80386		*Flags:*	of	df	if	tf	sf	zf	af	pf	cf
	▲	▲	▲			▲	–	–	–	▲	▲	▲	▲	▲

Purpose Adds two byte, word, or doubleword (80386 only) operands.

Syntax/Example

```
add al, immB                    add al, 2
add ax, immW                    add ax, 1024
add regB | memB, immB           add bl, 2
add regW | memW, immW           add [word bx], 1024
add regW | memW, immB           add cx, 2
add regB | memB, regB           add [byte bx], dl
add regW | memW, regW           add dx, bx
add regB, regB | memB           add bl, bh
add regW, regW | memW           add dx, [word bx]
```

80386 only:

```
add eax, immDW                  add eax, 65537
add regDW | memDW, immDW        add edx, 65537
add regDW | memDW, immB         add [dword bx], 2
add regDW | memDW, regDW        add edx, ecx
add regDW, regDW | memDW        add ecx, [dword bx]
```

Sample Code

```
DATASEG
var dd 01FFFEh            ; 131070 decimal
CODESEG
mov ax, [word var]       ; Load ax:dx with
mov dx, [word var + 2]   ;   doubleword value
add ax, [word var]       ; Add low-order word
adc dx, [word var + 2]   ; Add high-order word + cf
mov [word var], ax       ; Store ax:dx to
mov [word var + 2], dx   ;   doubleword value
```

Description Use `add` to add any two byte, word, or doubleword (80386 only) values stored in registers or in memory variables. (Both of the two operands can't be memory references.) The sum of the two operands is stored in the first operand. When adding multibyte values, follow `add` with `adc`, adding in a possible carry. The sample uses `add` with `adc` to add a doubleword value to itself.

See Also adc, sbb, sub

and
Logical AND

Processor:	8086/88	80286	80386	Flags:	of	df	if	tf	sf	zf	af	pf	cf
	▲	▲	▲		0	–	–	–	▲	▲	u	▲	0

Purpose Logically ANDs two byte, word, or doubleword (80386 only) values.

Syntax/Example

and *al, immB*	and al, 0Fh
and *ax, immW*	and ax, 0FF00h
and *regB	memB, immB*	and bl, 01h
and *regW	memW, immW*	and [word bx], 0800h
and *regW	memW, immB*	and cx, 0080h
and *regB	memB, regB*	and [byte bx], dl
and *regW	memW, regW*	and dx, cx
and *regB, regB	memB*	and bl, bh
and *regW, regW	memW*	and dx, [word bx]

80386 only:

and *eax, immDW*	and eax, 0FF000000h
and *regDW	memDW, immDW*	and edx, 0FFFF0000h
and *regDW	memDW, immB*	and [dword bx], 01h
and *regDW	memDW, regDW*	and edx, ecx
and *regDW, regDW	memDW*	and ecx, [dword bx]

Sample Code   and   dl, 0Fh   ; Set upper 4 MSDs to 0

Description Use **and** to perform a logical AND on the bits in any two byte, word, or doubleword (80386 only) values stored in registers or in memory variables. (Both of the two operands can't be memory references.) The corresponding bits in the first operand are set to 1 only if the bits in both of the operands equal 1. The sample uses **and** to set the first 4 bits in a byte register to 0.

See Also or, xor, test

bound
Check Array Index Against Bounds

Processor:	8086/88	80286	80386	Flags:	of	df	if	tf	sf	zf	af	pf	cf
		▲	▲		–	–	–	–	–	–	–	–	–

Purpose Verifies that an array index is within a specified range.

Syntax/Example   bound *regW, memDW*   bound si, [word bx]

80386 only:
bound *regDW, memQW*   bound esi, [qword bx]

Sample Code
```
DATASEG
LowBound  DW 100
highBound DW 199
CODESEG
P286
mov   si, 105          ; Load si with index value
bound si, [LowBound]   ; Check if index is in bounds
```

Description Assign the index value to the first operand and the address of the index range values to the second operand. This structure must contain two words (or, optionally, two doublewords on the 80386) with the lower value first (at the lower address). If the value of the first operand is not within the numeric range of these two values, a type 5 interrupt is automatically generated. Unfortunately, on ATs and compatibles, this interrupt is shared by the Print Screen function; therefore, you must trap and prevent Print Screen operations before using bound.

See Also iret

Bit Scan Forward   bsf

Processor:	8086/88	80286	80386		Flags:	of	df	if	tf	sf	zf	af	pf	cf
			▲			—	—	—	—	—	▲	—	—	—

Purpose Scans bits in LSD to MSD order.

Syntax/Example
bsf *regW, regW* | *memW*   bsf cx, dx
bsf *regDW, regDW* | *memDW*   bsf ecx, [dword var]

Sample Code
```
P386
mov dx, 0800h ; Set bit number 11 to 1
bsf cx, dx    ; Scan (cx = 000Bh)
jz  short @@10 ; Skip shift if all bits = 0
shr dx, cl    ; Shift dx by cl (dx = 0001)
@@10:
```

Description The first operand to bsf holds the result of scanning the second operand from right to left (starting at bit 0). If all bits are 0, then zf is set to 1, and the first operand is unchanged. If a 1 bit is located, then zf is set to 0, and the first operand is set to the bit number. The sample uses this value to shift a bit in dx into the LSD position.

See Also bsr

bsr

Bit Scan Reverse

	Processor:	8086/88	80286	80386		Flags:	of	df	if	tf	sf	zf	af	pf	cf
				▲			–	–	–	–	–	▲	–	–	–

Purpose   Scans bits in MSD to LSD order.

Syntax/Example   bsr *regW, regW | memW*   bsr cx, [word bx]
bsr *regDW, regDW | memDW*   bsr ecx, edx

Sample Code
```
P386
  mov dx, 0040h  ; Set bit number 6 to 1
  bsr cx, dx     ; Scan (cx = 0006h)
  jz  short @@10 ; Skip shift if all bits = 0
  shr dx, cl     ; Shift dx by cl (dx = 0001h)
@@10:
```

Description   The first operand to bsr holds the result of scanning the second operand from left to right (starting at the MSD). If all bits are 0, then zf is set to 1, and the first operand is unchanged. If a 1 bit is located, then zf is set to 0, and the first operand is set to the bit number. The sample uses this value to shift a bit in dx into the LSD position.

See Also   bsf

bt

Bit Test

	Processor:	8086/88	80286	80386		Flags:	of	df	if	tf	sf	zf	af	pf	cf
				▲			–	–	–	–	–	–	–	–	▲

Purpose   Copies a bit to the carry flag.

Syntax/Example
bt *regW | memW, immB*   bt ax, 14
bt *regW | memW, regW*   bt [word var], cx
bt *regDW | memDW, immB*   bt eax, 8
bt *regDW | memDW, regDW*   bt [dword var], ecx

Sample Code
```
P386
  mov dx, 0200h  ; Assign a test value to dx
  bt  dx, 9      ; Copy bit number 9 to cf
  jc  @@10       ; Test cf
  call procedure ; Call procedure if bit 9 = 0
@@10:
```

Description   The first operand to bt must be a word or doubleword register or memory reference. The second operand may be a word (0–15) or doubleword (0–

31) register or immediate value. Executing **bt** copies the bit from the first operand at the position specified by the second operand to **cf**. You can then use **jc** or **jnc** to test whether this bit was 1 or 0.

See Also   btc, btr, bts, test

Bit Test and Complement   btc

Processor:	8086/88	80286	80386 ▲		Flags:	of	df	if	tf	sf	zf	af	pf	cf
						—	—	—	—	—	—	—	—	▲

Purpose   Copies a bit to the carry flag and then complements the bit in the original value.

Syntax/Example

btc *regW | memW, immB*   btc ax, 14
btc *regW | memW, regW*   btc [word var], cx
btc *regDW | memDW, immB* btc eax, 8
btc *regDW | memDW, regDW* btc [dword var], ecx

Sample Code

```
P386
  mov dx, 0200h    ; Assign a test value to dx
  btc dx, 9        ; Copy bit number 9 to cf and complement
  jc  @@10         ; Test cf
  call procedure   ; Call procedure if bit 9 = 0
@@10:
```

Description   The operands and actions of **btc** are identical to **bt**, but after copying the specified bit to **cf**, that bit is complemented (toggled) in the original value. In the sample, this leaves **dx** equal to 0. Despite this, the zero flag is *not* set.

See Also   bt, btr, bts, test

Bit Test and Reset   btr

Processor:	8086/88	80286	80386 ▲		Flags:	of	df	if	tf	sf	zf	af	pf	cf
						—	—	—	—	—	—	—	—	▲

Purpose   Copies a bit to the carry flag and then resets the bit in the original value.

Syntax/Example

btr *regW | memW, immB*   btr [word var], 5
btr *regW | memW, regW*   btr dx, cx
btr *regDW | memDW, immB* btr [dword var], 6
btr *regDW | memDW, regDW* btr edx, ecx

Sample Code   P386

```
        mov   dx, OABCDh         ; Assign test value to dx
        mov   cx, 15            ; Assign bit number to cx
        btr   dx, cx            ; Copy bit to cf and reset
```

Description   The operands and actions of `btr` are identical to `bt`, but after copying the specified bit to `cf`, that bit is reset to 0 in the original value. In the sample, this changes `dx` to 02BCDh.

See Also   `bt, btc, bts, test`

---

bts

Bit Test and Set

Processor:	8086/88	80286	80386		*Flags:*	of	df	if	tf	sf	zf	af	pf	cf
			▲			−	−	−	−	−	−	−	−	▲

Purpose   Copies a bit to the carry flag and then sets the bit in the original value.

Syntax/Example
```
bts regW | memW, immB          bts dx, 4
bts regW | memW, regW          bts [word var], cx
bts regDW | memDW, immB        bts eax, 3
bts regDW | memDW, regDW       bts [dword var], edx
```

Sample Code   P386

```
        mov   dx, OABCDh         ; Assign test value to dx
        mov   cx, 14            ; Assign bit number to cx
        bts   dx, cx            ; Copy bit to cf and set
```

Description   The operands and actions of `bts` are identical to `bt`, but after copying the specified bit to `cf`, that bit is set to 1 in the original value. In the sample, this changes `dx` to 0EBCDh.

See Also   `bt, btc, btr, test`

---

call

Call Procedure

Processor:	8086/88	80286	80386		*Flags:*	of	df	if	tf	sf	zf	af	pf	cf
	▲	▲	▲			−	−	−	−	−	−	−	−	−

Purpose   Calls a subroutine procedure.

Syntax/Example
```
call nearTarget       call Here
call farTarget        call far ptr There
call regW             call bx
```

```
call memW          call [word bx]
call memDW         call [dword bx]

80386 only:
call regDW         call eax
call memFW         call [fword si]
```

Sample Code
```
call Times2        ; Call subroutine
jmp  Exit          ; Exit program

PROC Times2        ; Subroutine
add ax, ax         ; Add doubleword in
adc dx, dx         ;   ax:dx to itself
ret                ; Return from subroutine
ENDP
```

Description The `call` instruction pushes the address of the next instruction onto the stack and then jumps to the target location, causing the instructions in the subroutine procedure to begin executing. Usually, a `ret` instruction ends the subroutine, popping the return address from the stack and continuing the program with the instruction that follows the original `call`. In most programs, the target will be a label, marking the first instruction of the subroutine. But the target may also be a memory reference or a 16-bit register that holds the address of the subroutine. The sample calls a small subroutine `Times2`, which adds the value in `ax:dx` to itself. The `ret` instruction causes the program to continue from `jmp Exit`.

See Also `ret`

Convert Byte to Word   cbw

Processor:	8086/88	80286	80386		*Flags:*	of	df	if	tf	sf	zf	af	pf	cf
	▲	▲	▲			—	—	—	—	—	—	—	—	—

Purpose Extends a signed byte to a signed word.

Syntax/Example cbw *no operands*   cbw

Sample Code
```
mov al, -1         ; Set al to -1
cbw                ; Extend al to ax (ax = -1)
```

Description Use `cbw` to extend an 8-bit signed value in `al` to a 16-bit signed value of the same magnitude in `ax`. The instruction works by copying the MSD of `al` to all bits in `ah`, thus setting `ah` to 0FFh if `al` was negative (MSD = 1) or setting `ah` to 00h if `al` was positive (MSD = 0).

See Also `cdq`, `cwd`, `cwde`

cdq

Convert Doubleword to Quadword

Processor: 8086/88 80286 80386	*Flags:*	of	df	if	tf	sf	zf	af	pf	cf
▲		—	—	—	—	—	—	—	—	—

Purpose Extends a signed doubleword to a signed quadword.

Syntax/Example cdq *no operands* cdq

Sample Code
```
P386
 mov eax, -1     ; Set eax to -1
 cdq            ; Extend eax to eax:edx (eax:edx = -1)
```

Description Use cdq to extend a 32-bit signed value in eax to a 64-bit signed value of the same magnitude in the register pair eax:edx. The instruction works by copying the MSD of eax to all bits in edx, thus setting edx to 0FFFFFFFFh if eax was negative (MSD = 1) or setting edx to 0 if eax was positive (MSD = 0).

See Also cbw, cwd, cwde

clc

Clear Carry Flag

Processor: 8086/88 80286 80386	*Flags:*	of	df	if	tf	sf	zf	af	pf	cf
▲ ▲ ▲		—	—	—	—	—	—	—	—	0

Purpose Sets carry flag to 0.

Syntax/Example clc *no operands* clc

Sample Code
```
PROC Anyproc
; Procedure code
@@ErrExit:
 stc            ; Set carry (error)
 ret            ; Return to caller
@@NoErrExit:
 clc            ; Clear carry (no error)
 ret            ; Return to caller
ENDP AnyProc
```

Description Executing clc resets the carry flag to 0. As the sample code demonstrates, the instruction is often used to pass an error flag back from a subroutine, clearing cf if no error was detected.

See Also cmc, stc

Clear Direction Flag **cld**

Processor:	8086/88	80286	80386		Flags:	of	df	if	tf	sf	zf	af	pf	cf
	▲	▲	▲			—	0	—	—	—	—	—	—	—

Purpose   Clears direction flag to 0.

Syntax/Example   cld *no operands*   cld

Sample Code
```
DATASEG
s1 db 'Copy me'        ; Source string
s2 db 80 dup (?)       ; Destination string
CODESEG                ; Note: assume es = ds
mov cx, 4              ; Assign count to cx
mov si, offset s1      ; Address source with ds:si
mov di, offset s2      ; Address destination with es:di
cld                    ; Auto-increment si and di
rep movsb              ; Copy 4 chars from source to destination
```

Description   Use cld to reset the direction flag to 0. Always execute cld before a repeated string operation, which increments either or both si and di automatically if df = 0. The sample uses cld to prepare for a repeated movsb string instruction, copying 4 characters from string s1 to s2.

See Also   std

Clear Interrupt Flag **cli**

Processor:	8086/88	80286	80386		Flags:	of	df	if	tf	sf	zf	af	pf	cf
	▲	▲	▲			—	—	0	—	—	—	—	—	—

Purpose   Clears the interrupt-enable flag to 0.

Syntax/Example   cli *no operands*   cli

Sample Code
```
sti    ; Enable interrupts
hlt    ; Wait for interrupt to occur
cli    ; Disable interrupts
```

Description   Executing cli disables maskable interrupts from being recognized. To ensure proper PC operations, interrupts should not be disabled for long periods. The sample suggests one way to synchronize a program with an external event, pausing with hlt until an interrupt occurs and then immediately disabling interrupts.

See Also   sti

cmc

Complement Carry Flag

Processor:	8086/88	80286	80386	*Flags:*	of	df	if	tf	sf	zf	af	pf	cf
	▲	▲	▲		–	–	–	–	–	–	–	–	▲

Purpose Complements (toggles) the carry flag.

Syntax/Example cmc *no operands*   cmc

Sample Code
```
PROC Anyproc
; Procedure code
@@Exit:
  cmc    ; Complement error flag
  ret    ; Return to caller
ENDP
```

Description Use cmc to complement the carry flag, changing cf to 0 if it was 1 or to 1 if it was 0. One use for cmc is in a procedure that returns cf as an error flag but, because of other operations leaving cf in the opposite state, must toggle the carry flag before returning.

See Also clc, stc

cmp

Compare

Processor:	8086/88	80286	80386	*Flags:*	of	df	if	tf	sf	zf	af	pf	cf
	▲	▲	▲		▲	–	–	–	▲	▲	▲	▲	▲

Purpose Compares two operands.

Syntax/Example

cmp *al, immB*	cmp al, 2
cmp *ax, immW*	cmp ax, 1024
cmp *regB | memB, immB*	cmp bl, 2
cmp *regW | memW, immW*	cmp [word bx], 1024
cmp *regW | memW, immB*	cmp cx, 2
cmp *regB | memB, regB*	cmp [byte bx], dl
cmp *regW | memW, regW*	cmp dx, bx
cmp *regB, regB | memB*	cmp bl, bh
cmp *regW, regW | memW*	cmp dx, [word bx]

80386 only:

cmp *eax, immDW*	cmp eax, 65537
cmp *regDW | memDW, immDW*	cmp [dword si], 99123
cmp *regDW | memDW, immB*	cmp [dword bx], 2
cmp *regDW | memDW, regDW*	cmp edx, ecx
cmp *regDW, regDW | memDW*	cmp ecx, [dword bx]

Sample Code

```
cmp ax, cx      ; Compare ax and cx
je  @@10        ; Jump if ax = cx
inc ax          ; Increment ax if ax <> cx
@@10:
```

Description Use `cmp` to compare any two byte, word, or doubleword (80386 only) values. Both operands may not be memory references. Normally, you'll follow a `cmp` with a conditional jump instruction, taking appropriate action based on the result of the comparison. The sample uses `cmp` to test if registers `ax` and `cx` hold the same value. If not, `ax` is incremented. The `cmp` instruction works by subtracting the second operand from the first, throwing out the result, but saving the flags, which can then be tested. Consequently, when using `cmp` to determine how one value differs from another, assign the operands in the same order as the expression you need. For example, if you want to know whether `ax < bx`, use `cmp ax, bx` followed by `jl`.

See Also `cmps, sub`

Compare String

cmps cmpsb cmpsd cmpsw

Processor:	8086/88	80286	80386		Flags:	of	df	if	tf	sf	zf	af	pf	cf
	▲	▲	▲			▲	–	–	–	▲	▲	▲	▲	▲

Purpose Compare strings of values.

Syntax/Example

cmps *[es:]memB, memB*	`cmps    [byte dest], [byte source]`
cmps *[es:]memW, memW*	`cmps    [word es:si], [word di]`
cmpsb *no operands*	`cmpsb`
cmpsw *no operands*	`cmpsw`

80386 only:

cmps *[es:]memDW, memDW*	`cmps    [dword dest], [dword source]`
cmpsd *no operands*	`cmpsd`

Sample Code

```
DATASEG
s1 db 'Woe is me '
s2 db 'Woe is you'
CODESEG
ASSUME es: DGROUP       ; Tell TASM where es points
mov  si, offset s1      ; Address source string
mov  di, offset s2      ; Address destination string
mov  cx, 10             ; Assign count to cx
cld                     ; Auto-increment si, di
repe cmps [s1], [s2]    ; Find first mismatch
repe cmpsb              ; Note: same as above line
```

Description   The string comparison instructions compare two values in memory. Prefacing the instructions with repe or repne and storing a count value in cx builds instructions that can compare sequences of values. The first operand is the *source* and must be addressed by ds:si unless a segment override is used as in [es:label]. The second operand is the *destination* and must be addressed by es:di. The instructions subtract *[source]* − *[destination]*, discarding the result and saving the flags—similar to the way cmp works. In addition, if df = 0, si and di are advanced by the number of bytes being compared. If df = 1, the index registers are decremented.

Use cmps if you want Turbo Assembler to verify that the operands are addressable by ds:si or es:si and by es:di and also when you need to apply an es: override to the source operand. Or use the other three shorthand mnemonics if you don't want to specify explicit operands—cmpsb for byte comparisons, cmpsw for word comparisons, and cmpsd (80386 only) for doubleword comparisons. No matter what form of the instruction you use, it is still your responsibility to load si and di with the correct addresses. (For example, the last two lines in the sample, which finds the first mismatched character in two strings, produce the identical code.)

See Also   ins, insb, insd, insw, lods, lodsb, lodsd, lodsw, movs, movsb, movsd, movsw, outs, outsb, outsd, outsw, scas, scasb, scasd, scasw, stos, stosb, stosd, stosw

---

cwd   **Convert Word to Doubleword**

Processor:	8086/88	80286	80386	*Flags:*	of	df	if	tf	sf	zf	af	pf	cf
	▲	▲	▲		—	—	—	—	—	—	—	—	—

Purpose   Extends a signed word to a signed doubleword.

Syntax/Example   cwd *no operands*   cwd

Sample Code
```
mov ax, -1    ; Set ax to -1
cwd           ; Extend ax to ax:dx (ax:dx = -1)
```

Description   Use cwd to extend a 16-bit signed value in ax to a 32-bit signed value of the same magnitude in the register pair ax:dx. The instruction works by copying the MSD of ax to all bits in dx, thus setting dx to 0FFFFh if ax was negative (MSD = 1), or setting dx to 0 if ax was positive (MSD = 0).

See Also   cbw, cdq, cwde

Convert Word to Extended Doubleword **cwde**

	Processor:	8086/88	80286	80386		Flags:	of	df	if	tf	sf	zf	af	pf	cf
				▲			—	—	—	—	—	—	—	—	—

Purpose Extends a signed word to a signed extended doubleword.

Syntax/Example cwde *no operands* cwde

Sample Code
```
mov ax, -1      ; Set ax to -1
cwde            ; Extend ax to eax (eax = -1)
```

Description Use cwde to extend a 16-bit signed value in ax to a 32-bit signed value of the same magnitude in eax. The instruction works by copying the MSD of ax to all bits in the high word of eax, thus setting the high word to 0FFFFh if ax was negative (MSD = 1), or setting the high word to 0 if ax was positive (MSD = 0).

See Also cbw, cdq, cwd

Decimal Adjust After Addition **daa**

	Processor:	8086/88	80286	80386		Flags:	of	df	if	tf	sf	zf	af	pf	cf
		▲	▲	▲			u	—	—	—	▲	▲	▲	▲	▲

Purpose Adjusts numeric sum of two packed BCD digits to packed BCD format.

Syntax/Example daa *no operands* daa

Sample Code
```
mov al, 053h    ; Pack 5 and 3 into al
mov bl, 018h    ; Pack 1 and 8 into bl
add al, bl      ; al <- al + bl (al = 06Bh)
daa             ; Adjust result (al = 071h)
```

Description After adding two packed 8-bit bytes and placing the result in al, execute daa to convert the binary sum back to packed BCD format. If both af and cf equal 1, then the sum was greater than 99 decimal. (You can use this information to generate a carry in a multidigit addition.) If af = 1 but cf = 0, then the sum of the lower two digits was greater than 9 and a carry is automatically taken into account for the high digit of the result. (You can normally ignore this condition.) If both af and cf are 0, then no carries were generated (and daa does not change the value in al).

See Also aaa, aad, aam, aas, das

das

Decimal Adjust After Subtraction

Processor:	8086/88	80286	80386	Flags:	of	df	if	tf	sf	zf	af	pf	cf
	▲	▲	▲		u	–	–	–	▲	▲	▲	▲	▲

Purpose   Adjusts numeric difference of two packed BCD digits to packed BCD format.

Syntax/Example   das *no operands*   das

Sample Code
```
mov al, 007h    ; Pack 0 and 7 into al
mov bl, 014h    ; Pack 1 and 4 into bl
sub al, bl      ; al <- al - bl (al = 0F3h)
das             ; Adjust result (al = 093h)
```

Description   After subtracting two packed BCD values, place the result in al and execute das to convert the result back to packed BCD format. If both cf and af equal 0, then no borrows were needed during the subtraction. If cf = 0 and af = 1, then a borrow was needed for the lower 2 digits and the result is adjusted accordingly. (You can normally ignore this condition.) If cf = 1, then the result is a negative decimal complement and you can subtract 100 from the result in al to find the absolute value. In other words, if cf = 1 and al = 93h, as in the sample, the corrected value is −7, or (93 − 100).

See Also   aaa, aad, aam, aas, daa

dec

Decrement

Processor:	8086/88	80286	80386	Flags:	of	df	if	tf	sf	zf	af	pf	cf
	▲	▲	▲		▲	–	–	–	▲	▲	▲	▲	–

Purpose   Subtract 1 from a register or variable.

Syntax/Example   dec *regB | memB*   dec cl
dec *regW | memW*   dec [word var]

80386 only:
dec *regDW | memDW*   dec edx

Sample Code
```
mov  cx, 100    ; Assign count to cx
@@10:
call Anyproc    ; Call a procedure
dec  cx         ; Subtract 1 from count
jnz  @@10       ; Jump if cx > 0
```

Description   Use dec to decrease a byte, word, or doubleword (80386 only) register or memory value by 1. This is similar to subtracting 1 from unsigned values with sub, but faster. The sample demonstrates one way to construct a loop, calling Anyproc (not shown) 100 times and continuing past jnz only after dec finally decrements cx to 0.

See Also   inc

Unsigned Divide   div

Processor:	8086/88	80286	80386	Flags:	of	df	if	tf	sf	zf	af	pf	cf
	▲	▲	▲		u	—	—	—	u	u	u	u	u

Purpose   Divides two unsigned values.

Syntax/Example
div *regB* | *memB*   div dl
div *regW* | *memW*   div [word var]

80386 only:
div *regDW* | *memDW*   div [dword bx]

Sample Code
```
DATASEG
var dd 01FFFEh ; 131070 decimal
CODESEG
mov ax, [word var]       ; Load low word into ax
mov dx, [word var + 2]   ; Load high word into dx
mov bx, 1024             ; Load divisor into bx
div bx                   ; ax <- 131070 / 1024 (ax = 127)
```

Description   Use div to divide unsigned integer values. The operand refers to the divisor. The dividend registers are determined by the divisor size. Byte divisors are divided into ax, placing the quotient in al and the remainder in ah. Word divisors are divided into dx:ax (low-order word in ax), placing the quotient in ax and the remainder in dx. Doubleword divisors (80386 only) are divided into edx:eax (low-order doubleword in eax), placing the quotient in eax and the remainder in edx.

If the result of the division is greater than the maximum value the designated quotient register can hold—or if the divisor equals 0—then a type 0 interrupt is generated. Unless steps are taken to trap this interrupt, DOS will halt the program and display a divide error message. This is further complicated by the fact that, for 8086/88 processors, the interrupt return address is for the instruction following div, but, for 80286 and 80386 processors, the interrupt return address points to the div that caused the fault.

See Also   idiv

enter

Enter Procedure

						Flags:	of	df	if	tf	sf	zf	af	pf	cf
Processor:	8086/88	80286	80386				—	—	—	—	—	—	—	—	—
		▲	▲												

Purpose   Creates a stack frame for a procedure's local variables.

Syntax/Example

enter *immW, 0*   enter 2, 0
enter *immW, 1*   enter 8, 1
enter *immW, immB*   enter 0, 3

Sample Code

```
PROC AnyProc
  enter 8, 0     ; Reserve 8 bytes for local variables
; Procedure code
  leave          ; Reclaim reserved stack space
  ret            ; Return to caller
ENDP AnyProc
```

Description   Mostly used by high-level languages, enter prepares bp and subtracts from sp the number of bytes specified by the first operand, reserving space for variables on the stack, which can then be addressed by ss:bp. The second operand equals the nesting level and can be either an immediate 0 or 1 for fastest operation or a higher immediate value. The level is used by languages such as Pascal that allow true procedure nesting, providing a method for inner procedures to access local variables declared on outer levels. The sample shows how to use enter to reserve 8 bytes of stack space for variables. To recover this space, execute leave just before ret.

See Also   leave, ret

esc

Escape

						Flags:	of	df	if	tf	sf	zf	af	pf	cf
Processor:	8086/88	80286	80386				—	—	—	—	—	—	—	—	—
	▲	▲	▲												

Purpose   Passes instructions to a coprocessor.

Syntax/Example

esc *imm6, regB | regW*   esc 5, ax
esc *imm6, memAll*   esc 5, [var]

Sample Code

```
fld st(0)      ; Push operand
wait           ; Wait required for
esc 8, ax      ;   8087
```

Description   You can use esc to pass instructions to a coprocessor. The first operand represents the instruction's operation code. The second operand specifies a destination or source value for the coprocessor instruction. Because Turbo Assembler recognizes math coprocessor instruction mnemonics, `esc` is rarely of much practical use. If you do use `esc`, be aware that the 8087 requires a `wait` instruction before every math coprocessor instruction. Turbo Assembler automatically inserts `wait`s as needed—another reason to use coprocessor mnemonics instead of `esc`.

See Also   `wait`

Halt   hlt

Processor:	8086/88	80286	80386		Flags:	of	df	if	tf	sf	zf	af	pf	cf
	▲	▲	▲			—	—	—	—	—	—	—	—	—

Purpose   Halts until interrupt or reset.

Syntax/Example   hlt *no operands*   `hlt`

Sample Code
```
cli     ; Disable maskable interrupts
hlt     ; Pause until NMI or reset
sti     ; Enable maskable interrupts
```

Description   Execute `hlt` to pause until the next interrupt signal is acknowledged or until a reset signal is received. If maskable interrupts are disabled, `hlt` pauses the program until a reset signal or until a nonmaskable interrupt is acknowledged.

See Also   `cli, sti`

Signed Integer Divide   idiv

Processor:	8086/88	80286	80386		Flags:	of	df	if	tf	sf	zf	af	pf	cf
	▲	▲	▲			u	—	—	—	u	u	u	u	u

Purpose   Divides two signed values.

Syntax/Example
idiv *regB | memB*   `idiv dl`
idiv *regW | memW*   `idiv [word var]`

80386 only:
idiv *regDW | memDW*   `idiv [dword bx]`

Sample Code
```
mov ax, 100     ; Assign dividend to ax
mov bl, -3      ; Assign divisor to bl
```

```
idiv bl          ; al <- ax / bl (remainder in ah)
neg al           ; Find absolute value of al
```

Description   Use idiv to divide signed integer values. The operand refers to the divisor. The dividend registers are determined by the divisor size. Byte divisors are divided into ax, placing the quotient in al and the remainder in ah. Word divisors are divided into dx:ax (low-order word in ax), placing the quotient in ax and the remainder in dx. Doubleword divisors (80386 only) are divided into edx:eax (low-order doubleword in eax), placing the quotient in eax and the remainder in edx. The remainder always has the same sign as the original dividend.

The sample divides 100 decimal by −3, placing the quotient in al (0DFh) and the remainder in ah (01). Remember that negative values like 0DFh are expressed in two's complement form. To find the absolute value (3 in this case), use neg as in the sample.

If the result of the division is greater than the maximum value the designated quotient register can hold—or if the divisor equals 0—then a type 0 interrupt is generated. Unless steps are taken to trap this interrupt, DOS will halt the program and display a divide error message. This is further complicated by the fact that, for 8086/88 processors, the interrupt return address points to the instruction following div, but for 80286 and 80386 processors, the interrupt return address points to the div that caused the fault.

See Also   div

imul   **Signed Integer Multiply**

Processor:	8086/88	80286	80386		Flags:	of	df	if	tf	sf	zf	af	pf	cf
	▲	▲	▲			▲	−	−	−	u	u	u	u	▲

Purpose   Multiplies two signed values.

Syntax/Example
```
imul regB | memB                        imul [byte bx]
imul regW | memW                        imul cx
```

80286, 80386 only:
```
imul regW, immB                         imul cx, 9
imul regW, immW                         imul bx, 451
imul regW, regW | memW, immB            imul cx, [word bx], 3
imul regW, regW | memW, immW            imul ax, bx, 300
```

80386 only:
```
imul regDW | memDW                      imul [dword bx]
imul regDW, immB                        imul ebx, 10
imul regDW, immDW                       imul eax, 32769
imul regW, regW | memW                  imul bx, cx
```

```
imul regDW, regDW | memDW            imul ecx, [dword \bx]
imul regDW, regDW | memDW, immB       imul eax, edx, 12
imul regDW, regDW | memDW, immDW      imul eax, [dword bx], 35790
```

Sample Code
```
mov   al, 4          ; Multiplicand
mov   bl, -2         ; Multiplier
imul  bl             ; ax <- al * bl
                     ; (ax = 0FFF8h, cf = of = 0)
mov   al, 127        ; Multiplicand
mov   bl, -128       ; Multiplier
imul  bl             ; ax <- al * bl
                     ; (ax = 0C080h, cf = of = 1)
```

Description   Depending on the processor, imul has three basic formats, taking from one to three operands. Some forms require explicit registers. The simplest form multiplies a byte register or variable by al, placing the result in ax. A similar form multiplies a word register or variable by ax, placing the result in dx:ax (low-order word in ax). On the 80386 only, imul can multiply eax by a doubleword register or variable, placing the result in edx:eax. With all these forms, if both cf and of equal 0 after imul, then the high-order portion of the result is merely the sign extension of the low-order portion. In other words, as the first part of the sample shows, multiplying 4 * −2 sets ax to 0FFF8h. Because cf and of are 0, ah (0FFh) extends the sign of the 8-bit answer in al (0F8h), creating a full 16-bit value. When cf and of are both set to 1, as in the second part of the sample, then the result occupies the full width of the destination register—in this case ax, which equals the two's complement value 0C080h, or −16,256 in decimal, the product of 127 * −128.

80286 and 80386 processors expand on these basic forms with multiple-operand imul instructions. In the two-operand format, the first operand is the multiplicand; the second operand is the immediate byte or word multiplier. The product replaces the specified multiplicand register. In the three-operand format, the first operand specifies a destination register for the product, the second register holds the multiplicand, and the third operand is the immediate byte or word multiplier. The 80386 further expands these forms, allowing various combinations of doubleword registers, memory references, and immediate values. With all these variations, if cf and of are 0 after imul, then the product exactly fits within the specified destination register (always the first operand); otherwise, the product is too large for this register.

See Also   mul

imul

in

Input From Port

Processor:	8086/88	80286	80386		Flags:	of	df	if	tf	sf	zf	af	pf	cf
	▲	▲	▲			—	—	—	—	—	—	—	—	—

Purpose   Inputs values from ports.

Syntax/Example

```
in al, immB      in al, 14h
in al, dx        in al, dx
in ax, immB      in ax, 01Fh
in ax, dx        in ax, dx
```

80386 only:
```
in eax, immB     in eax, 0Fh
in eax, dx       in eax, dx
```

Sample Code
```
Ctrl8259 EQU 021h        ; 8259 masks port

in  al, Ctrl8259         ; Read 8259 enable masks
and al, EnableIRQ        ; Clear masked bit
out Ctrl8259, al         ; Write new 8259 masks
```

Description   The in instruction reads the value of a hardware port into al, ax, or eax (80386 only). As the sample shows, in is often used in conjunction with out and logical instructions such as and and or to examine and change bit switches at various port addresses in the computer. The simplest form of in reads a byte value into al from an immediate port address in the range 0–255. To access higher port addresses, specify the address in the dx register.

See Also   ins, out

inc

Increment

Processor:	8086/88	80286	80386		Flags:	of	df	if	tf	sf	zf	af	pf	cf
	▲	▲	▲			▲	—	—	—	▲	▲	▲	▲	—

Purpose   Adds 1 to a register or variable.

Syntax/Example

```
inc regB | memB        inc [byte bx]
inc regW | memW        inc dx
```

80386 only:
```
inc regDW | memDW      inc ecx
```

Sample Code

```
mov   dx, 0                  ; Initialize dx <- 0
@@10:
  call Anyproc               ; Call a procedure
  inc  dx                    ; dx <- dx + 1
  cmp  dx, 1000              ; Does dx = 1000?
  jne  @@10                  ; Jump if dx <> 1000
```

Description Use inc to increase a byte, word, or doubleword (80386 only) register or memory value by 1. This is similar to adding 1 to unsigned values with add, but faster. The sample uses inc to construct a simple loop, using dx as a control value to call a procedure Anyproc (not shown) 1000 times. (There may be more efficient ways to construct such a loop.)

See Also dec

Input From Port To String **ins insb insd insw**

Processor:	8086/88	80286	80386	*Flags:*	of	df	if	tf	sf	zf	af	pf	cf
		▲	▲		—	—	—	—	—	—	—	—	—

Purpose Inputs values from ports to a sequence of bytes, words, or doublewords in memory.

Syntax/Example

```
ins  di | memB, dx            rep ins [var], dx
ins  di | memW, dx            rep ins [word var], dx
insb no operands              rep insb
insw no operands              rep insw
```

80386 only:

```
ins  regDW | memDW, dx        rep ins [dword var], dx
insd no operands              rep insd
```

Sample Code

```
; ! NOTE: Don't run this sample !

mov cx, 100                  ; Number of words to read
mov dx, 049h                 ; Specify port address
mov di, offset s1            ; Address destination
cld                          ; Auto-increment di
rep insw                     ; Load string from port
```

Description As with all string instructions, the register assignments for ins and its shorthand forms insb, insd (80386 only), and insw are fixed, even if you specify address labels explicitly. The destination resister is always es:di, and the segment cannot be overridden. The port number must be placed in dx. (Don't forget to do this also for the shorthand mnemonics!) If df =

0, then `ins` increments `di`; if `df = 1`, `ins` decrements `di`. Normally, you'll preface `ins` with `rep`, repeating the instruction for the number of times specified in `cx` as illustrated in the sample.

See Also   `cmpsb, cmpsd, cmpsw, lods, lodsb, lodsd, lodsw, movs, movsb, movsd, movsw, outs, outsb, outsd, outsw, scas, scasb, scasd, scasw, stos, stosb, stosd, stosw`

---

int   **Call Interrupt Service Routine**

Processor:	8086/88	80286	80386		*Flags:*	of	df	if	tf	sf	zf	af	pf	cf
	▲	▲	▲			–	–	0	0	–	–	–	–	–

Purpose   Calls interrupt service routine by number.

Syntax/Example   int *3*   int 3
                       int *immB*   int 21h

Sample Code
```
DATASEG
message db 'Mastering Turbo Assembler', '$'
CODESEG
mov dx, offset message   ; Address message string
mov ah, 9                ; Specify DOS function number
int 21h                  ; Call DOS function handler
```

Description   Although there are two forms of `int`, they appear the same in programs. The first form is a special 1-byte code (0CCh) that debuggers typically use to replace instructions at specified breakpoints. You can insert this code yourself to cause most debuggers (Turbo Debugger included) to halt at various locations. The second form specifies a byte value as the interrupt number, which can range from 0 to 255, representing one of 256 four-byte vector pointer addresses stored in memory beginning at address 0000:0000. Executing `int` runs the interrupt service routine at the vectored address for this interrupt number. Just before this, the processor pushes onto the stack the flags and the return address, which are restored in the interrupt service routine by executing `iret`. In addition, the interrupt and trap flags are set to 0. (These two flags are restored by `iret`, and, because the flags are changed only for the interrupt service routine, some 8086 references incorrectly indicate that `if` and `tf` are not changed by `int`.)

See Also   `into, iret`

Interrupt On Overflow

into

Processor:	8086/88	80286	80386		*Flags:*	of	df	if	tf	sf	zf	af	pf	cf
	▲	▲	▲			—	—	▲	▲	—	—	—	—	—

Purpose   Generates a type 4 interrupt if of = 1.

Syntax/Example   into *no operands*   into

Sample Code
```
P386
imul ecx, [dword bx]    ; ecx <- ecx * [bx]
into                    ; Interrupt on overflow
```

Description   By installing an interrupt service routine for interrupt 4, you can use into to force execution of this code if the overflow flag is set by a previous operation. The instruction into behaves like int, pushing the flags and return address onto the stack, resetting tf and if, and jumping to the vector for interrupt 4. The interrupt code can then deal with the error and execute iret to resume program execution. The sample demonstrates how you might use into to detect an overflow from an imul instruction for an 80386 processor.

See Also   int, iret

Interrupt Return

iret iretd

Processor:	8086/88	80286	80386		*Flags:*	of	df	if	tf	sf	zf	af	pf	cf
	▲	▲	▲			▲	▲	▲	▲	▲	▲	▲	▲	▲

Purpose   Returns from an interrupt service routine.

Syntax/Example   iret *no operands*   iret

    80386 only:
    iretd *no operands*   iretd

Sample Code
```
PROC MyISR
   push ax          ; Save any changed registers
   sti              ; Enable maskable interrupts
; Procedure code
   iret             ; Return from interrupt
ENDP
```

Description   Execute iret as the last instruction in an interrupt service routine (ISR). The instruction pops the return address cs:ip from the stack and the flags, continuing the program from the point of the interruption. Use the same iret whether the interrupt was generated externally or internally by a fault condition such as an illegal division or by the int and into instructions.

On 80386-based systems only, `iretd` can be used to return to a 32-bit segment, popping the full-width `eip` extended instruction pointer from the stack.

See Also   `int, into`

---

j-condition   Jump Conditionally

Processor:	8086/88	80286	80386		Flags:	of	df	if	tf	sf	zf	af	pf	cf
	▲	▲	▲			—	—	—	—	—	—	—	—	—

Purpose   Jumps to a new location if certain flags are set and/or reset.

Syntax/Example   *condition shortTarget*   `jge @@30`

Sample Code
```
cmp ax, 1024    ; Compare ax and 1024
jb  @@20        ; Jump if ax < 1024
```

Description   All conditional jumps operate similarly and, therefore, are listed together here for easy reference. Also, although some of the mnemonics represent the same instructions (for example, `je` and `jz`), the mnemonics are listed separately. As Table 14-4 shows, certain flag settings control whether the jump is made. The target address of a conditional jump is a signed displacement of −128 to +127 bytes away from the address of the *following* instruction. On 80386 systems only, displacements may range from −32,768 to +32,767 bytes.

The sample demonstrates how to use a conditional jump after a `cmp` to test the value of a register. Comparing `ax` with 1,024 and following with `jb` jumps to the target address if the value of `ax` is *below* 1,024. Conditions that use the words "above" and "below" refer to unsigned comparisons; conditions that use the words "greater" and "less" refer to signed comparisons.

See Also   `jmp`

Table 14-4 *Conditional Jump Reference*

Instruction	Jump if ...	Flags
ja	above	(cf = 0) & (zf = 0)
jae	above or equal	(cf = 0)
jb	below	(cf = 1)
jbe	below or equal	(cf = 1) | (zf = 1)
jc	carry	(cf = 1)
jcxz	cx equals 0	—
jecxz	ecx equals 0	— (80386 only.)
je	equal	(zf = 1)
jg	greater	(sf = of) & (zf = 0)
jge	greater or equal	(sf = of)
jl	less	(sf <> of)
jle	less or equal	(sf <> of) | (zf = 1)
jo	overflow	(of = 1)
jp	parity	(pf = 1)
jpe	parity even	(pf = 1)
jpo	parity odd	(pf = 0)
js	sign	(sf = 1)
jz	zero	(zf = 1)
jna	not above	(cf = 1) | (zf = 1)
jnae	not above or equal	(cf = 1)
jnb	not below	(cf = 0)
jnbe	not below or equal	(cf = 0) & (zf = 0)
jnc	not carry	(cf = 0)
jne	not equal	(zf = 0)
jng	not greater	(sf<>of) | (zf = 1)
jnge	not greater or equal	(sf <> of)
jnl	not less	(sf = of)
jnle	not less or equal	(sf = of) & (zf = 0)
jno	not overflow	(of = 0)
jnp	not parity	(pf = 0)
jns	not sign	(sf = 0)
jnz	not zero	(zf = 0)

jmp

Jump Unconditionally

Processor:	8086/88	80286	80386		*Flags:*	of	df	if	tf	sf	zf	af	pf	cf
	▲	▲	▲			—	—	—	—	—	—	—	—	—

Purpose   Jumps to a new location.

Syntax/Example   jmp *shortTarget*   jmp short @@10
jmp *nearTarget*   jmp CloseBy

jmp

```
jmp farTarget        jmp far OverThere
jmp regW | memW      jmp bx
jmp memDW            jmp [dword bx]
```

80386 only:
```
jmp regDW            jmp ecx
```

Sample Code
```
or  bx, bx       ; Does bx = 0?
jnz Continue     ; Jump if bx <> 0
jmp Exit         ; Else jump to exit
Continue:
```

Description The `jmp` instruction causes program execution to continue at the address specified as a displacement from the instruction *following* the `jmp`. In assembly language programs, Turbo Assembler calculates the displacement from a label that you specify as the operand, automatically using the most efficient form of the instruction possible. There's rarely any good reason to calculate displacements manually.

When jumping to higher addresses, use the SHORT operator as in `jmp SHORT Nearby`, or Turbo Assembler will insert wasteful nop instructions to allow for the possibility that the address later will prove to be farther than about 128 bytes away.

In place of an explicit label, you can specify the target address in a register or via a memory reference. The 80386 allows extended registers to hold 32-bit offset addresses. This powerful ability is especially useful in creating "jump tables," which contain lists of locations to which control passes based on certain conditions.

See Also `j-condition`

lahf

Load Flags Into ah Register

Processor:	8086/88	80286	80386	*Flags:*	of	df	if	tf	sf	zf	af	pf	cf
	▲	▲	▲		—	—	—	—	—	—	—	—	—

Purpose Copies `sf`, `zf`, `af`, and `cf` to `ah`.

Syntax/Example `lahf` *no operands*   `lahf`

Sample Code
```
lahf             ; Load flags in to ah
test ah, 0Dh     ; Test sf, zf, cf
jnz  @@10        ; Jump if any flag = 1
```

Description Execute `lahf` to load the five flags sf(7), zf(6), af(4), pf(2), and cf(0) into the lower 4 bits of register `ah`. Bit numbers are shown in parentheses. After executing lahf, other bits in `ah` are undefined and may also change.

See Also `sahf`

Load Pointer and ds

lds

Processor:	8086/88	80286	80386	*Flags:*	of	df	if	tf	sf	zf	af	pf	cf
	▲	▲	▲		—	—	—	—	—	—	—	—	—

Purpose Loads pointer from memory into a register and ds.

Syntax/Example lds *regW, memDW* lds si, [bp + 4]

80386 only:
lds *regDW, memFW* lds edi, [bx]

Sample Code
```
push cs              ; Push segment
mov  ax, offset var  ; Load offset
push ax              ; Push offset
;
;
push bp              ; Save bp
mov  bp, sp          ; Address stack with bp
lds  si, [bp + 2]    ; Load pointer to ds:si
```

Description Use lds to load both a 16-bit general-purpose register (usually si) and the ds segment register with a 32-bit pointer stored in memory. The *memDW* operand may be any of the usual addressing modes, except for a direct address, which is not permitted. The 80386 can load a 48-bit pointer into an extended 32-bit register plus ds. The sample demonstrates how to pick up a pointer, perhaps passed to a subroutine by address on the stack. The first part of the sample pushes the segment cs and offset values of a variable (not shown) onto the stack; the second part uses lds along with bp to load ds:si with the pointer value.

See Also lea, les, lfs, lgs, lss

Load Effective Address

lea

Processor:	8086/88	80286	80386	*Flags:*	of	df	if	tf	sf	zf	af	pf	cf
	▲	▲	▲		—	—	—	—	—	—	—	—	—

Purpose Loads offset address of memory reference into a register.

Syntax/Example lea *regW, memW* lea bx, [bp + 2]

80386 only:
lea *regW | regDW, memW | memDW* lea edi, [dword bp + 2]

Sample Code

```
DATASEG
array db 80 dup (0)
CODESEG
lea     bx, [array + si]        ; Use this...
mov     bx, offset array        ; ...instead of these
add     bx, si                  ; two lines

lea     bx, [array + bp + si]   ; Use this...
mov     bx, offset array        ; ...instead of these
add     bx, bp                  ; three lines
add     bx, si
```

Description   Use lea to load the offset address, also called the effective address, into a word register or a doubleword register on 80386 systems. When you need to use a complex memory reference repeatedly—or when you need to load a register, usually bx, with the address of a table element perhaps for use with the xlat instruction—you can use lea to compute the offset address. The sample demonstrates how doing this can perform the work of two or three instructions. The first code line performs the same task as lines two and three; the fourth code line does the same job as the last three lines.

See Also   lds, les, lfs, lgs, lss

leave   Leave Procedure

Processor:	8086/88	80286	80386		*Flags:*	of	df	if	tf	sf	zf	af	pf	cf
		▲	▲			—	—	—	—	—	—	—	—	—

Purpose   Removes from the stack local variable space allocated by enter.

Syntax/Example   leave *no operands*   leave

Sample Code

```
PROC AnyProc
 enter 6, 0     ; Reserve 6 bytes for local variables
; Procedure code
 leave          ; Reclaim reserved stack space
 ret            ; Return to caller
ENDP AnyProc
```

Description   Just before a ret instruction, use leave to reclaim stack space previously allocated by enter at the start of a procedure. Usually, high-level language compilers use leave and enter to implement functions and procedures, but you can certainly use these instructions in pure assembly language programs, too. A leave performs the two steps mov sp, bp and pop bp, thus restoring the stack pointer and bp, which was pushed onto the stack by enter.

See Also   enter, ret

Load Pointer and es

les

	Processor:	8086/88	80286	80386		Flags:	of	df	if	tf	sf	zf	af	pf	cf
		▲	▲	▲			—	—	—	—	—	—	—	—	—

Purpose Loads pointer from memory into a register and es.

Syntax/Example les *regW, memDW*   les di, [bp + 4]

80386 only:
les *regDW, memFW*   les esi, [bx]

Sample Code
```
push ds            ; Push segment
mov  ax, offset var ; Load offset
push ax            ; Push offset
;
;
push bp            ; Save bp
mov  bp, sp        ; Address stack with bp
les  di, [bp + 2]  ; Load pointer to es:di
```

Description Use les to load both a 16-bit general-purpose register (usually di) and the es segment register with a 32-bit pointer stored in memory. The *memDW* operand may be any of the usual addressing modes, except for a direct address, which is not permitted. The 80386 can load a 48-bit pointer into an extended 32-bit register plus es. The sample demonstrates how to set es:di to point to a variable, perhaps passed to a subroutine by address on the stack. The first part of the sample pushes the segment ds and offset values of var (not shown) onto the stack; the second part uses les along with bp to load es:di with the pointer value.

See Also lds, lea, lfs, lgs, lss

Load Pointer and fs, gs

lfs lgs

	Processor:	8086/88	80286	80386		Flags:	of	df	if	tf	sf	zf	af	pf	cf
				▲			—	—	—	—	—	—	—	—	—

Purpose Loads pointer from memory into a register and fs (lfs) or into gs (lgs).

Syntax/Example
lfs *regW, memDW*   lfs di, [bp + 4]
lfs *regDW, memFW*   lfs esi, [bx]

lgs *regW, memDW*   lgs di, [bp + 4]
lgs *regDW, memFW*   lgs esi, [bx]

Sample Code
```
push cs                    ; Push segment
push 0                     ; Push high offset
push offset var            ; Push low offset
:
:
push bp                    ; Save bp
mov  bp, sp                ; Address stack with bp
lgs  edi, [bp + 2]         ; Load pointer to gs:edi
```

Description Use lfs and lgs to load a 16- or 32-bit offset pointer plus a 16-bit segment address value into any 16- or 32-bit register and either the **fs** or **gs** segment registers, available only on 80386 systems. Except for the ability to load 48-bit pointers, these two instructions are similar to lds and les and are typically used in procedures to access variables passed to subroutines by address on the stack.

See Also lds, lea, les, lss

lock   Lock the Bus

Processor:	8086/88	80286	80386		Flags:	of	df	if	tf	sf	zf	af	pf	cf
	▲	▲	▲			—	—	—	—	—	—	—	—	—

Purpose Asserts bus lock signal for next instruction.

Syntax/Example lock *no operands*   lock xchg [semaphore], al

Sample Code
```
; Note: Don't run this!
 mov dl, 1                    ; Set dl to 1
@@10:
 lock xchg [semaphore], dl    ; Exchange dl & memory
 or  dl, dl                   ; Does dl = 0?
 jz  @@10                     ; Jump until dl <> 0
```

Description Use lock as a prefix to instructions that reference memory shared by more than one processor. (PCs have single processors, so lock is rarely used in PC programming.) Typically, lock prefaces xchg on 8086/88 systems; movs, ins, and outs on 80286/386 systems; and adc, add, and, bt, btc, btr, bts, dec inc, neg, not, or, sbb, sub, and xor on 80386 systems when one operand is a memory reference. It's not necessary to preface xchg with lock on 80286/386 systems, which do this automatically.

The hypothetical sample shows a typical use for lock—setting a flag called a *semaphore* to prepare for exclusive use of a device or, perhaps, other memory blocks. The lock on the xchg prevents two processors from accessing the same byte; therefore, if dl is 0, the program can safely proceed while the other processor, which is running a similar or even the same routine, will pause until the first process again resets the semaphore to 0.

See Also   xchg

Load String   # lods lodsb lodsd lodsw

Processor:	8086/88	80286	80386		*Flags:*	of	df	if	tf	sf	zf	af	pf	cf
	▲	▲	▲			–	–	–	–	–	–	–	–	–

Purpose   Loads strings of values into the accumulator.

Syntax/Example

```
lods [es:]memB        lods    [byte source]
lods [es:]memW        lods    [word es:si]
lodsb no operands     lodsb
lodsw no operands     lodsw
```

80386 only:

```
lods [es:]memDW       lods    [dword source]
lodsd no operands     lodsd
```

Sample Code

```
mov si, offset string  ; Address string with ds:si
mov cx, MaxCount       ; Maximum loops to do
cld                    ; Auto-increment si
@@10:
lodsb                  ; al <- [ds:si]; si <- si + 1
call Subroutine        ; Call a procedure
loop                   ; Loop until cx = 0
```

Description   The operand to lods is always ds:si or, with a segment override, es:si. Even if the operand refers to a label by name, you still must initialize si to address this variable—all that Turbo Assembler can do is check that the variable you specify is actually in the expected segment. Most of the time, you'll use the shorthand mnemonics lodsb, lodsd (80386 only), and lodsw to load bytes, words, and doublewords into al, ax, and eax. Each time lods executes, if df = 0, si is incremented; if df = 1, si is decremented.

    The instruction is used most often in a loop that scans a string of values, as demonstrated in the sample. Register si is initialized to address a variable, cx is assigned the maximum number of loops to execute, and df flag is cleared so that lodsb will advance si. The loop then loads bytes at ds:si into al, calling a subroutine (not shown) and looping until cx equals 0.

    You can preface lods with repeat prefixes such as repe, but it makes little sense to do so as the effect is to load a single value into the accumulator, a job more easily performed with other instructions.

See Also   cmpsb, cmpsd, cmpsw, ins, insb, insd, insw, movs, movsb, movsd, movsw, outs, outsb, outsd, outsw, scas, scasb, scasd, scasw, stos, stosb, stosd, stosw

loop

Loop on cx

Processor:	8086/88	80286	80386		Flags:	of	df	if	tf	sf	zf	af	pf	cf
	▲	▲	▲			—	—	—	—	—	—	—	—	—

Purpose   Decrements cx and then jumps if cx is not 0.

Syntax/Example   loop *shortTarget*   loop StartLoop

Sample Code

```
 jcxz @@20            ; Skip loop if cx = 0
@@10:
 call Subroutine      ; Call a procedure
 loop @@10            ; cx <- cx - 1; jump if cx <> 0
@@20:
```

Description   This instruction is very handy for constructing loops that repeat for the number of times specified by register cx. At each loop execution, cx is decremented by 1. If this leaves cx not equal to 0, then a jump is made to the loop's target address, which must be no more than 126 bytes above (at a lower address than) the loop and no more than 127 bytes below (at a higher address). Because loop decrements cx *before* testing whether cx is 0, if cx = 0 at the start of a repeated section, that section will execute 65,536 times. To prevent this, precede the repeated section with jcxz as in the sample.

See Also   jcxz, loope, loopz, loopne, loopnz

loope loopz

Loop on cx While Equal

Processor:	8086/88	80286	80386		Flags:	of	df	if	tf	sf	zf	af	pf	cf
	▲	▲	▲			—	—	—	—	—	—	—	—	—

Purpose   Decrements cx and then jumps conditionally if cx is not 0. AND zf = 1

Syntax/Example   loope *shortTarget*   loope @@20
                    loopz *shortTarget*   loopz StartLoop

Sample Code

```
DATASEG
array      db '   ABCDEFG', 0
arraySize = $-array
```

```
CODESEG
  mov cx, arraySize        ; Assign array size to cx
  mov si, offset array     ; Address array with ds:si
  cld                      ; Auto-increment si
@@10:
  lods [byte array]        ; al <- [ds:si]; si <- si + 1
  cmp al, 32               ; Does al = 32?
  loope @@10               ; Jump while yes & cx <> 0
  je  AllBlank             ; Jump if string = all blanks
  dec si                   ; si addresses first nonblank
```

Description   Use either `loope` or `loopz`, both of which represent the same instruction, to decrement `cx` and jump to a target address if this leaves `cx` not equal to 0 and if `zf = 1`, presumably set or reset from a previous comparison. As with `loop`, the target must be within 126 bytes back and 127 bytes forward of `loope`. The sample shows how to use `loope` to scan a byte array. The array length is assigned to `cx`; the array address to `si`. Then a three-instruction loop loads successive array bytes into `al`, jumping to `@@10:` from the `loope` instruction if `cx` is not 0 and if the previous `cmp` found 32—the ASCII value for a blank character. After the loop, a `je` detects whether all characters in the string were blank. If not, `si` is decremented, thus pointing to the first nonblank character.

See Also   `loop, loopne, loopnz`

Loop on cx While Not Equal   **loopne loopnz**

Processor:	8086/88	80286	80386		*Flags:*	of	df	if	tf	sf	zf	af	pf	cf
	▲	▲	▲			—	—	—	—	—	—	—	—	—

Purpose   Decrements `cx` and then jumps conditionally if `cx` is not 0. *AND zf=0*

Syntax/Example   loopne *shortTarget*   `loopne @@Begin`
                     loopnz *shortTarget*   `loopnz @@110`

Sample Code
```
  mov cx, arraySize        ; Assign array size to cx
  mov si, offset array + arraySize - 1; Address end of array
  std                      ; Auto-decrement si
@@10:
  lods [byte array]        ; al <- [ds:si]; si <- si - 1
  cmp al, '.'              ; Does al = '.'?
  loopne @@10              ; Jump while no & cx <> 0
  jne  Exit                ; Jump if no '.' found
  inc si                   ; si addresses '.'
```

Description   These two mnemonics represent the same instruction and operate nearly identically to `loope` and `loopz`, except that the jump to a target address is made only if, after decrementing cx, this leaves cx <> 0 and if zf = 0. The sample uses loopne to locate a period in a file-name string, starting the scan at the end of the string and jumping to Exit (not shown) if no period is found or incrementing si to the period character if found.

See Also   loop, loope, loopz

lss   Load Pointer and ss

Processor:	8086/88	80286	80386	*Flags:*	of	df	if	tf	sf	zf	af	pf	cf
			▲		—	—	—	—	—	—	—	—	—

Purpose   Loads pointer from memory into a register and ss.

Syntax/Example
```
lss regW, memDW        lss si, [bp + 2]
lss regDW, memFW       lss edi, [bx]
```

Sample Code
```
mov [oldss], ss        ; Save old stack segment
mov [oldsp], sp        ;   and old stack pointer
lss sp, [newstack]     ; Load ss:sp with new values
;
;
mov sp, [oldsp]        ; Restore sp (interrupts disabled)
mov ss, [oldss]        ; Restore ss
```

Description   On 80386 systems, use lss to load a 16- or 32-bit offset pointer plus a 16-bit segment address value into any 16- or 32-bit register and the ss stack segment register. Normally, the offset value will be loaded into sp, but there's no restriction on using lss to load other registers. One way to use lss is to pick up the address of an alternative stack as the sample demonstrates.

See Also   lds, lea, les, lfs

mov   Move Data

Processor:	8086/88	80286	80386	*Flags:*	of	df	if	tf	sf	zf	af	pf	cf
	▲	▲	▲		—	—	—	—	—	—	—	—	—

Purpose   Moves values between registers or between registers and memory.

Syntax/Example
```
mov al, memB           mov al, [abyte]
mov ax, memW           mov ax, [aword]
mov memB, al           mov [abyte], al
```

```
mov memW, ax                            mov [aword], ax
mov regB | memB, regB | immB            mov dl, cl
mov regW | memW, regW | immW            mov [aword], 1024
mov regB, memB                          mov dl, [abyte]
mov regW, memW                          mov dx, [aword]
```

80386 only:

```
mov eax, memDW                          mov eax, [adword]
mov memDW, eax                          mov [adword], eax
mov regDW | memDW, regDW | immDW        mov edx, 99999
mov regDW, memDW                        mov edx, [adword]
```

Sample Code

```
DATASEG
var db 10 dup (0)       ; A 10-byte variable
CODESEG
 mov bx, 0              ; Initialize bx to 0
 mov cx, 10            ; Initialize cx to 10
@@10:
 mov [byte var + bx], cl  ; Copy cl to memory
 inc bx                 ; Increment pointer
 loop @@10              ; Loop on cx
```

Description

The mov instruction is probably the most heavily used of all instructions in 8086 programming. Various forms of mov allow transferring bytes, words, and doublewords (80386 only) between registers or between registers and memory, using all the usual memory-addressing modes.

There are a few restrictions on mov that are not evident from the syntax list. The direction of mov is from right to left—transferring the value of the second operand to the first. The value of the second operand is never affected. When both operands are registers, only one of those operands may be a segment register; therefore, it's legal to write mov es, ax and mov [aword], ds, but it's *not* legal to write mov ds, es. When one operand is a segment register, interrupts are disabled for the *next* instruction, allowing a mov to ss to be followed with a mov to sp, eliminating the danger that an interrupt signal will occur before the full stack pointer ss:sp is initialized. Another restriction is that both operands may not be memory references—all moves to and from memory must pass through a register. (See movs for an instruction that can move values between two memory locations.)

When one register operand is al, ax, or eax (80386 only), Turbo Assembler generates a faster form of mov. If the accumulator is free, you should use it in mov instructions to improve program performance.

The sample shows how mov is used to initialize registers, used here to store the successive values 10, 9, . . . , 1 in a variable. Another mov copies the value of cl to memory using base-addressing mode with bx.

See Also   movs, lods, stos

mov

movs movsb movsd movsw

Move String

Processor:	8086/88	80286	80386		Flags:	of	df	if	tf	sf	zf	af	pf	cf
	▲	▲	▲			—	—	—	—	—	—	—	—	—

Purpose   Moves strings of values directly between two memory locations.

Syntax/Example

movs *memB, [es:]memB*   movs [var1], [var2]
movs *memW, [es:]memW*   movs [var3], [es:si]
movsb *no operands*   movsb
movsw *no operands*   movsw

80386 only:
movs *memDW, [es:]memDW*   movs [edi], [es:var4]
movsd *no operands*   movsd

Sample Code

```
mov ax,@data          ; Initialize ds to address
mov ds,ax             ;  of data segment
mov es,ax             ; Make es = ds
ASSUME es:DGROUP      ; Tell tasm where es points
mov si, offset string ; Address source string
mov di, offset strcopy ; Address destination
mov cx, strlen        ; Assign count to cx
jcxz Exit             ; Don't copy if cx = 0!
cld                   ; Auto-increment si, di
rep movsb             ; Copy string to strcopy
```

Description   The movs instruction, plus its shorthand forms movsb, movsd (80386 only), and movsw, moves one value in memory directly to another memory location. The first operand must be es:di, addressing the destination for the move. The second operand must be ds:si or with a segment override es:si, addressing the source for the move. The extended 32-bit registers edi and esi may be used in 80386 programs. Executing movs copies 1 byte from the source location to the destination. After this, if df = 0, both si and di (or esi and edi) are advanced by the number of bytes being moved. If df = 1, the two registers are decremented by the number of bytes being moved. These register assignments are fixed—even, as in some of the examples, if you specify explicit labels, which Turbo Assembler will check to ensure that the variables are in the appropriate segments. It's still your responsibility to load di and si with the offset addresses of the variables. The shorthand forms of movs require no operands. There are no operational differences between the different mnemonics.

Usually, movs is prefaced with a rep prefix, repeating the instruction for the number of times specified in cx. As the sample shows, this lets you create powerful instructions to move blocks of memory from one place to another—in this case, copying string to strcopy. As a reminder, the instructions to initialize segment registers are also shown in the sample. Effectively using movs (as well as other string instructions) requires careful planning and control of segment registers.

See Also cmpsb, cmpsd, cmpsw, ins, insb, insd, insw, lods, lodsb, lodsd, lodsw, outs, outsb, outsd, outsw, rep, scas, scasb, scasd, scasw, stos, stosb, stosd, stosw

---

Move and Extend Sign   movsx

Processor:	8086/88	80286	80386		*Flags:*	of	df	if	tf	sf	zf	af	pf	cf
			▲			—	—	—	—	—	—	—	—	—

Purpose Moves signed values from smaller registers and memory locations into larger registers, extending the sign bit.

Syntax/Example
movsx *regW, regB* | *memB*   movsx dx, al
movsx *regDW, regB* | *memB*   movsx eax, [abyte]
movsx *regDW, regW* | *memW* movsx edx, dx

Sample Code
```
mov al, -1            ; al = -1
mov dx, 0             ; dx = 00000h
movsx dx, al          ; dx = 0FFFFh

mov [abyte], -1       ; [abyte] = -1
mov eax, 0            ; eax = 000000000h
movsx eax, [abyte]    ; eax = 0FFFFFFFFh

mov ax, -1            ; ax = -1
mov edx, 0            ; edx = 000000000h
movsx edx, ax         ; edx = 0FFFFFFFFh
```

Description On 80386 systems, use movsx to copy signed values with fewer numbers of bits to larger registers. For example, you can use movsx to load a word register such as ax with a byte value from memory and have the processor automatically initialize ah, extending the sign of the copied value as needed. The destination (first operand) to movsx must be a register. The source (second operand) may be a register or memory reference. The samples demonstrate how to use movsx to transfer values between dissimilar registers.

See Also mov, movs, movzx

movzx   Move and Extend Zero Sign

	Processor:	8086/88	80286	80386		Flags:	of	df	if	tf	sf	zf	af	pf	cf
				▲			—	—	—	—	—	—	—	—	—

Purpose   Moves unsigned values from smaller registers and memory locations into larger registers, zeroing the most significant digits.

Syntax/Example
```
movzx regW, regB | memB      movzx bx, [abyte]
movzx regDW, regB | memB     movzx edx, dl
movzx regDW, regW | memW     movzx edx, [aword]
```

Sample Code
```
mov al, 1            ; al = 1
mov dx, -1           ; dx = 0FFFFh
movzx dx, al         ; dx = 00001h

mov [abyte], 1       ; [abyte] = 1
mov eax, -1          ; eax = 0FFFFFFFFh
movzx eax, [abyte]   ; eax = 000000001h

mov ax, 1            ; ax = 1
mov edx, -1          ; edx = 0FFFFFFFFh
movzx edx, ax        ; edx = 000000001h
```

Description   On 80386 systems, use movzx to copy unsigned values with fewer numbers of bits to larger registers—similar to the way you can use movsx. For example, movzx can load an extended 32-bit register such as ecx with a word value from memory and have the processor automatically zero the upper 16-bits of ecx. The destination (first operand) to movzx must be a register. The source (second operand) may be a register or memory reference. The samples demonstrate how to use movzx to transfer values between dissimilar registers.

See Also   mov, movs, movsx

mul   Unsigned Multiplication

	Processor:	8086/88	80286	80386		Flags:	of	df	if	tf	sf	zf	af	pf	cf
		▲	▲	▲			▲	—	—	—	u	u	u	u	▲

Purpose   Multiplies two unsigned values.

Syntax/Example
```
mul regB | memB      mul bl
mul regW | memW      mul [aword]
```

80386 only:
```
mul regDW | memDW    mul ebx
```

Sample Code
```
DATASEG
multiplicand dw 1024
multiplier   dw 32
answer       dw 0
CODESEG
mov ax, [multiplicand]   ; Load multiplicand into ax
mul [multiplier]         ; dx:ax <- ax * multiplier
jc  Exit                 ; Jump if result > 16 bits
mov [answer], ax         ; Else store answer
```

Description
Unsigned multiplication in 8086 programming is considerably simpler than signed multiplication (see imul). The single operand to mul must be a general-purpose register or a memory reference, representing the multiplier. The size of the multiplier determines the location of the multiplicand and product. If the multiplier is a byte, then the multiplicand is al, and the product is deposited in ax. If the multiplier is a word, then the multiplicand is ax, and the result is placed in dx:ax with ax holding the low-order portion of the result. If the multiplier is a doubleword (80386 only), then the multiplicand is in eax, and the product appears in edx:eax, with the low-order 32 bits in eax. Overflow of the destination registers is not possible.

After mul, the of and cf flags can be used to determine the size of the result. Both flags are set to 1 if the product takes more bits than the specified source; otherwise, both flags are set to 0. Thus, if cf = 0 after mul bl, then ah is 0, and the 8-bit result fits in al. If cf = 1 after mul bx, then the result occupies the full 32-bit double register dx:ax. As the sample demonstrates, you can optionally test cf (or of) after mul to detect a result larger than the size of the original operands.

See Also
imul

Two's Complement Negation   **neg**

Processor:	8086/88	80286	80386		Flags:	of	df	if	tf	sf	zf	af	pf	cf
	▲	▲	▲			▲	–	–	–	▲	▲	▲	▲	▲

Purpose
Negates (forms two's complement) of a value.

Syntax/Example
neg *regB* | *memB*   neg [abyte]
neg *regW* | *memW*   neg ax

80386 only:
neg *regDW* | *regDW*   neg edx

Sample Code	`mov ax, 6`	`; Assign values to`
	`mov dx, 8`	`;   ax and dx`
	`sub ax, dx`	`; ax <- ax - dx (ax = 0FFFEh)`
	`jae @@10`	`; Jump if ax >= 0`
	`neg ax`	`; Find absolute value (ax = 0002)`
	`mov dl, '-'`	`; Display a minus sign`
	`mov ah, 2`	`;   via DOS function 2`
	`int 21h`	`; Call DOS`
	`@@10:`	`; Continue here`

Description   Apply neg to form the two's complement of a register or memory value. When the original value is a negative number in two's complement form, neg finds the absolute positive equivalent of the value. The instruction operates by subtracting the original value from 0, an operation that is logically equivalent to toggling all bits in the value from 0 to 1 and from 1 to 0, and then adding 1. As the sample demonstrates, if the result of a subtraction is negative, a minus sign can be sent to the standard DOS output file, and the result in ax can be negated. Not shown is the code after @@10: that would then write the absolute value of ax to the standard output, thus displaying the full negative number in decimal.

See Also   not

nop   No Operation

Processor:	8086/88	80286	80386		Flags:	of	df	if	tf	sf	zf	af	pf	cf
	▲	▲	▲			—	—	—	—	—	—	—	—	—

Purpose   Occupies 1 byte of machine code but has no operational effect.

Syntax/Example   nop *no operands*   nop

Sample Code	`jmp @@20`	`; Jump to forward label`
	`nop`	`; Inserted by Turbo Assembler...`
	`;`	
	`;`	
	`@@20`	`; ...if this label is within about`
		`;   128 bytes`

Description   Turbo Assembler inserts nop instructions to reserve bytes in cases where the exact size of an instruction is determined by code later in the program. For example, a jmp to a forward label is assumed to be 3 bytes long. But if the jmp destination proves to be within about 128 bytes, the assembler changes the jmp to a more efficient 2-byte form, leaving the unneeded third byte equal to a nop. (You can avoid this situation by prefacing the target address of forward labels with the **SHORT** operator.) Another use for nop is during debugging. If you want to remove an instruction, instead of quitting the debugger, loading your editor, making a modification, and reassembling, just poke a few `nop` bytes (90h) over the instruction. You can then run the program and examine the effects without this instruction in place—a useful debugging technique. Some references recommend using `nop` to adjust the timing of software loops, although because it is almost impossible to predict the exact timings of multiple instructions in 8086 programming—especially in an interrupt-driven computer system—this use of `nop` is dubious.

The `nop` instruction is identical to the instructions `xchg ax, ax` and `xchg eax, eax` (80386 only), both of which assemble to the same machine code as `nop`.

See Also   `xchg`

One's Complement Negation   **not**

Processor:	8086/88	80286	80386	*Flags:*	of	df	if	tf	sf	zf	af	pf	cf
	▲	▲	▲		—	—	—	—	—	—	—	—	—

Purpose   Toggles all 1 bits to 0 and all 0 bits to 1 in a value.

Syntax/Example
not *regB* | *memB*   not dh
not *regW* | *memW*   not dx

80386 only:
not *regDW* | *memDW* not [dword var]

Sample Code
```
DATASEG
false EQU 0             ; Value representing false
true  EQU -1            ; Value representing true
flag db true            ; Initialize flag to true
CODESEG
 cmp [flag], false      ; Is the flag false?
 je @@10                ; Jump if flag = false
 call Subroutine        ; Else call a subroutine
@@10:
 not [flag]             ; Toggle flag value
```

Description   Use `not` to toggle all 1 bits in a value to 0 and all 0 bits to 1. This is often useful for toggling the value of a true and false flag, as in the sample. (The referenced subroutine is not shown.)

See Also   `neg`

or

Logical OR

Processor:	8086/88	80286	80386	*Flags:*	of	df	if	tf	sf	zf	af	pf	cf
	▲	▲	▲		0	–	–	–	▲	▲	u	▲	0

Purpose

Logically ORs two byte, word, or doubleword (80386 only) values.

Syntax/Example

or *al, immB*	or al, 80h
or *ax, immW*	or ax, 01h
or *regB	memB, immB*	or bl, 0AAh
or *regW	memW, immW*	or [word bx], 0800h
or *regW	memW, immB*	or cx, 03h
or *regB	memB, regB*	or [byte bx], dl
or *regW	memW, regW*	or dx, dx
or *regB, regB	memB*	or bl, bh
or *regW, regW	memW*	or dx, [word bx]

80386 only:

or *eax, immDW*	or eax, 080000000h
or *regDW	memDW, immDW*	or edx, 0FFFF0000h
or *regDW	memDW, immB*	or [dword bx], 01h
or *regDW	memDW, regDW*	or edx, ecx
or *regDW, regDW	memDW*	or ecx, [dword bx]

Sample Code

```
mov ax, 01234h  ; ax = 01234h
and ax, 000FFh  ; ax = 00034h
or  ax, 08000h  ; ax = 08043h

or dx, dx       ; Does dx = 0?
jz Target       ; Jump if dx = 0
                ; Continue if dx <> 0
```

Description

Use **or** to perform a logical OR on the bits in any two byte, word, or doubleword (80386 only) values stored in registers or in memory variables. (Both of the two operands can't be memory references.) The corresponding bits in the first operand are set to 1 only if the bits in either or both of the operands equal 1. The first part of the sample uses **or** to set the MDS of a word value in **ax** to 1, after **ah** is zeroed by a previous **and** with a mask of 000FFh.

Another typical use for **or** is to test whether a value equals 0, as the second part of the sample demonstrates. ORing a value with itself sets the zero flag to 1, without changing the original value, only if all bits in the value are 0. Note that this also sets both **cf** and **of** to 0, a fact that might be useful in some circumstances.

See Also

and, xor

Output to Port   **out**

Processor:	8086/88	80286	80386	*Flags:*	of	df	if	tf	sf	zf	af	pf	cf
	▲	▲	▲		—	—	—	—	—	—	—	—	—

Purpose   Outputs values to ports.

Syntax/Example

out *immB, al*	out 14h, al
out *dx, al*	out dx, al
out *immB, ax*	out 01Fh, ax
out *dx, ax*	out dx, ax

80386 only:

out *immB, eax*	out 0Fh, eax
out *dx, eax*	out dx, eax

Sample Code

```
Ctrl8259 EQU 021h        ; 8259 masks port

in  al, Ctrl8259         ; Read 8259 enable masks
and al, EnableIRQ        ; Clear masked bit
out Ctrl8259, al         ; Write new 8259 masks
```

Description   The out instruction writes a value in al, ax, or eax (80386 only) to a hardware port. As the sample shows, out is often used in conjunction with in and logical instructions such as and and or to examine and change bit switches at various port addresses in the computer. (This is the same sample shown for in.) The simplest form of out writes a byte in al to an immediate port address in the range 0–255. To access higher port addresses, specify the address in the dx register.

See Also   in, outs

Output From String to Port   **outs outsb outsd outsw**

Processor:	8086/88	80286	80386	*Flags:*	of	df	if	tf	sf	zf	af	pf	cf
		▲	▲		—	—	—	—	—	—	—	—	—

Purpose   Outputs a sequence of bytes, words, or doublewords from memory to ports.

Syntax/Example

outs *dx, [es:]si | memB*	rep outs dx, [var]
outs *dx, [es:]si | memW*	rep outs dx, [word var]
outsb *no operands*	rep outsb
outsw *no operands*	rep outsw

80386 only:

```
outs dx, regDW| memDW      rep outs dx, [dword var]
outsd no operands          rep outsd
```

Sample Code

```
; Note: don't run this!

DATASEG
string db 'A string is a wonderful thing'
slen = $-string
CODESEG
mov si, offset string    ; Address string with ds:si
mov dx, <port number>    ; Assign port number to dx
mov cx, slen             ; Assign string length to cx
cld                      ; Auto-increment si
rep outsb                ; Send string to output port
```

Description

As with all string instructions, `outs` (and its shorthand forms `outsb`, `outsd` [80386 only], and `outsw`) register assignments are fixed, even if you specify address labels explicitly. The source resister is `ds:si` unless an `es:` override is used as in [`byte es:si`] or [`word es:var`]. The port number must be placed in `dx`. (Don't forget to do this also for the shorthand mnemonics.) If `df = 0`, then `outs` increments `si`; if `df = 1`, `outs` decrements `si` by the number of bytes being sent to the output port with each use of `outs`. Normally, you'll preface `outs` with `rep`, repeating the instruction for the number of times specified in `cx` as illustrated in the sample.

See Also

`cmpsb`, `cmpsd`, `cmpsw`, `ins`, `insb`, `insd`, `insw`, `lods`, `lodsb`, `lodsd`, `lodsw`, `movs`, `movsb`, `movsd`, `movsw`, `scas`, `scasb`, `scasd`, `scasw`, `stos`, `stosb`, `stosd`, `stosw`

pop

Pop from Stack

Processor:	8086/88	80286	80386		Flags:	of	df	if	tf	sf	zf	af	pf	cf
	▲	▲	▲			—	—	—	—	—	—	—	—	—

Purpose

Removes a word or doubleword (80386 only) from the stack.

Syntax/Example

```
pop regW         pop ax
pop memW         pop [word var]
pop es | ds | ss   pop es
```

80386 only:

```
pop regDW        pop ecx
pop memDW        pop [dword var]
pop fs | gs        pop gs
```

Sample Code	push ax	; Save ax on stack
	push bx	; Save bx on stack
	;	
	;	various instructions
	;	
	pop bx	; Restore saved bx value
	pop ax	; Restore saved ax value
	push cs	; Push cs onto the stack
	pop es	; Pop ds, making ds = cs

Description Execute pop to remove one word or doubleword (80386 only) value from the stack location addressed by ss:sp or by ss:esp on the 80386. After copying the stack value into the specified register, sp or esp are incremented by the number of bytes transferred. Having done this, the value above (at a lower address than) the new stack pointer is subject to being overwritten by other code.

The most common use for pop (see first part of sample) is to restore a register value previously inserted into the stack with push. Another use for pop is to load a segment register as in the second part of the sample, which sets es equal to cs. (Popping into the cs register is forbidden.) When popping values into a segment register, interrupts are temporarily disabled for the *next* instruction, thus allowing pop ss to be followed by pop sp without the danger that an interrupt will occur before the full stack pointer is initialized.

Often neglected is the ability to pop values into word and doubleword (80386 only) memory locations, using all memory-addressing modes. Thus, instructions such as pop [aword + bx + si] and pop [aword + si] are perfectly allowable, if somewhat unusual, commands.

See Also popa, popad, popf, popfd, push, pusha, pushad, pushf, pushfd

Pop All General-Purpose Registers   **popa**

Processor:	8086/88	80286	80386	*Flags:*	of	df	if	tf	sf	zf	af	pf	cf
		▲	▲		—	—	—	—	—	—	—	—	—

Purpose Removes registers di, si, bp, sp (discarded), bx, dx, cx, and ax from the stack.

Syntax/Example popa *no operands*   popa

Sample Code
```
PROC Anyproc
pusha             ; Save all general-purpose registers
;
;  Procedure code
;
popa              ; Restore general-purpose registers
ret               ; Return to caller
ENDP
```

Description   Use popa on 80286 and 80386 systems to pop the 16-bit registers di, si, bp, sp, bx, dx, cx, and ax in that order from the stack. Although the saved value for sp is removed from the stack, the value is not inserted into sp. Normally, you'll use popa after previously having executed pusha to push these same register values (in the opposite order). The instruction uses 16 bytes of stack space.

See Also   pop, popad, popf, popfd, push, pusha, pushad, pushf, pushfd

---

popad

Pop All General-Purpose Doubleword Registers

Processor:	8086/88	80286	80386		*Flags:*	of	df	if	tf	sf	zf	af	pf	cf
			▲			—	—	—	—	—	—	—	—	—

Purpose   Removes registers edi, esi, ebp, esp (discarded), ebx, edx, ecx, and eax from the stack.

Syntax/Example   popad *no operands*   popad

Sample Code
```
pushad            ; Save general-purpose 32-bit registers
;
; other code
;
popad             ; Restore saved registers
```

Description   Use popad on 80386 systems to pop the 32-bit registers edi, esi, ebp, esp, ebx, edx, ecx, and eax in that order from the stack. Although the saved value for esp is removed from the stack, the value is not inserted into esp. Normally, you'll use popad after previously having executed pushad to push these same register values (in the opposite order). The instruction uses 32 bytes of stack space.

See Also   pop, popa, popf, popfd, push, pusha, pushad, pushf, pushfd

Pop Flags

popf

Processor:	8086/88	80286	80386	Flags:	of	df	if	tf	sf	zf	af	pf	cf
	▲	▲	▲		▲	▲	▲	▲	▲	▲	▲	▲	▲

Purpose   Removes all flags from the stack.

Syntax/Example   popf *no operands*   popf

Sample Code

```
xor     ax, ax  ; Set ax = 0000
push    ax      ; Push ax onto stack
popf            ; Pop stack into flags, thus
                ;  resetting all flags to 0
```

Description   Execute popf to remove the top word from the stack and insert the bits in that word into the 8086 flags. Normally, you'll do this after previously executing pushf to push the flag values, perhaps to preserve the results of a comparison or other instruction. Another use for popf is to remove the flags from the stack in an interrupt service routine. You can also assign various bit values in a word register, push that register onto the stack, and then execute popf to transfer the bits to the flags, thus setting the flags to your new values.

See Also   pop, popa, popad, popfd, push, pusha, pushad, pushf, pushfd

Pop Extended Flags

popfd

Processor:	8086/88	80286	80386	Flags:	of	df	if	tf	sf	zf	af	pf	cf
			▲		▲	▲	▲	▲	▲	▲	▲	▲	▲

Purpose   Removes extended 80386 flags except vm and rf from the stack.

Syntax/Example   popfd *no operands*   popfd

Sample Code

```
pushfd          ; Save extended flags
;
; other code
;
popfd           ; Restore extended flags
```

Description   Execute popfd to remove the top two words from the stack and insert the bits in those words into the 80386 extended flag register. Normally, you'll do this after previously executing pushfd to push the extended flag values, perhaps to preserve the results of a comparison or other instruction. (See popf for other potential uses.) The 80386 vm (virtual 8086 flag, bit 17) and rf (resume flag, bit 16) are not changed by popfd.

See Also   pop, popa, popad, popf, push, pusha, pushad, pushf, pushfd

push   Push Onto Stack

Processor:	8086/88	80286	80386		*Flags:*	of	df	if	tf	sf	zf	af	pf	cf
	▲	▲	▲			—	—	—	—	—	—	—	—	—

Purpose   Transfers values to the stack.

Syntax/Example
```
push regW          push ax
push memW          push [word bx]
push cs | es | ds | ss   push cs
```

80286,80386 only:
```
push immB          push 0Fh
push immW          push 256
```

80386 only:
```
push regDW         push ecx
push memDW         push [dword bx]
push immDW         push 99999
push fs | gs       push gs
```

Sample Code
```
push ax          ; Save ax on stack
push bx          ; Save bx on stack
push cx          ; Save cx on stack
;
; other code that changes ax, bx, cx
;
pop cx           ; Restore original cx
pop bx           ; Restore original bx
pop ax           ; Restore original ax

P386
push 99999       ; Turbo Assembler incorrectly disallows this
;
db 066h, 068h    ; But you can code the instruction
dd 99999         ;  with these two lines
```

Description   Use push to transfer a word or doubleword (80386 only) to the stack. Executing push first decrements the stack pointer by 2 (or by 4 in the case of an 80386 doubleword push). Then the value of the specified operand is copied into the location addressed by ss:sp. Note that this causes the stack to grow toward lower-memory addresses. The most common use of push is to save register values onto the stack, as the first part of the sample demonstrates. Later, pop can be used to remove the saved values, restoring the original registers.

It is legal to push but not to pop the value of the code-segment register cs. Also, you can push values from memory, using all the usual addressing modes. Thus, instructions such as push [bx] and push [value + si] are legal but often neglected forms of the instruction. In addition, the 80286 and 80386 processors allow pushing immediate values, for example push 0 or push -1.

A bug in Turbo Assembler 1.0 prevents pushing 32-bit immediate values with instructions such as push 99999, which produces a "constant too large" error. To circumvent this presumably temporary problem, use the db and dd commands in the second part of the sample to insert the machine code for this instruction directly into your program.

See Also   pop, popa, popad, popf, popfd, pusha, pushad, pushf, pushfd

---

Push All General-Purpose Registers   **pusha**

Processor:	8086/88	80286	80386		*Flags:*	of	df	if	tf	sf	zf	af	pf	cf
		▲	▲			—	—	—	—	—	—	—	—	—

Purpose   Transfers registers ax, cx, dx, bx, sp, bp, si, and di to the stack.

Syntax/Example   pusha *no operands*   pusha

Sample Code
```
PROC Anyproc
pusha   ; Save general-purpose registers
;
; other code
;
popa    ; Restore registers
ret     ; Return to caller
ENDP
```

Description   Use pusha to push registers ax, cx, dx, bx, sp, bp, si, and di onto the stack in that order. The value pushed for sp is the value of sp *prior* to executing pusha. (This value is later discarded by popa, thus having no harmful effect on sp.) Normally, you'll follow pusha with popa to restore the saved registers, most often in a subroutine or interrupt service routine.

See Also   pop, popa, popad, popf, popfd, push, pushad, pushf, pushfd

pushad

Push All General-Purpose Doubleword Registers

Processor:	8086/88	80286	80386		Flags:	of	df	if	tf	sf	zf	af	pf	cf
			▲			—	—	—	—	—	—	—	—	—

Purpose Transfers registers `eax`, `ecx`, `edx`, `ebx`, `esp`, `ebp`, `esi`, and `edi` to the stack.

Syntax/Example pushad *no operands*   pushad

Sample Code
```
PROC Anyproc
pushad  ; Save 32-bit general-purpose registers
;
; other code
;
popad   ; Restore 32-bit registers
ret     ; Return to caller
ENDP
```

Description Use `pushad` to push the 80386 32-bit registers `eax`, `ecx`, `edx`, `ebx`, `esp`, `ebp`, `esi`, and `edi` onto the stack in that order. The value pushed for `esp` is the value of `esp` *prior* to executing `pushad`. (This value is later discarded by `popad`, thus having no harmful effect on `esp`.) Normally, you'll follow `pushad` with `popad` to restore the saved registers, most often in a subroutine or interrupt service routine.

See Also pop, popa, popad, popf, popfd, push, pusha, pushf, pushfd

pushf

Push Flags

Processor:	8086/88	80286	80386		Flags:	of	df	if	tf	sf	zf	af	pf	cf
	▲	▲	▲			—	—	—	—	—	—	—	—	—

Purpose Transfers the flags to the stack.

Syntax/Example pushf *no operands*   pushf

Sample Code
```
or ax, ax      ; Test whether ax = 0
pushf          ; Save result of comparison
;
; other code that may modify flags
;
popf           ; Restore result of "or"
jz Exit        ; Jump if ax was 0
```

Description Execute `pushf` to transfer the 8086 16-bit flag register to the stack. All flag bits as well as unused bits are pushed. You can pop this word into a general-purpose register or use popf to restore the saved flag bits, perhaps to recover the results of an earlier comparison.

See Also   pop, popa, popad, popf, popfd, push, pusha, pushad, pushfd

Push Extended Flags   **pushfd**

Processor:	8086/88	80286	80386	*Flags:*	of	df	if	tf	sf	zf	af	pf	cf
			▲		—	—	—	—	—	—	—	—	—

Purpose   Transfers the 80386 extended flags to the stack.

Syntax/Example   pushfd *no operands*   pushfd

Sample Code
```
P386
pushfd          ; Push extended flags
pop eax         ; Copy flags into eax
```

Description   Execute pushfd to transfer the 80386 32-bit extended flag register to the stack. All flag bits as well as unused bits are pushed. You can pop this doubleword into a general-purpose extended register or use popfd to restore the saved flag bits, perhaps to recover the results of an earlier comparison.

See Also   pop, popa, popad, popf, popfd, push, pusha, pushad, pushf

Rotate Left Through Carry   **rcl**

Processor:	8086/88	80286	80386	*Flags:*	of	df	if	tf	sf	zf	af	pf	cf
	▲	▲	▲		▲u	—	—	—	—	—	—	—	▲

Purpose   Rotates bits leftward through the carry flag.

Syntax/Example
rcl *regB* | *memB, 1*	rcl al, 1
rcl *regB* | *memB, cl*	rcl [abyte], cl
rcl *regW* | *memW, 1*	rcl [aword], 1
rcl *regW* | *memW, cl*	rcl bx, cl

80286, 80386 only:
rcl *regB* | *memB, immB*	rcl dl, 4
rcl *regW* | *memW, immB*	rcl [aword], 4

80386 only:

rcl *regDW* | *memDW, 1*	rcl eax, 1
rcl *regDW* | *memDW, cl*	rcl [dword bx], cl
rcl *regDW* | *memDW, immB*	rcl ecx, 4

Sample Code
```
mov cl, 4      ; Assign rotation count to cl
rcl ax, cl     ; Rotate ax left by count in cl
```

Description Use rcl to rotate the bits in word, byte, and doubleword (80386 only) registers and memory values to the left (toward the MSDs) including the carry flag cf as part of the orginal value. In other words, the old MSD shifts into cf, which shifts into the new LSD, while all other bits shift one position to the left. Repeating this action would eventually restore the original value and cf.

For all processors, the second operand specifies the number of bit rotations to perform. On the 8086 and 8088 processors, if the second operand is literal, it must equal 1. To rotate more than one bit, you must assign the rotation count to cl and specify this register as the second operand. The 80286 and 80386 processors allow you to use any immediate value as the second operand, for example as in rcl cx, 4 to rotate cx 4 bits left. The 80386 further extends these forms by allowing rotations involving 32-bit extended registers.

When the second operand is an immediate 1, after rcl the of flag equals the exclusive OR of cf and the MSD of the newly rotated value. Thus, if of = 1 after rcl reg|mem, 1, then the upper 2 bits of the original value were either 11 or 00. One way to use this knowledge is to stop a rotation as soon as a 1 bit appears in the rotated value's MSD. For example, if the original value in ax is 01000000b, executing rcl ax, 1 results in cf = 0 and ax = 10000000b, which sets of to 1, a condition that you can test with jo or jno. In all other cases, when the second operand to rcl is not an immediate 1, the of flag is not defined. Also, if the rotation count is 0, of and cf are left unchanged—an oddity of little practical value.

See Also rcr, rol, ror, sal, sar, shl, shr

---

rcr   **Rotate Right Through Carry**

Processor:	8086/88	80286	80386		Flags:	of	df	if	tf	sf	zf	af	pf	cf
	▲	▲	▲			▲u	–	–	–	–	–	–	–	▲

Purpose Rotates bits rightward through the carry flag.

Syntax/Example

rcr *regB* | *memB, 1*	rcr al, 1
rcr *regB* | *memB, cl*	rcr [abyte], cl
rcr *regW* | *memW, 1*	rcr [aword], 1
rcr *regW* | *memW, cl*	rcr bx, cl

80286, 80386 only:

```
rcr regB | memB, immB          rcr dl, 4
rcr regW | memW, immB          rcr [aword], 4
```

80386 only:

```
rcr regDW | memDW, 1           rcr eax, 1
rcr regDW | memDW, cl          rcr [dword bx], cl
rcr regDW | memDW, immB        rcr ecx, 4
```

Sample Code
```
mov cl, 2       ; Assign rotation count to cl
rcr ax, cl      ; Rotate ax right by count in cl
```

Description Use rcr to rotate the bits in word, byte, and doubleword (80386 only) registers and memory values to the right (toward the LSDs) including the carry flag cf as part of the original value. In other words, the old LSD shifts into cf, which shifts into the new MSD, while all other bits shift one position to the left. Repeating this action would eventually restore the original value and cf.

For all processors, the second operand specifies the number of bit rotations to perform. On the 8086 and 8088 processors, if the second operand is literal, it must equal 1. To rotate more than 1 bit, you must assign the rotation count to cl and specify this register as the second operand. The 80286 and 80386 processors allow you to use any immediate value as the second operand, for example as in rcr dx, 3 to rotate dx 3 bits right. The 80386 further extends these forms by allowing rotations involving 32-bit extended registers.

When the second operand is an immediate 1, after rcr the of flag equals the exclusive OR of the two MSDs of the newly rotated value. Thus, if of = 1 after rcr reg|mem, 1, then cf and the original MSD were different; otherwise, they were both equal to 1 or 0. Stated another way, of = 1 indicates a change in sign of the original value as a result of the rotation. In all other cases, when the second operand to rcr is not an immediate 1, the of flag is not defined. Also, if the rotation count is 0, of and cf are left unchanged—an oddity of little practical value.

See Also rcl, rol, ror, sal, sar, shl, shr

Repeat, Repeat While Equal   **rep repe repz**

Processor:	8086/88	80286	80386		Flags:	of	df	if	tf	sf	zf	af	pf	cf
	▲	▲	▲			—	—	—	—	—	—	—	—	—

Purpose Conditionally repeats a string instruction.

Syntax/Example
```
rep movs | movsb | movsw        rep movs [byte di], [byte es:si]
rep stos | stosb | stosw        rep stosw
repe cmps | cmpsb | cmpsw       repe cmps [word str1], [word str2]
```

```
repz cmps | cmpsb | cmpsw        repz cmpsb
repe scas | scasb | scasw        repe scasw
repz scas | scasb | scasw        repz scas [byte es:var]
```

80286, 80386 only:
```
rep ins | insb | insw            rep insb
rep outs | outsb | outsw         rep outs dx, [word es:si]
```

80386 only:
```
rep movs | movsd                 rep movs [dword edi], [dword esi]
rep stos | stosd                 rep stosd
rep ins | insd                   rep ins [dword var], dx
rep outs | outsd                 rep outs dx, [dword si]
repe cmps | cmpsd                repe cmpsd
repz cmps | cmpsd                repz cmps [dword str1], [dword str2]
repe scas | scasd                repe scasd
repz scas | scasd                repz scas [dword es:esi]
```

Sample Code

```
UDATASEG
string  db 80 dup (?)     ; Uninitialized variable
strlen  = $ - string      ; Length of string
CODESEG
mov ax, @data             ; Initialize es
mov es, ax                ;   segment register
ASSUME es:DGROUP          ; Tell tasm where es points
mov di, offset string     ; Address string with es:di
mov cx, strlen            ; Assign string length to cx
cld                       ; Auto-increment di
mov al, ' '               ; Assign ASCII value to al
rep stosb                 ; Fill string with blanks
```

Description

The three mnemonics rep, repe, and repz represent the same instruction prefix, which may be attached to any string instruction as shown in the examples and the sample code. Even though the mnemonics are identical, the effects differ depending on the string instruction that is prefaced. Use rep before movs, stos, ins, and outs—plus the shorthand mnemonics for these instructions. Use repe and repz before cmps and scas plus shorthand equivalents.

   The rep prefix repeats the string instruction that follows the number of times specified in cx. The repe and repz also repeat a string instruction by the value in cx but end the repetition if, after any iteration, zf = 0. Thus, you can use these two prefixes to repeat a string compare or scan for a certain number of times or until the string instruction locates a specific value. The lods instruction (and its shorthand mnemonics) may be repeated, although there is never any good reason to do so. (The result of a repeated lods instruction is to load the accumulator with one value after all repetitions are finished—there is no way to use the intermediate loaded values.)

See the various string instructions elsewhere in this chapter for more details and for the operands that you may use with instructions such as `cmps`, which, for brevity, are not repeated here. Also, although the repeat prefixes are listed here as not changing any flags, be aware that the string instructions following the prefixes can change flag settings.

See Also `cmps, ins, movs, outs, repne, repnz, scas, stos`

Repeat While Not Equal   # repne repnz

Processor:	8086/88	80286	80386		*Flags:*	of	df	if	tf	sf	zf	af	pf	cf
	▲	▲	▲			–	–	–	–	–	–	–	–	–

Purpose Conditionally repeats a string compare or scan instruction.

Syntax/Example

```
repne cmps | cmpsb | cmpsw      repne cmps [word str1], [word str2]
repnz cmps | cmpsb | cmpsw      repnz cmpsb
repne scas | scasb | scasw      repne scasw
repnz scas | scasb | scasw      repnz scas [byte es:var]
```

80386 only:

```
repne cmps | cmpsd             repne cmpsd
repnz cmps | cmpsd             repnz cmps [dword str1], [dword str2]
repne scas | scasd             repne scasd
repnz scas | scasd             repnz scas [dword es:esi]
```

Sample Code

```
DATASEG
string  db 'Thisstringhasn''tanyblanks'
strlen  = $ - string
CODESEG
mov ax, @data             ; Initialize es
mov es, ax                ;   segment register
ASSUME es:DGROUP          ; Tell tasm where es points
mov di, offset string + strlen - 1  ; Address end of string
mov cx, strlen            ; Assign string length to cx
std                       ; Auto-decrement di
mov al, ' '               ; Value to search for
repne scasb               ; Scan for blanks
jcxz Exit                 ; Exit if no blanks found
                          ; es:di addresses last nonblank
```

Description The `repne` and `repnz` prefixes, both of which represent the same machine code, repeat a `cmps` or `scas` string instruction (plus shorthand mnemonics) for the number of times specified in `cx` but end the repetitions early if an iteration sets `zf = 1`. For more details, see the notes for `repe` and `repz`, which operate similarly but recognize the opposite flag value for `zf`. The example demonstrates how to use `repne` to scan a string from back to front, leaving di addressing the last nonblank in the string or, if no blanks were found, jumping to label Exit (not shown).

See Also   cmps, ins, movs, outs, rep, repe, repz, scas, stos

repz   **Repeat While Zero**

	Processor:	8086/88	80286	80386	*Flags:*	of	df	if	tf	sf	zf	af	pf	cf
		▲	▲	▲		—	—	—	—	—	—	—	—	—

See   rep repe.

ret retf retn   **Return, Return Far or Near**

	Processor:	8086/88	80286	80386	*Flags:*	of	df	if	tf	sf	zf	af	pf	cf
		▲	▲	▲		—	—	—	—	—	—	—	—	—

Purpose   Returns from a subroutine procedure.

Syntax/Example

ret *no operands*	ret
retn *no operands*	retn
retf *no operands*	retf
ret immW	ret 8
retn immW	retn 16
retf immw	retf 4

Sample Code

```
PROC Anyproc
;
; procedure code
;
ret      ; Return to caller
ENDP Anyproc
```

Description   The three ret mnemonics are typically used as the final instruction of a procedure activated by call. Both ret and retn, which are synonyms for the same instruction, pop the 16-bit return address from the stack into register ip, continuing the program with the instruction that follows the call, which previously pushed this address onto the stack before activating the procedure. The retf instruction pops two words from the stack, assigning the first word to cs and the second to ip. Thus, the program continues in a different code segment. Use retf *only* if you made a *far* call to the subroutine, usually by using the instruction call FAR AnyProc.

When using simplified memory models (as in most of this book's example programs), it's probably best to use only ret. This lets Turbo

Assembler decide whether to assemble the code for `retf` or `retn` as needed and also to use the appropriate `call` instruction. You can force near and far calls and returns, but be aware that using `retf` when you should have used `retn` will undoubtedly cause a system crash sooner or later—probably sooner.

You may follow any of the three mnemonics with an unsigned value, which will be added to the stack pointer *after* the return address is popped. High-level languages such as Pascal use this form of `ret` to end procedures and functions to which parameters have been passed on the stack. Adjusting the stack pointer with `ret` lets the procedure itself remove the stacked parameters instead of leaving it to the calling code. Because the optional value added to `ret` is immediate (fixed), the method is not as helpful in languages such as C, which allow a variable number of parameters to be passed to functions.

See Also   `call`

Rotate Left   **rol**

Processor:	8086/88	80286	80386		Flags:	of	df	if	tf	sf	zf	af	pf	cf
	▲	▲	▲			▲u	–	–	–	–	–	–	–	▲

Purpose   Rotates bits leftward.

Syntax/Example
```
rol regB | memB, 1        rol al, 1
rol regB | memB, cl       rol [abyte], cl
rol regW | memW, 1        rol [aword], 1
rol regW | memW, cl       rol bx, cl
```

80286, 80386 only:
```
rol regB | memB, immB     rol dl, 4
rol regW | memW, immB     rol [aword], 4
```

80386 only:
```
rol regDW | memDW, 1      rol eax, 1
rol regDW | memDW, cl     rol [dword bx], cl
rol regDW | memDW, immB   rol ecx, 4
```

Sample Code
```
mov cl, 5              ; Load count into cl
rol [aword], cl        ; Rotate word left 5 times
```

Description   Use `rol` to rotate the bits in word, byte, and doubleword (80386 only) registers and memory values to the left (toward the MSDs). The old MSD shifts into the new LSD position while all other bits shift one position to the left. In addition, the old MSD is copied into `cf`. Repeating this action would eventually restore the original value but not necessarily restore `cf`.

(This is nearly identical to the way rcl operates, except that cf is not treated as an extra bit in the rotated value.)

For all processors, the second operand specifies the number of bit rotations to perform. On the 8086 and 8088 processors, if the second operand is literal, it must equal 1. To rotate more than 1 bit, you must assign the rotation count to cl and specify this register as the second operand. The 80286 and 80386 processors allow you to use any immediate value as the second operand, for example as in rol dx, 2 to rotate dx 2 bits left. The 80386 further extends these forms by allowing rotations involving 32-bit extended registers.

When the second operand is an immediate 1, after rol the of flag equals the exclusive OR of cf and the MSD of the newly rotated value. (See rcl for an expanded discussion of these flag values.) In all other cases, when the second operand to rcl is not an immediate 1, the of flag is not defined. Also, if the rotation count is 0, of and cf are left unchanged—an oddity of little practical value. Of more use might be the associated fact that, after every rol, cf equals the LSD of the newly rotated value.

See Also   rcl, rcr, ror, sal, sar, shl, shr

ror   Rotate Right

Processor:	8086/88	80286	80386		Flags:	of	df	if	tf	sf	zf	af	pf	cf
	▲	▲	▲			▲u	–	–	–	–	–	–	–	▲

Purpose   Rotates bits rightward.

Syntax/Example
```
ror regB | memB, 1          ror al, 1
ror regB | memB, cl         ror [abyte], cl
ror regW | memW, 1          ror [aword], 1
ror regW | memW, cl         ror bx, cl
```

80286, 80386 only:
```
ror regB | memB, immB       ror dl, 4
ror regW | memW, immB       ror [aword], 4
```

80386 only:
```
ror regDW | memDW, 1        ror eax, 1
ror regDW | memDW, cl       ror [dword bx], cl
ror regDW | memDW, immB     ror ecx, 4
```

Sample Code
```
mov cl, 8        ; Load count into cl
ror ax, cl       ; Rotate ax left 8 times
                 ; (Note: this is the same
                 ;  as xchg ah, al!)
```

Description Use `ror` to rotate the bits in word, byte, and doubleword (80386 only) registers and memory values to the right (toward the LSDs). The old LSD shifts into the new MSD position while all other bits shift one position to the right. In addition, the old LSD is copied into `cf`. Repeating this action would eventually restore the original value, but not necessarily restore `cf`. (This is nearly identical to the way `rcr` operates, except that `cf` is not treated as an extra bit in the rotated value.)

For all processors, the second operand specifies the number of bit rotations to perform. On the 8086 and 8088 processors, if the second operand is literal, it must equal 1. To rotate more than 1 bit, you must assign the rotation count to `cl` and specify this register as the second operand. The 80286 and 80386 processors allow you to use any immediate value as the second operand, for example as in `ror ah, 4` to rotate ah 4 bits right. The 80386 further extends these forms by allowing rotations involving 32-bit extended registers.

When the second operand is an immediate 1, after `ror` the `of` flag equals the exclusive OR of the two MSDs of the newly rotated value. Thus, if `of` = 1 after `ror reg|mem, 1`, then the original LSD and MSD bits were different; otherwise, these two end bits in the value were both equal to 1 or 0. In all other cases, when the second operand to `ror` is not an immediate 1, the `of` flag is not defined. Also, if the rotation count is 0, `of` and `cf` are left unchanged—an oddity of little practical value. Of more use might be the associated fact that, after every `ror`, `cf` equals the MSD of the newly rotated value.

See Also `rcl, rcr, rol, sal, sar, shl, shr`

Store ah Register to Flags   **sahf**

Processor:	8086/88	80286	80386		Flags:	of	df	if	tf	sf	zf	af	pf	cf
	▲	▲	▲			–	–	–	–	▲	▲	▲	▲	▲

Purpose Copies bits 7, 6, 4, 2, and 0 from `ah` to the marked flags.

Syntax/Example sahf *no operands*   sahf

Sample Code
```
xor ah, ah      ; Zero ah
sahf            ; Zero sf, zf, af, pf, cf
```

Description Execute `sahf` to store bits from `ah` into five flags. With bit numbers in parentheses, the affected flags are `sf` (7), `zf` (6), `af` (4), `pf` (2), and `cf` (0). Other flags are not affected. The instruction is sometimes used in conjunction with a math coprocessor.

See Also `lahf`

sal

Shift Arithmetic Left

Processor:	8086/88	80286	80386		*Flags:*	of	df	if	tf	sf	zf	af	pf	cf
	▲	▲	▲			▲u	–	–	–	▲	▲	u	▲	▲

Purpose   Shifts bits leftward.

Syntax/Example

sal *regB* | *memB*, 1	sal [abyte], 1
sal *regB* | *memB*, cl	sal ax, cl
sal *regW* | *memW*, 1	sal dx, 1
sal *regW* | *memW*, cl	sal [aword + bx], cl

80286, 80386 only:

sal *regB* | *memB*, immB	sal cx, 8
sal *regW* | *memW*, immB	sal [word bp + 4], 4

80386 only:

sal *regDW* | *memDW*, 1	sal edx, 1
sal *regDW* | *memDW*, cl	sal [dword es:di], cl
sal *regDW* | *memDW*, immB	sal [dword bx], 4

Sample Code

```
DATASEG
value dd 12345678      ; A doubleword value
CODESEG                ;  to be multiplied by 2
shl [word value], 1    ; Shift-low order word
rcl [word value + 2], 1 ; Shift high-order word
jc  Exit               ; Jump if overflow detected
```

Description   The sal and shl mnemonics are synonyms for the same instruction and generate the identical machine code. Normally, you'll use sal to multiply unsigned values by powers of 2 and shl to simply shift bits left into position. Using sal lends additional clarity to a program by indicating a mathematical shift, but you can use the two mnemonics interchangeably.

Executing sal or shl shifts the old MSD of the value into the carry flag. A zero bit shifts into the new LSD. Repeating this action eventually sets all bits in the specified register or memory location to 0.

When the second operand is an immediate 1, after shifting, of = 1 only if the new cf does not equal the new MSD. If of = 0, then the new cf and MSD bits are different. You might use this knowledge to detect a zero bit shifting into the MSD position of an initially nonzero value. When the second operand is not an immediate 1, of is not defined.

The sample shows how to use word shifts and rotations (see rcl) to multiply a doubleword value by 2. The initial shl shifts the low-order word, copying the MSD into cf. Then, rcl rotates the high-order word, shifting in cf to the new LSD (of the high-order word). Subsequent rcl instructions could be added to shift even larger multibyte values. If after the final rcl the carry flag equals 1, then an overflow has occurred.

See Also   rcl, rcr, rol, ror, sar, shl, shr

Shift Arithmetic Right

sar

Processor:	8086/88	80286	80386		Flags:	of	df	if	tf	sf	zf	af	pf	cf
	▲	▲	▲			▲u	–	–	–	▲	▲	u	▲	▲

Purpose Shifts bits rightward.

Syntax/Example

```
sar regB | memB, 1         sar bl, 1
sar regB | memB, cl        sar ch, cl
sar regW | memW, 1         sar [aword], 1
sar regW | memW, cl        sar [word bx], cl
```

80286, 80386 only:

```
sar regB | memB, immB      sar [byte bp + 2], 4
sar regW | memW, immB      sar dx, 4
```

80386 only:

```
sar regDW | memDW, 1       sar [dword bp - 8], 1
sar regDW | memDW, cl      sar eax, cl
sar regDW | memDW, immB    sar edx, 16
```

Sample Code

```
DATASEG
value dw 08000h         ; -32,768
CODESEG
mov cl, 4               ; Assign shift count to cl
sar [value], cl         ; Value = -2048 (-32,768/16)
```

Description Unlike sal and shl, which are synonyms, sar is *not* a synonym for shr. This often confuses people, but there's a good reason for the apparent discrepancy. The sar instruction shifts a register or memory value to the right, copying the old LSD bit into cf, but, unlike shr, sar *does not alter the old MSD bit.* By this action, the original sign of the shifted value remains unchanged; therefore, you can use sar to divide signed integers by powers of 2, while shr can divide only unsigned integers. The sample demonstrates how this works, using sar to divide −32,768 by 16, or 2^4.

When the second operand to sar is an immediate 1, of is set to 0. When the second operand is not an immediate 1, the effect on of is not defined.

When using sar to divide signed negative values in two's complement form by powers of 2, be aware that −1 (0FFFFh, for example) divided by 2 equals −1, not 0. Some references refer to this effect as "truncation toward negative infinity," suggesting that sar does not generate the same answers in all cases as idiv by powers of 2, which gives 0 for −1/2 (that is, "truncation toward zero").

See Also rcl, rcr, rol, ror, sal, shl, shr

sbb

Subtract Integers with Borrow

Processor:	8086/88	80286	80386		*Flags:*	of	df	if	tf	sf	zf	af	pf	cf
	▲	▲	▲			▲	–	–	–	▲	▲	▲	▲	▲

Purpose Subtracts integers, taking a possible borrow from a previous **sub** or **sbb** into account.

Syntax/Example

sbb *al, immB*	sbb al, 8
sbb *ax, immW*	sbb ax, 256
sbb *regB* | *memB, immB*	sbb [byte bx], 4
sbb *regW* | *memW, immW*	sbb [word si], 600
sbb *regW* | *memW, immB*	sbb dx, 3
sbb *regB* | *memB, regB*	sbb ah, al
sbb *regW* | *memW, regW*	sbb dx, ax
sbb *regB, regB* | *memB*	sbb cl, [byte bp + 4]
sbb *regW, regW* | *memW*	sbb ax, bx

80386 only:

sbb *eax, immDW*	sbb eax, 35
sbb *regDW* | *memDW, immB*	sbb ecx, 4
sbb *regDW* | *memDW, immDW*	sbb [dword bx], 18
sbb *regDW* | *memDW, regDW*	sbb [dword bx + si], eax
sbb *regDW, regDW* | *memDW*	sbb edx, [dword bp + 6]

Sample Code

```
DATASEG
v1 dd 87654321      ; A doubleword value
v2 dd 12345678      ; Value to subtract from v1
CODESEG
mov ax, [word v2]       ; Get low word of v2
mov dx, [word v2 + 2]   ; Get high word of v2
sub [word v1], ax       ; Subtract low words
sbb [word v1 + 2], dx   ; Subtract high words with borrow
```

Description After a **sub** or **sbb** on multibyte, word, or doubleword (80386 only) values, use **sbb** to subtract the higher-order portions of the values, taking a possible borrow into account. When you are not subtracting multipart values this way, always use **sub** instead, which does not take a borrow into account.

Usually, **sbb** is used as in the sample to subtract two large integers, in this case two doubleword values labeled **v1** and **v2**. First, the program loads **ax** and **dx** with the value of **v2**. Then **sub** subtracts the low-order words and **sbb** finishes the subtraction, subtracting the high-order words and taking a possible borrow from **sub** into account. (Note: Doubleword values can be subtracted directly on 80386 systems.)

See Also sub

Scan String

scas scasb scasd scasw

Processor:	8086/88	80286	80386		Flags:	of	df	if	tf	sf	zf	af	pf	cf
	▲	▲	▲			▲	–	–	–	▲	▲	▲	▲	▲

Purpose   Scans a string to search for specific values.

Syntax/Example

```
scas memB            scas [byte di]
scas memW            scas [word string]
scasb no operands    scasb
scasw no operands    scasw
```

80386 only:
```
scas memDW           scas [dword string]
scasd no operands    scasd
```

Sample Code
```
DATASEG
string db '2Bh or not 2Bh'   ; A string
strlen = $ - string          ; String Length
CODESEG
mov ax,@data         ; Initialize es
mov es,ax            ;  to address data segment
ASSUME  es:DGROUP    ; Tell tasm where es points
mov di, offset string ; Address string with es:di
mov cx, strlen       ; Assign length to cx
mov al, ' '          ; Assign search value to al
repne   scasb        ; Scan for first blank
;----- di now addresses the "o" in "or"
```

Description   As with all string instructions, register assignments are fixed for scas and the shorthand equivalent forms scasb, scasd (80386 only), and scasw. The instruction subtracts a byte, word, or doubleword value addressed by es:di and is usually used with repeat prefixes repe and repne to scan variables for specific values. Like cmp, the result of the subtraction is discarded—only the flags are retained. Byte values are subtracted from al; word values, from ax. On 80386 systems, doubleword values addressed by either es:di or es:edi are subtracted from eax. A segment override is not allowed; therefore, the string values must be stored in the segment addressed by es. After scas, if df = 0, then di (or edi) is incremented by the size of the specified operand—by 1 for bytes, 2 for words, and 4 for doublewords. If df = 1, then di (or edi) is decremented by the operand size.

   The sample uses scasb to scan a character string, looking for the first blank character. After this code executes, if cx equals 0, then no blanks were found. To search for the first character *not* matching the value in al, you would use the repe repeat prefix instead of repne.

See Also   cmpsb, cmpsd, cmpsw, ins, insb, insd, insw, lods, lodsb, lodsd, lodsw, movs, movsb, movsd, movsw, outs, outsb, outsd, outsw, stos, stosb, stosd, stosw

set-condition

Set Byte Conditionally

Processor: 8086/88 80286 80386   Flags: of df if tf sf zf af pf cf
                                ▲   —   —   —   —   —   —   —   —   —

Purpose
Stores a byte value to a register or to memory if the specified condition is true (byte stored = 1) or false (byte stored = 0).

Syntax/Example
set*condition regB* | *memB*   setae al

Sample Code
```
DATASEG
bits db 01101001b        ; Packed bits in a byte
bytes db 8 dup (?)       ; Eight bytes
CODESEG
P386
 mov bx, offset bytes    ; Address bytes with ds:bx
 mov ah, [bits]          ; Load packed bits into ah
 mov cx, 8               ; Assign loop count to cx
@@10:
 shl ah, 1               ; Shift 1 bit into cf
 setc [byte bx]          ; Set or reset unpacked byte
 inc bx                  ; Address next byte
 loop @@10               ; cx <- cx - 1; jump if cx <> 0
```

Description
On 80386 systems, follow a cmp instruction with any of the set-*condition* instructions listed in Table 14-5. You can also use these instructions after test or any other code that affects various flags. If the condition specified in the center column of the table is met according to the flag settings listed to the right, then the destination byte register or memory value is set to 1, indicating "true"; otherwise, the destination is set to 0. These conditions mirror those supported by the conditional jump instructions (see j-*condition* in this chapter) except for jcxz and jecxz, which have no equivalent set-*condition* instructions.

The sample demonstrates how to use setc to unpack the bits in a byte. On each pass through the loop, if the shr instruction shifts a 1 into cf, then setc sets the byte at [bx] to 1; otherwise, setc resets the byte to 0. After this loop finishes, the uninitialized bytes variable holds the eight values: 00 01 01 00 01 00 00 01.

See Also
j-*condition*

Table 14-5 *Conditional 80386 set-condition Reference*

Instruction	Set byte to 1 if . . . else set byte to 0	Flags
seta	above	(cf = 0) & (zf = 0)
setae	above or equal	(cf = 0)
setb	below	(cf = 1)
setbe	below or equal	(cf = 1)	(zf = 1)
setc	carry	(cf = 1)
sete	equal	(zf = 1)
setg	greater	(sf = of) & (zf = 0)
setge	greater or equal	(sf = of)
setl	less	(sf <> of)
setle	less or equal	(sf <> of)	(zf = 1)
seto	overflow	(of = 1)
setp	parity	(pf = 1)
setpe	parity even	(pf = 1)
setpo	parity odd	(pf = 0)
sets	sign	(sf = 1)
setz	zero	(zf = 1)
setna	not above	(cf = 1)	(zf = 1)
setnae	not above or equal	(cf = 1)
setnb	not below	(cf = 0)
setnbe	not below or equal	(cf = 0) & (zf = 0)
setnc	not carry	(cf = 0)
setne	not equal	(zf = 0)
setng	not greater	(sf <> of)	(zf = 1)
setnge	not greater or equal	(sf <> of)
setnl	not less	(sf = of)
setnle	not less or equal	(sf = of) & (zf = 0)
setno	not overflow	(of = 0)
setnp	not parity	(pf = 0)
setns	not sign	(sf = 0)
setnz	not zero	(zf = 0)

Shift Left **shl**

Processor:	8086/88	80286	80386		*Flags:*	of	df	if	tf	sf	zf	af	pf	cf
	▲	▲	▲			▲u	–	–	–	▲	▲	u	▲	▲

Purpose   Shifts bits leftward.

Syntax/Example

shl *regB | memB, 1*   shl [abyte], 1
shl *regB | memB, cl*   shl ax, cl
shl *regW | memW, 1*   shl dx, 1
shl *regW | memW, cl*   shl [aword + bx], cl

shl

80286, 80386 only:

```
shl regB | memB, immB        shl cx, 8
shl regW | memW, immB        shl [word bp + 4], 4
```

80386 only:

```
shl regDW | memDW, 1         shl edx, 1
shl regDW | memDW, cl        shl [dword es:di], cl
shl regDW | memDW, immB      shl [dword bx], 4
```

Sample Code
```
mov cl, 4        ; Assign shift count to cl
shl ax, cl       ; Multiply ax by 16 (2^4)
```

Description The shl and sal instructions generate the identical machine code. See the notes on sal for a description of how shl operates and the flags that are affected.

See Also rcl, rcr, rol, ror, sal, sar, shr

shld

Double-Precision Shift Left

Processor:	8086/88	80286	80386		Flags:	of	df	if	tf	sf	zf	af	pf	cf
			▲			u	–	–	–	▲	▲	u	▲	▲

Purpose Shifts bits of multiple values leftward.

Syntax/Example
```
shld regW | memW, regW, immB        shld ax, bx, 1
shld regDW | memDW, regDW, immB     shld [bx], eax, 2
shld regW | memW, regW, cl          shld bx, cx, cl
shld regDW | memDW, regDW, cl       shld [edi], edx, cl
```

Sample Code
```
DATASEG
v1 dd 00012345h       ; First 4 of 8 words
v2 dd 6789ABCDh       ; Second 4 of 8 words
CODESEG
P386
mov  cl, 8            ; Assign shift count to cl
mov  eax, [v2]        ; Load second 4 words into eax
shld [v1], eax, cl    ; Shift eax into [v1] cl times
shl  [v2], cl         ; Finish 64-bit shift by cl

;v1 = 01234567        ; Values after above code
;v2 = 89ABCD00        ;  is finished
```

Description On 80386 systems, use shld to shift double-precision values to the left. The first operand specifies the destination and may be a word or double-word register or memory reference. The second operand specifies the source bits that are shifted into the first operand. This value must be a word or doubleword register. The third operand specifies the number of shifts to perform and may be an immediate value from 0 to 31 or a value in register cl. Values greater than 31 are treated modulo 32.

The sample shows a typical use for shld. Two doubleword values v1 and v2 form a 64-bit variable in memory. Only four instructions are required to shift this variable left by any number of bits (up to 31)—8 in this sample. First, the shift count is loaded into cl. Then the second part of the value is loaded into eax. The shld instruction shifts the bits from eax into the doubleword value [v1], which also shifts to the left an equal number of times. The shl instruction finishes the shift by shifting [v2] by the same count in cl. The effect is to multiply in a very short time the full 64-bit double-precision value by 2^8 (256 decimal).

See Also shrd

Shift Right **shr**

Processor:	8086/88	80286	80386		*Flags:*	of	df	if	tf	sf	zf	af	pf	cf
	▲	▲	▲			▲u	–	–	–	▲	▲	u	▲	▲

Purpose Shifts bits rightward.

Syntax/Example
```
shr regB | memB, 1          shr [abyte], 1
shr regB | memB, cl         shr ax, cl
shr regW | memW, 1          shr dx, 1
shr regW | memW, cl         shr [aword + bx], cl
```

80286, 80386 only:
```
shr regB | memB, immB       shr cx, 8
shr regW | memW, immB       shr [word bp + 4], 4
```

80386 only:
```
shr regDW | memDW, 1        shr edx, 1
shr regDW | memDW, cl       shr [dword es:di], cl
shr regDW | memDW, immB     shr [dword bx], 4
```

Sample Code
```
mov ax, 10500    ; Assign value to ax
mov cl, 3        ; Assign shift count to cl
shr ax, cl       ; Divide 10500 by 8 (ax = 1312)
```

shr

Description   Executing shr shifts the old LSD of a byte, word, or doubleword (80386 only) value into the carry flag. A zero bit shifts into the new MSD. Repeating this action will eventually set all bits in the specified register or memory location to 0. Be aware that shr and sar are not synonyms, despite the fact that the counterpart instructions sal and shl are synonyms. (See these other instructions for more details.)

When the second operand to shr is an immediate 1, of is set to the MSD of the original value. When the second operand is not an immediate 1, the effect on of is not defined.

The sample demonstrates a common use for shr, dividing unsigned values by powers of 2. First, a value is loaded into ax, and the shift count is assigned to cl. Then shr shifts ax right by the number of times specified in cl. The result equals 10,500 divided by 2^3, or 1,312, dropping the remainder.

See Also   rcl, rcr, rol, ror, sal, sar, shl

shrd   Double-Precision Shift Right

Processor:	8086/88	80286	80386		Flags:	of	df	if	tf	sf	zf	af	pf	cf
			▲			u	–	–	–	▲	▲	u	▲	▲

Purpose   Shifts bits of multiple values rightward.

Syntax/Example
```
shrd regW | memW, regW, immB        shrd [bx], ax, 3
shrd regDW | memDW, regDW, immB     shrd [edi], edx, 4
shrd regW | memW, regW, cl          shrd ax, bx, cl
shrd regDW | memDW, regDW, cl       shrd eax, ebx, cl
```

Sample Code
```
shrd edx, ecx, 4     ; Shift bits in four
shrd ecx, ebx, 4     ;   general-purpose
shrd ebx, eax, 4     ;   registers by 4
shr  eax, 4
```

Description   On 80386 systems, use shlr to shift double-precision values to the right. The first operand specifies the destination and may be a word or doubleword register or memory reference. The second operand specifies the source bits that are shifted into the first operand. This value must be a word or doubleword register. The third operand specifies the number of shifts to perform and may be an immediate value from 0 to 31 or a value in register cl. Values greater than 31 are treated modulo 32.

You can use shrd to divide multiple-precision values by powers of 2. The sample demonstrates this idea by shifting 4 times left a 128-bit (16-byte) value held in registers eax, ebx, ecx, and edx with the highest-order portion of the value in `eax`. This divides the multiple-precision value by 2^4, or 16. For more information, read the notes to `shld`, which operates identically to `shrd` except for the direction of the shift.

See Also   `shld`

Set Carry Flag   `stc`

	Processor:	8086/88	80286	80386		Flags:	of	df	if	tf	sf	zf	af	pf	cf
		▲	▲	▲			–	–	–	–	–	–	–	–	1

Purpose   Sets the carry flag to 1.

Syntax/Example   `stc` *no operands*   `stc`

Sample Code
```
PROC Anyproc
; Procedure code
@@ErrExit:
  stc              ; Set carry (error)
  ret              ; Return to caller
@@NoErrExit:
  clc              ; Clear carry (no error)
  ret              ; Return to caller
ENDP AnyProc
```

Description   Executing `stc` sets the carry flag to 1. As the sample code demonstrates, the instruction is often used to pass an error flag back from a subroutine, setting `cf` if an error was detected. (This is the same example shown for `clc`.)

See Also   `clc, cmc`

Set Direction Flag   `std`

	Processor:	8086/88	80286	80386		Flags:	of	df	if	tf	sf	zf	af	pf	cf
		▲	▲	▲			–	1	–	–	–	–	–	–	–

Purpose   Sets the direction flag to 1.

Syntax/Example   `std` *no operands*   `std`

Sample Code
```
DATASEG
string db 10 dup (?)
strlen = $ - string
```

```
CODESEG
  mov ax,@data              ; Initialize es to address
  mov es,ax                 ;  of data segment
  ASSUME es:DGROUP          ; Tell tasm where es points
  mov cx, strlen            ; Assign string length to cx
  mov di, offset string + strlen - 1 ; di addresses string end
  std                       ; Auto-decrement di
@@10:
  mov al, cl                ; Assign next value to al
  stos [string]             ; Store al in string
  loop @@10                 ; cx <- cx - 1; jump if cx <> 0
```

Description   Use std to set the direction flag to 1. Always execute std (or the companion instruction cld) before a repeated string operation, which decrements either or both si and di automatically if df = 1. The sample demonstrates how to use std after first initializing cx to the length of a 10-byte string variable and addressing the end of the string with es:di. The three-instruction loop assigns successive values to al, which stos stores in the string, also decrementing di automatically because df = 1. The effect is to set string to the ten values 1, 2, . . . , 10.

See Also   cld

sti
Set Interrupt-Enable Flag

Processor:	8086/88	80286	80386		Flags:	of	df	if	tf	sf	zf	af	pf	cf
	▲	▲	▲			–	–	1	–	–	–	–	–	–

Purpose   Sets interrupt-enable flag to 1.

Syntax/Example   sti *no operands*   sti

Sample Code
```
cli     ; Disable maskable interrupts
;
; Code runs with maskable interrupts disabled
;
sti     ; Enable maskable interrupts again
```

Description   Executing sti sets the interrupt-enable flag if to 1, allowing the processor to recognize maskable interrupts. The instruction is commonly used as one of the first commands in an interrupt service routine, which begins running with if = 0. Setting if to 1 with sti allows interrupts to be recognized during execution of the ISR.

See Also   cli

Store String   stos stosb stosd stosw

Processor: 8086/88 80286 80386   Flags: of df if tf sf zf af pf cf
            ▲   ▲   ▲   —   —   —   —   —   —   —   —   —

Purpose   Stores strings of values into memory.

Syntax/Example
| | |
stos *memB*   stos   [byte destination]
stos *memW*   stos   [word destination]
stosb *no operands*   stosb
stosw *no operands*   stosw

80386 only:
stos *memDW*   stos   [dword destination]
stosd *no operands*   stosd

Sample Code
```
DATASEG
buffer db 512 dup (0ffh)
CODESEG
mov ax,@data           ; Initialize es to address
mov es,ax              ;   of data segment
ASSUME es:DGROUP       ; Tell tasm where es points
mov di, offset buffer  ; Address buffer with es:di
mov cx, 512 / 2        ; Assign buffer size / 2 to cx
xor ax, ax             ; Set ax to 0000
cld                    ; Auto-increment di
rep stosw              ; Fill buffer with 00 words
```

Description   Use stos or the equivalent shorthand mnemonics stosb, stosd (80386 only), and stosw to store strings of values in memory. Like all string instructions, register assignments are fixed even if you specify an explicit address label as the operand to stos. (The shorthand mnemonics do not require operands.) The instruction stores the value of al, ax, or eax (80386 only) to the location addressed by es:di. The size of the value stored depends on the size of the specified operand, unless you choose a shorthand mnemonic—stosb to store bytes, stosw to store words, and stosd to store 80386 doublewords. After the instruction executes, if df = 0, di is incremented by the size of the value stored—by 1 for bytes, 2 for words, or 4 for doublewords. If df = 1, then di is decremented by this amount.

Usually, stos is used with the rep repeat prefix along with a count value in cx to store values in multiple locations. As the sample demonstrates, this provides a fast and easy way to fill memory blocks with values, in this case, initializing a 512-byte buffer with zeros. Because the buffer size (512) is evenly divisible by 2, stosw is used instead of stosb, repeating for 256 instead of 512 times.

See Also   cmpsb, cmpsd, cmpsw, ins, insb, insd, insw, lods, lodsb, lodsd, lodsw, movs, movsb, movsd, movsw, outs, outsb, outsd, outsw, scas, scasb, scasd, scasw

sub

Subtract

Processor:	8086/88	80286	80386		Flags:	of	df	if	tf	sf	zf	af	pf	cf
	▲	▲	▲			▲	–	–	–	▲	▲	▲	▲	▲

Purpose   Subtracts integers.

Syntax/Example

```
sub al, immB                    sub al, 3
sub ax, immW                    sub ax, 1000
sub regB | memB, immB           sub dl, 5
sub regW | memW, immW           sub [word bx], 256
sub regW | memW, immB           sub bx, 8
sub regB | memB, regB           sub [byte es:di], dl
sub regW | memW, regW           sub cx, cx
sub regB, regB | memB           sub ah, al
sub regW, regW | memW           sub dx, [word bp + 4]
```

80386 only:

```
sub eax, immDW                  sub eax, 164532
sub regDW | memDW, immB         sub [dword bp - 8], 2
sub regDW | memDW, immDW        sub edx, 99999
sub regDW | memDW, regDW        sub [dword array + bx + di], edx
sub regDW, regDW | memDW        sub edi, ecx
```

Sample Code

```
DATASEG
v1 dd 155612          ; A doubleword value
v2 dd 35996           ; Value to subtract from v1
CODESEG
mov ax, [word v2]     ; Load low-order v2 into ax
sub [word v1], ax     ; Subtract low-order words
mov ax, [word v2 + 2] ; Load high-order v2 into ax
sbb [word v1 + 2], ax ; Subtract high-order words
```

Description   Use sub to subtract two signed or unsigned bytes, words, or doublewords (80386 only). The second operand is subtracted from the first, replacing the original value of the first operand. The sub instruction typically subtracts two values directly or begins a multiple-precision sequence that subtracts values larger than the maximum register size. When doing this, follow sub with one or more sbb instructions to complete the subtraction and take possible borrows into account. The sample demonstrates how this works, subtracting a doubleword value v2 from another doubleword value v1 and storing the result in v1. (Doublewords can be subtracted directly only on 80386 systems.)

See Also   sbb

Test Bits

test

Processor:	8086/88	80286	80386		Flags:	of	df	if	tf	sf	zf	af	pf	cf
	▲	▲	▲			0	–	–	–	▲	▲	u	▲	0

Purpose   Compares values, performing a logical AND.

Syntax/Example

```
test al, immB                    test al, 00001000b
test ax, immW                    test ax, 000Fh
test regB | memB, immB           test [byte bx], 080h
test regW | memW, immW           test dx, 01000h
test regB | memB, regB           test ah, cl
test regW | memW, regW           test ax, cx
```

80386 only:

```
test eax, immDW                  test eax, 02h
test regDW | memDW, immDW        test [dword bx + di], 04000000h
test regDW | memDW, regDW        test edx, ebx
```

Sample Code

```
mov  ax, -1          ; Load test value into ax
test ax, 08000h      ; Does MSD = 1?
jz   @@10            ; Jump if MSD <> 1
neg  ax              ; Else find absolute value
@@10:
```

Description   The test instruction is identical in every way to **and** except that the result of the logical AND operation is discarded—only the flags are retained, which can be inspected by a conditional jump. The most common use for test is to determine whether one or more bits equal 1 in byte, word, or doubleword values (80386 only). To demonstrate this, the sample loads a test value into **ax** and then applies test with the immediate value 08000h— in other words, a binary value with a 1 bit in the MSD position. If this value AND **ax** equals 0, thus setting **zf** to 1, then **ax**'s MSD must be 0; otherwise, **ax**'s MSD is 1. The **jz** instruction detects this condition, executing **neg** to find the absolute value of **ax** only if the value is a two's complement negative quantity (MSD = 1).

See Also   and

wait

Wait Until Not Busy

Processor:	8086/88	80286	80386		Flags:	of	df	if	tf	sf	zf	af	pf	cf
	▲	▲	▲			—	—	—	—	—	—	—	—	—

Purpose Waits until the processor's $\overline{\text{BUSY}}$ pin is inactive.

Syntax/Example wait *no operands*   wait

Sample Code
```
cstat dw 0              ; Coprocessor status word
CODESEG
; Turbo Assembler inserts a wait here automatically
fstsw [cstat]           ; Store status at cstat
wait                    ; Wait until finished
mov  ax, [cstat]        ; Load status into ax
```

Description Executing wait stops the processor until the $\overline{\text{BUSY}}$ pin becomes active (set to high), indicating that the attached device is *not* busy. The instruction is used typically to synchronize code with a coprocessor, allowing the program to continue only after finishing a calculation or other instruction. The 80287 and 80387 math coprocessors automatically synchronize with the main processor and do not require explicit waits. The 8087 math coprocessor requires a wait before every coprocessor instruction. Turbo Assembler automatically inserts wait's as required by the 8087. As the sample demonstrates, you may also have to *follow* a coprocessor instruction with wait when both the coprocessor and program instructions access the same memory locations. Because the coprocessor runs independently of the main processor, unless wait is used before the mov to ax, the program may attempt to read the value at cstat before the coprocessor finishes storing a value there. Although Turbo Assembler inserts a wait before the fstw instruction, to prevent all possibility of a conflict, you still have to add a following wait.

See Also esc

xchg

Exchange

Processor:	8086/88	80286	80386		Flags:	of	df	if	tf	sf	zf	af	pf	cf
	▲	▲	▲			—	—	—	—	—	—	—	—	—

Purpose Exchanges register values with other register and memory values.

Syntax/Example
```
xchg ax, regW            xchg ax, cx
xchg regW, ax            xchg bx, ax
xchg regB, regB | memB   xchg dh, dl
```

```
        xchg regB | memB, regB          xchg [byte bp + 4], ah
        xchg regW, regW | memW          xchg ax, bx
        xchg regW | memW, regW          xchg [word bx], dx
```

80386 only:
```
        xchg eax, regDW                 xchg eax, ebx
        xchg regDW, eax                 xchg ecx, eax
        xchg regDW, regDW | memDW       xchg edx, [dword bx + di]
        xchg regDW | memDW, regDW       xchg [dword var], eax
```

Sample Code
```
DATASEG
array    db 80 dup (?)      ; Addressed by [bx]
arraysize = $ - array       ; Size of array
newbx dw offset array       ; Place to hold bx
newcx dw arraysize          ; Place to hold cx
CODESEG
PROC Outer
call Inner                  ; Initialize/preserve bx, cx
;
; other code in procedure
;
PROC Inner
xchg bx, [newbx]            ; Initialize/restore bx
xchg cx, [newcx]            ; Initialize/restore cx
ret                        ; Return to caller
ENDP Inner
ENDP Outer
```

Description

Use xchg to exchange two byte, word, or doubleword (80386 only) values, which can be in registers or in memory locations. The two operands—of which at least one must be a register—exchange values without requiring the use of an intermediate value on the stack or in another register. The sample uses xchg to initialize and save the values of two registers bx and cx. The call to Inner at the beginning of the Outer procedure swaps the registers with two word variables. When the procedure finishes, the code falls through to Inner, again executing the two xchg instructions before returning to Outer's caller, thus restoring bx and cx to their original values, while storing the registers' *current* values. Later, when the procedure is again called, bx and cx will be loaded with the values they had at the end of the procedure's previous run, allowing the code to pick up where it left off.

Trivia department: The special form xchg ax,ax generates the identical machine code as a nop instruction—the single byte 90h.

See Also   lock, nop

xchg

xlat xlatb

Translate From Table

Processor:	8086/88	80286	80386		*Flags:*	of	df	if	tf	sf	zf	af	pf	cf
	▲	▲	▲			—	—	—	—	—	—	—	—	—

Purpose   Looks up (translates) a byte value from a table.

Syntax/Example

```
xlat memB          xlat [es:table]
xlatb no operands  xlatb
```

Sample Code

```
DATASEG
table db 120, 202, 100, 64, 98, 250, 14, 8
CODESEG
mov al, 3           ; Load index into al
mov bx, offset table  ; Address table with ds:bx
xlatb               ; Sets al to 64
```

Description   The xlat instruction translates a value in al to an associated value from a table of bytes. The table must be addressed by ds:bx or, using an es: override, by es:bx. The value in al represents an index into the table with the first table byte having the index value 0. Executing xlat loads the byte at ds:bx + al or es:bx + al into al. The sample demonstrates how this works; it loads al with the fourth byte (index = 3) from a small table, setting al to 64.

The plain xlat instruction does not require an operand. If you add an operand, it may refer to bx as in xlat [bx] and xlat [es:bx], or it may refer to the table by name as in xlat [table] and xlat [es:table]. No matter what form you choose, however, you still have to load bx with the offset address of the table—the instruction doesn't do this for you. The shorthand form xlatb, which performs identically to xlat, may not be used with an operand.

Some references suggest using lea to load bx with the effective address of a table element. For example, you could use the instruction lea bx, [matrix + si] to initialize bx to the offset address of two-dimensional matrix row indexed by si and then use xlatb to translate a column index in al to one of the bytes from that row. Another typical use for xlat is to translate ASCII characters to alternate symbols, perhaps to allow people to reprogram keyboards or to convert values to different character-set encodings.

See Also   lea

Exclusive OR

xor

Processor:	8086/88	80286	80386		Flags:	of	df	if	tf	sf	zf	af	pf	cf
	▲	▲	▲			0	–	–	–	▲	▲	u	▲	0

Purpose Logically exclusive ORs two byte, word, or doubleword (80386 only) values.

Syntax/Example
```
xor al, immB                    xor al, 0FFh
xor ax, immW                    xor ax, 08000h
xor regB | memB, immB           xor [byte bx], 01h
xor regW | memW, immW           xor cx, 0400h
xor regW | memW, immB           xor [word bp + 2], 10h
xor regB | memB, regB           xor ah, cl
xor regW | memW, regW           xor dx, cx
xor regB, regB | memB           xor ah, [byte bx]
xor regW, regW | memW           xor dx, dx
```

80386 only:
```
xor eax, immDW                  xor eax, 004000000h
xor regDW | memDW, immDW        xor edx, 0FFFFFFFFh
xor regDW | memDW, immB         xor [dword bx], 01h
xor regDW | memDW, regDW        xor eax, eax
xor regDW, regDW | memDW        xor edx, [dword bx + si]
```

Sample Code
```
xor ax, ax      ; Sets ax to 0000
xor bx, 0FFFFh  ; Forms one's complement of bx
```

Description Use xor to perform the logical exclusive OR operation to two byte, word, or doubleword (80386 only) values. The result of the operation replaces the value of the first operand. The second operand is often referred to as the *mask*. A typical use for xor is to toggle bits on and off, changing ones to zeros and zeros to ones. Also, due to the rules of the exclusive OR, because 1 can only result when the two original corresponding bits are different, performing xor on a register with itself sets that register to 0—a common 8086 technique that saves 1 byte. (The instruction mov ax,0 takes 3 bytes; xor ax,ax takes 2.)

See Also and, or, not

xor

Chapter *15 Turbo Assembler Reference*

In this Chapter

Symbols

Table 15-1 describes various italicized symbols used throughout this chapter while Table 15-2 describes in more detail the symbols for *warnclass*. The predefined symbols in Turbo Assembler are detailed in Table 15-3.

Table 15-1 *Symbols and Meanings*

Symbol	Meaning
I	either or
[ ]	optional*
. . .	a numeric series or continuation
[ ] . . .	a repeating optional element
::=	is equivalent to
align	byte I word I dword I para I page
argument	macro parameters
boundary	a power of 2 (e.g., 2, 4, 8)
class	*text* representing a segment classification
codesym	a code symbol (i.e., a label)
columns	number of columns
combine	at *expr* I common I memory I private I public I stack
condition	expression evaluating to true (<>0) or false (=0)
count	1, 2, . . . , 65535
datasym	a data symbol (i.e., a label)
definition	a directive element defined in the directive syntax
distance	near I far
dx	db I dd I df I dp I dq I dt I dw
entry point	a code label defining the start of a program
expr	numeric expression
fieldname	name of a record field name

Table 15-1 *Continued*

Symbol	Meaning
fields	any data allocation created by db, dw, etc.
filename	a file name with or without path and drive information
groupname	name of a multiple segment group
language	basic ǀ c ǀ fortran ǀ pascal ǀ prolog
macroname	name of a defined macro
memorymodel	tiny ǀ small ǀ medium ǀ compact ǀ large ǀ huge ǀ tpascal
memref	memory reference
name	an identifier such as MyData or YourCode
parameter	a replaceable dummy parameter
prefix	two-character local label prefix, normally @ @
recordname	name of a record data type
register	ax ǀ bx ǀ cx ǀ di ǀ ds ǀ dx ǀ es ǀ si ǀ (80386 only:) eax ǀ ebx ǀ ecx ǀ edi ǀ edx ǀ esi
rows	number of rows
segexpr	SEG *expr* (see SEG operator)
segmentname	name of a segment
segname	*segreg* ǀ *segmentname* ǀ *segexpr*
segreg	cs ǀ ds ǀ es ǀ ss
size	a whole number constant
statements	assembly language instructions or directives
structname	name of a structure
text	any sequence of characters
type	near ǀ far ǀ proc ǀ byte ǀ word ǀ dataptr ǀ dword ǀ fword ǀ pword ǀ qword ǀ tbyte ǀ *structname*
use	use16 ǀ use32
warnclass	aln ǀ ass ǀ brk ǀ icg ǀ lco ǀ opi ǀ opp ǀ ops ǀ ovf ǀ pdc ǀ pqk ǀ pro ǀ res ǀ tpi (See Table 15-2.)
width	a whole number constant

*Don't confuse the square brackets [ ], which surround optional items, with the square brackets used in a program's indirect memory references as in mov ax, [count].

Table 15-2 *Symbols for warnclass*

Symbol	Meaning
aln	segment alignment
ass	assumes 16-bit segment
brk	brackets needed
icg	inefficient code generation
lco	location counter overflow
opi	open IF conditional
opp	open procedure
ops	open segment
ovf	arithmetic overflow
pdc	pass-dependent construction
pqk	assuming constant for [const]
pro	protected-mode memory-write needs cs: override
res	reserved word
tpi	Turbo Pascal illegal construction

Table 15-3 *Turbo Assembler Predefined Symbols*

Symbol	Type	Description
@code	alias	Code segment name
@codesize	numeric (byte)	0 = small,compact model; 1 = other models
@cpu	numeric (word)	Enabled processor instructions; bit numbers (1 = on, 0 = off): 0—8086; 1—80186; 2—80286; 3—80386; 4, 5, 6—unused; 7—80286/386 protected mode; 8—8087; 9—unused; 10—80287; 11—80387; 12, 13, 14, 15—unused
@curseg	alias	Current segment name
@data	alias	Near data segment name
@datasize	numeric (byte)	Data memory model: 0 = tiny, small, medium; 1 = compact; 2 = huge
@fardata	alias	Far data segment name
@fardata?	alias	Far uninitialized data segment name
@filename	alias	Assembly file name as an equated symbol
@wordsize	numeric (byte)	Segment address size: 2 = 16 bit; 4 = 32 bit
??date	string	Today's date
??filename	string	Assembly file name as a character string
??time	string	Current time in DOS country-code format
??version	numeric (word)	Turbo Assembler version number: high byte = major revision numbers, low byte = minor revision numbers

Note: Equates of type *alias* represent other symbols. For example, @code represents the name of the current code segment—any place you can use a segment name, you can use an alias instead. Numeric equates represent whole number values—use them any place you would use another numeric equate. String equates represent unterminated character strings, which you can insert in db directives to create variables containing the file name, date, and time.

Operators

Operators are printed in Table 15-4 in uppercase to make them more visible. In programs, you may write operators in uppercase or lowercase. Table 15-5 lists possible SYMTYPE values. SYMTYPE is equivalent to MASM's .TYPE operator (with a leading period). The TYPE *operator* (without a leading period) returns a value as listed in Table 15-6. If positive, TYPE represents the *expr* size in bytes. If negative, TYPE represents a NEAR or FAR pointer. Turbo Assembler 1.0 requires MASM mode to be enabled before using TYPE. Despite appearances, TYPE is *not* equivalent to MASM's .TYPE operator.

Table 15-4 *Turbo Assembler Operators*

Symbol	Syntax	Description
( )	(*expr*)	evaluate expression
*	*expr* * *expr*	multiply
+	*expr* + *expr*	add
+	+*expr*	unary plus
−	*expr* − *expr*	subtract
−	−*expr*	unary minus
.	*memref.field*	structure member separator
/	*expr* / *expr*	divide
:	*segname* ǀ *groupname:expr*	segment override
?	*dx* ?	uninitialized data
[ ]	[*memref*]	indirect reference
AND	*expr* AND *expr*	logical AND
BYTE	BYTE [PTR] *expr*	8-bit byte data
DUP	*count* DUP (*expr* [,*expr*] . . .)	duplicate
DWORD	DWORD [PTR] *expr*	32-bit doubleword data
EQ	*expr* EQ *expr*	equals
FAR	FAR [PTR] *expr*	far-code address
FWORD	FWORD [PTR] *expr*	48-bit far-data pointer
GE	*expr* GE *expr*	greater than or equal
GT	*expr* GT *expr*	greater than
HIGH	HIGH *expr*	high order of
LARGE	LARGE *expr*	force offset to 32 bits
LE	*expr* LE *expr*	less than or equal
LENGTH	LENGTH *datasym*	length of (element count)
LOW	LOW *expr*	low order of
LT	*expr* LT *expr*	less than
MASK	MASK *recordname* ǀ *fieldname*	bit mask
MOD	*expr* MOD *expr*	modulo (division remainder)
NE	*expr* NE *expr*	not equal
NEAR	NEAR *expr*	near code address
NOT	NOT *expr*	one's complement

Table 15-4 *Continued*

Symbol	Syntax	Description
OFFSET	OFFSET *expr*	offset address
OR	*expr* OR *expr*	logical OR
PROC	PROC *codesym*	code procedure
PTR	*type* PTR *expr*	pointer to
PWORD	PWORD [PTR] *expr*	far-data pointer
QWORD	QWORD [PTR] *expr*	64-bit quadword data
SEG	SEG *expr*	segment address
SHL	*expr* SHL *count*	bit shift left
SHORT	SHORT *expr*	short code address
SHR	*expr* SHR *count*	bit shift right
SIZE	SIZE *datasym*	size in bytes
SMALL	SMALL *expr*	16-bit small offset
SYMTYPE	SYMTYPE *expr*	type of symbol (See Table 15-5.)
TBYTE	TBYTE [PTR] *expr*	80-bit tenbyte data
THIS	THIS *type*	assign current address
TYPE	TYPE *expr*	size of symbol (See Table 15-6.)
UNKNOWN	UNKNOWN *expr*	remove type information
WIDTH	WIDTH *record* ∣ *field*	record field bit width
WORD	WORD [PTR] *expr*	16-bit word data
XOR	*expr* XOR *expr*	logical exclusive OR

Table 15-5 *Possible SYMTYPE Values*

Bit Number	If bit = 1, then the symbol . . .
0	belongs to a code segment
1	belongs to a data segment
2	is a constant (i.e., an equate)
3	is a direct memory reference
4	is a register
5	is defined
6	(unused bit)
7	is external to module

Note: If bits 2 and 3 equal 0, then the symbol is an indirect memory reference such as [bx + si]. If all bits equal 0, then the symbol is not defined. (This condition produces an assembly error when using SYMTYPE in data allocation directives such as db and dw.)

Table 15-6 *Possible TYPE Values*

Value	Type Represented	Value	Type Represented
0	constant	8	QWORD
1	BYTE	10	TBYTE
2	WORD	OFFFh	NEAR
4	DWORD	OFFFh	FAR
6	FWORD or PWORD	n	number of bytes in a structure

Mode Equivalents

The MASM- and Ideal-mode equivalents are listed in Table 15-7.

Table 15-7 *MASM- and Ideal-Mode Equivalents*

MASM Mode	Ideal Mode
.186	P186
.286	P286
.286C	P286N
.286P	P286N
.287	P287
.386	P386
.386C	P386N
.386P	P386N
.387	P387
.8086	P8086
.8087	P8087
.ALPHA	DOSSEG
.CODE	CODESEG
COMMENT	(none)
.CONST	CONST
.CREF	%CREF
.DATA	DATASEG
.DATA?	UDATASEG
.ERR	ERR
.ERR1	ERRIF1
.ERR2	ERRIF2
.ERRB	ERRIFB
.ERRDEF	ERRIFDEF
.ERRDIF	ERRIFDIF
.ERRDIFI	ERRIFDIFI
.ERRE	ERRIFE
.ERRIDN	ERRIFIDN
.ERRIDNI	ERRIFIDNI
.ERRNB	ERRIFNB
.ERRNDEF	ERRIFNDEF
.ERRNZ	ERRIF
.FARDATA	FARDATA
.FARDATA?	UFARDATA
.LALL	%MACS
.LFCOND	%CONDS
.LIST	%LIST
.MODEL	MODEL
%OUT	DISPLAY

Table 15-7 *Continued*

MASM Mode	Ideal Mode
PAGE	%PAGESIZE
.RADIX	RADIX
.SALL	%NOMACS
.SEQ	(none)*
.SFCOND	%NOCONDS
.STACK	STACK
SUBTTL	%SUBTTL
.TFCOND	(none)
TITLE	%TITLE
.TYPE	SYMTYPE†
.XALL	(none)
.XCREF	%NOCREF
.XLIST	%NOLIST

*Turbo Assembler normally collects segments in sequential order as encountered during assembly. Use the DOSSEG (.ALPHA) directive to collect segments in alphabetic order. There is no Ideal-mode equivalent to the MASM .SEQ directive.

†This is an operator. All other symbols in this table are directives.

Directives

Most operators and directives are printed in Table 15-8 in uppercase to make them more visible. In programs, you may write operators and directives in uppercase or lowercase. Only Ideal-mode directives are listed in this table. See Table 15-7 for the equivalent MASM-mode directives.

Table 15-8 *Turbo Assembler Directives*

Directive Name Syntax	Directive Name Syntax
: Define near-code label *codesym*:	**%CREF** List cross references %CREF
= Define numeric equate *name* = *expr*	**%CREFALL** List all cross-reference symbols %CREFALL
ALIGN Align location counter ALIGN *boundary*	**%CREFREF** List only referenced symbols in cross reference %CREFREF
ARG Define procedural arguments ARG *arglist* [=*name*] [RETURNS *arglist*] *arglist* ::= *definition* [,*definition*] . . . *definition* ::= *name:typedef* *typedef* ::= *type* | PTR [*type*] | [*distance* [PTR [*type*]]]	**%CREFUREF** List only unreferenced symbols in cross reference %CREFUREF
ASSUME Set default segment register ASSUME *segreg:segmentname* [,*segreg:segmentname*] . . . ASSUME *segreg*:NOTHING [,*segreg*:NOTHING] . . . ASSUME NOTHING	**%CTLS** List listing controls %CTLS
%BIN Set listing object-code field width %BIN *size*	**DATASEG** Start new data segment DATASEG
CODESEG Start new code segment CODESEG [*name*]	**DB** Define byte [*name*] DB *expr* [,*expr*] . . .
COMM Define communal variable COMM *definition* [,*definition*] . . . *definition* ::= [*distance*] *name:type*[:*count*]	**DD** Define doubleword [*name*] DD [*type* PTR] *expr* [,*expr*] . . .
%CONDS List all conditional statements %CONDS	**%DEPTH** Set listing nesting depth level %DEPTH *size*
CONST Start of constant data segment CONST	**DF** Define farword pointer [*name*] DF [*type* PTR] *expr* [,*expr*] . . .
	DISPLAY Display string during assembly DISPLAY "*text*"

Table 15-8 *Continued*

Directive Name Syntax	Directive Name Syntax

DOSSEG
Enable standard DOS segment order
DOSSEG

DP
Define far 48-bit pointer
[*name*] DP [*type* PTR] *expr* [*,expr*] . . .

DQ
Define quadword
[*name*] DQ *expr* [*,expr*] . . .

DT
Define ten-byte variable
[*name*] DT *expr* [*,expr*] . . .

DW
Define word
[*name*] DW [*type* PTR] *expr* [*,expr*] . . .

ELSE
Start alternate conditional block
IF *condition*
statements
ELSE
statements
ENDIF

EMUL
Emulate coprocessor instructions
EMUL

END
End of source text
END [*entry point*]

ENDIF
End of conditional block
IF *condition*
statements
ENDIF

ENDP
End of procedure
ENDP [*name*]

ENDS
End of segment or structure
ENDS [*name*]

EQU
Equate symbol (*name*) to value (*expr*)
name EQU *expr*

ERR
Force error message
ERR

ERRIF
Force error if expr is true
ERRIF *condition*

ERRIF1
Force error if pass 1
ERRIF1

ERRIF2
Force error if pass 2
ERRIF2

ERRIFB
Force error if argument blank
ERRIFB *argument*

ERRIFDEF
Force error for defined symbol
ERRIFDEF *name*

ERRIFDIF
Force error for different arguments
ERRIFDIF *argument1, argument2*

ERRIFDIFI
Force error for different arguments ignoring case
ERRIFDIFI *argument1, argument2*

ERRIFE
Force error if expr is false
ERRIFE *expr*

ERRIFIDN
Force error for identical arguments
ERRIFIDN *argument1, argument2*

ERRIFIDNI
Force error for identical arguments ignoring case
ERRIFIDNI *argument1, argument2*

ERRIFNB
Force error if argument is not blank
ERRIFNB *argument*

ERRIFNDEF
Force error if symbol is not defined
ERRIFNDEF *name*

EVEN
Align code to even address
EVEN

EVENDATA
Align data to even address
EVENDATA

EXITM
Exit macro
EXITM

Table 15-8 *Continued*

Directive Name Syntax	Directive Name Syntax

EXTRN
Define external symbol
EXTRN *definition* [,*definition*] . . .
definition ::= *name:type*[:*count*]

FARDATA
Start of far data segment
FARDATA [*name*]

GLOBAL
Define global symbol
GLOBAL *definition* [,*definition*]
definition ::= *name:type*[:*count*]

GROUP
Define segment group
GROUP *name segmentname*
  [,*segmentname*] . . .

IDEAL
Switch to Ideal mode
IDEAL

IF
Assemble if condition is true
IF *condition*

IF1
Assemble if on pass 1
IF1

IF2
Assemble if on pass 2
IF2

IFB
Assemble if argument is blank
IFB *argument*

IFDEF
Assemble if symbol is defined
IFDEF *name*

IFDIF
Assemble if arguments differ
IFDIF *argument1, argument2*

IFDIFI
Assemble if arguments differ ignoring case
IFDIFI *argument1, argument2*

IFE
Assemble if expr equals 0 (is false)
IFE *expr*

IFIDN
Assemble if arguments are identical
IFIDN *argument1, argument2*

IFIDNI
Assemble if arguments are identical ignoring case
IFIDNI *argument1, argument2*

IFNB
Assemble if argument is not blank
IFNB *argument*

IFNDEF
Assemble if name is not defined
IFNDEF *name*

%INCL
List include files
%INCL

INCLUDE
Include separate file
INCLUDE "*filename*"

INCLUDELIB
Include library file during linking
INCLUDELIB "*filename*"

IRP
Insert repeated parameter
IRP *parameter, <text* [,*text*] . . . >
statements
ENDM

IRPC
Insert repeated parameter for characters
IRPC *parameter, text*
statements
ENDM

JUMPS
Enable conditional jump adjustments
JUMPS

LABEL
Define typed symbol
LABEL *name type*

%LINUM
Set listing line number field width
%LINUM *size*

%LIST
Listing on
%LIST

LOCAL
Define local symbol in macros
LOCAL *name* [,*name*] . . .

Table 15-8 *Continued*

Directive Name Syntax	Directive Name Syntax
LOCAL Define local symbol in procedures LOCAL *definition* [,*definition*] . . . [=*name*] *definition ::= name:type*[:*count*]	**NOJUMPS** Disable conditional jump adjustments NOJUMPS
LOCALS Enable local labels LOCALS [*prefix*]	**%NOLIST** Disable listing %NOLIST
MACRO Start macro definition MACRO *name* [*parameter* [,*parameter*] . . .]	**NOLOCALS** Disable local labels NOLOCALS
%MACS List macro expansions %MACS	**%NOMACS** List only code-generating macro statements %NOMACS
MASM Enable MASM-compatible assembly MASM	**NOMASM51** Disable MASM version 5.1 enhancements NOMASM51
MASM51 Enable MASM version 5.1 enhancements MASM51	**NOMULTERRS** Disable multiple errors per line NOMULTERRS
MODEL Select memory model MODEL *memorymodel* [,*language*]	**%NOSYMS** List no symbol table %NOSYMS
MULTERRS Enable multiple errors per line MULTERRS	**%NOTRUNC** Word-wrap long fields in listing %NOTRUNC
NAME Change module name NAME *filename*	**NOWARN** Disable warning message NOWARN [*warnclass*]
%NEWPAGE Start new listing page %NEWPAGE	**ORG** Set location counter origin ORG *expr*
%NOCONDS List no false conditional statements %NOCONDS	**P186** Enable 80186 instructions P186
%NOCREF List no cross reference %NOCREF [*name* [,*name*] . . .]	**P286** Enable all 80286 instructions P286
%NOCTLS List no listing controls %NOCTLS	**P286N** Enable 80286 non-protected-mode instructions P286N
NOEMUL Disable coprocessor emulation NOEMUL	**P287** Enable 80287 coprocessor instructions P287
%NOINCL List no include files %NOINCL	**P386** Enable all 80386 instructions P386

Table 15-8 *Continued*

Directive Name Syntax	Directive Name Syntax

P386N
Enable 80386 non-protected-mode
  instructions
P386N

P387
Enable 8087 coprocessor instructions
P387

P8086
Enable only 8086/88 instructions
P8086

P8087
Enable 8087 coprocessor instructions
P8087

%PAGESIZE
Set listing page height and width
%PAGESIZE [*rows*] [,*columns*]

%PCNT
Set listing segment:offset field width
%PCNT *width*

PNO87
Disable coprocessor instructions
PNO87

%POPLCTL
Pop listing controls from assembler stack
%POPLCTL

PROC
Define new procedure
PROC *name* [*distance*] [USES *reglist*]
  [*arglist*] [=*name*] [RETURNS *arglist*]
reglist ::= *register* [*register*] . . .
arglist ::= *definition* [,*definition*] . . .
definition ::= *name:typedef*
typedef ::= *type* | PTR [*type*] | [*distance*
  [PTR [*type*]]]

PUBLIC
Define public symbol
PUBLIC *name* [,*name*] . . .

PURGE
Delete macro definition
PURGE *macroname* [,*macroname*] . . .

%PUSHLCTL
Push listing controls onto assembler stack
%PUSHLCTL

QUIRKS
Enable MASM quirks
QUIRKS

RADIX
Set default radix
RADIX *expr*

RECORD
Define bit-field record
RECORD *name definition* [,*definition*] . . .
definition ::= *fieldname:width*[=*expr*]

REPT
Repeat statements
REPT *expr*
statements
ENDM

SEGMENT
Define segment
SEGMENT *name* [*align*] [*combine*] [*use*]
  ['*class*']

STACK
Start new stack segment
STACK [*size*]

STRUC
Define structure
STRUCT *name*
fields
ENDS [*name*]

%SUBTTL
Declare listing subtitle
%SUBTTL "*text*"

%SYMS
Enable listing symbol table
%SYMS

%TABSIZE
Set listing column tab width
%TABSIZE *width*

%TEXT
Set listing source field width
%TEXT *width*

%TITLE
Set listing title
%TITLE "*text*"

%TRUNC
Truncate long fields in listings
%TRUNC

UDATASEG
Start new uninitialized data segment
UDATASEG

Table 15-8 *Continued*

Directive Name Syntax	Directive Name Syntax
UFARDATA Start new uninitialized far data segment UFARDATA	**USES** Auto push and pop registers (language models only) USES *register* [*,register*] . . .
UNION Define union UNION *name* *fields* ENDS [*name*]	**WARN** Enable a warning message WARN [*warnclass*]

Bibliography

Borland International   *Turbo Assembler 1.0, Turbo Debugger 1.0, Turbo Pascal 5.0, Turbo C 2.0.* Scotts Valley, CA.

Programs in this book were tested with these numbered versions. *Turbo Assembler* and *Turbo Debugger* are sold as one package by most software distributors and include three references: *Turbo Debugger User's Guide, Turbo Assembler User's Guide,* and *Turbo Assembler Reference Guide. Turbo Pascal* and *Turbo C* are sold separately.

Brief   *Solution Systems.* Boston, MA.

I used Brief to write all the programs in this book as well as the text for the chapters. There are many good programming editors on the market, but you won't go wrong if you choose this one.

Campbell, Joe   *C Programmer's Guide to Serial Communications.* Indianapolis, IN: Howard W. Sams, 1987.

Every programmer who plans to write communications software in *any* language should read this superb book. Note: A C compiler is required—the author uses Aztec C, although your favorite compiler will probably work if you don't mind making a few alterations to the listings.

Duncan, Ray   *Advanced MS-DOS.* Redmond, WA: Microsoft Press, 1986.

This is one of the best MS-DOS programming books around. It contains many assembly language examples plus well-organized MS-DOS and IBM PC BIOS function references and includes an especially good chapter that explains how to write installable device drivers.

Intel Corporation   *iAPX 86/88, 186/188 User's Manual—Programmer's Reference.* Santa Clara, CA, 1986.

Serious assembly language programmers should consider purchasing this and the next two technical references from Intel, makers of the 8086, 8088, 80186, 80286, and 80386 processors—among other products. Despite errors here and there, the references list complete details about machine-code bit formats and instruction timings—data that you may need for detailed assembly language work. Helpful pseudocode listings describe how individual instructions operate. You probably won't find these references in book stores; for more information, write to: Intel Literature Sales, P.O. Box 58130, Santa Clara, CA 95052-8130.

Intel Corporation   *80286 and 80287 Programmer's Reference Manual.* Santa Clara, CA, 1987.

Intel Corporation   *80386 Programmer's Reference Manual.* Santa Clara, CA, 1987.

Jensen, K., and Wirth, N.   *Pascal User Manual and Report*, 2nd ed. New York: Springer-Verlag, 1974.

This is the book that started the Pascal ball rolling. Now seriously out of date, the reference is useful primarily as a general guide to designing portable programs in "standard" Pascal that you plan to optimize with assembly language using the methods discussed in chapter 12. Beware: Some "standard" procedures such as `get` and `put` are not supported by Turbo Pascal.

Kernighan, B., and Ritchie, D.   *The C Programming Language*, 2nd ed. Englewood Cliffs: Prentice Hall, 1988.

Every beginning C programmer should read this tutorial from cover to cover. Like the "Jensen and Wirth" Pascal guide, "Kernighan and Ritchie" (the popular alternate title for the book) is especially useful as a guide to designing portable programs in "standard" C that you plan to optimize with assembly language using the methods discussed in chapter 13.

Microsoft Corporation   *Microsoft Macro Assembler 5.1 Reference.* Redmond, WA, 1987.

If you have Turbo Assembler, you don't need to purchase the Microsoft Macro Assembler. But if you don't mind paying for two assemblers, the MASM references are well written and make useful additions to your programming library. Note: MASM does not support Turbo Assembler's Ideal mode.

Strauss, Edmund   *80386 Technical Reference.* New York, NY: Brady, 1987.

A general guide to the 80386, this book duplicates much of the material in the Intel *80386 Programmer's Reference Manual.* Even so, you'll find some good information here on using protected-mode instructions.

Swan, Tom   *Mastering Turbo Pascal 4.0*, 2nd ed. Indianapolis, IN: Howard W. Sams, 1988.

See chapter 14, "Pascal Meets Assembly Language," for more information about adding in-line assembly language to Turbo Pascal. Note: This chapter was written before Turbo Assembler existed.

Tanenbaum, Andrew S.   *Operating Systems: Design and Implementation.* Englewood Cliffs, NJ: Prentice-Hall, Inc., 1987.

Beyond a doubt, this is one of the best (maybe *the* best) book ever written about multitasking, multiuser operating systems. The text is witty and accurate but highly technical at times. Although the content is aimed at C programmers and contains very little assembly language code, understanding the book's content is a prerequisite to getting started with 80386 protected-mode programming of multitasking operating systems.

The Waite Group   *The Waite Group's MS-DOS Papers*. Indianapolis, IN: Howard W. Sams, 1988.

Many assembly language examples and interesting tidbits from several different authors make for interesting reading. It contains useful hints about IBM PC and assembly language programming.

Answers to Exercises

Chapter 1

1-1 Machine language, an improper synonym for assembly language, refers to the binary code that drives a computer processor; therefore, machine code is a better term.

1-2 Most computer languages are high level. C, Pascal, BASIC, and others, while varying in many ways, are all considered to be high-level languages. Machine code is the lowest of low-level languages. Assembly language is somewhere in between, giving programmers a way to program the CPU directly while taking advantage of features normally found in high-level languages.

1-3 Individual assembly language instructions translate (assemble) directly to single machine codes. Individual high-level language statements usually translate (compile) to many machine codes.

1-4 Machine code is cumbersome because many codes depend on their position in a program or refer to fixed addresses in memory. Modifying machine code directly is impractical. Early programmers had no choice in the matter because there weren't any computer languages—not even assembly language—in the dawn of the computer age.

1-5 Debuggers such as Turbo Debugger help programmers fix broken programs by running the code at slow speed, stopping at various locations, and letting people examine processor registers and memory values. These same features provide ways to examine the inner workings of programs, too, and can help prevent system crashes.

1-6 A register is a small amount of memory located inside the CPU and directly affected by certain machine-code instructions.

1-7 A flag is a single bit of memory located inside the CPU and, like registers, directly affected by certain machine-code instructions.

1-8   Ideal mode assembles faster than MASM mode. Ideal mode syntax is easier to understand and use than MASM mode. Ideal mode adds features that are especially useful for writing stand-alone assembly language programs.

1-9   Advantages of assembly language include the promise (but not the guarantee) of top speed and the ability to control directly the CPU and peripheral devices attached to the computer.

1-10   Many disadvantages are often cited about assembly language. The major disadvantage is the difficulty of transferring assembly language programs from one processor to another. Doing so usually means writing the program over from scratch.

Chapter 2

2-1   Header: 1–6; Equates: 7–11; Data: 12–24; Body: 25–39; Closing: 40.

2-2   `prCodes.`

2-3   There are 14 comments in Program 2-1. Did you miss the comment in line 8?

2-4   Turbo Assembler allows either a dash (–) or a forward slash (/). Turbo Linker allows only a forward slash.

2-5
```
tasm -zi bugaboo
tlink /v bugaboo
```

2-6   Turbo Assembler creates object code. Turbo Linker further processes object-code files to create executable programs. The purpose of object code is to allow programmers to write and assemble large programs in separate pieces, or modules. Turbo Linker can join multiple modules to create the finished code file.

2-7   An error is fatal—the resulting object code will not link or run. A warning is not fatal—the resulting object code might link and run. If you receive an error, you should examine and fix the line identified by the number in parentheses. If you receive a warning, you should probably do the same, unless you are certain, based on your intimate knowledge of the program, that the warning may be safely ignored.

2-8   A .COM code file organizes its data, code, and stack in one memory segment. An .EXE code file separates the program's data, code, and stack into separate memory segments. Writing .EXE programs takes a little more work than writing .COM programs. Programs in .COM format always occupy 64K of memory. Programs in .EXE format occupy only as much memory as they need.

2-9
```
tasm -l listme
type listme.lst>prn
```

OR

```
tasm -l-c listme
type listme.lst>prn
```

2-10   Assembly language programs do not end—they hand over control to another program, usually COMMAND.COM.

2-11   DB reserves space for one or more byte variables in memory. You can use DB to reserve space for single and multiple bytes, plus one or more character strings.

Chapter 3

3-1   Binary digit

3-2   There are 8 bits in a byte and 2 bytes in a word. There are 4 words in a quadword.

3-3   MSD—most significant digit; LSD—least significant digit; MSB—most significant byte; LSB—least significant byte.

3-4
```
     0110 1011 1111 1001
 +   1010 1011 1100 1000
   1 0001 0111 1100 0001
```

3-5
```
    6BF9
 +  ABC8
   117C1
```

3-6 $(2 \times 2 \times 2 \times 2 \times 2 \times 2 \times 2) = 128$. 2^7 is the power of column number 7, the seventh column from the right. Did you remember that the rightmost column (lsb) is number 0?

3-7   3ECA = $(3 \times 4096) + (14 \times 256) + (12 \times 16) + (10 \times 1) = 16,704$
2F78 = $(2 \times 4096) + (15 \times 256) + (7 \times 16) + (8 \times 1) = 12,152$
2F78 = 0010 1111 0111 1000

3-8   AND mask = 0010 1100
OR mask   = 1100 0000
XOR mask = 1000 0000

Did you remember that bits are numbered from right to left, starting with 0? If not, see Figure 3-1 and try again.

3-9

```
       a??? ab??    (a = bits 3,7; b = bit 2; ? = to preserve)
AND    0111 0111    (AND mask)
       0??? 0b??    (result of AND)
OR     1000 1000    (OR mask)
       1??? 1b??    (result of OR)
XOR    0000 0100    (XOR mask)
       1??? 1B??    (result of XOR; B = NOT b)
```

3-10 $(6 \times 2048 \times 8) = 98{,}304$.

3-11

Original Value	One's Complement	Two's Complement
1011 1111	0100 0000	0100 0001
0000 0001	1111 1110	1111 1111
1000 0000	0111 1111	1000 0000
1110 0001	0001 1110	0001 1111
1111 1111	0000 0000	0000 0001

3-12

```
1111 1001   (original signed value)
0000 0110   (one's complement)
0000 0111   (two's complement)
```

Forming the two's complement of 1111 1011 equals 7, indicating that the original binary value is -7 in two's complement notation.

3-13 Six bits can express values up to $(2*2*2*2*2*2) - 1$, or 63. Nine bits can express up to $(2*2*2*2*2*2*2*2*2)$, or 512, including 0.

3-14

```
0011 1001 × 4 = 1110 0100   (shift left 2 times)
        57 × 4 = 228        (in decimal)

1001 1100 / 8 = 0001 0011   (shift right 3 times)
       156 / 8 = 19         (in decimal)
```

You can't multiply 0101 0101 by 8 accurately using left shifts because the result is larger than 8 bits.

Chapter 4

4-1 The minimum size of a segment is 16 bytes because a segment must begin on a 16-byte boundary in memory—therefore, segments must either overlap or be separated by at least 16 bytes. The maximum size of a segment is 65,536 bytes (roughly 64K).

4-2
```
xor ax, ax
sub ax, ax
mov ax, 0
and ax, 0
```

```
        mov  cl, 16
        shl  ax, cl      ; or shr
```

4-3
```
        push dx          ; Push dx onto stack
        pop  ax          ; Pop value of dx into ax
```

4-4 neg forms the two's complement of a byte or word; not forms the one's complement of a byte or word.

4-5
```
        mov  cl, 17
        rcl  ax, cl      ; or rcr
```

The rcl and rcr instructions treat cf as though it were the 17th bit of a word (or the 9th bit of a byte). Therefore, these are the only two instructions that can rotate a value back to its original state and preserve cf.

4-6
```
        mov  dh, ah      ; Copy original value to dh from ah
        mov  cl, 4       ; Prepare to execute 4 shifts
        shr  dh, cl      ; Shift upper 4 bits right
        mov  dl, ah      ; Copy original value to dl from ah
        and  dl, 0Fh     ; Strip all but lower 4 bits
```

4-7
```
        mov  cl, 3       ; Prepare to execute 3 shifts
        shl  dh, cl      ; Shift bit 5 into cf
        jc   BitIsSet    ; Jump only if cf = 1
```

4-8
```
        jl   Target      ; Jump if less to Target
        jnl  Continue    ; Jump if not less to Continue
        jmp  Target      ; Jump if less to Target
        Continue:
```

4-9
```
        xor  bx, 0FFFFh  ; One's complement of bx
        inc  bx          ;  plus 1 forms two's complement
```

4-10
```
        mov  ax, ax
```

OR

```
            jmp short next:
        next:
```

4-11 A string repeat prefix repeats one of the four string instructions cmps, lods, scas, and stos by the number of times specified in cx. When used with cmps and scas, the repetitions stop when zf indicates that the comparison or scan condition failed.

4-12
```
        xor  cx, cx
        rep  scasb       ; Or repe or repz
```

Chapter 5

```
5-1    mov     ax, 1             ; Immediate data
       xor     cx, cx            ; Register data
       mov     bx, [index]       ; Memory data
```

```
5-2    inc     [bankBalance]          ; Direct addressing
       sub     [word bx], 5           ; Register-indirect ([bx]) addressing
       mov     ax, [bp + 10]          ; Base addressing
       and     [byte si + 6], 0Fh     ; Indexed addressing
       mov     [word bx + di + 2], 0  ; Base-indexed addressing
```

```
5-3    DATASEG
       aByte   db      0
       aWord   dw      0
       aString db      'This is a string'
       UDATASEG
       aBuffer db      1024 DUP (?)
```

```
5-4            mov     di, offset aBuffer   ; Address aBuffer with di
               mov     cx, 1024             ; Assign loop count to cx
               cld                          ; Auto-increment di
       @@10:
               mov     al, cl               ; Assign value to al
               stosb                        ; Store al in aBuffer[di]
               loop    @@10                 ; Loop until cx = 0
               ret                          ; Return to caller
```

```
5-5    tasm module
       tasm program
       tlink program module     ; Or tlink program + module
```

5-6 The linker can extract only the modules it needs. Using the extended dictionary option speeds linking.

5-7 PUBLIC directives export procedure, numeric constant, and variable labels from one module to others. EXTRN imports these same kinds of symbols into a module.

5-8 The jmp refers to the second @@40: local label (the one under the je instruction) because the global Repeat: label blocks the view of the first @@40: from jmp. Remember that local labels extend only up and down to the nearest global label.

5-9 The MaxCount, YesAnswer, and BufferSize equates can be exported in a PUBLIC directive. If you didn't include YesAnswer in your answer, remember that characters in assembly language are just numbers expressed in ASCII in the program text.

```
5-10   s1      db      20 DUP (?)
       s2      db      '12345678901234567890'
```

```
s3      db      'abcdefghij'
        db      'klmnopqrst'
```

The last two lines create a single string variable with 20 characters because variables are stored sequentially in memory.

5-11
```
tasm printer
tasm getdata
tasm readtext
tasm YourProgram
tlink YourProgram,,, mta
```

Or, for the link step:

```
tlink YourProgram printer getdata readtext strings strio
```

5-12
```
tlib /E mta -+printer
tlib /E mta -+getdata
tlib /E mta -+readtext
```

5-13
```
CODESEG
        jmp     short @@10      ; Jump over data
Flag    db      0fh             ; Store byte in code segment
@@10:
        mov     dh, [cs:Flag]   ; Load byte into dh
```

Storing data in the code segment this way is not usually necessary (and is, perhaps, unwise). Still, the technique is available if you need it. To refer to the byte requires using the segment override instruction prefix `cs:`.

5-14
```
quotable    db    '"This ''string'' can''t have "too" many'
            db    ' quotes," she said.'
```

There are several possible answers, but this answer works. For space reasons and for demonstration purposes, this answer is listed on two lines. You could declare the entire string on one line.

Chapter 6

6-1
```
STRUC   Time
    hours       db      0       ; 0-23
    minutes     db      0       ; 0-59
    seconds     db      0       ; 0-59
ENDS
```

6-2 Assuming the default field values are 0:

```
DATASEG
TenThirtyFortyFive Time <10,30,45>
FourteenHundred     Time <14>      ; Or <14,,> or <14,0,0>
SixteenThirty       Time <16,30>  ; Or <16,30,> or <16,30,0>
Midnight            Time <>       ; Or <0,0,0>
```

6-3
```
DATASEG
theTime    Time   <>
oldTime    Time   <>


CODESEG
; set the time to 15:45:12
mov     [theTime.hours], 15
mov     [theTime.minutes], 45
mov     [theTime.seconds], 12


; Increment the hour
inc     [theTime.hours]


; Reset the time to 00:00:00 (assumes es = data segment)
xor     ax, ax                ; ax <- 0000
mov     di, OFFSET theTime    ; Address theTime with es:di
cld
stosw   ; Zero hours and minutes fields
stosb   ; Zero seconds


; Copy theTime to oldTime
mov     al, [theTime.hours]
mov     [oldTime.hours], al
mov     al, [theTime.minutes]
mov     [oldTime.minutes], al
mov     al, [theTime.seconds]
mov     [oldTime.seconds], al
```

6-4

00001011	(hex)	= 4113
10000000	(binary)	= 128
1234	(hex)	= 4660
4321d	(decimal)	= 4321
FACE	(label!)	= not a value
00FF	(hex)	= 255

6-5
```
DATASEG
f1      dt      2.5
f2      dt      88.999
f3      dt      0.141
bcd1    dt      125000
bcd2    dt      1250500
```

The largest possible binary-coded-decimal number is 20 digits long, or 99,999,999,999,999,999,999.

6-6
```
DATASEG
WordArray        dw        45 DUP (0)        ; 90 bytes
DoubleArray      dd        100 DUP (0)       ; 400 bytes
Buffer1024       db        1024 DUP (0)      ; 1024 bytes
BCDArray         dt        75 DUP (0)        ; 750 bytes
```

6-7
```
DATASEG
index    dw      0        ; Word array index
CODESEG
; WordArray
mov      bx, [index]           ; Get index value
shl      bx, 1                 ; Multiply by 2
add      bx, OFFSET WordArray  ; Add to array address


; DoubleArray
mov      bx, [index]             ; Get index value
shl      bx, 1                   ; Multiply by 4
shl      bx, 1
add      bx, OFFSET DoubleArray  ; Add to array address


; Buffer1024
mov      bx, [index]             ; Get index value
add      bx, OFFSET Buffer1024   ; Add to array address


; BCDArray
mov      bx, [index]             ; Get index value
mov      ax, bx                  ; Save in ax temporarily
mov      cl, 3                   ; Assign shift count
shl      bx, cl                  ; Multiply index by 8
shl      ax, 1                   ; Multiply index by 2
add      bx, ax                  ; Finish multiply by 10
add      bx, OFFSET BCDArray     ; Add to array address
```

6-8
```
STRUC    FourBytes
  byte1          db      ?
  byte2          db      ?
  byte3          db      ?
  byte4          db      ?
ENDS     FourBytes


STRUC    TwoWords
  loWord         dw      ?
  hiWord         dw      ?
ENDS     TwoWords


UNION    ByteWordDWord
  asBytes        FourBytes       <>
  asWords        TwoWords        <>
  asDWord        dd              ?
ENDS     ByteWordDWord
```

```
        DATASEG
        v1      ByteWordDWord   <>
        CODESEG
        mov     ah, [v1.asBytes.byte3]
        mov     ax, [v1.asWords.hiWord]
        mov     bx, offset v1.asDWord
        mov     ax, [bx]
        mov     dx, [bx + 2]
```

6-9   RECORD inventory location:3, status:1, quantity:5, vendor:4

This record occupies one word because more than 8 bits are specified. The range of values for each field are:

```
location = 0 to 7
status   = 0 to 1
quantity = 0 to 31
vendor   = 0 to 15
```

6-10 maskLocation   =   MASK location
          maskStatus   =   MASK status
          maskQuantity   =   MASK quantity
          maskVendor   =   MASK vendor

```
        DATASEG
        inv     inventory       <>
        CODESEG
        ; Set location  to 3
                and     [inv], NOT maskLocation ; Punch hole in record
                or      [inv], 3 SHL location   ; Insert 3 into hole

        ; Set status to 1
                or      [inv], maskStatus       ; Set single bit = 1

        ; Add 6 to quantity field
                mov     ax, [inv]               ; Load record into ax
                and     ax, maskQuantity        ; Isolate quantity field
                mov     cl, quantity            ; Assign shift count to cl
                shr     ax, cl                  ; Move value to right
                add     ax, 6                   ; Add 6 to value
                shl     ax, cl                  ; Shift back into position
                and     ax, maskQuantity        ; Limit value (optional)
                and     [inv], NOT maskQuantity ; Punch hold in value
                or      [inv], ax               ; Insert new quantity

        ; Load vendor field into dh
                mov     dx, [inv]               ; Load record into dx
                and     dx, maskVendor          ; Isolate vendor field
                mov     cl, vendor              ; Assign shift count to cl
                shr     dx, cl                  ; Move to right of dx
                xchg    dh, dl                  ; Swap result from dl into dh
```

```
              ; Toggle the status field
                      xor       [inv], maskStatus         ; 0 -> 1; or 1 -> 0

              ; Zero all fields in the record
                      xor       ax, ax                    ; Set ax = 0000
                      mov       [inv], ax                 ; Set inv = ax
```

6-11 There are several possible answers to this question, the following being one of the simplest. To save space here, ADDHEX.ASM does not flag errors, as it probably should. See the CONVERT program in chapter 6 for hints on how you can improve ADDHEX. Assemble and link the program with the commands:

```
tasm addhex
tlink addhex,,, mta
```

Program Answers-1 *ADDHEX.ASM*

```
 1:  %TITLE "Sum of Two Hex Values"
 2:
 3:            IDEAL
 4:            DOSSEG
 5:            MODEL    small
 6:            STACK    256
 7:
 8:            DATASEG
 9:
10:  exitCode       DB        0
11:  prompt1        DB        'Enter value 1: ', 0
12:  prompt2        DB        'Enter value 2: ', 0
13:  string         DB        20 DUP (?)
14:
15:            CODESEG
16:
17:            EXTRN    StrLength:proc
18:            EXTRN    StrWrite:proc, StrRead:proc, NewLine:proc
19:            EXTRN    AscToBin:proc, BinToAscHex:proc
20:
21:  Start:
22:            mov      ax, @data              ; Initialize ds to address
23:            mov      ds, ax                 ;   of data segment
24:            mov      es, ax                 ; Make es = ds
25:
26:            mov      di, offset prompt1     ; Address prompt #1
27:            call     GetValue               ; Prompt for input
28:            push     ax                     ; Save first value
29:            mov      di, offset prompt2     ; Address prompt #2
30:            call     GetValue               ; Prompt for input
31:            pop      bx                     ; Get first value
```

```
32:            add      ax, bx                 ; ax <- sum of values
33:            mov      cx, 4                  ; Request 4 digits
34:            mov      di, offset string      ; Address string
35:            call     BinToAscHex            ; Convert ax to string
36:            call     StrWrite               ; Display answer
37: Exit:
38:            mov      ah, 04Ch               ; DOS function: Exit program
39:            mov      al, [exitCode]         ; Return exit code value
40:            int      21h                    ; Call DOS. Terminate program
41:
42: ; GetValue: di = address of prompt; output: ax = value entered in hex
43: PROC     GetValue
44:            call     StrWrite
45:            mov      di, offset string
46:            mov      cl, 4
47:            call     StrRead
48:            call     NewLine
49:            call     StrLength
50:            mov      bx, cx
51:            mov      [word bx + di], 'h'
52:            call     AscToBin
53:            ret
54: ENDP     GetValue
55:
56:            END      Start                  ; End of program / entry point
```

6-12 See lines 16–17 and 31–32 in Program 6-2, VERSION.ASM, if you are having trouble with this one.

Chapter 7

7-1
```
mov  ah, 1             ; Specify DOS "Character Input" function
int  21h               ; Call DOS. Character returned in al

mov  ah, 7             ; Specify DOS "Unfiltered input without echo"
int  21h               ; Call DOS. Character returned in al

mov  ah, 8             ; Specify DOS "Filtered input without echo"
int  21h               ; Call DOS. Character returned in al
```

7-2
```
@@10:
         mov      ah, 7             ; Unfiltered input without echo
         int      21h
         cmp      al, 27            ; ASCII Esc
         je       Exit              ; Exit on Esc key
         cmp      al, 'a'           ; Check for lowercase letter
         jb       @@20
         cmp      al, 'z'
         ja       @@20
```

```
            sub     al, 'z' - 'Z'   ; Convert to uppercase
@@20:
            mov     dl, al          ; Assign character to dl
            mov     ah, 2           ; Character output function number
            int     21h             ; Call DOS to write character
            jmp     @@10
```

In the sub instruction, instead of 'z' - 'Z', you can also use 'a' - 'A' or just 32.

7-3
```
        PROC    EscKey
            push    ax              ; Save ax on stack
            mov     ah, 11          ; Get input status
            int     21h             ; Call DOS
            or      al, al          ; Does al = 0? (i.e., no key waiting)
            je      @@10            ; Jump if so (zf = 1)
            mov     ah, 7           ; Unfiltered input without echo
            int     21h             ; Call DOS to get key press
            cmp     al, 27          ; Does al = Esc?
            je      @@20            ; Jump if al = Esc (zf = 1)
@@10:
            or      al, 1           ; Set zf = 0
@@20:
            pop     ax              ; Restore saved ax
            ret                     ; Return to caller
        ENDP    EscKey
```

There are other good solutions. For example, the second je can be replaced with a jmp short @@20 as zf is already set or cleared correctly by the previous cmp. There's no need to reset zf to 0 if al does not equal 27. As this shows, juggling flags can be tricky. Run tests in Turbo Debugger if you're having trouble understanding how the code works.

7-4 Replace the cmp and je instructions just above label @@10: in the answer to question #7-3 with:

```
or      al, al          ; Does lead-in = 0?
jne     @@20            ; No, so exit (can't be F1)
int     21h             ; Call DOS to get second key press
cmp     al, 03Bh        ; Does al = F1 code?
jmp     short @@20      ; Exit with zf properly set
```

7-5 A handle is a 16-bit number that represents a logical file. DOS lets you specify handles to direct a program's I/O to and from various logical files. DOS preassigns five handles.

7-6 Filter programs read from the standard input file and write to the standard output file; therefore, their input and output can be piped together with other filters to create complex commands out of relatively simple programs. DOS supplies three standard filters: SORT, FIND, and MORE.

7-7
```
DATASEG
string  db      'I hate meeses to pieces'
strlen  =       $ - string
```

7-8
```
; al=char to display; changes bx, dx, di

PROC    FillScreen
        push    ax              ; Save ax on stack for later use
        mov     dh, 24          ; Initialize dh to maximum row
@@10:
        mov     dl, 79          ; Initialize dl to maximum column
@@20:
        pop     ax              ; Get character to display
        push    ax              ; Save character on stack again
        push    dx              ; Save dx--changed by ScPokeChar
        call    ScPokeChar      ; Display one character
        pop     dx              ; Restore dx
        dec     dl              ; Subtract 1 from column number
        jns     @@20            ; Jump if dl >= 0
        dec     dh              ; Subtract 1 from row number
        jns     @@10            ; Jump if dh >= 0
        pop     ax              ; Restore original ax value
        ret                     ; Return to caller
ENDP    FillScreen
```

This subroutine demonstrates how to save values temporarily on the stack. Each time through the loop at label @@20:, the character is popped from the stack and then immediately pushed for the next pass. In this way, the stack serves as a temporary holding place for the variable—an especially useful technique when all registers are used for other purposes. The initial push at the start and the pop at the end are both required to make this method work.

7-9
The following is not a complete program. To test the code, add the instructions at appropriate places to a copy of EXESHELL.ASM from chapter 2.

```
Red     EQU     4       ; Value for red attribute
White   EQU     7       ; Value for white attribute


DATASEG
message         db      'ERROR: Dumb mistake detected', 0

CODESEG
EXTRN ScReadXY:proc, ScPokeStr:proc, StrLength:proc
EXTRN ScSetBack:proc, ScSetFore:proc, ScBright:proc
EXTRN ScBlink:proc
```

```
         mov    al, Red             ; Assign red color to al
         call   ScSetBack           ; Set background to red
         mov    al, White           ; Assign white color to al
         call   ScSetFore           ; Set foreground to white
         call   ScBright            ; Make it whiter than white
         call   ScBlink             ; Blink foreground
         mov    di, offset message  ; Address message with es:di
         call   StrLength           ; Set cx = length of message
         call   ScReadXY            ; Get current cursor location
         mov    si, offset message  ; Address message with ds:si
         call   ScPokeStr           ; Display message at cursor
```

7-10   ScInit.

7-11
```
 PROC    YesNo
         push   ax                  ; Save ax on stack
@@10:
         call   GetCh               ; Get key press
         je     @@10                ; Reject function and control keys
         cmp    al, 'y'             ; Does key = lowercase y?
         je     @@99                ; Jump if yes
         cmp    al, 'Y'             ; Does key = uppercase Y?
@@99:
         pop    ax                  ; Restore saved ax from stack
         ret                        ; Return to caller
 ENDP    YesNo
```

Chapter 8

8-1   The advantages include:

- ▶ Macros can reduce repetition
- ▶ Macros can clarify assembly language
- ▶ Macros let you customize Turbo Assembler

The disadvantages are:

- ▶ Macros can hide effects on register values
- ▶ Macros can increase assembly time

8-2
```
 MACRO   Startup
         mov    ax, @data   ;; Initialize segment registers
         mov    ds, ax      ;; ds and es to address the program's
         mov    es, ax      ;; data segment
 ENDM    Startup
```

8-3   1) Any nonzero value represents true; 2) only zero represents false; and 3) 1 or −1 typically represent true.

8-4 Comments preceded with double semicolons are not written to a listing file created with the /l option during assembly. Comments preceded by single semicolons are listed each time the macro is used in the program. A double semicolon can reduce listing file size and, therefore, decrease printing time.

8-5 Use the PURGE directive to throw away a macro definition.

8-6 You don't specify parameter types in macro definitions. Parameter types depend on how the parameters are used inside the macro.

8-7
```
MACRO   stz                     ;; Set zf flag = 1
        push    ax              ;; Save ax on stack
        lahf                    ;; Load flags into ah
        or      ah, 040h        ;; Set bit 6 (zf)
        sahf                    ;; Store ah to flags
        pop     ax              ;; Restore ax
ENDM    stz

MACRO   clz                     ;; Clear zf flag = 0
        push    ax              ;; Save ax on stack
        lahf                    ;; Load flags into ah
        and     ah, 0BFh        ;; Clear bit 6
        sahf                    ;; Store ah to flags
        pop     ax              ;; Restore ax
ENDM    clz
```

8-8
```
;----- Macro definition
MACRO   AssignSeg       reg, value
        push    ax
        mov     ax, value
        mov     reg, ax
        pop     ax
ENDM    AssignSeg

;----- Assign color video buffer address to es
AssignSeg       es, 0B800h
```

8-9
```
INCLUDE "FLOAT.MAX"
INCLUDE "BIOSMAC.TXT"INCLUDE "CUSTOM.MAX"
```

Did you remember the quotes required around file names in Turbo Assembler's Ideal mode?

8-10
```
True            =       -1
False           =       0
;HasFastCrt     =       True    ; For PCs
HasFastCrt      =       False   ; For plain MS-DOS systems

PROC    WriteAChar
IF HasFastCrt
```

```
            call     ScPokeChar         ; Fast write to x,y
     ELSE
            cmp      al, ' '            ; Reject control codes
            jae      @@HFC10            ; Jump if not a control
            mov      al, '.'            ; Char to display for controls
     @@HFC10:
            cmp      dh, 24             ; Does row = maximum?
            jne      @@HFC20            ; Jump if not
            cmp      dl, 79             ; Does column = maximum?
            je       @@HFC99            ; Exit to prevent scroll!
     @@HFC20:
            xchg     dx, bx             ; Preserve requested x,y
            call     ScReadXY           ; Get current cursor position
            push     dx                 ; Save current position
            xchg     bx, dx             ; Restore requested x,y
            call     ScGotoXY           ; Position the cursor
            mov      dl, al             ; Assign character to dl
            MS_DOS   2                  ; Call DOS output char function
            pop      dx                 ; Restore saved cursor position
            call     ScGotoXY           ; Put cursor back where it was
     ENDIF
     @@HFC99:
            ret                         ; Return to caller
     ENDP     WriteAChar
```

The answer to this problem is trickier than it seems at first. Because ScPokeChar ignores the cursor position, poking characters directly into the video memory buffer, the DOS replacement code must read and restore the cursor to its original position. Also, because writing a character to the bottom right corner causes the display to scroll up one line, the code must prevent characters from being displayed at this position. Because control codes such as carriage returns and line feeds cause actions when written via DOS but not ScPokeChar, control codes must be converted to another character (in this case, a period). Obviously, then, the two routines can't be 100% identical, and the best you can do is come close.

Chapter 9

9-1　Closing a file writes or flushes to disk any data held in DOS buffers, updates the entry for this file in the disk directory, and releases the file handle for use with other files.

9-2　Opening a file is required before you can read and write data in the file. Unless an error occurs, when DOS opens a file, it returns a file handle that you can subsequently use to refer to the opened file.

9-3
```
     DATASEG
     prompt         db        'File? ', 0
     string         db        65 dup (0)
```

```
        CODESEG
        ; Input : none
        ; Output: cf = 0 : ax = file handle, string = file name
        ;         cf = 1 : ax = error code (or 0 if no file entered)
        ; Regs  : ax, cx, di
        PROC    OpenFile
                mov     di, offset prompt    ; Address prompt string
                call    StrWrite             ; Display prompt
                mov     di, offset string    ; Address input string
                mov     cx, 64               ; Limit to 64 characters
                call    StrRead              ; Get file name
                call    StrLength            ; Check length in cx
                jcxz    @@10                 ; Exit if length = 0
                mov     dx, di               ; Address string with ds:dx
                mov     ah, 03Dh             ; DOS Open-File function
                mov     al, 2                ; 2 = Read/Write access
                int     21h                  ; Call DOS to open file
                ret                          ; Return (cf = result)
        @@10:
                xor     ax, ax  ; No error code in this case
                stc             ; Set carry to indicate file is not open
                ret             ; Return to caller
        ENDP    OpenFile
```

9-4
```
        ; Input  : bx = file handle; dx = address of file name
        ; Output : File flushed and reopened. (Location changed to
        ;          beginning of file.) cf = 0:no errors; cf = 1:error
        ; Regs   : ax
        PROC    FlushFile
                mov     ah, 03Eh             ; DOS Close-File function number
                int     21h                  ; Call DOS to close the file
                jc      @@99                 ; Exit on errors
                mov     ah, 03Dh             ; DOS Open-File function
                mov     al, 2                ; 2 = Read/Write access
                int     21h                  ; Call DOS to open file
        @@99:   ret                          ; Return (cf = result)
        ENDP    FlushFile
```

9-5
```
        ; Input  : cx = record size; ax = record number; bx = file handle
        ;          : ds:dx = address of buffer
        ; Output : cf = 1:error (ax = code); cf = 0:success
        ; Regs   : ax
        PROC    ReadRecord
                push    cx                   ; Save record size
                push    dx                   ; Save buffer address
                mul     cx                   ; ax:dx <- ax * cx
                mov     cx, dx               ; cx <- MSW of result
                mov     dx, ax               ; dx <- LSW of result
                mov     ah, 042h             ; DOS Seek-File function
                mov     al, 0                ; Seek from beginning of file
                int     21h                  ; Position file pointer
```

```
              jc      @@99            ; Exit on errors
              mov     ah, 03Fh        ; DOS Read-File function
              pop     dx              ; Retrieve buffer address
              pop     cx              ; Retrieve record size
              int     21h             ; Read cx bytes from file
      @@99:   ret                     ; Return to caller
      ENDP    ReadRecord
```

9-6
```
      ; Input  : cx = record size; bx = file handle
      ;        : ds:dx = address of buffer
      ; Output : cf = 1:error (ax = code); cf = 0:next record loaded
      ; Regs   : cx, dx
      PROC    ReadNextRec
              push    cx              ; Save record size
              push    dx              ; Save buffer address
              mov     dx, cx          ; dx <- cx
              xor     cx, cx          ; Zero upper half of value
              mov     ah, 042h        ; DOS Seek-File function
              mov     al, 1           ; Seek from current position
              int     21h             ; Position file pointer
              mov     ah, 03Fh        ; DOS Read-File function
              pop     dx              ; Retrieve buffer address
              pop     cx              ; Retrieve record size
              int     21h             ; Read cx bytes from file
              ret                     ; Return to caller
      ENDP    ReadNextRec
```

9-7
```
      ; Input  : ah = option letter e.g., 'P' (case sensitive)
      ; Note   : Must have called GetParams earlier
      ; Output : cf = 1:not found; cf = 0:option (e.g., -P) found
      ; Regs   : al, cx, di
      PROC    OptionLetter
              call    ParamCount      ; dx = number of parameters
              mov     cx, dx          ; Transfer num to cx
      @@10:
              jcxz    @@99            ; Exit if all params checked
              dec     cx              ; Count number params done
              push    cx              ; Save count on stack
              call    GetOneParam     ; Get param addr in di
              call    StrLength       ; Get length of param string
              cmp     cx, 2           ; Test string length
              pop     cx              ; Restore count from stack
              jb      @@10            ; Jump if length < 2 chars
              mov     al, '-'         ; al = '-'; ah = option letter
              scasw                   ; Compare ax with [ds:di]
              jnz     @@10            ; Jump if compare fails
              clc                     ; Clear carry
              ret                     ; Return success!
      @@99:   stc                     ; Set carry
              ret                     ; Return failure
      ENDP    OptionLetter
```

9-8
```
; Add these variables to DR.ASM between lines 18 and 19
oneDot          DB        '.', 0            ; Single dot string
oneBlank        DB        ' ', 0            ; Single blank string


; Insert this procedure between lines 129 and 130 and also insert
; a call ExpandName instruction between lines 117 and 118


; Input  : ds:di addresses file name in directory DTA
; Output : name expanded, e.g., xxx.txt --> xxx    txt
PROC    ExpandName
        mov     si, offset OneDot       ; Address '.' string
        call    StrPos                  ; Is there a '.' here?
        jnz     @@05                    ; Jump if no
        cmp     dx, 0                   ; But is '.' at front?
        jne     @@10                    ; Jump if no
@@05:
        call    StrLength               ; Get string length
        mov     dx, cx                  ; And assign to dx
        jmp     short @@20              ; Skip delete steps next
@@10:
        mov     cx, 1                   ; Number of chars to delete
        call    StrDelete               ; Delete '.' (if there)
@@20:
        mov     si, offset OneBlank     ; Address ' ' string
@@30:
        call    StrLength               ; Get string length
        cmp     cx, 12                  ; Is length = 12 yet?
        je      @@99                    ; Exit if yes
        call    StrInsert               ; Insert blank into string
        jmp     @@30                    ; Repeat until done
@@99:
        ret                             ; Return to caller
ENDP    ExpandName
```

9-9
```
; Insert into KOPY.ASM between lines 115 and 116:


        mov     al, [oneByte]       ; Get input byte
        cmp     al, ' '             ; Is byte >= ' '?
        jge     @@Continue          ; Jump if yes (not a control)
        cmp     al, 13              ; Is byte a carriage return?
        je      @@Continue          ; Jump if yes
        cmp     al, 10              ; Is byte a line feed?
        je      @@Continue          ; Jump if yes
        mov     al, ' '             ; Change controls to blanks
        mov     [oneByte], al       ; Store char back in variable
@@Continue:
```

9-10
```
; Add these lines to DR.ASM between lines 18 and 19
comExtn         DB        '.COM', 0         ; .COM file extension
exeExtn         DB        '.EXE', 0         ; .EXE file extension
```

```
; Replacement for Action procedure in DR.ASM, lines 116-128
        PROC    Action
                push    si                      ; Save si
                mov     di, offset dirData + FileName    ; Address file name
                mov     si, offset comExtn      ; Check for .COM extensions
                call    StrPos                  ; Is '.COM' there?
                jz      @@05                    ; Jump if yes
                mov     si, offset exeExtn      ; Check for .EXE extensions
                call    StrPos                  ; Is '.EXE' there?
                jnz     @@99                    ; Exit if no
        @@05:

                call    ExpandName              ; OPTIONAL: see answer to question #9-8

                call    StrWrite                ; Write file name
                call    StrLength               ; Tab to next column
                sub     cx, 16
                neg     cx
        @@10:
                mov     ah, 2
                mov     dl, ' '
                int     21h
                loop    @@10
        @@99:   pop     si                      ; Restore si
                ret                             ; Return to caller
        ENDP    Action
```

Chapter 10

10-1   External interrupts can occur at any time; therefore, changing a register could destroy a value being used by the interrupted program.

10-2   An iret instruction pops the flags and return address off the stack, resuming the program with the instruction just after the place where the interruption occurred.

10-3   The cli instruction disables maskable interrupts. The sti instruction enables maskable interrupts. Both instructions operate by clearing and setting the interrupt-enable flag if. In an ISR, a cli instruction could appear anywhere but is unnecessary because interrupts are disabled when the ISR begins to run. An sti instruction should appear near the beginning of the ISR if you want interrupts to be recognized during the ISR's execution. Placing an sti before iret is always unnecessary because ending the interrupt restores the if flag to its previous state.

10-4
```
DATASEG
    oldSeg  dw      ?       ; Stores original vector segment
    oldOfs  dw      ?       ; Stores original vector offset
```

```
CODESEG

;----- Install new vector
push    ds                      ; Save ds register
push    es                      ; Save es register
mov     ax, 351Ch               ; Get interrupt 1C vector
int     21h                     ; Call DOS for vector
mov     [oldSeg], es            ; Save segment value
mov     [oldOfs], bx            ; Save offset value
mov     ax, 251Ch               ; Set interrupt 1C vector
push    cs                      ; Make ds = cs to address
pop     ds                      ;  the new ISR, placing full
mov     dx, offset NewISR       ;  address into ds:dx
int     21h                     ; Set new interrupt vector
pop     es                      ; Restore es
pop     ds                      ; Restore ds

;----- Restore original vector
push    ds                      ; Save ds, changed below
mov     ax, 251Ch               ; Set interrupt 1C vector
mov     dx, [oldOfs]            ; Get saved offset value
mov     ds, [oldSeg]            ; Get saved segment value
int     21h
pop     ds                      ; Restore ds
```

10-5 Yes, but you have to execute an `sti` instruction to set the interrupt-enable flag, allowing maskable interrupts to be recognized.

10-6
```
sti                     ; Enable interrupts
mov     al, 020h        ; End-of-interrupt value
out     020h, al        ; Output to 8259 port
```

10-7
```
PROC    PrintScreen
        int     5       ; Call "hardware" interrupt 5
        ret             ; Return to caller
ENDP    PrintScreen
```

10-8 When a divide fault occurs, causing an interrupt type 0 signal, the 8086/88 processors push the address of the next instruction after the `div` or `idiv` that caused the fault. The 80286/386 processors push the address of the divide instruction.

10-9
```
int 3           ; Set breakpoint
```

10-10
```
;----- Set trap flag (tf)
push    bp                      ; Save bp
pushf                           ; Push flags onto stack
mov     bp, sp                  ; Address stack with bp
or      [word bp], 0100h        ; Set tf in saved flags
popf                            ; Restore flags from stack
pop     bp                      ; Restore bp
```

Chapter 11

11-1 There would be 8 digits in a hypothetical packed 4-byte BCD value (2 digits per byte). There would be 6 digits in a hypothetical 6-byte unpacked BCD value (1 digit per byte). The `dt` directive allocates 10 bytes. At 2 digits per byte, that's enough room to hold up to 20 packed BCD digits.

11-2
```
mov     al, 079h        ; Assign packed BCD to al
mov     ah, al          ; Copy value to ah
mov     cl, 4           ; Assign shift count to cl
shr     ah, cl          ; Shift BCD MSD to LDS position
and     al, 00Fh        ; Mask other digit in al
aad                     ; Convert unpacked BCD to binary
```

The trick here is to convert the packed BCD byte in `al` to unpacked form in `ax` (1 digit per byte), using `shr` and `and` instructions to manipulate the bits. With the data in this format, `aad` converts the value to binary in `ax`.

11-3
```
GLOBAL  string:Byte     ; or, GLOBAL string:Byte:25
GLOBAL  count:Word
GLOBAL  BCD:TByte
```

The string `GLOBAL` definition can also be `string:Byte:25`, although it's not necessary in this case to specify the exact length of the string variable.

11-4
```
DATASEG
cubes db 0, 1, 8, 27, 64, 125, 216 ; cubes of 0 to 6
CODESEG
mov al, cl              ; Copy index in cl to al
mov bx, offset cubes    ; Address table with ds:bx
xlat                    ; Translate al from table
```

11-5 `ASSUME` tells Turbo Assembler where a specified segment register points. Using `ASSUME` lets the assembler verify that references to named variables are logical.

11-6
```
SEGMENT MoreData Page Public 'DATA'
MyWord  dw      1234h
ENDS    MoreData

CODESEG
mov     ax, MoreData    ; Address MoreData segment
mov     ds, ax          ;   with ds
ASSUME  ds:MoreData     ; Tell Turbo Assembler where ds points
mov     ax, [MyWord]    ; Load ax with value of MyWord
```

11-7 `GROUP` combines multiple segments that have different names and, possibly, different classes, into one segment up to 64K long. To group the four listed segments under the name `DataGroup`, use the command:

```
GROUP DataGroup SomeData, MoreData, TableSeg, StringSeg
```

Then you can address the data in the grouped segment by first initializing
a segment register to the start of the group:

```
mov      ax, DataGroup
mov      ds, ax
ASSUME   ds:DataGroup
```

11-8 The definition for KbFlag in the BIOSData segment can also be LABEL Kb-
Flag Byte. Execute these commands to assemble, link, and run the program, which calls a procedure in the STRIO library module:

```
tasm capslock
tlink capslock,,, mta
capslock
```

```
%TITLE "Test CapsLock Key"
        IDEAL
        DOSSEG
        MODEL    small
        STACK    256


SEGMENT BIOSData at 0040h
        ORG      017h
KbFlag  db       ?
ENDS    BIOSData


        DATASEG
CapsString      db       'CapsLock is: ', 0
CapsOn          db       'ON', 0
CapsOff         db       'OFF', 0


        CODESEG
        EXTRN    StrWrite:proc
Start:
        mov      ax, BIOSData            ; Address BIOSData segment
        mov      es, ax                  ;   with es
        ASSUME   es:BIOSData             ; Tell tasm where es points
        mov      bl, [KbFlag]            ; Load keyboard flag into bl
        mov      ax, @data               ; Initialize ds and es
        mov      ds, ax                  ;   to default data segment
        mov      es, ax
        ASSUME   ds:@data, es:@data      ; Tell tasm where es,ds point
        mov      di, offset CapsString   ; Address string with di
        call     StrWrite                ; Display string
        mov      di, offset CapsOn       ; Address "ON" with di
        test     bl, 040h                ; Test keyboard flag bit
        jnz      @@10                    ; Jump if bit <> 0
        mov      di, offset CapsOff      ; Else address "OFF" with di
```

```
@@10:
        call    StrWrite            ; Display "ON" or "OFF"
        mov     ax, 04C00h          ; DOS function: Exit program
        int     21h                 ; Call DOS. Terminate program

        END     Start        ; End of program / entry point
```

11-9

```
P286N
PROC    ISR286
        pusha               ; Push all general-purpose registers
;
; Other code goes here
;
        popa                ; Pop all general-purpose registers
        iret                ; Return from interrupt
ENDP    ISR286
```

11-10 This problem reduces to two tasks: Transfer a certain bit to the carry flag and then either do nothing to the original bit bt, complement the bit btc, reset the bit btr, or set the bit bts. The following shows how to accomplish these tasks for bit 3. Other bits require different mask values, but the code is the same.

```
;-----  To transfer bit 3 (mask = 0008h) to cf:

        test    dx, 08h         ; zf <- result; cf <- 0
        jz      @@10            ; Jump if bit = 0
        stc                     ; Else set carry
@@10:

;-----  Then, to complement, reset and set bit 3:

        xor     dx, 08h         ; Complement bit 3
        and     dx, NOT 08h     ; Reset bit 3
        or      dx, 08h         ; Set bit 3
```

Chapter 12

12-1 *Critical code* refers to program statements that account for most of a program's total execution time.

12-2 A profiler monitors a running program and prepares statistics that can help identify the program's critical code.

12-3
```
InLine( $F8 );   { clc -- clear carry flag }
InLine( $F9 );   { stc -- set carry flag }

PROCEDURE clc; InLine( $F8 );   { clear carry flag }
PROCEDURE stc; InLine( $F9 );   { set carry flag }
```

12-4
```
PUBLIC  PlayBall
PROC    PlayBall  FAR
        ret                 ; Return to caller
ENDP    PlayBall
```

Did you remember to declare this procedure FAR, required because of the Pascal {$F+} declaration?

12-5
```
{$L NEWSTUFF.OBJ}
PROCEDURE OldStuff; EXTERNAL;
FUNCTION OlderStuff : Integer; EXTERNAL;
```

12-6 Using the TPASCAL memory model adds push bp and mov bp,sp instructions to every procedure, whether or not these instructions are needed to address parameters on the stack. The advantage of the TPASCAL memory model is the ability it gives you to use simplified segment directives DATASEG and CODESEG in external modules. The alternative is to declare segments manually with SEGMENT directives, also requiring the use of ASSUME to inform the assembler to which memory segments cs, ds, and es refer.

12-7 Plain constants and types such as Months, MaxLevel, and Esc identifiers can't be imported into an assembly language module. The other declarations can be imported into a data segment this way:

```
SEGMENT DATA word public
        EXTRN AreaCode : WORD, YourName : BYTE, Score : WORD
        EXTRN SalesPerMonth : WORD
ENDS    DATA
```

12-8 In the Pascal program:

```
PROCEDURE WriteASCII; FORWARD;
{$L ASCII.OBJ}
```

In the object-code module:

```
SEGMENT CODE byte public
ASSUME  cs:CODE, ds:DATA
EXTRN   WriteASCII : NEAR
PROC    AnyProc NEAR
        mov     ax, ' a'        ; Pass character as word
        push    ax              ;  on stack
        call    WriteASCII      ; Call Pascal procedure
        ret
ENDP    AnyProc
ENDS
```

12-9
```
mov     ax, [word LongValue]
mov     dx, [word LongValue + 1]
ret
```

12-10 The assembly language module, TESTASM.ASM:

```
                IDEAL
                MODEL   TPASCAL
                CODESEG
                PUBLIC  LotsOfParams

        PROC    LotsOfParams    NEAR
                ARG a:Word, b:Word, Number:dword, char:dword
                mov     cx, [a]            ; Load a into cx
                mov     dx, [b]            ; Load b into dx
                les     di, [Number]       ; Address Number with es:di
                add     [word es:di], 5    ; Add 5 to number
                les     si, [char]         ; Address ch with es:si
                mov     al, [byte es:si]   ; Load ch into al
                ret                        ; Return to caller
        ENDP    LotsOfParams

                END                        ; End of module
```

The Pascal program, TESTPAS.PAS:

```
PROGRAM TestPas;
VAR     Score : Integer; ch : char;
{$L TESTASM.OBJ}
PROCEDURE LotsOfParams( a, b : Integer; VAR number : Integer;
   VAR ch : char ); EXTERNAL;
BEGIN
   ch := 'A';
   score := 100;
   Writeln( 'Before score = ', score );
   LotsOfParams( 1, 2, score, ch );
   Writeln( 'After score = ', score )
END.
```

Chapter 13

13-1 The two methods of adding assembly language to C programs are: in-line asm statements and external functions. In-line statements require Turbo C to compile the entire program into an .ASM text file and then assemble and link this file separately. External functions are assembled separately and then linked with a compiled Turbo C program in .OBJ code-file format.

13-2 External functions must save and restore si and di (if these registers are used), but only if another function using register variables calls the external code. It is never necessary to save and restore si and di in C functions that use in-line asm statements. In that case, Turbo C automatically saves and restores these registers while also turning off register variables, thus preventing any possibility of a conflict.

13-3 To compile this program, save as CFLAGS.C and enter `tcc cflags`.

```c
#pragma inline
#include <stdio.h>

void showflags();

main()
{
    showflags();
}

void showflags()
{
    unsigned int theflags;

    printf("- - - - O D I T S Z - A - P - C\n");
    asm pushf                       /* push flags onto stack */
    asm pop [theflags]              /* pop flags into the flags */
    asm mov cx, 16                  /* assign loop count to cx */
Again:
    asm rol [Word ptr theflags], 1  /* rotate bit to LSD position */
    asm push cx                     /* save loop count on stack */
    printf("%d ", (theflags & 1));  /* display value of LSD */
    asm pop cx                      /* restore saved loop count */
    asm loop Again                  /* repeat until done */
    printf("\n");                   /* start new output line */
}
```

13-4 `asm lea bx, MyThings.OneThing`

13-5 Use the `-S` option (the `S` must be in uppercase) to compile a program to assembly language text. For example, to compile CHECKERS.C, you could use the command:

```
tcc -S checkers
```

The result is a file named CHECKERS.ASM containing the program in assembly language form. The danger of this command is that any existing CHECKERS.ASM file is erased with no prior warning.

13-6 Using Turbo C as a front end to Turbo Linker:

```
tasm /ml func1
tasm /ml func2
tcc -c main
tcc -ms main.obj func1.obj func2.obj
```

Or, to link directly, replace the fourth line with:

```
tlink \tc\lib\cOs main func1 func2, main,, \tc\lib\cs
```

13-7   `ARG source:DWord, destination:DWord, sourcelen:Word`

13-8   `#include <stdio.h>`

```c
extern void copystring( unsigned char far * source,
    unsigned char far * destination,
    int sourcelen );

char *source = 'Source';
char *destination = 'Destination';

main()
{
    printf("Before destination: %s\n", destination);
    copystring( source, destination, 6 );
    printf("After destination : %s\n", destination);
}
```

13-9   `%TITLE "Copy String External C Function"`

```
        IDEAL
        MODEL   small

        CODESEG

        PUBLIC  _copystring

PROC    _copystring     NEAR

        ARG source:DWord, destination:DWord, sourcelen:Word

        push    bp                  ; Save bp
        mov     bp, sp              ; Address params with bp
        mov     cx, [sourcelen]     ; Load length into cx
        jcxz    @@99                ; Exit if cx = 0
        push    ds                  ; Save ds on stack
        les     di, [destination]   ; Address dest with es:di
        lds     si, [source]        ; Address source with ds:si
        cld                         ; Auto-increment si, di
        rep     movsb               ; Copy source chars to dest
        pop     ds                  ; Restore ds
@@99:
        pop     bp              ; Restore bp
        ret                     ; Return to caller
ENDP    _copystring

        END                     ; End of module
```

13-10   `DATASEG`

```
string1         db      'A Source String', 0
s1len           =       $ - string1
```

```
string2          db        'A Destination String', 0

CODESEG
;
;
mov      ax, s1len - 1             ; Load string length into ax
push     ax                        ; Push length parameter
push     ds                        ; Push dest segment address
mov      ax, offset string2        ; Push dest offset address
push     ax
push     ds                        ; Push source segment address
mov      ax, offset string1        ; Push source offset address
push     ax
call     _copystring               ; Call external function
add      sp, 10                    ; Remove parameters from stack
```

Index

continued

continued

continued

continued

continued

continued

Special Disk Offer

To save time and avoid typing mistakes, you can order all the programs in this book on disk for only $20, postage paid. (For foreign orders, add $5 for postage and handling.) Fill in and mail the order form below or, for faster service, telephone today. With your order, you'll receive:

- One 5¼-inch 360K double-sided MS-DOS or PC-DOS floppy disk.
- Complete source code to program listings.
- Additional instructions on disk.

To order, call (717)627-1911, 9 a.m. to 5 p.m., Eastern time, or write to:

Swan Software
Mastering Turbo Assembler Disk
P.O. Box 206
Lititz, PA 17543

Howard W. Sams & Company assumes no liability with respect to the use or accuracy of the information contained on this diskette.

- -

Disk Order Form

Swan, *Mastering Turbo Assembler*, #48435

Name _____

Address _____

City/St/Zip _____

Telephone _____

☐ Check or money order for $20 enclosed (Pennsylvania residents,
   add 6% sales tax). Make checks payable to Swan Software.

☐ Bill my credit card   ☐ Visa   ☐ MasterCard

Card Number _____ Exp. Date _____

Signature _____

Price of $20 includes postage to anywhere in the United States or to an APO number. Foreign orders, add $5 for postage and handling. Pennsylvania residents must add 6% sales tax ($1.20). Allow 2 weeks for checks to clear.

Swan Software, Mastering Turbo Assembler Disk
P.O. Box 206, Lititz, PA 17543